This is the third in a series of companions to major philosophers that Cambridge will be issuing in the next few years. Each volume will contain specially commissioned essays by an international team of scholars, together with a substantial bibliography and will serve as a reference work for students and nonspecialists. One aim of the series is to dispel the intimidation such readers often feel when faced with the work of a difficult and challenging thinker.

The fundamental task of philosophy since the seventeenth century has been to determine whether the essential principles of both knowledge and action can be discovered by human beings unaided by an external agency. No one philosopher has contributed more to this enterprise than has Immanuel Kant, whose *Critique of Pure Reason* (1781) shook the very foundations of the intellectual world. Kant argued that the basic principles of natural science are imposed on reality by human sensibility and understanding, and hence human beings can also impose their own free and rational agency on the world.

This volume is the only available systematic and comprehensive account of the full range of Kant's writings and the first major overview of his work to be published in more than a dozen years. An internationally recognized team of Kant scholars explore Kant's conceptual revolution in epistemology, metaphysics, philosophy of science, moral and political philosophy, aesthetics, and the philosophy of religion. The volume also traces the historical origins and consequences of Kant's work.

New readers and nonspecialists will find this the most convenient, accessible guide to Kant currently in print. Advanced students and specialists will find a conspectus of recent developments in the interpretation of Kant.

THE CAMBRIDGE COMPANION TO

KANT

OTHER VOLUMES IN THIS SERIES OF CAMBRIDGE
COMPANIONS:

AQUINAS *Edited by* NORMAN KRETZMANN *and*
ELEONORE STUMP
ARISTOTLE *Edited by* JONATHAN BARNES
DESCARTES *Edited by* JOHN COTTINGHAM
FOUCAULT *Edited by* GARY GUTTING
FREUD *Edited by* JEROME NEU
HEGEL *Edited by* FREDERICK BEISER
HEIDEGGER *Edited by* CHARLES GUIGNON
HOBBES *Edited by* TOM SORRELL
HUME *Edited by* DAVID FATE NORTON
HUSSERL *Edited by* BARRY SMITH *and* DAVID
WOODRUFF SMITH
LEIBNIZ *Edited by* NICHOLAS JOLLEY
LOCKE *Edited by* VERE CHAPPELL
MARX *Edited by* TERRELL CARVER
MILL *Edited by* JOHN SKORUPSKI
NIETZSCHE *Edited by* BERND MAGNUS
PLATO *Edited by* RICHARD KRAUT
SARTRE *Edited by* CHRISTINA HOWELLS
SPINOZA *Edited by* DON GARRETT

The Cambridge Companion to
KANT

Edited by Paul Guyer

CAMBRIDGE
UNIVERSITY PRESS

Published by the Press Syndicate of the University of Cambridge
The Pitt Building, Trumpington Street, Cambridge CB2 1RP
40 West 20th Street, New York, NY 10011-4211, USA
10 Stamford Road, Oakleigh, Melbourne 3166, Australia

© Cambridge University Press 1992

First published 1992
Reprinted 1992, 1993, 1994 (twice), 1995, 1996

Printed in the United States of America

Library of Congress Cataloging-in-Publication Data is available

A catalogue record for this book is available from the British Library

ISBN 0-521-36587-2 hardback
ISBN 0-521-36768-9 paperback

CONTENTS

List of contributors   *page* vii

Method of citation   x

Introduction: The starry heavens and the moral law   1
PAUL GUYER

1 Kant's intellectual development: 1746–1781   26
FREDERICK C. BEISER

2 The Transcendental Aesthetic   62
CHARLES PARSONS

3 Functions of thought and the synthesis of intuitions   101
J. MICHAEL YOUNG

4 The transcendental deduction of the categories   123
PAUL GUYER

5 Causal laws and the foundations of natural science   161
MICHAEL FRIEDMAN

6 Empirical, rational, and transcendental psychology:
   Psychology as science and as philosophy   200
GARY HATFIELD

7 Reason and the practice of science   228
THOMAS E. WARTENBERG

8 The critique of metaphysics: Kant and traditional
   ontology   249
KARL AMERIKS

v

9 Vindicating reason   280
   ONORA O'NEILL

10 Autonomy, obligation, and virtue: An overview of
   Kant's moral philosophy   309
   J. B. SCHNEEWIND

11 Politics, freedom, and order: Kant's political
   philosophy   342
   WOLFGANG KERSTING

12 Taste, sublimity, and genius: The aesthetics of nature
   and art   367
   EVA SCHAPER

13 Rational theology, moral faith, and religion   394
   ALLEN W. WOOD

14 The first twenty years of critique: The Spinoza
   connection   417
   GEORGE DI GIOVANNI

   Bibliography   449

   Index   472

CONTRIBUTORS

KARL AMERIKS is Professor of Philosophy at the University of Notre Dame. He has written widely on Kant and other figures in German philosophy. He is the author of *Kant's Theory of the Mind: An Analysis of the Paralogisms of Pure Reason* (Oxford University Press, 1982), and will soon publish a selected translation of Kant's *Lectures on Metaphysics* in The Cambridge Edition of the Works of Immanuel Kant (forthcoming).

FREDERICK C. BEISER teaches at Indiana University. He is the author of *The Fate of Reason: German Philosophy from Kant to Fichte* (Harvard University Press, 1987). He is currently editing *The Cambridge Companion to Hegel.*

GEORGE DI GIOVANNI is Professor of Philosophy at McGill University. He has written widely on Kant and German idealism. With H. S. Harris, he edited and translated *Between Kant and Hegel: Texts in the Development of Post-Kantian Idealism* (State University of New York Press, 1985), and he has also edited *Essays on Hegel's Logic* (State University of New York Press, 1990).

MICHAEL FRIEDMAN is Professor of Philosophy at the University of Illinois–Chicago. He is the author of *Foundations of Space–Time Theories: Relativistic Physics and Philosophy of Science* (Princeton University Press, 1983), and of numerous articles on Kant's philosophy of mathematics and science, some of which will be included in his *Kant on the Exact Sciences* (Harvard University Press, forthcoming).

PAUL GUYER is Professor of Philosophy at the University of Pennsylvania. He is the author of *Kant and the Claims of Taste* (Harvard

vii

University Press, 1979) and *Kant and the Claims of Knowledge* (Cambridge University Press, 1987); he also edited *Essays in Kant's Aesthetics* (University of Chicago Press, 1982) with Ted Cohen. He is general co-editor of The Cambridge Edition of the Works of Immanuel Kant (forthcoming).

GARY HATFIELD is Professor of Philosophy at the University of Pennsylvania. He is the author of *The Natural and the Normative: Theories of Spatial Perception from Kant to Helmholtz* (MIT Press, 1990), as well as of numerous papers in the history of philosophy and the philosophy of psychology.

WOLFGANG KERSTING is Professor of Philosophy at the University of Hannover. He has published widely in moral, legal, and political philosophy. His books include *Die Ethik in Hegels "Phänomenologie des Geistes"* (Hannover, 1974), *Wohlgeordnete Freiheit: Immanuel Kants Rechts- und Staatsphilosophie* (Walter de Gruyter, 1984), *Niccolo Machiavelli: Leben-Werk-Wirkung* (Beck, 1986), and *Die politische Philosophie des Gesellschaftsvertrags* (Wissenschaftliche Buchgesellschaft, 1991).

ONORA O'NEILL is Professor of Philosophy at the University of Essex. Her works include *Acting on Principle: An Essay on Kantian Ethics* (Columbia University Press, 1975), *Faces of Hunger* (Blackwell, 1986), and *Constructions of Reason: Explorations of Kant's Practical Philosophy* (Cambridge University Press, 1989).

CHARLES PARSONS is Professor of Philosophy at Harvard University. He has made contributions to logic, philosophy of logic, and philosophy of mathematics. Some of his papers in the latter two areas as well as on Frege and Quine are included with two studies of Kant's philosophy of mathematics in his *Mathematics in Philosophy* (Cornell University Press, 1983).

EVA SCHAPER is Professor of Philosophy at the University of Glasgow. She has written on a wide range of issues in aesthetics and its history. She is the author of *Prelude to Aesthetics* (George Allen & Unwin, 1968) and *Studies in Kant's Aesthetics* (Edinburgh University Press, 1979), and has also edited *Pleasure, Preference, and Value: Studies in Philosophical Aesthetics* (Cambridge University Press, 1983).

J. B. SCHNEEWIND is Professor of Philosophy at the Johns Hopkins University. He has worked extensively in the history of both British and continental moral philosophy. His publications include *Backgrounds of English Victorian Literature* (Random House, 1970), *Sidgwick's Ethics and Victorian Moral Philosophy* (Oxford University Press, 1975) and *Moral Philosophy from Montaigne to Kant* (Cambridge University Press, 1990). He also edited *Mill: A Collection of Critical Essays* (Anchor Books, 1968).

THOMAS E. WARTENBERG is Associate Professor of Philosophy at Mount Holyoke College. He is the author of *The Forms of Power: From Domination to Transformation* (Temple University Press, 1990).

ALLEN W. WOOD is Professor of Philosophy at Cornell University. His books include *Kant's Moral Religion* (Cornell University Press, 1970), *Kant's Rational Theology* (Cornell University Press, 1978), *Karl Marx* (Routledge & Kegan Paul, 1981), and *Hegel's Ethical Thought* (Cambridge University Press, 1990). He also translated, with Gertrude S. Clarke, Kant's *Lectures on Philosophical Theology* (Cornell University Press, 1978). He is general co-editor of The Cambridge Edition of the Works of Immanuel Kant (forthcoming).

J. MICHAEL YOUNG is Professor of Philosophy at the University of Kansas. He has published articles on Kant's epistemology and philosophy of mathematics, and has translated Kant's *Lectures on Logic* for The Cambridge Edition of the Works of Immanuel Kant (forthcoming).

METHOD OF CITATION

Citations to Kant's texts are generally given parenthetically, although some additional references are included in the notes to the essays. Two forms of citation are employed. Citations to the *Critique of Pure Reason* are located in the customary manner by reference to the pagination of Kant's first ("A") and second ("B") editions. Where both A and B page numbers are provided, the passage cited is included in both editions; otherwise the passage occurs only in the one edition cited. In most instances, reference to the title of the *Critique of Pure Reason* is omitted. All other passages are located by volume and page number, given in arabic numerals separated by a colon, in the standard critical edition of Kant's works, *Kant's gesammelte Schriften*, edited by the Königlichen Preußischen (later Deutschen) Akademie der Wissenschaften (Berlin: Georg Reimer [later Walter de Gruyter], 1900–); in addition, if Kant divided the work in question into numbered sections, his section number precedes the volume and page of the *Akademie* edition. These references are preceded by a short title for the work in question unless the context obviates the need for that. Several authors have followed the *Akademie* edition citation with a citation of an English translation of the work, although, because most modern English translations include the *Akademie* edition pagination, it is not always necessary to do so. Each essay provides information about the translations used in that essay.

The following lists, in alphabetical order, the short titles of Kant's works (with date of original publication in parentheses) which are employed throughout the volume. Note 8 to Chapter 8 includes a list of additional abbreviations for Kant's lectures on metaphysics, which are cited only in that chapter.

Conflict	*Conflict of the Faculties* (1798)
Dissertation	*Dissertation on the Forms and Principles of the Sensible and Intelligible Worlds* (1770)
Dreams	*Dreams of a Spirit-Seer* (1766)

Enlightenment	*Answer to the Question: What Is Enlightenment?* (1784)
False Subtlety	*The False Subtlety of the Four Syllogistic Figures* (1762)
FI	*First Introduction to the Critique of Judgment* (posthumous)
Groundwork	*Groundwork of the Metaphysics of Morals* (1785)
Judgment	*Critique of Judgment* (1790)
Lectures	*Lectures on Philosophical Theology* (posthumous)
Living Forces	*Thoughts on the True Estimation of Living Forces* (1747)
Logic	*Immanuel Kant's Logic: A Handbook for Lectures* (edited by G. B. Jäsche) (1800)
Metaphysical Foundations	*Metaphysical Foundations of Natural Science* (1786)
Morals	*Metaphysics of Morals* (1797)
Negative Quantities	*Attempt to Introduce the Concept of Negative Quantities into Philosophy* (1763)
Nova dilucidatio	*A New Exposition of the First Principles of Metaphysical Cognition* (1755)
Observations	*Observations on the Feeling of the Beautiful and Sublime* (1764)
Only Possible Basis	*The Only Possible Basis for a Demonstration of the Existence of God* (1763)
Orientation	*What Does It Mean to Orient Oneself in Thought?* (1786)
Perpetual Peace	*Towards Perpetual Peace* (1795)
Physical Monadology	*The Joint Use of Metaphysics and Geometry in Natural Philosophy, the First Example of which Contains the Physical Monadology* (1756)
Practical Reason	*Critique of Practical Reason* (1788)
Prize Essay	*Investigation of the Clarity of the Principles of Natural Theology and Morals* (1764)
Progress	*What Is the Real Progress That Metaphysics Has Made in Germany since the Time of Leibniz and Wolff?* (edited by F. T. Rink) (1804)
Prolegomena	*Prolegomena to Any Future Metaphysics That Shall Come Forth as Scientific* (1783)
Pure Reason	*Critique of Pure Reason* (1781/1787)
R	*Reflexionen* (Kant's marginalia)
Regions	*On the Ultimate Ground of the Differentiation of Regions in Space* (1768)

Religion	*Religion within the Limits of Reason Alone* (1793)
Theodicy	*On the Failure of all Philosophical Attempts at a Theodicy* (1791)
Theory and Practice	*On the Old Saying: That May Be Right in Theory But Does Not Work in Practice* (1793)
Universal History	*Ideas towards a Universal History from a Cosmopolitan Point of View* (1784)
Universal Natural History	*Universal Natural History and Theory of the Heavens* (1755)

Introduction: The starry heavens and the moral law

In what may be his single most famous passage, the first sentence of which was even inscribed on his tombstone, Immanuel Kant concluded his *Critique of Practical Reason* (1788) thus:

Two things fill the mind with ever new and increasing admiration and awe, the more often and steadily we reflect upon them: *the starry heavens above me and the moral law within me.* I do not seek or conjecture either of them as if they were veiled obscurities or extravagances beyond the horizon of my vision; I see them before me and connect them immediately with the consciousness of my existence. The first starts at the place that I occupy in the external world of the senses, and extends the connection in which I stand into the limitless magnitude of worlds upon worlds, systems upon systems, as well as into the boundless times of their periodic motion, their beginning and continuation. The second begins with my invisible self, my personality, and displays to me a world that has true infinity, but which can only be detected through the understanding, and with which . . . I know myself to be in not, as in the first case, merely contingent, but universal and necessary connection. The first perspective of a countless multitude of worlds as it were annihilates my importance as an *animal creature*, which must give the matter out of which it has grown back to the planet (a mere speck in the cosmos) after it has been (one knows not how) furnished with life-force for a short time. The second, on the contrary, infinitely elevates my worth, as an *intelligence*, through my personality, in which the moral law reveals to me a life independent of animality and even of the entire world of the senses, at least so far as may be judged from the purposive determination of my existence through this law, which is not limited to the conditions and boundaries of this life but reaches into the infinite.   (*Practical Reason*, 5:161–2)

Like many philosophers from the time of René Descartes and Thomas Hobbes onward, Kant tried to explain both the possibility of the new scientific knowledge, which had culminated in the mathe-

1

matical worldview of Isaac Newton, and the possibility of human freedom. Unlike mechanists and empiricists from Hobbes to David Hume, Kant did not try to reduce human freedom to merely one more mechanism among those of a predictable nature, but, unlike rationalists from Descartes to Gottfried Wilhelm Leibniz and Christian Wolff, Kant was not willing to ground human freedom on an alleged rational insight into some objectively perfect world only confusedly grasped by the senses. Instead, Kant ultimately came to see that the validity of both the laws of the starry skies above as well as the moral law within had to be sought in the legislative power of human intellect itself. It took Kant a long time to transcend the solutions of his predecessors, and perhaps he never fully clarified the nature of his own solution. Nonetheless, the idea to which he was ultimately drawn was the recognition that we can be certain of the foundations of physical science because we ourselves impose at least the basic form of scientific laws upon the nature that is given to us by our senses, yet that precisely because we ourselves impose the basic laws of science upon our world we are also free to look at the world from a standpoint in which we are rational agents whose actions are chosen and not merely predicted in accordance with deterministic laws of (as we would now say) biology, psychology, or sociology. But in neither case, Kant ultimately came to recognize, is our freedom complete. Although we can legislate the basic forms of laws of nature, and indeed bring those laws ever closer to the details of nature through increasingly concrete conceptualizations, we can do so only asymptotically and must wait upon nature itself to fill in the last level of detail – which, because of the infinite divisibility and extendability of matter in space and time, nature will never quite do. And although we can autonomously legislate laws of reason for our actions, we must ultimately also look to nature, not only outside us but also within us, for cooperation in realizing the ends of those actions.

For Kant, then, his profound recognition of our legislative power in both science and morals, in both theoretical and practical reason, always had to be reconciled with an equally deep sense of the contingency of our success in both theory and practice. Even though he was hardly a conventionally religious thinker, Kant retained a sense of the limits of human powers of mind that is often missing from the wilder optimism of some of his rationalist predecessors as well as idealist successors. In spite of his sense of human limits, however, Kant radically and irreversibly transformed the nature of Western thought. After he wrote, no one could ever again think of either science or morality as a matter of the passive reception of entirely external truth or reality. In reflection upon the methods of science, as well as in many particular areas of science itself, the recognition of our own input into the world we claim to know has become inescapable. In the practical sphere, few can any longer take seriously the idea that moral reasoning consists in the discovery of external norms – for instance, objective perfections in the world or the will of God – as opposed to the construction for ourselves of the most rational way to conduct our lives both severally and jointly. Of course not even a Kant could have single-handedly transformed the self-conception of an entire culture; but at least at the philosophical level of the transformation of the Western conception of a human being from a mere spectator of the natural world and a mere subject in the moral world to an active agent in the creation of both, no one played a larger role than Immanuel Kant.

This extraordinary revolution was accomplished by a most unlikely individual. Unlike those of his predecessors such as Leibniz or John Locke who were men of means familiar with the corridors of power in the great European capitals and active in the political and religious struggles of their day, Kant was born into narrow straits in a small city virtually at the outermost limits of European civilization. Although Königsberg, where Kant was born into an artisan family in 1724, was a Hanseatic trading city with English connections as well as the administrative center of East Prussia, it was hardly London or Paris or Edinburgh or Amsterdam (the German city of Königsberg no longer exists, having been leveled in World War II and replaced with the Russian naval base Kaliningrad). Its university, which Kant entered at the age of sixteen after a preparatory education financially supported by the family's Pietist pastor and where he then spent most of his life, was barely more than a glorified high school, and even so Kant had to struggle in the poverty of a *Privatdozent* paid by the head (he quickly learned how to make his lectures very popular, however) until he was finally appointed to a proper chair in metaphysics at the age of forty-six. And after the decade of frequent publication which led to that appointment in 1770, Kant fell into a decade of silence which must have persuaded many that his long wait for a chair even at such a provincial university had been fully deserved. Yet from this dreary background there erupted a philosophical volcano the likes of which the world has rarely seen. Beginning in 1781, when he was already fifty-seven years old, Kant published a major work almost every year for more than a decade and a half. Foremost, of course, are his three great *Critiques,* the *Critique of Pure Reason* (1781, substantially revised in 1787), offering a new foundation for human knowledge and demolishing virtually all of traditional metaphysics; the *Critique of Practical Reason* (1788), inextricably linking human freedom to the moral law while attempting to reconstruct the most cherished ideas of traditional metaphysical belief on a practical rather than theoretical foundation; and the *Critique of Judgment* (1790), ostensibly bringing the seemingly disparate topics of aesthetic and teleological judgment into Kant's system but also struggling to refine and even substantially revise some of Kant's most basic conceptions about theoretical and practical reason and the relation between them. But these works were accompanied by a flood of others: In the *Prolegomena to Any Future Metaphysics That Shall Come Forth as Scientific* of 1783, Kant attempted to make the ideas of the first *Critique* accessible to a broader public while defending them from the first onslaught of criticism. He wrote several essays on the nature of enlightenment and the role of reason in history, including *Ideas towards a Universal History* and *What Is Enlightenment?* in 1784 and the *Conjectural Beginning of Human History* and *What Does it Mean to Orient Oneself in Thought?* of 1786. In the *Groundwork of the Metaphysics of Morals* of 1785, he made his boldest brief for the purity of the moral law and the certainty of human freedom. In the *Metaphysical Foundations of Natural Science* of 1786, he attempted to reconstruct Newtonian physics on the *a priori* basis offered by the principles of human knowledge demonstrated in the *Critique of Pure Reason.* In *Religion within the Limits of Reason Alone* of 1793 and *Conflict of the Faculties* of 1798, Kant argued firmly for the primacy of philosophy over religion in both its theoretical and institutional forms. And finally, in 1797, in the work at which he had been aiming most of his life, the *Metaphysics of Morals,* divided into a *Theory of Right* or political philosophy and *Theory of Virtue* or normative ethics, Kant demonstrated that his formal principle of morality justifies the use of coercion in the state yet simultaneously places strict limits on the ends the state can justifiably pursue by coercive means. He also demonstrated that the same principle implies a detailed series of ethical duties to ourselves and others that go beyond the limits of positive legislation in such a state. Even after all this work had been done, Kant continued to work at the foundations of scientific theory, trying to bring the basic principles of the *Metaphysical Foundations of Natural Science* into closer contact with physical reality, as well as with the latest advances in the sciences of chemistry as well as physics. The book that was to result from this work, however, remained incomplete before the wane of his powers and his death a few weeks short of his eightieth birthday in 1804. (The surviving sketches of this work have been known as the *Opus postumum* since their publication early in this century.) Any one of these works – produced in spite of a daily load of three or four hours lecturing on subjects like anthropology and geography as well as metaphysics, ethics, and rational theology – would have made Kant a figure of note in the history of modern philosophy; together, they make him the center of that history.

As the whole of the book that follows can serve as only an introduction to the great range of Kant's work, it would certainly be hopeless to attempt to introduce the reader to all of it here. What follows will be only the briefest of sketches of the evolution of Kant's thought to help the reader situate what is offered in the essays of this collection.

Kant first came to attention with several scientific works: on graduation from the university in 1747 he published *Thoughts on the True Estimation of Living Forces*, a piece on the debate between Leibnizians and Cartesians on the proper measure of forces; and at the time of his return to the university as a *Privatdozent* in 1755, after eight years as a household tutor for several East Prussian landowners, he published two more scientific works, the *Universal Natural History and Theory of the Heavens*, in which he showed how a system of heavenly bodies could have arisen out of an unformed nebula by purely mechanical means (what later became known as the Kant–Laplace cosmology), as well as a less important Latin dissertation on fire. In that same year he also published his first philosophical work, another Latin treatise, the *Principiorum primorum cognitionis metaphysicae nova dilucidatio* or *New Exposition of the*

First Principles of Metaphysical Knowledge. This treatise, only thirty pages in length, is pregnant with Kant's philosophical future, for in it Kant revealed what was to become his lifelong preoccupation with the fundamental principles of natural science on the one hand and the problem of human freedom on the other. The positions for which the then thirty-one-year-old philosopher argued were far from his mature positions, but of great significance nonetheless. On the theoretical side, Kant accepted the basic rationalist enterprise of deriving the principle of sufficient reason from purely logical considerations (although he departed from the details of the proofs offered by Wolff and his follower Alexander Gottlieb Baumgarten, on whose textbooks of metaphysics and ethics Kant was to lecture for his entire career), but he also tried to show that this principle led to results precisely the opposite of those Leibniz and his followers had drawn from it. In particular, manifesting his future concern with the justification of the concept and principle of causation long before he had become familiar with Hume, Kant argued that the principle of sufficient reason implied rather than excluded real causation and interaction among substances, and that it even gave rise to a refutation of idealism. In this work Kant also introduced the first version of his critique of the ontological argument, that paradigmatic rationalist attempt to move directly from the structure of concepts to the structure of reality itself. On the practical side, Kant took the side of Leibnizian compatibilism between free will and determinism rather than the radical incompatibilism of the anti-Wolffian Pietist philosopher Christian August Crusius. (Kant's mature work on freedom of the will consists of a perhaps never quite completed attempt to reconcile the Leibnizian insight that we can only be responsible for actions produced in accordance with a law with the Crusian insight that responsibility requires a radical freedom of choice not compatible with the thoroughgoing predictability of human action.) Kant's major works of the 1750s were completed with another Latin scientific treatise, the *Physical Monadology,* in which he introduced the conception of attractive and repulsive forces that was to be essential to his attempts to provide a foundation for physical theory for the remainder of his life.

The philosophical work of the 1750s pointed Kant in the direction of a number of conclusions he subsequently wanted to establish. It turned out, however, that this work could not serve as a foundation for the later version of those conclusions, because Kant came to reject completely the rationalist methodology on which that work was based. Much of the 1760s was devoted to the demolition of rationalism, particularly of its two assumptions that all philosophical principles could be discovered by essentially logical methods alone and that the principles thus arrived at automatically give us insight into the ontology of objective reality. Kant's search for an alternative philosophical method in this decade was less successful than his demolition of all previous methods, however. In a work published in 1763, *The Only Possible Basis for a Demonstration of the Existence of God*, Kant deepened the critique of the ontological argument already suggested in 1755. He accompanied that critique with an attack upon the two other forms of proof of the existence of God that had still enjoyed currency in eighteenth-century debates, the argument from the existence of a contingent creation to some necessary cause of it (what he called the "cosmological" argument) and the argument from design, the argument that the orderly form of the world we observe around us can be explained only by the activity of an intelligent designer (what he called the argument from "physicotheology"). Yet Kant still argued that there was an *a priori* proof for the existence of God available, which had been overlooked by his predecessors: God could be demonstrated as the necessary ground of even the mere possibility of existence. Kant's confidence in this argument turned out to be a last gasp of rationalism. Later that same year, in his *Attempt to Introduce the Concept of Negative Quantities into Philosophy*, Kant introduced a fundamental distinction between *logical* and *real* opposition – a distinction of the kind that exists between a proposition and its negation on the one hand, and two physical forces trying to push a single object in opposite directions on the other. He intimated not only that this could be extended into a general distinction between logical and real relations, but also that all causal and existential relations would have to be understood as real rather than logical relations, so could never be demonstrated by any purely logical means alone. But this result, reminiscent of Hume but more likely to have been influenced by Crusius at this point in time, left room for the conclusion that philosophy could have no distinctive nonanalytical yet not merely empirical methodology at all, a danger evident in Kant's essay *On the Clarity of the Principles of Natural Theology and Ethics* published the following year (1764). Here Kant argued that, contrary to the dream of all rationalist philosophers since Descartes, philosophy could not use the same method as mathematics. Mathematics could begin with definitions and then prove indubitable results by constructing objects in accordance with those definitions and performing various operations upon them; philosophy, however, could never begin with definitions but only with "certain primary fundamental judgments" the analysis of which could lead to definitions as its conclusion, not its commencement. The origin and source of the certainty of these fundamental judgments remained obscure. In language reminiscent of both Crusius as well as British moral sense philosophers such as Francis Hutcheson (both of whom were influential for Kant at this time), he could say only that metaphysics had to begin with "certain inner experience, that is, by means of an immediate evident consciousness" that could give reliable information about the nature of a reality without immediately yielding "the whole essence of the thing" (2:286). At this point, it seems fair to say, Kant had hardly replaced the rejected method of the rationalists with a concrete proposal of his own for grounding first principles of either theoretical or practical reasoning.

This embarrassment remained evident in Kant's peculiar *Dreams of a Spirit-Seer* of 1766, which engaged in a lengthy examination of the spiritualist fantasies of the Swedish mystic Emanuel Swedenborg for the polemical purpose of showing that rationalist arguments for the simplicity, immateriality, and immortality of the soul offered by such philosophers as Wolff and Baumgarten were not any better grounded in empirical evidence. Like the essay *Negative Quantities*, the *Dreams of a Spirit-Seer* then concluded with the negative result that only empirical claims about "relations of cause and effect, substance, and action" could serve as starting points for philosophy, "but that when one finally comes to fundamental relations, then the business of philosophy is at an end, and we can never understand through reason how something can be a cause or have a force, but these relations must merely be derived from experience" (2:370). However, Kant completed this work with one point that was to remain unchallenged in all his subsequent thought about morality. All the metaphysical attempts to prove the immortality of the soul have been motivated by the need to allow for the reward of virtuous deeds performed in ordinary life, he argued, but are entirely unnecessary because only a morality that can motivate us to perform our duty without either promise of reward or fear of punishment is truly virtuous. Kant asked,

Is it good to be virtuous only because there is another world, or are actions rather not praised because they are good and virtuous in themselves? Does not the heart of man contain immediate moral precepts, and must one in order to motivate his disposition in accordance with all of these here always set the machinery of another world to work? Can one properly be called upright and virtuous who would gladly yield to his favorite vices if only he were not terrified of a future punishment, and would one not rather say that he avoids the expression of evil but nourishes a vicious disposition in his soul, that he loves the advantage of the simulation of virtuous action but hates virtue itself?

Obviously these questions needed no answer; so Kant could conclude that it is "more appropriate for human nature and the purity of morals to ground the expectation of a future world on the sensations of a well-disposed soul than to ground its good behavior on the hope of another world" (2:372–3). This insistence that virtue must move us by itself and that faith in religious doctrines of immortality and providence must not be the basis for morality but only a consequence of it were to reverberate in Kant's work for the rest of his life.

The *Dreams of a Spirit-Seer* thus reduced the need for a new method for metaphysics by freeing morality of the need for a positive metaphysical foundation altogether, although Kant was subsequently to recognize that morality requires at least a metaphysical proof that freedom is not impossible and that at least a "groundwork" for the metaphysics of morality was required. And the task of providing certain foundations for the Newtonian worldview without appealing to the method of mathematics still remained. Kant took a first step toward providing the latter if not the former in his next two works, an essay *On the Primary Ground of the Differentiation of Regions in Space* in 1768 and the *Dissertation on the Forms and Principles of the Sensible and Intelligible Worlds*, which he defended on his inauguration, at long last, as Professor of Metaphysics in 1770. In the first of these, Kant argued that the fact that two objects such as right- and left-handed gloves or screws could be described by identical conceptual relations but nevertheless be incongruent demonstrated that their orientation toward the axes of an

absolute space was an irreducible fact about them, and thus proved
the validity of the Newtonian conception of absolute space rather
than the Leibnizian reduction of space to more primary and independent properties of substances. But the metaphysical possibility as
well as the epistemology of Newtonian absolute space remained a
mystery until Kant solved it in the inaugural dissertation by arguing
that the human mind possesses two fundamentally distinct capacities of sensibility and intellect, not the single faculty for more or less
clear and distinct thought that Leibniz and Wolff and all their followers had supposed, and that the existence of a unique and absolute
space – and time – in which all the objects of our experience can be
ordered reflects the inherent form of our capacity for sensible experience itself. Thus Kant took the fateful first step of arguing that the
possibility and indeed the certainty of the spatiotemporal framework of Newtonian physics could be secured only by recognizing it
to be the form of our own experience, even though this meant that
the certainty of the foundations of Newtonian science could be pur-
chased only by confining them to objects as we experience them
through the senses – "appearances" or "phenomena" – rather than
those objects as they might be in themselves and known to be by a
pure intellect – "noumena." Thus Kant argued that absolute space is
"not some adumbration or schema of the object, but only a certain
law implanted in the mind by which it coordinates for itself the
sensa that arise from the presence of the object" (§4, 2:393). As for
the further principles of the scientific worldview as well as the metaphysics of morality, however, the *Dissertation* did not merely fail to
demonstrate any progress, but in some ways even regressed from the
critical position of the 1760s. A metaphysical insight that all of the
substances of the world constitute a single whole could be grounded,
Kant claimed, in intellectual insight into their dependence on a
common extramundane cause (God, of course). More purely in-
tramundane or immanent foundations for science, such as the maxims that *"All things in the universe take place in accordance with
the order of nature," "Principles are not to be multiplied beyond
what is absolutely necessary,"* and *"No matter at all comes into
being or passes away,"* he could only introduce as mere *"principles
of convenience"* (§30, 2:419). Morality, finally, Kant was suddenly
prepared to treat as a matter requiring metaphysical, indeed "dog-

matic" insight into "some exemplar only to be conceived by the pure intellect and which is a common measure for all other things insofar as they are realities." Kant continued:

> This exemplar is NOUMENAL PERFECTION. This perfection is what it is either in a theoretic sense or in a practical sense. In the first sense it is the highest being, GOD, in the second sense it is MORAL PERFECTION. So *moral philosophy*, in as much as it supplies the first *principles of critical judgment*, is cognized only by the pure intellect and itself belongs to pure philosophy. And the man who reduced its criteria to the sense of pleasure or pain, Epicurus, is very rightly blamed. . . .   (§9, 2:396)

Kant was certainly to retain the idea that morality could not be grounded in empirical facts about what is pleasurable and what is painful, and that its principle must come from pure reason instead; but any sense that recognition of such a principle required metaphysical cognition of a reality lying beyond ourselves, as knowledge of God does, was ultimately to be banished from his thought. This meant that the inaugural dissertation had left entirely untouched all the work of grounding foundational principles for scientific knowledge beyond its abstract spatiotemporal framework, as well as the task of explaining both the nature of moral knowledge and the possibility of freedom in spite of the scientific worldview.

Kant struggled with these unresolved difficulties for a decade and then adopted the extraordinary objective of eliminating the lingering noumenal metaphysics of the inaugural dissertation from the foundations of both science and morality and showing how all of the fundamental principles of both science and morality, like the form of space and time, are products of our own thought alone, although we cannot just ruthlessly impose these principles upon the data of our senses but must engage in a never-ending task of accommodating them to the particularity of experience. It would be misleading to suppose, however, that Kant had clearly formulated the idea of accomplishing this objective in his three great *Critiques* before commencing their composition; in fact, the evidence strongly suggests that Kant had no idea that a *Critique of Practical Reason* would be required when he first finished the *Critique of Pure Reason*, and still had no idea that a *Critique of Judgment* would be needed even when the *Critique of Practical Reason* had been finished. Each of the latter two *Critiques* revises as well as extends the insights of its predecessors. Indeed, for all its appearance of systematicity, Kant's thought was in a state of constant evolution throughout his life.

The evolution of Kant's mature thought obviously begins with the *Critique of Pure Reason* as first published in 1781, which turned out not to be the complete foundation for both science and morality that Kant originally intended it to be, but which certainly remained the basis for all that followed. The agenda for this work is enormous but can be brought under the two headings suggested by our opening quote. On the one hand, Kant aims to provide a general foundation for the laws of science, a metaphysics of experience that will generalize the approach taken to space and time alone in the *Dissertation* by showing that there are also concepts of the understanding and principles of judgment, including general forms of the laws of the conservation of matter, universal causation, and universal interaction, which can be shown to be certain by their *a priori* origin in the structure of human thought itself, although the cost of this certainty is that we must also recognize "that our representation of things, as they are given to us, does not conform to these things as they are in themselves, but rather that these objects, as appearances, conform to our manner of representation" (B xx). On the other hand, the very fact that the universal validity of the foundational principles of the scientific worldview, including that of universal causation, can be proved only for the appearances of things means that we can at least coherently consider the possibility that things as they are in themselves may not be governed by these laws, indeed may be governed by other laws; in particular, we can coherently consider that at the deepest level we ourselves are free agents bound only by the laws of morality and not by the deterministic laws of nature. Kant sums up this complex result thus:

On a hasty overview of this work one will believe himself to perceive that its use is only *negative,* namely that we can never dare to exceed the bounds of experience with speculative reason, and that is indeed its first use. But this then becomes *positive* if one becomes aware that the principles with which speculative reason dares to exceed its bounds would not in fact have the inevitable result of *extending* but, more closely considered, that of *restricting* our use of reason, in that they would really extend the bounds of sensibility, to which they actually belong, to everything, and so threaten to obstruct the pure (practical) use of reason. Thus a critique, which limits the former, is so far to be sure *negative,* but, insofar as it also removes a hindrance that threatens to restrict or even destroy the latter use of reason, is in fact of *positive* and very important use, as soon as one is convinced that it yields an entirely necessary practical use of pure reason (the moral use), in which it is unavoidably extended beyond the limits of sensibility, but thereby requires no help from speculative reason, but must nevertheless be secured from its opposition in order not to land in contradiction with itself.

(B xxiv–xxv)

Or as Kant more succinctly but also more misleadingly puts it, "I must therefore suspend *knowledge* in order to make room for *belief,*" or, as it is often translated, *"faith"* (B xxx). This is misleading if it is taken to mean that Kant intends to argue that knowledge must be limited in order to allow us some nonrational basis for belief about important matters of morality. Rather, what Kant means is that the limitation of the foundational principles of the scientific worldview to the way things appear to us is necessary not only in order to explain its own certainty but also in order to allow us to conceive of ourselves as rational agents who are not constrained by the deterministic grip of nature but can freely govern ourselves by the moral law as practical reason (although certainly not all forms of religious faith) requires.

The steps that Kant goes through in order to secure this result are intricate, and some of them will be treated in much more detail in what follows. The barest sketch will have to suffice here. Kant begins in the "Transcendental Aesthetic," or theory of sensibility, by reiterating the argument of 1770 that all of our particular experiences of objects, or empirical intuitions, necessarily come to us in spatiotemporal form, and also that we have *a priori* insight into the uniqueness and infinitude of space and time, both of which can be explained only on the supposition that space and time are the pure forms of our intuition of all objects originating in the structure of our own sensibility, not anything derived from the independent properties of objects as they are in themselves. In the *Prolegomena* of 1783 and second edition of the *Critique* of 1787, Kant supplements this with a specific argument that the propositions of mathematics, especially geometry, are nontautologous and informative, or synthetic rather than analytic, yet are known *a priori,* which can also be explained only on the supposition that they describe the structure of subjective forms of intuition rather than independent properties of objects (see especially A 47–8 / B 64–5).

In the "Transcendental Analytic," or theory of understanding, Kant extends this argument by showing that in addition to *a priori* forms of intuition there are also *a priori* concepts of the pure understanding, or categories, as well as *a priori* principles of judgment that are necessary conditions for our own thought of objects rather than principles derived from any particular experience of those objects. Kant's argument for this result proceeds through several stages. First, he argues that the fact that our knowledge of objects always takes the form of *judgment* and that judgment has certain inherent forms, discovered by logic, implies that there must be certain basic correlative concepts necessary for thinking of the *objects* of those judgments (the "metaphysical deduction"). Next, he tries to argue that our very certainty of the numerical identity of our self throughout all our different experiences implies that we must connect those experiences according to rules furnished by the understanding itself, which are none other than the same categories required by the logical forms of judgment (the "transcendental deduction"). Finally, and most convincingly, he tries to show in detail that the ability to make objective judgments about objects given in space and time (which are missing from most of the transcendental deduction) requires that we bring them under concepts of extensive and intensive magnitude and under principles of conservation, causation, and interaction (the "system of principles," especially the "analogies of experience"). And indeed, Kant finally argues, the ability to make determinate temporal sense of our own experiences considered even as merely subjective states requires that we see them as caused by such a law-governed realm of external objects (the "refutation of idealism"). Kant describes the underlying assumption of this extended argument thus:

However exaggerated, however absurd it may sound to say that the understanding is itself the source of the laws of nature, thus of the formal unity of nature, such an assertion is nevertheless right and appropriate to the object, namely experience. To be sure, empirical laws as such can by no means derive their origin from pure understanding, just as little as the immeasurable multiplicity of appearances can be adequately comprehended from the pure form of sensible intuition. But all empirical laws are only particular determinations of the pure laws of understanding, under which and in accor-

dance with the norm of which they are first possible and the appearances
assume a lawful form, just as all appearances, in spite of the diversity of
their empirical form, must nevertheless always be in accord with the conditions of the pure form of sensibility.   (A 127–8)

In the longest part of the work, the "Transcendental Dialectic,"
Kant then argues that most of the doctrines of traditional metaphysics are fallaciously derived by attempting to use concepts of the understanding without corresponding evidence from sensibility. These are
fallacies, he adds, into which we do not just happen to fall but to
which we are pushed by reason's natural inclination to discover a
kind of completeness in thought that the indefinitely extendable
bounds of space and time can never yield. Thus we mistake the
logical simplicity of the thought of the self for knowledge of a simple, immaterial, and immortal soul (the "paralogisms of pure reason"), and we think that the mere idea of a ground of all possibility
(the "ideal of pure reason") is equivalent to knowledge of the necessary existence of such a ground. (Kant now brings his critique of the
ontological argument to bear on the one possible basis for a demonstration of the existence of God that he had spared in his work of
that title of 1763.) Little can be salvaged from these misguided metaphysical doctrines, but the case is somewhat different with the metaphysical paradoxes that Kant describes under the title of "antinomies of pure reason." Operating without any notice of the need for
evidence from the senses and thus of the limits of sensibility, pure
reason manages to convince itself both that the world must be finite
in space and time and that it must also be infinitely extended in both
dimensions, that the division of substances must yield smallest possible particles yet that it cannot, that there must be a causality of
freedom in addition to the mechanism of nature yet that there can
be no such thing, and finally that there must be a necessary being at
the ground of the series of contingent existences yet again that there
cannot be so. The first two paradoxes may simply be set aside by
recognizing that space and time are, again, nothing but the forms of
our own intuitions, and that things as they are in themselves, which
reason takes itself to know, are thus neither spatially nor temporally
finite nor infinite. But the case is different with the last two antinomies. Here, no longer dealing with quantitative concepts that are
necessarily linked to the structure of sensibility, Kant argues that

while we can conceive of the empirical or phenomenal world only as a realm of contingent existences entirely governed by causal laws of nature, we can at least coherently consider that the realm of things in themselves lying behind the appearances of the empirical world not only contains a necessary being but, more important, contains free and not merely determined actions. Thus, Kant claims, the critique of traditional metaphysics at least leaves open the *possibility* of freedom. Then he can conclude:

We require the principle of the causality of appearances among themselves in order to seek and to be able to provide natural conditions for natural occurrences, i.e., causes in appearance. If this is conceded and is not weakened through any exception, then the understanding, which in its empirical employment sees in all events nothing but nature and is justified in so doing, has everything that it can require, and physical explanations can proceed unhindered on their way. Now it does not do the least violence to this, if one assumes, even if it is otherwise only imagined, that among natural causes there are also some that have a faculty that is intelligible only in that their determination to action never rests on empirical conditions, but on mere grounds of reason, though in such a way that the *action in the appearance* from this cause is in accord with all the laws of empirical causality.   (A 545 / B 573)

Kant concludes, therefore, that we can at least consistently conceive of events that fit into the seamless web of natural causality yet are also the products of the free exercise of the rational agency of natural agents considered as they are in themselves. In thinking of ourselves as moral agents, we can think of ourselves in precisely this twofold way.

It is not clear whether Kant thought it would be necessary to say more about freedom when he finished the *Critique of Pure Reason;* but he shortly realized that it was. A further proof, indeed a theoretical proof, that freedom is not just possible but actual is one of the two main items on the agenda of the *Groundwork of the Metaphysics of Morals* of 1785, along with a clear formulation of the fundamental law of morality itself and a sketch of how such a principle would give rise to the specific set of duties that Kant had always intended to describe in a metaphysics of morals. Kant argued that the concepts of good will and duty, which could be derived from ordinary consciousness, and the concept of a categorical imperative, which could be derived from popular moral philosophy, but also his own conception of humanity as an end in itself whose free agency must always be preserved and when possible enhanced, all give rise to the fundamental moral principle that one should act only on maxims or policies of action that could be made into a universal law or assented to, made into an end of their own, by all agents who might be affected by the action. Such a principle Kant characterizes as the law of pure practical reason, reflecting the requirements that are imposed on actions not from any external source but from the nature of reason itself. But he also argued that in order to know that we are actually bound by such a moral principle, we must know that we really are rational agents capable of freely acting in accordance with the principle of pure reason regardless of what might be predicted on the basis of our passions and inclinations, indeed our entire prior history and psychology. Kant thus now felt compelled to prove that human freedom is not just possible but actual. Although he initially suggests that the very idea of ourselves as agents implies that we conceive of ourselves as acting under rules of our own choice, he attempts to go beyond this in order to deliver a metaphysical proof of the actuality of freedom. He argues that in ourselves as well as all other things we must distinguish between appearance and reality. He then equates this distinction with one between that which is passive and that which is active in ourselves, which he in turn equates with the distinction between sensation and reason. Thus Kant infers that we must assign to ourselves a faculty of reason rooted in our nature as things in themselves and thus free to act without constraint by the causal laws governing mere appearance. Kant concludes:

A rational being must therefore regard itself as an *intelligence* (therefore not from the side of its lower powers) as belonging to the world of understanding, not of sense; thus it has two standpoints from which it can consider itself and know the laws of the use of its powers, thus of all of its actions, *first*, insofar as it belongs to the world of senses, under natural laws (heteronomy), *second*, as belonging to the intelligible world, under laws which, independent from nature, are not empirical but grounded in reason alone.   (4:452)

Unfortunately, in spite of his attempt to avoid such a problem, Kant's argument is circular. It derives our possession of a spontaneous and efficacious faculty of reason from our membership in the world of things in themselves precisely by construing that world as an *intelligible* world – that is to say, nothing less than a world conceived to be essentially rational and understood by reason itself. In other words, Kant's argument – not for the content but for the actuality and efficacy of pure practical reason – violates one of the most fundamental strictures of his own *Critique of Pure Reason*. It depends on interpreting our ultimate reality not as noumenon in a merely *"negative* sense" but as noumenon in a *"positive* sense," that is, not just something that is *not* known through sensibility but something that *is* known through pure reason (B 307).

Kant never doubted that he had correctly formulated the content of pure practical reason through the requirement of the universal acceptability of the maxims of intended actions, but he quickly recognized the inadequacy of the *Groundwork*'s proof that we actually have a pure practical reason. He thus radically revised his approach to the problem of freedom in the *Critique of Practical Reason*, published only three years later in 1788. Kant does not call this work a critique of *pure* practical reason like the earlier critique of pure theoretical reason, because whereas the point of the former work was to show that theoretical reason oversteps its bounds when it tries to do without application to empirical data, in the case of practical reason the point is precisely to show that it is *not* limited to application to empirically given inclinations and intentions but has a pure principle of its own. Kant now surrenders the objective of giving a theoretical proof of the efficacy of pure practical reason, however. While both the *Groundwork* and the new *Critique* agree that a will bound by the moral law must be a free will and that only a free will can be bound by the moral law, what has come to be known as his "reciprocity thesis" (5:28–9), Kant's strategy is now not to prove that we are bound by the moral law by offering a theoretical proof that we possess a free will but rather simply to argue that we must possess a free will because of our indubitable recognition that we are in fact bound by the moral law. "The thing is strange enough and has no parallel in the entire remainder of practical reason," Kant admits; nevertheless, he insists:

The *a priori* thought of a possible universal law-giving . . . without borrowing anything from experience or any external will, is given as an unconditioned law. . . . One can call the consciousness of this fundamental law a fact of reason, since one cannot speciously derive it from any antecedent data of reason, e.g., the consciousness of freedom (since this is not antecedently given to us), rather since it presses itself upon us as a synthetic *a priori* proposition, which is not grounded in any intuition, whether pure or empirical, although it would be analytic if one presupposed the freedom of the will. . . . But in order to regard this law as *given* without misinterpretation one must well note that it is not an empirical fact but the sole fact of pure reason. . . .   (5:31)

Theoretical philosophy can prove the possibility of freedom of the will, Kant continues to believe, but not its actuality; this can follow only from our firm consciousness – our conscience, one might say – of being bound by the moral law itself. If we have a pure practical reason, there is no problem explaining how it binds us, precisely because the law that binds us comes from within ourselves and not from anywhere else, not from any other will, not the will of a Hobbesian sovereign nor even from the will of God; but our proof that we have such a pure practical reason is precisely our recognition that we bind ourselves by its law.

Although the proof of the actuality of freedom can only appeal to our conviction of our obligation under the moral law, Kant has no hesitation about the power of our freedom. Kant is more convinced than ever that the scope of our freedom is unlimited, that no matter what might seem to be predicted by our prior history we always retain the freedom to make the morally correct choice, even if the very history of our empirical character itself must be revised in order to make our freely chosen action compatible with natural law:

The same subject, who is also conscious of himself as thing in himself, considers his own existence, *so far as it does not stand under conditions of time,* as itself determinable only through laws that he gives himself through reason, and in this his existence nothing is antecedent to his determination of his will, but every action and every determination of his existence changing in accord with his inner sense, even the entire course of his existence as a sensible being is never to be regarded in his consciousness of his intelligible existence as anything but the consequence and never the determining ground of his causality as *noumenon.*   (5:97–8).

The *Critique of Practical Reason* also includes Kant's attempt to reconstruct two of the most cherished doctrines of traditional metaphysics, the existence of God and the immortality of the soul. He argues that morality enjoins on us not just the effort to be motivated by duty alone but also the end of attaining happiness in proportion to our virtue. Moral motivation alone may be the sole unconditioned good, but it is not the complete or highest good until happiness in proportion to our worthiness to be happy through our virtue is added to it. But we have no reason to believe that we can approach purity of will in our terrestrial life spans alone, or that our virtue will be accompanied with proportionate happiness by natural mechanisms alone. We must thus postulate, although always as a matter of practical presupposition and never as a theoretical doctrine, that our souls can reach purity in immortality and that there is a God to redress the natural disproportion between virtue and happiness. But Kant always insisted that these practical postulates could never enter into our motivation to be moral, and that they would undermine the purity of that motivation if they did; they rather flesh out the conditions presupposed by the rationality of moral action and so allow us to act on that pure motivation without threat of self-contradiction.

Kant remained content with this doctrine for the remainder of his life, but the problem of freedom continued to gnaw at him; and as he refined his solution to the problem of freedom he refined his theory of the foundations of science as well. The evidence for this further struggle is found in his last great critique, the *Critique of Judgment* of 1790. This work ostensibly deals with the rational foundations of two forms of judgment not considered in Kant's previous work, aesthetic judgments of taste about natural or artistic beauty and sublimity and teleological judgments about the role of purpose in natural organisms and systems; but Kant's reflections on these two species of what he calls reflective judgment touch on larger issues as well.

Kant begins the work with a reflection upon the role of the ideal of systematicity in the attempt to move from the abstract level of the categories to concrete knowledge of empirical laws of nature. Whereas the *Critique of Pure Reason* had assigned the search for systematicity to the faculty of reason, suggesting that it is required for the sake of completeness but has nothing to do with the truth of empirical laws themselves, the *Critique of Judgment* assigns it to the faculty of reflective judgment, suggesting that we can never get from the categories to particular empirical laws except by trying to place individual hypotheses in the context of a system of such laws. Because such a system is always an ideal that is never actually completed, however, this implies that the search for empirical law is necessarily open-ended, that we can approach but never actually reach certainty about any individual law of nature as well as completeness in the whole system of such laws. This was a perspective that Kant attempted to explore further in his *Opus postumum*, which fittingly itself remained incomplete.

Kant then introduces the more specific subjects of aesthetic and teleological judgment with the claim that there is a "great abyss" between the concepts of nature and of freedom that must yet be bridged (5:195). Since in the *Critique of Practical Reason* he had argued that the domination of reason over the world of sense must be complete, it is not immediately apparent what gulf Kant has in mind, but his meaning gradually emerges. In the first half of the work, the *Critique of Aesthetic Judgment,* Kant is concerned to show that the existence and power of freedom are not just accessible to philosophical theory but can be made palpable to us as embodied and therefore feeling human beings as well. His argument in the case of the experience of the sublime is obvious. Vast and powerful objects in nature exceed the grasp of our imagination and understanding, but our indifference to their threats of intellectual and even physical injury is an exhilarating revelation of the power and primacy of practical reason within ourselves. Kant's argument about beauty is more complex, however. The experience of beauty is initially characterized as one in which sensibility or imagination and understanding reach a state of harmony without the constraint of any concept, moral concepts of the good included. But then it turns out that in virtue of its very freedom from constraint by such concepts the experience of beauty can serve as a symbol of our freedom in morality itself and make this freedom palpable to us. In addition, although as it were our first layer of pleasure in natural beauty is free of any antecedent interests, the very fact that nature offers us beauty without intervention of our own is some evidence that it is hospitable to our own interests, those of morality included, and we take additional pleasure in the realization of this fact. Here Kant does not treat us as simply dominating nature by our reason, but rather more contingently finding that our reason allows us to be at home in nature.

Kant's argument about teleological judgment is even more complicated, and, although the force of Kant's treatment of organisms has certainly been undercut by the success of the Darwinian theory of evolution, the *Critique of Teleological Judgment* remains profoundly revealing of Kant's philosophical sensibility. Kant argues that organisms require us to see the parts as the cause of the whole but also the whole as the cause of its parts. The latter requirement violates the unidirectional nature of our conception of mechanical causation – we cannot conceive how a whole that comes into being only gradually from its parts can nevertheless be the cause of the properties of those parts (here is where the theory of natural selection removes the difficulty). And so, Kant argues, we can explain the relation only by supposing that the nature of the parts is determined by an antecedent *conception* of the whole employed by a designer of the organism, although we can never have theoretical evidence of the existence of such an intelligence. Next Kant argues that we cannot suppose an intelligent designer to have acted without a *purpose* as well as a *plan*, but that the only kind of nonarbitrary purpose that we can introduce into natural systems and indeed into nature as a system as a whole is something that is an end in itself – which can be nothing other than human freedom, the sole source of intrinsic and unconditioned value. Besides all of humankind's merely natural ends, desires, and conceptions of happiness that are of no more value than any other creature's and to which nature is not in any case particularly hospitable, "there remains as that which in respect to nature can be the final purpose that lies beyond it and in which its ultimate purpose can be seen only [mankind's] formal, subjective condition, namely [our] capacity to set our own ends in general" (§83, 5:431). Mankind is "the only natural being in whom a super-sensible faculty (of *freedom*) can be known," and only as "the subject of morality" can humanity constitute a "final purpose to which the whole of nature is teleologically subordinated" (§84, 5:435–6). Again, Kant subtly revises his earlier point of view: Human freedom is not to be seen just as a force entirely external to nature, but as the ultimate aim of nature itself.

Kant is still careful to insist that this is not a perspective that can be justified by theoretical or scientific reasoning, but rather a point of view that is at least compatible with scientific reasoning and recommended for its value to practical reason. But his expression of this caution in the *Critique of Judgment* also suggests a subtle shift in his view of the status of scientific law itself. In his first two critiques, Kant had argued that the application of the fundamental principles of theoretical knowledge and thus the foundations of science to the world of experience was without exception, indeed as he called it "constitutive" of the phenomenal realm, and that there could be room for a conception of human freedom only because we could also regard ourselves as things in themselves whose nature is not determined by the laws of appearance. Now, however, Kant suggests another view, namely the idea that *both* the causal laws of nature *and* the laws of reason that guide our freely chosen actions are "regulative principles" that we bring to nature. He argues that an antinomy can be avoided only by supposing that the "maxim of reflection" that "All generation of material things and their forms must be estimated as possible according to merely mechanical laws" and the maxim that "Some products of material nature cannot be estimated as possible according to merely mechanical laws," that they instead require "an entirely different law of causality, namely that of final causes" are both "regulative principles for the investigation" of nature (§70, 5:387). He thus suggests that the deterministic perspective of the mechanical worldview is not something that we can simply impose on nature, but a perspective that we bring to bear on it just as we do the perspective of freedom itself. The latter perspective Kant now also explicitly describes as a regulative ideal:

Although an intelligible world, in which everything would be actual solely because it is (as something good) possible, and even freedom itself as the formal condition of such a world, is an excessive concept, which is not suitable to determine any constitutive principle, an object and its objective reality: Nevertheless in accordance with the constitution of our (partially sensible) nature and faculty it serves for us and all rational creatures standing in connection with the sensible world, insofar as we can represent ourselves in accordance with the constitution of our reason, as a universal *regulative* principle, which does not determine the constitution of freedom as the form of causality objectively, but rather, and with no less validity than if this were the case, makes the rule of actions in accordance with this idea a command for everyone.   (§76, 5:404)

Here Kant not only suggests that we cannot give a theoretical proof of the existence of freedom, but also that we do not even have to regard it as a metaphysical fact about some purely noumenal aspect of our being at all, and can instead bring the principle of practical reason as a rule for actions to bear on our natural existence, something we can do precisely because the deterministic picture of natural causation necessary for scientific explanation and prediction is also only a perspective that we ourselves bring to bear on nature. Because the presuppositions of both science and morality are both principles that we ourselves bring to bear on nature, Kant finally recognizes, they must ultimately be compatible.

Having finally reached this recognition so late in his career, Kant never worked out the details, although that may have been the last thing he was trying to do in the latest stage of his work on the *Opus postumum* just before his death. Nor is it clear that any philosopher since has taken up the challenge of fleshing out this suggestion. Perhaps that is the most vital task Kant leaves for us.

For the benefit of the reader I will conclude this introduction with a brief guide to the essays that follow. In the first one, Frederick Beiser offers an account of Kant's philosophical development up until the publication of the *Critique of Pure Reason*. The next seven essays are primarily devoted to that work itself. Charles Parsons addresses Kant's theory of space and time and his conception of mathematics in the "Transcendental Aesthetic"; Michael Young considers Kant's attempt to derive the categories from the forms of judgment in the "metaphysical deduction"; and I assess Kant's strategy and success in the "transcendental deduction." Michael Friedman considers Kant's treatment of causation in the first *Critique* and in later work as well. Next, Gary Hatfield evaluates the role of psychology in Kant's theory of experience. Two essays then consider the topics in the "Transcendental Dialectic": Thomas Wartenberg considers Kant's positive doctrine of reason as the source of regulative ideals, and Karl Ameriks reviews Kant's critique of traditional metaphysics but also shows how considerable aspects of that metaphysics remained central to Kant's thought. In the next essay, Onora O'Neill effects the transition from the *Critique of Pure Reason* to Kant's practical philosophy by examining Kant's conception that reason can vindicate itself without falling into either Cartesian foundationalism or the kind of relativism that now predominates so much of our intellectual scene; the analysis is based on passages from the final part of the first *Critique*, the "Methodology," but applies to practical reason as well if not indeed primarily. The next two essays then address Kant's practical philosophy directly: J. B. Schneewind shows how the idea of autonomy, the idea that moral law can arise only from our own reason, is central to the development of Kant's ethics; Wolfgang Kersting shows how Kant's conception of political authority arises from the fundamental idea of human freedom and discusses the limits that places on the proper scope of politics as well. Eva Schaper considers Kant's theory of aesthetic judgment, discussing Kant's theories of the sublime and of artistic genius as well as beauty. This is followed by Allen Wood's analysis of Kant's philosophy of religion, which is naturally focused on Kant's complex view of the prospects for founding religion in reason alone. Finally, George di Giovanni discusses some of the responses to Kant that were offered in Germany in the first two decades after the publication of the *Critique of Pure Reason*, showing how such figures as Friedrich Jacobi, Karl Leonhard Reinhold, Gottlob Ernst Schulze (Aenesidemus), Johann G. Fichte, and Friedrich Wilhelm Schelling struggled to overcome the dualisms we will have seen to be central to Kant's philosophy, such as the distinction between intuition and concept and between appearance and thing in itself, setting the stage for much of the nineteenth-century philosophy that was to follow.

1 Kant's intellectual development: 1746–1781

I. THE PROBLEM OF METAPHYSICS IN EIGHTEENTH-CENTURY GERMANY

Kant's early philosophical career before the publication of the *Critique of Pure Reason* in May 1781 was dominated by an unhappy love affair. "I have had the fate to be in love with metaphysics," Kant wrote ruefully in 1766,[1] "although I can hardly flatter myself to have received favors from her." This preoccupation with metaphysics provided the leitmotif, and indeed the underlying drama, behind Kant's early intellectual development. We can divide his career into four phases according to whether he accepted or rejected the blandishments of his mistress. The first phase, from 1746 to 1759, is the period of infatuation. During these years Kant's chief aim was to provide a foundation for metaphysics. Accordingly, he developed a rationalist epistemology that could justify the possibility of knowledge of God, providence, immortality, and the first causes of nature. The second phase, from 1760 to 1766, is the period of disillusionment. Kant broke with his earlier rationalist epistemology and inclined toward skepticism, utterly rejecting the possibility of a metaphysics that transcends the limits of experience. The third phase, from 1766 to 1772, is a period of partial reconciliation. Kant returned to metaphysics in the belief that he could finally provide it with a firm foundation; he then sketched his plans for a modest ontology. The fourth and final phase, from 1772 to 1780, is the period of divorce. By 1772 Kant realized that his renewed confidence in metaphysics could not resolve one fundamental problem: How are synthetic, *a priori* principles valid of experience if they are not derived

26

from it? From 1772 he began to formulate his mature critical doctrine about the possibility of metaphysics.

In any intense and prolonged love affair we do not always see the beloved in the same light. He or she takes on many different guises, even identities, according to our mood. Kant's love affair with metaphysics was no exception. There is no single specific meaning that we can give to "metaphysics" in Kant's philosophical development. Metaphysics had many meanings: It was a science of the limits of human reason, an ontology of the first predicates of being, speculation about God, providence, and immortality, or a study of the first causes and most general laws of nature. We can give one general meaning to all these different senses: It is the eighteenth-century sense of metaphysics as the *Haupt-* or *Grundwissenschaft*, the science of the first principles or most universal properties of things.[2] Yet that is obviously much too vague. What truly unites these various projects is more Kant's abiding concern and interest in all of them: to determine the ends and limits of human reason.

Kant's concern with metaphysics was neither new nor original, but typical of philosophers in Germany in the middle of the eighteenth century. The possibility of metaphysics had been one of the central problems of German philosophy ever since the end of the seventeenth century. This problem arose when the old Aristotelian metaphysics, which had dominated German intellectual life in the seventeenth century, was thrown back on the defensive by the growth of the new sciences. The geometrical method of Cartesian physics, and the inductive-mathematical method of Newton, had undermined both the concepts and methods of the old Aristotelianism. The scholastic forms had been banished from physics as so many occult qualities; and the deductive method of syllogistic reasoning was dismissed as fruitless. Metaphysics, it therefore seemed, was doomed to extinction, the legacy of a moribund scholasticism. Leibniz and Wolff attempted to respond to this crisis by demanding that metaphysics imitate the mathematical method that had been used with such success in the natural sciences. If metaphysics only proceeded *more geometrico*, beginning with clearly defined terms and then rigorously deducing theorems from them, they argued, then it too would be able to walk down the road toward science. But, beginning in the 1720s, the methodology of the Leibnizian-Wolffian school encountered stiff opposition from such Pietist philosophers as J. F. Budde, J. Lange, A. F. Hoffmann, A. Rüdiger and A. C. Crusius. According to the Pietists, the method of philosophy should be empirical and inductive rather than mathematical and deductive; the philosopher cannot construct concepts according to definitions, like the mathematician, but must analyze concepts given to him in experience. The dispute between the Wolffians and Pietists about the proper method of metaphysics continued well into the late 1740s and the early 1750s – the very period in which Kant began his intellectual career at the University of Königsberg.[3] The debate finally came to a head in 1761 when the Academy of Sciences in Berlin posed a prize competition dealing with the following question: "Whether the metaphysical truths in general, and especially the first principles of natural theology and morals, are capable of the same degree of proof as geometrical truths, and if they are not capable of such proof, what is the nature of their certainty, and to what degree can they achieve it, and is such certainty sufficient for conviction?" Some of the foremost minds of Germany wrote contributions for this competition, among them Tetens, Mendelssohn, Lambert and, of course, Kant himself.[4]

The problem of metaphysics became even more critical when some apparently irresolvable conflicts arose between the new mathematics and the metaphysics of the Leibnizian-Wolffian school. Although Leibniz and Wolff championed the mathematical method in philosophy, their attempt to place metaphysics upon a firm foundation became deeply embarrassed when they found themselves locked in heated debates with Newtonian and Cartesian mathematicians. There were three disputes between the mathematicians and metaphysicians in eighteenth-century Germany.[5] The first was the notorious debate between the Leibnizians and Cartesians concerning the proper measure of force, which began at the close of the seventeenth century and continued well into the eighteenth century until D'Alembert's *Traité de dynamique* of 1747. The new geometrical physics of Descartes analyzed all physical properties in terms of extension; and among these properties was force, which was measured strictly in terms of the "quantity of motion," the speed multiplied by the mass (MV). The Leibnizians, however, insisted that there is something more to a body than its extension: namely its inherent living force, which was the striving of a body to reproduce from within itself the quantity of motion that it received from external causes (MV^2). The second dispute was the debate between the Leibnizians and Newtonians concerning the existence of monads, which became official in 1747 with a prize competition of the Berlin Academy of Sciences. It was a simple theorem of mathematics that space, and everything within it, was infinitely divisible; but the Leibnizians contended that all bodies ultimately consisted in simple indivisible parts or monads. The third dispute was the famous debate between the Leibnizians and Newtonians on the nature of space, which began with Leibniz's correspondence with Clarke in 1715. While the mathematicians insisted upon the absolute status of space to ensure *a priori* certainty to their theorems, the Leibnizians maintained that space consists only in the assemblage of all real and possible distances between things. These debates were widely known in eighteenth-century Germany, so much so that Euler said that everyone in court could talk about little else.[6] They were indeed notorious when they became the chief point of friction between the Newtonian Academy of Sciences in Berlin and the Leibnizian-Wolffian school. Although these debates were often technical, they raised fundamental epistemological issues about the value of metaphysics and the limits of the mathematical method. The metaphysicians accused the mathematicians of extending their methods beyond their proper domain, and of treating fictions (for example, absolute space) as if they were realities; the mathematicians, for their part, charged the metaphysicians with reviving useless scholastic subtleties and with interfering with the autonomy of science. These debates were of the first importance for the formation of Kant's philosophy. Kant was constantly preoccupied with them from his first published work in 1746 until the publication of the *Critique of Pure Reason* in 1781. They provided all the materials for his antinomies, whose solution eventually led him to his transcendental idealism.[7]

We can understand the young Kant's early devotion to metaphysics only if we consider the general predicament of the Leibnizian-Wolffian philosophy in the early decades of the eighteenth century. Wolff's philosophy had a profound symbolic significance in early eighteenth-century Germany: It represented the very vanguard of the *Aufklärung*, the attempt to establish the authority of reason in all walks of life, whether in the state, the church, the universities, or society at large. Predictably, then, Wolff's philosophy would come under severe criticism from Pietist quarters, which saw rationalism as a threat to the faith. And, sure enough, as early as the 1720s, Lange, Budde, Rüdiger and Hoffmann had mounted a concerted campaign against the Wolffian philosophy. The essence of their polemic was that the new mathematical method of the Wolffian philosophy ends of necessity in atheism and fatalism.[8] Because that method discovered mechanical causes for everything, they argued, it left no room for freedom, the basis of morality, or for miracles, the foundation of the faith. Although their campaign against Wolff had lost steam in the 1730s, it received new impetus in the 1740s and 1750s through the writings of C. A. Crusius. With a rigorous epistemology, Crusius systematized and strengthened many of the Pietists' objections against Wolff. The thrust of Crusius's criticisms of Wolff's rationalism was that the basic principles of our thought cannot be demonstrated by reason, and that reason cannot provide us with any knowledge beyond sense experience.[9] The net effect of the Pietists' campaign was to present the Wolffians with a dilemma: either a rational skepticism or an irrational fideism. We can explain Kant's early devotion to metaphysics from his desire to escape this dilemma. Only metaphysics, the young Kant believed, could rescue the *Aufklärung*'s faith in reason from the attacks of the Pietists. Only it could provide a rational justification for our moral and religious beliefs, and thus a middle path between skepticism and fideism. Yet Kant was all too keenly aware that it was necessary to provide a new foundation for metaphysics, and that the old defenses of the Wolffian school had begun to collapse after all the attacks mounted upon them. The essential task of Kant's philosophy in the 1750s was therefore set: how to provide a new foundation for metaphysics in the face of Crusius's criticisms.

II. KANT'S EARLY METAPHYSICS, 1746–1759

Despite their apparent diversity, there is a single aim to all of Kant's major early writings, those he wrote from 1746 to 1759, the period between his doctoral dissertation and the onset of his criticism of rationalism in the early 1760s.[10] This aim was to provide a foundation for the metaphysics of nature. Such was the goal not only of Kant's first explicitly epistemological work, the *Nova dilucidatio* of 1755, but also of his basic writings on natural philosophy, the *Gedanken von der wahren Schätzung der lebendigen Kräfte* (*Thoughts on the*

True Estimation of Living Forces, 1746–7), the *Allgemeine Natur-geschichte und Theorie des Himmels* (*Universal Natural History and Theory of the Heavens*, 1755), and the *Monadologica physica* (*Physical Monadology*, 1756).

According to Kant, the task of the metaphysics of nature is to discover the inner forces of things, the first causes of the laws of motion and the ultimate constituents of matter. Unlike empirical physics, which determines by observation the mechanics of nature, the laws of external motions, the metaphysics of nature determines by reason the dynamics of nature, the laws of its inner forces. This program for a "metaphysics of nature" was first developed by Leibniz in his *Specimen dynamicum*. In his polemic against the purely mechanical physics of the Cartesians, Leibniz argued the need for a more dynamic or "metaphysical" approach to nature.[11] The essence of matter was not simply extension, he contended, but inner living force. The aim of the young Kant was to fulfill Leibniz's program, to put the dynamics of nature upon a firm foundation.

Such was the goal of Kant's first published work, his *Gedanken von der wahren Schätzung der lebendigen Kräfte* (Living Forces). In the very beginning of this work Kant tells us explicitly that his aim is to make the doctrine of living forces "certain and decisive," and that to do so he intends to investigate "some of the metaphysical conceptions of the powers of bodies" (§1). Later on, he complains that metaphysics has hitherto not been placed upon a firm foundation, and that it remains only on "the threshhold of science" (§19). It has suffered from those who are more ready to speculate and expand knowledge than to place it upon a firm foundation. To determine the precise validity of Leibniz's doctrine of living force, Kant had to resolve the dispute between the Cartesians and Leibnizians about the proper measurement of force. He attempted to do so by distinguishing between two kinds of motion, the free motion of a body that would continue to infinity if it were not stopped by some resistance, and the impressed motion of a body that would continue only as long as some external force acted upon it (§15–18, 114–21). While the Cartesian measurement was valid for impressed motions, where a body had a power only proportionate to the cause of motion (hence MV), the Leibnizian measurement was valid for free motions, where a body's inner force multiplied the power it received from the cause of motion (hence MV^2) (§119). In making this distinction, Kant believed that he had provided a secure foundation for Leibnizian dynamics *and* a definite place for the mathematical approach to nature of the Cartesians. Kant then drew some important methodological conclusions from his resolution of the debate. First, he insisted that we should not overgeneralize from the evidence available to us, as if the measurement of one form of motion is true of motion in general (§§87–9). We must always compare the premises and conclusions of our reasoning to make sure that the premises are sufficient to entail the conclusion. Second, and most important, we must distinguish between the mathematical (Cartesian) and the metaphysical (Leibnizian) approaches to nature (§§114–15). Each is valid for its respective kind of motion. The dispute between the Leibnizians and Cartesians arose only because they suffered from the common assumption that mathematics alone could discover the living forces of nature, when in truth it can determine only those forces arising from external causes. So important were these methodological points to the young Kant that he regarded his whole treatise as little more than a discourse on method (§88). The issue between the Leibnizians and Cartesians, he stressed, concerned not a matter of fact but only the *ratio cognoscendi* (§50).

Kant's early concern with the metaphysics of nature also appears in the major work of his early years, his *Allgemeine Naturgeschichte und Theorie des Himmels (Universal Natural History)*. It is in this work that Kant expounds what later became known as the Kant–Laplace hypothesis of the origin of the universe. Kant's stated aim in this work is to find a mechanical explanation of the origin of the universe, and in particular of the systematic order of the solar system (the facts that the orbits of the planets all fall in the same plane, that they all move in the same direction, and so on) (1:221, 334). To achieve this end, Kant had to take issue with no less than Newton himself. Newton had argued that the systematic order of the solar system was the result of "the immediate hand of God," because the space between the planets is empty and therefore cannot have a material cause. Kant admits that we cannot avoid such a supernatural hypothesis *if* we assume that the present order of the universe is eternal, for then no material cause could have produced it. If, however, we assume that the space was originally filled with some primal mass, then we can explain how the systematic order arose from the forces of attraction and repulsion working upon it. To avoid a supernaturalistic hypothesis like Newton's, Kant argues that we must add the dimension of natural history to cosmology (1:262–3, 339–41). We must recognize that what appears to be given and eternal in nature, such as the systematic order of the solar system, is in fact the product of a long history. Prima facie, Kant's argument seems to have little to do with his attempt to find a foundation for dynamics. He seems much more concerned simply to extend and confirm the principles of Newtonian mechanics. Yet in his very attempt to extend the principles of mechanics Kant was returning to his metaphysical program. For at the very heart of the natural history that must supplement mechanics lies his dynamic view of matter. The fact that the systematic order of the universe arises from the laws governing matter shows that matter has within itself a striving to create order and harmony. It does not have this order and harmony imposed upon it by some external supernatural cause, but develops it from within according to its own inherent laws. Hence Kant stresses how matter consists in creative force, how it is a veritable "phoenix of nature" that creates new order from its very decay (1:314, 317, 321). The nub of Kant's argument in the *Universal Natural History*, then, was that the mechanical conception of nature could be extended to explain the universe only if it were supplemented with a dynamic view of matter; in other words, empirical physics has for its foundation a metaphysics of nature.

Kant's preoccupation with the metaphysics of nature continued with his *Monadologica physica* (*Physical Monadology*), which appeared in 1756. The aim of this tract is, again, to provide a foundation for dynamics, and in particular to establish the existence and fundamental laws of monads, the ultimate units of force and basic constituents of matter. In the preface, Kant expressly warns against those who would banish metaphysics from the sphere of natural philosophy (1:475–6). If we confine ourselves only to the available evidence, then we fail to discover the source and cause of the laws. Metaphysics is indispensable to natural philosophy, for it alone determines the ultimate parts of matter and how they interact with one another. Kant then proceeds to argue that all physical bodies consist in monads, whose activity consists in their repulsive and attractive forces. In virtue of their attractive forces bodies form solid masses, while in virtue of their repulsive forces they occupy space. The external occasion for this tract was the controversy concerning the existence of monads provoked by the Berlin Academy in 1747. For the young Kant, this dispute was all the more reason to make another careful distinction between the methods of mathematics and those of metaphysics. He attempted to resolve this dispute by arguing that geometry deals with space, which is indeed infinitely divisible, whereas metaphysics deals with the substance that fills this space, which is indivisible. Because space is not a substance but only the appearance of its external relations, the divisibility of space does not imply the divisibility of the substances that compose it (1:479–80; Prop. IV, V).

Kant's early concern with the foundation of metaphysics is most explicit in his *Nova dilucidatio* (*New Exposition*), an expressly epistemological treatise that attempts to clarify the first principles of reason. A thorough examination of the conditions and limits of knowledge, Kant believed as early as 1755, was crucial if metaphysics were to be provided with a proper foundation. In this work Kant defends some of the central tenets of Leibnizian-Wolffian rationalism, even if he often criticizes some of the arguments of Leibniz and Wolff. Like Leibniz and Wolff, Kant attempts to reduce the foundation of knowledge down to a few self-evident first principles. He disagrees with Wolff that there can be a single first principle of all knowledge, because the first principle of all true affirmative propositions cannot be the first principle of all true negative propositions, and conversely (Prop. I). Nevertheless, Kant does think that he can narrow the foundations of knowledge down to two fundamental principles, 'Everything that is, is' for true affirmative propositions, and 'Everything that is not, is not' for true negative propositions (Prop. II). Nothing more clearly reveals Kant's early rationalism than his adherence to Leibniz's "predicate-in-notion" principle, according to which a judgment is true if the predicate follows from, or is "contained in," the notion of the subject (Prop. IV). This principle means that all true judgments are analytic, so that we can, if only in principle, determine their truth through reason alone by an analysis of the subject term. Following in the footsteps of Wolff, though disagreeing with the details of his argument, Kant then attempts to derive the principle of sufficient reason from the principle of identity. Nothing is true without a sufficient reason, Kant argues, because there must be something about a subject that excludes the opposite predicate from being true of it (Prop. V). On this basis Kant proceeds to derive the analogous principle that there must be some reason or cause for everything that exists (Prop. VIII). This deduction of the principle of sufficient reason was the cornerstone of Kant's early rationalism, for it meant that reason could justify the main principle behind our knowledge of matter of fact, the principle of causality. In other words, to use Kant's later terminology, the principle of causality was analytic rather than synthetic *a priori*. Kant was very far here from his later recognition of the problem of the synthetic *a priori*. The *Nova dilucidatio* represents the high noon of Kant's early rationalism, the very antithesis of his later critical doctrines.

Granted that the attempt to find a foundation for dynamics was Kant's dominant early ambition, we must ask ourselves why he embarked on this search in the first place. What value did a metaphysics of nature have for him? What purpose could it serve? To the young Kant, a metaphysics of nature seemed to be the only middle path between the occultism of Pietistic *Naturphilosophie* and the mechanism of Cartesian physics. Kant clearly had little sympathy for the *Naturphilosophie* of Thomasius and his followers, which saw the working of the supernatural in the most ordinary events of nature, and which rejected the use of the mathematical method. Nevertheless, for all its rigor and mathematical precision, he could not entirely agree with the mechanical conception of nature of the Cartesians. Like Leibniz, Kant seemed to fear the moral and religious consequences of the Cartesian physics, which reduced all of nature down to a machine, to an inert matter that consisted in nothing more than extension.[12] In such a view of nature there did not seem to be any place for mind or spirit. The mind was either a machine inside nature or a ghost outside it. The young Kant, however, decidedly rejected both dualism and mechanism.[13] He argued in the *Living Forces* that a vitalistic conception of matter provided a means of explaining the interaction between the mind and body, without postulating a mysterious preestablished harmony, and without reducing the mind to a machine (§§5–6). The great attraction of a metaphysics of nature, then, was that it provided for a monistic, naturalistic *Weltanschauung* without the damaging moral and religious consequences of a mechanical materialism.

Now that we have considered the first phase of Kant's development, we are compelled to reject two of the most common opinions concerning the young Kant. The first opinion is that Kant was a

Wolffian in his early years.[14] Although Kant certainly sympathized with the aims of Wolff's metaphysics, and although he defended some of the central tenets of its rationalism, he was never a devoted disciple of Wolff. As early as 1746 Kant insisted upon the need for independent thought, free from partisan disputes and the authority of great names.[15] And, indeed, his own independence from the Wolffian school emerges time and again. Thus he was extremely critical of some of Wolff's arguments, such as his demonstration of a *vis motae*, his version of the ontological proof of God's existence, and his deduction of the principle of sufficient reason. Although Kant agreed with Wolff that philosophy should follow a rigorous demonstrative method, he argued that the Wolffians had taken their mathematical method too far in applying it to the domains of natural philosophy; Kant's distinction between the mathematical and metaphysical method was indeed an implied criticism of the Wolffian school.[16] The second opinion is that the young Kant was a "dogmatic" metaphysician. Kant himself seems to sanction this view, given his famous phrase about his early "dogmatic slumbers."[17] Yet, in all likelihood, these slumbers were only a short nap that Kant took in 1770.[18] If by "dogmatism" we mean the procedure by which pure reason makes claims to knowledge without a previous criticism of its powers, then it becomes highly misleading to apply this term to the young Kant. As we have seen, from the very beginning of his career Kant was concerned with the foundations and limits of knowledge. Such epistemological concerns were a necessary consequence of his attempt to provide a foundation for metaphysics. Although the young Kant did believe that it was possible to attain knowledge through pure reason, he did so only as a result of his investigation into its principles. We must be on our guard, then, in making a distinction between a "precritical" and a "critical" Kant. This should be a distinction between Kant before and after the first *Critique*, not a distinction between a dogmatic and a critical Kant, or a metaphysical and epistemological Kant.

III. KANT'S TURBULENT DECADE, 1760–1769

Although Kant struggled to find a new foundation for metaphysics in the 1750s, he never doubted its aims, its underlying rationalism, and still less its very possibility. The problem was only one of laying the foundation with sufficient care, and then it would be able to cross over the threshold of science. The writings of the 1760s mark a fundamental shift away from this attitude. The earliest works of this decade are much more critical of the whole enterprise of metaphysics. They cast doubt upon its syllogistic logic, its prospects of achieving mathematical certainty, and its use in supporting morality. Although Kant continued to try to find a new foundation for metaphysics until 1764, he had become skeptical of its rationalist methodology. His attempt to replace its rationalist with a more empiricist methodology eventually gave way in 1765 to a complete skepticism about the very possibility of metaphysics. By 1766 Kant had reformulated the very task of metaphysics: Its aim was to provide not a knowledge of God, providence, and immortality, but a science of the limits of human reason. Metaphysics was no longer the queen of the sciences, but only the handmaiden to ethics.

The onset of Kant's more critical attitude toward metaphysics was his *Die falsche Spitzfindigkeit der vier syllogistischen Figuren* (*The False Subtlety of the Four Syllogistic Figures*), which appeared in 1762. This short tract was a sharp critique of traditional scholastic logic, which had been the backbone of metaphysics for centuries. Kant had such a low opinion of the foundations of the traditional logic that he called it "a colossus with its head in the clouds and feet of clay." He accused the older logicians of having engaged in pointless subtleties that betrayed the very purpose of logic, which was not to complicate but to simplify the first principles of knowledge (§5; 2:56). The main target of Kant's criticism was the traditional classification of the syllogism into four chief forms or "figures." According to Kant, this classification is completely specious, because there is only one pure form, of which the others are only hybrid variations. The starting point of Kant's argument is his analysis of syllogistic reasoning into a form of mediate judgment, where we attribute a characteristic to a thing in virtue of some characteristic or middle term that is a characteristic of a characteristic; for example, we can attribute spirituality to the human soul if we know that the human soul is rational, and that everything rational is spiritual. Here the characteristic of rationality – a characteristic of spirituality – is the mediating term that allows us to attribute spirituality to the human soul. Proceeding from this premise, Kant maintains that there are only two fundamental rules of inference: "The characteristic of a characteristic of a thing is a characteristic of the thing itself" for positive judgments; and "What contradicts the characteristic of a thing contradicts the thing itself" for negative judgments (§2; 2:49). Both of these rules are perfectly exemplified, Kant argues, in the first figure of the syllogism, that which takes the form 'A is B; B is C; therefore, A is C' (§4; 2:51). The other forms are indeed correct insofar as they produce valid conclusions; but they are not "pure forms" insofar as they do not have two premises and a conclusion. Rather these forms are impure because they require a hidden third premise, which is the inversion of the other two (§4; 2:51–55). What concerns us here is neither the details nor the validity of Kant's argument but the central premise behind it, namely its identification of reasoning with a form of judgment. This was part of Kant's more general theory, announced at the close of his tract (§6; 2:57–61), that the "higher faculty of knowledge" can be analyzed into forms of judgment. Rejecting the traditional classification of the faculty of knowledge into concepts, judgments, and syllogisms, Kant argued that concepts are only a form of immediate judgment as syllogisms are a form of mediate. This analysis clearly prepared the ground for the later "metaphysical deduction" of the categories in the first *Critique*. By considering the genesis of that view in the *False Subtlety*, we can see that Kant arrived at his identification of the understanding with judgment not by uncritically accepting, but by sharply attacking the traditional logic.[19]

The critical attitude of the *False Subtlety* only grew in Kant's next work in the 1760s, *Der einzig mögliche Bewisgrund zu einer Demonstration des Daseins Gottes* (*The Only Possible Basis for a Demonstration of the Existence of God*), which appeared in late 1762. This work continues Kant's early attempts to provide a foundation for metaphysics. Kant intends to give a solid basis for rational theology by laying down the materials for an irrefutable proof of God's existence. But, in attempting to show that this is "the only possible proof of God's existence," Kant engages in a critique of rational theology, a critique so thoroughgoing that it betrays his increasing lack of confidence in metaphysics. Kant's growing skepticism about metaphysics emerges in the preface to this work. Here he says that it is fortunate that providence has not made our happiness depend upon the subtleties of a metaphysical demonstration of the existence of God (2:65–6). "The natural common understanding" (*der natürlichen gemeinen Verstand*) can find sufficient reasons for the existence of God simply by contemplating the order, beauty, and harmony of nature, for it is highly improbable that this could arise without an intelligent and beneficent creator. If, however, we wish to have a demonstrative certainty of God's existence, then we have to throw ourselves into "the bottomless abyss of metaphysics," which is indeed "a dark sea without shores and lighthouses." All the later arguments against rational theology in the first *Critique* are clearly laid down in the *Only Possible Basis*. Just as in the first *Critique*, Kant criticizes the traditional ontological proof on the grounds that existence is not a predicate. Because the same thing with all its properties can either exist or not exist, adding existence to a thing does not give it any new properties. The Cartesian ontological proof fails to recognize this point, however, for if existence is not a predicate it also cannot be the predicate of the most perfect being (2:72–3, 156–7). Again anticipating the first *Critique*, Kant attacks the traditional cosmological arguments on two grounds: First, all the evidence from the order, beauty, and harmony of nature permits us to infer only a wise craftsmen who shaped matter, but not a creator of matter itself (2:124–5); and, second, all that we can infer from such evidence is that there is a wise, powerful, and beneficent creator, not that there is an infinite, omniscient, and omnipotent God (160–1). The main thrust of Kant's arguments against rational theology in the *Only Possible Basis* was directed against its teleology, its belief that everything useful in nature gives evidence for providence. Relying upon his conception of matter developed in the *Universal Natural History*, Kant argues that all the order, beauty, and harmony of nature cannot be evidence for its direct creation by God, because it is derivable from the inherent laws of matter itself (96–103). All that does depend upon the direct will of God is the creation of matter itself, for its organization and structure is derivable from its inner forces. With this argument Kant had virtually abolished traditional natural theology, for he had effectively banished the supernatural from the sphere of material nature and eliminated all need to infer a supernatural cause. Although he still insisted that God creates the concept of matter itself, he had pushed the activity of the divine even farther into the irrelevant beyond. Unintentionally, he had supported the arguments of those materialists who had insisted upon the self-sufficiency of matter.[20]

Kant's major methodological work on metaphysics in the 1760s was his so-called *Prize Essay, Untersuchung über die Deutlichkeit der Grundsätze der natürlichen Theologie und der Moral (Investigation of the Clarity of the Principles of Natural Theology and Morals)*, which he completed in the autumn of 1762, shortly after the *Only Possible Basis*. In this work Kant abandons his previous hopes for a dogmatic or demonstrative certainty. Metaphysics, he argues, must resign itself to not attaining the same degree of certainty and clarity as mathematics. The *Prize Essay* also marks a major break with Kant's earlier rationalism, and in particular his use of the geometrical method in metaphysics. Although in the 1750s Kant insisted upon distinguishing between the methods of mathematics and metaphysics, he still argued *more geometrico* in the *Nova dilucidatio* and *Monadologica physica*, beginning with definitions and axioms and deducing specific theorems from them. He believed that the mathematical method, though of no use in helping us to discover the ultimate forces and particles of nature, still provided the model of demonstrative certainty for metaphysics. In the *Prize Essay*, however, Kant finally broke with his former faith in the mathematical method. Rather than applying a deductive mathematical method, he now argued, metaphysics should do the very opposite: It should follow the inductive empirical method of the natural sciences. Kant came to this new conclusion by making a sharper and broader distinction than hitherto between the mathematical and metaphysical method – a distinction that he was later to build upon in the first *Critique*. According to this distinction, the method of mathematics is *synthetic*, beginning with universal concepts formed according to definitions and then deriving specific conclusions from them. The method of metaphysics, however, is *analytic*, starting from the analysis of a concept into its specific components and then gradually forming universal conclusions (§1; 2:276–8). The mathematician can follow a synthetic method since he creates his concepts and then deduces only what he has placed within them; the metaphysician, though, must follow an analytic method since his concepts are given to him in ordinary language. Because his concepts are so vague, they cannot be represented *in concreto*; and because they are given and complex, many features will escape his attention; hence the metaphysician cannot attain the same degree of certainty as the mathematician (§§2–4; 2:278–83). Although Kant doubts that metaphysics can attain the same degree of certainty as mathematics, he still believes that it can attain a sufficient degree of certainty provided that the metaphysician follows the proper method. In particular, he should follow two guidelines: (1) Rather than beginning with a general definition, he should determine all the essential characteristics of a concept that can be attributed to it with certainty; (2) after determining that these characteristics are indeed simple and independent of one another, he should use them, and them alone, as the basis for all further deductions (2:285–6). In thus beginning from specific evidence and then gradually ascending to a more universal conclusion, the method of metaphysics should resemble that of Newtonian science (286).

Kant's critique of rationalism continued in his next published work, *Versuch den Begriff der negativen Grössen in die Weltweisheit einzuführen* (*An Attempt to Introduce the Concept of Negative Quantities into Philosophy*). While the *Prize Essay* had criticized the attempt to employ the mathematical method in philosophy, this work pressed home the attack upon rationalism by questioning one of its most fundamental principles: that reason could express and explain the fundamental qualities and relations of our experience. The starting point of Kant's critique was his attempt to introduce the mathematical notion of a negative quantity into philosophy. A negative quantity expressed the concept of a *real* opposition, which was distinct from that of *logical* opposition. Logical opposition consists in contradiction, the affirmation and denial of one and the same predicate of a thing. Here one predicate is the negation of the other; and the result of affirming them both of the same thing is nothing. Real opposition, on the other hand, consists in two opposing forces, tendencies, or quantities whose effects cancel each other; for example, the forces making a body move in opposite directions, equal degrees of heat and cold, equal amounts of attractive and repulsive force. In these cases both of the opposing terms are positive and can be predicated of the same thing; and the result of their opposition is not nothing but something, namely that the body does not move but stays at rest. Kant maintained that he could apply the concept of real opposition throughout our experience. We could apply it to the realm of psychology (pain is negative pleasure), moral philosophy (vice is negative virtue), and physics (repulsion is negative attraction) (2:179–88). Kant fully realized the important implications of such a broad application of this concept. It meant that the entire range of our experience could not be expressed or explained in strictly rational terms according to the principle of contradiction. We could no longer regard the realm of our immediate experience, as the Leibnizians did, simply as so many confused representations of reason. Rather than differing only in degree, the spheres of reason and experience would differ in kind. Here then Kant had laid the foundation for his later distinction between reason and sensibility in the first *Critique.* But Kant saved his most potent objection against rationalism until the close of his essay. Mocking those metaphysicians who claim to know so much through pure reason, Kant asks them to explain according to the law of identity how one thing can produce another (2:201–4). He understands how one thing follows another according to the law of identity, since then it is only a matter of analyzing one term to see that the other is involved in it. But he cannot understand how one thing gives rise to something else as cause and effect where both terms are logically distinct; for example, how God's will can be the cause of the world, or how the motion of one body produces the motion of another. If we analyze God's will we cannot find any reason for the creation of the world; and if we analyze the notion of the one body we cannot find the reason for the motion of the other. Hence the relationship of cause and effect, the fundamental constituent of our knowledge of matter of fact, cannot be reduced to the principle of identity. Here Kant had anticipated, though without possessing the terminology, the central question of the first *Critique:* How are synthetic *a priori* judgments possible?

Although the *Prize Essay* and *Negative Quantities* were sharply critical of rationalism, they did not question the possibility of metaphysics. On the contrary, Kant still believed that if only metaphysics would follow the method of Newtonian physics, then it would be sure to travel down the road to science. Yet, probably sometime in late 1764 or early 1765, Kant's views underwent a very marked and radical change. This emerges from Kant's remarks to his copy of his 1764 treatise *Beobachtungen über das Gefühl des Schönen und Erhabenen (Observations on the Feeling of the Beautiful and Sublime),* which were written around this time. If we closely examine these remarks, then we find that Kant had come to a decidedly negative view about not only the possibility but even the desirability of metaphysics (20:181). His thought had undergone nothing less than a complete revolution, for he had now arrived at a totally new conception of the ends of reason. Rather than devoting itself to speculation about God, providence, immortality, and the ultimate forces and particles of nature, reason should concern itself first and foremost with the ends of life. The final end of all inquiry, Kant tells us, is to know "the vocation of man" (41, 45, 175). To ensure that reason fulfills its proper end, Kant envisages a method of skeptical doubt that will undermine the pretences of speculation and direct enquiry into what is useful for human life (175). Kant then redefines the task of metaphysics itself. It should be not speculation about things transcending our sense experience, but "a science of the limits of human reason" (181).

What brought about such a fundamental shift in attitude? What made Kant so drastically redefine the role of reason and his entire conception of metaphysics? There can be little doubt that it was the influence of Rousseau. Throughout his remarks to the *Observations* Kant struggles with Rousseau's critique of the arts and sciences in the first and second *Discours*. Rousseau had convinced him that, at least in their present state, the arts and sciences were indeed doing more to corrupt than promote morals. They could become a source of good to humanity only if they were redirected in their ends. In a famous passage Kant bluntly states his debt to Rousseau and indicates how he made him rethink the ends of reason:

I am myself by inclination a seeker after truth. I feel a consuming thirst for knowledge and a restless desire to advance in it, as well as a satisfaction in every step I take. There was a time when I thought that this alone could constitute the honor of mankind, and I despised the common man who knows nothing. Rousseau set me right. This pretended superiority vanished and I learned to respect humanity. I should consider myself far more useless than the common laborer if I did not believe that one consideration alone gives worth to all others, namely to establish the rights of man.   (20:44).

It is important to see, however, that Kant did not simply accept *tout court* Rousseau's critique of culture. He also regarded it as a challenge. Rousseau had maintained in the first and second *Discours* that the advantage of reason in modern society had not ennobled but enslaved man, insofar as the arts and sciences had created artificial and insatiable needs and desires that made one person dependent upon others.[21] Kant agreed with Rousseau that, understood simply in an instrumental sense as a power of determining means to ends, reason could indeed enslave man; but he countered that it was wrong to restrict reason to such a role. The essence of his reply to Rousseau essentially consists in a new theory about the ends of reason. Kant argues that if reason is not to be the source of the moral corruption of man, then it should be redirected in two ways. First, the end of reason should be practical rather than theoretical, so that it serves humanity rather than fostering vain and idle speculations. Second, reason should be not an instrument of satisfying our desires, but a faculty of moral ends, indeed the source of universal moral laws. Rousseau himself had suggested this line of thought in the *Social Contract* with his theory of the general will. Thus, partly in reaction to Rousseau, and partly under his influence, Kant had developed the view of reason as a faculty of ends that is so characteristic of his later moral philosophy. This new conception of reason allowed him to say that it would not enslave but liberate man. Indeed, it would be the source of the very moral autonomy that Rousseau was so anxious to protect.[22]

What was so wrong with metaphysics that it had contributed to the decline of morals? It is important to see that Kant's criticism of metaphysics in the remarks to the *Observations* is not only ad hominem, directed against the vanity of those metaphysicians who think that they are better than the common man because they can engage in sophisticated reasoning. Rather, it undermines the very purpose behind the traditional metaphysics. The motivation for metaphysics was to provide a rational foundation for religion and morality by giving demonstrations for the existence of God, providence, and immortality. Morality, in particular, was dependent upon our knowledge of the universe as a whole. If we were to determine the fundamental duties of man, the metaphysicians believed, then we first had to know "the vocation of man" (*die Bestimmung des Menschen*), his place in the creation, the role that God had assigned him on earth; and then we had to determine the basic principles of natural law, which had been laid down in the providential order created by God. In the remarks to the *Observations*, however, Kant had come to doubt both the need for, and value of, such a foundation of morality. The fundamental source of morality, he now believed,[23] was freedom itself, the power of the will to prescribe universal laws.

The problem with metaphysics, then, was that it projected the source of morality into the world outside us, renouncing our own freedom and alienating us from our own powers. Like so many of the arts and sciences, it made us ignore the true source of virtue, which lay within ourselves. It had in its own way contributed to that malaise Rousseau had so trenchantly exposed in all his works: "Man is born free but everywhere he is in chains." In making this criticism of metaphysics, Kant already adumbrated a central theme of the first *Critique:* that metaphysics hypostasizes our own human creations.

The crowning work of the 1760s was Kant's *Träume eines Geistersehers (Dreams of a Spirit-Seer)*, which appeared in 1766. This work represents the height of Kant's growing disaffection with metaphysics. All the critical forces that had been mounting in the earlier writings of the 1760s now reach their climax in a complete skepticism toward metaphysics. So profound is Kant's disillusionment that he likens metaphysics to the dreams of the visionary or spirit-seer. Both metaphysicians and spirit-seers are accused of chasing imaginary will-of-the-wisps and living in a private world of their own imagination (2:342, 256). The main weapon of Kant's new skepticism is an empiricist criterion of knowledge, which makes him dismiss all speculation that transcends the bounds of experience as so much illusion and self-deception. One of the saddest casualties of this ruthless skepticism is his earlier metaphysics of vital forces. The postulate of immaterial forces within matter, he says, is only "the refuge of a lazy philosophy," because it stops short the attempt to explain things through mechanical causes (331). Kant no longer has any hope that, if he only follows the right method, the metaphysician will be able to provide us with knowledge of God, providence, and immortality. He now rejects the inductive method of the *Prize Essay* as much as the deductive method of his earlier works (358–9). If the attempt to move from universal premises to specific conclusions succeeds only by smuggling empirical data, the attempt to proceed from the specific facts of experience to general principles fails to answer the basic question why these facts exist in the first place. Although the skepticism of the *Dreams* is sometimes seen as the fundamental break with Kant's earlier devotion to metaphysics,[24] the truth of the matter is that it simply completes the program set down in the remarks to the *Observations*. Here, as in the *Observations*, Kant's skepticism is motivated by a moral end. The aim of skepticism is to expose the vanity and conceit of speculation, so that we direct our efforts to finding what is truly useful to man. This skepticism shows us, Kant maintains, that metaphysics is not necessary to the happiness of man (368–73). We do not need a demonstrative knowledge of God, providence, and immortality to provide a foundation for morality. For morality should be an end in itself, regardless of the prospects of eternal rewards, and regardless of whether or not the soul is immortal. Rather than basing morality on metaphysics, we should do the very reverse: base metaphysics on morality. For it is only our moral sentiments, Kant argues, that sustains our interest in metaphysics. The moral skepticism of the *Dreams* clearly anticipates many of the later doctrines of the mature critical philosophy, most conspicuously the doctrine of practical faith. It indeed helps us to explain one of the apparently paradoxical features of the critical philosophy: its harsh empiricist strictures upon the limits of knowledge and its sympathy toward moral and religious belief. Both of these seemingly conflicting features of the critical philosophy are the necessary result of Kant's earlier moral skepticism in the *Dreams*.

IV. RETURN TO METAPHYSICS, 1770–1772

Although Kant had sharply criticized metaphysics in the *Dreams of a Spirit-Seer*, he was far from abandoning it. On the contrary, his interest in the method and aims of metaphysics only gained in intensity after 1766. This is perfectly clear from the letters that Kant wrote to Lambert, Mendelssohn, and Herder in the period immediately after the *Dreams*. In December 1765 Kant wrote to Lambert that, "after many upheavals," he had finally found the method to resolve those problems in metaphysics that arise from not having a universally accepted criterion of knowledge. All his recent work, he assured Lambert, revolved around "the method of metaphysics." Such, indeed, was Kant's devotion to this problem that he had planned to write a book by Easter titled "Die Methode der Metaphysik" (10:52–3). Then, in April 1766, Kant told Mendelssohn that so far was he from regarding metaphysics as trivial or dispensable that he believed the well-being of the human race depended upon it. He insisted, however, that skepticism was indispensable, because it was necessary to undermine the dogmatic pretensions of metaphysics before anything constructive could be achieved. If a healthy understanding needed only a doctrine of method, the corrupt illusions of metaphysics required something more, "a cartharticon" (10:67–8). Finally, in May 1768, Kant wrote his former pupil Herder that his chief interest was still "to determine the proper ends and limits of human powers and desires," a preoccupation that was now leading him to write "a metaphysics of morals" (10:70–1). In these letters Kant does not fully explain either the aims or the method of his new metaphysics. Nevertheless, the context and content of his remarks would suggest that he had in mind the metaphysical program that he outlined in the *Dreams*, namely a science of the limits of human reason. From 1766 to 1768, then, there is no indication that Kant had departed from the direction of his thought imparted to him by Rousseau in 1765.

It is therefore surprising, indeed extremely puzzling, to find that, in August 1770, Kant appears to revive a speculative metaphysics in his inaugural dissertation, *De mundi sensibilis atque intelligibilis forma et principiis dissertatio* (*Dissertation on the Form and Principles of the Sensible and Intelligible Worlds*). The conception of metaphysics that Kant outlines in this work seems to be the complete negation of that in the *Dreams*. The aim of metaphysics is not to determine the limits of human reason, but to give us a rational knowledge of the intelligible world. Rather than limiting reason to sense experience, the metaphysician should prevent the ideas of sensibility from trespassing into the domain of pure reason. The basis of Kant's new metaphysics was his distinction between two faculties of knowledge, sensibility and rationality (*intellectus*). Sensibility is the receptivity of a subject by which it is affected by objects in experience; rationality is the activity of the subject by which it creates representations not given to the senses. Whereas the object of sensibility is phenomena, the object of rationality is noumena (§3). Sensibility consists in both matter and form: The matter is the content of sensation; the form is the specific manner in which sensations are organized according to a natural law of the mind. The form of sensibility consists in two *a priori* forms of intuition: space and time. Reason, on the other hand, consists in certain *a priori* concepts that are necessary conditions of thinking any object whatsoever; namely existence, necessity, substance, and cause (§8). These concepts are not acquired from experience; nor are they innate, however, because they are acquired from thinking about the inherent laws of our own mental activity (§8). Such a sharp distinction in kind between reason and sensibility marked Kant's final and definitive break with the rationalist tradition, which saw the distinction between these faculties as only one of degree. That Kant would eventually make this break was perfectly predictable from the course of his thought in the 1760s. His distinction between reason and sensibility is the final product of his distinction between existence and essence in the *Only Possible Basis,* and his distinction between logical and real opposition in the *Negative Quantities.* Yet what is so surprising now is that Kant builds a new metaphysics upon this distinction – a distinction that undermines the rationalist epistemology behind his old metaphysics. Kant tells us explicitly in the *Dissertation* that while sensibility gives us knowledge only of how things appear to us, reason provides us with knowledge of things as they are in themselves (§4). Moreover, he claims that, to give us knowledge of noumena, the concepts of reason do not require application or verification in experience (§§26, 29). Metaphysics, as Kant now defines it, is that philosophy which contains "the first principles of the use of the pure intellect" (§8). The use of the pure intellect is said to be twofold: One is *elenctic,* preventing sensible concepts from interfering with intellectual; and the other use is *dogmatic,* providing some archetype or exemplar that serves as a measure of all other things insofar as they are realities (§9). All in all, it seems difficult to imagine a more complete reversal of the skepticism of the *Dreams.* After ridiculing a dogmatic metaphysics Kant now seems to be in the grip of a Platonic fervor, which gives him insight into a purely intelligible world transcending the world of phenomena. Within the space of two years, from May 1768 to August 1770, the moral skeptic has apparently become a metaphysical enthusiast.

What had happened? How do we explain this sudden revival of metaphysics after Kant's skepticism in the *Dreams?* These questions have been the cause of much gnashing of teeth and wringing of hands among Kant scholars. Some regard it as a mystery better passed over in silence, while others have devised the most elaborate hypotheses.[25] It is indeed difficult to explain the genesis of the *Dissertation* since we have so little material for the years 1768 to 1770. Yet, if we carefully examine the *Dissertation,* and if we study the

Reflexionen for the years immediately before and after it, then we find that, contrary to all the appearances, there is really no break with the program of 1766. Strange as it might seem, the *Dissertation* was not the rejection but the fruition of the *Dreams.*

In the first place, it is important to see that the metaphysics prescribed in the *Dissertation* is not the same as that proscribed in the *Dreams.* Kant's new metaphysics is first and foremost an ontology, a system of the most general attributes or predicates of things. This ontology does not speculate about a distinct kind of entities, but simply determines the necessary laws by which our reason can think any object whatsoever. Although Kant sometimes loosely speaks of his noumena as if they were a kind of entity, we must be careful not to reify them. They are not a type of existing thing, but simply the forms or structures to which any existing or possible thing must conform. It is because the laws of reason do not refer to any existing thing that Kant is not worried about the problem of their verification or application in experience. The metaphysics that Kant wished to banish in the *Dreams*, however, was speculation about the world of spirits. Kant argued that reason could never answer questions about how spirits communicate and interact with one another, how they exist in space, or how they interact with the body. These are not questions that Kant attempts to answer in the *Dissertation.* Indeed, so far was Kant from encouraging such speculation in the *Dissertation* that he continued to discourage it. Thus he again denies that we can have any knowledge of spiritual substances, of either their relations among themselves or to external bodies (§17). He also says that the principles of the intelligible world do not concern the kind of substance – whether material or immaterial – but only the forms of any kind (§16). Rather than contradicting the program of 1766, then, the metaphysics of the *Dissertation* only continues it. For it does not attempt to extend knowledge into the unknown spiritual world; and its ontology does nothing more than determine those concepts that are necessary limits and conditions of reason.

This reading of the *Dissertation* is more than amply confirmed by the *Reflexionen* written in 1769 and 1770.[26] Without exception, we find that throughout these reflections Kant only develops the proto-critical conception of metaphysics that he had in 1766. The object of metaphysics, he writes,[27] is to determine the first principles or basic concepts of our reason. Metaphysics should be an ontology, though not an ontology in the traditional sense of a science about some kind of thing.[28] Rather, its aim should be to determine the conditions under which it is possible to think any object whatsoever according to reason. Its concepts are neither ectypes nor archetypes, but concepts about the conditions under which anything can be thought (*Bedingungsbegriffe*).[29] In all the reflections for these years Kant insists that the principles of metaphysics have not an objective but only a subjective validity insofar as they do not refer to any properties of things but only the conditions under which anything can be thought.[30] With the benefit of hindsight we can see Kant groping toward what he will later call "transcendental philosophy." This was the ultimate fruit of the skeptical program of the *Dreams*.

There are, however, some considerations that would seem to weigh against this reading of the *Dissertation*. For is not the intelligible or noumenal world also the realm of God, freedom, and immortality? The first *Critique* gives us every reason to think so. And, if this is the case, are we not justified in regarding the noumenal world as a realm of spiritual beings after all? There are indeed some passages from the *Reflexionen* that give evidence for this interpretation.[31] Yet a closer look at these passages reveals that, as a spiritual realm, Kant gives the intelligible or noumenal world a strictly moral meaning, just as he had done in the *Dreams of a Spirit-Seer*.[32] We are told explicitly by Kant on several occasions that the only law we know to be true of the intelligible world is the moral law. The *mundus vere intelligibilis* is the *mundus moralis*. The only datum that we have of the intelligible world, Kant says,[33] is that of our awareness of freedom. Hence it is the principles of freedom that constitute the *formae mundi intelligibilis*. The concept of God is valid, Kant further explains,[34] only insofar as it is based upon moral laws. We cannot prove this concept *a priori*, but are allowed to infer it only insofar as it is a precondition of the highest good. These passages from the *Reflexionen* then provide us with the context to interpret Kant's remarks about the dogmatic use of reason in the *Dissertation*. In postulating certain exemplars of perfection, the dogmatic use of reason gives us not constitutive but regulative principles. They do not state what does exist, but what ought to exist. Such a usage is dogmatic not in the sense that it speculates about entities beyond experience, but in the sense it is certain according to *a priori* principles, namely the first principle of morality.

If the metaphysics of the *Dissertation* is not incompatible with the moral skepticism of the *Dreams*, it still seems implausible that it could derive from it. Yet this is in fact the case. Some of the central tenets of the *Dissertation* were the product of Kant's earlier moral skepticism. In the years immediately after the *Dreams* Kant attempted to find ways of strengthening his new skepticism. He eventually discovered a new strategy to expose the pretentions of metaphysics. This was to prove both the thesis and antithesis of some metaphysical subject, a practice that clearly foreshadows the antinomies of the first *Critique*. It was while constructing such arguments in 1769, Kant later said,[35] that "a great light" dawned upon him. That great light was most probably the distinction between reason and sensibility. Kant saw that this distinction could finally resolve the persistent conflicts between metaphysics and mathematics. In the very first section of the *Dissertation*, for example, he uses it to reconcile the conflict between the mathematician and metaphysician regarding the infinite divisibility of space. The distinction between reason and sensibility, noumena and phenomena, could give an equal and independent validity to the claims of both metaphysics and mathematics. Hence that distinction, the very cornerstone of the *Dissertation*, is, at least in part, the product of the moral skepticism of the *Dreams*. Prima facie, there would seem to be a straightforward conflict between the moral skepticism of the *Dreams*, which attempts to limit reason to experience, and the propaedeutic criticism of the *Dissertation*, which aims to prevent sensibility from encroaching upon the sphere of reason. And yet they are only different strategies of the same enterprise. The fundamental aim of the moral skepticism of the *Dreams* was to protect our basic moral values against rampant speculation. In the late 1760s, however, Kant saw that this goal demanded preventing sensible ideas from being applied to noumena more than limiting reason to sense experience. For if the thesis of the infinite divisibility of space and time, and of the infinite series of cause and effect, were extended beyond the sphere of sensibility to the noumenal world they would jeopardize two of our essential moral beliefs: namely immortality, which presupposes the simplicity of the soul, and freedom, which requires spontaneous causes. It is indeed no accident that in the late 1760s Kant had already sketched his solution to not only the mathematical but also the dynamical antinomies.[36] Kant was determined that the fundamental principle of the noumenal world – the principle of freedom – had to be saved at all costs against the encroachments of a scientific method that extended its principles beyond the limits of experience. The propadeutic criticism of the *Dissertation* was, then, only a new strategy of the moral skepticism of the *Dreams*, the response of that skepticism to the dangers of materialism and determinism.

V. THE SILENT DECADE, 1770–1780

If the 1760s were Kant's turbulent decade, then the 1770s have been called with justice "the silent decade." In contrast to the 1760s Kant wrote very little in these years. Other than the *Dissertation* there were a few essays on education, *Zwei Aufsätze, betreffend das Philanthropin* (*Two Essays Concerning the Philanthropic Academy*) (1776–7), and an article on anthropology, "Von den verschiedenen Rassen der Menschen" (*On the Different Races of Mankind*) (1775). But that was all. Many of Kant's contemporaries were puzzled, even disturbed, by his silence. Yet what Kant needed most was peace and solitude. For this was the decade of his intense labor on the *Critique of Pure Reason*. Unfortunately, we have few sources to document the stages in the writing of the *Critique*. There are Kant's letters to his former student Marcus Herz; some students' notes from lectures given around 1775; and the *Reflexionen*, among them the set known as the *Duisburg Nachlaß*. But even these sources cast but a dim light upon the darkness. Kant's letters give only the most scanty information; the lecture notes are of dubious reliability; the *Reflexionen* cannot be precisely dated; and the *Duisburg Nachlaß* is a cipher.[37]

The starting point for any consideration of the 1770s remains the *Dissertation*. This work brought Kant close to the threshold of the critical philosophy. Several of its most important teachings anticipate the first *Critique*: the distinction in kind between reason and sensibility, the theory of space and time as *a priori* forms of sensibility, the *a priori* concepts constitutive of the intellect, and the limitation of metaphysics to an ontology of pure concepts. Yet if Kant had approached the threshold of the critical philosophy he certainly had not passed over it. The *Dissertation* still had not posed the fundamental problem of the *Critique*, the possibility of synthetic *a priori* judgments; and it had not formulated the central thesis of transcendental idealism, that the objects given to us in experience are only appearances of "things in themselves."[38] The *Dissertation* was at best, then, only a halfway house on the difficult road toward the *Critique*.

We can now arrive at such a conclusion, though, only with the benefit of hindsight. In 1770 Kant saw things differently. On September 2, 1770, Kant wrote J. H. Lambert, one of the philosophers in Germany he admired most, asking him for his comments on the *Dissertation*. Although Kant readily admitted that much in his tract was still crude and vague, he expressed satisfaction with his general position. "For around a year now I flatter myself that I have arrived at those concepts that I will surely have to expand but never have to change; by their means all manner of metaphysical questions can be examined according to certain and easy criteria and, insofar as they are resolvable at all, can be decided with certainty" (10:93). Yet such optimism was to be shortlived. For in his October 13 reply to Kant Lambert posed a question that would undermine the *Dissertation* and begin that train of reflections that would eventually lead to the first *Critique*. Lambert said that he found Kant's sharp dualism between reason and sensibility troublesome, for he could not understand how such distinct faculties could cooperate (10:100). He then implied that there would have to be some interchange between them because the concepts of ontology must be applicable to phenomena (103). In effect, then, Lambert had posed the question: How do we know that the pure *a priori* concepts of metaphysics are applicable to experience?

Lambert's question seems to have plagued Kant for well over a year.[39] The first result of his reflections on this question was his celebrated February 2, 1772, letter to Marcus Herz, where Kant first poses the fundamental problem of the critical philosophy. In this letter Kant began by telling Herz of his plans to publish soon a work titled *Die Grenzen der Sinnlichkeit und der Vernunft*, which would consist of two parts, one theoretical and the other practical. While thinking through the first part, Kant observed that he was still missing something important, something that constituted "the key to the secret of the hitherto still obscure metaphysics" (10:124). He now felt that it was necessary to raise the question: "On what basis does a representation relate to its object?" This is an especially acute problem, Kant argued, for the *a priori* concepts of the understanding.

It is easy to answer this question in the case of empirical concepts, for these are only the manner in which the subject is affected by objects given to it, so that the representation will be an effect that corresponds to its cause. There is also no difficulty in the case of mathematical concepts, because here the mind creates its objects in the very act of knowing them, so that there is nothing in the object not thought in the concept. Yet our understanding is in possession of *a priori* concepts that are not the cause of their objects nor the effect of objects given in experience. The problem then arises: How do *a priori* representations correspond to objects if they do not create or derive from them (124–6)? Kant flatly rejected the previous solutions to this problem offered by Plato, Malebranche, and Leibniz, which postulated some intuition of the divine or a preestablished harmony (126). Such metaphysical ideas were no better than a deus ex machina. They explained the obscure by the more obscure and begged the question of how we could have knowledge of God or the preestablished harmony. Kant believed that he had made considerable progress toward the solution of this problem (126–7). In searching for the origin of our intellectual knowledge, he classified all the concepts of "transcendental philosophy" according to a few fundamental principles of the understanding. Kant was so satisfied with the progress of his inquiries that he felt confident that, within the next three months, he could write a "Kritik der reinen Vernunft" (critique of pure reason).

Yet we know, again thanks to hindsight, that such optimism was unfounded. The letter to Herz shows that Kant was still very far from a solution to his problem. His proposed solution determines at best only the origin of our *a priori* concepts, but not their justification, their application to experience. In other words, to use Kant's later terminology, he had provided only a "metaphysical" and not a "transcendental deduction." Kant still had not arrived at the crucial distinction between the *quid juris* and *quid facti*, the question of the justification and that of the origin of knowledge. He seemed to think that to determine the origin of a concept is to determine its justification.

It was probably shortly after his letter to Herz that Kant was aroused from his "dogmatic slumber" by his recollection of Hume.[40] Kant had been aware of Hume's skepticism since at least the summer of 1759, for J. G. Hamann had told him about it in a letter written in June of that year (10:15). He had probably read a translation of the *Essays* and *Enquiries* by the early 1760s,[41] because he refers to Hume in both his announcement of his lectures for the winter semester of 1765–66 (2:311) and in his *Observations on the Feeling of the Beautiful and the Sublime* (2:253). Herder, who had heard Kant lecture from 1762 to 1764, said that Hume was one of his most frequently cited authors.[42] There are indeed striking parallels between Hume's and Kant's criticism of rationalism in 1763 and 1766, because Kant uses the same example as Hume in criticizing the rationalist interpretation of the principle of causality.[43] Nevertheless, it is unlikely that Hume exerted his decisive influence in the 1760s. Kant's criticism of rationalism could have come from more indigenous sources, most notably Crusius; and, in any case, Kant was not exactly slumbering in the 1760s with regard to the presuppositions of rationalism. Kant's "dogmatic slumbers" most probably took place from 1770 to 1772, between the *Dissertation* and his letter to Herz. In using this expression, Kant was probably referring to his confident belief that the *Dissertation* was his final position. A recollection of Hume would have been most fitting after 1772, for it would have helped Kant to formulate in more powerful and precise terms the problem he stated to Herz. If Hume's doubts about causality were duly generalized, then they implied that *a priori* concepts could be neither demonstrated *a priori* nor verified in experience. In other words, to use the terminology that Kant evolved at this time, these concepts appeared in judgments that were neither analytic *a priori* nor synthetic *a posteriori* but synthetic *a priori*. The influence of Hume is most visible, then, in Kant's later formulation of the criticial problem: "How are synthetic *a priori* judgments possible?" What perhaps sparked the memory of Hume was a translation of James Beattie's *An Essay on the Nature and Immutability of Truth*, which appeared in its German version in 1772.[44] Beattie's *Essay* contained long summaries of Hume, and in particular important passages from the *Treatise* that had not been translated before.

It was perhaps Kant's recollection of Hume that convinced him that he was very far from a solution to the difficulty confronting him. In any case, the hope that he could write a "Kritik der reinen Vernunft" by the summer of 1772 soon dissipated. In his next letter to Marcus Herz, written toward the end of 1773, Kant had to admit that his work had created more problems than he had anticipated. He explained that he wanted to create "a wholly new science," and that such a project demanded much effort in creating a new method, terminology, and classification of concepts (10:137). Still, Kant hoped to complete his work by the following Easter. Once again, though, Kant was compelled to shelve these plans. On November 24, 1776, nearly three years later, he wrote to Herz that, although he had amassed huge amounts of material and had never worked more systematically and persistently, his project was still not complete. Kant again referred to the problems of creating a completely new system of philosophy. He was pleased to report, though, that he now had the major obstacles behind him and expected to be finished by the next summer (10:185–6). But, as if he realized that this was much too optimistic, Kant asked Herz not to have too high expectations, as this was only added pressure. And, sure enough, Kant was still far from finished. His following letters to Herz, those written August 20, 1777 and April 1778, continue in a similar vein. Kant again says that the difficulties of his project prevent its completion; and he proposes two new dates for publication, both of them soon forgotten (10:195–8, 214–16).

Just how far Kant had come in his thinking by the middle of the 1770s is shown by the *Duisburg Nachlaß*, some fragments written in 1775.[45] These manuscripts reveal that Kant had already arrived at most of the fundamental ideas of the *Critique*. They sketch in very rough form some of the ideas of the transcendental deduction and analogies. Kant has already formulated the concept of objectivity of the deduction, analyzing the concept of an object into a rule of synthesis;[46] and he has stated its central critical conclusion – namely, that synthetic *a priori* concepts are possible only as necessary conditions of experience.[47] The standpoint of the *Dissertation* is now far behind Kant. *A priori* concepts do not give knowledge without application to experience; and understanding and sensibility are not opposed to each other but cooperate to provide the conditions of knowledge.

If Kant had made great progress by 1775, his project was still far from complete. What is missing in the *Duisburg Nachlaß* is the detailed argumentation of the *Critique*. The problem of supplying that argumentation, along with Kant's frail health and academic duties, is sufficient to explain the further five years he needed for the completion of the *Critique*. It was only on May 1, 1781 that Kant could write to Herz that a book by him would soon appear under the title *Kritik der reinen Vernunft*.

Now that we have surveyed Kant's intellectual development since 1746 it would be pleasant to describe the publication of the *Critique* as a happy ending, as the crowning conclusion of Kant's career. But this is a temptation that we should firmly resist. Kant's most creative decade, the 1780s, was still to come. If the critical philosophy had been born, it still had to mature. Its later shape and structure – the division into three *Critiques* with the *Critique of Judgment* as the keystone – was to become fully clear to Kant only in the late 1780s. In the end, the story of Kant's intellectual development stops only with his death. For, well into the 1790s, Kant was thinking about the foundations of metaphysics, and he was constantly changing his ideas. The flames of his old love affair burned on until the bitter end.

NOTES

1 See *Dreams*, 2:367.
2 See J. C. Adelung, *Versuch eines vollständigen grammatisch-kritischen Wörterbuches der Hochdeutschen Mundart* (Leipzig, 1777), Theil III, p. 488, "Metaphysik."
3 On the intellectual context of Königsberg in the early eighteenth century, see Benno Erdmann, *Martin Knutzen und seine Zeit* (Leipzig, 1876).
4 The prize for the competition went to Mendelssohn's *Abhandlung über die Evidenz in metaphysischen Wissenschaften* (Berlin, 1764); Kant's contribution won the *Accessit*. Lambert's contribution to the competition was never published or even submitted. It was later published by Karl Bopp in *Kant-Studien, Ergänzungshefte* 36 and 42 (1915, 1918) under the title "Über die Methode die Metaphysik, Theologie und Moral richtiger zu beweisen." On the general context behind the debate about the mathematical method, see G. Tonelli, "Der Streit über die mathematische Methode in der Philosophie in der ersten Halfte des 18 Jahrhunderts und die Entstehung von Kants Schrift ueber die Deutlichkeit," *Archiv für Philosophie* 9 (1959): 37–66.
5 Concerning these disputes, see E. Cassirer, *Das Erkenntnisproblem in der Philosophie und Wissenschaft der neueren Zeit* (Berlin, 1911), vol. III, pp. 442–521, esp. 472–85; and Irving Polonoff, "Force, Cosmos, Mo-

nads and Other Themes of Kant's Early Thought," *Kant-Studien, Ergän-zungsheft* 107 (1973): 6–21, 77–89.

6 Leonhard Euler, *Lettres à une Princesse d'Allemagne* (Leipzig, 1770), vol. II, 218–19.

7 On the importance of the antinomies for the formation of the critical philosophy, see Benno Erdmann's introduction to his *Reflexionen Kants zur kritischen Philosophie* (Leipzig, 1885), pp. xxiv–xlvii; and Norbert Hinske, *Kants Weg zur Transcendentalphilosophie* (Stuttgart, 1970), pp. 97–133.

8 See, for example, J. F. Budde, *Bedencken über die Wolffianische Philosophie* (Freiburg, 1724), pp. 1–5, 10–12, 15, 21; J. Lange, *Bescheidene und ausführliche Entdeckung der falschen und schädlichen Philosophie in dem Wolffianischen System der Metaphysik* (Halle, 1724), pp. 34–57, 130–49, 177–80, 211–43, esp. 62–6 and *Placidae Vindiciae: Modestae Disquisitionis de Systemate Philosophiae Novo* (Halle, 1723). The Pietist battle against Wolff is described in detail by Max Wundt, *Die deutsche Schulphilosophie im Zeitalter der Aufklärung* (Hildesheim, 1964), pp. 230–64.

9 On Crusius's critique of rationalism, see his *Entwurf der nothwendigen Vernunftwahrheiten* (Leipzig, 1745) §§33–8, 72, 235.

10 There are conflicting interpretations of the aims of the young Kant. There are those who stress the primacy of Kant's epistemological concerns even in his early natural philosophy. See, for example, E. Cassirer, *Kants Leben und Lehre* (Berlin, 1921) pp. 25–6, 48–9, and H. de Vleeschauwer, *The Development of Kantian Thought* (London, 1962), pp. 15–26. There are also those who see Kant's primary concern as natural philosophy rather than epistemology. See, for example, A. Drews, *Kants Naturphilosophie als Grundlage seines Systems* (Berlin, 1894), pp. iii–iv, and Polonoff, "Force, Cosmos, Monads," p. 60. Some completely ignore Kant's early writings on natural philosophy because they are not relevant to his epistemological concerns; see, for example, Friedrich Paulsen, *Versuch einer Entwicklungsgeschichte der kantischen Erkenntnistheorie* (Leipzig, 1875), pp. 1–3. This debate is sterile, however, resting upon artificial distinctions between disciplines. Once we recognize that Kant's primary aim in his early writings was to provide a foundation for a metaphysics of nature, then it follows that his concerns were necessarily both epistemological and scientific.

11 On Leibniz's use of the term "metaphysical" in this context, see his *Discours de Metaphysique*, §§10, 18, in *Die philosophischen Schriften von G. W. Leibniz*, ed. C. J. Gerhardt (Berlin, 1880), vol. IV, pp. 434, 444.

12 Concerning Kant's rejection of "materialism" and "Freigeisterei," see

the Preface to the *Universal Natural History*, I, 1:229, 231, and the "Scholion" to Propositio XII of the *Nova dilucidatio*, 1:495.

13 Concerning Kant's rejection of dualism, see *Living Forces*, §§5, 6, 1:19–21. In the *Nova dilucidatio*, however, Kant began to take a different position toward the relationship between mind and body. See §3, 1:412–16.

14 This opinion is held by, for example, Paulsen, *Versuch einer Entwicklungsgeschicte der kontischen Erkenntnistheorie*, p. 29, and Keith Ward, *The Development of Kant's View of Ethics* (Oxford, 1972), p. 5.

15 See the Preface to the *Living Forces*, 1:1–16. [Publication of *Living Forces* began in 1746 but dragged on until 1747. (P.G.)]

16 It is important to recognize, however, that Wolff himself had his reservations about applying the mathematical method to natural philosophy. He sometimes distinguished between the philosophical and mathematical method. See, for example, *Vernunftige Gedanken von den Würkungen der Natur* (Halle, 1725), pp. 12–13, 18, and *Uebrige theils noch gefundene kleine Schriften und Einzelne Betrachtungen zur Verbeserung der Wissenschaft* (Halle, 1755), pp. 286–92. But it would be wrong to argue, as does Polonoff, "Force, Cosmos, Monads," p. 73, that Kant was only a follower of Wolff in distinguishing between mathematics and metaphysics. For Kant's polemic in the *Gedanken* is clearly directed across Wolffians who overextend the mathematical method in natural philosophy.

17 See Kant, *Prolegomena*, Preface, 4:260–1.

18 As Lewis White Beck has rightly put it. See his *Early German Philosophy* (Cambridge, Mass., 1969), p. 439.

19 The most notable exponent of this common view was Hegel. See his *Enzklopädie der philosophischen Wissenschaften* §42 in *Werke in Zwanzig Bänden*, ed. E. Moldenhauer and K. Michel (Frankfurt, 1971), Vol. VIII, 117. Cf. *Geschichte der Philosophie* 20:345.

20 Kant's concept of matter as a self-organizing force was on a par with that of the early English free-thinkers, such as Toland and Collins. On their conception of matter and the early reaction to it, see Margaret C. Jacob, *The Radical Enlightenment: Pantheists, Freemasons and Republicans* (London, 1981), pp. 29–62.

21 See Rousseau, *Discours sur l'origine et les fondements de l'inégalité parmi les hommes*, ed. J. Roger (Paris, 1971), pp. 209, 216–17.

22 On the importance of Rousseau for the development of Kant's moral philosophy around 1765, see J. Schmucker, *Die Ursprünge der Ethik Kants* (Meisenheim, 1961), pp. 143–252, and R. L. Velkley, *Freedom and the End of Reason* (Chicago, 1989), pp. 61–88.

23 See 20:31, 138, 145. Cf. *R* 6598, 6610, 6672, 19:103, 107, 129.

24 See, for example, W. H. Werkmeister, *Kant: The Architechtonic and Development of his Philosophy* (London, 1980), p. 43.

25 Concerning some of these speculations, see Beck, *Early German Philosophy*, p. 457.

26 The dating of these materials is fortunately not subject to much doubt. See Adickes's comments on their dating in 14:xxxviii–xix.

27 *R* 3946, 17:359.

28 *R* 3931, 17:353; Cf. *R* 3946, 17:359; and *R* 3959, 17:367.

29 *R* 3978, 17:373–4.

30 *R* 3949, 17:361; *R* 3952, 17:362–3; *R* 3917, 17:343; *R* 3938, 17:355; *R* 3954, 17:363; *R* 4369, 17:521–2.

31 *R* 4254, 17:483–4; *R* 4108, 17:418; *R* 4349, 17:516.

32 See *Dreams*, 2:334–7.

33 *R* 4349, 17:516; *R* 4375, 17:525; *R* 4261, 17:486; *R* 4291, 17:498; *R* 4254, 17:483–4.

34 *R* 4349, 17:516.

35 *R* 5037, 18:69.

36 See *R* 4334, 17:509; *R* 4336, 17:510; *R* 3922, 17:346–7.

37 Concerning the dubious reliability of some of the lecture notes, see Kant's August 28 and October 20, 1778 letters to Beck, 10:195–8, 214–16. Concerning the debate about the dating of the *Vorlesungen über Metaphysik*, see Benno Erdmann's articles, "Eine unbeachtet gebliebene Quelle zur Entwicklungsgeschichte Kant's" and "Mittheilungen über Kant's metaphysischen Standpunkt in der Zeit um 1774," *Philosophische Monatshefte* 19–20 (1883): 129–44, 65–97. Erdmann's case for dating these manuscripts around 1774 was effectively demolished by Paul Menzer in "Die Entwicklungs-geschichte der kantischen Ethik in den Jahren 1760–65," *Kant-Studien* 3 (1894): 41–104, 56, 57, 64–65. Because the dating of this material is so uncertain, I have decided not to consider it in my account of Kant's development in the 1770s.

38 Concerning Kant's failure to develop transcendental idealism in the *Dissertation*, see Paul Guyer, *Kant and the Claims of Knowledge* (Cambridge, 1987), pp. 11–24.

39 On the influence of Lambert on Kant's philosophical development at this time, see L. W. Beck, "Lambert and Hume in Kant's Development from 1769 to 1772," *Essays on Hume and Kant* (New Haven, Conn., 1978), pp. 101–10.

40 The arguments for placing Hume's influence in the 1760s were sharply criticized by Benno Erdmann in his "Kant und Hume um 1762," *Archiv für Geschichte der Philosophie* 1 (1888): 62–77, 216–30. In placing Hume's influence in the 1770s, I follow Beck, *Essays*, pp. 101–10 and

Early German Philosophy, pp. 464–5, and De Vleeschauwer, *The Development of Kantian Thought*, pp. 64–5.

41 This translation was by J. G. Sulzer and appeared under the title *Philosophische Versuche über die menschliche Erkenntnis* (Hamburg and Leipzig, 1755). This edition included translations of both the *Enquiries*.

42 See Herder, *Briefe zur Beförderung der Humanität*, in *Sämmtliche Werke*, ed. B. Suphan (Berlin, 1881), vol. XVII, 404 and vol. XVIII, 325.

43 On these parallels, see Cassirer, *Erkenntnisproblem*, vol. II, 606–9.

44 See James Beattie, *Versuch über die Natur und Unveränderlichkeit der Wahrheit* (Leipzig, 1772).

45 On the *Duisburg Nachlaß*, see Guyer, *Kant and the Claims of Knowledge*, pp. 25–70, and Theodor Haering, *Der Duisburg'sche Nachlaß und Kants Kriticismus um 1775* (Tübingen, 1910).

46 See Haering, *Nachlaß*, *Blatt* 15 (19)(22), *Blatt* 8(4).

47 Ibid., *Blatt* 17 (3–4); *Blatt* 12 (9); *Blatt* 18 (10).

2   The Transcendental Aesthetic

Among the pillars of Kant's philosophy, and of his transcendental idealism in particular, is the view of space and time as *a priori* intuitions and as forms of outer and inner intuition respectively. The first part of the systematic exposition of the *Critique of Pure Reason* is the Transcendental Aesthetic, whose task is to set forth this conception. It is then presupposed in the rest of the systematic work of the *Critique* in the Transcendental Logic.

I

The claim of the Aesthetic is that space and time are *a priori* intuitions. Knowledge is called *a priori* if it is "independent of experience and even of all impressions of the senses" (B 2). Kant is not very precise about what this "independence" consists in. In the case of *a priori* judgments, it seems clear that being *a priori* implies that no particular facts verified by experience and observation are to be appealed to in their justification. Kant holds that necessity and universality are criteria of apriority in a judgment, and clearly this depends on the claim that appeal to facts of experience could not justify a judgment made as necessary and universal.[1] Because Kant is quite consistent about what propositions he regards as *a priori* and about how he characterizes the notion, the absence of a more precise explanation has not led to its being regarded in commentary on Kant as one of his more problematic notions, even though a reader of today

I wish to thank the editor for his comments on an earlier version, for his explanation of his own views, and for his patience. I am also indebted to the participants in a seminar on Kant at Harvard University in the fall of 1989.

would be prepared at least to entertain the idea that the notion of *a priori* knowledge is either hopelessly unclear or vacuous.

It is part of Kant's philosophy that not only judgments but also concepts and intuitions can be *a priori*. In this case the appeal to justification does not obviously apply. It is harder to separate what their being *a priori* consists in from an explanation that Kant offers, that they are contributions of our minds to knowledge, "prior" to experience because they are brought to experience by the mind. However, I believe a little more can be said. For a representation to be *a priori* it must not contain any reference to the content of particular experiences or to objects whose existence is known only by experience. *A priori* concepts and intuitions are in a way necessary and universal in their application (so that their content is spelled out in *a priori* judgments). In fact, Kant apparently holds that if a concept is *a priori*, its objective reality can be established only by *a priori* means; that seems to be Kant's reason for denying that change and physical motion are *a priori* concepts.[2] Although this consideration leads into considerable difficulties, they do not affect the apriority of the concepts of space and time or of mathematics.

The concept of intuition requires more discussion. Kant begins the Aesthetic as follows:

In whatever manner and by whatever means a mode of knowledge may relate to objects, *intuition* is that through which it is in immediate relation to them.   (A 19 / B 33)

Later he writes of intuition that it "relates immediately to the object and is singular," in contrast with a concept, which "refers to it mediately by means of a feature which several things may have in common" (A 320 / B 377). To this should be compared the definition of intuition and concept in his lectures on Logic:

All modes of knowledge, that is, all representations related to an object with consciousness, are either *intuitions* or *concepts*. The intuition is a singular representation (*repraesentatio singularis*), the concept a *general* (*repraesentatio per notas communes*) or *reflected* representation (*repraesentatio discursiva*).[3]

An intuition, then, is a singular representation; that is, it relates to a single object. In this it is the analogue of a singular term. A concept is general.[4] The objects to which it relates are evidently those that fall under it. That it is a *repraesentatio per notas communes* is just what the *Critique* says in saying that it refers to an object by means of a feature (*Merkmal*, 'mark') which several things may have in common.

In both characterizations in the *Critique*, an intuition is also said to relate to its object "immediately." Kant gives little explanation of this "immediacy condition," and its meaning has been a matter of controversy. It means at least that it does not refer to an object by means of marks. It seems that a representation might be singular but single out its object by means of concepts; it would be expressed in language by a definite description. One would expect such a representation not to be an intuition. And in fact, in a letter to J. S. Beck of 3 July, 1792, Kant speaks of "the black man" as a concept (11:347). Apparently he does not, however, have a category of singular non-immediate representations, that is, singular concepts. He says that the division of concepts into universal, particular, and singular is mistaken. "Not the concepts themselves, but only their use, can be divided in that way."⁵ Kant does not say much about the singular use of concepts, but their use in the subject of singular judgments is evidently envisaged. The most explicit explanation is in a set of student notes of his lectures on logic, where after talking of the use of the concept *house* in universal and particular judgments, he says,

Or I use the concept only for a single thing, for example: This house is cleaned in such and such a way. It is not concepts but judgments that we divide into universal, particular, and singular.⁶

Thus it is not clear that there are singular representations that fail to satisfy the immediacy condition.

Assuming that there are none, it does not follow that the immediacy condition is just a "corollary" of the singularity condition, as Jaakko Hintikka maintained in his earlier writings.⁷ The fact that the only "intrinsically" singular representations are intuitions follows from the singularity and immediacy conditions only together with the further substantive thesis that it is only the "use" of concepts that can be singular. Moreover, we have so far said little about what the immediacy condition means.

Evidently concepts are expressed in language by general terms. It would be tempting to suppose that, correlatively, intuitions are expressed by singular terms. This view faces the difficulty that Kant's conception of the logical form of judgment does not give any place to singular terms. In Kant's conception of formal logic, the constituents of a judgment are concepts, and concepts are general. We are inclined to think of the most basic form of proposition as being 'a is F' or 'Fa', where 'a' names an individual object, to which the predicate 'F' is applied. How is such a proposition to be expressed if it must be composed from general concepts? Evidently the name must itself involve a singular use of a concept. Kant does offer examples involving names as cases of singular judgments,[8] but also judgments of the form 'This F is G'.[9] Kant's acceptance of the traditional view that in the theory of inference singular judgments do not have to be distinguished from universal ones (A 71 / B 96) implies that the subject concept in a singular judgment can also occur in an equivalent universal judgment.[10]

Relation to an object not by means of concepts, that is to say not by attributing properties to it, naturally suggests to us the modern idea of direct reference. That that was what Kant intended has been proposed by Robert Howell.[11] It appears from the above that Kant's view must be that judgments cannot have any directly referential constituents, and indeed it has been persuasively argued that Kant has to hold something like a description theory of names.[12] This is not a decisive objection, however, because intuitions are not properly speaking constituents of judgments. This conclusion still leaves some troubling questions, particularly concerning demonstratives. If we render the form of a singular judgment as 'The F is G', then the question arises how we are to understand statements of the form 'This F is G' or even those of the form 'This is G'. The latter form might plausibly (at least from a Kantian point of view) be assimilated to the former, on the ground that with 'this' is implicitly associated a concept, in order to identify an object for 'this' to refer to. But now how are we to understand the demonstrative force of 'this' in 'This F is G'? It only shifts the problem to paraphrase such a statement as 'The F here is G'. Although there is no doubt something conceptual in the content of 'this' or 'here' (perhaps involving a relation to the observer), in many actual contexts it will be understood and interpreted with the help of perception. It is hard to escape the conclusion, which seems to be the view of Howell,[13] that in such a context intuition is essential not just to the verification of such a judgment and to establishing the nonvacuity of the concepts in it, but also to understanding its content. But it would accord with Kant's general view that the manifold of intuition cannot acquire the unity that is already suggested by the idea of intuition as singular representation without synthesis according to concepts, that one should not be able to single out any portion of a judgment that represents in a wholly nonconceptual way.

In the Aesthetic, the logical meaning of the immediacy condition that we have been exploring is not suggested. Following the passage cited previously Kant says that intuition is that

> to which all thought as a means is directed. But intuition takes place only in so far as the object is given to us. This again is only possible, to man at least, in so far as the mind is affected in a certain way.   (A 19 / B 33)

The capacity for receiving representations through being affected by objects is what Kant calls sensibility; that for us intuitions arise only through sensibility is thus something Kant was prepared to state at the outset. It appears to be a premise of the argument of the Aesthetic; if not Kant does not clearly indicate there any argument of which it is the conclusion.[14]

An earlier proposal of my own, that immediacy for Kant is direct, phenomenological presence to the mind, as in perception,[15] fits well both with the opening of the Aesthetic and the structure of the Metaphysical Exposition of the concept of space (see Section II of this essay). One has to be careful because this "presence" has to be understood in such a way as not to imply that intuition as such must be sensible, since that would rule out Kant's conception of intellectual intuition,[16] and of course that human intuition is sensible was never thought by Kant to follow immediately from the meaning of 'intuition'. That this is what the immediacy condition means can probably not be established by direct textual evidence.[17] What is in any case of more decisive importance is the question what role immediacy in this sense might play in the parts of Kant's philosophy where intuition plays a role, particularly his philosophy of mathematics. The intent of Hintikka, apparently shared by some other writers on pure intuition whose views are not otherwise close to Hintikka's,[18] is to deny that pure intuition as it operates in Kant's philosophy of mathematics is immediate in this sense at all, whether by definition or not. Whether this is true is a question to keep in mind as we proceed.

II

I now turn to the argument of the Aesthetic. The part of the argument called (in the second edition) the Metaphysical and Transcendental Expositions of the concepts of space and time (§§2–3 (through B 41), 4–5) argues that space, and then time, are *a priori* intuitions. The further conclusions that they are forms of our sensible intuition, that they do not apply to things as they are in themselves and are thus in some way subjective, are drawn in the "conclusions" from these arguments (remainder of §3, §6) and in the following "elucidation" (§7) and "general observations" (§8, augmented in B). The framework is Kant's conception of "sensibility," the capacity of the mind to receive representations through the presence of objects:

By means of outer sense, a property of our mind, we represent to ourselves objects as outside us, and all without exception in space.   (A 22 / B 37)

"Outside us" cannot have as its primary meaning just outside our *bodies*, because the body is in space and what is inside it is equally an object of outer sense.[19]

Kant alludes at the outset to what is in fact the background of all his thinking about space (and to a large extent time as well): the issue between what are now called absolutist and relationist conceptions of space and time, represented paradigmatically by Newton and Leibniz:

What, then, are space and time? Are they real existences? Are they only determinations or relations of things, yet such as would belong to things even if they were not intuited?   (A 23 / B 37)

Early in his career Kant's view of space was relationist and basically Leibnizian. This was what one would expect from the domination of German philosophy in Kant's early years by Christian Wolff's version of Leibniz's philosophy. Kant was, of course, influenced from the beginning by Newton and was never an orthodox Wolffian. In 1768 in *Regions in Space*, he changed his view of space in a more Newtonian direction;[20] this was the first step in the formation of his final view, which is in essentials set forth in the *Dissertation* of 1770.

The Metaphysical Exposition of the Concept of Space gives four arguments, the first two evidently for the claim that space is *a priori*, the second two for the claim that it is an intuition.

(i) The first argument claims that "space is not an empirical concept which has been derived from outer experiences" (A 23 / B 38). The representation of space has to be presupposed in order to "refer" sensations to something outside me or to represent them as in characteristic spatial relations to one another.

This argument might seem to prove too much, if its form is, "In order to represent something as *X*, the representation of *X* must be presupposed." If that is generally true, and if it implies that *X* is *a priori*, the argument would show that all representations are *a priori*.

Kant seems, rather, to be claiming that the representation of space (as an individual, it will turn out from the third and fourth arguments) must be presupposed in order to represent particular spatial relations. The argument should be seen as aimed at relationism. Leibniz would be committed to holding that space consists of certain relations obtaining between things whose existence is prior both to that of space and to these relations. However, it seems open to the relationist to say that objects and their spatial relations are interdependent and mutually conditioning.[21] The argument is stronger if it is viewed as calling attention to the fact that it is the spatial character of objects that enables us to represent them as distinct from ourselves and from each other. This is not the plain meaning of the text. That it may be Kant's underlying intention, however, is suggested by a parallel passage in the *Dissertation*:

For I may not conceive of something as placed outside me unless by representing it as in a place which is different from the place in which I myself am, nor may I conceive of things outside one another unless by locating them at different places in space.   (§15A, 2:402)

(ii) The second argument claims that space is prior to appearances, in effect to things in space:

We can never represent to ourselves the absence of space, though we can quite well think it as empty of objects.   (A 24 / B 38–9)

In what sense of "represent" can we not represent the absence of space? The existence of space is not necessary in the most stringent sense; in whatever sense we can think things in themselves, we can think a nonspatial world. On the other hand, Kant has to claim more than that we are incapable, as a "psychological" matter, of imagining or representing in some other way the absence of space.[22]

Kant's conclusion will be that space is in some way part of the content of any intuition, and in that way any kind of representation that allows representing the absence of space will not be intuitive. Thus he says that it is "the condition of the possibility of appearances" (A 24 / B 39). I doubt that one can single out at the outset, independent of the further theory Kant will develop, a notion of representation in which we can't represent the absence of space.

That space is a fundamental phenomenological given that in some way can't be thought away is a very persuasive claim. But it would take a whole theory to explain what it really means, and Kant seems to have to appeal to more theory in order to explicate it himself. We can think its absence, but we can't give content to that thought in the sense of "content" that matters: relation to intuition. But that way of putting the point presupposes not only the claim that outer intuition is spatial, but the claim that concepts require intuition in order not to be empty.

Kant says we can think space without objects. This is in one way obviously true; for example, it is what we do in doing geometry. It is not clear, however, that Kant means to appeal to geometry at this point, and if he does one could, at least from a modern point of view, object to his claim on the ground that in geometry we are dealing with a mathematical abstraction, not with physical space (or at least that it is then a substantive scientific, and in the end empirical, question whether our description of space fits physical reality). In any event, it is not clear that the thought of space without objects is not really just the thought of space with objects about which nothing is assumed. This understanding, which seems weaker than what Kant intended, is sufficient for Kant's claim that space is *a priori* but possibly not for his case against relationism.

(iii–iv) The third and fourth arguments of the Metaphysical Exposition are, as I have said, concerned to show that space is an intuition. Strictly, the claim is that this is true of the "original representation" of space (B 40), because from Kant's point of view there clearly must be such a thing as the concept of space, to be a constituent of judgments concerning space.[23]

Part of Kant's claim, what is emphasized in the third argument, is that the representation of space is singular. This has a clear and unproblematic meaning. That when it refers to the space in which we live and perceive objects, or to the space of classical physics, "space" is singular is an obvious datum of what one might call grammar; moreover, its having reference in the former usage surely rests on the fact that there is a unique space of experience, and it is reasonable to suppose that the uniqueness of space in classical physics derives from this.

It is abstractly conceivable, however, that we could have characterized space in some conceptual way from which uniqueness would *follow* (as might be the case with a conception of God in philosophical theology). Then we would have, not an intuition but a singular use of a concept. Kant clearly intends to rule out this possibility. Now this would be, if not exactly ruled out, rendered idle if Kant could claim that the representation of space is not only singular but also immediate in the sense of one of the interpretations mentioned above, of involving presence to the mind analogous to perception. Kant seems to be saying that when he begins the fourth argument with the statement, "Space is represented as an infinite *given* magnitude" (B 39; cf. A 25). In any event Kant needs, and clearly intends to claim, a form of immediate knowledge of space; otherwise the question would arise whether what he has said about the character of the representation of space does not leave open the possibility that there is just no such thing.

Kant also claims that the representation of a unitary space is prior to that of spaces, which he conceives as parts of space. (The modern mathematical notion of space, roughly a structure analogous to what is considered in geometry, is not under consideration.) Spaces in this sense can only be conceived as *in* "the one all-embracing space" (A 25 / B 39); unlike a concept, the representation of space contains "an infinite number of representations *within* itself" (B 40).

Whatever the precise sense of 'immediate' in which Kant's thesis implies that the representation of space is immediate, there is a phenomenological fact to which he is appealing: places, and thereby objects in space, are given in a one space, therefore with a "horizon" of surrounding space. The point is perhaps put most explicitly in the *Dissertation:*

The concept of space is a singular representation comprehending all things *within itself,* not an abstract common notion containing them *under itself.*

For what you speak of as several places are only parts of the same boundless space, related to one another by a fixed position, nor can you conceive to yourself a cubic foot unless it be bounded in all directions by the space that surrounds it.   (§15B, 2:402)

This way of putting the matter has the virtue of describing a sense in which space is given as infinite (better, "boundless") that does not commit Kant to any metrical infinity of space (that is, the lack of any upper bound on distances), although his allegiance to Euclidean geometry did lead him to affirm the metrical infinity of space. Kant says that space is given as "boundless"; he also wishes to say that, without the aid of the intuition of space, no concept would accomplish this:

A general concept of space . . . cannot determine anything in regard to magnitude. If there were no limitlessness in the progression of intuition, no concept of relations could yield a principle of their infinitude.   (A 25)

Kant does not, so far as I can see, argue in the Aesthetic that the infinity of space could not be yielded by "mere concepts" at all, still less that no infinity at all could be obtained in that way. His arguments seem at most to say that "a general concept of space" could not do this and are not in my view of much interest. It seems very likely that from Kant's point of view there can be a conceptual representation whose content would in some way entail infinity (that of God would again be an example[24]). From a modern point of view, we can describe (say, by logical formulas) types of structure that can have only infinite instances; an axiomatization of geometry would be an example. Such a description would use logical resources unknown to Kant, and that he would have recognized the possibility of a purely conceptual description of *mathematically* infinite magnitude is doubtful.[25] But even if he did, there would be the further question of constructing it, which would be the equivalent for Kant of showing its existence in the mathematical sense. Construction is, of course, construction in intuition. By the "progression of intuitions" in the preceding quotation (A 25), Kant presumably means some succession of intuitions relating to parts of space each beyond or outside its predecessor; such a succession would "witness" the boundlessness of space. A similar appeal to intuition is needed also for the construction of numbers, so that arithmetic does not yield a representation of infinity whose nonempty character can be shown in a "purely conceptual" way.

What is accomplished by the Metaphysical Exposition? Kant makes a number of claims about space of a phenomenological character that seem to me on the whole sound. That space is in some way prior to objects, in the sense that objects are experienced as *in* space, and in the sense that experience does not reveal objects, in some way not intrinsically spatial, that stand in relations from which the conception of space could be constructed, seems to me evident. The same holds for the claim that space as experienced is unique and boundless (in the sense explained previously).

Furthermore, it seems to me that these considerations do form a formidable obstacle that a relationist view such as Leibniz's has to overcome. However, they are not a refutation of such a view, because phenomenological claims of this kind would not suffice to show that, in our objective description of the physical world, we would not in the end be able to carry out a reduction of reference to space to reference to relations of underlying objects such as Leibniz's individual substances (monads).

It is another question how much of a case Kant has yet made for the stronger claims of his theory of space. Regarding the claim that space is *a priori*, part of the content of this is surely that *propositions* about space will be known *a priori*, and it is hard to see so far that anything very specific has been shown to have this character. But the propositions in question will be primarily those of geometry, and we have not yet examined the Transcendental Exposition or other evidence concerning Kant's view of geometry.

The kind of considerations brought forth in the Metaphysical Exposition also hardly rule out possible naturalistic explanations. It could be objected that our experience is spatial because we have evolved in a physical, spatiotemporal world. Such an explanation would of course presuppose space, but it would be empirical in that it made use of empirical theories such as evolution (or some alternative naturalistic account). It would view the inconceivability of the absence of space as a fact about human beings. In a way it could not have been otherwise: Beings of which it is not true would not be human beings in the sense in which we use that phrase. But although we can't conceive *how* it could turn out to be wrong, it is in some way abstractly possible that it *should* turn out to be wrong; some change in the world, which our present science is incapable of envisaging, could lead us to experience the world (and ourselves) as, say, in two spaces instead of one.

Now we should probably understand the claims made in the Metaphysical Exposition as ruling out the kind of naturalistic story just sketched. When Kant says that the representation of space "*must* be presupposed" in one or another context, the necessity he has in mind is something stricter than the natural necessity that is the most stringent that one could expect to come out of the naturalistic story. This does not change the philosophical issue, since the naturalist would respond that insofar as they make this strong claim, the claims of the Metaphysical Exposition are dogmatic. I shall leave the issue at this point, because the notion of necessity will come up at some further points in the discussion of the Aesthetic, in particular in connection with geometry.

Because I have said that the Metaphysical Exposition, although it poses a real difficulty for relationism, does not refute that view, we should not leave it without noting that it does not contain Kant's whole case against the relationist position. Kant's break with relationism came in *Regions in Space* in 1768. There he refers to an essay by Euler which argues for absolute space on the basis of dynamical arguments that go back to Newton.[26] Kant says that Euler's accomplishment is purely negative, in showing the difficulty the relationist position has in interpreting the general laws of motion, and that he does not overcome the difficulties of the absolutist position in the same domain (2:378). Kant then deploys his own argument, the famous argument from "incongruent counterparts." Although this argument does not occur in the *Critique*, it is used for different purposes in other later writings of Kant, up to the *Metaphysical Foundations of Natural Science* of 1786.[27]

By incongruent counterparts Kant means bodies, in his examples three-dimensional, that fail to be congruent only because of an opposite orientation. (The same term could be applied to figures representing their shapes.) One can think of right and left hands, with some idealization, as such bodies. He considers them "completely like and similar" (2:382), in particular in size and the manner of combination of their parts. Yet their surfaces cannot be made to coincide "twist and turn [it] how one will," evidently by continuous rigid motion. Nonetheless, Kant considers the difference to be an internal one, and he says:

Let it be imagined that the first created thing were a human hand, then it must necessarily be either a right hand or a left hand. In order to produce the one a different action of the creative cause is necessary from that, by means of which its counterpart could be produced.   (2:382–3)

Kant claims that the Leibnizian view could not recognize this difference, because it does not rest on a difference in the relations of the parts of the hands. He concludes that the properties of space are prior to the relations of bodies, in accordance with the conception of absolute space and contrary to relationism.

Kant's claim has been defended in our own time by noting that the existence of incongruent counterparts depends on *global* properties of the space.[28] We can already see this by a simple example: In the Euclidean plane, congruent triangles or other figures can be asymmetrical; they can be made to coincide by a motion only if it goes outside the plane into the third dimension. Similarly, it is the three-dimensionality of space (which Kant emphasizes) that prevents incongruent counterparts from being made to coincide; this could be accomplished if they could "move" through a fourth dimension. Moreover, in some spaces topologically differing from Euclidean space, called nonorientable spaces (a Möbius strip would be a (two-dimensional) example), the phenomenon could not arise.

Relationist replies to an argument based on these considerations are possible, but I shall not pursue the matter further here.[29]

III

I now turn to the Transcendental Exposition.

I understand by a transcendental exposition the explanation of a concept, as a principle from which the possibility of other *a priori* synthetic knowledge can be understood.   (B 40)

The claim of the Transcendental Exposition is that taking space to be an *a priori* intuition is necessary for the possibility of *a priori* synthetic knowledge in geometry.

It is therefore a premise of this argument that geometry is synthetic *a priori*. Kant clearly understood geometry as a science of space, the space of everyday experience and of physical science. Thus for us, it would be very doubtful that geometry on this understanding is *a priori*;[30] indeed, the development of non-Euclidean geometry and its application in physics were, historically, the main reasons why Kant's theory of geometry and space came to be rejected. With regard to geometry, as with mathematics in general, Kant, however, does not see a need to argue that it is *a priori*; it is supposed to follow from the obvious fact that mathematics is necessary (B 14–15). In this, Kant was in accord with the mathematical practice of his own time. The absence of any alternative to Euclidean geometry, and the fact that mathematicians had not sought for sophisticated verifications of the axioms of geometry, cohered with the absence of an available way of interpreting geometry so as to give space for the kind of distinction between "pure" and "applied" geometry that would imply that only the latter makes a commitment as to the character of physical space.[31]

It seems that there should not be any particular problem with Kant's assertion that characteristic geometric truths are synthetic, so long as we understand geometry as the science of space. But we must now, as we have not before, take account of the analytic–synthetic distinction. Kant gives the following explanation:

In all judgments in which the relation of a subject to the predicate is thought . . . , this relation is possible in two different ways. Either the predicate B belongs to the subject A, as something which is (covertly) contained in this concept A; or B lies outside the concept A, although it does indeed stand in connection with it. In the one case I entitle the judgment analytic, in the other synthetic.   (A 6–7 / B 10)

When a concept is "contained" in another may not be very clear. As a first approximation, we can say that a proposition is analytic if it can be verified by analysis of concepts. Kant thinks of such analysis as the breaking up of concepts into "those constituent concepts that have all along been thought in it, although confusedly" (A 7 / B 11); this would give rise to a narrower conception of what is analytic than has prevailed in later philosophy.

Kant suggests as a criterion of *synthetic* judgment that in order to verify it is necessary to appeal to something outside or beyond the subject concept. This may be experience, if the concept has been so derived, as in Kant's example "All bodies are heavy" (B 12, also A 8), or if experience is otherwise referred to. In the case of mathematical judgments it is, on Kant's view, pure intuition.

In arguing that mathematical judgments are synthetic, Kant emphasizes the case of arithmetic, where he seems (reasonably, in the light of history) to have anticipated more resistance. The geometrical example that he gives, that the straight line between two points is the shortest (B 16), might be more controversial than some alternatives, which either involve existence or had given rise to doubt. The parallel postulate of Euclidean geometry would meet both these conditions. It is hard to see how by analysis of the concept "point external to a given line" one could possibly arrive at the conclusion that a parallel to the line can be drawn through it, unless it is already built into the concept that the space involved is Euclidean. The latter way of looking at such a proposition, however, is alien to Kant.

We can well grant Kant's premise that geometrical propositions are synthetic; the hard questions about the analytic–synthetic distinction arise with arithmetic and with nonmathematical subject matters. But his view of geometry as synthetic *a priori* is tied to the mathematical practice of his own time. If we make the modern distinction between pure geometry as the study of certain structures of which Euclidean space is the oldest example, but which include not only alternative metric structures but also affine and projective spaces, and applied geometry as roughly concerned with the question which of these structures correctly applies to physical space (or space-time), then it is no longer clear that pure geometry is synthetic; at least the question is bound up with more difficult questions about the analytic–synthetic distinction and about the status of other mathematical disciplines such as arithmetic, analysis, and algebra; and the view that applied geometry is *a priori* would be generally rejected.

If we do grant Kant's premises, however, then the conclusion that space is an *a priori* intuition is, if not compelled, at least a very natural one. That it is precisely *intuition* that is needed to go beyond our concepts in geometrical judgments might be found to require more argument, particularly since he does admit the possibility of synthetic *a priori* judgments from concepts.[32] That empirical intuition will not do is implied by the premise that geometry is *a priori* and therefore necessary.

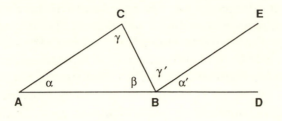

Figure 2.1

Kant does supply such an argument in his account of the construction of concepts in intuition, in the context of describing the difference between mathematical and philosophical method, to which we will now turn. This account has rightly been seen as filling a gap in the argument of the Aesthetic.[33] It has been the focus of much of the discussion in the last generation about Kant's philosophy of mathematics.

To construct a concept, according to Kant, is "to exhibit *a priori* the intuition that corresponds to the concept" (A 713 / B 741). An intuition that is the construction of a concept will be a single object, and yet "it must in its representation express universal validity for all possible intuitions that fall under the same concept" (ibid.). It is clear that Kant's primary model is geometrical constructions, in particular Euclidean constructions.[34]

It is construction of concepts that makes it possible to prove anything nontrivial in geometry, as Kant illustrates by the problem of the sum of the angles of a triangle. The proof proceeds by a series of constructions: One begins by constructing a triangle ABC (see Figure 2.1), then prolonging one of the sides AB to D, yielding internal and external angles whose sum is two right angles, then drawing a parallel BE dividing the external angle, and then observing that one has three angles α', β, γ', whose sum is two right angles and which are equal respectively to the angles α, β, γ of the triangle.[35]

In this fashion, through a chain of inferences guided throughout by intuition, he [the geometer] arrives at a fully evident and universally valid solution of the problem.   (A 716–7 / B 744–5)

Intuition seems to play several different roles in this description of a proof. The proof proceeds by operating on a constructed triangle, and the operations are further constructions. They are constructions *in*

intuition; space is, one might say, the field in which the constructions are carried out; it is by virtue of the nature of space that they
can be carried out. Postulates providing for certain constructions are
what, in Euclid's geometry, play the role played by existence axioms
in modern axiomatic theories such as the axiomatization of Euclidean geometry by Hilbert. But not all the evidences appealed to in
Euclid's geometry are of this form; in particular, objects given by the
elementary Euclidean constructions have specific properties such as
(to take the most problematic case) being parallel to a given line. On
Kant's conception, these evidences must also be intuitive. A third
role of intuition (connected with the first) is that we would represent
the reasoning involving constructive operations on a given triangle
as reasoning with *singular terms* (to be sure depending on parame-
ters). Kant clearly understood this reasoning as involving singular
representations. Free variables, and terms containing them, have the
property that Kant requires of an intuition constructing a concept, in
that they are singular and yet also "express universal validity" in the
role they play in arguing for general conclusions.[36]

A difficult question concerning Kant's view is whether the role of
intuition can be limited to our knowledge of the axioms (including
the postulates providing constructions), so that, to put the matter in
an idealized and perhaps anachronistic way, in the case of a particular proof such as the one just discussed, the conditional whose antecedent is the conjunction of the axioms and whose consequent is the
theorem would be analytic. Such a view seems to be favored by
Kant's statement that "all mathematical inferences proceed in accordance with the principle of contradiction":

For though a synthetic proposition can indeed be discerned in accordance
with the principle of contradiction, this can only be if another synthetic
proposition is presupposed, and if it can be discerned as following from this
other proposition.   (B 14)

These remarks have generally been taken to imply that it is only
because the axioms of geometry are synthetic that the theorems are.[37]
On the other hand, Kant describes the proof that the sum of the angles
of a triangle is two right angles as consisting of "a chain of inferences
guided throughout by intuition." Interpretations of Kant's theory of
construction of concepts by Beth, Hintikka, and Friedman have all
taken that to mean that, according to Kant, mathematical proofs do

not proceed in a purely analytical or logical way from axioms.[38] It is clear (as has been given particular emphasis by Friedman), that had Kant believed that they do, the Aristotelian syllogistic logic available to him would not have provided for a logical analysis of the proofs. In fact, one anachronistic feature of the question whether the conditional of the conjunction of the axioms and the theorem is analytic, is that our formulation of such a conditional would use polyadic logic and nesting of quantifiers, devices that did not appear in logic until the nineteenth century.

It is not literally true that Kant could not have formulated such a conditional; it is not that these logical forms could not be expressed in eighteenth-century German.[39] But it would be more plausible to suppose that Kant thought of mathematical reasoning in terms of which he had at least the beginnings of an analysis. What we would call the logical structure of the basic algebraic language, in which one carries out calculations with equations whose terms are composed from variables and constants by means of function symbols, was well enough understood in Kant's time. Such calculations are described by Kant as "symbolic construction."[40] And of course Kant would not describe the inference involved in calculation as logical. Friedman has illuminated a lot of what Kant says about geometry by the supposition that basic constructions in geometry work in geometric reasoning like basic operations in arithmetic and algebra. And in a language in which generality is expressed by free variables, and "existence" by function symbols, the conditional of the conjunction of the geometric axioms and a theorem could indeed not be formulated, so that the question whether it is analytic, or logically provable, could not arise.

We do not have to decide this issue, because in any event Kant's account of mathematical proof gives clear reasons for regarding geometrical knowledge as dependent on intuition. Nonetheless the Transcendental Exposition is probably not intended to stand entirely on its own independently of the Metaphysical Exposition. That the intuition appealed to in geometry is ultimately of space as an individual does not follow just from a "logical" analysis of mathematical proof[41] or even from the observation that what is constructed are spatial figures. Kant presumably meant here to rely on the third and fourth arguments of the Metaphysical Exposition.

Before I turn to the further conclusions that Kant draws from his arguments, I should comment briefly on the Metaphysical and Transcendental Expositions of the concept of Time. These discussions bring in no essentially new considerations. The arguments of the Metaphysical Exposition parallel those of the Metaphysical Exposition of Space rather closely. Because there is not obviously any mathematical discipline that relates to time as geometry relates to space, one may be surprised that a Transcendental Exposition occurs in the discussion of time at all. That time has the properties of a line (i.e., a one-dimensional Euclidean space) Kant evidently thinks synthetic *a priori*, and he appeals to properties of this kind (A 31 / B 47).[42] Kant also adds that "the concept of alteration, and with it the concept of motion, as alteration of place, is possible only through and in the representation of time" (B 48). The concepts of motion and alteration are, for Kant, dependent on experience,[43] which makes Kant's statement here misleading, but he did allow synthetic *a priori* principles whose *content* is not entirely *a priori* (B 3).

Some writers on Kant have thought that Kant thought that *arithmetic* relates to time in something close to the way in which geometry relates to space. This view finds no support in the Transcendental Exposition or in corresponding places in the *Dissertation*.[44] Though time and arithmetic do have an internal connection, it is difficult to describe and not really dealt with in the Aesthetic.[45]

IV

I now want to turn to the conclusions Kant draws from his discussion of time and space in the Aesthetic. The one with which Kant begins is the most controversial, and in some ways the most difficult to understand:

> Space does not represent any property of things in themselves, nor does it represent them in their relations to one another. That is to say, space does not represent any determination that attaches to the objects themselves, and which remains when abstraction has been made of all the subjective conditions of intuition.   (A 26 / B42)

Kant's distinction between appearances and things in themselves has been interpreted in very different ways, and accordingly the question what Kant's fundamental arguments are for holding that "space does not represent any property of things in themselves" is controversial.

A second conclusion Kant draws is that "space is nothing but the form of all appearances of outer sense," or, as he frequently expresses it, the form of outer intuition or of outer sense. One might mean by "form of intuition" a very general condition, which might be called formal, satisfied by intuitions or objects of intuition. This is part of Kant's understanding of the notion. One must distinguish between the general disposition by which intuitions represent their objects as spatial, and what space's being a form of intuition entails about the *objects* of outer intuition, that they are represented as in space, and that they stand in spatial relations that obey the laws of geometry. The latter seems properly called the form of appearances of outer sense. Kant's doctrine of pure intuition is that this form is itself known or given intuitively.

That outer intuition has a "form" in this sense does not by itself imply that space is subjective or transcendentally ideal. It seems that intuitions might have this "form" and the form be itself given intuitively without its following that the form represents a contribution of the subject to outer representation and knowledge of outer things.[46] Kant, however, denies this. Space is "the subjective condition of sensibility, under which alone outer intuition is possible for us" (A 26 / B 42). Kant's arguments, both in the Aesthetic and in corresponding parts of the *Prolegomena*, are based on the idea that the fact that *a priori* intuition is possible can only be explained if the form of intuition derives from *us*, as we will see. Two different things are to be explained, one specific to the Aesthetic and one not: First, the fact that there is *a priori intuition* of space, second, the fact that there is synthetic *a priori knowledge* concerning space, in particular in geometry. Of course, the existence of such knowledge is one of Kant's arguments for *a priori* intuition. But in arguing for the subjectivity of space Kant appeals specifically to *a priori* intuition rather than to synthetic *a priori* knowledge. Thus even in the Transcendental Exposition he writes:

How, then, can there exist in the mind an outer intuition which precedes the objects themselves, and in which the concept of these objects can be determined *a priori*? Manifestly, not otherwise than in so far as the intuition has its seat in the subject only, as the formal character of the subject, in virtue of which, in being affected by objects, it obtains *immediate represen-tation*, that is *intuition*, of them, and only so far, therefore, as it is merely the form of outer *sense* in general.   (B 41)

Kant appeals to the same consideration in arguing that space and time are not conditions on things in themselves:

> For no determination, whether absolute or relative, can be intuited prior to the existence of the things to which they belong, and none, therefore, can be intuited *a priori*.   (A 26 / B 42)

> Were it [time] a determination or order inhering in things themselves, it could not precede the objects as their condition, and be known and intuited *a priori* by means of synthetic propositions. But this last is quite possible if time is nothing but the subjective condition under which all intuition can take place in us.   (A 33 / B 49)

Kant thus argues on the same lines both to the conclusion that *a priori* intuitions do not apply to things in themselves and to the conclusion that space and time are forms of intuition.

In the presentation of the argument in §§8–9 of the *Prolegomena*, Kant makes clearer that what is advanced is a consideration specific to intuition:

> Concepts, indeed are such that we can easily form some of them *a priori*, namely such as to contain nothing but the thought of an object in general; and we need not find ourselves in an immediate relation to an object.
>   (4:282)

Thus with regard to *a priori* intuition, there is a problem about its very possibility; with regard to *a priori* concepts, the problem arises only from the fact that to have "sense and meaning" they need to be applicable to intuition, and at this stage it is not evident that the intuition has to be *a priori*.[47]

Why should it be obvious that *a priori* intuition, which "precedes the objects themselves," must "have its seat in the subject only"? It is tempting to see this in causal terms: There could not be any causal basis for the conformity of objects to our *a priori* intuitions unless this basis is already there with the intuition itself. We could imagine Kant arguing as Paul Benacerraf does in a somewhat related context:[48] We can't understand how our intuitions yield knowledge of objects unless there is an adequate causal explanation of how they conform to objects, and in the case of *a priori* intuitions, such an explanation is impossible unless the mind is causally responsible for this conformity.

It would be rash to suppose that Kant never thought in this way, and many commentators, perhaps most eloquently P. F. Strawson in his conception of the "metaphysics of transcendental idealism,"[49] have read Kant as saying that the mind literally makes the world, along the way imposing spatial and temporal form on it.

Two views about intuition that we have already considered, that an intuition has something like direct reference to an object, and that an intuition involves phenomenological presence of an object, may be of some help here. There can't be direct reference to an object that isn't there; thus there may be puzzlement as to how an object can be intuited "prior" to its existence (whatever exactly "prior" means here). We have to ask exactly what the object of the intuition is. That to whose existence the *a priori* intuition is prior is presumably an empirical object. But then maybe the answer is that that object, strictly speaking, *isn't* intuited prior to its existence (and perhaps that it can't be), so that the proper object of the intuition is a form instantiated by it rather than the object itself. Then the claim becomes that the only way in which the form of a not-yet-present object can be intuited is if this form is contributed by the subject. It is not clear to me how the force of this claim is specific to intuition or how it is more directly evident than other applications of the Copernican hypothesis.

The phenomenological-presence view seems to me to defeat the literal sense of the claim in Kant's argument. Imagination being immediate in the required sense, immediacy of a representation does not imply the existence of its object at all, so that it seems it can perfectly well be "prior" to it. Again, however, a general claim about *a priori* knowledge survives this observation: Kant can reply that if, in an imaginative thought experiment, I have intuition from which formal properties of objects can be learned, the only assurance that these properties will obtain for subsequent empirical intuitions of what was imagined is if the form is contributed by me.

We have to examine more closely the meaning of the conclusion that things in themselves are not spatial or temporal; this might offer hope of greater insight into Kant's argument. This leads us, however, into one of the worst thickets of Kant interpretation: the concept of thing in itself and the meaning of Kant's transcendental idealism. Since, according to Kant, transcendental idealism finds support from arguments offered in the Analytic and Dialectic as well as the Aesthetic, we can in the present discussion deal with only one aspect of the issues.

One might begin by distinguishing the claim that we do not know that things, as they are in themselves, are spatial (or that our knowledge of things as spatial is not knowledge of things as they are in themselves) from the claim that things as they are in themselves are not spatial. A long-running debate concerns the question whether Kant's arguments might prove, or at least lend plausibility to, the first claim and yet not prove the second, although it is often suggested by Kant's language. Kant, it has been claimed, leaves open the possibility, traditionally called the "neglected alternative," that although we don't *know* that things in themselves are spatial, or that they have the spatial properties and relations we attribute to them, nonetheless, without its being even possible for us to know it, they really are in space and have these properties and relations.⁵⁰ Kant might reply to this objection by appealing to the arguments of the Antinomies, particularly the Mathematical Antinomies.⁵¹ That would, however, leave him apparently making a dogmatic claim in the Aesthetic, with no indication that an important part of its defense is deferred.

A more interesting reply is that when the concept of thing in itself and Kant's argument in the Aesthetic are properly understood, it will be clear that the "neglected alternative" is ruled out. One understanding of the contrast of appearances and things in themselves would be that our intuitions represent objects as having certain properties and relations, but in fact they don't have them. Kant occasionally comes close to saying this:

What we have meant to say is ... that the things we intuit are not in themselves what we intuit them as being, nor their relations so constituted in themselves as they appear to us.   (A 42 / B 59)

It is hard to see how, on this view, Kant avoids the implication that our "knowledge" of outer objects is *false:* The objects we perceive are perceived as spatial, but "in themselves," as they really are, they are not spatial. One might call this general view of the relation of appearances and things in themselves the Distortion Picture. It arises naturally from viewing things in themselves as real things, of which Kant's *Erscheinungen* are ways these things appear to us. It identifies how things are in themselves, in Kant's particular sense, with how they really are.[52]

This view certainly rules out the "neglected alternative." But it seems to do so by fiat. It is difficult to see how, on this interpretation, the thesis that things in themselves are not spatial is supported by argument.[53] Indeed, if the idea that things in themselves are spatial merely means that their relations have the formal properties that our conception of space demands, the thesis that they are not is pretty clearly incompatible with the unknowability of things in themselves. Space has to be what is represented in the intuition of space, as it were as so represented.

A plausible line of interpretation with this result, favored by several passages in the Aesthetic (e.g., that from B 41 quoted before), might be called the Subjectivist view. This is what is expressed in Kant's frequent statements that empirical objects are "mere representations."[54] A better way of putting it might be that for space and time and therefore for the objects in space and time, the distinction between object and representation collapses, or that an "empirical" version of the distinction can only be made in some way within the sphere of representations.[55] According to this view, the neglected alternative is ruled out because there would be a kind of category mistake in holding that things in themselves, as opposed to representations, are spatial.

Paul Guyer, in his discussion of the Aesthetic's case for transcendental idealism, relies heavily on an interpretation of an argument from geometry in the General Observations to the Aesthetic. I see his interpretation as making this argument turn on just such a subjectivist view. Commenting on Kant's first conclusion concerning space, Guyer says that Kant assumes that

> it is not possible to know independently of experience that an object genuinely has, on its own, a certain property. Therefore space and time, which are known *a priori*, cannot be genuine properties of objects and can be only features of our representations of them.[56]

Guyer objects to this assumption on the ground that one might conceivably know, because of constraints on our ability to perceive, that any object we perceive will have a certain property; our faculties would restrict us to perceiving objects that independently have the properties in question, so that it would not follow that the objects cannot "on their own" have them.

According to Guyer, Kant nonetheless relies on this assumption because he conceives the necessity of the spatiality of objects and their conformity to the laws of geometry as absolute; he holds not merely

(1) Necessarily, if we perceive an object x, then x is spatial and Euclidean; but rather

(2) If we perceive an object x, then necessarily, x is spatial and Euclidean.[57]

This has to be a condition on the nature of the objects, not merely a restriction on what objects we can perceive. Hence, according to Guyer, this view commits Kant to the view that spatial form is imposed on objects by us.

Guyer discerns an appeal to (2) in the second clause of the following remark:

If there did not exist in you a power of *a priori* intuition, and if that subjective condition were not also at the same time, as regards its form, the universal *a priori* condition under which alone the object of this outer intuition is itself possible; if the object (the triangle) were something in itself, apart from any relation to you, the subject, how could you say that what necessarily exist in you as subjective conditions for the construction of a triangle must of necessity belong to the triangle itself? (A 48 / B 65)

Here the first "necessarily" can express the kind of necessity expressed in (1), but the second necessity does not have the form of being conditional on the subject's construction, intuition, or perception.

Guyer states that the absolute necessity claimed in (2) "can be explained only by the supposition that we actually *impose* spatial form on objects."[58] It is, indeed, a reason for not resting with the "restriction" view that Guyer regards as the major alternative.[59] Apart from its relevance to questions about the distinction between appearances and things in themselves, the point is relevant also to another controversial point: whether Kant's argument for transcendental idealism in the Aesthetic makes essential appeal to geometrical knowledge, or whether it needs to rely only on the kind of considerations presented in the Metaphysical Exposition. Clearly the Metaphysical Exposition yields at best conditional necessities of the general form of (1); an argument from absolute necessity to transcendental idealism has to rely on geometry. In my view, Guyer's exegesis of the argument from the General Observations is quite convincing, and this argument is clearer than what can be gleaned from the arguments that proceed more directly from *a priori* intuition (i.e., B 41, A 26 / B 42, and *Prolegomena* §§8–9, all commented on earlier in this essay).[60]

The claim (2), however, is more defensible than Guyer allows, at least with regard to geometry: The content of geometry has to do with points, lines, planes, and figures that are in some way forms of objects, and not with our perception. If we accept the usual conception of the necessity of mathematics, what will be necessary will be statements about these entities. There is nothing in the content of these statements to make their necessity conditional on our perceiving or intuiting them. Thus it seems to me likely that Kant was not sliding from conditional necessity to absolute necessity, but rather applying the idea that mathematics is necessary, which he would have shared with his opponents, to the case of the geometry of space. The objection to this is the now standard one, that we do not have reason to believe that the geometry of actual space obtains with such mathematical necessity.

Even if we grant Kant this premise, however, it is questionable that he attains the "apodeictic proof" of his Copernican principle that he claims. Whether the essential assumption is *a priori* intuition or "absolute" necessity, in either case the claim must be that nonapplication to things in themselves is the only possible *explanation*. The merit of the Subjectivist view is that it offers a view of appearances as objects that fits with that explanation.

The Subjectivist view does not directly imply the Distortion view, but can lead to it naturally. The relation depends on how one thinks of the *object* of representations. If appearances are representations, it is natural to think of things in themselves as their objects. And Kant clearly sometimes does think of them that way, as for example in places where he says that the notion of appearance requires something which appears:

. . . We must yet be in a position to think [objects] as things in themselves; otherwise we should be landed in the absurd conclusion that there can be appearance without anything that appears.   (B xxvii)

The same conclusion also, of course, follows from the concept of an appearance in general; namely, that something which is not in itself appearance must correspond to it.   (A 251)

But if the object of our empirical representations is a thing in itself, and these representations represent their objects as spatial, then we have the Distortion view. But this conception of the object of representations is not the only one that Kant deploys even within the Subjectivist conception, as one can see from the discussions of the concept of object in the A deduction (esp. A 104–5) and the Second Analogy (A 191 / B 236).

I would like now to introduce a third possible meaning of the nonspatiotemporality of things in themselves, what I will call the Intensional view. According to this view, the conclusion from the argument of the Aesthetic is that the notions of space and time do not represent things as they are in themselves, where, however, "represent" creates here an intensional context, so that in particular it does not entitle us to single out things in themselves as a kind of thing, distinct from appearances. The manner in which we know things is not "as they are in themselves," but rather "as they appear." But talk of "appearances" and "things in themselves" as different objects is at best derivative from the difference of modes of representation. However, there is an inequality between the two, in that representation of an object as it appears is full-blooded, capable of being knowledge, whereas representation of an object as it is in itself is a mere abstraction from conditions, of intuition in particular, which make such knowledge possible.

Assuming that it has been shown that knowledge of things as spatial is not knowledge of them as they are in themselves, on this view there cannot be a further question whether things as they are in themselves are spatial; either "things in themselves are not spatial" merely repeats what has already been shown, or it presupposes that there is a kind of thing called "things in themselves."

This is a philosophically attractive idea, and it is supported by many passages where Kant expresses the distinction as that of considering objects as appearances or as things in themselves, as in the following striking remark:

But if our Critique is not in error in teaching that the object is to be taken *in a twofold sense*, namely as appearance and as thing in itself; if the deduction of the concepts of understanding is valid, and the principle of causality therefore applies only to things taken in the former sense, namely, insofar as they are objects of experience – these same objects, taken in the other sense, not being subject to the principle – then there is no contradiction in supposing that one and the same will is, in the appearance, that is, in its visible acts, necessarily subject to the law of nature, and so far *not free*, while yet, as belonging to a thing in itself, it is not subject to that law, and is therefore *free*.   (B xxvii–xxviii)

Gerold Prauss has supported a version of this view by a careful textual analysis of Kant's manner of speaking about things as they are in themselves.[61] Prauss acknowledges, however, that Kant's way of speaking is far from consistent and that his usage often lays him open to the interpretation of things in themselves as another system of objects in addition to appearances. In fact, Kant often says in virtually the same place things that seem to support the Intensional view, and things that contradict it.[62] I shall not go into the many questions the Intensional view raises. In spite of the foregoing passage from the preface to the second edition, it has often been claimed that this understanding of the distinction will not suffice for the purposes of Kant's moral philosophy, and indeed Kant's ethical writings contain passages that would be very difficult to square with it. Clearly, it is beyond the scope of this essay to go into such matters.

We do, however, have to consider whether the Intensional view can offer a sensible interpretation of Kant's arguments for his conclusions in the Aesthetic. The difficulty lies in the fact, noted above, that Kant in the statement of his conclusions understands the form of sensibility as contributed entirely by the subject, so that the spatiality of objects and their geometrical properties are due entirely to ourselves.[63] This is sometimes expressed in the language of the Subjectivist view, as in the claim that *a priori* intuition "contains nothing but the form of sensibility" (*Prolegomena* §9, 4:282). That is to say, it is not just conditioned by my own subjectivity, so that it therefore represents them in a way that, in particular, would not be shared by another mind whose forms of intuition were different, but it is conditioned *entirely* by my own subjectivity. This is the essential element of the conclusion that Guyer draws from the argument from the necessity of geometry in the General Observations. It is very naturally interpreted by the Subjectivist view of objects.

It is not clear, however, that either the conclusion that spatiality arises entirely from the subject or the Subjectivist view of empirical objects is incompatible with the Intensional view, which should perhaps be seen primarily as an interpretation of the conception of thing in itself. A difficulty that has been raised for it is the following: According to it, we know certain objects in experience, and we can think these very objects as they are in themselves. But our very individuation of objects is conditioned by the forms of intuition and the categories. How can we possibly have any basis for even thinking of, for example, the chair on which I am sitting "as it is in itself," when there is no basis for the assumption that reality as it is in itself is divided in such a way that any particular object corresponds to this chair? The only possible reply to this objection is the one suggested by Prauss: When one considers *this chair* as it is in itself, "this chair" refers to an empirical object, so that its consideration as an appearance is presupposed.[64] So long as there is *some* distinction between empirical objects and representations, this way of understanding talk of things in themselves is available. The conclusion that the Intensional view is most concerned to resist, that there is a world of things in themselves "behind" the objects we know in experience, is not forced by Kant's subjectivist formulations, unless one takes the conditioning by our subjectivity in a causal way. It seems to me clear that Kant intended to avoid taking it in that way, but a discussion of the matter would be beyond the scope of a treatment of the Aesthetic.

This is not to deny that Kant's conclusion is more subjectivist than many who are sympathetic to Kant's transcendental idealism will be comfortable with. The modern idea of the "relativity of knowledge," that all our knowledge is unavoidably conditioned by our own cognitive faculties, or language, or "conceptual scheme," so that we can't know or even understand how the world would "look" from outside these (for example from a "God's eye view") no doubt owes important inspiration to Kant.[65] In his conception of forms of intuition, Kant claimed to identify aspects of the content of our knowledge that are conditioned entirely by our own subjectivity but are still knowledge of objects, reflected in the most objective physical science. That one should be able to identify such a "purely subjective" aspect of objective knowledge is surprising and even paradoxical. Even granted *a priori* knowledge of necessary truths about space, I have found Kant's arguments in the Aesthetic for this conclusion less than apodeictic. But that premise does give them enough plausibility so that it is not surprising that more modern views that reject this particular radical turn of Kant's transcendentalism also reject the premise.

The Aesthetic is of course not the only place where Kant argues for transcendental idealism or says things bearing on its meaning. In particular, the Analytic probably contributed more to the development of the modern conception just alluded to. I should end by emphasizing once again the very limited scope of the present discussion of transcendental idealism.

NOTES

The *Critique of Pure Reason* is quoted in Kemp Smith's translation, sometimes modified. I use the following other translations:

Dissertation. Trans. G. B. Kerferd in Kant, *Selected Pre-Critical Writings*, ed. Kerferd and D. E. Walford. Manchester, U.K.: Manchester University Press, 1968. This volume contains the *Akademie* pages in the margins.

Prolegomena. Trans. Lewis White Beck, revising earlier translations. New York: Liberal Arts Press, 1950. Also contains *Akademie* pages.

Regions in Space. Trans. D. E. Walford in Kerferd and Walford, eds., *Pre-Critical Writings.*

Theology lectures (*Religionslehre Pölitz*). Trans. Allen W. Wood and Gertrude M. Clark as *Lectures on Philosophical Theology*. Ithaca, N.Y.: Cornell University Press, 1978.

Translations other than those cited here are my own.

1 The relevant kind of universality is "strict universality, that is . . . that no exception is allowed as possible" (B 3); thus it itself involves necessity.
2 For change, see B 3, but Kant is not entirely consistent; compare A 82 / B 108.
3 *Logic*, ed. Jäsche, §1 (9:91)
4 "It is a mere tautology to speak of general or common concepts" (*Logic* §1, Note 2, 9:91).
5 *Logic* §1, Note 2 (9:91). Alan Shamoon argues persuasively that this view is directed against Meier and thereby against Leibniz. See "Kant's Logic," unpublished Ph.D. Dissertation, Columbia University, 1979, ch. 5.

Appreciation of this remark of Kant, and of Kant's conception of singular judgments, derives mainly from Manley Thompson, "Singular Terms and Intuitions in Kant's Epistemology," *Review of Metaphysics* 26 (1972–3): 314–43.

6 *Wiener Logik* (1795), 24:909. Shamoon, in commenting on this passage, remarks that a judgment is singular, and its subject concept has singular use, if it has in the subject a demonstrative or the definite article. (See Kant's Logic, p. 85.)

7 "Kantian Intuitions," *Inquiry* 15 (1972): 341–5, p. 342. In his principal discussion of the matter, "On Kant's Notion of Intuition (*Anschauung*)," in Terence Penelhum and J. J. Macintosh, eds., *The First Critique* (Belmont, Calif., Wadsworth, 1968), pp. 38–53, Hintikka does not say explicitly how he understands the immediacy condition or its role, but indicates that he thinks the singularity condition gives a sufficient definition. But cf. note 11 of "Kant's Transcendental Method and his Theory of Mathematics," *Topoi* 3 (1984): 99–108.

8 'Caius is mortal' in *Logic* §21, note 1 (cf. A 322 / B 378), also in *Logik Pölitz* (1789, 24:578); 'Adam was fallible', in R. 3080 (16:647).

9 In addition to the passage from the *Wiener Logik* cited above, 'This world is the best' in R 3173 (16:695).

10 Kant gives the example 'God is without error; everything which is God is without error' in R. 3080 (16:647).

11 "Intuition, Synthesis, and Individuation in the *Critique of Pure Reason*," *Noûs* 7 (1973): 207–32, p. 210.

12 Thompson, "Singular Terms and Intuitions," p. 335; Shamoon, Kant's Logic, pp. 110–11.

13 "Intuition, Synthesis, and Individuation," p. 232.

14 A remark at B 146 is translated by Kemp Smith as "Now, as the Aesthetic has shown, the only intuition possible to us is sensible." The German reads simply, "Nun ist alle uns mögliche Anschauung sinnlich (Aesthetik)." The remark does not make clear that Kant is doing more than simply refer to the Aesthetic as the place where that thesis was stated and explained.

If it is the conclusion of argument rather than an assumption of Kant, then the argument is not explicitly pointed to in the Aesthetic. The most plausible theory about what such an argument might be would give it a form similar to that of the second edition Transcendental Exposition of the Concept of Space: Geometry is (in some sense to be explicated) intuitive knowledge; this is possible only if the intuition involved is sensible; therefore human intuition is sensible. As an argument for the existence of *a priori* sensible intuition this might possibly be discerned in the text of the Aesthetic. But something further would be needed to get to the conclusion that *all* human intuition is sensible.

Although I have not systematically studied the use of the terms

Anschauung and *intuitus* in Kant's earlier writings, it seems clear that they emerge as central technical terms in the 1768–70 period, when Kant makes the sharp distinction between sensibility and understanding and makes the decisive break with the Leibnizian views of space and sense-perception. Especially noteworthy is the fact that Kant's early formulation of his views on mathematical proof in the "*Investigation of the Clarity of the Principles of Natural Theology and Ethics*" (2:272–301), although it already makes the connection between mathematics and sensibility, does not use the term *Anschauung* in the principal formulation of its theses. It occurs only a few times in the entire essay.

I would conjecture, then, that in Kant's development the use of *Anschauung* as a technical term and the thesis that human intuition is sensible emerged more or less simultaneously and that he did not articulate theories in terms of the notion of intuition in abstraction from, or before formulating, the latter thesis.

15 "Kant's Philosophy of Arithmetic" (1969), in *Mathematics in Philosophy: Selected Essays* (Ithaca, N.Y.: Cornell University Press, 1983), p. 112.

16 Cf. B 72 and elsewhere. A fuller explanation of the divine understanding as intellectual intuition is given in the theology lectures (28:1051, trans. p. 85).

17 Two passages in the *Dissertation* are highly suggestive:

> For all our intuition is bound to a certain principle of form under which form alone something can be *discerned* by the mind immediately or as *singular*, and not merely conceived discursively through general concepts.   (§10, 2:396)

> That there are not given in space more than three dimensions, that between two points there is only one straight line, ... etc. – these cannot be concluded from some universal notion of space, but can only be seen in space itself as in something concrete.   (§15C, 2:402–3)

Both, it seems to me, support the claim that intuition is immediate in the sense at issue. The punctuation of the Latin in the first passage, however, suggests that *singulare* is being offered as explication of *immediate*, and thus rather goes against the claim that the connection between immediacy and "seeing" obtains by definition. It is not, on the other hand, something for which Kant *argues*.

18 For example Robert Pippin, *Kant's Theory of Form* (New Haven, Conn.: Yale University Press, 1982), ch. 3.

19 Although I don't know of specific comments by Kant on "proprioceptive" sensations, it follows that such objective content as they have would belong to outer sense.

20 This essay is generally represented as (temporarily) completely buying

the Newtonian position. Reasons for caution on this point, in my opinion justified, are given in William Harper, "Kant on Incongruent Counterparts," in James Van Cleve and Robert E. Frederick, eds., *The Philosophy of Right and Left: Incongruent Counterparts and the Nature of
Space* (Dordrecht: Kluwer, 1991).

21 As was apparently urged against Kant by Eberhard's associate J. G. E.
Maass; see Henry Allison, *Kant's Transcendental Idealism* (New Haven,
Conn.: Yale University Press, 1983), p. 84, and *The Kant–Eberhard Controversy* (Baltimore: The Johns Hopkins University Press, 1973), pp. 35–
6.

22 This psychologistic reading has been advocated by some commentators,
e.g., Kemp Smith (*A Commentary to Kant's 'Critique of Pure Reason'*
(2d ed. London: Macmillan, 1923), p. 110). It is somewhat encouraged by
the German: "Wir können uns niemals eine Vorstellung davon machen,
daß kein Raum sei." Although our inability to imagine the absence of
space is not what Kant is ultimately after, it is of course an indication of
it, and has some force as a plausibility argument.

23 In fact, he ought to distinguish between what he calls the "general
concept of space" (A 25), which would apply to portions of space, and the
concept that applies uniquely to the "one and the same unique space" (A
25 / B 39). The latter could, however, be a "singular use" of the former,
although that would oblige us to view it as expressed by a demonstrative
attached to the word "space" in its general meaning.

Kant in the *Dissertation* speaks more freely of "the concept of space"
and writes, e.g., "The concept of space is therefore a pure intuition. For it
is a singular concept, . . ." (§15C, 2:402); whereas in the *Critique* he
writes "Consequently, the original representation of space is an a priori
intuition, not a concept" (B 40). How far this represents an actual difference of view on Kant's part and how much it is a matter of more careful
formulation, I do not know. Even in the second edition of the *Critique*
Kant titles the section we are discussing "Metaphysical Exposition of
the Concept of Space." (This contrast between the *Dissertation* and the
Critique was noted by Kirk Dallas Wilson, "Kant on Intuition," *Philosophical Quarterly* 25 (1975): 247–65, p. 250.)

24 In his theology lectures, however, Kant discusses the "mathematical
infinity" of God and says that "the concept of the infinite comes from
mathematics, and belongs only to it" (28:1017, trans. p. 48). To say that
God is infinite in this sense is to compare his magnitude with some
unit. Because the unit is not fixed, one does not derive an absolute
notion of the greatness of God, even in some particular dimension (such
as understanding). It is doubtful that from Kant's point of view the
statement that God is infinite in this sense is free from reference to

intuition. Kant also considers the notion of God as "metaphysically infinite": "In this concept we understand perfections in their highest degree, or better yet, without any degree. The *omnitudo realitatis* [All of reality] is what is called metaphysical infinity" (28:1018, trans. p. 49). Kant concludes that the term "All of reality" is more appropriate than "metaphysical infinity." (A briefer remark with the same purport is in Kant's letter to Johann Schultz of 25 November 1788, 10:557.)

I would conclude that although a purely conceptual characterization of God does *entail* that God is infinite, in what Kant considered the proper sense this implication cannot be drawn out without intuition.

25 On this point see section II of Michael Friedman, "Kant's Theory of Geometry," *Philosophical Review* 94 (1985): 455–506, which contains an interesting discussion of these passages. Compared to my own discussion in the text, Friedman downplays the phenomenological aspect.

26 Leonhard Euler, "Réflexions sur l'espace et le tems," *Mémoires de l'académie des sciences de Berlin*, 1748; *Opera omnia*, series 3, vol. 2 (Geneva 1942), pp. 376–83.

Kant's own final position about absolute space is presented in the *Metaphysical Foundations*, according to which absolute space is a kind of Idea of Reason. The manner in which he discusses the question, both briefly in the 1768 essay and more fully in the *Metaphysical Foundations*, should dispel a somewhat misleading impression created by the exposition in the Aesthetic, from which a reader could easily conclude that in developing his theory of space and time, Kant was not concerned with the considerations about the foundations of mechanics that were central to the debate between Leibniz and Newton and have played a central role in debates about relationist and absolutist or substantivalist views down to the present day. (See Michael Friedman, "The Metaphysical Foundations of Newtonian Science," in R. E. Butts, ed., *Kant's Philosophy of Physical Science* (Dordrecht: D. Reidel, 1986), pp. 25–60; cf. section IV of Friedman's essay in the present book.)

27 In §15C of the Dissertation, Kant appeals to incongruent counterparts in arguing that the representation of space is an intuition (2:403). In §13 of the *Prolegomena* (4:285–6) and more briefly in the *Metaphysical Foundations* (4:483–4), it is offered further as a consideration in favor of the view that space is a form of sensibility not attaching to things in themselves. It has been maintained that Kant's different uses of the argument are inconsistent (for example, Kemp Smith, *Commentary*, pp. 161–6). A thorough discussion of Kant's use of the argument, which undertakes to rebut this accusation, is Jill Vance Buroker, *Space and Incongruence: The Origins of Kant's Idealism* (Dordrecht: D. Reidel, 1981), chs. 3–5.

28 See Graham Nerlich, "Hands, Knees, and Absolute Space," *Journal of Philosophy* 70 (1973): 337–51; also Buroker, *Space and Incongruence*, ch. 3.

29 For two recent mathematically and physically informed treatments, see John Earman, *World Enough and Space-Time* (Cambridge, Mass.: MIT Press, 1989), ch. 7, and Harper, "Kant on Incongruent Counterparts." Both concentrate on the argument of *Regions in Space* but also have something to say about the later versions. Harper is more sympathetic, especially to the claim of the *Dissertation* and later writings that intuition is needed to distinguish incongruent counterparts. Harper's paper contains a number of references to further literature. Earman's discussion places the argument in the context of the development of the absolutist–relationist controversy from Newton to the present day.

30 In fact, that the geometry of space is empirical was held a generation after Kant by the great mathematician C. F. Gauss.
   Kant's view that it is only in transcendental philosophy that it is established that mathematics yields genuine knowledge of objects probably implies that although it is a synthetic *a priori* truth that physical space is Euclidean, this is not intuitively evident in the way geometrical truths are. (Cf. Friedman, "Kant's Theory of Geometry," p. 469 and n. 20, also p. 482 n. 36.) But I do not see that there could be a Kantian argument for the conclusion that physical space is Euclidean that did not take as a premise that space as intuited, as described in the Aesthetic, is Euclidean.

31 In the second edition of the *Critique* (B 15) and even more in the *Prolegomena* Kant talks of "pure mathematics." I know of only one use of this phrase in the first edition (A 165 / B 206) (but *mathesis pura* occurs in the *Dissertation*; see note 44 in this chapter). Kant does not say explicitly with what nonpure mathematics he is contrasting it, but the A 165 / B206 passage suggests that the contrast is with applied mathematics, although he does not use that term there or, so far as I know, elsewhere in the *Critique*. Additional evidence that that is the contrast Kant intends is that he distinguishes pure from applied *logic* (A 52–3 / B 77–8) and contrasts pure with applied mathematics in a note to his copy of the first edition of the *Critique* (R XLIV, 23:28). (I owe the latter observation to Paul Guyer; cf. *Kant and the Claims of Knowledge* (Cambridge University Press, 1987), p. 189. I am also indebted here to Michael Friedman.)

32 The modern discussion of the analyticity or syntheticity of arithmetic might be taken to show that the fact that arithmetic is not analytic in Kant's particular sense does not show that it depends on intuition. So long as one holds to the conception of geometry as the science of space, it is not clear how to apply this line of thought to geometry.

33 For example by Hintikka. It does not follow that it is to be read as

independent of the connection between intuition and perception or sensibility. The latter view is effectively criticized in Mirella Capozzi Cellucci, "J. Hintikka e il metodo della matematica in Kant," *Il Pensiero* 18 (1973): 232–67.

34 The importance of Euclid for Kant's philosophy of mathematics was stressed by Hintikka; see in particular "Kant on the Mathematical Method" (1967), in *Knowledge and the Known* (Dordrecht: D. Reidel, 1974). Particular Euclidean constructions are stressed by Friedman, "Kant's Theory of Geometry."

35 This proof occurs in Euclid, *Elements*, Book I, Prop. 32. (I have borrowed notations from Michael Friedman. I am grateful to Jotham Parsons for his assistance with Figure 2.1.)

36 This analogy was first noted by E. W. Beth, "Über Lockes 'allegemeines Dreieck'," *Kant-Studien* 48 (1956–7): 361–80.

37 See for example Lewis White Beck, "Can Kant's Synthetic Judgments Be Made Analytic?" (1955), in *Studies in the Philosophy of Kant* (Indianapolis: Bobbs-Merrill, 1965), pp. 89–90. In his work *Prüfung der kantischen Critik der reinen Vernunft*, Vol. I (Königsberg, 1789), Kant's pupil Johann Schultz, who was professor of mathematics at Königsberg and who clearly discussed philosophy of mathematics with Kant, seems to have understood Kant's view in this way. His argument for the synthetic character of geometry is largely, and his argument for the synthetic character of arithmetic is almost entirely, based on the fact that these sciences require synthetic axioms and postulates. Regarding arithmetic, however, there are clear differences between Kant and Schultz (see "Kant's Philosophy of Arithmetic," pp. 121–3).

38 Beth, "Über Lockes 'allgemeines Dreieck' "; Hintikka, "Kant on the Mathematical Method" and other writings; Friedman, "Kant's Theory of Geometry." Interestingly, Kurt Gödel expresses this view in an unpublished lecture draft from about 1961 (thus conceivably influenced by Beth but not by the others).

39 Formulations of axioms and postulates for geometry that would lend themselves to expressing such a conditional are given by Schultz, *Prüfung*, Vol. I, pp. 65–7.

40 A 717 / B 745. It is not possible for me to go into this notion or how Kant understands the role of intuition in arithmetic and algebra. See "Kant's Philosophy of Arithmetic"; also Thompson, "Singular Terms and Intuitions," sec. IV; J. Michael Young, "Kant on the Construction of Arithmetical Concepts," *Kant-Studien* 73 (1982): 17–46; Friedman, "Kant on Concepts and Intuitions in the Mathematical Sciences," *Synthese* 84 (1990): 213–257.

41 An influential recent tradition of discussion of Kant's theory of construc-

tion of concepts, represented by Beth, Hintikka, and Friedman, ignores the more "phenomenological" side of Kant's discussion of these matters. Beth and Hintikka in fact reduce the role of pure intuition in mathematics to elements that would, in modern terms, be part of logic. Hintikka draws the conclusion, natural on such a view, that Kant's view that all our intuitions are sensible is inadequately motivated. (See "Kant's 'New Method of Thought' and His Theory of Mathematics" (1965), *Knowledge and the Known*, pp. 131–2.)

The same tendency is present in Friedman's writings, but because geometry gives particular constructions, there is a clear place in his account for the intuition of space. (See "Kant's Theory of Geometry," pp. 496–7.) He also gives an extended account of the role of time, even in geometry.

For discussion of Friedman's views, I am much indebted to Ofra Rechter. I regret that time and the format of this essay have not permitted me to do them justice here.

42 That "different times are not simultaneous but successive" is perhaps a way of formulating the fact that instants of time are linearly ordered.

43 For motion see A 41 / B 58, also *Prolegomena* §15 (4:295), for alteration B 3. The problems surrounding these views are discussed (with references to other literature) in my "Remarks on Pure Natural Science," in Allen W. Wood, ed., *Self and Nature in Kant's Philosophy* (Ithaca, N.Y.: Cornell University Press, 1984), pp. 216–27.

44 In fact, the latter text seems to give this role to "pure mechanics": "Hence PURE MATHEMATICS deals with *space* in GEOMETRY, and *time* in pure MECHANICS" (§12, 2:397). For a view of what Kant might have meant by this statement, see Friedman, "Kant on Concepts and Intuitions," §5.

45 Relevant texts are the argument for the syntheticity of "7 + 5 = 12" (B 15–16), the characterization of number as the "pure schema of magnitude" (A 142–3 / B 182), and Kant's letter to Schultz of 25 November 1788 (10:554–8). For two related but still differing interpretations of the connection, see "Kant's Philosophy of Arithmetic," secs. VI and VII, and Friedman, "Kant on Concepts and Intuitions."

46 Some later writers influenced by Kant seem to have taken the idea of a form of intuition in this way. This is not to say that the form represents things as they are in themselves in Kant's or some other sense; rather it means merely that whether this is so is a further question.

47 Kant could presumably argue that the subjectivity of space is needed to explain synthetic *a priori* knowledge in geometry by appealing to the "Copernican" hypothesis that "we can know *a priori* of things only what we ourselves put into them" (B xviii). The more specific claim about intuition Kant evidently thought more directly evident. Thus

Kant says of the Copernican hypothesis that "in the *Critique* itself it will be proved, apodeictically not hypothetically, from the nature of our representations of space and time and from the elementary concepts of the understanding" (B xxii n.).

48 "Mathematical Truth," *Journal of Philosophy* 70 (1973): 661–79.

49 *The Bounds of Sense* (London: Methuen, 1966), Part Four.

50 This claim has a long history in writing about Kant; see Allison, *Kant's Transcendental Idealism*, pp. 110–14, and Kemp Smith, *Commentary*, pp. 113–14.

51 Cf. A. C. Ewing, *A Short Commentary on Kant's Critique of Pure Reason* 2d ed. (London: Methuen, 1950), p. 50.

52 Such an identification may be encouraged by §4 of the *Dissertation*, where Kant writes "Consequently it is clear that things which are thought sensitively are representations of things *as they appear*, but things which are intellectual are representations of things *as they are* (2:392). This remark is, however, the conclusion of an argument that Kant would have disclaimed in application to space and time in the *Critique*, appealing to the variability of the "modification" of sensibility in different subjects, as Paul Guyer points out (*Kant and the Claims of Knowledge*, p. 341). Also, the formulation itself seems to be criticized in the *Critique* (A 258 / B 313); see Gerold Prauss, *Kant und das Problem der Dinge an sich* (Bonn: Bouvier, 1974), p. 59 n. 13. Still, the passage encourages the idea that the Distortion Picture is the view with which Kant started when he first came to the view that space is a form of sensibility representing things as they appear.

53 Indeed, it may lead to actual inconsistency, as Robert Howell, who seems to adopt this view, argues in "A Problem for Kant," in Esa Saarinen, Risto Hilpinen, Ilka Niiniluoto, and Merrill Provence Hintikka, eds., *Essays in Honour of Jaakko Hintikka* (Dordrecht: D. Reidel, 1979), pp. 331–49.

54 Such statements are, however, rare in passages added in the second edition, and the argument where this conception is most strongly relied on in its simple form, the "refutation of idealism" in the Fourth Paralogism, is omitted; in the new Refutation empirical objects are more clearly distinguished from representations.

55 As Kant suggests in the Second Analogy, A 191 / B 236.

56 *Kant and the Claims of Knowledge*, p. 362.

57 Ibid., p. 366.

58 Ibid., p. 361.

59 Regarding the power of *a priori* intuition as "the universal a priori condition under which alone the *object* of this outer intuition is *itself* possible" (emphasis mine) hardly squares with the restriction view.

60 Guyer seems to suppose that the argument he derives from the General Observations is the same argument as that of the passages cited. That seems to me doubtful. He does, however, point to other passages in Kant's writings where he is pretty clearly arguing from necessity.

61 *Kant und das Problem der Dinge an sich,* ch. 1.

62 As Manfred Baum remarks concerning B 306–8 in "The B-Deduction and the Refutation of Idealism," *Southern Journal of Philosophy* 25 supplement (1987): 89–107, p. 90. The Phenomena and Noumena chapter seems to me on the whole to favor the Intensional view, but not consistently, as Baum rightly observes.

63 It is this that gives rise to the temptation to think of the matter causally, which in turn leads naturally to the idea of "double affection," which the Intensional view avoids.

64 *Kant und das Problem der Dinge an sich,* pp. 39 ff.

65 It is in turn reflected in Kant commentary, for example in Allison's idea of "epistemic conditions," which underlies his interpretation of Kant's transcendental idealism.

3 Functions of thought and the synthesis of intuitions

The Transcendental Analytic of the *Critique of Pure Reason* has three main sections: the Metaphysical Deduction, the Transcendental Deduction, and the Analytic of Principles. The second and third sections have spawned much lively controversy, both interpretive and substantive. The first, by contrast, has generated little interest. Most readers have thought it clear what Kant means to establish here, and how. Most have also thought it plain that his argument is a failure, unworthy of continued exploration.

I will not try to defend the argument of the Metaphysical Deduction. I will try to show that this section of the *Critique* contains material of considerable importance, however. First I will summarize Kant's argument (I) and review some of the difficulties with it (II). Then I will discuss the notion of synthesis, trying to show that the Metaphysical Deduction helps to shed light on this important but otherwise obscure notion (III). Finally, I will comment briefly on the central contention of the Metaphysical Deduction (IV).

I. KANT'S ARGUMENT

The Metaphysical Deduction[1] is officially titled "The Clue to the Discovery of All Pure Concepts of the Understanding." In it, Kant is concerned with the concepts that are fundamental to all knowledge and so are called categories (A 79–80 / B 105). As his title suggests, he makes two claims. One is to have identified the categories systematically and hence exhaustively. The other is to have shown that they are pure concepts, and, indeed, that they are merely intellectual, having their origin solely in the understanding.

The first claim gets considerable emphasis. Kant compares his endeavor to that of Aristotle, who likewise tried to identify the concepts fundamental to all knowledge, but who did so in a "rhapsodic" and "haphazard" way, "merely pick[ing] them up as they came his way" (A 81 / B 106–7). Kant claims by contrast to proceed systematically, developing his categories "from a common principle" (ibid.). This makes it possible to show "why just these concepts and no others" qualify as categories (A 81 / B 107; compare B 109). It makes it possible, accordingly, to identify the categories exhaustively and with certainty, since the "completeness and articulation of this system yield a criterion of the correctness and genuineness of all its components" (A 65 / B 90).

Kant's second claim gets less emphasis, but it is actually more fundamental, since it points to the "common principle" from which the categories are said to be developed. He claims that the categories are pure concepts, ones "in which there is nothing that belongs to sensation" (A 20 / B 34). He claims, indeed, that they are merely intellectual concepts. They do not derive, that is, from what is given in our intuition of individual things, not even from the forms of such intuition, space and time. They stem instead from the structure of judgment, or from the nature of the understanding, which is the faculty of judgment (A 69 / B 94).

Kant's view, more fully stated, is that the categories have their origin in "the function of thought in judgment" (A 70 / B 95). It is the task of general logic, he holds, to give a systematic account of the various "moments" of this function. Abstracting from any content a judgment may have, and considering merely its form, logic establishes "that the function of thought in judgment can be brought under four heads, each of which contains three moments" (ibid.). These moments – which commentators usually refer to as forms of judgment, but which Kant typically calls the logical functions of judgment (B 128, 143), or the moments or relations of thought in judgment (A 73 / B 98) – are represented in the familiar table (Table 3.1; A 70 / B 95).

Kant's claim, now, is that the categories, which are concepts fundamental to all our knowledge, have their roots in these logical functions of judgment. He claims, indeed, that the categories "*are* these functions of judgment, insofar as they are employed in the determination of the manifold of a given intuition" (B 143, my emphasis; see also B 128). There are just as many categories as there are functions

Table 3.1

	I	
	Quantity of judgments	
	Universal	
	Particular	
	Singular	
II		**III**
Quality		*Relation*
Affirmative		Categorical
Negative		Hypothetical
Infinite		Disjunctive
	IV	
	Modality	
	Problematic	
	Assertoric	
	Apodictic	

of thought, accordingly; they are represented in a second table (Table 3.2), whose structure is supposed to be based on that of the first (A 80 / B 106).

These two tables give rise to a multitude of questions and difficulties. Before turning to these, however, we should consider more closely Kant's contention that the categories *are* the functions of judgment employed in a certain way. This is plainly the central contention of the Metaphysical Deduction. It underwrites the claim that the categories are pure and merely intellectual by establishing that they "have their seat in the pure understanding" (A 81 / B 107). It also supports the claim that the categories form a complete system by indicating how they "trace their origin to the understanding" (ibid.), and in particular to the functions of judgment, which "specify the understanding completely and yield an exhaustive inventory of its powers" (A 79 / B 105).

Kant develops his contention in a few dense and very difficult pages (A 76–9 / B 102–5). The backdrop for these pages is his insistence that we can have knowledge only of those things of which we can have sensible intuition, and that knowledge of such things requires apprehension of the manifold of sensible intuition through which they are given to us. (Cf. A 19 / B 33 and A 50 / B 74ff.) In the

Table 3.2

	I	
	Of Quantity	
	Unity	
	Plurality	
	Totality	
II		III
Of Quality		*Of Relation*
Reality		Of Inherence and Subsistence
		(*substantia et accidens*)
Negation		Of Causality and Dependence
		(cause and effect)
Limitation		Of Community (reciprocity be-
		tween agent and patient)
	IV	
	Of Modality	
	Possibility–Impossibility	
	Existence–Nonexistence	
	Necessity–Contingency	

Transcendental Aesthetic he has discussed the forms of sensible intuition, space and time. Now he adds that knowledge requires more than the mere intuition of a manifold in space and time. It also requires that this intuited manifold "be gone through in a certain way, taken up, and connected" (A 77 / B 102). The act of doing this, of "putting different representations together and of grasping what is manifold in them in one cognition" (A 77 / B 103), Kant labels "synthesis." Synthesis plays an essential role in knowledge, he argues, for it is what provides our concepts with content. As far as content is concerned, "no concepts can first arise by way of analysis" (A 77 / B 103). On the contrary, synthesis is "that which first gathers the elements for cognition and unites them to form a certain content." And hence it is "what first gives rise to cognition" (ibid.).

Having introduced the notion of synthesis, Kant proceeds to build his central contention around it. Again there is an important backdrop. Kant has said a few pages earlier that in every judgment "there is a concept which holds of many representations, and which among this many comprehends a given representation, which is then immediately related to an object" (A 68 / B 93). In the judgment that bodies are divisible, for instance, the concept of something divisible, which holds of many things, is "related in particular to the concept of body, and this again to certain appearances that present themselves to us" (A 68–9 / B 93). In judgment, accordingly, "a higher representation, which comprehends under itself this representation and others, is used for cognition of the object, and thereby many possible cognitions are drawn together in one" (A 69 / B 94). With this in mind Kant says that judgments are "functions of unity among our representations" (ibid.). As the *Logic* has it, judgment is "the representation of the unity of the consciousness of various representations, or the representation of their relation insofar as they constitute a concept" (*Logic* §17, 9:101).

Kant's central contention, now, is that these functions of thought, through which we unify representations in a judgment, also give unity to the synthesis of the manifold of intuition. Besides being ways in which we bring representations *under* concepts, they are also ways in which we "bring *to* concepts, not representations, but the *pure synthesis* of representations" (A 78 / B 104,). They are concepts "which give unity to this pure synthesis, and which consist solely in the representation of this necessary synthetic unity" (A 79 / B 104). Summing up, Kant therefore says that the

same function that gives unity to the various representations *in a judgment* also gives unity to the mere synthesis of various representations *in an intuition*. ... Thus the same understanding, through the same operations by which in concepts, by means of analytical unity, it produced the form of a judgment, also brings a transcendental content into its representations by means of the synthetic unity of the manifold in intuition in general. ...

(A 79 / B 104–5)

Insofar as they serve to give unity to the synthesis of intuition, the functions of thought are said to constitute pure concepts of the understanding, or categories.

II. DIFFICULTIES

To a modern reader it is likely to seem that Kant's argument rests on an impoverished logical theory and perhaps on a flawed conception of logic as well. Kant believes that logic is a strictly formal discipline, which "abstracts from all content of cognition of the under-

standing . . . and deals with nothing but the mere form of thought"
(A 54 / B 78; see also *Logic* Intro. I, 9:11–16). He also believes that
logic as he knows it is "a closed and completed body of doctrine" (B
viii), which may not legitimately be altered in any substantive way.
Given familiar attacks by Quine and others,[2] Kant's view on the first
point is likely to strike a modern reader as naive. Given developments in logical theory over the last century, his view on the second
point is likely to seem embarrassingly shortsighted.

On the first point one can expect interesting controversy, since
attacks on the view that logic deals with fixed and purely formal
principles stem from a thoroughgoing empiricism that Kant would
no doubt seek to reject. On the second point, however, the issue is
likely to seem uncontroversial. It is true that Kant does not accept
the logic of his day uncritically. In the one logical work that he
himself published, for example, he attacks the doctrine of the four
syllogistic figures,[3] and in several places he criticizes traditional
logicians for focusing on categorical propositions and inferences, to
the neglect of hypothetical and disjunctive ones.[4] Unfortunately,
however, he is not consistent in heeding his own point. Contrary to
his own insistence, for example, he continues to take the categorical
proposition as paradigmatic.[5] But in any case, his logical theory is
plainly impoverished. It deals, at best, with only a small fragment of
propositional logic. It also provides no explicit treatment of quantification, the implicit treatment being limited to categorical propositions. Most important, his logic does not allow for the representation of multiplace predicates or of the complex quantificational
structures that are the engines of mathematical reasoning.[6]

It is obvious, then, that Kant's logical theory is limited. It is not so
obvious what bearing this has on the Metaphysical Deduction.
Kant's central contention is that there are fundamental structures of
thought in judgment, and that these provide unity to the pure synthesis of the manifold of intuition. It is unclear whether developments
in logical theory do anything more than simply alter our understanding of what those structures are.[7] To get more clear about this, we
will need to focus on the central contention itself, ignoring for the
moment the limitations of Kant's logical theory.

A second group of difficulties has to do not with Kant's logical
theory but with the use he makes of it in constructing his table of
the logical functions of judgment. As we have seen, Kant can claim

that his second table is systematic only because he takes for granted that his first one is. Curiously, however, he offers no explanation of the idea or principle behind the first table. He simply presents it, treating it as well established, even while granting that it "seems to depart in some, though not in any essential respects, from the technical distinctions recognized by logicians" (A 70–1 / B 96). Critics, including Hegel,[8] have charged that there is no explanation to give: that Kant's list of the functions of judgment, like Aristotle's list of categories, has been developed empirically and "rhapsodically." In a well-known and much admired study, Klaus Reich has tried to refute this charge. His effort has failed to gain acceptance, however.[9]

If the principle behind Kant's first table is unclear, so too are many of its details. Kant makes several "observations" designed to "guard against any possible misunderstanding" (A 71 / B 96), but his comments often serve only to confuse matters. Explaining why he includes singular judgments as a separate "moment" under the heading of quantity, for example, Kant concedes that "in the employment of judgments in syllogisms, singular judgments can be treated like those that are universal" (ibid.).[10] He argues, though, that if we consider a singular judgment "as cognition in general, in respect of the quantity it has in comparison with other cognitions, it is certainly different from generally valid judgments . . . and in a complete table of the moments of thought in general deserves a separate place" (A 71 / B 96–7). His point is presumably that judgments are rightly treated in logic not merely as components of a syllogism, but also in their own right, "as cognition in general."[11] It is unclear, however, just what it is to consider a judgment "as cognition in general," and why singular judgments, thus considered, have to be distinguished from universal ones.

A similar problem emerges in Kant's explanation of why infinite judgments are included alongside affirmative and negative ones under the heading of quality. Kant notes that the judgment, "The soul is nonmortal," is quite different from the negative judgment, "The soul is not mortal." He maintains that it should not be treated as an affirmative judgment whose predicate happens to involve negation, however. The distinction is clear enough. What is not clear, once again, is why this pertains to the logical form of the judgment, and why infinite judgments are to be regarded as coordinate with affirmative and negative ones. In his attempt to clear the matter up, unfortunately, Kant seems to contradict his own view. He concedes that infinite judgments are "rightly classified" with affirmative ones in general logic (A 72 / B 97). He insists that they have to be recognized as a separate class in transcendental logic (A 71 / B 97), however, or in "a transcendental table of all moments of thought in judgments" (A 73 / B 98). This implies that the logical functions of judgment are identified within transcendental logic, the discipline that deals with the categories. On Kant's own view, however, as we have noted, these functions are supposed to be identified within general logic, thus providing the "clue" that transcendental logic can utilize to develop the table of categories.

A third group of difficulties has to do with Kant's table of categories and its relationship to the table of the functions of judgment. The correlation between the two tables is in many cases obscure. It is far from obvious, for instance, why the function of thought manifested in the singular judgment is correlated with the category of totality rather than that of unity.[12] Apart from saying that the categories are the functions of judgment employed in a certain way, Kant says little about the correlations in general. In the few comments he does make about the structure of the table of categories, moreover, he refers only to considerations internal to that table, asserting that the third category under each heading "arises from the combination of the second category with the first" (B 110). Allness or totality, by way of illustration, is said to be "nothing other than manyness considered as unity" (B 111). Kant insists that the third category is not for this reason "merely derivative," because combination of the first and second concepts to produce the third "requires a special act of the understanding, which is not the same as that which is exercised in the first and the second" (ibid.). It is unclear what this "special act" is, however, and how it bears on the relationship between the categories and the functions of thought in judgment.[13]

A fourth group of difficulties, finally, has to do neither with the logical theory that forms the backdrop to Kant's central contention, nor with the use that he makes of that theory in constructing his two tables, but with the central contention itself. Kant asserts that the logical functions of thought also constitute concepts that must be applicable to the things given in sensible intuition. It is hard to see why he should think this.

Kant's contention seems to stem from two underlying views. He holds, as we have noted, that we can have knowledge of things only insofar as they can be given to us in sensible intuition. He also holds that knowledge resides in judgments. His view, it appears, is that when we put these two points together, we see that our intuition of things must somehow conform to the logical functions of judgment, and that these functions therefore constitute fundamental concepts to which all objects of knowledge must conform – that is, "concepts of an object in general" (B 128), or categories.

At first glance, Kant's contention may seem to be that the things we intuit must conform to the functions of judgment if we are to be capable of making any judgments about them. If that were his claim, though, his contention would be either trivial or absurd. If we are to make categorical judgments about things given in intuition, then we must of course be able to represent them as subjects and to attribute predicates to them. But this is merely to repeat, trivially, that we must be able to make categorical judgments about them. It is not to say that there is some determinate categorical feature that things must possess if we are to identify them as subjects of predication. If Kant meant to make this latter claim, moreover, his contention would be absurd, even on his own view. For this claim implies that we cannot make judgments except about the things that exhibit the categorical features. This would contradict Kant's view that logic is topic-neutral, that it "abstracts from all content of cognition" and "treats of the form of thought in general" (A 55 / B 79). It would also imply that we cannot even make judgments about things that we cannot intuit; yet it is judgments of this sort that are the subject matter of the Transcendental Dialectic.

What Kant means to claim, it seems plain, is that things must possess categorical features as a condition, not of our making judgments about them, but of our having knowledge of them. As he says, the categories apply to the things we intuit because "only through [them] is it possible to *know* anything *as an object*" (A 92 / B 125). But this gives rise to another difficulty. Even if we suppose that there are such categorical features, it is hard to see why they should be connected in any way with the logical functions of judgment. Suppose, for instance, as Strawson has argued,[14] that we cannot attain knowledge of the subjects about which we judge unless we can, in general, reidentify a thing as the same thing we intuited on another occasion. Suppose, too, that this requires that we be able to identify the subjects of our judgments as things that persist through time, and that change in regular ways. It may be true that things have to possess such features in order to be objects of knowledge for us. It does not follow that these features are identical with, or even that they must somehow correspond to, the logical functions of thought in judgment.[15]

Kant's central contention seems quite implausible, then. Yet before we abandon it, we should perhaps look more carefully at what he says about synthesis. In the last few paragraphs I have been speaking of the categories, as commentators typically do, as concepts *under* which things intuited must fall. What Kant says, however, is that they are concepts that give unity to the synthesis of intuition, through which intuition is brought *to* concepts. It may be worthwhile to explore this distinction, and the notion of synthesis around which it revolves.

III. THE NOTION OF SYNTHESIS

Discussions of the notion of synthesis usually focus on the Transcendental Deduction, where Kant links it to the notion of apperception or self-consciousness. He actually introduces the notion in the Metaphysical Deduction, however, in a passage summarized earlier; and when he does so, he links it not to claims about self-consciousness but to claims about conceptual content. As I will show, Kant's remarks connect the notion of synthesis with important logical and epistemological doctrines. By drawing on these connections we can clarify the notion of synthesis. Conceivably this will shed light on the central contention of the Metaphysical Deduction. In any case, it will help to clarify a notion that is central to the Transcendental Deduction.

Kant says, as we have seen, that "as to content, no concepts can first arise by way of analysis" (A 77 / B 103). Synthesis is what "gathers the elements for cognition and unites them in a certain content," and synthesis, therefore, is what "first gives rise to cognition" (A 77–8 / B 103). To understand the notion of synthesis we must therefore understand Kant's views concerning conceptual content.

It is natural to suppose that a concept's content is simply the collection of predicates that are, in Kant's standard metaphor, "contained" within it. In interpreting the notion of content it is natural, accordingly, to draw on what Kant says about analytic judgments. Kant holds, as we know, that any one concept will typically contain others.[16] Any concept, that is, will typically contain various predicates, which hold conjointly of its instances. Kant calls the contained predicates "partial concepts," since each of them does hold of the very same things that the containing concept does, yet it is only by being conjoined that they serve to identify those things. He notes, moreover, that these partial concepts may be related in two ways (Logic Intro. VIII, 9:59). They may be independent of one another and hence simply coordinate. In the concept of a human being, for example, the predicate "is an animal" and "is rational" would presumably be coordinate. It may also be the case, however, that one predicate holds of the things conceived just because another does, and hence that one is subordinate to another. In our example, the predicate "is an animal" would presumably have subordinate to it the predicate "has a body," and this in turn would presumably have subordinate to it the predicate "is a material thing," and so on. Conceptual analysis, as Kant understands it, reveals or clarifies such contained predicates, along with their relations of coordination and subordination, thereby rendering the main concept distinct. Analytic judgments are ones that express the results of such analysis.

It seems natural, then, to identify the content of a concept with what analysis reveals: the collection of predicates that are contained in a concept, related coordinately and subordinately. This is essentially what is said in the Logic (§7, 9:95). As far as it goes, moreover, this is in fact Kant's view. Two points need to be made, though, if we are to understand the view correctly.

First, though analysis may uncover the content of a concept, conceptual content cannot be defined as what analysis reveals. For not all concepts can be analyzed, according to Kant. We can analyze concepts that are given, ones that we find ourselves employing even though we are not yet clear what predicates they contain. Indeed, the notion of analysis is defined by reference to such concepts. But some concepts are made rather than given. With concepts of this sort, which Kant thinks are characteristic of mathematics and natural science, we begin, as it were, by legislating the conditions a thing must satisfy to qualify as an instance of the concept in question. In mathematics, for example, we give a definition, whereas in empirical science we establish the criteria by which things of a certain kind are to be identified.

We then proceed to determine what further predicates hold of the things in question, not by uncovering what was implicit in our initial concept, but instead by adding predicates to that concept, either by constructing it and producing a demonstration (in mathematics) or by observing instances of the concept (in empirical science).[17] With concepts that are "made" in this way, analysis is impossible, then, because there is nothing to uncover. Here we do not begin with the whole concept and proceed to clarify the predicates it contains. Rather, we begin by laying down a few predicates, to which we then add. With concepts that are made, as the *Logic* has it,

I begin with the parts and proceed toward the whole. Here there are as yet no marks; I acquire them only through synthesis. From this synthetic procedure emerges synthetic distinctness, . . . which actually extends my concept as to content through what is added as a mark over and above the concept in (pure or empirical) intuition. (Intro. VIII, 9:63)

Kant's discussion of the distinction between concepts given and concepts made is intriguing in several respects. One wonders, for example, why mathematical demonstration or empirical observation should add predicates to our *concept* of a thing, "as parts of the complete possible concept" (ibid.), rather than simply adding to our *knowledge* of the things conceived.[18] The important point just now, however, is that even if a concept is made rather than given, it will still contain various predicates (at a minimum, those that establish the conditions a thing must satisfy to qualify as an instance). It seems natural to suppose, therefore, that with any concept, given or made, its content will be the various predicates it contains. As far as it goes, moreover, this is in fact Kant's view. But a second point needs to be made if we are to understand the view properly.

At several points in the *Critique* Kant distinguishes between the content of a concept and its (mere) logical form.[19] At several points, too, he links the content of a concept with that concept's matter.[20] Now the matter of a concept, on Kant's view, is just its object: the individual things that we conceive, as opposed to the predicates through which we conceive those things (*Logic* §2, 9:91). Kant holds, however, that the only individual things that we can identify are those that can be given to us in sensible intuition (A 19 / B 33). His view, accordingly, is that concepts have content, not merely because they contain various predicates, but also because those predicates are

tied to what can be given in sensible intuition. The predicates themselves exhibit a certain structure insofar as they hold conjointly of the
things conceived, and insofar as they are related to one another coordinately and subordinately. This structure constitutes the logical form
of the concept. Apart from their relation to sensible intuition, however, and to the individuals we can represent through it, the predicates constitute *merely* the logical form of a concept. Should it be
impossible to link them to sensible intuition, that form would be
empty or without content. As Kant also puts it, the concept would
"be without sense, that is, without meaning" (A 240 / B 299).

Kant is not merely stipulating that concepts will be said to have
content only if things of the kind conceived are given in intuition.
His claim is rather that things intuited somehow figure in an essential way in the concept itself. Apart from this relation to things
intuited, the concept would be merely an empty shell, which could
not serve as a basis for knowledge. In thinking it we would merely
have "played with representations" (A 155 / B 195).

It is not the business of logic to investigate the conditions under
which concepts can be related to sensible intuition and hence have
content, because logic "abstracts from all content of cognition, that
is, from all relation of cognition to the object" (A 55 / B 79). In the
Critique, however, this relation is of central concern. When Kant
introduces the notion of synthesis and says that synthesis "gathers
the elements for cognition and unites them in a certain content"
(A 77–8 / B 103), his aim is to explain this relation. The notion of
synthesis is supposed to make clear how it is that intuition enters
into concepts and provides them with content that they would otherwise lack.

These claims are initially puzzling. We can see their point, however, if we take as our guide some of what Kant says about mathematical concepts. It is characteristic of such concepts, according to
him, that they "contain an arbitrary synthesis that admits of *a priori*
construction" in intuition (A 729 / B 757). In saying that the synthesis is *arbitrary*, Kant echoes the point made earlier, namely that
mathematical concepts are made, not given. In saying that what is
arbitrary is a *synthesis*, he makes the point that is of interest right
now. Reflection on an example will help to clarify that point.

If asked to say what a triangle is, we might first say that it is
something that is a figure, is rectilinear, and is three-sided. As far as

it goes, moreover, this is quite correct, since any triangle will have to satisfy all three of these predicates. It is a mistake to suppose that we are specifying the content of the concept merely by listing such predicates, however, for the content consists not in the mere conjunction of such predicates but rather, to put it roughly, in what we think through those predicates; and this is something that cannot be conveyed merely by the listing of further predicates. For something to be a figure, for instance, is not merely for it to satisfy further predicates. It is for there to be certain lines, and for these lines to be so related as to constitute a figure. To be rectilinear, moreover, is for these lines, taken individually, to be straight. To be three-sided is for these lines, taken jointly, to be a collection of three. To convey what is thought through the predicates, and to make plain how they are related to one another, requires, as Kant would say, that we posit objects that constitute the thing we are conceiving.

From a modern viewpoint, the point of importance here would be considered a logical one. Kant thinks of concepts as one-place predicates that contain, as their partial concepts, other one-place predicates. Accordingly, he thinks of the propositions that specify these partial concepts – analytic propositions, in case the concepts are given – as universal categoricals, having the form

$$(x) \ (Tx{\rightarrow}Fx), \ (x) \ (Tx{\rightarrow}Rx), \ (x) \ (Tx{\rightarrow}TSx), \ \text{etc.}$$

To specify all the partial concepts that a concept contains would be to state a series of such propositions. Equivalently, it would be to state a single proposition with a compound predicate, of the form

$$(x) \ [Tx{\leftrightarrow}(Fx \ \& \ Rx \ \& \ TSx \ \& \ \cdots)].$$

The point of importance, now, is that we cannot specify the content of the concept of a triangle by a proposition of this form. For something to be a triangle is not merely for it to satisfy certain predicates. It is for there to be three line segments, suitably joined. More carefully, it is for there to be three noncolinear points, joined by line segments, and for the composite entity constituted by those line segments to be identical with the thing in question.[21] What is required, therefore, is a proposition of the form[22]

$$(x) \ \{Tx{\leftrightarrow}(\exists w) \ (\exists y) \ (\exists z) \ [Pw \ \& \ Py \ \& \ Pz \ \& \ \sim C(w,y,z) \ \&$$
$$(wy \cup yz \cup zw = x)]\}.$$

Kant would not make the point in this way, of course. As noted in II, his logic does not allow for such nesting of existential quantifiers, nor for multiplace predicates. He sees, however, that we cannot specify the content of mathematical concepts merely by listing the partial concepts they contain.[23] When he says that "mathematical definitions are constructions of concepts" that "contain an arbitrary synthesis" of things intuited (A 729–30 / B 757–8), he is making the point in his own way. We cannot capture the content of a mathematical concept merely by listing *predicates* that the instances of that concept must satisfy. Instead, we must posit *objects* and represent them as standing in certain relations. Representing such objects involves intuition. In Kant's characteristic phrase, it involves representing a manifold, or multiplicity, in intuition. This manifold of things also has to be represented as related in certain ways, so as to constitute the thing we are conceiving. In Kant's phrase, the manifold also has to be "gone through in a certain way, taken up, and connected" (A 77 / B 102) "Synthesis" is simply Kant's term for this form of representation, and it is in this sense that synthesis gives a mathematical concept its content.[24]

Modern logic helps to elucidate the importance of Kant's notion of synthesis. It is important to realize, though, that Kant's view of the matter is in important ways quite different. From a modern viewpoint, the content of the concept of a triangle cannot be captured by the conjoining of one-place predicates, requiring instead nested existential quantifiers. The claims represented by those quantifiers need not be true, however, in order for us to express the content of the concept and to prove things about what is conceived. Should there fail to be three points, for instance, we can still state the definition of a triangle, and we can still produce proofs about the properties of triangles. But Kant views the matter quite differently. What we express by means of the nested existential quantifiers, he thinks of as involving the intuition of a manifold. Should the requisite intuition be lacking, the concept would therefore have no content and could not serve as a basis for reasoning and for knowledge, even in mathematics.[25] He says, accordingly, that concepts "have no meaning if no object can be given for them, or at least for the elements of which they are composed" (A 139 / B 178).

IV. KANT'S CENTRAL CONTENTION

It is clear from the foregoing discussion that the Metaphysical Deduction contains important material. That material merits more attention than it has received, and more than I have been able to give it. For the moment, nonetheless, the discussion in III will have to suffice. The question at hand is whether that discussion gives us any insight into the argument of the Metaphysical Deduction. The question, most importantly, is whether it lends plausibility to Kant's central contention that the categories are simply the logical functions of thought in judgment, employed in the determination of the sensible manifold.

The answer, I think, is negative. The discussion in III helps us to gain perspective on the argument of the Metaphysical Deduction. It helps us to see, in particular, that Kant conceives of his argument as part of an endeavor to revise the dogmatic metaphysics of his predecessors, notably Leibniz. It also makes it plain, however, that Kant did not carry his revisions as far as he should have.

Leibniz took it for granted that knowledge is to be expressed in the form of categorical judgments. He argued, moreover, that there must be a basis in reality for the truth of all true categoricals, and that this basis must lie in the individuals that are the real subjects of such judgments. These individuals can provide the needed basis, he argued, only if the concept of each individual contains all the predicates truly attributable to it. Each individual must therefore be the object of what Leibniz calls a "complete concept." Indeed, since a predicate can hold true of an individual only if it is contained in its complete concept, an individual is to be understood as nothing but the object of such a concept. From this claim many of the familiar tenets of Leibnizian metaphysics – that individuals are ungenerable and indestructible, that they are incapable of real interaction, etc. – follow quite directly.[26]

Leibniz realized, of course, that the knowledge we can gain by analysis of concepts is actually quite meager, and that for any but the most general truths we have to base our judgments on experience. He believed that this is merely because the complete concepts of these things are infinitely complex, however, whereas our powers of analysis are finite. Because of our limitations, the complete concepts of things always remain for the most part obscure to us, allow-

ing us to see that things have various properties, but not to work out
the infinitely complex chain of reasons. In appealing to experience,
what we are appealing to is just these obscure concepts of things.

Kant insists, contrary to Leibniz, that experience does not consist
merely of confused concepts. It also involves sensible representations, which are fundamentally different from concepts, being ways
in which we find ourselves affected, not ways in which we think
about what affects us. Leibniz's fundamental error, Kant thinks, was
to fail to understand the nature of this difference, and to fail to
realize that for us, as well as for any intelligence we can comprehend, knowledge depends essentially on sensible representations.[27]
We cannot identify individuals except by means of sensibility. We
cannot have significant knowledge of individuals, either, except insofar as our concepts involve a synthesis – along the lines suggested in
III – of the sensible representations through which we apprehend
them. Leibniz was wrong, therefore, to "intellectualize" (A 271 / B
327) the objects of experience. There may be no contradiction, perhaps, in the notion of an intellect that does not depend on sensibility, one whose intuition is intellectual and whose knowledge rests
merely on the analysis of concepts. But we cannot claim to comprehend what such an intellect would be like. Neither can we use the
notion of such an intellect as a basis for determining what things
must be like "in themselves."

The proper task of metaphysics, and its proper method, are thus
quite different from what Leibniz supposed. We are not to abstract
from the limitations of human knowledge in order to determine
what things must be like "in themselves." On the contrary, we are
to recognize those limitations, and we are to determine what our
representation of things must be like if, given our limitations, we are
to be capable of having knowledge. We are to determine, more specifically, what sort of synthesis must underlie our concepts of things
if those concepts are to have content that will provide the basis for a
body of genuine knowledge. We cannot argue, for example, as Leibniz thought he could, that individuals must be objects of complete
concepts if truth is to have a basis in reality. We can show, however,
Kant argues in the First Analogy of Experience (A 182–9, B 224–32),
that if we are to have knowledge of the individuals we experience,
we have to be able to represent those individuals as things having a
substratum that endures through all change. We cannot determine

the nature of substance, as Leibniz supposed. We can show that we have to be able to identify something substantial in our intuition of individuals, however, if knowledge of them is to be possible.

As these last remarks suggest, the differences between Kant's metaphysics and Leibniz's do not become fully apparent until the Analytic of Principles, where Kant inquires into the various types of synthesis that "schematize" our fundamental concepts of things, thereby providing those concepts with their content. One aim of the Metaphysical Deduction, however, is to lay the foundations for this later inquiry. In the Metaphysical Deduction, accordingly, Kant introduces the notion of synthesis and states his doctrine that synthesis provides the content of concepts. He makes it plain, too, that this requires a break from the Leibnizian tradition; for he insists that metaphysical concepts are empty unless we view them, not as concepts of the properties of things "in themselves," but as concepts "which consist solely in the representation of [the] necessary synthetic unity" through which intuition provides content for our concepts (A 79 / B 104).

On the one hand, then, the Metaphysical Deduction constitutes an important step in Kant's endeavor to revise the methods of Leibnizian metaphysics. On the other hand, ironically, it also reveals Kant's continuing commitment to a characteristically Leibnizian line of thought. As we have noted, Leibniz thought he could determine the nature of substance by reflecting on the structure of the categorical judgment. Kant denies this. He continues to suppose, however, that the structure of judgment provides the "clue" to the basic concepts of metaphysics. Indeed, rather than rejecting Leibniz's view on this point he tries instead to generalize it. He insists that we should attend not only to the form of the categorical judgment but also to those of the hypothetical and the disjunctive. He insists, more generally, that we should attend to all the functions of thought in judgment, not just those that have to do with the moment of relation.[28]

If we examine Kant's treatment of individual categories, it seems plain that he does not proceed in the way that his "clue" requires. Consider, once again, the concept of substance. Leibniz might claim, with some plausibility, to have derived his doctrine concerning substance from the form of the categorical judgment. His notion of a substance is that of an individual to which predicates may be attributed, after all, and in his metaphysics he simply attempts to determine what individuals must be like if they are to provide the basis for judgments attributing predicates to them. On Kant's view, by way of contrast, the notion of substance is not that of an individual to which predicates are attributed. Instead, it is that of a substratum, of something that underlies individuals and that persists even as they come to be or pass away. It is simply implausible for Kant to claim that this concept of substance is somehow derived from the form of the categorical judgment.

The difficulty is not one merely of detail. Having insisted that we can have knowledge only insofar as our concepts involve a synthesis of intuitions, Kant rightly concludes that metaphysics will be possible only as an inquiry into the nature of the synthesis that is required if those concepts are to make possible knowledge of the things we experience. It is clear, of course, that such knowledge will reside in judgments. There is no reason to suppose that the logical structure of judgment will provide a clue to the nature of the synthesis that will make knowledge possible, however. From his own point of view, then, Kant's continuing commitment to this Leibnizian line of thought is a mistake, one that he for the most part ignores, thankfully, when he actually develops his system of categories in the Analytic of Principles.

NOTES

Translations from Kant's texts are my own, though to facilitate location of passages in the *Critique*, I follow the translation by Norman Kemp Smith (Second Impression, with corrections; London: Macmillan, 1963) as closely as possible.

1 A 66–83, B 91–116. At B 159 Kant refers to this section as the "metaphysical deduction," and the name has become standard.
2 See, e.g., W. V. O. Quine, *Philosophy of Logic* (Englewood Cliffs, N.J.: Prentice-Hall, 1970), ch. 7.
3 "Die falsche Spitzfindigkeit der vier syllogistischen Figuren" (The False Subtlety of the Four Syllogistic Figures) (2:45–61). The *Logic* that appears in *Ak.* 9 was prepared for publication, at Kant's request late in life, by G. B. Jäsche, and there is controversy about its accuracy in reflecting Kant's views. Cf. T. Boswell, "On the Textual Authenticity of Kant's *Logic*," *History and Philosophy of Logic* 9 (1988): 193–203.

4 See B 140–1, A 304–5 / B 360–1, and *Logic* §25 n.2, 9:105–6, §29 n., 9:107–8, and §60 n.2, 9:122.

5 This is evident, for example, in the passage (summarized above) where Kant states his view that judgments are functions of unity among our representations. Kant tries to formulate his definition of judgment in such a way as to include hypothetical and disjunctive judgments (B 140–1 and *Logic* §17, 9:101). He likewise tries to formulate the principle of the syllogism so that it will cover hypothetical and disjunctive inferences as well as categorical ones (*Logic*, §§57–61, 9:120–3). Neither effort is very clear or successful, however.

6 As we will see in III, Kant is aware that his logical theory cannot represent such inferences. Indeed, his notion of synthesis, and his view that mathematical inference rests on construction of concepts in intuition, reflect this awareness.

7 P. F. Strawson argues, in *The Bounds of Sense* (London: Methuen, 1966, esp. pp. 80–2), that there are two ideas fundamental to modern logic, those of truth-functional composition and of quantification, and that we cannot derive categories from either. His conclusion turns out to be correct, I think, but his argument ignores Kant's insistence that the categories are not concepts under which intuited things must fall, but concepts that give unity to the synthesis through which intuition is brought to concepts. See below, end of II and III.

8 G. W. F. Hegel, *Enzyklopädie der philosophischen Wissenschaften im Grundrisse*, Theil I (Die Wissenschaft der Logik), 3rd edition (1830), §42.

9 Klaus Reich, *Die Vollständigkeit der kantischen Urteilstafel* (Berlin: Richard Schoetz, 1932), esp. pp. 46 ff. Reich's presentation is controversial because he bases his development of the functions of judgment on Kant's assertion that judgment "is nothing but the manner in which given modes of knowledge are brought to the objective unity of apperception" (B 141). While not rejecting this characterization, most readers doubt that general logic, as opposed to transcendental logic, can properly draw on this feature of judgment. In addition, Reich's narrative account of why we have the various functions of judgment, though not implausible, fails to show why other accounts, different in structure and content, might not equally well be given.

A new work on the table of judgments, *Die Urteilstafel*, by Reinhard Brandt (forthcoming from Felix Meiner Verlag) has been announced, but I have not been able to see a copy.

10 Kant's point is that a singular judgment functioning as minor premise in a syllogism – e.g., 'All men are mortal, Socrates is a man, therefore Socrates is mortal' – can be treated as though it were universal. But the point is more limited, and more complex, than Kant suggests, as indicated by the fact that singular judgments cannot function as major premises.

11 This point is made by Manley Thompson, "Unity, Plurality, and Totality as Kantian Categories," *Monist* 72 (1989), pp. 169–89, esp. pp. 170–1.

12 This issue has been much discussed. For an insightful treatment see Thompson, ibid.

13 For a critical discussion of Kant's table of categories that explores the table in some detail see Jonathan Bennett, *Kant's Analytic* (Cambridge: Cambridge University Press, 1966), pp. 84–99.

14 Strawson, *The Bounds of Sense*, Part Two.

15 For development of this point, see Strawson, ibid., pp. 74–82.

16 According to the *Logic*, analysis terminates with the identification of concepts that are simple and unanalyzable. See Intro. VIII 9:59.

17 See *Logic* Intro. VIII, 9:63–4, and §§99–105, 9:140–3, as well as "The Discipline of Pure Reason in Its Dogmatic Employment" in the first *Critique*, esp. A 727 / B 755 ff.

18 The point is not unimportant, because the definition of judgment in the *Logic* (§17, 9:101) says that every judgment, and hence even a synthetic one, represents the subject and the predicate as combined "insofar as they constitute a concept."

19 See A 43 / B 60–1, A 239 / B 298, A 262 / B 318, A 289 / B 346, A 572 / B 600, A 709 / B 737. In related passages Kant identifies having content with having an object and says that in concepts that have no object we think, but our thought is empty. We have "merely played with representations" (A 155–6 / B 194–5), and our concepts are "without sense, that is, without meaning" (A 240 / B 299). See also A 55 / B 79, A 62–3 / B 87, B 146–7 and A 139 / B 178.

20 Sometimes "matter" and "content" appear to be treated as equivalent terms, as in *Logic* §5 n.1, 9:94 and at A 6 / B 9. But Kant's view seems rather to be that having matter, or an object, is a necessary condition for having content, as in the argument at A 77 / B 102.

21 This is a standard modern view of how to define a triangle, which Kant would not accept; for as Manley Thompson has insisted in correspondence, Kant holds that we do not intuit points but only lines, points being the conceived limits of line segments (see A 169 / B 211). To develop the point in Kant's way would complicate the matter, but it would not affect the point I am seeking to make.

22 The definition will actually be more complex than this, because the same point needs to be made again for at least one of the predicates employed. For three points not to be colinear, for instance, is for there not to be a line segment on which all three are located. Hence $\sim C(w,y,z)$ would have to be replaced by something of the form $\sim(\exists u)(Lu \,\&\, \ldots)$.

23 See Frege's comments on Kant toward the end of the *Foundations of Arithmetic* (German text with English translation by J. L. Austin (Oxford: Blackwell, 1959), pp. 99ff.). Frege observes that Kant "seems to

think of concepts as defined by giving a simple list of characteristics in no special order; but of all ways of forming concepts, that is one of the least fruitful" (p. 100). He does not see that Kant's notion of synthesis represents an attempt to characterize a more "fruitful" way of defining a concept.

24 That Kant's views about mathematics reflect his awareness of what we would view as the logical complexity of mathematical concepts has been stressed by Michael Friedman in his influential paper, "Kant's Theory of Geometry," *Philosophical Review* 94 (1985): 455–506. My approach to the notion of synthesis owes much to Friedman's work.

25 Friedman develops this point at length, ibid.

26 See Leibniz's *Discourse on Metaphysics*, §viii and following. That Kant understands Leibniz's view in this way is indicated in his discussion of that view in the Amphiboly of the Concepts of Reflection (A 260 / B 316ff.).

27 In addition to the Amphiboly of the Concepts of Reflection, see also A 43 / B 60–1ff. and A 50 / B 74f.

28 Kant's attempt to generalize Leibniz's view on this point parallels his attempt to generalize the problem that Hume had discovered with the concept of causality (B 19–20).

4 The transcendental deduction of the categories

I

In the preface to the first edition of the *Critique of Pure Reason*, published in 1781, Kant wrote:

I know of no investigations that would be more important for getting to the bottom of the faculty that we call understanding and at the same time for determining the rules and limits of its employment than those that I have undertaken in the second part of the Transcendental Analytic, under the title of the *Deduction of the Pure Concepts of the Understanding*; they have also cost me the most, but not, I hope, unrewarded effort.   (A xvi)[1]

However, the initial response to Kant's argument, which he also titled the "transcendental deduction of the categories" (A 85 / B 117), was largely one of incomprehension, and in the preface to the *Metaphysical Foundations of Natural Science*, published in 1786, Kant himself acknowledged that precisely "that part of the *Critique* which should have been the clearest was the most obscure, or even revolved in a circle" (4:474 n.). So in the second edition of the *Critique*, published the following year, Kant completely rewrote the transcendental deduction. He claimed that this revision touched only the manner of *"presentation,"* not the "propositions themselves and their grounds of proof" (B xxxvii–xxxviii). But in spite of Kant's efforts at clarification, the intervening two centuries have brought little agreement in the interpretation of the deduction, even on the fundamental question of whether the two editions of the *Critique*, in 1781 and 1787, try to answer the same question by means of the same argument. The last three decades alone have brought forth dozens of competing interpretations or "reconstructions" of Kant's transcendental deduction.[2]

Problems of interpretation begin with the question of exactly what thesis the transcendental deduction is supposed to prove, for what Kant first announces as the goal to be reached and what he subsequently describes as the conclusion he has established are by no means identical.

At the outset of the exposition of the transcendental deduction in the *Critique of Pure Reason*, Kant introduces a famous distinction between "the question about that which is rightful (*quid juris*) and that which concerns the fact (*quid facti*)" (A 84 / B 116), and says that a deduction is required to answer the *quid juris* when experience alone cannot afford a proof of the "objective reality" of a concept, a proof that a concept has a legitimate employment. He then states:

> But among the many concepts that make up the very complicated web of human cognition there are some that are determined for pure *a priori* employment (completely independent of all experience), and these always require a deduction of their authority; for proofs from experience are never sufficient for the propriety of such an employment, but one must yet know how these concepts can relate to objects that they yet derive from no experience. I therefore call an explanation of the way in which concepts can relate *a priori* to objects their *transcendental deduction*.   (A 85 / B 117)

This passage begins with the premise that there *are a priori* concepts, and maintains that a transcendental deduction is required only to establish that these *a priori* concepts do apply *to objects*. Logically speaking, this question would be at least adequately answered by a proof that there are *some* objects that can be considered to be independent of our representations – an assumption that Kant appears to make when he says that "representation in itself . . . does not produce its object as far as *existence* is concerned" (A 92 / B 125) – to which these *a priori* concepts of subjective origin nevertheless necessarily apply.

Yet as Kant continues, it soon becomes clear that he intends to prove more than that certain concepts, our *a priori* knowledge of which can be assumed, apply to *some* objects that are in some sense distinct from our mere representations of them. Kant claims that the problem of a transcendental deduction arises for the categories of the understanding in a way in which it does not for space and time as the pure forms of intuition. He says this is so because, whereas *all* appearances or empirical intuitions are *given* to us already in spatial and temporal form, the applicability of any *concept, a fortiori* any *a priori* concept, to all empirical intuitions is not in the same way manifest in anything immediately given (A 89–90 / B 121–2; see also A 93 / B 126).[3] Because of this difference, Kant claims, "a difficulty manifests itself here that we did not encounter in the field of sensibility, namely how *subjective conditions of thinking* should have *objective validity*, i.e., yield conditions of the possibility of all cognition of objects" (A 89–90 / B 122). Here it is suggested that what must be shown is not that the categories are legitimately applied to *some* objects independent of our representations but that they necessarily apply to *all* objects of knowledge. This difference may be marked by Kant's change from the claim that the *objective reality* of the categories must be deduced (A 84 / B 116) to the claim that their *objective validity* must be demonstrated. Kant does not offer formal definitions of these terms, but usually employs them in contexts which suggest that a concept has *objective reality* if it has at least *some* instantiation in experience but *objective validity* only if it applies to *all* possible objects of experience.

To further complicate matters, sometimes Kant suggests that the deduction not only must show that concepts antecedently assumed to be known *a priori* have objective validity, not just objective reality, but must even prove that there *are* such concepts in the first place. This emerges in his statement of strategy at the outset of the deduction, when he implies that the proof must begin by showing that experience of objects requires concepts at all: "But all experience contains in addition to the intuition of the senses, through which something is given, a *concept* of an object that is given or appears in the intuition: thus concepts of objects in general will lie at the basis of all empirical cognition as *a priori* conditions" (A 93 / B 126). This should appear puzzling, since an earlier section of the *Critique*, the so-called metaphysical deduction, has already argued that twelve particular *a priori* concepts of the understanding are necessary in order to apply the logical functions of judgment to objects.[4] Either Kant is now intimating that this preliminary argument needs to be redone, or else he is suggesting the strategy necessary to exploit the earlier result, namely that he must now argue that all experience does take the form of judgments about objects, in which case the *a priori* concepts that are the conditions of the possibility of judgment will become the necessary conditions of experience itself.

If this is so, however, then the difference between Kant's questions of objective *reality* and objective *validity*, between proving that the categories apply to *some* objects as contrasted to our representations and proving that they apply to all experiences as such, all possible "data for a possible experience" (A 119), therefore even our own representations, becomes pressing.

If Kant's point is to prove that the categories necessarily apply to objects considered in contrast to our mere representations or subjective states as such, then one strategy for the deduction naturally suggests itself, namely to show that the categories necessarily apply to objects precisely by showing that it is by means of their application to objects that the contrast between objects and merely subjective representations is made. But if the point of the deduction is to show that there can be no experiences that are not subject to the categories, then the strategy that proves the objective reality of the categories by using them to contrast objects to mere representations cannot be employed, for it places mere representations outside the domain of the categories. Another strategy must be found that does not make the application of the categories only to objects itself the basis for contrasting representations and objects. At the same time, however, because the contrast between subjective states and external objects does seem fundamental to Kant's conception of knowledge (as well as to most other theories of knowledge), the way in which the categories are applied to all possible experiences cannot make it impossible to preserve the contrast, in particular, cannot end up by converting all of our representations *into* objects of the kind to which they are ordinarily contrasted.

We shall see that these considerations cause serious problems for Kant. One strategy he attempts to exploit for the transcendental deduction does indeed treat the categories as conditions for knowledge of objects as contrasted to merely subjective representations, and ends up by leaving the latter outside the domain of the categories altogether. An alternative strategy attempts to avoid this problem by making the categories into necessary conditions of *self-consciousness* itself, or what Kant calls "apperception," and then suggesting that they are *a fortiori* also conditions for the representation of any objects through the medium of subjective states of which we are self-conscious (see A 107, A 113, B 116, B 133). But this strategy in turn runs two risks. First, unless it shows that self-consciousness itself requires knowledge of objects, it runs the risk of leaving the categories as merely necessary conditions for the possible knowledge of objects, not showing that they actually do apply to any objects; thus, Kant's question about objective reality may go unsolved. Second, there is also the danger that Kant can identify the categories as the necessary conditions for self-consciousness only by equating self-consciousness with knowledge of objects and deriving the categories from the latter, thereby not only reverting to the first strategy but in addition now blocking the possibility for the contrast between mere representations and objects altogether.

In the theory of knowledge offered by the *Critique of Pure Reason* as a whole, Kant does avoid these shoals. In the sections on the "Analogies of Experience" (A 176–218 / B 218–65) he shows that judgments about the temporal relations of states of objects can be made only by contrasting them to the temporal relations of merely subjective states by use of such categories as substance and causation. In the "Refutation of Idealism" (B 274–9), he suggests that judgments about the temporal relations of even merely subjective states require their correlation but not identification with objective states subsumed under these categories. He thus shows that the categories can be applied to both subjective states and external objects without collapsing the difference between them, and also proves that judgment about the former requires knowledge of the latter, that self-consciousness requires knowledge of objects but does not collapse into it. Kant can only establish these connections, however, by bringing into consideration conditions for the confirmation of empirical judgment that go beyond the more abstract theses of the transcendental deduction. Indeed, although the arguments of the transcendental deduction are supposed to prepare the way for this theory of empirical knowledge, they frequently risk undermining it.[5]

II

In a famous letter to his former student Marcus Herz written at the outset of his work on the *Critique of Pure Reason*, Kant asserted that the problem of the categories had been ignored in previous philosophy, including his own.[6] This was misleading. From the beginning of his philosophical career, Kant had tried to prove the necessity of certain intellectual *principles*, particularly principles of the conservation of substances, about the possibility of real action of one substance on another, and about the real community of substances. In his earliest purely philosophical work, the *New Exposition of the First Principles of Metaphysical Cognition* (the *Nova dilucidatio*) of 1755, Kant had argued against Leibniz and his Wolffian followers that such principles were entailed rather than excluded by the principle of sufficient reason, which like his predecessors he attempted to derive from logical grounds.[7] In his 1763 *Attempt to Introduce Negative Quantities into Philosophy*, however, Kant introduced a fundamental distinction between *real* and *logical* relationships, on the basis of which he argued, in a manner reminiscent of Hume,[8] that principles of causality could never be derived from logical relations alone.[9] After this, however, Kant had no clear strategy for the proof of the principle of causality or other substantive rather than merely logical principles of thought. And this embarrassment was reflected in his inaugural dissertation of 1770. Here Kant made one passing reference to metaphysical *concepts* – "possibility, existence, necessity, substance, cause, etc., together with their opposites"[10] – but did not explain the connection between these and the appearances of objects presented to us in space and time. And he was so unclear about the proper status of the *principles* he had always wanted to establish, particularly the principles of universal causality and the conservation of substance, that he could only call them "principles of convenience," "conditions under which it seems to the intellect easy and practicable to use its own perspicacity." He did assert that *"if we depart from them scarcely any judgment about a given object would be permitted to our intellect,"*[11] but he offered no explanation of this claim. In other words, in the period up to 1770, Kant had not simply overlooked the problem of the categories; rather, he just did not know how to solve it.

Yet when Kant wrote his letter to Herz, he was confident that he would publish his book on the methods and limits of metaphysics within three months (10:127). In fact, it was nine years before he published the *Critique of Pure Reason*, and he was still struggling with the transcendental deduction up to the publication of its second edition six years later. So whatever insight Kant had in 1772 still had plenty of wrinkles to be ironed out. Nevertheless, we can say in the most general terms that Kant had realized that the way out of his impasse lay in connecting the *principles* he had always wanted to establish with the pure *concepts* of the understanding and in interpreting the latter as conditions for conceiving and judging of any objects of experience at all. If the pure concepts of the understanding could be shown to be conditions for any experience of objects but also to carry the principles along with them, then the validity of the principles could be rooted in the very possibility of experience of objects. And how could the pure concepts of the understanding be shown to be necessary conditions for any experience of objects at all? By providing an argument for the unsupported assertion that Kant had made at the end of the inaugural dissertation – namely by demonstrating that the categories really are the only conditions under which *"judgment about a given object would be permitted to our intellect."* Kant's strategy thus became to use the categories as the link between the idea of making any judgments about objects, on the one hand, and the substantive principles of causation and conservation which he had always wanted to prove, on the other.

This strategy brings us back to a fundamental question we have so far deferred, namely the question of exactly what Kant means by a category of pure understanding. We can now appreciate that what he means by a category is, in fact, just a concept of an object, or more precisely a general feature of any determinate concept of an object, which allows the application of a judgment to that object.

Some of Kant's most general comments define a category simply as a concept by means of which mere intuitions can be thought or represented *as an object.* For instance, this early reflection states that "Categories are the universal actions of reason, by means of which we think an object in general (to the representations, appearances)" (R 4276, 17:492).[12] More often, however, Kant suggests that the categories are the necessary conditions for conceiving of intuitions as representing *the object of a judgment.* His idea appears to be that since a judgment expresses a certain relation among its component representations, for instance it contains a predicate that it assigns to a subject, the *object* of the judgment must be represented as having parts or aspects represented by those syntactically distinct components of the judgment; in the case of a subject–predicate judgment, for example, something in the object must be represented as the *substance* corresponding to the *subject-concept* in the judgment and something else as the *property* corresponding to the *predicate* in the judgment. The categories are the concepts by means of which we organize our intuitions in order to make them accessible to judgments in this way.[13]

Numerous passages in Kant's published writings and his notes suggest this general picture. The key paragraph of the section of the *Critique of Pure Reason* in which he first discusses the categories, for instance, suggests that the categories are simply concepts by means of which we introduce into our intuitions the structure needed for us to make judgments apply to those intuitions:

The same function that gives unity to the different representations *in a judgment* also gives unity to the mere synthesis of different representations *in an intuition*, and indeed through the very same actions by means of which in concepts, through analytical unity, it produced the logical form of a judgment, it also, by means of the synthetic unity of the manifold in intuition in general, brings a transcendental content into its representations. . . .

(A 79 / B 104–5)

The "transcendental content" that is added to the manifold of intuitions appears to be a conceptualization of the latter in a form that allows it to become an object for a judgment. The same thought is present in a number of Kant's reflections. Thus Kant writes: "The logical condition of the judgment is the relation to the subject, etc.; the concept of a thing through this logical function is the category" (R 5555, 18:231),[14] and "The category is therefore the *concept of an object in general, so far as it is determined* in itself *in respect of a logical function of judgments a priori* (that one must think through this function of combination of the manifold in its representation) (R 5932, 18:392)."[15] Finally, the recapitulation of the transcendental deduction in the *Prolegomena to Any Future Metaphysics*[16] suggests a similar view:

The given intuition must be subsumed under a concept, which determines the form of judging in general in respect to the intuition . . . such a concept is a pure *a priori* concept of the understanding, which does nothing but merely determine an intuition in the way in general in which it can serve for judging.

(*Prolegomena* §20, 4:300)

All of these passages suggest that the categories are simply those general concepts by means of which our intuitions are converted into representations of objects of judgments.

In other places, however, Kant suggests that the role of the categories is not just to make *possible* the application of judgments and their logical structures to objects, but to make that application *determinate* or to *constrain* it in certain ways. Here his idea appears to be that as far as logic itself is concerned, it makes no difference which feature of an object is represented by the subject-concept, for instance, and which by the predicate, or whether what is represented by the subject-concept on one occasion is represented by the predicate on another, but that the function of a *category* such as that of substance is to ensure that the logical function of subject–predicate judgment is used in a certain way, such that there is something, namely a substance, which must always be a subject, and other things, namely accidents, which must always be represented by predicates.[17] Such a view is clearly expressed in a paragraph added to the introduction to the transcendental deduction in the second edition of the *Critique:*

First, I must only still add the *explanation of the categories*. They are concepts of an object in general, by means of which its intuition is regarded as *determined* in regard to one of the *logical functions* of judging. Thus the function of the *categorical* judgment was the relation of the subject to the predicate, e.g., all bodies are divisible. Only in regard to the merely logical employment of the understanding it remains undetermined which of the two concepts one is to give the function of the subject and which that of the predicate. For one can also say: Something divisible is a body. Through the concept of substance, however, if I bring the concept of a body under it, it is determined that its empirical intuition in experience must always be considered only as subject, never as mere predicate; and so with all the other categories.   (B 128)

Logic does not care what serves as the subject and what as the predicate of a judgment, as long as these roles are filled in some way or other; but the categories, for reasons that therefore cannot arise from the logic of judgment alone, carve our experience up into entities that, for instance, must always be subjects of judgment, or substances, and aspects that must always be predicated of such substances.

This view does not just suddenly appear in the 1787 revision of the

Critique; it can be found alongside the other view all along. Thus Kant wrote in 1773:

First there must be certain titles of thought, under which appearances in themselves can be brought: e.g., whether they are to be regarded as magnitude or as subject or as ground or as whole or merely as reality (figure is no reality). On this account I cannot regard whatever I want in the appearance as either subject or predicate, rather it is determined as subject or respectively as ground. Therefore [it is determined] what sort of logical function in regard to another is really valid of one appearance, whether that of magnitude or of the subject, therefore which function of judgment. For otherwise we could use logical functions arbitrarily without demonstrating or even perceiving that the object is more suitable for one rather than the other.

(*R* 4672, 17:635–6)

Here Kant's claim is that the function of the "titles of thought" is not just to allow judgments to be made about objects of our experience but to constrain *how* we make such judgments about them, to make our use of the logical forms of judgment nonarbitrary. The same view appears ten years later:

Category is the necessary unity of consciousness in the composition of the manifold of representations (intuition), so far as it makes possible the concept of an object in general (in contrast to the merely subjective unity of the consciousness of the perceptions). This unity in the categories must be necessary. E.g., logically a concept can be either subject or predicate. An object, however, considered transcendentally, presupposes something that is necessarily only subject and something else that is only predicate.

(*R* 5931, 18:390–1)[18]

Again the claim is that categories are required in order to make the combination of concepts into judgments nonarbitrary.

This ambiguity in Kant's very definition of the categories obviously creates the possibility of a fundamental bifurcation in his strategy for their transcendental deduction. On the one hand, the idea that the categories are just concepts that make the logically distinct forms and components of judgment applicable to our intuitions allows for a simple form of argument on which the necessary applicability of the categories follows directly from the premise that we make any sort of judgments about our intuitions at all. Kant was occasionally tempted by such a form of argument. But Kant's conception of the categories as extralogical constraints upon the employment of the merely logical functions of judgment obviously calls for more complicated argumentation. Kant's point seems to be precisely that intuitions cannot be formed into concepts of objects in any logically possible way. Merely adding the information provided by the forms of intuition to that yielded by the logical functions of judgment would not be enough. But then the need for such constraint must be explained and a source for it discovered. Much of the obscurity in Kant's actual expositions of the transcendental deduction is due precisely to the fact that he did not explicitly distinguish these two conceptions of the categories, and thus did not clearly distinguish the two strategies for deduction that they require. We will also see that he appealed to several distinct sources of extralogical necessity, a special conception of self-consciousness on the one hand and a special conception of objects on the other, as the ground for the requirement of extralogical categories. Each of these strategies has its problems, however. If the extralogical constraint in the categories arises from their role in contrasting objects to mere representations, then it may not be obvious how the universality of their application is to be preserved; but if it arises from the nature of self-consciousness itself, then it may be difficult to see how the distinction between merely subjective representations and the representation of objects is to be preserved.

Before we can finally see how these issues arise in the actual arguments of the transcendental deduction, however, there is one more question about the categories to consider. This is the question about the *number* of the categories. Both the *Critique* and the *Prolegomena*, of course, assert that there are *twelve* different categories corresponding to the *twelve* logical functions of judgments. This opinion is closely tied to the conception of the categories as simply the "transcendental content" that makes the logical functions of judgment applicable to intuitions. Thus, in the *Critique of Pure Reason* Kant follows the claim that there is one function that determines both the unity of representations in a judgment and in an intuition with the claim that "In such a way there arise exactly as many pure concepts of understanding, which apply *a priori* to objects of intuition in general, as there . . . were logical functions in all possible judgments" (A 79 / B 105; see also *Prolegomena* §21, 4:302). This passage is followed by Kant's well-known tables of the logical functions of judgment and of categories (see Tables 3.1 and 3.2 in the preceding essay).

According to these tables, every judgment is characterized by quantity (which in any given case can be universal, particular, or singular), quality (it can be affirmative, negative, or infinite), relation (it can be categorical, hypothetical, or disjunctive), and modality (it can be problematic, assertoric, or apodictic) (A 70 / B 95; *Prolegomena* §21, 4:302–3). Correspondingly, Kant holds, there are twelve categories or transcendental concepts of objects in general as opposed to functions of judgment: the three categories of quantity, namely unity, plurality, and totality; three categories of quality, namely reality, negation, and limitation; three categories of relation, namely substance or inherence and subsistence, cause or causality and dependence, and community or reciprocity between agent and patient; and finally three categories of modality, namely possibility, existence, and necessity (A 80 / B 106; *Prolegomena* §21, 4:303). These categories are supposed to describe twelve different ways of conceiving of objects that are necessary in order to make the twelve different logical functions of judgment applicable to them.

There are obviously problems with the list of categories. What is the difference, for instance, between "reality" as a category of "quality" and "existence" as a category of "modality"? In ordinary usage, these are surely coextensive if not synonymous. But we do not have to pare down the table of categories on our own, for Kant himself frequently gives shorter lists of the categories. In fact, in many passages Kant suggests that there are not *twelve* but only *five* categories. In R 4672, as we saw, Kant suggests that the basic "titles of thought" are just *magnitude, reality, subject, ground,* and *whole* (17:634). *Reflexion* 4385 (1771) also lists five (or six) basic concepts, though it substitutes a modal concept for the concept of magnitude:

The metaphysical concepts are: 1. Possible, 2. Being (2b. Necessity), 3. One added to another (Whole), 4. One in another (Substance), 5. One through another (Ground). The last three are real relations. The unity of the many: a. of the whole, b. the unity of predicates in one subject or c. of consequences through a ground.   (17:528)[19]

But a nearby passage suggests that the modal concept of possibility more accurately applies to the concept of a thing than to the thing itself, and thus casts doubt on whether it should be included among the basic concepts of *objects* in general (R 4371, 17:523). This would leave four basic categories, namely existence, substance, whole, and ground. Finally, a great many passages suggest there are really only three basic concepts of the understanding or, as Kant sometimes calls them, "categories of synthesis" (R 4476, 17:565), namely the concepts of substance, causality, and composition or wholeness or the relation of part to whole – in other words, just the three categories *of relation*.[20] In one of his most extensive outlines of the *Critique of Pure Reason*, Kant also suggests that the whole of the content of a "Transcendental Theory of Experience" is exhausted by the three concepts of "something as substance," of "every condition of the world [as] a consequence," and of "all appearances together making one world" or whole (R 4756, 17:702 [1775–7]).

How can Kant so prominently assert that there are twelve categories and yet so often list only five, four, or even three? He offers no explicit answer to this question. Yet it is not too difficult to provide the answer. Even if we adopt only the weaker conception of categories as just the concepts necessary to apply the logical functions of judgment to objects, we can quickly see that we do not need twelve different ways of conceiving of objects in order to be able to apply all twelve logical functions of judgment to them. In order to be able to apply the several logical functions of quantity (all, some, one) to objects, we simply need to be able to apply the single category of *determinate magnitude* to the manifold of our intuitions. Of course, there will be an infinite number of particular magnitudes into which we might carve up our intuitions, which might support an indefinite variety of judgments of the form "All ..." or "Some ..." or "One ..."; but these will be different determinations of the more general determinable *magnitude*, not alternatives to the latter. Likewise, in order to apply both logically affirmative and negative judgments to objects, we need only the basic category of the *reality* of objects; negative judgments, in particular, are not made in virtue of the *presence* of a special property, namely "negation," in objects, but rather simply in view of the *absence* of reality or of the satisfaction for whatever turns out to be our criterion for reality.[21]

However, the three categories of substance, causation, and composition (or, as Kant later substitutes for this, interaction) are clearly distinct. This makes plausible Kant's claim that it is only by virtue of the three independent conceptions of objects as substances, as standing in relations of cause and effect, and as parts of wholes, that we can employ the categorical, hypothetical, and disjunctive forms of judgment – which are, it may be noted, really distinct *kinds*[22] of judgment and not just distinct *values* of a single kind of judgment, as might be held in the cases of the functions of quantity and quality.[23]

Finally, it can be argued that the concepts of *modality* are not properly additional concepts *of objects* at all. The assertion of existence is represented by the ascription of reality to the concept of an object, or, if one likes, to the object itself; but that is already taken care of by the category of reality under the heading of quality. Possibility and necessity, however, do not have to be conceived of as properties of objects at all, but rather as properties ascribed to our judgments about objects in virtue of our application of the genuinely objective categories to them. We can argue, for instance, that the judgment '*a* is F' is necessary because *a*'s being F is a *causal consequence* of its being something else, say G. And Kant himself seems to admit as much when he says that "The modality of judgments is a quite peculiar function of them, which . . . contributes nothing to the content of the judgment (for besides magnitude, quality, and relation there is nothing more that constitutes the quality of a judgment" (A 74 / B 100). Instead, judgments of modality say something about the status of our direct assertions about objects, and do not themselves describe any additional properties of objects.[24]

Unraveling Kant's contradictory statements about the number of the categories, then, ought to lighten the burden of the transcendental deduction. We really do not need to prove the objective validity of twelve distinct *a priori* concepts of objects in general, but only of five general concepts: reality, magnitude, substance, cause, and the fluctuating fifth category, sometimes described as just the general idea of a whole made of parts and sometimes described as the more particular idea of interaction among the parts of a whole. But as we shall now see, even with this lightened burden Kant's task remains hard enough.

III

We can now turn to Kant's actual expositions of the transcendental deduction. The next three sections will offer a chronological account of the evolution of the transcendental deduction in the 1780s.

The first edition transcendental deduction offers a preliminary and then a final exposition of its argument (A 98). These two expositions at first appear to present radically different arguments. The preliminary exposition begins by offering an account of the conditions that are necessary for knowledge of an object, thus apparently assuming that we do have knowledge of objects. It then tries to show that one of the key conditions necessary for cognition of an object, namely a concept or rule that "represents the necessary reproduction of a manifold of given appearances, thus the synthetic unity in the consciousness of them" (A 106), can only have its "transcendental ground" in a consciousness of the representation of the necessary numerical identity of the *self* throughout its various representations, or "transcendental apperception" (A 107). Conditions for this unity of self-consciousness are thus also necessary conditions for knowledge of objects; and Kant maintains that there are "*a priori* rules" (A 108) for the transcendental unity of apperception that are therefore *a priori* rules for cognition of objects as well. In the subsequent, "systematic" (A 115) presentation of the argument, Kant omits the preliminary analysis of knowledge of an object, and begins directly with the claim that "We are conscious *a priori* of the thoroughgoing identity of our self with respect to all representations that can ever belong to our cognition" (A 116). He then proceeds to assert that there is an *a priori* synthesis of representations that is presupposed by this *a priori* consciousness, and that this *a priori* synthesis is a product of the faculty of understanding, which thus contains "*a priori* cognitions," namely the categories (A 119), which apply to all the constituents of the transcendental unity of apperception and thus to the objects we represent by means of them. In fact, once Kant has introduced the concept of transcendental apperception into the preliminary exposition of the deduction, the two expositions are practically identical. The original assumption that there is some kind of necessity directly implied by the concept of an *object* becomes otiose and the existence of *a priori* rules of the understanding is instead derived solely from the examination of the conditions for the occurrence of the transcendental unity of apperception.

The fundamental difficulties in the two versions of the argument are also the same. First, the justification of the claim that the transcendental unity of apperception is an *a priori* certainty of the numerical identity of the self requiring a synthesis of representations according to *a priori* rules is unclear, and the identification of these rules with the categories is asserted without adequate defense. Sec-

ond, the connection between the transcendental unity of apperception and *objects* of our cognition distinct from our representations of
them is also unclear. Perhaps, as in the preliminary exposition, Kant
means throughout simply to assume that we do have knowledge of
such objects, and intends to prove only that there are necessary
conditions for such knowledge, namely the categories that are alleged to be necessary conditions for the transcendental unity of
apperception itself. But he certainly does not prove that the transcendental unity of apperception itself *requires* knowledge of objects
distinct from the self, and he thus seems to omit what might have
seemed a natural step in proving the objective reality of the categories: that they do in fact apply to at least *some* objects distinct from
our own representations. Yet Kant also fails to suggest that anything
in addition to the categories is required for knowledge of objects,
and this runs the risk of equating transcendental apperception with
an experience consisting *exclusively* of knowledge of objects, thus
leaving no room for the distinction between mere representations
and cognition of objects.

The preliminary exposition contains some additional problems of
its own. Kant begins with a premise that he asserts is crucial to
everything that follows. This is the claim that all representations,
whether of other objects or inner states, nevertheless belong to
inner sense, and thus that the only way to represent a *manifold* or
multiplicity of representations is by "distinguishing the time in the
series of impressions one upon another" – that is, by representing
the representations as occurring at successive moments (A 99). He
then exploits this premise of the temporal successiveness of all
manifolds of representation to develop a theory of threefold synthesis: Items in a temporally successive manifold must be successively *apprehended* (A 99–100); previously apprehended items
must somehow be *reproduced* alongside later ones if connections
among them are to be recognized (A 100–2); and, finally, there
must be some *concept* in virtue of which the connection of several
successive representations as representations of the *same* object is
recognized (A 103).

Stated thus, Kant's three conditions seem unobjectionable and
sufficient to prove that the recognition of a temporally extended
manifold of data requires *some concept or other* in virtue of which it
can be recognized that the successively apprehended items do repre-

sent some one object.²⁵ But Kant adds two assumptions to this initial analysis. The first may be unwarranted but harmless for the further course of the deduction, but the second is more troubling. First, Kant does not just assume that it is necessary that we be able to reproduce earlier members of a manifold *if* we are to succeed in cognizing an object by means of that manifold, a merely conditional necessity that would not imply that we must be able to succeed in cognizing an object by means of any particular manifold, but rather makes the stronger, unconditional claim that *any* given manifold must necessarily yield knowledge of an object. Only this stronger assumption leads to Kant's conclusion "that there must be something that itself makes this reproduction of appearances possible by being the *a priori* ground of its necessary synthetic unity" (A 101). This introduces an *a priori* ground into Kant's argument too early and too easily.

Second, Kant makes a very strong assumption about the function of the concept of an object in the third stage, the synthesis of recognition in a concept. He claims that the application of a concept of an object to a manifold of representations expresses a kind of necessity in their connection that can only be explained by an *a priori* ground. His initial explication of the role of a concept of an object may seem innocuous:

We find, however, that our thought of the relation of all cognition to its object brings along with it something of necessity, since it is regarded as that which is opposed to our cognitions being determined at will or arbitrarily rather than *a priori* in certain ways, since, insofar as they are to be related to an object they must also necessarily agree with each other in relation to it, i.e. have that unity which constitutes the concept of an object.   (A 104–5)

However, the necessity that Kant describes could just be the *conditional* necessity that *if* a group of representations are to represent, say, a chair, then there had better be among them representations of a seat, back, and legs, or, to use his own example, that *if* a group of representations is to represent a body then there had better be among them representations of extension, shape, and impenetrability (A 106). Without further explanation, it is not obvious why such necessities could not be thought of as analytical consequences of mere definitions of types of objects. That is, given how we understand the terms "chair" or "body," it follows that an object *must* have certain properties *if* it is to be properly called a chair or body.

But Kant clearly thinks that the application of a concept of an object to a manifold of representations expresses a deeper necessity than this, for his next step is to claim that the unity furnished by the concept of an object "is impossible if the intuition cannot be generated through such a function of synthesis according to a rule that makes the reproduction of the manifold necessary *a priori* " (A 105). The kind of necessity that he sees as following from the concept of an object cannot be grounded in something arbitrary like a definition, but requires a "transcendental condition":

All necessity is always grounded in a transcendental condition. There must therefore be found a transcendental ground of the unity of consciousness in the synthesis of the manifold of all our intuitions, thus of concepts of objects in general, thus of all objects of experience, without which it would be impossible to think any object for our intuitions: for this is nothing more than the something the concept of which expresses such a necessity of synthesis.   (A 106)

In fact, Kant seems to have in mind not the conditional necessity that an object must have certain properties if it is to be classified in a certain way, but rather an absolute necessity that any given manifold of representations be able to be regarded as constituting an object. He then introduces the transcendental unity of apperception as the sole possible ground for a necessity of this sort: "Now this original and transcendental condition is none other than *transcendental apperception*" (A 107–8). Yet he has provided no reason for us to think that our experiences of objects must not just be *experiences of necessity* of the kind that can be construed as analytical implications of merely empirical concepts, but rather must themselves somehow *be necessary experiences*, the necessity of which requires some deep explanation. His argument to this point runs aground on a confusion about necessity, a confusion between the necessity that experiences of a certain type of object include certain characteristic representations and the necessity *that we experience objects* in any given manifold. And this in turn suggests not merely that Kant begs his original question about the objective reality of the categories by simply assuming that we *do* experience objects to which the categories can apply, but that he makes the even stronger initial assumption that we *necessarily* experience objects, and derives the *a priori* necessity of certain rules of the understanding from this necessity.

Once Kant has introduced the concept of the transcendental unity of apperception, however, this confusion too may become irrelevant, since this notion itself carries with it certain claims about necessity that are independent of what may have preceded it and that might yet suffice to prove everything Kant wants about the categories. Kant's basic argument from the premise of the transcendental unity of apperception is quite straightforward, and at this point the differences between the preliminary and systematic expositions become minor. I will draw on both in what follows.

(1) The fundamental premise of the argument is that all representations, regardless of what particular empirical significance they may subsequently be discovered to have, are necessarily recognized to belong to oneself: I thus have *a priori* knowledge that all of my representations, whatever they may represent, belong to my single, numerically identical self. Kant reiterates this premise numerous times. For instance,

Now no cognitions can take place in us, no connection and unity among them, without that unity of consciousness which precedes all data of intuitions and in relation to which alone all representation of objects is possible. This pure, original, unchangeable consciousness I will call *transcendental apperception*. . . . The numerical unity of this apperception therefore lies *a priori* at the ground of all concepts. . . .   (A 107)

All possible appearances belong, as representations, to the entire possible self-consciousness. From this, however, as a transcendental representation, numerical identity is inseparable, and *a priori* certain, since nothing can come into cognition except by means of this original apperception. (A 113)

All intuitions are nothing for us and concern us not in the least unless they can be taken up into consciouness. . . . We are conscious *a priori* of the thoroughgoing identity of our self in regard to all representations that can ever belong to our cognition, as a necessary condition of the possibility of all representations (since these can represent something in me only insofar as they belong with all others to one consciousness . . .) This principle stands firm *a priori*.   (A 116)

No matter what else we may come to know about or by means of any given representation, Kant holds, we are necessarily able to recognize that it is one among all of our other representations, or a part of our numerically identical self.

(2) Next, Kant assumes the transcendental unity of apperception is not just an *analytical* unity, but a *synthetic* unity.[26] That is, all of the different representations that are known *a priori* to belong to a numerically identical self do not just share a common mark, such as being designated by the expression "mine," but rather share such a common mark on the basis of some other connection that holds among them:

> For only insofar as I assign all perceptions to one consciousness (of original apperception) can I say of all perceptions: that I am conscious of them. There must therefore be an objective ground, i.e., one that can be understood *a priori* prior to all empirical laws of the imagination, on which the possibility, indeed the necessity of one law stretching through all appearances rests. . . .   (A 122)

(3) But if the transcendental unity of apperception implies the existence of a synthetic connection among all possible representations that is independent of their empirical content and thus of any empirical syntheses or connections that may be established among them, then there must be an *a priori* synthesis that connects them all together; and this *a priori* synthesis must have its own, *a priori* rules. Kant states these key assumptions twice. He states the first alone in his systematic exposition of the deduction, where he writes "This synthetic unity however presupposes a synthesis, or includes one, and if the former is to be necessary *a priori*, then the latter must also be an *a priori* synthesis" (A 118). He explicitly asserts both the existence of an *a priori* synthesis of all possible representations as well as the existence of *a priori* rules for this synthesis in the preparatory exposition:

> But just this transcendental unity of apperception constitutes out of all possible appearances that can ever come together in one experience a connection of all these representations according to laws. For this unity of consciousness would be impossible if in the cognition of the manifold the mind could not become conscious of the identity of the function by means of which it connects it synthetically in one cognition. Therefore the original and necessary consciousness of the identity of oneself is at the same time a consciousness of an equally necessary synthesis of all appearances according to concepts, i.e., according to rules that not only make them necessarily

reproducible but also thereby determine an object for their intuition, i.e., the concept of something in which they are necessarily connected: For the mind could not possibly think the identity of itself in the multiplicity of its representations, and indeed think this *a priori*, if it did not have before its eyes the identity of its action, which subjects all synthesis of apprehension (which is empirical) to a transcendental unity. . . .   (A 108)

All possible representations, regardless of their particular empirical significance, are subjected to an *a priori* synthesis with its own *a priori* rules in virtue of their mere subjection to the transcendental unity of apperception.

(4) But the fundamental source of all combination is the faculty of understanding, and the *a priori* rules required for the *a priori* synthesis implied by the transcendental unity of apperception can be nothing other than the most fundamental rules of the faculty of understanding, namely the categories:

But the possibility, indeed even the necessity of these categories rests on the relation that the entire sensibility and with it all possible appearances have to original apperception, in which everything necessarily accords with the conditions of the thoroughgoing unity of self-consciousness, i.e., must stand under universal functions of synthesis, namely the synthesis according to concepts in which alone apperception can demonstrate *a priori* its thoroughgoing and necessary identity.   (A 111–12)

Apperception requires a synthesis of all possible representations that is distinct from whatever empirical syntheses may ultimately reveal their empirical significance, and the rules of this *a priori* synthesis are nothing other than the categories (see also A 119).

(5) Finally, Kant points out that the necessary conditions for the synthesis of all representations per se in the transcendental unity of apperception are also necessary conditions for the representation of any *objects* by means of those representations:

The *a priori* conditions of a possible experience in general are at the same time conditions of the possibility of the objects of experience. Now I assert that the . . . categories are nothing other than the *conditions of thinking in a possible experience*, just as *space and time* contain the *conditions of intuition* for that same experience. Therefore they are also fundamental concepts for thinking objects in general for appearances, and therefore have *a priori* objective validity; which was that which we really wanted to know.

(A 111)

Thus Kant's argument concludes: (1) all possible representations belong to a single, numerically identical self; (2) this is a synthetic connection of representations, which (3) requires an *a priori* synthesis among them, (4) the rules of which are none other than the categories, which are therefore (5) necessary conditions for the representation of any objects by means of the representations that themselves belong to the numerically identical self.

Kant's argument is ultimately simple, but the problems with it are serious. The most serious problems come at the beginning. Here it may appear plausible for Kant to assume that no matter what I may discover about the empirical significance of any of my representations, and indeed prior to any discoveries about their empirical significance, I must at least know that I *have* those representations, and thus those representations must already satisfy some minimal conditions for self-knowledge. But in fact Kant offers no defense of this claim, and it cannot stand up to scrutiny. To be sure, when I set out to investigate the empirical significance of a series of representations I take myself to have had, it must at least *seem* to me that I have in fact had those representations; but in some cases it may turn out that I cannot make empirical sense of a manifold of representations except by concluding that I could not have had certain representations – for example, could not have correctly made certain observations – after all. I must begin with the *belief* that I have had a certain manifold of representations, but genuine *knowledge* that I have actually experienced all the representations in this manifold may have to await successful empirical interpretation of this initial impression. And if that is so, then I do not in fact have *a priori* knowledge of my numerical identity throughout a given manifold of representations independently of any *empirical* synthesis of them. *A fortiori*, it is not clear that I must have a set of rules for an *a priori* synthesis of them that is independent of my eventual empirical synthesis of them. If this is so, the successful deduction of the categories will have to show that they have a necessary role in any *empirical* synthesis of the manifold of representations rather than in a putative *a priori* synthesis of them.[27]

Second, the connection between the unity of apperception and knowledge of *objects* remains unclear. As we saw, Kant clearly infers that *necessary* conditions for the unity of apperception are also *necessary* conditions for the representation of objects that are distinct from our own representations of them. But this of course does not imply that we must actually represent any such objects, therefore that the categories actually do apply to any such objects. In other words, it seems to prove only the conditional thesis that the categories are necessary if we are to experience objects as well as merely subjective representations, but not yet to show that we are actually justified in applying the categories to such objects, or, in the terms of Section I, to show that the categories actually have objective reality.

Yet Kant assumes that he has shown that the categories provide not only necessary but also *sufficient* conditions for the representation of objects distinct from our own representations. He defines the general concept of an object that is distinct from our representations, but is yet not assumed to be a thing in itself, as the concept of the "transcendental object" of experience (A 109). He then says:

Now this concept cannot contain any determinate intuition, and therefore concerns nothing other than that unity which must be found in a manifold of cognition insofar as it stands in relation to an object. But this relation is nothing other than the necessary unity of consciousness, thus also the synthesis of the manifold through a common function of the mind for connecting it in one representation. Now since this unity must be regarded as *a priori* necessary (for otherwise the cognition would be without an object), the relation to a transcendental object, i.e., the objective reality of our empirical cognition, rests on the transcendental law that all appearances, insofar as objects are to be given to us through them, must stand under *a priori* rules of their synthetic unity, according to which their relation in empirical intuition is alone possible, i.e., that they stand under conditions of necessary unity of apperception in experience just as they must stand under the formal conditions of space and time in mere intuition. . . .   (A 109–10)

This suggests that the conditions of the unity of apperception alone suffice to constitute the concept of the transcendental object, which might equally well be called the transcendental concept of an object or the framework for conceiving of objects as contrasted to mere representations. But this is profoundly problematic. First, it ignores the idea that there is an essential difference between the self and its representations on the one hand and the objects they may represent on the other. For this suggests that even if the conditions for the possibility of apperception are also necessary conditions for the representation of objects, there must be some additional condition necessary to represent objects that is not a condition for self-consciousness as such. Yet if we were to ignore this requirement and grant Kant's present claim that the conditions for the unity of apperception are sufficient for the representation of objects, then it would become obscure how we can ever represent mere conditions of the *self* without also representing an object. In other words, Kant's present claim seems neither adequately to explain why we must represent any objects distinct from the self nor, if we do, then how we can represent the mere self as contrasted to objects. In light of these problems, the endgame problem, that Kant does not adequately show that the rules of the *a priori* synthesis of apperception are really the *categories*, seems minor.

IV

Perhaps in recognition of these unresolved difficulties with the concept of the transcendental unity of apperception, in the years immediately following the publication of the first edition of the *Critique of Pure Reason* Kant attempted to accomplish his proof of the objective validity of the categories without any reference to apperception at all. This approach is evident in the *Prolegomena to Any Future Metaphysics* of 1783 and in a compact but suggestive footnote in the preface to the *Metaphysical Foundations of Natural Science* of 1786, as well as in several sketches that have been assigned to the period 1783–4, and thus represent either preparatory notes for the *Prolegomena* or further reflections on it.[28]

In the *Metaphysical Foundations of Natural Science*, Kant suggests that the deduction of the categories could be accomplished "virtually through a single inference from the precisely determined definition of a *judgment* in general (of an action, through which given representations first become cognition of an object)." By such a definition of judgment, however, Kant cannot mean any connection of representations by means of a merely logical function of judgment, but rather one in which "through the concept of the understanding an object is thought as *determined* with regard to one or another function of judgment" (4:475 n.), or an act of the mind in which it is made determinate *which* logical function of judgment must be employed on a given manifold of intuition.

This is made clearer in the *Prolegomena*, where the key to Kant's deduction of the categories is a distinction between a merely subjective connection of perceptions, in which the logical functions of judgment *are* employed but are employed entirely arbitrarily, and a connection of perceptions that is objectively valid, which Kant interprets to mean universally and necessarily valid. Kant's basic contention is that in the latter case there must be *a priori* concepts of the understanding that make the employment of the logical functions of judgment nonarbitrary, and that this is the role of the categories. In section 22, Kant argues that the "sum" of the matter is that all thinking is "uniting representations in one consciousness," which is "the same as judging, or referring representations to judgment in general"; and all instances of judgment employ the logical functions of judgment. But judgments may be "either merely subjective, if they relate representations to the consciousness in one subject alone . . . or objective, if they unite representations in a consciousness in general, i.e., necessarily." The latter kind of judgments give rise to experience, which "consists in the synthetic connection of appearances (perceptions) in one consciousness, so far as this is necessary" (4:304–5).

Kant formalizes this distinction by means of a contrast between "judgments of perception," which "hold good only for us" and employ "only the logical connection of perceptions in a thinking subject," and "judgments of experience," which assert the "necessary universal validity" of the connection of perceptions that is expressed through the logical function of judgment (§18, 4:298). Such a claim of necessary universal validity always depends upon a "pure concept of the understanding, under which the perception is subsumed," that is, a category, which therefore cannot simply be an objectified form of a merely logical function of judgment but is instead an extralogical concept that somehow makes the use of the merely logical functions of judgment nonarbitrary:

The judgment of experience must add something beyond the sensible intuition and its logical connection . . . in a judgment, which determines the synthetic judgment as necessary and hereby as universally valid; and this can be nothing other than that concept, which represents the intuition as determined in regard to one form of judgment rather than another.

(§21a, 4:304)

Kant's argument to this point is excessively abstract, but he offers several examples in an attempt to clarify it. In the *Metaphysical Foundations of Natural Science*, Kant argues that logic alone is entirely indifferent to our choice of concepts for subjects and predicates, and that only the extralogical concept of *substance* determines that certain intuitions must always be regarded as logical subjects and others as predicates:

E.g., in the categorical judgment: *The stone is hard*, the *stone* is employed as subject and *hard* as predicate, yet in such a way that the understanding is permitted to reverse the logical function of this judgment and say: something hard is a stone; on the contrary, if I represent it to myself as *determined* in the *object* that in every possible determination of an object the *stone* . . . must be thought of as subject, but the hardness only as predicate, then the same logical function of judgment now becomes a *pure concept of the understanding* of objects, namely as *substance* and *accident*. (4:475 n.)

By itself logic affords the possibility of conceiving of subject and predicates, but does not require that there be anything that can *only* be thought of as a subject and never as a predicate; this is an extralogical requirement for conceiving of determinate, nonarbitrary objects, and requires the extralogical conception of substances – that is, necessary subjects – and their accidents. In the *Prolegomena*, Kant attempts to construct a similar argument in the case of the hypothetical form of judgment: Logic alone merely affords the possibility of distinguishing between antecedents and consequents but does not itself determine that one concept must necessarily figure in the antecedent of a judgment and another in the consequent; that is the function of the extralogical concept of cause and effect. "Let such a concept be the concept of a cause, then it determines the intuition that is subsumed under it, e.g., the intuition of air, in regard to judging in general, namely that the concept of air in regard to its expansion serves in the relation of antecedent to consequent in a hypothetical judgment" (§20, 4:300).[29]

This kind of argument has a certain intuitive plausibility, but Kant hardly works it out in sufficient detail to be persuasive. At least as Kant presents it, it depends on a problematic conception of judgments of experience as universally true, where that means not merely intersubjectively acceptable but also necessarily true. Such an understanding of empirical judgment would certainly be difficult to sell to an empiricist such as Hume, although it is no one other than Hume whom Kant is attempting to answer in the *Prolegomena*.[30]

V

Perhaps with this difficulty in mind, Kant reverted to the premise of apperception for his new version of the deduction in the second edition of the *Critique*. In fact, one can see this new version as attempting to combine the earlier idea of apperception with the new understanding of judgment developed from 1783 to 1786. But this combination remains uneasy.

The B-deduction begins (§15) with the general claim that all "combination (*conjunctio*) of a manifold in general" (B 129) is an act of "spontaneity" or "self-activity of the subject," specifically "an act of the understanding" (B 130). In several summaries of the transcendental deduction written after 1787, Kant suggests that the objective validity of the categories in all synthesis could be derived directly from this simple premise.[31] Here, however, Kant clearly intends this general claim only to prepare the way for the more specific claim that all combinations of the manifold presuppose the fundamental form of synthesis that is contained in the transcendental unity of apperception, to be introduced in section 16. However, an additional thesis that Kant introduces before moving from the general to the specific claim obscures the intended relationship between the categories and the unity of apperception in all that follows. Instead of simply claiming that, because all combination stems from the understanding, it therefore necessarily employs the pure categories of that faculty, Kant argues that "the concept of combination" involves a concept of the unity of the manifold that *precedes* all specific categories. As he puts it,

This unity, which precedes *a priori* all concepts of combination, is not [the] category of unity . . . ; for all categories are grounded in logical functions of judgment, but in these connection, thus the unity of given concepts, is already thought. The category therefore already presupposes combination. We must therefore seek this unity . . . somewhere higher. (B 131)

This higher form of unity preceding all categories is obviously meant to be the transcendental unity of apperception. But what Kant

has argued now seems to imply that, although the use of the categories must presuppose the transcendental unity of apperception, the
latter precedes the use of the categories and is therefore independent
of it. The entire project of showing that the categories apply to all
the objects of the transcendental unity of apperception precisely
because apperception itself presupposes the use of the categories is
therefore endangered.

In section 16, Kant reiterates the basic claims of the first-edition
argument about apperception. He argues that "the *I think* must *be
able* to accompany all my representations" (B 131–2), or that "all of
the manifold of intuition has a necessary relation to the *I think* in
the same subject in which this manifold is found" (B 132). He then
argues that this connection of all possible representations to a single
self cannot be the merely *analytic* unity furnished by some common
mark, for there is no single impression of the self in all possible
representations: "The empirical consciousness, which accompanies
different representations, is in itself diverse and without relation to
the identity of the subject" (B 133) (here Kant is directly following
Hume). Instead, "the *analytic* unity of apperception is only possible
under the presupposition of some *synthetic* one": "This thoroughgoing identity of the apperception of a manifold given in intuition
contains a synthesis of representations, and is only possible through
the consciousness of this synthesis" (B 133). Kant then asserts, as in
the first edition, that we have genuine *a priori* knowledge of the
necessary connection of all representations to this single self and
that there must therefore be an *a priori* synthesis of the understanding to which the unity of apperception is due: "Synthetic unity of
the manifold of intuitions, as given *a priori,* is thus the ground of the
identity of apperception itself, which precedes *a priori* all *my* determinate thoughts" (B 134); and this "combination" is "solely an arrangement of the understanding" (B 135). No more than in the first
edition, however, does Kant defend the claim that the synthetic
unity of apperception is actually "given *a priori*" rather than depending upon empirical synthesis of the manifold of intuition.

Because Kant has claimed that an *a priori* combination due to the
faculty of understanding underlies the unity of apperception, we
might expect him to introduce directly the categories as at A 119;
however, perhaps the argument of section 15 bars him from so doing.
In any case, the next few sections now attempt a much more invo-

luted route to the objective validity of the categories. In sections 17–19, Kant attempts to establish a connection between apperception and knowledge of objects. His arguments, however, endanger the strategy of arguing from necessary conditions of apperception to necessary concepts of objects by instead simply identifying apperception with judgments about objects and deriving the conditions for the former from the latter.

In section 17, Kant introduces the idea of "an *object* as that in the concept of which the manifold of a given intuition is *united*" (B 137). This could be taken to be a deflationary definition of an object: Although one might have thought that an object was something distinct from any merely subjective connection of representations, requiring something in addition to the latter, Kant would now be defining an object as constituted by any conceptual connection of the manifold of intuition whatever, even if it did not involve any such contrast with the subject. In this case, Kant's next claim would hold: "Consequently the unity of consciousness is that which alone constitutes the relation of representations to an object, thus their objective validity" (B 137). However, in this case Kant's original task of proving that categories that are subjective in origin necessarily apply to objects that are distinct from the self would seem to have been forgotten. But if that task is not to be forgotten, and Kant is not to rest content with a deflationary conception of an object of knowledge, then at this point in the argument he should be arguing only that the conditions for the unity of apperception – which still remain to be discovered – are *necessary* conditions for knowledge of objects, not, as he seems to be suggesting, *sufficient* conditions.

This excessive assumption would be only a minor problem if Kant were now successfully to derive necessary conditions for the unity of apperception, which, because the unity of apperception is itself a necessary condition for knowledge of objects, would in turn be necessary conditions for knowledge of objects. However, the argument of section 18 does not do this. In fact, Kant now proceeds as if cognition of *objects* were itself the necessary condition of the unity of apperception, and thus as if the *a priori* conditions for the unity of apperception could be derived from conditions for the knowledge of objects instead of vice versa. As he puts it, "The *transcendental unity* of apperception is that unity through which everything in a given manifold is united in a concept of the object" (B 139). The project of discovering conditions for apperception that will also be necessary conditions for cognition of objects is thus entirely inverted. Consequently, section 19, like the *Prolegomena*, contrasts judgments as assertions of *"necessary unity"* with merely subjectively valid relations of representations, and implies that there must be *a priori* grounds in the understanding for such necessary unity. To be sure, Kant says that he does not mean "that these representations *necessarily* belong *to each other* in empirical intuition, but that they belong to each other *in virtue of the necessary unity* of apperception in the synthesis of intuitions" (B 142). But because the unity of apperception has just been identified with cognition of objects, this still seems to base his argument on a controversial definition of knowledge of an object. The argument of the B-deduction, in other words, has collapsed into that of the *Prolegomena* precisely at the crucial point where necessary conditions for cognition of objects should have been derived from independently discovered conditions for the possibility of apperception itself.

The argument of section 20, which is supposed to crown Kant's deduction, only compounds his embarrassment. He claims that "the manifold given in a sensible intuition" is subject to the synthetic unity of apperception, and then that "the act of the understanding by which the manifold of given intuitions . . . is brought under an apperception in general is the logical function of judgment," therefore that "all the manifold, so far as it is given in one empirical intuition, is *determined* in respect of one of the logical functions of judgment. . . . Now the *categories* are nothing other than these functions of judgment" (B 143). In part, this argument seems unobjectionable and indeed a successful circumvention of the confusion about the connection between apperception and objects in sections 17–19: It just asserts that the unity of apperception is itself expressed by means of judgments and must therefore employ the logical functions or structure of judgments. However, now Kant's insistence that the categories are not just semantic equivalents of the logical functions of judgment but extralogical *constraints* on the use of the merely logical functions of judgment, the key to his argument in the *Prolegomena*, has gone by the boards. We may have a noncontroversial argument that apperception takes the logical form of judgment, but we are still without any argument that apperception depends upon the categories.

At this point, we might conclude that in spite of all the effort Kant devoted to the transcendental deduction, he failed to establish a firm connection between the unity of apperception and the categories, and that the continuing interest of the *Critique of Pure Reason* must lie elsewhere. Before we leave the B-deduction, however, we must note one more puzzle about it, for the solution to this puzzle does point to Kant's ultimately successful argument for the categories. At the outset of section 21, Kant claims that the preceding argument has only made a "beginning of a *deduction* of the pure concepts of the understanding" by showing that the categories are the necessary conditions of the "empirical consciousness of a given manifold of one intuition" (B 144), and that the "*a priori* validity [of the categories] in regard to all objects of our senses" remains to be demonstrated in order to complete the deduction (B 145).[32] The completion of the argument, he then asserts (§26), lies in recognizing that the unity of *space* and *time* themselves require a synthesis of the understanding. For the purposes of the Transcendental Aesthetic the unity of space and time – that is, the fact that all regions of space constitute parts of a single all-inclusive space and all moments of time parts of a single all-inclusive time – could be treated as if merely given. But in fact this kind of unity, like any other, must be due to the combinatory activity of the understanding (B 160–1). And because nothing can be presented to us that is not presented to us as occupying some determinate region of space or time or both, therefore nothing can be presented to us by our senses that is not subject to the combinatory activity of the understanding and thus the categories: "Consequently all synthesis, even that through which perception itself is possible, stands under the categories . . . and [the categories] therefore hold *a priori* of all objects of experience" (B 161). Now debate has raged about whether this introduction of space and time into the deduction merely makes the general or abstract conclusion of section 20 more specific, by introducing reference to the specifically human forms of intuition that is lacking in the earlier part of the argument, or whether it really removes some fundamental restriction on the universal applicability of the categories in the first half of the argument.[33] What has not been noticed, however, is that there is a major disparity between the way in which Kant describes the conclusion of the deduction in sections 20 and 21 and the premise from which he set out in section 16. In sections 20 and 21, Kant speaks of the conditions of the unity of the manifold in *a* or *one* given manifold, suggesting that some additional consideration is needed to remove this restriction and prove that *all* of our intuitions can in fact be unified in a *single* manifold. But in section 16, he set out from the claim that *all* of our intuitions are in fact unified in the transcendental unity of apperception. If this claim were valid, then there would be no need for any additional proof that *all* of our intuitions can in fact be synthesized under the categories, and the introduction of space and time in section 26 would indeed be nothing more than the specification of a more abstract description of the unity of all our possible experience already contained in the concept of the transcendental unity of apperception. Indeed, the unity of apperception might itself be interpreted as a ground for the original assumption of the unity of space and time, rather than vice versa.

So why does Kant restrict his result in sections 20 and 21, and appeal to the unity of space and time for a conclusion that should already have followed from the original unity of apperception? We can only conjecture that Kant does this out of a tacit recognition that all is not well with his concept of apperception, that at some level he recognizes that his claim that we have *a priori* certainty of the numerical identity of the self in all its possible representations is not unimpeachable, and that he looks to the unity of space and time as a less controversial ground for the proof of the universal objective validity of the categories.

In any case, the unity of apperception plays no further role in Kant's accounts of the transcendental deduction after 1787. Moreover, the heart of Kant's subsequent arguments for the objective validity of the categories lies precisely in showing that the use especially of the relational categories of substance, causation, and interaction are necessary conditions for objective knowledge of the determinate positions of objects and events in a *single, objective space and time*. This is the brunt of his argument in the section of the *Critique* following the transcendental deduction, the "Analytic of Principles" and especially its discussion of the "Analogies of Experience." But here we must rest with the hint that Kant's closing statement that the synthesis of the understanding employing the categories is the necessary condition for the unity of perception of objects in space and time, which would be redundant if his original claim about the necessary unity of apperception were to be maintained, is

in fact the key to his eventual success in demonstrating the indispensable role of the categories of quantity, substance, causation, and
interaction in our objective experience.

Formally speaking, the transcendental deduction is a failure, and
at best sets the agenda for the detailed demonstration of the role of
the categories in the determination of empirical relations in space
and especially time in the following sections of the *Critique of Pure
Reason*. Nevertheless, the transcendental deduction also completely
transformed the agenda of modern philosophy. While he had difficulty initially spelling it out, Kant clearly perceived that there was
some inescapable connection between self-knowledge and knowledge of objects, and this completely undermined the Cartesian assumptions that we could have a determinate knowledge of our inner
states without any knowledge of the external world at all and that
we had to discover some means of inferring from the former to the
latter. And while Kant had difficulty in distinguishing between the
categories as merely logical functions of judgment and as extralogical constraints on judgment, he nevertheless clearly saw that
both self-knowledge and knowledge of objects were intrinsically
judgmental and necessarily involved logical structures as well as
empirical inputs. This completely undermined the Lockean and
Humean project of discovering the foundations of all knowledge and
belief in the empirical input of sensation and reflection alone. Progress in philosophy is rarely dependent upon the formal soundness of
an argument, but on the compelling force of a new vision, and from
this point of view the transcendental deduction was a total success,
turning Cartesian rationalism and Lockean empiricism into mere
history and setting new agendas for subsequent philosophical movements from German idealism to logical positivism and the linguistic
philosophy of our own times.

NOTES

1 For the *Critique of Pure Reason*, I follow the text edited by Raymund
   Schmidt, *Immanuel Kant: Kritik der reinen Vernunft*, 2d rev. ed. (Hamburg: Felix Meiner Verlag, 1930). All translations from Kant's German
   writings are my own; translations of his Latin writings will be cited
   where necessary.
2 There will be no space for a systematic review of the literature on the

transcendental deduction here. Any attempt at such a review, however, would have to take account of at least the following works: H.-J. De Vleeschauwer, *La Déduction transcendentale dans l'oeuvre de Kant*, Vol. 2 (Antwerp: De Sikkel, 1936) and Vol. 3 (1937); Klaus Reich, *Die Vollständigkeit der kantischen Urteilstafel*, 3d ed. (Hamburg: Felix Meiner, 1986); Graham Bird, *Kant's Theory of Knowledge* (London: Routledge & Kegan Paul, 1962), pp. 110–48; Robert Paul Wolff, *Kant's Theory of Mental Activity* (Cambridge, Mass.: Harvard University Press, 1963), pp. 59–202; Jonathan Bennett, *Kant's Analytic* (Cambridge: Cambridge University Press, 1966), pp. 71–138; D. P. Dryer, *Kant's Solution for Verification in Metaphysics* (London: George Allen & Unwin, 1966), pp. 108–54; P. F. Strawson, *The Bounds of Sense* (London: Methuen, 1966), pp. 72–117; Stefan Körner, "The Impossibility of Transcendental Deductions," in L. W. Beck, ed., *Kant Studies Today* (LaSalle, Ill.: Open Court, 1967), pp. 230–44; Dieter Henrich, "The Proof-Structure of Kant's Transcendental Deduction," *The Review of Metaphysics* 22 (1969): 640–59; Richard Rorty, "Strawson's Objectivity Argument," *The Review of Metaphysics* 24 (1970): 207–44; Eva Schaper, "Arguing Transcendentally," *Kant-Studien* 63 (1972): 101–16, and "Are Transcendental Deductions Impossible?" in L. W. Beck, ed., *Kant's Theory of Knowledge* (Dordrecht: D. Reidel, 1974), pp. 3–11; W. H. Walsh, *Kant's Criticism of Metaphysics* (Edinburgh: Edinburgh University Press, 1975), pp. 35–96; Karen Gloy, *Die Kantische Theorie der Naturwissenschaft* (Berlin: Walter de Gruyter, 1976), pp. 63–120; Dieter Henrich, *Identität und Objektivität* (Heidelberg: Carl Winter, 1976); Karl Ameriks, "Kant's Transcendental Deduction as a Regressive Argument," *Kant-Studien* 69 (1978): 273–87; Malte Hossenfelder, *Kants Konstitutionstheorie und die Transzendentale Deduktion* (Berlin: Walter de Gruyter, 1978); Ralph C. S. Walker, *Kant* (London: Routledge & Kegan Paul, 1978), pp. 74–86; Reinhold Aschenberg, *Sprachanalyse und Transzendentalphilosophie* (Stuttgart: Klett-Cotta, 1982), pp. 103–97 (includes extensive bibliography); Patricia Kitcher, "Kant on Self-Identity," *The Philosophical Review* 91 (1982): 41–72; Henry E. Allison, *Kant's Transcendental Idealism* (New Haven, Conn.: Yale University Press, 1983), pp. 133–72; Hansgeorg Hoppe, *Synthesis bei Kant* (Berlin: Walter de Gruyter, 1983); Manfred Baum, *Deduktion und Beweis in Kants Transzendentalphilosophie* (Königstein: Hain bei Athenäum, 1986), pp. 45–172; Wilfried Hinsch, *Erfahrung und Selbstbewußtsein* (Hamburg: Felix Meiner Verlag, 1986); Paul Guyer, *Kant and the Claims of Knowledge* (Cambridge: Cambridge University Press, 1987), pp. 73–154; Richard E. Aquila, *Matter in Mind: A Study of Kant's Transcendental Deduction* (Bloomington: Indiana University Press, 1989); Wolfgang Carl, *Der schweigende Kant: Die*

Entwürfe zu einer Deduktion der Kategorien vor 1781 (Göttingen: Vandenhoeck & Ruprecht, 1990); and Hubert Schwyzer, *The Unity of Understanding* (Oxford: Clarendon Press, 1990). Surveys of the literature on the transcendental deduction may also be found in Anthony Brueckner, "Transcendental Arguments I," *Noûs* 17 (1983): 551–75, and "Transcendental Arguments II," *Noûs* 18 (1984): 197–225, as well as *Kants transzendentale Deduktion und die Möglichkeit von Transzendentalphilosophie*, herausgegeben vom Forum für Philosophie Bad Homburg (Frankfurt am Main: Suhrkamp, 1988).

3 It may seem strange for Kant to argue that space and time, unlike the categories, do not need a transcendental deduction, when the Transcendental Aesthetic includes a "transcendental exposition" of the concepts of space and time (B 40–1 and B 48–9) as well as a merely "metaphysical exposition." But it should be noted that those "transcendental expositions" were added only in the second edition, while the claim that the categories but not space and time need a transcendental deduction originates from the first edition. Kant's incomplete revision of his text creates a problem here.

4 See the essay by Michael Young in this book.

5 I will not be able to consider the development of Kant's theory of knowledge beyond the confines of the transcendental deduction in this essay, but have done so in *Kant and the Claims of Knowledge*, Parts III and IV. Kant's treatment of causation also receives detailed examination in the essay by Michael Friedman, the next essay in this book.

6 Letter of 21 February 1772, 10:129–35. Translations may be found in Arnulf Zweig, *Kant: Philosophical Correspondence 1759–99* (Chicago: University of Chicago Press, 1967), pp. 70–6, and G. B. Kerferd and D. E. Walford, trans., *Kant: Selected Pre-Critical Writings and Correspondence with Beck* (Manchester, U.K.: Manchester University Press, and New York: Barnes & Noble, 1968), pp. 111–18.

7 See especially *Nova dilucidatio*, Proposition XII (1:410–12), where Kant directly confronts the Leibnizians by arguing that the reality of causation between distinct substances is not excluded by the principle of sufficient reason but is instead precisely what that principle entails.

8 It is a matter of continuing scholarly debate whether this essay was written under the *influence* of Hume, or represented Kant's entirely independent arrival at a conclusion similar to Hume's. I have no room to pursue this dispute here.

9 See especially 2:202–3.

10 *On the Form and Principles of the Sensible and Intelligible Worlds (Dissertation)*, §8, 2:395. Translation from G. B. Kerferd and D. E. Walford, p. 59.

11 *Dissertation*, §30, 2:418. Kerferd and Walford, pp. 89–90.

12 The term "reflection" (*Reflexion*, abbreviated *R*) is used to designate the notes Kant wrote in the interleaved copies of the textbooks from which he taught as well as certain other notes written on separate sheets of paper (the so-called *Lose Blätter*, or loose leaves), often the backs of letters that Kant had received. Building on earlier work by Benno Erdmann and Rudolf Reicke, Erich Adickes edited, numbered, and dated these in volumes 14–19 of *Kants gesammelte Schriften*. The reflections on metaphysics, namely those found in or connected with Kant's copies of Baumgarten's *Metaphysica*, the text he used for his metaphysics lectures, are found in volumes 17 and 18; volume 14 contains his reflections on natural science, volumes 15 and 16 the reflections on logic, and volume 19 the reflections on moral philosophy, political philosophy, and philosophy of religion; of course there are overlaps, especially between Kant's notes on metaphysics and his notes on moral philosophy. Among other factors such as style, content, ink, and handwriting, Adickes used the dates of letters on which Kant had written to determine the chronology of the notes. Although Adickes's dating of some individual items has been questioned, there is no general alternative to his general chronology, and it is widely accepted as a supplement to the chronology of Kant's published works for determining the evolution of his thought. The present reflection, *R* 4276, is assigned to the period 1770–1, and thus may represent the first stage of Kant's preoccupation with the problem of the categories after the presentation of the inaugural dissertation.

13 In fact, Kant distinguishes between the pure categories, which we may regard as the semantic correlatives of the syntactical features of judgments, and the schemata for the categories (or, as modern commentators usually say, schematized categories), which are conceptions of relations that can be discerned in intuition and serve as the semantic correlatives of the logical functions of judgment (See A 139 / B 178). Kant does not draw this distinction in his discussions of the categories prior to the *Critique of Pure Reason*, but ultimately needs to introduce it in order to explain how we can have at least *concepts* if not *knowledge* of objects of which we have no intuitions (such as God or the free will).

14 Adickes was not able to determine whether the note from which this sentence comes was written in the late 1770s or in the early 1780s.

15 See also *R* 5933, 18:392. These notes are from 1783–4.

16 This is the work Kant published in 1783 in order to overcome the initially adverse reception of the *Critique*. It is much shorter, and was intended to be more popular. But in order to achieve this end, Kant chose to use an "analytical" rather than "synthetical" method (4:263), which in practice consisted of assuming from the outset that mathematics and

pure physics consisted of synthetic *a priori* knowledge, and arguing that the pure intuitions and pure categories were the conditions of this knowledge. We shall see in Section IV that this caused him to adopt an unsatisfactory approach to the transcendental deduction in that work, which may also have infected his treatment of the deduction in 1787.

17 A similar conception of a distinction between logical and extralogical conceptions of the categories has recently been advanced by T. K. Swing, "Kant's Conception of the Categories," *Review of Metaphysics* 43 (1989): 107–32.

18 Kant goes on to maintain that the same things hold with respect to the categories of ground (*Grund*) and community (*Gemeinschaft*).

19 This list is also reminiscent of *Dissertation* §8, where Kant listed as the concepts of metaphysics "possibility, existence, necessity, substance, cause, etc., together their opposites or correlates" (2:395).

20 Among many examples, see *R* 4493, 17:571; *R* 4496, 17:573; *R* 4674, 17:645–7; *R* 5284, 18:143; *R* 5286, 18:143; and *R* 5289, 18:144.

21 Kant subsequently argued that there are an infinite number of *degrees* of reality, or that reality admits of "intensive magnitude" (A 166–76 / B 207–18), but this does not imply that there is more than one *category* of quality, namely reality itself.

22 This is particularly evident from the fact that categorical judgments are atomic, linking concepts that are not themselves judgments, whereas the hypothetical and disjunctive judgments are molecular, linking components that are themselves judgments.

23 There are problems, to be sure, about whether the relation of cause and effect is the *only* relation that will license the use of the hypothetical form of judgment, or whether there can be noncausal forms of dependence also expressed by this form of judgment, and about whether there is any connection between the idea of a *logical* disjunction and the relation of parts in a whole. But these problems need not concern us here.

24 Even if one wants to admit modality among the genuine categories of objects, one needs to add only one modal concept to the concept of existence itself. For if one takes the concept of possibility as primary, then one can define necessity by negation ("It is necessary that . . ." is equivalent to "It is not possible that not . . .") or vice versa. Then one would end up with a list of six categories: existence, magnitude, the three relational categories, and one additional modal category.

25 For further discussion of this point, see my "Psychology in the Transcendental Deduction," in Eckart Förster, ed., *Kant's Transcendental Deductions: The Three "Critiques" and "Opus postumum"* (Stanford, Calif.: Stanford University Press, 1989), pp. 47–68.

26 This terminology is more prominent in the second than in the first edition, but the point is already assumed in the first.

27 For a more extended version of this criticism, see my *Kant and the Claims of Knowledge*, pp. 139–49.

28 The most important of these are *R* 5923 and *R* 5932. For reasons of space, however, only the two published texts from the period between the two editions of the *Critique* will be discussed.

29 See also Kant's discussion of the sun and the stone at 4:301 n.

30 See 4:257–9.

31 See *What Real Progress Has Metaphysics Made in Germany since the Time of Leibniz and Wolff?*, 20:271, and letter to J. S. Beck, 16 October 1792, 11:376.

32 Dieter Henrich drew attention to this two-staged structure of the deduction in his 1969 article "The Proof-Structure of Kant's Transcendental Deduction" (see note 2 above). Virtually every work on the transcendental deduction since then has attempted to offer some account of the two stages; Henrich has replied to some of these proposals in Burkhard Tuschling, ed., *Probleme der "Kritik der reinen Vernunft": Kant-Tagung Marburg 1981* (Berlin: Walter de Gruyter, 1984), pp. 41–96. I will now suggest, however, that it is deeply problematic *whether* Kant should ever have suggested that there are two stages to the deduction.

33 This is Henrich's view.

5   Causal laws and the foundations of natural science

I

In the Transcendental Analytic Kant develops a characteristically striking – and at the same time characteristically elusive – conception of the causal relation. Thus, for example, in a preliminary section (§13) to the transcendental deduction Kant introduces the problem by remarking that, with respect to the concept of cause, "it is *a priori* not clear why appearances should contain something of this kind" (A 90 / B 122); for, as far as sensibility is concerned, "everything could be situated in such disorder that, e.g., in the succession of appearances nothing offered itself that suggested a rule of synthesis – and thus would correspond to the concept of cause and effect – so that this concept would therefore be entirely empty, null, and without meaning" (A 90 / B 123). A memorable paragraph then follows:

If one thought to extricate oneself from the difficulty of this investigation by saying that experience unceasingly offers examples of such rule-governedness of appearances, which [examples] provide sufficient inducement for abstracting the concept of cause therefrom and thereby simultaneously prove the objective reality of such a concept, then one is failing to observe that the concept of cause can absolutely not arise in this way. Rather, it must either be grounded completely *a priori* in the understanding or be entirely abandoned as a mere chimera. For this concept positively requires that something A be such that something else B follow from it *necessarily* and *in accordance with an absolutely universal rule*. Appearances certainly provide cases in which a rule is possible according to which something customarily occurs, but never that the result is *necessary*. To the synthesis of cause and effect there consequently also belongs a dignity that one absolutely cannot express empirically: namely, that the effect is

161

not merely joined to the cause, but rather is posited *through* it and results *from* it. The strict universality of the rule is certainly not a property of empirical rules, which, through induction, can possess nothing but comparative universality: i.e., extended utility. Thus, the use of the pure concepts of the understanding would be entirely altered if one wanted to treat them only as empirical products.   (A 91–2 / B 123–4)[1]

A very strongly anti-Humean conception of the causal relation appears to be expressed here.

First, Kant appears clearly to assert that there is a *necessary connection* between cause and effect: An effect B does not simply follow its cause A as a matter of fact (it is not merely "joined" to A); rather, B necessarily follows A (it in some sense "results *from*" A). Thus, Kant appears to be explicitly endorsing just the kind of necessary connection, efficacy, or nexus between cause and effect that Hume notoriously rejected. Moreover, that Kant thought himself to be contradicting Hume on precisely this point seems clear from the Introduction to the *Prolegomena*, where Kant describes Hume's problem as follows:

> *Hume* proceeded principally from a single, but important concept of metaphysics – namely, from that of the *connection of cause and effect* (and thus also its derivative concepts of force, action, etc.) – and he challenged reason, which pretends to have given birth to this concept of itself, to speak and answer him with what right she thinks that something could be so constituted that, if it is posited, something else must necessarily also be posited thereby – for this is what the concept of cause says. He proved incontrovertibly that it is entirely impossible for reason to think such a combination *a priori* and from concepts, for such a combination contains necessity; but it absolutely cannot be conceived why, because something is, something else must also necessarily be, and thus how the concept of such a connection can be introduced *a priori*.   (4:257)[2]

And Kant's strategy in the *Prolegomena* also seems clear: The concept of causality *is* the concept of a necessary connection between two events.[3] But Hume has shown that this cannot be a merely logical or analytic necessity arising purely from reason alone (purely "from concepts"). We can show, however, that there is nonetheless a *synthetic* necessity here arising from the conditions of objective judgment in a possible experience, and thus Hume's doubts are answered.

A second anti-Humean strand also appears to be clearly expressed in our passage from section 13 of the *Critique of Pure Reason*. Not only is the connection between cause and effect necessary, it also obtains in accordance with a "strictly" or "absolutely" universal rule – where the universality in question here is contrasted with merely "empirical" or "comparative" universality derived through induction. This contrast is explained in section 2 of the Introduction to the *Critique:*

Experience never provides true or strict, but only assumed or comparative *universality* (through induction) for its judgments, so that one must properly say: So far as we have observed until now no exception is found for this or that rule. . . . Empirical universality is thus only an optional [*willkürlich*] augmentation of validity from that which holds in most cases to that which holds in all – as, e.g., in the proposition: All bodies are heavy. Where, on the other hand, strict universality essentially belongs to a judgment, this indicates a particular source of knowledge for such, namely a faculty of *a priori* knowledge.   (B 3–4)

Thus, if event A causes event B, we know that this relation is universal: Events of the same kind as A are necessarily followed by, or result in, events of the same kind as B.[4] We know this, moreover, not solely on the basis of inductive considerations, that is, from repeated observation of events of type A being followed by events of type B. For, according to Kant, such merely inductive considerations can never ground the strictly universal judgment that *all* events of type A are followed by events of type B: What we are entitled to say here, strictly speaking, is only that all events of type A observed so far have been followed by events of type B. Hence, neither the necessity nor the true or strict universality involved in the causal relation can be grounded empirically.[5]

The conception of causality that emerges from the passages we have been considering therefore appears to be the following. To say that event A causes event B is to say, first, that there is a universal rule or law of the form: Events of type A are followed by events of type B.[6] Yet, because experience alone can never show that such a rule or law is *strictly* universal, the judgment that A causes B must be grounded, additionally, in an *a priori* source or faculty of knowledge. The latter is of course the understanding, with its *a priori* conditions of objective judgment in a possible experience. Thus, after our judgment is thereby grounded *a priori*, we are entitled to assert, with true or absolute universality, that *all* events of type A are followed by events of type B. And this means, finally, that we are also entitled to assert that all events of type A are *necessarily* followed by events of type B. In other words, the causal relation is understood in terms of strictly universal causal laws, which latter, in turn, are characterized as necessary. From section 13 of the Transcendental Analytic it would then appear that Kant's task there is precisely to show – contra Hume – that this conception of causality actually applies to our experience of nature. Kant must show that there are such necessary and more than merely inductive causal laws, and he must explain how the *a priori* conditions of judgment in a possible experience serve to ground such laws and to secure their special status.

Yet this description of the task of the Transcendental Analytic has been almost universally rejected or dismissed by twentieth-century commentators – at least in the English-speaking world. According to the virtually unanimous opinion of these commentators, we must sharply distinguish between the universal *principle* of causality of the Second Analogy – namely the principle that every event B has a cause A – and particular causal laws: particular instantiations of the claim that all events of type A are followed by events of type B. The former principle is in fact a necessary truth holding as a universal transcendental law of nature in general, and this principle is in fact proved in the Transcendental Analytic. The Transcendental Analytic does not, however, establish that particular causal laws are themselves necessary. Indeed, as far as particular causal laws are concerned, the Transcendental Analytic is in basic agreement with Hume: They are established by induction and by induction alone.[7]

Such a strong separation of particular causal laws from the universal causal principle then leads naturally to the idea that the Transcendental Analytic is not really concerned with particular causal laws at all. We know *a priori* that every event B has a cause A, but this implies nothing whatsoever concerning the *repeatability* of the sequence A-B – nor, therefore, does anything follow concerning the existence of regularities or laws connecting events of the same kind as A with events of the same kind of B.[8] Putting the point in a somewhat different way, because the universal causal principle is powerless to secure the necessity of particular causal laws, it is equally unable to guarantee their existence: This is a purely empirical matter best left to the progress of science and experience.[9]

The idea that particular causal laws are to be strongly separated from the universal causal principle, so that neither their necessity nor even their existence is thought to follow from that principle, clearly has much to recommend it.

First of all, Kant uses necessity and genuine or strict universality (which, as I have urged in section I of this essay, inevitably go hand in hand) as "sure criteria" of *a priori* knowledge. Thus, in the passage cited above from B 3–4 of the Introduction to the *Critique*, I omitted the surrounding context:

> What is in question here is a characteristic by which we can surely distinguish a pure from an empirical cognition. To be sure, experience teaches us that something is constituted in such and such a way, but not that it cannot be otherwise. *First*, then, if a proposition is found that is thought simultaneously with its *necessity*, then it is an *a priori* judgment; and if, beyond this, it is also derived from no judgment except that which itself, in turn, is valid as a necessary proposition, then it is absolutely *a priori*. *Second:* Experience never provides true or strict, but only assumed or comparative *universality* (through induction) for its judgments. . . . Thus, if a judgment is thought in strict universality – i.e., so that no exception whatsoever is allowed as possible – then it is not derived from experience but valid absolutely *a priori*. . . . Necessity and strict universality are therefore sure criteria of an *a priori* cognition, and also belong inseparably together.

If particular causal laws are necessary and strictly universal, it would then seem to follow that they are nonempirical and absolutely *a priori* as well. But Kant surely does not intend to say that particular causal laws are known *a priori*.

Indeed, Kant himself takes great pains in the Transcendental Analytic carefully to distinguish the pure or universal laws of nature in general – namely the principles of the understanding – from all more specific laws of nature:

> Nature, considered merely as nature in general, is dependent on these categories, as the original ground of its law-governedness (as nature viewed for-

mally). Pure understanding is not, however, in a position, through mere categories, to prescribe to appearances any *a priori* laws other than those which are involved in a *nature in general*, that is, in the law-governedness of all appearances in space and time. Particular laws, because they concern empirically determined appearances, can *not be completely derived* therefrom [*können davon nicht vollständig abgeleitet werden*], although they one and all stand under them. Experience must come into play in order to become acquainted with the latter *as such* [*überhaupt*]; but only the former *a priori* laws provide instruction concerning experience in general, and concerning that which can be cognized as an object of experience.   (B 165)[10]

And Kant makes substantially the same distinction in section 36 of the *Prolegomena:*

> There are many laws of nature that we can only know by means of experience; but we can become acquainted with the law-governedness in the connection of appearances, i.e., nature in general, through no experience, because experience itself requires such laws, on which its possibility is based *a priori*.   (4:318–19)

> We must, however, distinguish empirical laws of nature, which always presuppose particular perceptions, from the pure or universal natural laws, which, without being based on particular perceptions, contain merely the conditions of their necessary uniting in an experience – and with regard to the latter nature and possible experience are entirely and absolutely one and the same; and, since in nature law-governedness rests on the necessary connection of appearances in an experience (without which we could cognize absolutely no object of the sensible world at all) – and therefore rests on the original laws of the understanding – it thus at first indeed sounds strange, but is nonetheless certainly true, if with the regard to the latter I say: *The understanding does not extract its laws (a priori) from, but prescribes them to, nature.*   (320)

Kant explicitly restricts the idea of an *a priori* prescription by the understanding to the "pure or universal" laws of nature in general: All more particular laws are known only on the basis of experience.

Second, Kant distinguishes between universal transcendental laws of the understanding and particular empirical laws of nature even more sharply in the *Critique of Judgment*. He there appears to suggest, in fact, that the understanding by itself is entirely powerless with respect to empirical laws. Thus, in section 4 of the First Introduction Kant writes:

We have seen in the *Critique of Pure Reason* that the whole of nature as the totality of all objects of experience constitutes a system according to transcendental laws, namely such that the understanding itself provides *a priori* (for appearances, in so far as they are to constitute an experience, bound together in one consciousness). For precisely this reason, experience must also constitute a system of possible empirical cognitions, in accordance with universal as well as particular laws, so far as it is in general possible objectively considered (in the idea). For this is required by the unity of nature according to a principle of the thoroughgoing combination of all that is contained in this totality of all appearances. So far, then, experience in general is to be viewed as a system according to transcendental laws of the understanding and not as a mere aggregate.

But it does not follow therefrom that nature is also a system *comprehensible* to the human faculty of cognition in accordance with *empirical laws*, and that the thoroughgoing systematic coherence of its appearances in an experience – and thus experience as a system – is possible for men. For the manifoldness and inhomogeneity of the empirical laws could be so great, that it would certainly be possible in a partial manner to connect perceptions into an experience in accordance with particular laws discovered opportunely, but it would never be possible to bring these empirical laws themselves to unity of affinity under a common principle – if, namely, as is still possible in itself (at least so far as the understanding can constitute *a priori*), the manifoldness and inhomogeneity of these laws, together with the corresponding natural forms, were so infinitely great and presented to us, in this respect, a crude chaotic aggregate and not the least trace of a system, although we equally had to presuppose such a system in accordance with transcendental laws. (20:208–9)

It appears, then, that the law-governedness of nature under universal transcendental laws of the understanding does not at all guarantee that nature is also governed by particular empirical laws.

In section 5 of the published Introduction Kant makes the same point with respect to the universal causal principle and the particular causal laws that fall under it:

In the grounds of the possibility of an experience we certainly find, in the first place, something necessary, namely the universal laws without which nature in general (as object of the senses) cannot be thought; and these rest on the categories, applied to the formal conditions of all intuition possible for us, in so far as it is likewise given *a priori*. The faculty of judgment is determinative under these laws; for it has nothing to do but subsume under given laws. For example, the understanding says: Every alteration has its cause (universal law of nature); the transcendental faculty of judgment has nothing further to do except to supply the condition of subsumption under the exhibited concept of the understanding *a priori:* and this is the succession of the determinations of one and the same thing. For nature in general (as object of possible experience) the former law is cognized as absolutely necessary. But the objects of empirical cognition are still determined in many modes besides this formal time-condition – or, as far as one can judge *a priori,* are so determinable – so that specifically different natures can still be causes in infinitely manifold ways, besides what they have in common as belonging to nature in general; and every one of these modes must (according to the concept of a cause in general) have its rule – which is a law and therefore carries with it necessity – although, according to the constitution and limitations of our cognitive faculty, we can absolutely not comprehend this necessity. Thus, with respect to its merely empirical laws, we must think in nature the possibility of an infinite manifoldness of empirical laws, which for our insight are yet contingent (cannot be known *a priori*); and, with respect to them, we judge the unity of nature in accordance with empirical laws and the possibility of the unity of experience (as a system according to empirical laws) as contingent.   (5:182–3)

Here Kant appears to separate the universal causal principle from particular causal laws as strongly as one could wish. The principle that every event B has a cause A is indeed *a priori* and necessary. Yet particular causal laws – particular instantiations (via particular empirical concepts) of the generalization that all events of type A are followed by events of type B – are left completely undetermined by the causal principle. Such particular causal laws can only be found empirically and, accordingly, cannot (so far as our understanding can judge) be viewed as either *a priori* or necessary. Indeed, as far as our understanding can determine *a priori,* it appears to be an entirely contingent fact that nature is governed by any empirical laws at all.[11]

A final reason for strongly separating particular causal laws from the universal principle of causality is that otherwise Kant's argument for the causal principle in the Second Analogy appears to be vulnerable to a classical charge of non sequitur. According to this charge, as articulated most clearly and forcefully by Lovejoy,[12] what the argument of the Second Analogy actually shows is that in any single given instance of objective succession (as contrasted with merely subjective succession due to changes in the subject rather than the object) the order of the succeeding states must be represented as fixed or determinate – as "bound down" or irreversible. For example, given that a particular ship is in fact moving downstream on a particular occasion, its states higher up in the stream must be represented as determinately preceding its states lower down – and not vice versa. But from this nothing at all follows concerning the repeatability of such a sequence or its conformity to causal uniformities:

> But all this has no relation to the law of universal and uniform causation, for the manifest reason that a proof of the *irreversibility* of the sequence of my perceptions in a *single instance* of a phenomena is not equivalent to a proof of the necessary *uniformity* of the sequence of my perceptions in *repeated instances* of a given *kind* of phenomenon. Yet it is the latter alone that Hume denied and that Kant desires to establish.   (pp. 300–1)

Hence, if the Second Analogy is understood as arguing from the determinacy or irreversibility of particular objective sequences to the existence of general causal laws or uniformities, then Kant has indeed committed "one of the most spectacular examples of the *non-sequitur* which are to be found in the history of philosophy" (p. 303).

It is therefore entirely natural – particularly in view of Kant's explicit separation of empirical causal laws or uniformities from the transcendental universal principle of causality just considered – to respond to this charge of non sequitur by insisting that Kant himself makes no such inference. Kant is not trying to derive the existence of general causal laws or uniformities at all; his concern, rather, is to provide an account of objective determinacy as such: to explain what distinguishes determinate objective sequences of events from merely subjective and indeterminate succession of perceptions. Kant argues that the distinction in question cannot be explained in virtue of mere psychological association of ideas (for this, in the end, can yield only subjective succession), nor can it be explained in virtue of the correspondence of our representations to some independent object or thing in itself existing outside of or "behind" our representations (for neither the object nor the correspondence can possibly be known by us). Instead, Kant argues, the distinction can only be explained in virtue of the subsumption of our perceptions under an *a priori* concept of the understanding: namely the concept of causality. More precisely, determinate objective sequences are just those that are subsumed under the *schema* of causality – the *a priori* representation of necessary or determinate succession in time.

On this kind of interpretation there is thus no further requirement concerning the existence of empirical causal laws or uniformities. Kant's answer to Hume does not consist in proving a principle of the uniformity of nature, but rather in demonstrating that the concept of causality (together with its schema) is of *a priori* origin and, at the same time, that this *a priori* concept necessarily applies to our experience (for otherwise determinate objective succession cannot be represented). And the application of the *a priori* concept of causality to our experience does not result in general causal laws or uniformities (for these are the responsibility of reason and reflective judgment), but rather in particular determinate sequences of individual objective events – from which general causal laws or uniformities may then be derived empirically by standard inductive procedures.[13]

III

In spite of its many advantages, however, the strong separation of empirical causal laws from the transcendental principle of causality maintained by the preceding interpretation does not cohere at all well with much of what Kant explicitly says in the Transcendental Analytic.

Consider, first of all, the transcendental principle of causality itself: Every event B has a cause A. What does it mean for A to be the cause of B? As I observed in I, Kant appears clearly to hold that there must be a law or regularity in virtue of which all events of the same kind as A are followed by or result in events of the same kind as B.[14] For Kant, then, if particular individual events occur in a determinate objective succession in virtue of the (schema of the) concept of causality, then they *also* are subsumed under a general causal law or uniformity – a point that stands out most clearly, perhaps, in the following important passage from the Second Analogy:

Thus, if I perceive that something happens then in this representation it is contained, first, that something precedes, because it is precisely in reference to this that the appearance acquires its time-relation: namely, to exist after a preceding time in which it was not. But it can acquire its determinate temporal position in this relation only insofar as something is presupposed in the preceding state upon which it always – i.e., in accordance with a rule – follows. It then follows, first, that I cannot reverse the order and place that which happens prior to that upon which it follows, and second, that if the preceding state is posited, this determinate event inevitably and necessarily follows. (A 198 / B 243–4)[15]

To say that B has a cause A is therefore, at the same time, to say that B is related to A by a uniformity or causal law; and it thereby follows that the universal causal principle must assert the existence of particular causal laws or uniformities as well.

Moreover, if the universal causal principle asserts the existence of particular causal laws or uniformities, it must also assert their necessity. In the passages just considered from the Second Analogy, Kant of course intimately links causal uniformity with necessity, and this is also explicitly emphasized in his discussion of the category of necessity in the Postulates of Empirical Thought:

Now there is no existence that can be cognized as necessary under the condition of other given appearances except the existence of effects from given causes in accordance with laws of causality. Therefore, it is not the existence of things (substances), but only that of their state whereof necessity can be cognized – and indeed from other states that are given in perception, in accordance with empirical laws of causality. . . . Therefore, necessity concerns only the relations of appearances according to the dynamical law of causality and the possibility thereupon grounded of inferring *a priori* from some given existence (a cause) to another existence (the effect).

(A 227–8 / B 279–80)

Once again, therefore, particular "empirical laws of causality" – in accordance with which alone any particular effect can be "inferred *a priori*" from any particular cause – are very closely linked with the universal transcendental principle of causality ("*the* dynamical law of causality"). What this passage clearly suggests, in fact, is that the possibility of particular causal laws is somehow grounded in the transcendental principle.

Indeed, although Kant explicitly and carefully distinguishes the universal transcendental principles of the understanding from particular empirical laws of nature in the Transcendental Analytic, he is just as explicit in his claim that particular empirical laws are somehow made possible by – are grounded in or determined by – the transcendental principles. And it is clear, in addition, that it is precisely in virtue of this kind of grounding that even empirical laws too somehow count as necessary:

> Even natural laws, when they are considered as principles of the empirical employment of the understanding, at the same time carry with themselves an expression of necessity and thus at least the suggestion of a determination from grounds that hold *a priori* and antecedent to all experience. Yet all laws of nature without distinction stand under higher principles of the understanding, in that they merely apply these to particular cases of appearance. These principles alone therefore give the concept that contains the condition, and as it were the exponent, of a rule in general; but experience gives the case that stands under the rule.   (A 159 / B 198)[16]

The same point is made, even more strongly perhaps, in Kant's concluding remarks on the analogies of experience:

> By nature (in the empirical sense) we understand the connection of appearances according to their existence, in accordance with necessary laws, that is, in accordance with rules. There are thus certain laws, in fact *a priori* laws, that first make a nature possible. Empirical laws can obtain, and be discovered, only by means of experience, and indeed in virtue of these original laws through which experience itself first becomes possible. Our analogies therefore properly present the unity of nature in the connection of all appearances under certain exponents, which express nothing other than the relation of time (insofar as it comprehends all existence within it) to the unity of apperception, which can take place only in the synthesis according to rules.   (A 216 / B 263)

Here Kant asserts that, although particular laws of nature are of course discovered empirically ("by means of experience"), this very discovery takes place "*in virtue of* these original laws through which experience itself first becomes possible." Together with the first passage, then, this suggests that particular laws of nature are not obtained or derived *solely* empirically.[17]

Now, if particular laws of nature are somehow grounded in or made possible by the transcendental principles of the understanding, it follows that even empirical laws too must have a more than merely inductive status. The explicit discussion of induction in the Second Analogy is especially relevant to this issue:

> To be sure, this appears to contradict all observations that have always been made concerning the procedure of our understanding, according to

which we are only first guided by the observed and compared concurrent sequences of many events following upon preceding appearances to discover a rule according to which certain events always follow upon certain appearances, and we are thereby first induced to make for ourselves the concept of cause. On such a basis this concept would be merely empirical, and the rule that it provides – that everything which happens has a cause – would be precisely as contingent as experience itself: its universality and necessity would then be only imputed, and would have no true universal validity, since they would not be grounded *a priori* but only on induction.

(A 195–6 / B 240–2)

Neither the universal causal principle nor any particular causal law falling under it has a merely inductive status, for both cases are characterized by a necessity and a (strict) universality that no merely empirical considerations can explain.

That particular empirical laws or uniformities are subsumed under the *a priori* concept of causality in such a way that they thereby become necessary and acquire a more than merely inductive status, is explicitly stated in section 29 of the *Prolegomena*:

In order to make a trial with *Hume's* problematic concept (his *crux metaphysicorum*) – namely the concept of cause – I am first given *a priori* by means of logic the form of a conditional judgment in general, namely to use a given cognition as ground and the other as consequent. It is possible, however, that a rule of relation is met with in perception, which says that upon a certain appearance another constantly follows (although not conversely); and this is a case for me to use the hypothetical judgment and to say, e.g., that if a body is illuminated long enough by the sun then it becomes warm. Here there is certainly not yet a necessity of connection – nor, therefore, the concept of cause. But I continue and say: If the above proposition, which is merely a subjective connection of perceptions, is to be a proposition of experience, it must be viewed as necessary and universally valid. But such a proposition would be that the sun is, through its light, the cause of heat. The above empirical rule is now viewed as a law – and, indeed, not as valid merely for appearances, but for them on behalf of a possible experience, which requires completely [*durchgängig*] – and thus necessarily – valid rules.   (4:312)

The rule of uniformity according to which illuminated bodies happen to become warm is at first merely empirical and inductive; if it is to count as a genuine law of nature, however, this same empirical uniformity must be subsumed under the *a priori* concept of causality, whereupon it then becomes necessary and strictly universal. It would appear, therefore, that the principle of causality makes experience possible precisely by somehow injecting necessity (and thus strict universality) into particular causal laws.

The upshot of these considerations is that particular causal laws, for Kant, have a peculiar kind of mixed status: They result from a combination of inductively observed regularities or uniformities with the *a priori* concept (and principle) of causality. Insofar as particular causal laws merely record observed regularities they are contingent and *a posteriori;* insofar as they subsume such regularities under the *a priori* principle of causality, however, they are necessary – and even, in a sense, *a priori*. Kant explicitly remarks upon this peculiar mixed status in an important footnote to section 22 of the *Prolegomena:*

> But how does this proposition, that judgments of experience are to contain necessity in the synthesis of perceptions, agree with the proposition I have in many ways often urged above, that experience as *a posteriori* cognition can yield merely contingent judgments? If I say that experience teaches me something, then I always mean only the perception that lies within experience – e.g., that heat always follows upon the illumination of a stone by the sun – and thus the experiential proposition is always so far contingent. That this heating necessarily results from the illumination by the sun is in fact contained in the judgment of experience (in virtue of the concept of cause), but I do not learn this through experience; on the contrary, experience is first generated through this addition of the concept of the understanding (of cause) to perception.   (305)[18]

It follows that Kant recognizes at least two distinct types of necessity (and thus apriority). The transcendental principles of the understanding are absolutely necessary and *a priori:* they are established entirely independent of all perception and experience. Empirical laws that somehow fall under these transcendental principles are then necessary and *a priori* in a derivative sense. They, unlike the transcendental principles themselves, indeed depend partially on inductively obtained regularities (and thus on perception), yet they are also in some sense grounded in or determined by the transcendental principles and thereby acquire a necessary and more than merely inductive status.[19]

What has made the problem so difficult, however, is that we are left quite in the dark concerning the precise nature of this "grounding."

How do the transcendental principles inject necessity into empirical laws of nature so as to secure them a more than merely inductive status? *How* do judgments that merely record observed regularities or uniformities become truly and "strictly" universal via the addition of the concept of causality? The unfortunate fact is that Kant does very little to explain — or even to illustrate — this crucially important relationship between transcendental principles and empirical laws of nature in either the first *Critique* or the *Prolegomena*. In particular, the example of the sun causing heat through the illumination of a stone seems quite unhelpful here; for it is so far entirely unclear how this specific causal connection is related to the universal causal principle. To be sure, the former certainly constitutes a particular instance of the kind of causal connection attributed generally by the latter; but this instantial relation is of course completely trivial, and does nothing at all to explain how the law in question is grounded *a priori* so as to obtain a nonempirical necessity.

IV

In an unpublished *Reflexion* written somewhere between 1776 and the early 1780s, Kant illustrates the transition from merely empirical rules to necessary laws discussed in 29 of the *Prolegomena* with a more interesting and, I think, more significant example:

> Empirically one can certainly discover rules, but not laws — as Kepler in comparison with Newton — for to the latter belongs necessity, and hence that they are cognized *a priori*. Yet one always supposes that rules of nature are necessary — for on that account it is nature — and that they can be comprehended *a priori*; therefore one calls them laws by way of anticipation. The understanding is the ground of empirical laws, and thus of an empirical necessity, where the ground of law-governedness can in fact be comprehended *a priori*: e.g., the law of causality, but not the ground of the determinate law. All metaphysical principles of nature are only grounds of law-governedness.   (R 5414, 18:176)[20]

Kant here illustrates the transition from "rules" to "laws" — along with the correlative notion of a grounding of empirical laws through the transcendental principles of the understanding — by the transition from Kepler's laws of planetary motion to the Newtonian law of universal gravitation that is derived therefrom. And this suggests that the law of universal gravitation is paradigmatic of the peculiar kind of mixed status Kant attributes to genuine empirical laws.

It is significant, furthermore, that in the *Prolegomena* itself Kant illustrates the claim of section 36, that "*the understanding does not extract its laws (a priori) from, but prescribes them to, nature,*" in section 38 immediately following, by precisely the law of universal gravitation. Moreover, according to section 37, this illustration is to show:

> that laws, which we discover in objects of sensible intuition, especially if they are cognized as necessary, are indeed held by us to be such as the understanding has placed there, although they are equally similar otherwise in all respects to natural laws that we ascribe to experience.   (320)

And thus it appears that the law of gravitation has just the kind of mixed status illustrated in section 29 and the footnote to section 22 by the example of the sun warming a stone.[21]

Kant's fullest discussion of the law of universal gravitation is found in the *Metaphysical Foundations of Natural Science* of 1786, which is devoted to an exposition of "pure natural science" or "the pure doctrine of nature." The principles of pure natural science are expounded in four chapters, corresponding to the four headings of the table of categories from the first *Critique*.[22] Of particular importance are the principles of pure natural science expounded in the third chapter or Mechanics, which thus correspond to the relational categories of substance, causality, and community. These principles, parallel to the three analogies of experience, are given by Kant as the three "Laws of Mechanics": (1) the principle of the conservation of mass or quantity of matter, (2) the law of inertia ("Every body persists in its state of rest or motion, in the same direction and with the same speed, if it is not necessitated through an external cause to leave this state" – 4:543), (3) the principle of the equality of action and reaction. And it is clear, moreover, that Kant views these as synthetic *a priori* principles – very closely related to the transcendental relational principles themselves.[23]

Of even greater importance, from the present point of view, is the fourth chapter or Phenomenology, which corresponds to the modal categories of possibility, actuality, and necessity, and which has as its aim the transformation of *appearance* [*Erscheinung*] into *experience* [*Erfahrung*]. More specifically, its aim is to transform *apparent motions* into *true motions*. Here it appears that Kant is following the lead of Book III of Newton's *Principia*, which applies the laws of motion to the observable, so far merely relative or apparent motions in the solar system so as to derive therefrom the law of universal gravitation and, at the same time, to establish a privileged frame of reference (the center of mass frame of the solar system) relative to which the notion of true (or absolute) motion is first empirically defined.[24] In particular, Kant outlines a procedure for applying the Laws of Mechanics expounded in the previous chapter so as to subject the given appearances (namely, apparent motions) to the modal categories in three steps or stages.[25]

In the first stage, we record the observed relative motions in the solar system of satellites with respect to their primary bodies and the fixed stars: the orbits of the moons of Jupiter and Saturn, the orbits of the planets with respect to the sun, and the orbit of Earth's moon. We begin, then, with precisely the empirical "phenomena" that initiate Newton's argument for universal gravitation. We note that all such observed relative motions are described by Kepler's laws, and we subsume these so far merely apparent motions under the category of *possibility*.

In the second stage, we assume that these relative motions approximate to true motions (from a modern point of view, that the aforementioned frames of reference approximate, for the purpose of describing these motions, to inertial frames of reference), and we then can apply Kant's law of inertia (Newton's first and second laws of motion) to infer that the relative accelerations in question manifest an "external cause" or *impressed force* directed toward the center of each primary body. Moreover, it now follows purely mathematically from Kepler's laws that these given forces – together with the true accelerations engendered thereby – satisfy the inverse-square law. Accordingly, we now subsume these true orbital motions (inverse-square accelerations) under the category of *actuality*.

In the third and final stage, we apply the equality of action and reaction (Newton's third law of motion) to conclude that these true accelerations are *mutual* – equal and opposite – and also to conclude that gravitational acceleration is directly proportional to mass. To infer the latter result from the equality of action and reaction we need to assume, in addition, that *all* bodies in the solar system – not merely the satellites in question – experience inverse-square accelerations toward each primary body (and thus, in effect, that gravitational attraction is *universal*), and we also need to apply the third law of motion directly to these mutual interactions of the primary bodies (and thus, in effect, to assume that gravitational attraction acts *immediately* at a distance).[26] Given these assumptions and our previous results the law of universal gravitation now follows deductively: Each body experiences an inverse-square acceleration toward each other body, which, in addition, is directly proportional, at a given distance, to the mass of the body toward which it accelerates. Moreover, we are now – and only now – in a position rigorously to estimate the masses of the various primary bodies in the solar system so as rigorously to determine the center of mass frame of the solar system. Finally, because the true motions can now be explained precisely as motions relative to this privileged frame of reference, we are also now in a position to discharge the provisional assumption of stage 2 – namely that the relative motions of stage 1 closely approximate to true motions.[27] The inverse-square accelerations resulting thereby – which are universal, everywhere mutual, and directly proportional to mass – are subsumed under the category of *necessity*.

From Kant's point of view the significance of our three-stage procedure is to be understood in the following way. We begin the argument with Kepler's laws, and these are initially mere empirical regularities obtained solely by induction. At this stage, then, we have mere appearances or "judgments of perception" – analogous to the purely empirical circumstance that heat customarily follows the illumination of a body. Hence, to obtain genuinely objective experience we need to apply the transcendental principles of the understanding to our given appearances. More precisely, we need to apply the more specific "metaphysical" principles of pure natural science, which realize or instantiate the transcendental principles of the understanding via the empirical concept of matter.[28] When these principles are applied to our given initial "phenomena," however, the law of universal gravitation results uniquely and deductively: There is no *further* room, that is, for inductive or hypothetical underdetermination or uncertainty.

In this way, Kepler's at first merely inductive or empirical regularities are transformed into something radically new: a law that, despite its obvious dependence on initial empirical data, depends *also* on synthetic *a priori* principles and thereby acquires a more than merely inductive status. That the law of universal gravitation acquires a more than merely empirical status in this fashion is emphatically reemphasized in the unpublished fragments constituting Kant's *Opus postumum:*

> It is, namely, a remarkable appearance in the field of science that there was a moment where its progress appeared to be terminated, where the ship lay at anchor and there was nothing further to be done for philosophy in a certain field. *Kepler's* three analogies had enumerated the phenomena of orbital motion of the planets completely, although still only empirically, and mathematically described them without yet providing an intimation of the *moving forces*, together with their law, which may be the cause thereof.
> Instead of Kepler's *aggregation* of motions containing empirically assembled rules, Newton created a principle of the system of moving forces from active causes. Unity (22:521)

> The *laws* of motion were sufficiently established through Kepler's three analogies. They were altogether mechanical. Huygens knew also the composite, yet derivative motion through the forces that flee or continually strive toward the center (*vis centrifuga et centripeta*); but as close as both [were] . . . yet all that was erected was mere empiricism of the doctrine of motion and always a universal and properly so-called principle was lacking: i.e., a concept of reason from which one could infer *a priori*, as from a cause to an effect, a law of force-determination; and this explanation was given by Newton. . . . (22:528–9)

Thus these fragments from 1799–1800 appear to make essentially the same point as *Reflexion* 5414 cited previously.[29]

Finally, the three-stage procedure by which the law of universal gravitation is derived from Kepler's laws also yields the result that the former law is in an important sense necessary. The relevant notion of necessity here is in fact just the "empirical" or "material" necessity explained in the Postulates of Empirical Thought:

> 1. That which agrees with the formal conditions of experience (according to intuition and concepts), is *possible.*
> 2. That which connects with the material conditions of experience (sensation), is *actual.*
> 3. That whose connection with the actual is determined in accordance with universal conditions of experience, is (exists as) *necessary.*
> (A 218–19 / B 265–6)

And, as we have seen, the law of universal gravitation satisfies this notion of necessity exactly: It is determined in connection with the actual (namely Kepler's laws, provisionally viewed as recording true motions as in stage 2) in accordance with universal conditions of experience (namely the transcendental principles of the understanding, as further specified to yield the metaphysical principles of pure natural science).[30]

This example also illuminates the relationship between the third postulate of empirical thought and the principle of causality. In his discussion of the third postulate Kant characterizes the relationship between the principle of causality and the categories of modality as follows:

Everything that happens is hypothetically necessary; this is a principle that subordinates the alterations in the world to a law – i.e., a rule of necessary existence – without which nature would absolutely not occur. Therefore, the proposition: Nothing happens through blind chance (in mundo non datur casus), is an a priori law of nature. So also is the proposition: No necessity in nature is blind, but always a conditioned and therefore intelligible [verständliche] necessity (non datur fatum). Both are such laws through which the play of alterations is subordinated to a nature of things (as appearances) – or, what is the same thing, to the unity of the understanding, in which they can alone belong to an experience, as the synthetic unity of appearances. These two principles belong among the dynamical principles. The first is properly a consequence of the principle of causality (under the analogies of experience). The second belongs to the principles of modality, which add to the causal determination the concept of necessity, which, however, stands under a rule of the understanding.   (A 228 / B 280-1)

This suggests that, whereas the principle of causality says that every event is related to a preceding event by an empirical causal law, the third postulate of modality indicates a procedure by which empirical causal laws are themselves related to the a priori principles of the understanding so as to confer on them both necessity and intelligibility. Thus, whereas Kepler's laws empirically describe the temporal evolution of the motions of the heavenly bodies quite adequately, only their explanation within the theory of universal gravitation makes them both necessary and intelligible (and the relevant standard of intelligibility is provided via the transcendental principles of the understanding).

V

We have now seen how an empirical law of nature can be related to – can be grounded in or determined by – synthetic *a priori* principles so as to acquire thereby a necessary and more than merely inductive status. Strictly speaking, however, we have not yet seen how empirical laws are grounded in or determined by the transcendental principles of the understanding, for the synthetic *a priori* principles to which we have so far appealed are the metaphysical principles of pure natural science. How do these metaphysical principles themselves relate to the transcendental principles of the understanding? How exactly do the former constitute an instantiation or realization of the latter?

The relationship between transcendental principles and the more specific metaphysical principles is illustrated in the following important passage from section 5 of the published Introduction to the *Critique of Judgment:*

> A transcendental principle is that through which is represented *a priori* the universal condition under which alone things can be objects of our cognition in general. On the other hand, a principle is called metaphysical if it represents *a priori* the condition under which alone objects, whose concept must be empirically given, can be further determined *a priori*. Thus, the principle of the cognition of bodies as substances and as alterable substances is transcendental, if it is thereby asserted that their alterations must have a cause; it is metaphysical, however, if it is thereby asserted that their alterations must have an *external* cause: Because in the first case bodies may be thought only through ontological predicates (pure concepts of the understanding), e.g., as substance, in order to cognize the proposition *a priori*; but in the second case the empirical concept of a body (as a movable thing in space) must be laid at the basis of the proposition – however, as soon as this is done, that the later predicate (motion only through external causes) belongs to body can be comprehended completely *a priori*. (5:181)

A closely related contrast is found in section 15 of the *Prolegomena:*

> Universal natural science [contains] purely discursive principles (from concepts), which constitute the philosophical part of the pure cognition of nature. But there is still also much in it that is not entirely pure and independent of empirical sources: such as the concept of *motion*, of *impenetrability* (on which the empirical concept of matter rests), of *inertia*, etc., which prevents it from being able to be called an entirely pure natural science;

moreover, it extends only to the objects of outer sense, and thus yields no example of a universal science of nature in the stricter sense – for the latter must bring nature in general under universal laws, whether it concerns the object of outer sense or that of inner sense (the object of physics as well as psychology).   (4:295)

The connection between these two passages then lies in the circumstance that only thinking beings – or, more generally, living beings – possess *inner* principles of causality.

Kant strongly emphasizes this last point in his Observation to the Proof of the law of inertia in the *Metaphysical Foundations:*

The inertia of matter is and signifies nothing else but its *lifelessness* as matter in itself. *Life* means the capacity of a *substance* to act on itself from an *inner principle*, of a *finite substance* to alter itself, and of a *material substance* to determine itself to motion or rest as alteration of its state. Now we are acquainted with no other inner principle of a substance to alter its state except *desire* – and, in general, no other inner activity except *thinking* and that which depends thereupon: *feeling* of pleasure or displeasure and *appetite* or willing. But these grounds of determination and actions absolutely do not belong to the representations of outer sense and thus not to the determinations of matter as matter. Therefore all matter as such is *lifeless.* This, and nothing more, is what the proposition of inertia says.   (4:544)

Thus, the metaphysical principles of pure natural science apply only to the activities and powers of nonliving, nonthinking beings: beings represented solely through predicates of outer sense. The transcendental principles of the understanding, by contrast, apply to all beings without distinction – where, for example, inner principles of causality (appropriate to living beings) are just as permissible as external causes.

It certainly does not follow, however, that the transcendental principles extend also to nonspatial substances – to objects *solely* of inner sense, as it were. For Kant consistently denies that the concept of substance can be meaningfully applied to objects of mere inner sense (such as the soul), and clearly asserts that "in order to provide something permanent in intuition corresponding to the concept of *substance* (and thereby to verify the objective reality of this concept), we require an intuition of *space* (of matter), because space alone is determined as permanent, but time, and therefore everything in inner sense, continually flows" (B 291). Therefore all substances, even those falling only under the transcendental concept of a nature in general, must be spatial.[31]

Indeed, as is well known, Kant himself insists upon the spatiality of all substances in his marginal notes to the First Analogy in his copy of the first edition of the *Critique*. In particular, at A 182 he writes:

> Here the proof must be so developed that it applies only to substances as phenomena of outer sense, and therefore from space – which, together with its determinations, exists at all times.
>
> In space all alteration is motion; for, were there another [determination] in the relation, then, according to the concept of alteration, the subject would still have to endure. Thus, everything in space would have to vanish together. (*R* LXXX, 23:30)[32]

Kant's thought seems to be that if substance could alter in some way other than through motion then it would be possible for all substances to vanish – and thus substance would not be conserved.

What Kant has in mind here becomes clearer through a comparison with the Observation to the Proof of the law of conservation of mass or quantity of matter in the *Metaphysical Foundations*. Kant's point there is that only that whose quantity consists of spatial parts external to one another can be proved to satisfy the conservation law; for only in this case does decrease in quantity occur by division – that is, by the relative *motion* of the spatial parts – rather than by diminution. Only spatial division (via relative *motion*), as opposed to the diminution or mere decrease in degree characteristic of a purely intensive magnitude, necessarily conserves the total quantity of the magnitude thereby divided. By contrast, the permanence of a merely intensive magnitude, such as would belong solely to inner sense, cannot be proved:

> It is therefore no wonder if the permanence of substance can be proved of the latter [matter] but not of the former [the soul], for in the case of matter it already flows from its *concept* – namely that it is to be movable, which is possible only in space – that that which has a quantity in it contains a multiplicity of realities external to one another, and thus of substances; and therefore the quantity of substance can only be diminished by division, which is not vanishing – and the latter in [matter] would also be impossible according to the law of continuity. On the other hand, the thought I is absolutely *no concept* but only inner perception, and absolutely nothing can

therefore be inferred from it (outside of the sheer distinction of an object of inner sense from that which is thought merely as object of outer sense) – thus, the permanence of the soul as substance can also not be inferred.

(4:543)

Thus, for example, clarity of consciousness in inner sense has an intensive magnitude and hence a degree, but nothing precludes its vanishing – that is, its continuous diminution to nothing (542).[33]

Spatiality – and hence conservation of total quantity via division (through relative motion) into smaller parts that are themselves spatial substances – is therefore a necessary property of all substances falling under the transcendental concept of a nature in general. The more specific metaphysical concept of a body or material substance then results from this by the addition of the empirically given properties of impenetrability and weight: the two fundamental forces of repulsion and attraction. Thus in the Anticipations of Perception Kant speaks, from the point of view of transcendental philosophy, of "the *real* in space (I may here not call it impenetrability or weight, because these are empirical concepts)" (A 173 / B 215). And in the Postulates of Empirical Thought Kant provides the following interesting example of a thinkable, but not in fact empirically given, realization of the relational categories:

A substance that would be permanently present in space, yet without filling it (as that intermediate thing between matter and thinking being that some have wanted to introduce); or a particular fundamental power [*Grundkraft*] of our mind to *intuit* the future in advance (and not merely to infer it, for example); or finally a capacity of our mind to be in community of thought with other men (as distant as they may be). . . .   (A 222 / B 270)[34]

It follows that substances falling only under the transcendental concept of nature in general indeed take up or *occupy* space, but they do not necessarily *fill* space; this latter property results only by the addition of the empirical concept of impenetrability – "on which the empirical concept of matter rests."[35]

We are now in a position, finally, to see, at least in outline, how the transcendental principles of the understanding function as the highest laws of nature "under which all others stand." The key point is that the transcendental concept of a nature in general is not *entirely* indeterminate: It does not simply say that nature consists of some otherwise entirely indeterminate substances obeying some otherwise entirely indeterminate empirical causal laws. Rather, the transcendental principles depict a world with a particular character: a world of spatially extended substances consisting of spatial parts that always count as substances in turn (the total quantity of substance is thereby always conserved via division and recombination of such spatial parts), a world whose substances change their states always in response to (internal or external) powers or causes, and a world whose spatially separated substances are in thoroughgoing interaction with one another (and thus always act on one another through external causes). It is clear, moreover, that this world depicted by the transcendental principles is closely modeled on the central empirical example Kant consistently takes to be paradigmatic here: namely the system of heavenly bodies as described by the Newtonian theory of universal gravitation.

Nevertheless, as we have seen, the transcendental concept of a nature in general is certainly much more abstract than that of a Newtonian system of masses; and to reach the latter from the former we in fact need to add specifically empirical content in two successive steps or stages. First, we need further to specify the transcendental principles of the understanding to the metaphysical principles of pure natural science. These result by the addition of the empirical concept of matter – and, in particular, the empirical concepts of impenetrability and weight (resting on the two fundamental forces of repulsion and attraction) – which has the effect of restricting our attention to nonliving material substances or massive bodies and thereby transforming the analogies of experience into the Newtonian laws of motion. Second, we need to apply the resulting principles of pure natural science to the initially merely empirical or inductive regularities codified in Kepler's laws in the manner I sketched in IV. Once this is done, however, the Newtonian theory of universal gravitation results uniquely and deductively.

I suggest that we now see, at least in outline, how the peculiarly Kantian conception of a grounding of empirical laws by transcendental principles of the understanding is supposed to work. It is not that empirical laws are somehow derived from the transcendental principles as their deductive consequences. This, as Kant himself repeatedly emphasizes, is impossible. Rather, empirical laws are to be thought of as framed or nested, as it were, within a sequence of progressively more concrete and empirical instantiations or realizations of the transcendental principles: a sequence consisting of progressively more concrete and empirical natures or worlds. The most abstract such world is just that depicted by the transcendental concept of a nature in general – a world of interacting spatial substances; the next world is that described by the metaphysical principles of pure natural science – a world of nonliving, purely material substances interacting via the two fundamental forces in accordance with the Newtonian laws of motion; the next world is that described by the Newtonian theory of gravity – a world of massive bodies interacting in accordance with the law of universal gravitation; and so on. The notion of an *a priori* grounding is then expressed by the idea that, although purely empirical data play a necessary and unavoidable role in this procedure, the framing or nesting of such data within the transcendental concept of a nature in general is to result – at least in principle – in a unique and determinate description of the empirical world that thereby acquires a more than merely empirical status.

It is in this way, I suggest, that *all* empirical judgments are ultimately to be grounded in the transcendental principles for Kant. Thus, for example, particular judgments of objective succession asserting that event A precedes event B are grounded in empirical causal laws asserting that all events of the same kind as A are followed by or result in events of the same kind as B; these latter are themselves grounded in higher empirical laws; and these in turn – in the manner just illustrated – are ultimately grounded in the transcendental principles. And it is along these lines, I suggest, that Lovejoy's charge of non sequitur discussed in II should be met. Kant is not arguing, that is, from a neutral and uncontroversial conception of particular objective succession to the existence of general causal laws or uniformities – this would of course be a non sequitur indeed. Rather, Kant is relying upon his own characteristic conception of objective empirical judgment, a conception according to which genuinely objective empirical judgments are simply impossible without a grounding in progressively more abstract laws of nature terminating in the transcendental principles themselves.

VI

It remains briefly to consider the role of reason or reflective judgment in the articulation and determination of empirical causal laws.

We saw in II of this essay that the faculty of reflective judgment does in fact play an absolutely central role here, but the precise nature of this role is not yet entirely clear. In particular, it is not yet clear whether Kant's discussion of reflective judgment supports the kind of strong separation of empirical causal laws from the universal causal principle considered in II, or, on the other hand, whether it is perhaps more in harmony with the alternative interpretation I outlined in III–V.

Let us begin by reconsidering the passage from section 4 of the First Introduction to the *Critique of Judgment* cited in II. The first point to notice is that Kant does not say there that the faculty of reflective judgment is the ground of particular empirical laws themselves, but, rather, that reflective judgment is required to secure the *systematicity* of such laws. The problem left unsettled by the understanding is not that empirical laws may not exist at all, as it were, but only that they may fail to constitute a system:

For the manifoldness and inhomogeneity of the empirical laws could be so great, that it would certainly be possible in a partial manner to connect perceptions into an experience in accordance with particular laws discovered opportunely, but it would never be possible to bring these empirical laws themselves to unity of affinity under a common principle . . .

(20:209)

Hence, the task of reflective judgment is to systematize the manifold of particular empirical laws so as to bring these laws to "unity of affinity." The crucial problem, then, is to understand what "unity of affinity" means here.

Kant explains his thinking further in the next section of the First Introduction, where the principle of reflective judgment is first officially stated:

Now it is clear that the reflective judgment could not undertake in accordance with its nature to *classify* the whole of nature according to its empirical variety, if it did not presuppose that nature itself *specifies* its transcendental laws according to some principle. This principle can now be no other than that of the suitability to the faculty of judgment itself, to find sufficient affinity in the immeasurable manifoldness of things in accordance with empirical laws in order to bring them under empirical concepts (classes) and these under more universal laws (higher species) and thus to be able to attain to an empirical system of nature.   (20:215)

The peculiar principle of the faculty of judgment is therefore: *nature specifies its universal laws to empirical* [laws], *in accordance with the form of a logical system, on behalf of the faculty of judgment.*   (20:216)

I assume that the "universal laws" referred to in the official statement of the principle of reflective judgment are the same as the "transcendental laws" mentioned in the immediately preceding paragraph; and, if this is correct, the principle of reflective judgment therefore states that empirical laws are brought to systematic "unity of affinity" precisely by being somehow related to the transcendental principles of the understanding – which latter are thereby "specified" to empirical laws.

We saw previously that the *Metaphysical Foundations* depicts a procedure by which the transcendental principles are in fact further specified empirically so as to yield the principles of pure natural science and to ground thereby the law of universal gravitation. This procedure results in the very highest concept or species of empirical classification (the empirical concept of matter) and the very highest empirical law (the law of gravitation) which governs all matter as such regardless of all differences among more specific types of matter. And, in this way, the most general framework of empirical natural science is secured. But what about more specific empirical laws governing more specific subspecies of matter – such as the laws of chemistry, for example? As far as the *Metaphysical Foundations* is concerned, all such more specific empirical laws remain entirely unaccounted for, and we are therefore left with no idea how *these* laws are grounded in the transcendental principles. We are left with no idea, that is, how the combination of metaphysical principles and mathematical constructions that (uniquely) determines the law of gravitation can be further extended so as to ground or determine any more specific empirical law.

Indeed, it is for precisely this reason that Kant himself despairs of the properly scientific status of chemistry in the *Metaphysical Foundations:*

So long, therefore, as there is still for chemical actions of matters on one another no concept to be discovered that can be constructed – that is, no law of approach or withdrawal of the parts of matter can be specified according to which, perhaps in proportion to their density and the like, their motions and all the consequences thereof can be made intuitive and presented *a priori* in space (a demand that will only with great difficulty ever be fulfilled) – chemistry can be nothing more than a systematic art or experimental doctrine, but never a proper science. For its principles are merely empirical and allow of no presentation *a priori* in intuition. Consequently, they do not in the least make the principles of chemical appearances conceivable according to their possibility, for they are not susceptible to the application of mathematics.   (4:470)

Thus, the laws of chemistry remain merely empirical (and thus so far merely inductive) so long as we do not yet have a properly grounded mathematical force law analogous to the law of gravitation.

It follows that the empirical laws of chemistry do not yet count as necessary:

Any whole of cognition that is systematic can indeed thereby be called *science*, and, if the connection of cognition in this system is an interconnection of grounds and consequences, even *rational* science. If, however, the grounds or principles themselves are still in the end merely empirical – as, for example, in chemistry – and the laws from which the given facts are explained through reason are mere laws of experience, then such laws or principles carry with them no consciousness of their *necessity* (are not apodictically certain), and thus the whole [of cognition] does not deserve the name of science in the strict sense. – Chemistry should thus be called systematic art rather than science.   (486)

Yet reason requires that *all* empirical science must eventually be brought into connection with pure natural science so as to secure thereby the appropriate kind of necessity (the problem is simply that this has not yet been done for chemistry):

In accordance with demands of reason, every doctrine of nature must finally lead to [pure] natural science and terminate there, because such necessity of laws is inseparably joined to the concept of nature and therefore must certainly be comprehended. Hence, the most complete explanation of given appearances from chemical principles still always leaves behind a certain dissatisfaction, because one can cite no *a priori* grounds for such principles which, as contingent laws, have been learned merely from experience. (469)

It is particularly noteworthy that these passages explicitly deny that *systematic form* alone is sufficient for the required type of necessity: We need, in addition, "*a priori* grounds" analogous to those we have considered in IV and V.

All of this seems to me to be perfectly consistent with Kant's discussion of necessity and contingency in the passage from §5 of the published Introduction to the *Critique of Judgment* cited in II. Kant's point there is that the vast majority of empirical laws have not yet been grounded in the transcendental principles of the understanding. Indeed, since the manifoldness of empirical laws is potentially infinite, we can imagine such a grounding for the *totality* of empirical laws only as the regulative ideal of a complete science we can only continually approach but never fully attain. Hence, from the point of view of our (finite) understanding, most empirical laws must remain contingent, although we nonetheless remain equally aware of the demand of reason for their eventual *a priori* grounding and hence their necessity:

Specifically different matters can still be causes in infinitely manifold ways, besides what they have in common as belonging to nature in general; and every one of these modes must (according to the concept of a cause in general) have its rule – which is a law and therefore carries with it necessity – although, according to the constitution and limitations of our cognitive faculty, we can absolutely not comprehend this necessity. Thus, with respect to its merely empirical laws, we must think in nature the possibility of an infinite manifoldness of empirical laws, which for our insight are yet contingent (cannot be known *a priori*); and, with respect to them, we judge the unity of nature in accordance with empirical laws and the possibility of the unity of experience (as a system according to empirical laws) as contingent. (5:183)

Kant is not, as I read him, here asserting that the necessity of empirical laws depends on reflective judgment rather than on the understanding. Empirical necessity can derive from nowhere else than an *a priori* grounding in the principles of the understanding such as we have attempted to articulate above, and the point of the present passage is simply to emphasize that the vast majority of empirical laws have not yet received *this* kind of grounding. The task of reflective judgment is not somehow to provide a kind of necessity that the understanding itself cannot provide, but rather to systematize the potentially infinite multiplicity of empirical laws under more and more general empirical laws so as to approximate to the *a priori* necessity issuing from the understanding and from the understanding alone.

More precisely, the relationship between the transcendental principles of the understanding and the faculty of reflective judgment is, I think, best understood as follows. The principles of pure natural science – which represent, as it were, the closest possible specification of the transcendental principles – articulate the empirical concept of matter and thereby ground the law of universal gravitation. In this way, the highest concept of empirical classification and the most general empirical law are brought into immediate contact with the principles of the understanding.[36] Yet the vast majority of empirical laws (and thus the overwhelming majority of empirical phenomena) still remain unaccounted for: They have so far received no transcendental grounding whatsoever. The task of reflective judgment is then to furnish methodological principles – of parsimony, continuity, simplicity, and so on[37] – which guide the procedure of organizing lower level empirical concepts (and laws) into a classificatory system. Only when such a classificatory system is ideally completed, so that *all* empirical concepts (and laws) are brought into determinate relation with the highest concept of empirical classification (and thus, in the end, with the principles of the understanding as well), will the totality of empirical laws thereby receive a transcendental grounding. And, although such an ideal complete science will of course never actually be attained, the principle of reflective judgment nonetheless demands that we continually strive to approach it as far as is possible. In this sense, the faculty of reflective judgment operates under the transcendental presupposition that *"nature specifies its universal laws to empirical* [laws], *in accordance with the form of a logical* [classificatory] *system. . . ."*

There is a final complication that is well worth mentioning here. It so happens that the modern foundations of some of the most important of the more empirical branches of natural science – first the quantitative science of heat and later the new physical chemistry of Lavoisier – were just being established during the last third of the eighteenth century. It so happens, furthermore, that Kant himself was following these new developments with ever increasing interest. In particular, it appears that Kant was well acquainted with the key advances in the quantitative science of heat, with Wilhelm Scheele's theory of radiant heat and Joseph Black's theory of latent and specific heats, by the early to middle 1780s.[38] And, what turns out to be even more decisive, Kant was led officially to embrace the new physical chemistry of Lavoisier by the mid-1790s. It is clear, moreover, that, whereas the chemistry to which Kant denies a prop-

erly scientific status in the *Metaphysical Foundations* is the traditional phlogistic chemistry of Georg Stahl, the revolutionary new
theory of Lavoisier led Kant to a fundamental reconsideration of the
status of chemistry.[39] Kant was led thereby, in the *Opus postumum*,
to a reconsideration of the philosophical foundations of natural science (where he contemplates a new chapter of the critical system to
be titled *Transition from the Metaphysical Foundations of Natural
Science to Physics*) and, in the end, to a fundamental reconsideration
of the nature and scope of transcendental philosophy itself. A further
consideration of these matters, however, lies far beyond the scope of
the present discussion.[40]

NOTES

1 All translations from Kant's writings are my own.
2 The problem: "how I am to understand *that, because something is, something else should be!*" is first raised by Kant in his *Attempt to Introduce
   the Concept of Negative Magnitude into Philosophy* of 1763 (2:202). This
   essay is concerned with distinguishing "logical opposition" and "real
   opposition," "logical grounds" from "real grounds." The point is that
   causal connection, for example, cannot be understood as mere logical
   connection, but only as an essentially distinct type of "real" connection.
3 Compare B 5: "the concept of cause itself so obviously contains the
   concept of a necessity of the connection with an effect and a strict
   universality of the rule, that it would be entirely lost if one wanted to
   derive it, as *Hume* did, from a repeated association of that which happens with that which precedes and the custom (and thus the subjective
   necessity) arising therefrom of connecting representations."
4 Compare Kant's characterization of the causal relation in the Second
   Analogy: "In accordance with such a rule, in that which in general
   precedes an event there must lie the conditions for a rule according to
   which this event follows always and necessarily" (A 193 / B 238–9);
   "that which follows or happens must follow according to a universal
   rule from that which was contained in the previous state" (A 200 / B
   245); "in that which precedes the condition is to be met with, under
   which the event always (i.e., necessarily) follows" (A 200 / B 246).
   Clearly, only types or kinds of events can follow one another *always* –
   that is, universally.
5 Compare part II of section IV of Hume's *Enquiry:* "As to past *experience,*
   it can be allowed to give *direct* and *certain* information of those precise
   objects only, and that precise period of time, which fell under its cogni-

zance: but why this experience should be so extended to future times, and to other objects, which, for aught we know, may be only in appearance similar; this is the main question on which I would insist. . . . These two propositions are far from being the same, *I have found that such an object has always been attended with such an effect*, and *I foresee, that other objects, which are, in appearance, similar, will be attended with similar effects.*"

6 Some examples of such rules or laws given by Kant are: at a freezing temperature the liquid state of water is followed by the solid state (B 162–3); the position of a drifting ship higher up in the course of a stream is followed by its position lower down (A 192–3 / B 237–8); in the presence of a hot stove the cool air in a room becomes warm (A 202 / B 247–8); when scooped out from a larger vessel into a narrow glass a horizontal surface of water becomes concave (A 204 / B 249); heat follows the illumination of a stone by the sun (*Prolegomena*: 4:305). I here ignore the complication that not all causes literally precede their effects: What matters here is only that each instance of the causal relation is *associated* with a rule or law of temporal succession.

7 See H. J. Paton, *Kant's Metaphysic of Experience* (New York, 1936); G. Bird, *Kant's Theory of Knowledge* (London, 1962); R. P. Wolff, *Kant's Theory of Mental Activity* (Cambridge, Mass., 1963); L. W. Beck, "Once More into the Breach: Kant's Answer to Hume, Again," *Ratio* 9 (1967): 33–37, reprinted in *Essays on Kant and Hume* (New Haven, Conn., 1978), and "A Prussian Hume and a Scottish Kant," ibid.; W. A. Suchting, "Kant's Second Analogy of Experience," *Kant-Studien* 58 (1967): 355–69; G. Buchdahl, "The Kantian 'Dynamic of Reason' with Special Reference to the Place of Causality in Kant's System," in L. W. Beck, ed., *Kant Studies Today* (LaSalle, Ill., 1969), *Metaphysics and the Philosophy of Science* (Oxford, 1969), and "The Conception of Lawlikeness in Kant's Philosophy of Science," in L. W. Beck, ed., *Kant's Theory of Knowledge* (Dordrecht, 1974); J. Van Cleve, "Four Recent Interpretations of Kant's Second Analogy," *Kant-Studien* 64 (1973): 69–87; G. Brittan, *Kant's Theory of Science* (Princeton, N.J., 1978); H. Allison, *Kant's Transcendental Idealism* (New Haven, Conn., 1983); P. Guyer, *Kant and the Claims of Knowledge* (Cambridge, 1987), and "Kant's Conception of Empirical Law," *Proceedings of the Aristotelian Society, Supplementary Volume* 64 (1990): 221–42. A notable exception to this trend is A. Melnick, *Kant's Analogies of Experience* (Chicago: 1973) – see esp. §18; even Melnick appears to agree, however, that causal laws are established solely on the basis of empirical or inductive evidence.

8 Paton disassociates regularity and repeatibility from the causal principle in vol. 2, ch. 45, §7 of *Kant's Metaphysic of Experience*. Beck, in "Prus-

sian Hume and Scottish Kant," sharply distinguishes the "every-event-some-cause" principle from the "same-cause-same-effect" principle; he argues that while Hume raises doubts concerning both, Kant intends only to vindicate the first in the Transcendental Analytic. However, this interpretation has been articulated most clearly, and in its most explicit and developed form, by Buchdahl; see, in particular, "Dynamic of Reason," V–VII.

9 Note that Kant himself holds, as we have seen, that generalizations supported only inductively cannot qualify as *laws*, strictly speaking, at all; for mere inductive generalizations do not and cannot possess genuine or strict universality. And thus Kant himself explicitly asserts that necessity and genuine or strict universality "belong inseparably together" (B 4). Compare the Preface to the *Metaphysical Foundations of Natural Science:* "the word nature already carries with it the concept of laws, and the latter carries with it the concept of the *necessity* of all determinations of a thing that belong to its existence" (4:468). (I am indebted to Graciela De Pierris for emphasizing the importance of this point to me.)

10 From the second edition transcendental deduction; in the first edition we find a similar separation: "Although we learn many laws through experience, these are nonetheless only particular determinations of yet higher laws, among which the highest (under which all others stand) originate *a priori* in the understanding itself, and are not borrowed from experience but rather provide appearances with their law-governedness, and precisely thereby make experience possible. . . . To be sure, empirical laws as such can in no way derive their origin from pure understanding – no more than the immeasurable manifold of appearances can be adequately comprehended from the pure form of sensibility" (A 126–7).

11 These passages from the two introductions to the *Critique of Judgment* are therefore especially emphasized by Buchdahl as providing clear support for his interpretation of the relationship between the transcendental principle of causality and particular empirical causal laws. For Buchdahl both the existence and the necessity of particular causal laws falls entirely within the province of reflective judgment (or the regulative use of reason). The purely regulative maxims of reflective judgment govern the *search* for particular causal laws – which search has no *a priori* guarantee of success; and the necessity (or "empirical lawlikeness") of particular causal laws depends solely on their place in a *systematic* structure of such laws (namely an empirical scientific theory) – where the existence of this kind of systematic structure is again seen as a purely regulative demand of reason rather than as a constitutive requirement of the understanding. Compare Guyer, "Empirical Law."

12 A. Lovejoy, "On Kant's Reply to Hume," *Archiv für Geschichte der Philosophie* (1906): 380–407, reprinted in M. Gram, ed., *Kant: Disputed Questions* (Chicago, 1967), pp. 284–308 – page references are given parenthetically in the text to this edition.

13 This kind of interpretation has been defended most clearly and explicitly by Buchdahl, and also especially by Beck and Allison. See the references cited in note 7, and also Beck, "Is There a Non Sequitur in Kant's Proof of the Causal Principle?" *Kant-Studien* 67 (1976): 385–9, reprinted (as "A Non Sequitur of Numbing Grossness?") in *Essays on Kant and Hume.* With respect to the principle of uniformity and Lovejoy's objection, see Beck, "Prussian Hume and Scottish Kant," p. 126: "It has often been objected that Kant's Second Analogy does nothing to support the principle same-cause-same-effect [for example, by Lovejoy]. This is true, but it was not Kant's purpose there to support *that* principle; he was concerned only with the principle every-event-some-cause. . . ." Compare Allison's treatment, in which he appears closely to follow Buchdahl's interpretation: *Kant's Transcendental Idealism*, pp. 228–34.

14 See the passages cited in note 4; moreover, it is evident from note 6 that all of Kant's own causal examples involve universal relations between types or kinds of events.

15 Thus, Kant clearly asserts that objective succession of events is determinate or irreversible *and* that this kind of determinacy essentially involves general laws or uniformities in virtue of which the succeeding event always or invariably follows in relevantly similar cases. It is no wonder, then, that this is the very passage where Lovejoy purports to find his "spectacular" non sequitur: see "On Kant's Reply to Hume," p. 303.

16 Compare the continuation of A 127 cited in note 10: "Yet all empirical laws are only particular determinations of the pure laws of the understanding, under which and in accordance with the norm of which they first become possible, and the appearances take on a lawful form – just as all appearances, notwithstanding the manifoldness of their empirical form, nonetheless also must always be in accordance with the condition of the pure form of sensibility" (A 127–8). The problem, of course, is to understand precisely what "particular determinations" means here.

17 Note also that in the passage at B 165 cited in II Kant says: "Particular laws, because they concern empirically determined appearances, can *not be completely derived* [from the transcendental principles], although they one and all stand under them" – and he thus suggests that particular empirical laws are somehow *partially* so "derived." For a different perspective, compare Buchdahl's discussion of B 165 and A 159 / B 198: "Dynamic of Reason," pp. 355–60.

18 Compare the footnote to §20 at 301. Buchdahl and Guyer are almost alone among recent commentators in explicitly recognizing that empirical laws, for Kant, are somehow both necessary and contingent. Both insist, however, that necessity pertains to empirical laws solely in virtue of reason or reflective judgment; as far as the understanding is concerned, such laws are entirely inductive and contingent. For Buchdahl see "Dynamic of Reason," pp. 340–6, 365–6; for Guyer see "Empirical Law" and also *Claims of Knowledge*, p. 241 (including footnote 7 thereto on p. 447).

19 Note that in the passage from B 3–4 cited in II in the present essay Kant distinguishes two types of *a priori* judgments: such that are "thought simultaneously with [their] necessity," and such that are "derived from no judgment except that which itself, in turn, is valid as a necessary proposition" and are therefore "absolutely *a priori*." Empirical laws, since they are *partially* derived from purely contingent observations of regularity, then satisfy the first characterization but not the second. See also Kant's remarks in the following paragraph, which again suggest that even empirical rules need to be grounded in principles valid "absolutely *a priori*."

20 Buchdahl remarks upon *R* 5414, although from a completely different point of view, on p. 130 of "The Conception of Lawlikeness."

21 Section 38 of the *Prolegomena* also presents serious difficulties of interpretation, which are discussed in M. Friedman, "Kant on Space, the Understanding, and the Law of Gravitation: *Prolegomena* §38," *The Monist* 72 (1989): 236–84.

22 Compare Kant's observations on the table of categories in §11 (added to the second edition of the *Critique*) at B 110, together with the footnote thereto referring to the *Metaphysical Foundations*.

23 Compare the discussion of the synthetic *a priori* principles of pure natural science at B 17–18, B 20 n, and §15 of the *Prolegomena*. The relationship between these "metaphysical" principles and the transcendental principles of the understanding is further discussed in the next section of this essay.

24 Thus, for example, it is only after establishing the center of mass frame of the solar system in Proposition XI of Book III that Newton can settle the issue of heliocentrism in Proposition XII. Compare Kant's remarks on this at B xxii n.

25 For an attempt to articulate in detail this reading of the Phenomenology of the *Metaphysical Foundations*, see M. Friedman, "The Metaphysical Foundations of Newtonian Science," in R. Butts, ed., *Kant's Philosophy of Physical Science* (Dordrecht, 1986), pp. 25–60, "*Prolegomena* §38," and "Kant and Newton: Why Gravity Is Essential to Matter," in P.

Bricker and R. Hughes, eds., *Philosophical Perspectives on Newtonian Science* (Cambridge, Mass., 1990).

26 For further discussion of the crucial importance of these two additional assumptions of *universality* and *immediacy*, see the references cited in note 25.

27 A delicate issue arises here, for we can also now show that the relative motions of stage one *cannot* be exactly true: Kepler's laws fail due to the planetary perturbations. Yet this does not compromise the strictly deductive character of the foregoing argument, I think. For first, what is derived at stage 2 is the *existence* of an inverse-square force directed toward the center of each primary body – and this remains exactly true at stage 3 as well; and second, we infer the properties of this force from the statement that satellites approximately obey Kepler's laws *and would exactly obey them if the force in question were the only force acting –* and this statement also remains exactly true at stage 3 (where we show that the deviations from Kepler's laws result *entirely* from the perturbing gravitational forces due to the other primary bodies in the system).

28 This instantiation yields, in particular, *a priori* arguments (Kant's Propositions 7 and 8 of the second chapter or Dynamics) for the two crucial assumptions of *universality* and *immediacy* required in the third or final stage of the Newtonian argument. For further discussion see the references cited in note 25. Again, the relationship between the transcendental principles and the more specific metaphysical principles will be further discussed in the next section of this essay.

29 There are many more such fragments in the *Opus postumum:* For further citations and discussion, see M. Friedman, "Transition from the Metaphysical Foundations of Natural Science to Physics," in *Kant and the Exact Sciences* (Cambridge, Mass.: 1992).

30 For further discussion of this notion of "empirical" or "material" necessity, also in the context of Kant's perspective on the Newtonian argument for universal gravitation, see W. Harper, "Kant on the A Priori and Material Necessity," in Butts, ed., *Kant's Philosophy of Physical Science*, pp. 239–72.

31 Allison argues that "the occupation of space or spatiality" necessarily belongs to the transcendental concept of substance – *Kant's Transcendental Idealism*, pp. 210–12; I cannot endorse everything he there says about the relation of the transcendental concept of substance to that of the *Metaphysical Foundations*, however.

32 Kemp Smith comments on this *Reflexion* on p. 361 of his *Commentary to Kant's 'Critique of Pure Reason'* (London, 1923).

33 Compare the "Refutation of Mendelssohn's Proof of the Permanence of the Soul" at B 413–15. Kant makes the same point in a marginal note to

A 183: "In the soul there is no quantum of substance possible. Therefore also nothing which one could determine through any predicate and call permanent" (R LXXXIV, 23:31).

34 Kant goes on to insist, of course, that this thinkable realization of the relational categories is in no way *really possible*, for any such particular realization must occur via *empirical* concepts whose "possibility must either be known *a posteriori* or empirically or it absolutely cannot be known at all" (A 222 / B 270). Nevertheless, this kind of nonactual but thinkable realization of the categories is still consistent with the *formal* conditions of intuition and thought – and is thus *so far* possible. Compare the discussion in the Amphiboly at A 290–2 / B 347–9.

35 For the contrast between *occupying* space [*einen Raum einnehmen*] and *filling* space [*einen Raum erfüllen*], see the Observation to the first Definition of the Dynamics of the *Metaphysical Foundations* at 4:497. The property of occupying a space belongs to all spatial or extended things as such (even to mere geometrical figures). The property of filling a space, on the other hand, belongs only to the impenetrability of matter and leads, in Proposition 1 immediately following, to the fundamental force of repulsion.

36 I do not intend to deny that the faculty of reflective judgment plays an essential role here as well; on the contrary, I assume that reflective judgment is necessarily presupposed in any process of empirical concept-formation whatsoever – including the formation of the empirical concept of matter itself. Indeed, Kant himself suggests a necessary role for (the regulative use of) reason in the genesis of the theory of gravitation at A 662–3 / B 690–1. A fuller discussion of this important matter will have to wait for another occasion however.

37 See the list of "maxims of the faculty of judgment" in section 5 of the published Introduction to the *Critique of Judgment* at 5:182, and compare the discussion of maxims of the regulative use of reason at A 652–63 / B 680–91,

38 Scheele's *Chemische Abhandlung von der Luft und dem Feuer* appeared in 1777. Black's work was done in 1757–64, but remained unpublished until 1803; Kant probably learned of it via A. Crawford's *Experiments and Observations on Animal Heat*, published in 1779 and reported to the continent by J. H. Magellan in 1780. (For an attempt to document Kant's evolving awareness of these developments, see Friedman, "Transition," III.) It seems to me to be quite likely that these advances in the quantitative science of heat constitute the immediate background to many of Kant's favorite examples of causal laws from the critical period, including the illuminated stone of the *Prolegomena*: compare note 6 above (as Paton points out – *Kant's Metaphysic of Experience* p. 284, n. 2 – the example

of the concave surface of water in a glass from A 204 / B 249 is derived from experiments of J. A. Segner in 1751 on surface-tension that constituted an early contribution to the theory of capillarity).

39 It is clear from the Preface to the second (1787) edition of the first *Critique* at B xii–xiii, and also from the chemical examples discussed in the Appendix to the Transcendental Dialectic at A 645–6 / B 673–4 and A 652–3 / B 680–1, that Kant still held to Stahlian chemistry in the critical period. Lavoisier's *Traité élémentair de chimie* appeared in 1789 and was translated into German in 1792; an important German textbook by C. Girtanner also appeared in 1792. Although Kant officially endorses Lavoisier in print only in 1797, it appears from his correspondence that this endorsement actually occurred by 1795 at the latest. (Again, for further discussion and documentation, see Friedman, "Transition.")

40 For an examination of the *Transition* project of the *Opus postumum* in light of Kant's evolving knowledge of the chemical revolution – and, in particular, in the context of Kant's heroic attempt to harmonize these new developments with the essentially Newtonian model of the foundations of natural science of the critical period – see Friedman, "Transition."

6 Empirical, rational, and transcendental psychology: Psychology as science and as philosophy

Although Kant never developed a theoretical psychology of his own, he discussed psychological topics throughout his life. These discussions ranged from early, brief remarks on mind–body interaction in the *True Estimation of Living Forces* (§§5–6, 1:20–1) of 1747 to the relatively late, extended treatment of the faculties of cognition in the *Anthropology*, published from Kant's lecture notes under his supervision in 1797.[1] In his lectures on metaphysics, from the 1760s onward, he followed common practice and regularly discussed what he and his contemporaries called "empirical" and "rational" psychology (records of these lectures survive through student notes: 28:59–122, 221–301, 583–94, 670–90, 735–75, 849–74, 886–906). And in the preface to his *Metaphysical Foundations of Natural Science* (1786) he examined the question of whether empirical psychology could ever achieve a scientific status like that of physics, notoriously answering that it could not (4:471). For our purposes, however, the central problems pertaining to Kant's relation to psychology arise in the *Critique of Pure Reason*. In the *Critique* Kant distinguished his philosophical aim from that of empirical psychology. He also investigated the possibility of empirical and especially of rational psychology. In addition, and problematically, he adopted, even in the avowedly philosophical portions of the work, an implicitly psychological vocabulary. Because of his extensive use of this vocabulary, interpreters have, from the instant of the *Critique's* publication, disputed the extent to which Kant rested his arguments on psychological ground.[2]

Efforts to determine Kant's explicit and implicit relation to psychology face two problems. The first owes to the fact that in Kant's time psychology was not an established science with an accepted

200

body of doctrine; it was a science in the making, and its creators disagreed over how it should be made. Many authors, including Christian Wolff and his followers, treated psychology as the rational and empirical study of an immaterial, substantial soul; Kant began with this conception, but he ultimately supported a conception of psychology as a natural science, according to which all mental phenomena are subject to natural law.[3] The problem, then, is that of distinguishing instances in which Kant uses the term "psychology" according to his own definition from those in which he follows the usage of his contemporaries. The second problem is that of determining whether the *Critique* contains its own "transcendental psychology" divorced from empirical and rational psychology, and if it does, whether this is a merit or a demerit. Interpreters of Kant are divided over both questions. Those who judge the presence of psychology to be a demerit tend to deemphasize the psychological discussions in the *Critique*; others, however, are happy to find a full-blown empirical psychology in that work. Although this is not the place for a full review of psychological interpretations of Kant or an assessment of what has been called "psychologism," it is fitting to investigate Kant's reasons for distinguishing his transcendental philosophy from empirical (and rational) psychology, and to examine how he used psychological vocabulary in his philosophical work.

I organize the psychological topics of the first *Critique* under four headings: the refutation of traditional rational psychology as given in the Paralogisms; the contrast between traditional empirical psychology and the transcendental philosophy of the Deduction; Kant's appeal to an implicit psychology in his taxonomy and theory of cognitive faculties throughout the *Critique*; and his new definitions of and support for empirical and rational psychology in the Doctrine of Method.

I. REFUTATION OF RATIONAL PSYCHOLOGY

Kant's vigorous attack on traditional rational psychology in the Paralogisms of Pure Reason constitutes his most extensive explicit discussion of psychology in the *Critique*.[4] Kant defined rational psychology, or the "rational doctrine of the soul" (*rationale Seelenlehre*), as the science of the object of inner sense, or the "I": "the expression 'I', as a thinking being, indeed signifies the object of that psychology which may be entitled the 'rational doctrine of the soul', provided I seek to learn nothing more of the soul than what can be inferred independently of all experience (which determines me more specifically and *in concreto*) from this concept 'I', so far as it is found in all thought" (A 342 / B 400). As he succinctly put it, "I think" is "the sole text of rational psychology, from which the whole of its teaching must be developed" (A 343 / B 401). Kant dismissed the objection that the assertion 'I think', being based on inner experience, is itself empirical, contending that it abstracts from any specific object of perception, and so is not "empirical knowledge," but rather "knowledge of the empirical in general" (ibid.). As portrayed by Kant, rational psychology first applies the metaphysical concept of substance to its text, and then argues from the substantiality of the soul to its immateriality, from its simplicity to its incorruptibility, from its identity through time to continuity of personhood, and thence to the soul's spirituality and immortality (A 345 / B 403).

The only name Kant mentions in connection with rational psychology in either version of the Paralogisms is Moses Mendelssohn's. In the B version of the Paralogisms Kant credits Mendelssohn for raising and removing an objection to the traditional argument for the soul's immortality. According to the traditional argument, the soul, being simple, cannot cease to exist as bodies do, through the separation of its parts; Mendelssohn added a further argument to block the objection that a simple being might cease to exist simply by vanishing (B 413–14).[5] The unembellished argument from simplicity to incorruptibility and immortality had been common fare in previous rational psychology (as Kant well knew); indeed, such arguments belonged to its special province. Thus Wolff, in his *Psychologia empirica* (1st ed., 1732), argued from the empirical fact of consciousness to the conclusion that the soul exists (§§11–21). But he reserved for his *Psychologia rationalis* (1st ed., 1734) demonstrations that "body cannot think" because it cannot represent (§44), and that "the soul cannot be material" (§47); from these conclusions he further argued that "the soul is a simple substance" (using as a premise that it cannot communicate with – induce motion in – body, §46). His assertion of the soul's simplicity, along with an elaboration of the requisites for the continuity of one's personhood (cf. A 361–5), figured prominently in his alleged proof of the soul's immortality (§§729–47).[6] Similarly, Wolff's disciple Alexander Baumgarten argued in his *Metaphysica*

(1st ed., 1739) that, because the human soul is characterized by a single power, the power of representation (§744), it must be simple; from this conclusion he further reasoned that it "has no quantitative magnitude," and therefore that "the physical corruption of the human soul is intrinsically impossible (§§15, 705); i.e., the human soul is absolutely physically incorruptible" (§746). The latter conclusion figured crucially as a premise in his demonstration of the soul's immortality (§781).[7] Such arguments were not original with Wolff (earlier versions had been discussed by Descartes and Leibniz), nor were they limited in Kant's time to Wolff's followers (or to Mendelssohn): Christian Crusius in his *Entwurf der nothwendigen Vernunft-Wahrheiten* (1745), a work whose subject was limited to *a priori* metaphysics, including "metaphysical pneumatology" (or rational psychology), argued from the premise that the soul is a simple substance to the conclusion that it is incorruptible (§§473–4).[8]

Kant sought to expose the illegitimacy of these traditional arguments by showing that they exceed the bounds of possible experience and hence advance claims that transcend the domain of possible metaphysical knowledge. Thus, in the A version of the Paralogisms he begins his examination of the arguments of rational psychology with the following reminder, to which he repeatedly refers: "In the analytical part of the Transcendental Logic we have shown that pure categories, and among them that of substance, have in themselves no objective meaning, unless they rest on an intuition and can be applied to the manifold of this intuition as functions of synthetic unity" (A 348–9). He goes on to argue that although the "I" is the *logical* subject of all our thoughts, it cannot be regarded as a substance because it cannot be given in intuition; the pure category of substance can be properly applied only to objects that can be given in experience, that is, to objects of possible experience (A 349–50). Similarly, the claim of rational psychology, that the soul is simple, may be granted with respect to the "I" as the formal unity of thought (that is, as the formal concept of the unity of representations in a single subject), but this formal concept cannot be made to yield the conclusion that the soul is a simple substance (A 351–6). For, Kant contends, the logical unity of the "I" does not lead analytically to its substantial simplicity: The unified self might, for all we know, arise "from a collective unity of different substances acting together" (A 353 – though presumably not from mere organized matter, B 419–20); the claim of rational psychology that the unity of thought arises from a simple substance is synthetic. For the purposes of rational psychology it would not do to base this synthetic proposition in experience, for experience cannot ground the necessity that rational psychology, as a science of reason, demands. In any case, the simple substance supposed to be the substratum of thought lies outside experience, as its putative substratum. For the latter reason, the proposition that the soul is simple could not be synthetic and *a priori*, given the earlier reminder that synthetic *a priori* knowledge is limited by the requirement that the categories must be applied to intuition, that is, to objects of possible experience (A 353). As Kant explains, the rational psychologist confuses the unity of the "I" as a formal condition of thought with the supposed ontological simplicity of the soul as a substance (A 354–5). Kant repeats these arguments in abbreviated form in B. (Of course, there are important differences between the two versions of the Paralogisms on other matters.)

In the end, Kant contended that although traditional rational psychology has no doctrine to teach, once criticized it can play two roles in the Critical Philosophy: It can serve to *discipline* the impulses of speculative reason by reminding us that both materialism and spiritualism are unfounded metaphysically (B 421; see also A 379, 383); and its idea of the soul as simple can serve a regulative function in the investigation of inner experience (A 672 / B 700).

II. THE DEDUCTION: TRANSCENDENTAL PHILOSOPHY VS. EMPIRICAL PSYCHOLOGY

In the Transcendental Deduction Kant sought to establish the existence and objective validity of the categories (see Chapter 4 of this book). His arguments for these conclusions were not psychological, or so he claimed. In stark contrast with the most noteworthy of his eighteenth-century predecessors and contemporaries, Kant denied that empirical psychology was of use in answering philosophical questions about what he termed the "origin" and "validity" of cognitive claims. Although in neither version of the Deduction does he discuss empirical psychology in depth, in both he clearly distinguishes the aims and methods of transcendental philosophy from those of empirical psychology.[9]

The belief that the empirical study of the mind can importantly inform investigations of the characteristics and limitations of human cognition was widely shared by Kant's contemporaries, even when these contemporaries disagreed on other fundamental matters. David Hume is the most familiar of the authors who advocated using, as he termed it, a "science of human nature" to ground explanations of human cognition. Having marshaled skeptical arguments against the view that human reason can ground assertions of matters of fact that go beyond current evidence, he turned to empirically based associationistic psychology in order to explain human tendencies to form beliefs, and proceeded to reduce the principles governing belief-formation about matters of fact to three laws of association.[10] Moreover, the very Wolff who adopted a modified Leibnizian ontology of the soul as a spiritual substance nevertheless contended that empirical psychology is more fundamental than rational psychology in establishing doctrines about human cognition. He advocated taking an empirical approach toward the fundamental cognitive powers of the soul, and even toward the principles of logic.[11] Later, Johann Tetens undertook to investigate the "human understanding" using the method of "observation," a method he credited to Locke and to recent "psychologists" working toward an empirical theory of the soul (*Erfahrungs-Seelenlehre*).[12] By contrast, Crusius stands out among Kant's immediate predecessors because he denied that empirical psychology was relevant to his philosophical investigation of human reason; he argued that his investigation was metaphysical, that metaphysics seeks propositions known with absolute necessity, and that consequently it must proceed in an *a priori* manner (*Entwurf*, §459; cf. *Pure Reason*, A 848 / B 876).

Kant explicitly sets the project of the Deduction apart from empirical psychology at the beginning of his discussion. He acknowledges that empirical study might be of use in determining the "occasioning causes" by which the pure categories and forms of intuition are "first brought into action," and he credits Locke with performing the service of showing that they arise only with experience. He continues, however, by explaining that because a deduction of the categories must justify their *a priori* applicability (that is, their applicability independent of experience), the Deduction itself cannot use principles drawn from experience:

A *deduction* of the pure *a priori* concepts can never be obtained in this manner; it does not lie anywhere along this path, for in view of their subsequent employment, which must be entirely independent of experience, the pure concepts must be in a position to show a certificate of birth quite other than that of descent from experiences. This attempted physiological derivation, which cannot properly be called a deduction because it concerns a *quaestio facti*, I shall therefore entitle the explanation of the possession of pure cognition. It is therefore clear that the only deduction that can be given of the pure concepts is one that is transcendental, not empirical, and that the latter type of deduction, in respect to pure *a priori* concepts, is nothing but an idle pursuit, which could occupy only those who have failed to grasp the completely peculiar nature of these modes of cognition. (A 86–7 / B 119)

At first blush this passage may not seem pertinent to empirical psychology; it contrasts a transcendental deduction with an empirical or *physiological* explanation. But Kant here, as elsewhere, employs the term "physiology" to mean the "science of nature" in general; in accordance with this usage, he equates empirical psychology with the "physiology of inner sense" (A 347 / B 405). Kant several times reiterates the point that the empirical laws of inner sense – that is, the laws of empirical psychology – cannot serve to ground the Deduction (or its subarguments). At two places in the A Deduction he argues that the "laws of association," which are merely empirical laws, cannot provide the needed account of the necessary synthetic unity of apperception (A 100, 121). In the B Deduction he makes a similar point in distinguishing the empirical unity of consciousness, based on association, from "original" unity of consciousness, by stressing the contingency of the empirically based unity and thus its unsuitability for explaining the necessity and universality of the original or "objective" unity of consciousness (B 139–40). In the B Deduction he also distinguishes the transcendental synthesis of the imagination, which he ascribes to the "productive" imagination, from the synthesis produced by the "reproductive" imagination under the aegis of the empirical laws of association; the former, which concerns the *a priori* grounds for the applicability of the categories to sensibility (and hence to all objects of possible experience), he ascribes to transcendental philosophy, and the latter to the field of psychology (B 152).

Kant believed that empirical psychology, owing to its empirical status, could not serve as the basis for his deduction of the categories.

So much is clear. But it may also be that, independently of this problem, Kant found the distinctive content of empirical psychology – its mode of conceptualizing mental processes – to be conceptually incapable of serving the purposes of the Deduction. Although he did not explicitly distinguish the problem of the empirical status of empirical psychology from the problem of its conceptual inadequacy, it will be useful for us to distinguish and develop both problems.

Kant held that a deduction serves to answer what he, in accordance with the juridical terminology of his day, called the "question of right" (*quid juris*) as opposed to the "question of fact" (*quid facti*).[13] In a legal case, the question of fact asks, for example, who has possession of a piece of property, while the question of right demands the grounds for legal title to it. In the Deduction, the "right" under dispute pertains to the propriety of applying the categories in an *a priori* manner. As Kant puts it: "among the various concepts which form the highly complicated web of human knowledge, there are some that are destined for pure *a priori* employment (completely independent of all experience), and their right to be so employed always demands a deduction; because proofs from experience do not suffice to legitimize this kind of employment, we are faced with the problem of how these concepts can relate to objects that they do not derive from any experience" (A 85 / B 117). From this passage, the insufficiency of empirical proofs for establishing the *a priori* applicability of the categories may seem quite straightforward: What is demanded is justification for applying the categories independently of experience – ipso facto, empirical considerations, which essentially include an appeal to experience, cannot meet this demand.

But as these very passages, and indeed the subsequent development of the Deduction, make clear, Kant's reason for banishing empirical proofs and hence empirical psychology from the deduction of the categories is not merely that they are empirical and hence do not pertain to the *a priori*; it is rather that because they are empirical they cannot meet the standards of justification demanded by the Deduction. For what needs to be established is the *objective validity* of any *a priori* employment of the categories (A 89 / B 122), as well as the necessity and universal validity of principles derived from the categories, such as the law of cause (A 90–2 / B 122–4; A 766–7 / B 794–5). But as Kant remarks in the Introduction, "experience never confers on its judgments true or strict, but only assumed and comparative universality, through induction, so that properly one can only say: So far as we have observed up to now, there is no exception to this or that rule. If, then, a judgment is thought with strict universality, that is, so that no exception whatsoever is allowed as possible, it is not drawn from experience, but is valid absolutely *a priori*" (B 3–4). The same holds for necessity (B 3; see also A 91 / B 124). Consequently no empirical investigation, and hence no finding of empirical psychology, could support the claim that the categories have necessary and universal validity. As Kant further observes, it is for this reason that empirical laws of association, which govern the connections among representations, cannot serve to explain the necessary connectability of representations, or what Kant calls the synthetic unity of apperception (A 100, 121; B 151–2).

Kant does not make explicit the second of the aforementioned reasons that empirical psychology cannot serve the needs of the Deduction (namely conceptual inadequacy), but it lies implicit in his division between questions of fact and questions of right. Kant considered empirical psychology to be a branch of natural science, the branch that investigates the laws of inner sense – that is, the laws that govern the sequence of representations present to the mind. The only laws of empirical psychology Kant explicitly mentions are the laws of association. In the Deduction his only explicit criticism of these laws is that they are empirical and hence cannot explain the possibility of necessary judgments. But even if the laws could be established universally and necessarily Kant would still reject them from the Deduction, for such laws could do no more than describe the sequence of representations in inner sense in terms of mere causal sequences. The laws of association are couched in the language of natural law, which is a language of factual relations. But the Deduction requires an argument cast in the language of right or entitlement, for it aims to show that the application of the categories to all possible experience is justified. A natural law showing that the categories apply necessarily to all possible experience would not show this application to be justified, any more than in Kant's moral theory a universal and necessary natural law that caused one to act in accordance with the moral law, and did so independently of one's grasp of the moral law, would make one's actions moral.

The reasons Kant gives for rejecting empirical considerations from moral theory interestingly parallel the two sorts of considerations given here for rejecting empirical psychology from the Deduction. In both the first and second *Critiques* Kant at first rejects practical principles of action based on desire or inclination merely on the grounds that they are empirical and hence unable to serve in a true science of morality possessed of necessity, observing that such a science must be established *a priori* (*Pure Reason*, A 54–5 / B 79; *Practical Reason*, 5:21–2). But in fact, he also held that even if the laws of desire could be known to hold universally and necessarily they still would not provide a suitable basis for morality, for their content would be "physical" rather than moral (*Practical Reason*, 5:26) and they would be unable to specify what ought to be done, being limited to what necessarily and universally is done (A 549–50 / B 577–8). Similarly, a universal and necessary law of association would merely show that all representations *are* connected according to a rule, but it would not justify the objective validity of the law of cause, for that would require showing that the mind *is entitled* to require that all representations be so connected. Perhaps because, in his view, the principles of desire and the laws of association could be rejected on the grounds that they are empirical and hence lack necessity, Kant devoted little attention to showing that as laws of nature they could not in any case yield a moral law or answer the question of epistemic right. Nonetheless, it is reasonable to conclude that in each case even if the laws were necessary, they could not speak to the matters in question.

III. THE FIRST *CRITIQUE:* AN EXERCISE IN TRANSCENDENTAL PSYCHOLOGY?

Although Kant himself was clear in denying the possibility of traditional rational psychology and in expounding the irrelevance of empirical psychology to his project in the first *Critique*, there have been readers of this work, from the time of its publication down to the present, who have contended that it is primarily a work in psychology. Assessments of the precise character of this psychology have varied, as have judgments about its propriety for Kant's purposes. Some have held the psychology to be empirical in spite of Kant's protests, others have suggested that the psychology purports to be noumenal, while still others have assigned it its own transcendental status. Further, some have contended that it was proper for Kant to ground his work in empirical psychology, even though he did not recognize this fact, while others have found Kant's (alleged) use of psychological concepts in the Aesthetic and Deduction to reveal a deep-seated conceptual confusion, a confusion ultimately labeled "psychologism." Finally, those who judge the psychology to be noumenal object that it violates Kant's prohibition of claims to know the noumenal self.[14]

Evidence that Kant engaged in psychology has not seemed difficult to find. For beyond the few passages of the Paralogisms and the Deduction canvassed in our investigation of Kant's negative claims about psychology, both the Aesthetic and Deduction liberally invoke terms and concepts that seem prima facie equivalent to those used in the empirical and rational psychology of his contemporaries. Thus, he distinguishes between "inner" and "outer sense" as two sources of knowledge (A 22 / B 37), thereby seemingly subscribing to the scholastic distinction, adopted by Baumgarten, between external senses such as touch and vision and an internal sense directed toward states of the mind itself. The Aesthetic and Analytic posit a division of the cognitive faculties into sensibility, imagination, understanding, judgment, and reason, thereby echoing similar divisions in scholastic and Wolffian psychology.[15] Further, having asserted that geometry must be based on *a priori* intuition, and in connection with his own distinction between the "form" and "matter" of intuition, Kants asks: "How, then, can there be inherent in the mind an outer intuition, which precedes the objects themselves, and in which the concept of these objects can be determined *a priori?*", a question that seems to require that an innate causal sensory mechanism be specified, such as seems in fact to be posited by Kant's answer to the question: "Manifestly, not otherwise than insofar as the intuition has its seat in the subject only, as the formal disposition of the subject to be affected by objects, and thereby to obtain *immediate representation*, that is, *intuition*, of them; therefore only as the form of outer *sense* in general" (B 41). In the Deduction Kant introduces premises that ascribe a special activity to imagination and understanding, that of synthesis, and he writes as if this activity were a causal process in the mind: "By *synthesis*, in its most general meaning, I understand the act of putting different representations together, and of grasping their multiplicity in one cognition"

(A 77 / B 103). Of course, he places great weight on the requirement that representations be connectable through a synthesis, which he expresses as the demand for a unity of apperception.

At one point Kant claims to have direct knowledge, seemingly through introspection, of the self as the subject of the synthetic activities underlying the unity of apperception. In a discussion of the Third Antinomy, he asserts:

Man, however, who knows all the rest of nature solely through the senses, knows himself also through pure apperception, and indeed in acts and inner determinations that he cannot reckon among the impressions of the senses. He is thus to himself, on the one hand phenomenon, and on the other hand however, in respect of certain faculties, a purely intelligible object, because the acts of these faculties can in no way be classed with the receptivity of sensibility. We entitle these faculties understanding and reason. . . .

(A 546–7 / B 574–5)

However problematically and atypically, Kant here asserts outright that he knows himself as a purely intelligible object. More typically, he maintains that the only knowledge we have of ourselves is empirical; yet even in making this point he nonetheless allows that we have "consciousness" of the self as the locus of the synthesizing activity:

in the transcendental synthesis of the manifold of representations in general, and therefore in the synthetic original unity of apperception, I am conscious of myself, not as I appear to myself, nor as I am in myself, but only *that* I am. This *representation* is a *thought*, not an *intuition*. Now in order to *know* ourselves, there is required in addition to the act of thought, which brings the manifold of every possible intuition to the unity of apperception, a determinate mode of intuition whereby this manifold is given. . . . The consciousness of one's self is thus far from being a cognition of one's self. . . .   (B 157–8)

Even here, Kant is willing to assert that "I exist as an intelligence which is conscious solely of its power of combination" (B 158), an assertion it would be difficult to justify except by appeal to consciousness of the self as synthesizer. Additional passages in which Kant seems to ground his assertions in a sort of reflective introspection are not difficult to find, as when he begins the Introduction to the second edition of the *Critique* with the remark that "long practice has made us attentive to and skilled at separating" the elements of cognition that "our own faculty of cognition" adds to the "raw material" provided by the senses; that is, by long practice we can become skilled at separating pure from empirical cognition (B 1–2).

The central arguments of the *Critique* exhibit, then, at least four seemingly psychological features: (1) the division of the mind into cognitive faculties (inner and outer sense, imagination, understanding, judgment, and reason); (2) the positing of apparently innate mental structures, such as the forms of intuition or the categories; (3) the appeal to mental activities such as synthesis in explaining the conditions on the possibility of experience, and hence in "deducing" the validity of the categories; and (4) the apparent appeal to introspection in establishing the existence of the synthesizing activity of apperception, and in making other distinctions, such as that between empirical and pure cognition. We need to consider whether some or all of these instances are correctly classified as psychological, and what would follow if they are.

Let us consider points (3) and (4) in tandem. On one construal of these points, Kant becomes subject to the charge that in describing the synthetic activity of understanding, he purports to describe the noumenal activity of the self, thereby violating his own stated prescription against claims to know noumena; he also becomes guilty of describing such activity on the basis of experience, in violation of his assertion that noumena lay beyond the pale of experience. In fact I have found only one passage in which Kant claims to have *knowledge* of the self as an intelligible object (the one already quoted). It is plausible to suppose that in discussing the Third Antinomy, with its assertion that we can "think" the noumenal self, Kant in a momentary lapse overstepped his bounds and claimed that this thinking of the noumenal self amounts to "knowing" it as an intelligible object. But even if, as here suggested, one discounts the noumenal reading of synthesis, that would not remove all difficulty. For it is clear that Kant distinguishes the transcendental synthesis entailed by the unity of apperception from the merely empirical synthesis known through inner sense and hence available as phenomenon. Indeed, the transcendental synthesis presumably could not be phenomenal, for it is the process by which the phenomena of inner sense are first constituted. But if the transcendental synthesis is neither phenomenal nor noumenal, what is its status?

One way of answering this question is to assign the transcendental synthesis, and indeed the forms of intuition and the categories, their own "transcendental" status, making them neither objects of inner sense (and empirical psychology) nor noumenal processes (and objects of rational psychology). Such a strategy of course requires determining how, precisely, a "transcendental" process should be conceived. We may further consider the possibility that the forms of intuition and the categories (from item 2) are themselves neither objects of empirical psychology nor features of the noumenal self, and ask whether they, along with the attendant division of the faculties (as in item 1), should also be assigned a transcendental status.

How might one decide whether items (1)–(4) constitute a transcendental psychology, or indeed a psychology of any kind? One way to determine whether something is psychological is to delimit a domain of subject-matter as psychological and to consider whether the target items belong to that domain. At the time of Kant the domain of psychology was denominated in various ways. Some took its subject-matter to be soul (considered as a simple substance), while others took its object to be mental phenomena, or those phenomena available to "inner sense." In either case, the considerations previously reviewed disqualify transcendental psychology from membership in the domain of psychology proper. The subject-matter of Kant's transcendental investigation is epistemic. In investigating the cognitive faculties, the forms of intuition, the categories, and the transcendental synthesis Kant is seeking conditions for knowledge; his investigation is directed neither at the soul as a simple substance nor at the phenomena of inner sense. It remains to be considered whether in carrying out this investigation he was forced to rely on psychology.

Kant stresses the epistemic character of his investigation in an oft-quoted passage from the Preface to the first edition. He observes that his search for the "rules and limits" of the understanding has both an objective and a subjective side.

The one refers to the objects of pure understanding, and is intended to demonstrate and render comprehensible the objective validity of its *a priori* concepts; just for that reason it is also essential to my purposes. The other seeks to investigate the pure understanding itself, its possibility and the cognitive faculties upon which it rests, and so examines it in its subjective aspect; although this latter exposition is of great importance for my chief purpose, it is not essential to it. For the chief question always remains: What and how much can the understanding and reason know apart from all experience? and not: How is the faculty of thought itself possible?

(A xvi–xvii)

Here Kant distinguishes the investigation of "cognitive faculties" and of "the faculty of thought itself" from the explication of the objective validity of knowledge claims, and particularly (as becomes clear) of claims to synthetic *a priori* knowledge.

Despite Kant's own clear statement that his enterprise is aimed at determining conditions and constraints on knowledge, he obviously did refer to the "subjective" side of the investigation quite regularly, as evidenced by our items (1)–(4). So even if the cognitive subject-matter Kant considers is epistemic as opposed to psychological, perhaps he nonetheless relied on psychological concepts and modes of explanation in constructing his exposition, or explanation, of the possibility of synthetic *a priori* knowledge.

One way to determine whether his explanations are psychological is to consider whether he appeals to psychological argumentation when introducing such concepts as that of a form of intuition or a category. Does he appeal to the data of inner sense? Does he invoke a ready-made psychological theory? The answer, I think, is that however much he may have been indebted to suggestions from psychological theory in his own understanding of the concepts he introduced, his arguments for introducing them were not psychological but transcendental. Although it is notoriously difficult to state the essence of such arguments, it is clear how the arguments proceeded in practice. Kant argued by elimination from a set list of candidate explanations of the possibility of a given cognitive achievement; by considering whether each of the explanations was adequate to the task of explaining this achievement, he arrived at the conclusion that only one such explanation was. By way of example, consider his argument from the second edition version of the Aesthetic for introducing space as a form of sensibility:

Geometry is a science that determines the properties of space synthetically and yet *a priori*. What, then, must the representation of space be, in order that such knowledge of it may be possible? It must in its origin be intuition; for from a mere concept no propositions can be obtained that go beyond the concept – as happens in geometry (Introduction, V). But this intuition must be *a priori*, that is, it must be met with in us prior to any perception of an object, and must therefore be pure, not empirical, intuition. For geometrical propositions are one and all apodictic, that is, are bound up with the consciousness of their necessity; for instance, that space has only three dimensions. Such propositions cannot be empirical or [in other words] judgments of experience, nor can they be derived from such judgments (Introduction, II).   (B 40–1)

In the quotation, Kant considers three possible bases for geometry. It might be based on the analysis of concepts, in which case it would be analytic; it might be based on experience, and thus be synthetic *a posteriori*; or it might be synthetic *a priori*. He rules out the first of these possibilities, that geometry is analytic, by contending that geometry cannot be based on concepts alone; he later explains that geometrical demonstrations always depend upon a process of construction that requires an essential appeal to intuition, and hence goes beyond the mere analysis of concepts (A 712–38 / B 740–66). Against the second possibility, Kant argues that the intuitions in question must be pure, not empirical, in order to explain the apodictic certainty of geometry. Kant therefore concludes that geometry must have a synthetic *a priori* foundation in intuition; not in an actual intuition given before experience, but in an *a priori* constraint on any possible intuiton, which requires that all "outer" intuitions conform to the space of Euclid's geometry (see Chapter 2 in this book). His claim is not, then, that a certain form of intuition is innate – a claim about the psychological development of individuals presumably to be grounded in empirical study of the abilities of infants and young animals – but that a certain form of intuition must be posited because it provides the only means of explicating actual geometrical knowledge (see 11:79). Similarly, in the Deduction he attempts to show that the categories provide conditions for the very possibility of experience (see Chapter 4). Again, it would be irrelevant to argue that the categories are innate, for such an argument could only support an empirical claim about the psychological development of an individual; it could not establish that the categories are necessary for determining the synthesis required by the unity of apperception.

If it belongs to philosophy rather than to psychology to investigate the conditions for synthetic *a priori* knowledge, by examining and ruling out on conceptual grounds various candidate explications of the possibility of such knowledge, then Kant was right to call his investigation "transcendental philosophy" rather than "transcendental psychology." Of course, even in arguing for his transcendental philosophy Kant surely must appeal to experience to ground some basic claims, for example, that we experience in space and time, that we are finite intelligences, that we have sensations and feelings. But this sort of "empirical" data was accepted even by Crusius, the most avowedly aprioristic metaphysician of Kant's time (*Entwurf*, §§425–6). And reasonably so. If it were otherwise, any sort of reflection on human experience whatsoever would count as "empirical," effectively rendering all philosophy empirical by stipulation. For the purpose of reading and interpreting Kant, and for many other purposes, we are well advised to distinguish between treating reflection on ordinary experience as a minimal starting point for philosophy and adopting an empirical approach when formulating and confirming explanatory theses in philosophy. Kant argued that his Critical Philosophy could not take the latter approach; he took the legitimacy of the former for granted.

Nevertheless, Kant's transcendental program has implications for psychology, or at least for empirical science, even if it was not psychological in its fundamental aim nor in its mode of argument. For Kant claimed to establish, through his arguments for space as the form of outer intuition, that physical space must be the space of Euclid. Notoriously, this claim came under attack in the nineteenth century by Bernard Riemann, Hermann Helmholtz, and others.[16] Under this attack Kant's claim about the spatial form of intuition must either be pared back to a psychological claim about the character of human sensory experience independent of the character of physical space – thereby undercutting Kant's conception of the relationship between the grounds for geometry *per se* and the grounds for its application to physical space (B 147; A 165–6 / B 206; A 224 / B 271; A 239 / B 299) – or it must be accepted as a claim about the character of perceptual and physical space that turned out to be empirical, not *a priori*, contingent, not necessary, and indeed, as is widely held, false. However this may be, Kant's transcendental program might nevertheless have psychological implications for our own day, if it should turn out that psychology can produce a science of cognition, as some have suggested. In the end, the psychological relevance of the *Critique* may depend upon whether psychology develops in such a way that Kant's transcendental suggestions about the structure of cognition can be appreciated.

IV. KANT'S OWN RATIONAL AND EMPIRICAL PSYCHOLOGY

Although we have examined Kant's attempts to set transcendental philosophy apart from empirical psychology, we have yet to examine his considered view of whether empirical psychology can attain the status of science.[17] Perhaps his most notorious remarks on this subject are those from the preface to the *Metaphysical Foundations of Natural Science,* to the effect that empirical psychology will never be a proper science. While we must give these remarks their due, they should not be allowed to obscure Kant's basic position that the phenomena of empirical psychology are strictly bound by the law of cause just as are the phenomena of physics. Let us first consider this latter aspect of Kant's position as it is expressed in the first *Critique* and the *Prolegomena.*

In the third chapter of the Transcendental Doctrine of Method Kant laid out his conception of the systematic relations among the various branches of philosophy. In the body of the *Critique* he had, of course, discussed various branches of philosophy, including metaphysics and rational psychology, but under their traditional descriptions. Now, with a completed critique of pure reason extant, he proceeds to outline the "architectonic of pure reason," which he defines as the art of constructing systems of all knowledge arising from pure reason (A 832 / B 860). This chapter contains some mildly paradoxical branches of "pure philosophy," that is, of the part of philosophy that, in contrast with empirical philosophy, is based solely in pure reason. For, having argued against the possibility of metaphysics traditionally conceived, Kant proceeds to set forth the possibility of a new systematic metaphysics and he includes among its branches a new "rational psychology" containing *a priori* principles governing the phenomena of inner sense. The branches of philosophy he now describes draw their metaphysical principles, at least in the case of the metaphysics of nature, from the Analytic of Principles in the *Critique;* these include the principle of the permanence of substance and the law of cause.

In his architectonic, Kant first divides pure philosophy from empirical philosophy. He subdivides pure philosophy in turn into (i) the propadeutic investigation of pure reason itself, which he terms "criticism" and of which the *Critique* is an example, and (ii) "the system of pure reason (science), the whole body (true as well as illusory) of philosophical cognition arising out of pure reason [presented] in systematic connection, which is entitled *metaphysics*" (A 841 / B 869). Metaphysics divides into practical and speculative parts, or into a metaphysics of morals and a metaphysics of nature. The latter has two branches, the first being transcendental philosophy, which "treats only of the understanding and of reason itself, in a system of all concepts and principles that relate to objects in general, without taking account of objects that may be given": it provides such *ontology* as is available in Kant's reconstituted discipline of metaphysics. The second branch is the "physiology of pure reason," that is, the rational physiology (or science of nature) of given objects, or of objects that can be given in experience. This pure or rational physiology again has two branches, transcendent and immanent; the first pertains to "that connection of objects of experience which transcends all experience" – here, presumably, is an instance of one of the illusory branches of philosophical cognition Kant has mentioned – and the second pertains to the cognition of nature "insofar as its cognition can be applied in experience" (A 845 / B 873). Transcendent physiology thus includes the empty speculative disciplines of rational cosmology (the connection of nature as a whole) and rational theology (the relation of nature as a whole to a being above nature).

Immanent rational physiology thus provides the only substantive *a priori* principles that pertain to nature as an object of possible experience. The only worked out version we have of this body of doctrine is that found in the *Metaphysical Foundations of Natural Science*. Here Kant applies principles from the Analytic of Principles to the (empirically derived) concept of motion and purports thereby to derive two of Newton's laws of motion in an *a priori* manner. Yet in the Methodology, Kant announces the possibility not only of a rational physics, but also of a rational psychology.[18] This rational psychology would set *a priori* conditions on the object of inner sense, that is, on the succession of representations in time. In the *Critique* Kant does not give any indication of the content of his reconstituted version of rational psychology. But in the *Prolegomena* he gives one hint. In the second part, which treats pure natural science, he characterizes what he terms "a universal science of nature in the strict sense": "Such a science must bring nature in general, whether it regards the object of the external senses or that of the internal sense (the object of physics as well as psychology), under universal laws." Universal natural science comprises the objects of both physics and psychology. Kant admits that there are only a few principles with the required generality, but he is able to name two: "the propositions that 'substance is permanent', and that 'every event is determined by a cause according to constant laws' . . . These are actual universal laws of nature, which subsist completely *a priori*" (*Prolegomena*, §15, 4:295). Although Kant does not go on to give examples of these principles as applied to inner sense, presumably• the persistence of the "I" as the ground of the empirical unity of the self – not as a simple, spiritual being, but merely as a permanent substratum in time – is an example of the first principle, and the law (or laws) of association of representations is an example of the second principle. In any event, it is evident that Kant is committed to the view that the representations of inner sense, no less than the objects of outer sense, are subject to universal natural laws.

At first blush, Kant's commitment to universal laws of psychology may seem hard to square with his opinion, expressed in the preface of the *Metaphysical Foundations of Natural Science*, that empirical psychology is far removed from "the rank of what may properly be called natural science" (4:471). Upon closer examination, however, it becomes apparent that his denial of scientific status to psychology did not result from any doubt that there are universal natural laws in psychology; rather, it resulted from specific methodological requirements he imposed on any "proper" science, together with his beliefs about the applicability of these requirements to psychology.

Kant would admit nothing to the rank of science whose subject-matter could not be handled mathematically. As he puts it, "in every special doctrine of nature only so much science proper can be found as there is mathematics in it" (4:470). Every proper science also has a pure or rational part that "grounds" the empirical part, and the principles of which apply *a priori* to objects of possible experience. Kant argues that the restriction of science to that which can be treated mathematically follows from the basic condition that in order for a rational special science to apply *a priori* to objects, it must specify *a priori* conditions not only for concepts of its objects, but also for their intuition. (Recall that for Kant no object can be given without an intuition.) As he puts it, "in order to cognize the possibility of determinate natural things, and hence to cognize them *a priori*, there is further required that the intuition corresponding to the concept be given *a priori*, that is, that the concept be constructed." But, he further contends, "rational cognition through the construction of concepts is mathematical" (4:470). Here he seems to rely on his general doctrine that mathematical concepts must be constructed in intuition. From this doctrine it does not, however, follow immediately that any constructed concept must be mathematical. The doctrine only tells us that mathematics requires *a priori* construction, not that all *a priori* constructions are mathematical. But it is difficult to imagine any basis other than the *a priori* structure of the forms of intuition for "constructing" objects *a priori*, and Kant in effect equates the *a priori* forms space and time, in light of their "formal" characteristics, with the objects of the mathematical sciences, namely, those of geometry and arithmetic.

Granting for the sake of argument that science requires mathematization, let us pursue Kant's argument that psychology (whether rational or empirical) admits no mathematical construction of its objects. He argues that the "empirical doctrine of the soul" cannot achieve the rank of natural science,

because mathematics cannot be applied to the phenomena of internal sense and their laws, unless one might want to take into consideration merely the law of continuity in the flow of internal changes in inner sense. But the enlargement of cognition so attained would bear much the same relation to that which mathematics provides for the doctrine of body, as the doctrine of the properties of the straight line bears to the whole of geometry. For the pure inner intuition in which the soul's appearances are to be constructed is time, which has only one dimension.   (4:471)

The problem is not that there are no laws of psychology, but that such laws apparently cannot be constructed *a priori* except through the minimally informative construction of time as a line. But if no *a priori* construction is possible, psychology can at best be empirical, and can never admit of the necessity and universality that befits science.

This argument is problematic for reasons internal to the Kantian perspective and also because of the constraints it places on empirical science. Internally, it is not clear that the only *a priori* mathematical result pertaining to internal sense is that of the "straight line" of continuity in time. Indeed, Kant himself, in the Anticipations of Perception, invites one such *a priori* application, in arguing that "in all appearances, the real that is object of sensation has intensive magnitude, that is, a degree" (B 207). Rational psychology apparently can declare that sensations have a degree. This in itself is no great advance over the establishment of continuous linear flow in accordance to law. There would be an advance, however, if it were possible to construct *a priori* a relation between intensity and the laws of succession in time, such as might be expected in a law of association according to which sensations with similar intensity become associated. This task would, however, presumably seem as hopeless to Kant as did the *a priori* construction of the specific laws of attraction and repulsion between "matters," laws that might constitute an *a priori* chemistry (4:470–1).

But granting that psychology cannot construct its laws *a priori*, does that preclude it from the status of science? Why could psychology not discover mathematical laws through empirical research? If it did so, its doctrine could meet one of the prime requirements of science in Kant's day (and our own), for the laws could be used to order systematic explanations; that is, if the laws were mathematical, even if empirically discovered, observed (or expected) phenomena could be derived from them mathematically. The sole problem on this eventuality is that the specific laws, because of their empirical basis, would not be known with universality and necessity, and so would not, in Kant's view, count as science. On the grounds Kant stated in the *Metaphysical Foundations*, nothing can be a science whose basic structure cannot be constructed *a priori*, as the laws of physics were in that work. The requirement of *a priori* constructibility may seem too great a restriction on empirical science, for it would banish from the domain of natural science any body of doctrine, no matter how mathematically well ordered its explanations, whose principles could not be constructed *a priori*. In any event, it turns out that the reason Kant ruled out the possibility of a scientific psychology was not a claim that mathematics could not be applied to inner sense at all, but that it could not be applied *a priori*. Indeed, given what he says in the Anticipations of Perception, it is plausible to suppose that he believed mathematics could be applied to the matter of perception. Consequently, if one is willing to accept that there can be sciences whose laws cannot be constructed *a priori* but are empirically discovered, Kant has provided no argument against a mathematical science of psychology of that type.

Be that as it may, Kant had a further methodological reason for pessimism about the prospects of empirical psychology. He doubted that experiments could be carried out on the phenomena of inner sense. He argued that such experiments are impossible either on ourselves or through the observation of others. We cannot conduct them on ourselves because "the manifold of inner observation is separated only by mere thought-division, but cannot be kept separate and connected again at will" (4:471). Presumably Kant is here contrasting the case of experimentation with external objects, in which the objects can be manipulated repeatedly at will, with the case of internal sense, in which the will cannot directly determine the flow of representations. By saying that the objects of inner sense can be separated "only by mere thought-division," he may be claiming that such manipulations of the phenomena of internal sense as can be performed will be mere imaginary thought-experiments. This argument is not compelling. Consider a possible study of the associative law of contiguity. Although one cannot cause pairs of sensations to be presented to inner sense in temporal contiguity merely by willing that it be so, one can will that external objects be presented to one's senses in such a way that pairs of similar sensations are presented to inner sense in the appropriate manner; one can then cause one of the pair to be presented at a later time, in order to test whether there arises an expectation of the other member of the pair. Moreover, it is difficult to see why such experiments could not be carried out on others besides one's self. However, Kant contends that "even less does another thinking subject submit to our investigations in such a way as to be conformable to our purposes, and even the observation itself alters and distorts the state of the object observed" (4:471). The plausibility of this remark depends on what the subject is being asked to do. One might expect subjects to be willing to submit to an experiment of the sort just envisioned. Furthermore, Kant's charge that the observation distorts the object observed may apply only to some cases. If one is investigating the cognition of divination or of distraction (examples from the *Anthropology*, 7:187, 206), Kant seems right. He might also be right if one is asking subjects to report the apparent size of objects (the attitude taken by the subject in such cases can be all important, as writers contemporary to Kant were aware).[19] But simpler aspects of visual experience might well be made the subject of report without distortion, within appropriate bounds of precision. At any rate, significant numbers of Kant's near contemporaries believed they were, and subsequent investigations in psychophysics support their contention.[20]

In any case, Kant's methodological pessimism should not be allowed to obscure his certainty that there are psychological laws governing the phenomena of inner sense. Perhaps ironically, the nineteenth and early twentieth centuries have seen a complete reversal of the methodological picture painted by Kant. Precise mathematical measurements became possible in psychophysics, and experimental techniques were applied with considerable success in studies of sensory perception and of simple memory tasks. And although the Kantian faith that there are proper laws of inner sense, or of the combination of representations, remained strong within psychology throughout the century following Kant, the twentieth century has seen a radical shift from the search for simple, universal laws for combining mental representations, toward a search for the particular mechanisms that underlie distinct cognitive abilities such as depth perception by means of stereoscopic vision or short-term memory for letters and numbers.

Thus, neither Kant's account of the shortcomings of empirical psychology nor his implied conception of the systematic structure of the science (in terms of simple universal laws) has proved lasting. By contrast, his criticisms of rational psychology were devastating, and that discipline never really revived. Ultimately, though, his most permanent contribution may be his distinction between his own philosophical project in the Deduction and the aims of empirical, natural-scientific psychology. That distinction and its descendants, such as the more recent distinction between the "logical space of reasons" and the "logical space of causes,"[21] mark out a fundamental divide between the natural science of mental processes and investigation of the logical, conceptual, and justificatory order of thought. The latter division remains controversial, which is to say that the question of the ultimate viability of the Kantian distinction remains contested. But the most important philosophical contributions often take the form, not of definitive solutions to a problem, but of setting a problem space. Kant's most lasting contribution to psychology as science and as philosophy may well be of this important kind.

NOTES

1 The method of citation for Kant's works is described in the frontmatter of the present volume. The works of other authors are cited by short title in the text when practical; complete titles are given in the attendant note. I am responsible for all translations, though for Kant's works I have consulted and sometimes partially adopted the standard translations as listed in the references.
2 General treatments of psychology in Kant's works include Jürgen Bona Meyer, *Kants Psychologie* (Berlin, 1870); Kurt Burchardt, *Kants Psychologie im Verhältnis zur transzendentalen Methode* (Berlin, 1911); Vladimir Satura, *Kants Erkenntnispsychologie*, Kantstudien Ergänzungshefte no. 101 (Bonn: Bouvier, 1971); and Patricia Kitcher, *Kant's Transcendental Psychology* (New York: Oxford University Press, 1990).
3 The most extensive discussion of psychology in the time of Kant is Max Dessoir, *Geschichte der neueren deutschen Psychologie*, 2d ed. (Berlin, 1902). Kant's discussion of natural laws in psychology is examined in section IV herein. On his early views on the soul and their subsequent development, see Karl Ameriks, *Kant's Theory of Mind: An Analysis of the Paralogisms of Pure Reason* (Oxford: Oxford University Press, 1982).
4 Recent discussions of Kant's attack on rational psychology include Jonathan Bennett, *Kant's Dialectic* (Cambridge: Cambridge University Press, 1974), chs. 4–6; Alfons Kalter, *Kant's vierter Paralogismus: Eine entwicklungsgeschichtliche Untersuchung zum Paralogismenkapitel der ersten Ausgabe der Kritik der reinen Vernunft* (Meisenheim am Glan: Anton Hain, 1975); W. H. Walsh, *Kant's Criticism of Metaphysics* (Edinburgh: Edinburgh University Press, 1975), §31; Ameriks, *Kant's Theory of Mind*; Henry E. Allison, *Kant's Transcendental Idealism: An Interpretation and Defense* (New Haven, Conn.: Yale University Press, 1983), ch. 13; and Kitcher, *Kant's Transcendental Psychology*, ch. 7.
5 Moses Mendelssohn, *Phädon* (1767; 2d ed., 1768; 3d ed., 1769), Zweytes Gespräch, and appendix to second edition, in his *Gesammelte Schriften*, F. Bamberger and L. Strauss, eds. (Berlin, 1932), 3.1:89–101, 131–5; and "Abhandlung von der Unkörperlichkeit der menschlichen Seele" (1785), dritte Betrachtung, ibid., 3.1:171–6.
6 The citations and quotations are from Christian Wolff, *Psychologia empirica methodo scientifica pertractata, qua ea, quae de anima humana indubia experientiae fide constant, continentur*, new ed. (Frankfurt and

Leipzig, 1738) and *Psychologia rationalis methodo scientifica pertractata, qua ea, quae de anima humana indubia experientiae fide innotescunt, per essentiam et naturam animae explicantur*, new ed. (Frankfurt and Leipzig, 1740).

7 Citations and quotations from Alexander Gottlieb Baumgarten, *Metaphysica*, 7th ed. (Halle, 1779).

8 Christian August Crusius, *Entwurf der nothwendigen Vernunft-Wahrheiten, wiefern sie den zufälligen entgegen gesetzet werden* (Leipzig, 1745).

9 The role of psychology in the Deduction has been much discussed, as is apparent from these selected references: Norman Kemp Smith, *A Commentary to Kant's "Critique of Pure Reason,"* 2d ed. (London: Macmillan, 1923), pp. 234–48; H. J. De Vleeschauwer, *La Déduction transcendentale dans l'oeuvre de Kant*, 3 vols. (Antwerp: De Sikkel, 1934–7), passim; Robert Paul Wolff, *Kant's Theory of Mental Activity* (Cambridge, Mass.: Harvard University Press, 1963), pp. 100–2, 176–7; Jonathan Bennett, *Kant's Analytic* (Cambridge: Cambridge University Press, 1966), pp. 111–17; P. F. Strawson, *The Bounds of Sense: An Essay on Kant's Critique of Pure Reason* (London: Methuen, 1966), pp. 93–7; W. H. Walsh, "Philosophy and Psychology in Kant's Critique," *Kantstudien* 57 (1966): 186–98; Dieter Henrich, *Identität und Objektivität: Eine Untersuchung über Kants transzendentale Deduktion* (Heidelberg: Carl Winter, 1976); Paul Guyer, "Psychology and the Transcendental Deduction," in Eckart Förster, ed., *Kant's Transcendental Deductions: The Three "Critiques" and the "Opus postumum"* (Stanford, Calif.: Stanford University Press, 1989), pp. 47–68; and Kitcher, *Kant's Transcendental Psychology*, chs. 3–6.

10 Hume's program for investigating the origin of belief through a science of human nature is put forward in his *Treatise of Human Nature* (London, 1739–40), Introduction (see also Bk. 1, pt. 1, §§1–3 and Bk. 1, pt. 3), and *Inquiry Concerning Human Understanding* (London, 1748), §§1–3.

11 Prolegomena to *Empirical Psychology*, §9, as translated from Wolff's *Psychologia empirica* by Robert J. Richards in his "Christian Wolff's Prolegomena to Empirical and Rational Psychology: Translation and Commentary," *Proceedings of the American Philosophical Society* 124 (1980): 227–39.

12 Johann Nicolas Tetens, *Philosophische Versuche über die menschliche Natur und ihre Entwickelung*, 2 vols. (Leipzig, 1777), 1:iii–iv.

13 On this juridical distinction and Kant's use of it, see Dieter Henrich, "Kant's Notion of a Deduction and the Methodological Background of the First *Critique*," in Förster, ed., *Kant's Transcendental Deductions*, pp. 29–46.

14 The literature relevant to the question of the proper role of psychology in

Kant's first *Critique* is vast. Early writers who attributed latent psychological content to the work, to one effect or another, include Karl Leonard Reinhold, *Versuch einer neuen Theorie des menschlichen Vorstellungsvermögens* (Prague, 1789), pp. 65–7, and *Briefe über die kantische Philosophie*, 2 vols. (Leipzig, 1790–92), 2:25; Johann Gottlieb Fichte, "Zweite Einleitung in die Wissenschaftslehre" (1797), in his *Sämtliche Werke*, ed. I. H. Fichte, 8 vols. (Berlin, 1845–6), 1:471–9; Jakob Friedrich Fries, *Neue oder anthropologische Kritik der Vernunft*, 2d ed., 3 vols. (Heidelberg, 1828), 1:20–6, 28–30; Johann Friedrich Herbart, *Lehrbuch zur Einleitung in die Philosophie* (Königsberg, 1813), preface, §§126–7, in his *Sämtliche Werke*, ed. K. Kehrbach and O. Flügel, 19 vols. (Langensalza, 1887–1912), 4:9–10, 208–13. Studies devoted to the proper role of psychology in Kant include Meyer, *Kants Psychologie*; Burchardt, *Kants Psychologie im Verhältnis zur transzendentalen Methode*; Satura, *Kants Erkenntnispsychologie*, appendix; Gary Hatfield, *The Natural and the Normative: Theories of Spatial Perception from Kant to Helmholtz* (Cambridge, Mass.: The MIT Press/Bradford Books, 1990), ch. 3; and Kitcher, *Kant's Transcendental Psychology*. Recent authors expressing discomfort at Kant's psychologizing tendencies include Strawson, *Bounds of Sense*, pp. 15–16, 32, and Bennett, *Kant's Analytic*, pp. 6–8. The term "psychologism" apparently was coined by Johann Eduard Erdmann to refer, not to Kant's own alleged psychologizing, but to the psychological interpretation of Kant's theory of knowledge advanced by F. E. Beneke: Erdmann, *Grundriss der Geschichte der Philosophie*, 2d ed., 2 vols. (Berlin, 1870), 2:636.

15 Kant divides sensibility from understanding at A 21–2 / B 35–6; he distinguishes a separate faculty of imagination at A 94 and B 151; and he distinguishes separate faculties of understanding, judgment, and reason at A 75 / B 100 (note) and A 130 / B 169. Baumgarten distinguishes inner from outer sense at *Metaphysica*, §535. On the division of the cognitive faculties by Wolff, see *Psychologia empirica*, pt. I, §§1–3 and *Psychologia rationalis*, §I, chs. 1–4; by Baumgarten, *Metaphysica*, §§535, 557, 606, 624, and 640. Wolff and Baumgarten posit many additional cognitive faculties, and Kant discusses some additional cognitive faculties in his *Anthropology*, Bk. I.

16 On the psychological implications of Kant's doctrine that Euclid's space is the form of outer intuition and on Helmholtz's attack on Kant's position, see Hatfield, *Natural and Normative*, ch. 3, §4 and ch. 5, §5, and the literature cited there.

17 Studies of Kant's views on the scientific status of psychology include Meyer, *Kants Psychologie*, ch. 6, §3; Edward Franklin Buchner, *A Study of Kant's Psychology with Reference to the Critical Philosophy*, Psychologi-

cal Review Monograph Supplement no. 4 (New York, 1897); Hans Ehrenberg, *Kritik der Psychologie als Wissenschaft: Forschungen nach den Systematischen Principien der Erkenntnislehre Kants* (Tübingen, 1910); Theodore Mischel, "Kant and the Possibility of a Science of Psychology," *The Monist* 51 (1967): 599–622; Satura, *Kants Erkenntnispsychologie,* ch. 2; David E. Leary, "Immanuel Kant and the Development of Modern Psychology," in William R. Woodward and Mitchell G. Ash, *The Problematic Science: Psychology in Nineteenth Century Thought* (New York: Praeger, 1982), pp. 17–42.

18 Kant's contemporaries noticed that he included legitimate versions of rational and empirical psychology in his architectonic division of the sciences. His division of the sciences in the first *Critique* is summarized in a review of his *Grundlegung zur Metaphysik der Sitten,* in the *Allgemeine Literature-Zeitung* (1785), 2:21–3; his distinction between two types of rational psychology is addressed in Karl C. E. Schmid, *Empirische Psychologie,* 2d ed. (Jena, 1796), pp. 22–4.

19 Joseph Priestley, *Geschichte und gegenwärtiger Zustand der Optik, vorzüglich in Absicht auf den physikalischen Theil dieser Wissenschaft,* trans. G. S. Klügel (Leipzig, 1775–76), pp. 493–4; Johann Samuel Traugott Gehler, *Physikalisches Wörterbuch, oder Versuch einer Erklärung der vornehmsten Begriffe und Kunstwörter der Naturlehre,* 6 vols. (Leipzig, 1787–96), 2:537–42.

20 Priestley, who surveyed a great body of optical literature, described several reports of perceptual experience as produced under specified conditions, including observations on afterimages (*Geschichte,* pp. 450–1), on depth perception with one eye (496), on the windmill illusion (498–9), and on the perception of motion (501–3). He reported Robert Smith's quantitative estimate, given certain explanatory assumptions, of the magnitude of the moon illusion (507–8), and he described Tobias Mayer's mathematically expressed measurements of visual acuity (487). On Mayer, see Eckart Scheerer, "Tobias Mayer – Experiments on Visual Acuity (1755)," *Spatial Vision* 2 (1987): 81–97. The standard survey of the modern history of experiments on perception remains Edwin G. Boring, *Sensation and Perception in the History of Experimental Psychology* (New York: Appleton-Century-Crofts, 1942), and of experimental psychology in general, Boring, *History of Experimental Psychology,* 2d ed. (New York: Appleton-Century-Crofts, 1950).

21 Richard Rorty, *Philosophy and the Mirror of Nature* (Princeton, N.J.: Princeton University Press, 1979), p. 141, and especially Wilfrid Sellars, "Empiricism and the Philosophy of Mind," as printed in his *Science, Perception and Reality* (London: Routledge & Kegan Paul, 1963), pp. 127–96, on pp. 131, 144–5, 166–9.

THOMAS E. WARTENBERG

7   Reason and the practice of science

Kant's philosophy is often characterized as an attempt to provide the metaphysical foundation for Newtonian science. In such a characterization, the revolutionary metaphysical stance that Kant develops in the *Critique of Pure Reason*, based on a distinction between appearances and things in themselves, is seen as the result of his commitment to show the legitimacy of Newtonian science in a manner that still leaves space for morality and religious belief. His well-known dictum that he had "found it necessary to deny *knowledge* [of reality in itself], in order to make room for *faith*" (B xxx)[1] bears witness to the legitimacy of this characterization of the Kantian project.

Such a description of the *Critique* leaves open, however, the question of Kant's more general beliefs about the philosophy of science. In this chapter, I shall show that Kant advocates a more empirically minded philosophy of science than could be anticipated from his views on Newtonian physics. In particular, I will show that Kant presents an account of the use of theoretical concepts in the development of scientific theories under the rubric of the "regulative use of reason." The understanding of science that Kant presents under this title has a great deal in common with the pragmatic understanding of scientific practice, in which the fallibility of particular scientific theories is stressed. Once the regulative use of reason is taken into account, it becomes clear that Kant views the scientific enterprise in a more empirical and less aprioristic manner than has been commonly thought.

In memory of Wilfrid Sellars.

I want to thank Jay Garfield for reading a draft of this chapter. His challenging and insightful comments helped me understand the issues I discuss more clearly than I had previously.

228

I

One of the central characteristics of science for Kant is its use of nonempirical concepts in its theories. Kant uses the term "idea" to refer to such nonempirical concepts, claiming that ideas are crucial to the scientific enterprise.

These concepts of reason [i.e., ideas] are not derived from nature; on the contrary, we interrogate nature in accordance with these ideas, and consider our knowledge as defective so long as it is not adequate to them.

(A 646–7 / B 673–4)

In order to understand the significance of this claim, we need to consider Kant's general use of the term "idea." Kant defines the term "idea" in the following manner: "A concept formed from notions and transcending the possibility of experience is an *idea* or concept of reason" (A 320 / B 377). Ideas are concepts that are generated by reason and not by experience. They are concepts that cannot be adequately instantiated within experience. As such, they form a diverse assemblage of concepts, since reason generates concepts for various different purposes of its own.[2]

The group of ideas upon which Kant primarily focuses his attention in the body of the Dialectic of the first *Critique* are the three transcendental ideas – self, world, and God. The central argument of the Dialectic is that traditional metaphysics treats these ideas as if they referred to objects and attempts to determine in an *a priori* manner certain basic features of such objects. The critical aspect of the *Critique* involves the claim that such attempts are necessarily illicit since they seek to extend knowledge to objects that lie beyond the bounds of empirical knowledge.

In the passage quoted earlier, however, Kant uses the term "idea" in a different manner and gives a very different appraisal of the importance of ideas. The ideas that Kant is discussing are what I shall call *theoretical ideas* – that is, concepts that are used within scientific theorizing, but whose use is not justified by means of a reference to experience itself. It is a central feature of scientific theories that they employ concepts that are not derived directly from experience. In fact, many of these concepts are in principle not observable. Kant refers to such theoretical concepts as ideas in order to highlight their special nature. Because such concepts are not capable of empirical instantiation, it makes sense to call them "ideas" – that is, concepts that reason generates and that are not derived from experience.

The use of theoretical ideas within scientific practice is a feature of science that Kant sees as requiring a special justification. This is because the use of theoretical ideas cannot be legitimated in the same way as the use of empirical concepts. In the Analytic, Kant argues that empirical concepts function as rules for cognizing the unity of a given empirical intuition: "an *object* is that in the concept of which the manifold of a given intuition is *united*" (B 137). As this quotation makes clear, Kant views empirical concepts as specifying the nature of empirical objects and, in so doing, providing a means of seeing an intuition as unified despite the presence of a sensory manifold. This is a view of the nature of empirical concepts that lies at the heart of the *Critique* and that constitutes an important aspect of its revolutionary teaching concerning objectivity. The crucial point, for my purposes, is that empirical concepts have a legitimate use because they serve as unifiers of perceptual data.

The theoretical concepts in terms of which scientific theories are formulated – theoretical ideas – are not directly related to the sensory manifold. As a result, their use is problematic. Kant needs to show why reason is justified in using these ideas in its attempt to attain knowledge of the phenomenal world. Since ideas cannot have adequate empirical instantiations, treating them as having empirical content seems highly problematic.

Kant begins his solution to this problem by pointing out that theoretical ideas, like empirical concepts, do function as unifiers. The difference lies in the items that are unified by ideas: "Just as understanding unifies the manifold in the object by means of concepts, so reason unifies the manifold of concepts by means of ideas. . . " (A 644 / B 672). The unity that is achieved through the use of theoretical ideas in science, Kant claims, is a unity of the knowledge of the understanding, that is, of ordinary empirical knowledge. In other words, reason, by using ideas, provides a way of seeing ordinary knowledge as more unified than it would otherwise be.

But what justifies reason's search for unity among the manifold items of knowledge produced by the understanding? Kant points out that the use of these ideas seems to result from reason's own demand that it try to unify empirical knowledge. In order to make it clear that this interest in tidying up knowledge is one that reason simply has for its own purposes, Kant calls it the "logical use of reason." Kant's use of the word "logical" is meant to have the force that we associate with the word "methodological." It indicates that this use of reason is brought about by an interest that reason has in producing unity in the manifold of knowledge produced by the understanding, so that this use of reason is one in which reason is simply trying to put its own house in order.

But if this unity is thought of as constituted solely by an interest of reason, it would have only *subjective* validity. By claiming that this principle has only subjective and not objective validity, one would be stating that this use of reason was simply a piece of methodological advice that reason imposed upon itself. It would be illegitimate to attribute any more validity to this use of reason than that. In particular, there would be no justification for claiming that knowledge necessarily would meet this particular interest of reason in unity. Kant seems to endorse this view in the following passage:

But one sees from this that the systematic or rational unity of the manifold knowledge of understanding is a *logical* principle. Its function is to assist the understanding by means of ideas . . . and thus to secure coherence as far as it is possible. But to say that the constitution of objects or the nature of the understanding which knows them as such, is in itself determined to systematic unity, and that one can in a certain measure postulate this unity *a priori*, without reference to such an interest of reason . . . that would be a *transcendental* principle of reason, and would make the systematic unity necessary, not only subjectively and logically, as method, but objectively also.   (A 648 / B 676)

Kant's use of the subjunctive mode in making this statement should make one cautious in attributing the stated view to Kant as his own. While Kant clearly distinguishes between the logical and transcendental uses of this principle of reason, it is not clear whether he really denies transcendental status to such a use of reason. Kant is clear, however, that a transcendental use of this principle stands in need of further argumentation.

If Kant is taken to deny the validity of a transcendental use of the principle of reason, then he would be claiming that the theoretical ideas generated by scientific theorizing do not have objective validity, a justified application to nature or the understanding. While such ideas are used by reason for its own purposes, such a use would have to be distinguished from an interpretation of these ideas in which it was claimed that either inner or outer nature is such that it must necessarily correspond to the structure posited by such ideas. Kant would then sound very much like an instrumentalist in the philosophy of science. That is, he would be claiming that theoretical terms have a role to play in science as unifiers of concepts and laws that genuinely refer to empirical reality but that theoretical terms do not themselves refer to such reality. They are generated as conveniences for our own use, but it would be a serious theoretical error to view them as providing us with more adequate knowledge of empirical reality than that which we acquire from the use of nontheoretical empirical concepts.[3]

It is a fundamental mistake to interpret Kant as an instrumentalist in regard to theoretical ideas. Indeed, Kant argues that the logical use of reason makes sense only in light of a transcendental principle according to which the products of scientific reasoning can be viewed as providing a description of objective, though phenomenal, reality.

> How there could be a logical principle of the rational unity of rules cannot in fact be conceived unless a transcendental principle were also presupposed whereby such a systematic unity necessarily inhering in the objects was likewise assumed as *a priori* and necessary.   (A 651 / B 679)

Kant here states that the logical use of reason requires some transcendental backing. His considered view is that the logical use of reason to unify our knowledge is a legitimate practice only because it is grounded by an item of transcendental knowledge.

No sooner is Kant's view of the use of theoretical ideas within science stated than it seems to run afoul of some of the most basic claims that Kant makes about the scope of *a priori* and empirical knowledge. As I have already pointed out, Kant argues in the Dialectic of the first *Critique* that any attempt to use reason to generate knowledge of objects independently of experience is necessarily illicit. The only *a priori* knowledge that is available to human beings is limited to the general structure of experience and the empirical objects that make up the phenomenal world. Since Kant goes on to claim that reason has only a regulative and not a constitutive role in regard to knowledge, it seems impossible to attribute to him the view that reason does provide a transcendental grounding for scientific practice. Such an attribution would seem to go against Kant's own strictures on what reason is able to achieve in the absence of experience.

In the balance of this chapter, I will show that Kant's claims about a transcendental grounding of scientific practice do not violate his general denial that reason is capable of providing *a priori* knowledge. Once the specific claims that Kant makes about the regulative use of reason are understood, it will be clear that, although he attributes transcendental knowledge to reason as the basis for scientific practice, such knowledge does not amount to an illegitimate extension of our *a priori* knowledge beyond its legitimate bounds.

II

In order to see why Kant's account of the regulative use of reason provides a necessary element of his general critical program, we need to begin by looking more carefully at exactly what is involved in the regulative use of reason. According to Kant, the regulative use of reason involves the adoption of three different principles: those of genera, specification, and affinity. It is these principles that admit of both a logical and a transcendental use. In the latter use, these principles are genuine items of metaphysical knowledge that reason generates *a priori*. Together, they constitute the *idea of a completely adequate system of scientific knowledge*. This system is the goal of scientific practice and specific scientific theories are attempts to describe an aspect of that system. In order to explain how these principles generate the idea of such a system, I shall look carefully at Kant's presentation of them.

Kant begins his discussion of the regulative use of reason with a consideration of the principle of genera, devoting more time to this principle than to the others. The logical principle of genera asserts that there must be enough unity among species concepts that they can be unified into a genus. The example that Kant uses to explain this principle is the idea of a fundamental power of the human mind, an idea that Kant sees as playing an important role in empirical psychology. The concept of a fundamental power is an idea because it is not a concept that is derived from experience; rather, it is a concept that is introduced in order to unify the existing knowledge of the human mind. At the logical level, the principle of genera asserts that the different powers of the human mind – "sensation, consciousness, imagination, memory, wit, power of discrimination, pleasure, desire, etc." (A 649 / B 677) – should be compared with one another in order to detect various unities among them.

One has to enquire whether imagination combined with consciousness may not be the same thing as memory, wit, the power of discrimination, and perhaps even identical with understanding and reason.   (A 649 / B 677)

At this level, all that the principle of genera asserts is that scientific inquirers should attempt to unify the concepts employed within their theories as much as possible. It suggests that they should search for some theoretical idea that would allow them to reduce the complexity of their empirical concepts and theories.

The logical principle of genera can be represented as a heuristic maxim for the scientist in the following manner:

> Develop a conceptual structure that will reduce the complexity of empirical knowledge by searching for generic concepts and laws of which known empirical concepts and laws will be specifications.

Such a logical principle is a piece of advice that reason gives to itself in its role as scientific investigator. It tells itself that it would be convenient to be able to reduce the manifold of empirical laws to a unity by means of the use of a theoretical idea. Such a piece of methodological advice makes no pretense of being anything more than a suggestion that reason makes to itself, a piece of theoretical advice that reason gives itself, for its own convenience in handling the knowledge provided by the understanding. It does not claim that empirical concepts are of such a nature that this unification must be possible, but only advises reason to attempt such unifications wherever they might be possible.

Kant does think, however, that there is a use of the concept of a fundamental power in which reason does more than simply try to find such unity among empirical concepts as might be discovered. This is the transcendental employment of understanding in which such a unity is simply assumed.

Reason presupposes the systematic unity of the manifold powers, on the ground that particular laws of nature fall under more general laws, and that parsimony of principles is not only an economic principle of reason, but is an inner law of nature. (A 650 / B 678)

In this passage, Kant states quite clearly that, in the transcendental employment of the understanding, the idea of a fundamental power is treated as a concept that accurately describes the nature of the mind even though the actual theory that would articulate such a unity has yet to be discovered. That is, even though empirical psychology has not yet produced a specific scientific theory that demonstrates how the various powers of the mind are to be unified under the idea of a fundamental power, the transcendental employment of the understanding proceeds on the assumption that such a unification will necessarily be forthcoming. And this is so despite the fact that the specific nature of the unification is not yet known.

Kant claims that this is a case in which reason is asserting that its own product – a theoretical idea – does apply to the phenomenal world, that the powers of the mind are reducible to a fundamental power. Such a use of the idea goes beyond the limits allowed by a methodological interpretation of the regulative use of reason.

The logical principle of genera therefore needs to be supplemented with a transcendental principle that clearly states that the phenomenal world has a structure that accords with the demand of reason that empirical concepts be unifiable. The *transcendental principle of genera* is an item of transcendental knowledge supplied by reason and can be specified as follows:

> Inner and outer nature have such regularity that the concepts that we use to describe them must be capable of unification into a highest genus.

This principle is a transcendental principle in that it posits knowledge of the phenomenal world that reason is able to achieve independently of experience. It is this principle that guides the scientific attempt to produce experimental results that would confirm the idea that there is a fundamental power of the human mind.

Because I have been claiming that the regulative use of reason is really Kant's general view of the philosophy of science, it may seem strange that Kant points to the use of the idea of a fundamental power within transcendental philosophy as an example of how the principle of genera functions. Kant's choice of this example can be made more plausible by pointing out that Kant thought of empirical psychology as requiring this idea. It also suggests that Kant thought of philosophy itself as requiring something like scientific canons of rationality.

But even if this example seems strange, we can turn to other, less problematic examples in which Kant ties the use of the principle of genera to some of the scientific advances of his time. The examples that he cites are from the chemistry of his day and involve a theory in which chemical substances are thought to be composed of the four basic elements: pure air, pure earth, pure fire, and pure water. Kant characterized these elements as ideas because of their purity. Because empirical substances will always contain some mixture of these pure elements, the concepts of the elements are ideas – that is, concepts that do not allow of an adequate empirical instantiation (A 646 / B 674). Kant illustrates the importance of the transcendental principle of genera by means of an example involving the chemical theory in which these ideas figure:

> It was already a great advance when chemists could reduce all salts to two main genera, acids and alkalies. . . . One might believe that this is merely an economical contrivance that reason uses to save itself all possible trouble [i.e., to simply involve the logical principle of genera]. . . . But such a selfish purpose can very easily be distinguished from the [regulative use of the] idea. For in conformity with the [regulative use of the] idea everyone presupposes that this unity of reason accords with nature itself, and that reason – without being able to determine the limits of this unity – does not here beg but command [i.e., the transcendental principle of genera is involved].
>
> (A 652–3 / B 680–1)

This passage demonstrates the correctness of my contention that Kant believes that the use of ideas in scientific theorizing entails a rejection of an instrumentalist conception of science. He claims that the results of the attempt to unify scientific concepts are taken to be true of nature and that this shows that the demand of reason for such unity is not merely subjectively valid. Indeed, Kant explicitly rules out the merely logical interpretation of the use of reason as not adequate as a justification of scientific practice.

This passage also stresses an important aspect of Kant's theory that allows him to claim that the regulative use of reason involves a fundamentally different use of *a priori* knowledge than that which he attributes to the understanding. Although it is true that Kant thinks that science requires the assumption that nature accord with reason's interest in unity, he also thinks that, as we saw in the case of the idea of a fundamental power of the human mind, the way in which nature satisfies this demand cannot be specified *a priori.*

In this respect, reason's demand for systematic unity is different from the understanding's demand for unity in the sensory manifold. In the Analytic, Kant argued that it was possible to anticipate the precise nature of the unity that concepts would have to embody as a result of the fact that they served to unify the sensory manifold. The categories, schemata, and principles of the understanding provide specific *a priori* knowledge concerning the nature of the unity that will be brought about by using empirical concepts to unify the perceptual manifold. We know *a priori*, for example, that our experience is of a single world of interacting substances.

Although Kant does attribute *a priori* knowledge to reason in virtue of the use of ideas within science to unify the knowledge provided by the understanding, he denies that this knowledge is schematizable in the way that the categorial knowledge of the understanding is. That is, although reason is able to supply the ideal of a completely adequate system of scientific knowledge, it cannot anticipate the manner in which empirical knowledge will achieve this systematic structure.[4]

Understanding this distinction allows us to see one reason for calling this use of reason *regulative* as opposed to *constitutive.*[5] Although there is a tendency to think of regulative principles as *regulating* a practice without explicitly guaranteeing its success – that is, as simply methodological advice or what Kant terms "logical" principles – this is not the contrast that Kant attempts to draw by the use of this terminology. His use of the term "regulative" characterizes the knowledge of reality determined by this principle of reason "as synthetic *a priori* propositions, that have objective but indeterminate validity" (A 663 / B 691). That is, in characterizing the use of reason as regulative rather than constitutive, Kant is making reference to the relation of this use of reason to empirical objects, phenomena. Kant is claiming that this use of reason is not constitutive of such objects. The principles of understanding are, by themselves, sufficient to constitute the objective domain that Kant refers to with the terms "appearances" and "phenomena." The transcendental principle of genera does not supplement our knowledge

of phenomena in the sense of providing any other intrinsic characteristic that objects need to embody in order for them to be objects of
our experience. The transcendental principle of genera does, however, provide us with knowledge about relations among the concepts
we use for characterizing these objects. For this reason, Kant claims
that such knowledge is regulative rather than constitutive.[6] By making this distinction, however, Kant is not claiming that the transcendental knowledge supplied by reason is not essential to understanding the nature of our knowledge, only that reason's contribution to
the framework of knowledge does not involve the actual constitution of the objects that we know.

III

So far, I have only looked at Kant's discussion of the principle of
genera. In so doing, I have gone beyond a mere characterization of
this principle in an attempt to show that Kant holds that it has a
transcendental as well as logical use. But in order to fill out Kant's
view of the methodology of natural science, it is important to understand how he conceives of the function of the two other principles of
reason that make up the idea of a completely adequate system of
scientific knowledge.

The second principle of reason in its regulative use is that of
specification. This principle states that it is always possible to differentiate a generic concept into two or more specific ones. As in the
case of the principle of genera, Kant introduces this second principle
by distinguishing a logical use of that principle from a transcendental one. Discussing the different temperaments that scientists actually have, some searching for unity and others for differences, Kant
proceeds to discuss the logical principle of specification:

This latter mode of thought is evidently based upon a logical principle that
aims at the systematic completeness of all knowledge – prescribing that, in
beginning with the genus, I descend to the manifold that may be contained
thereunder, in such fashion as to secure extension for the system. . . . This
law of specification can be expressed: *entium varietates non temere esse
minuendas* [the variety of entities is not to be thoughtlessly reduced].

(A 655–56 / B 683–4)

Kant points out that scientists often proceed by attempting to show
that an empirical genus really conceals two or more different species

under its scope. A modern example of such a scientific advance would be the discovery that a given empirical substance such as uranium actually has two or more different isotopes. In fact, Kant gives an example, once again drawn from the chemistry of his day, that is very similar to this one.

> That absorbent earths are of different kinds (chalk and muriatic earths) required for its discovery an antecedent rule of reason that made it into an assignment for the understanding to seek for the difference that it assumes to be so richly present in nature.   (A 657 / B 686)

In giving this example, however, Kant goes beyond the attempt to legitimate the logical principle of specification. In fact, he states that this scientific discovery requires more than the logical principle of specification, for that principle does not entail that nature itself would satisfy the understanding's attempt to further differentiate its empirical concepts.

That Kant does think that the logical principle of specification requires a transcendental principle for its grounding can be seen in the following quotation:

> One can easily see, however, that also this logical law would be without meaning and application if a transcendental *law of specification* did not undergird it, a law that to be sure does not demand of the things that can be objects for us an actual *infinity* in relation to their difference.
>
> (A 656 / B 684)

Kant's discussion of the transcendental principle of specification raises an important issue. One of the problems with the use of the idea of the world that Kant criticized in the Antinomies was that it involved the concept of infinity. As Zeno's paradoxes had already demonstrated some two thousand years earlier, the concept of infinity presents real problems to the philosopher. If one posits an actual infinity as necessarily contained under a concept, it makes it impossible for a human being to think such a concept, given the finite nature of our lives and understandings.

Kant's solution is to say that infinity should be understood as a task rather than as a given entity. In the present context, this means that the transcendental principle of specification sets an infinite task for the understanding, namely that of producing more and more specific concepts for the generic ones in its scientific theories. So, once again, Kant is attributing to reason a role in directing the understanding to look for specific sorts of unities in its experience. The point of the principle of specification is to direct the understanding to look in its experience for regularities that support specifications of its generic concepts.

It is worth noting that Kant thinks of himself as having solved a problem about the nature of scientific investigation by seeing the two principles of genera and specification as both aspects of the regulative use of reason. There are two different tasks that scientists might identify with the essence of scientific activity. The first task is that of seeking to provide an overarching law that allows empirically distinct laws to be seen as specifications of a single generic one. Many examples of scientific progress can be thought of as proceeding from this drive toward unity, and the covering law theory of science seems to accept such a view.[7] However, scientific practice also proceeds by means of detailed observation and the establishment of differences. Learning that things that appear to be the same actually have different microstructures is certainly one way in which science proceeds. It therefore might seem that science is constituted by two contradictory drives, one toward unity and one toward diversity.

Kant's manner of presenting this dispute about scientific methodology shows that there is no need to decide which view is the correct one about the essence of scientific activity. Kant's theory of the regulative use of reason avoids this trap by claiming that both parties to the dispute have a grasp of a truth that can be comprehended in the more encompassing view that Kant himself puts forward. All that is required is that we see a drive for unity and a drive for differentiation as both equally necessary to the development of a completely adequate system of scientific knowledge. Both groups of scientists – those who see themselves as unifiers and those who see themselves as differentiators – have necessary but complementary roles to play in the project of science. An adequate model of science cannot recognize only one of these two aspects of scientific practice.

The third and final principle that Kant sees as a necessary component of the regulative use of reason is that of affinity. The example he gives to explain it is very interesting and I will quote it at length.

The affinity of the manifold (as, notwithstanding its diversity, coming under a principle of unity) refers not only to things, but still more to their properties and powers. Thus, for instance, if at first our not yet fully corrected experience presents the orbit of the planets as circular, and if we subsequently detect discrepancies, we trace the discrepancies to that which can change the circle, in accordance with a fixed law, through all the infinite intermediate degrees, into one of these divergent orbits. That is to say, we assume that the movements of the planets, which are not circular, will more or less approximate to the properties of a circle; and thus we come upon the idea of an ellipse. . . . Thus, under the guidance of these principles, we discover a unity in the generic forms of the orbits and thereby a unity in the cause of all the laws of planetary motion, namely, gravitation.

(A 662–3 / B 690–1)

Kant here presents the development of Newtonian physics as an example of the regulative use of reason, specifically of the principle of affinity. The principle of affinity states that the differences among generic concepts will be such as to modify themselves gradually. In the example, this means that the deviations from circular orbits in planetary motion are assumed to be slight, so that it becomes rational to see if they are ellipses. Kant's claim is that the principle of affinity gives the scientist a means of viewing deviations from an ideal as themselves admitting of a systematic specification. He goes so far as to claim that this principle of reason had a necessary role to play in the discovery of the law of universal gravitation.

It is noteworthy that Kant claims in this passage that the discovery of universal gravitation was something that took place as a result of the regulative use of reason. Because Kant took Newtonian physics to be the paradigm of a scientific theory and thought that many aspects of the theory were in fact capable of *a priori* justification,[8] his claim that the theory of universal gravitation requires the assumption of a transcendental principle of affinity shows the importance that Kant attributed to the regulative use of reason. He saw this use of reason as central to the method whereby scientific hypotheses were formulated and then tested.

These three principles – of genera, specification, and affinity – collectively amount to Kant's delineation of the systematic structure to which our knowledge of nature aspires. Together, they specify the idea of what I have called "a completely adequate system of scientific knowledge." This is an idea because it posits a completeness in our knowledge along three different axes, a completeness that can characterize only an ideal outcome of the process of scientific investigation. Our actual scientific knowledge of the world, even though it employs theoretical ideas in its formulation, can never attain the infinite structure posited by this idea. Such a structure can be viewed only as a task that science seeks to realize, not as an object that it actually possesses. We must understand attempts at scientific investigation of the world to involve a progressive articulation of the completely adequate system of scientific knowledge. Only in light of the structure posited by such an ideal, can we see science as a rational undertaking.

IV

In the previous section, I have shown that Kant believes that scientific theorizing, insofar as it employs theoretical ideas, requires transcendental principles that articulate the ideal explanatory system to which our actual knowledge of the world only approximates. The three principles of genera, specificity, and affinity together constitute this idea of an ideally adequate system of scientific knowledge. I now want to pull together the claims that Kant makes about the role of ideas in scientific practice.

In order to do this, I shall once again use some comments that Kant makes about the actual nature of scientific practice. Kant claims that theoretical ideas are actually used as a basis for "interrogating nature." Citing the experiments of Galileo, Torricelli, and Stahl as evidence, and pointing out that, in each case, these scientists approached nature armed with theories that they had developed in order to put them to an empirical test, Kant argues that such a use of reason is central to scientific method:

Reason has insight only into that which it produces according to its own design, and, proceeding with principles of its own judgment according to fixed laws, it must require nature to answer its own questions, rather than allowing nature to lead it by a string.   (B xiii)

This passage contains a picture of scientific practice that is at odds with the dominant empiricist view of science according to which science proceeds by means of the simple collection of observed regularities in experience. Kant claims that the important scientific advances made by Galileo, Torricelli, and Stahl do not conform to such a model. While experience – or, more precisely, experimentation – did play an important role in their scientific advances, the importance of experimentation for the legitimation of scientific theories requires an explicit acknowledgment of the role of ideas.

This is because the ideas actually provide the scientist with specific instructions about what to look for when he turns to experience via experimentation. Experience without the guidance of ideas would be a rather passive affair in which the scientist merely accumulated observations made from nature. Kant's central point is that science is an activity in which reason takes an active role as the interrogator of nature. It assumes this role by generating ideas that specify the particular sorts of regularities that the scientist ought to look for by means of experimentation. Ideas allow scientists to anticipate regularities that they can then seek to produce by means of experiments.

This view of scientific practice treats experimentation as a crucial element in science. However, in so doing it stresses the fact that scientific experimentation is a specific goal-directed activity that takes place in light of ideas – that is, concepts that are not themselves generated by experience. When a scientist conceives of an experiment, she does so in light of ideas that specify the sort of experience that ought to be looked for in the experiment. Experiments are not simple observations of the phenomenal world, but directed interrogations of nature that take place in accordance with goals set up by the practice of science itself. Kant's theory of the regulative use of reason stresses the role of experimentation in science while contesting a simplistic understanding of that role.

Perhaps a good way to capture Kant's claims about the importance of ideas in science is to paraphrase his famous dictum about the relation between concepts and intuitions – "Thoughts without content are empty, intuitions without concepts are blind." (A 51 / B 75) – and to say that science without experimentation is empty, experimentation without ideas is blind. Only by seeing science as involving the use of ideas as a means of guiding experimentation can we develop an adequate understanding of the nature of scientific practice.

Reason in its regulative role, then, functions to provide the scientist with the focused attention toward nature that is characteristic of scientific experimentation. From Kant's point of view, the actual practice of science, in which theoretical ideas are tested by means of experimentation, belies the claim that these ideas are mere heuristic or calculational devices. A theory of scientific practice needs to acknowledge the fact that science proceeds by actually searching out specific sorts of experiences *in light of ideas* with the express purpose of showing that these ideas do have empirical confirmation in that they predict the presence of certain uniformities that can be demonstrated empirically.

But this means that the theoretical ideas, although they do not have empirical instances, do have an immanent use – that is, they play a role in the elaboration of experience. The ideas are legitimated by the discovery, through the directed attention of the scientific inquirer via experiments, that certain regularities posited by the idea do obtain in nature. It is this role of ideas that Kant highlights in his account of the nature of scientific practice.

By showing the importance of experimentation to scientific practice, Kant presents a view of science that makes the validity of specific scientific theories depend on actual experience. In this regard, his theory is not simply aprioristic but recognizes the importance of experience in the confirmation of scientific theories. By pointing out that scientific theorizing involves experimentation, Kant is making the more radical point that specific experiences are sought out in order to show the validity of theoretical ideas. This is clearly an account of the use of experimental testing in science that distinguishes Kant's view of science from a more aprioristic account. It shows that Kant takes science to be an enterprise whose specific products attain validity by being tested against empirical data.

The idea of a completely adequate system of scientific knowledge is what legitimates scientific experimentation. It provides reason with an idea that it seeks to realize by means of specific scientific theories. The theoretical ideas that it uses are guides to reason in its attempt to figure out what the systematic structure of our knowledge really is. They provide reason with a specific focus to use when it turns to the empirical world in order to produce the empirical regularities that constitute the basis of our empirical knowledge of the world.

This is because the regulative principles of reason provide us with an understanding of what the aim of science really is. By specifying the goal of scientific understanding as the realization of a completely adequate system of knowledge, the regulative principles posit a set of connections among the elements of knowledge that are essential to understanding the nature of knowledge. For Kant, scientific practice is an attempt to exhibit the systematic interconnection among the items that constitute knowledge. Such systematic interconnection is, however, crucial to understanding what the enterprise of knowledge is all about. Knowledge of the world is not simply a set of facts, as it sometimes seemed to the empiricists; it is a complex structure of statements whose interconnections Kant articulates by means of the idea of systematicity.

V

Having shown that Kant thinks that the regulative use of reason involves the attribution of transcendental knowledge to reason itself, let me now examine an objection to my reconstruction of his view. Kant specifically states that a transcendental deduction of the ideas of reason is not possible (A 669 / B 697). Doesn't this entail that my account of the transcendental status of the regulative use of reason must be mistaken?

In answering this objection, it is important to be clear about which ideas Kant means when he denies the possibility of their deduction. The ideas for which Kant claims that no deduction is possible are the three transcendental ideas: self, world, and God. It is not at all surprising to find Kant claiming that these ideas cannot be given a deduction, for these ideas do not refer to objects that we can experience. Indeed, the bulk of the Dialectic is directed to showing the problems that arise when one thinks of these ideas as referring to objects and thus as the sorts of things about which we could have *a priori* knowledge.

Nevertheless, Kant does think that these ideas can be salvaged, so long as we understand that what they refer to is not an actually existing object, but rather a type of systematic unity among the knowledge that we do have. In fact, the theory of the regulative use of reason is his attempt to show that the dialectical errors of reason can be thought of as reason's own misunderstanding of its legitimate drive for systematic understanding of the external world and its own faculties. Because Kant thinks that reason cannot simply be mistaken in its activities, he posits the regulative use of reason as the appropriate correlate to reason's illicit drive for substantive *a priori* knowledge of the transcendental ideas of reason.[9]

Hence nothing that Kant says about the impossibility of a transcendental deduction of the transcendental ideas should be taken to deny that ideas have an important, indeed a necessary role to play in the constitution of experience. By calling this role regulative, Kant is simply seeking to make us aware that this role is very different from the role that reason was alleged to have in the claims of traditional metaphysics. These ideas do not refer to special objects that lie beyond the bounds of possible experience, but rather characterize the ideal structure to which our knowledge of empirical objects aspires.

There is another problem with Kant's view that is worth looking at. Let us grant that Kant is right to claim, as he does in his argument for the transcendental principle of genera (A 653–4 / B 681–2), that experience is only possible if there is a certain amount of uniformity in that which presents itself to our senses. By what right can Kant claim that it is possible to guarantee that nature has precisely the correct amount of unity (as well as difference and affinity) to be conceptualized by our scientific practice?

This is a difficult problem. The first step in answering it is to recall that Kant is not claiming that we have any precise knowledge of exactly what such a systematic structure amounts to empirically. The question might then be put in the following way: Could we conceive of a situation in which we would discover that science was not a rational manner in which to approach the worlds of inner and outer nature? Could we have an experience in which we discovered that nature was not, in fact, systematic?

Kant would answer this question in the negative. We might find out that particular scientific theories did not yield correct answers. Indeed, we often do find this out. However, Kant's claim is that science is constituted as a social practice in such a way that the idea of finding out that it won't work is impossible. The aim of science is to exhibit the systematic connections among items of knowledge that make knowledge an explanatory enterprise. While we may be frustrated in our attempts to actually produce such unity, no experience will ever tell us that we should not keep on trying. Indeed, no such experience can even be imagined without it also destroying the very idea of experience itself providing us with knowledge of the world in which we live.

In this sense, Kant's argument concerning the regulative use of reason is part and parcel of his transcendental project. Kant's aim is to demonstrate that empirical knowledge presupposes a general framework within which specific empirical claims can be situated. The regulative use of reason, by specifying the structure of a completely adequate system of scientific knowledge, provides the context within which specific scientific theories are located. Only on the supposition that science is seeking to develop theories that will result in the creation of such a system of empirical knowledge can science be seen as a rational practice whose product is knowledge of the structure of the phenomenal world.

VI

My aim in this chapter has been to demonstrate that Kant's view of scientific practice includes a greater awareness of the role that experience plays in science than has commonly been thought. In particular, I have shown that Kant's account of the regulative use of reason comprises a theory concerning the testing of hypotheses involving the use of theoretical ideas. Kant's claim is that such a scientific methodology makes sense only on the presupposition that the regularities of nature can be adequately captured by the systematic structure of our scientific theories. Only in light of this idea does it make sense for human beings to use scientific methods to determine the nature of the phenomenal world.

As a result of this argument, the regulative use of reason is seen to be an insightful and challenging account of the nature of scientific activity that occupies a central place in Kant's transcendental philosophy. Scientific activity, by means of which reason seeks to display the systematic structure of our knowledge of nature, is an essential part of Kant's understanding of the enterprise of human knowledge for which he provides a transcendental framework. By paying attention to this neglected aspect of Kant's account of the nature of empirical knowledge, one comes to see that, despite his championing of certain *a priori* aspects of the project of epistemology, Kant was sensitive to the manner in which human empirical knowledge is an ongoing and self-correcting enterprise in which experience plays a central role.

NOTES

1 All translations from the *The Critique of Pure Reason* are my own modifications of those of Norman Kemp Smith, *Immanuel Kant's Critique of Pure Reason* (London: Macmillan, 1933).
2 For a more complete discussion of the types of concepts that Kant classifies as ideas, see my unpublished doctoral dissertation, "Reason and Truth in Kant's Theory of Experience" (Ann Arbor, Mich.: University Microfilms, 1977), ch. 3.
3 Körner discusses this possibility in *Kant* (Harmondsworth, U.K.: Penguin, 1955), pp. 124–5. He points out that Kant's later treatment of the ideas "as-if" they were true of the world points toward such an interpretation.
4 Kant does hold that there is something analogous to a schematization of the idea, namely an *analogon* via the idea of a maximum (A 665 / B 693).
5 My previous discussion should have made it clear that there are other reasons why Kant calls this use of reason "regulative." Specifically, this use of reason is regulative in that it gives specific directives to the understanding about what sorts of regularities to look for in its experience.
6 Kant also uses the regulative-constitutive distinction within the Analytic in order to characterize the difference between the dynamical and mathematical categories. See A 179–80 / B 222–3.
7 This view is common among empiricist philosophers of science.
8 See the essay by Michael Friedman in this volume.
9 Kant's view here is akin to Descartes's claim in the *Meditations* that, since God is not a deceiver, there must be a positive use to perceptual ideas despite their seemingly deceptive character when taken to be representations of the actual structure of reality.

8   The critique of metaphysics: Kant and traditional ontology

Kant's attitude toward metaphysics and ontology is ambiguous in his Critical work. On the standard view of the *Critique of Pure Reason*, the positive and negative aspects of this attitude map neatly onto the two major sections of that work. After that first section presents a "Transcendental Analytic" of the understanding, or a "metaphysics of experience," which legitimates the use of certain pure concepts necessary for structuring our spatiotemporal knowledge, a Transcendental Dialectic is provided to expose fallacies that theoretical reason entangles itself in when it extends itself beyond experience. Just prior to that Dialectic, Kant also inserts an "Appendix" on "concepts of reflection" that sketches how the restriction of our use of pure concepts to the domain of experience limits the general claims of the traditional ontology of the Leibnizian system. These attacks would appear to complement each other. Whereas the specific errors of rational psychology, rational cosmology, and rational theology are exposed in the core of the Dialectic, the critique of ontology and the general discussions of the operations of "reflection" and "reason" suggest a principle of closure for dismissing all claims of our theoretical reason that would stray beyond a merely immanent spatiotemporal field.

On this view, there is little positive theoretical doctrine in the latter half of the *Critique;* at the most it is noted that Kant's discussion of the antinomies in cosmology can be seen as offering support for the doctrine of transcendental idealism. And even this discussion can be seen as making a negative point about a negative doctrine – that is, as showing merely that we run into contradictions if we take

Special thanks for assistance on this essay are due to Steven Naragon, Paul Guyer, Alison Laywine, and Eric Watkins.

our spatiotemporal knowledge to apply to things in themselves. But while the treatment of transcendental idealism is a high point of the Dialectic, by itself it is not sufficient for explaining Kant's entire mature attitude to the tradition. In the *Dissertation* (1770) he had already claimed the ideality of space and time, but this hardly stopped him from making numerous specific positive assertions about the "intelligible form" of things in themselves. In the *Critique of Pure Reason*, he reversed himself by challenging such assertions – and with such effectiveness that the general notion of a rejection of transcendent metaphysics met with more approval than Kant's own attempt to resuscitate pure philosophy in the form of a metaphysics of experience. However, this approval has rarely rested on a close scrutiny of Kant's own discussion, and often it has left unconsidered the possibility (which will be emphasized in what follows) that even in his late work there are significant limits to Kant's criticism of the tradition.

A proper understanding of Kant's criticism requires recalling the general outline of his new account of the dialectic of reason, but to evaluate that criticism it is also important to compare this account with the whole range of particular claims that Kant as well as the tradition had made previously. To determine how far the criticism really goes, one needs to look beyond the surface structure of the Dialectic and back to all the specific ontological issues of the traditional discussion. Hence, after an introductory outline of the Dialectic of the first *Critique* (readers familiar with Kant may skip over this and move directly to section II), I will turn in more detail to a few less familiar texts where some neglected aspects of the contrast between Kant and his Leibnizian predecessors can be explored most directly.

I

The Dialectic proposes a general pattern for the errors of transcendent metaphysics. The pattern is not exactly what one might first expect, namely the error of simply employing categories apart from their specific spatiotemporal schematization, for example by making claims about substance without considerations of permanence. This is an error, but by itself it is accidental in the double sense of being neither fully systematic nor imposed by any special force. For

Kant, the dialectical errors of reason are anything but accidental. They involve special representations, called Ideas of reason, which are systematically organized and give rise to inferences with a special "unavoidable" force, as if they were a "natural and inevitable illusion" (A 298 / B 355).[1]

The content of the Ideas is determined by ordered variations of the idea of something unconditioned, an idea that comes from making the general "logical maxim" of reason, namely to seek the condition of any particular conditioned judgment, into a "real principle" so that "a unity [of reason] is brought to completion." One thereby assumes that "if the conditioned is given, the whole series of conditions ... which is therefore itself unconditioned, is likewise given, that is, contained in the object and its connection" (A 308 / B 364). This is a fallacy because the analytic connection of a given concept to its logical ground is not the same as the synthetic connection of a given thing and its real ground.[2] Yet there is a force allegedly making this assumption "inevitable," namely the naturalness of taking "the subjective necessity of a connection of our concepts, which is an advantage of the understanding, for an objective necessity in the determination of things in themselves" (A 297 / B 353).

The "connection of concepts" Kant has in mind here comes from what he takes to be the peculiar office of reason to connect representations in chains of syllogisms. Thus: "We may presume that the form of syllogisms [Vernunftschluss] ... will contain the origin of special a priori concepts which we may call pure concepts of reason, or transcendental ideas, and which will determine according to principles how understanding is to be employed in dealing with experience in its totality" (A 321 / B 378). The "determination of things in themselves" that he has in mind here amounts to the thought of an unconditioned item, or set of items, corresponding to each of the syllogistic "forms," viz., an unconditioned, i.e., unpredicable, subject of categorical syllogisms, an unconditioned, i.e., first, object for "the hypothetical synthesis of the members of a series," and an unconditioned, i.e., exhaustive, source for "the disjunctive synthesis of the parts in a system" (A 323 / B 379).

To this ambitious scheme Kant immediately adds a further systematic proposal. He holds that the "unconditioned subject" corresponds to the absolute "unity of the thinking subject," that the unconditioned first item of the series of hypothetical syllogisms corresponds to the "absolute unity [i.e., either an absolutely first item or a total series] of the series of appearance," and that the unconditioned ground of the disjunctive syntheses is "the absolute unity of the condition of all objects of thought in general" (A 334 / B 391). Even more specifically, the thought of an unconditioned subject is taken to lead to the Idea of an immortal self, that of the unconditioned appearance is taken to lead to the contradictory Idea of a completely given whole of appearances (and thereby the notion of the mere phenomenality of the natural world, which allows the Idea of transcendental freedom), and the notion of an unconditioned source for thought is taken to lead to the Idea of "a being of all beings," God (A 336 / B 393; cf. B 395 n.).

These proposed connections are just the first layers of Kant's ingenious architectonic. The Ideas are determined further by the table of categories, so that the subject is considered as unconditioned qua substance, quality, quantity, and modality (hence there are four paralogisms of rational psychology), and the whole of appearances as unconditioned qua quantity, quality, causality, and modality (hence there are four antinomies of rational cosmology).

More specifically, in the Paralogisms Kant challenges rationalist arguments from the mere representation of the I to *a priori* claims that the self is substantial, simple, identical over time, and independent of other beings. Kant's ultimate concern is with showing that the unique and ever available character of the representation of the I, which is central to his own philosophy as an indication of the transcendental power of apperception, should not mislead us into claims that it demonstrates a special spiritual object, necessarily independent of whatever underlies other things. But although Kant properly stresses that our theoretical self-representation does not provide an intuition of the soul as a special phenomenal or noumenal object, his exposure of certain fallacies does not directly undermine all traditional rationalist claims about the self.[3]

In the attack on rational cosmology in the Antinomies, Kant "skeptically" contrasts pairs of *a priori* claims about the composition, division, origination, and relation of dependence of existence "of the alterable in the field of appearance" (A 415 / B 443). Roughly, the theses are: The set of appearances is finite in age and spatial extent, composed of simples, containing uncaused causality and a necessary being. The antitheses are: It is given as infinite in age and extent, divisible without end, and without uncaused causality or a necessary being impinging on it. Kant challenges these particular assertions by pointing out ways that the indirect arguments for them fail, since the denial of the opposite claim does not entail the assertion of the original claim. Thus one can escape the antinomies by avoiding the general assumption that either, because no endless series is given, there must be an end in composition, division, generation, and so forth or, because no end can be given as unconditioned, there must be an unconditioned series given without end. This solution is clearest for the last two antinomies, where Kant treats the causal and modal status of an appearance in general just as he does the phenomenal characterization of the self: It is an *a priori* truth that we can go on without end in seeking empirical acts of causality impinging on it, and empirical beings upon which it is dependent, and yet this does not yield a given unconditioned series because it always leaves open a possible involvement with some (nongiven) nonempirical causality and nondependent being. But although Kant can distinguish this result from dogmatic claims that there must be, or that there cannot be, a first causality and a nondependent being, he still leaves open (for grounding elsewhere) both the assertion that there must be *a priori* laws governing phenomena and the idea that there is some ground for assuming something beyond phenomena. His discussions still presume, as Leibniz would want, that all items within the spatiotemporal field are thoroughly governed by a principle of sufficient reason, and also, as Newton would want, that they are located in irreducible (although not absolutely real) forms of space and time.

Just as one should not be wholly taken in by the antirationalist tone of the Dialectic, one also should not assume that its architectonic has an entirely rigid structure. Like much of the *Critique*, it was the product of a series of hasty rearrangements,[4] and the final product contains some surprising oddities. The discussion of the Idea of God largely ignores the table of categories, while the treatments of the self and of the world often seem to pick arbitrarily from that table, each using just four of the six main headings (quantity, quality, substance, cause, community, and modality). Thus the issue of the agency of the self, which was considered a proper categorical topic in notes prior to the *Critique*, disappears from the discussion of rational psychology, while the question of the substantiality of phenomena in general is not posed directly (see A 414 / B 441). Furthermore, it is unclear why the notion of an unconditioned starting point for categorical syllogisms should lead to an ultimate subject considered only psychologically – that is, specifically as thinking, just as it is unclear why the nature of the thinking subject should not be considered (as it was by many rationalists) as just a part of the general theory of the world. The discussion of rational cosmology supposedly is to consider the world only as appearance (which is not the same as already assuming that it is only appearance), while the discussion of the subject can, and does, shift between regarding it as a phenomenon or as something beyond appearances. This distinction is not cleanly maintained, however, because sometimes (e.g., in the consideration of the simplicity of the components of the world) arguments about cosmology introduce nonphenomenal considerations (albeit in a way to be criticized – but the same is true in the Paralogisms), and sometimes (in the second and third Antinomies; cf. A 463 / B 491) they focus on psychological examples after all.

These oddities do not present such a severe problem if it is not assumed that the three Ideas need to be approached in fully parallel ways. And in fact this is not a fair assumption, since Kant makes clear that he has very different views about the Ideas. Whereas he argues that rationalist claims about the self are fallaciously inflated, he does not do much within the *Critique* to rule out the idea of a consistent, albeit very formal and negative, pure theory of the ultimate nature of the self, for example as necessarily immaterial and rational. Cosmological claims, on the other hand, get us into contradictory theses that are resolvable only by transcendental idealism, because we supposedly cannot say that the world is either of finite or of given infinite magnitude.[5] Here the problem is not one of a lack of knowledge or detail; rather, for certain questions (e.g., "How old is the world in itself") there is simply no sensible answer about an ultimate nature (because there is no quantity of this sort "in itself"). But this pattern of argument applies at best to only the first antinomy; for most cosmological issues, a fairly extensive rational doctrine (of phenomenal laws and noumenal possibilities) is allowed and is outlined in part in the *Metaphysical Foundations of Natural Science*.[6] Finally, the theological Idea is like the psychological one in not leading to contradictions, but also somewhat like the cosmology in providing a relatively full doctrine of

attributes, although for Kant their instantiation is left without support until one shifts from theoretical to moral–practical considerations. We thus gain from rational theology the "transcendental
ideal" of a perfect and necessary being, even if speculative arguments all fail to establish its existence.[7]

II

In view of all these reservations, one can expect some remnants of
the tradition to elude Kant's attack, even if it is unclear where one
might best seek them. Two clues will be pursued here. First, in order
to gain a fuller sense of Kant's view on the range of issues at stake in
the tradition, I will refer briefly to his direct comments on Leibniz in
the *Critique*'s "Amphiboly of Concepts of Reflection" (A 260–92 / B
316–49) and in the late draft on *What Real Progress Has Metaphysics Made in Germany since the Time of Leibniz and Wolff?* (1804).
Second, in order to treat one of these issues in some detail and from a
new perspective, I will focus on a central theme from Kant's extensive lectures on Baumgarten's Leibnizian metaphysics.

In the Amphiboly, Kant organizes his remarks in terms of four
major Leibnizian doctrines: (a) the principle of the identity of indiscernibles, (b) the principle of sufficient reason, (c) the monadology
and doctrine of preestablished harmony, and (d) the doctrine of the
ideality of space and time. The last issue applies to all the rest. For
Kant, even though Leibniz holds spatiotemporal determinations to
be derivative, he is a transcendental realist about space and time:
"Leibniz conceived space as a certain order in the community of
substances, and time as the dynamic sequence of their states" (A
275 / B 331). Once Kant rejects this conception, as he does in the
Transcendental Aesthetic, he can argue against (a) that otherwise
indiscernible substances can differ simply with respect to space and
time. The same point holds against (b), although initially Kant
expresses it not explicitly in terms of the notion of sufficient reason, but rather in terms of the general idea that logical and real
opposition are not to be equated, and that this cannot be appreciated when things are considered simply through the understanding
(A 264f. / B 320f.; A 273 / B 329; but cf. *Progress*, 20:282). Finally,
against (c), Kant presents not so much a counterargument as rather
a hypothesis, namely that Leibniz was led to the monadology be-

cause he could not conceive the inner states of substances in spatiotemporal terms but only in terms of simple founding properties, which we are supposedly aware of as representative states. This last conception is attacked, of course, in Kant's doctrine that even our inner sensibility is an appearance – not a self-illuminating intuition but a datum requiring for its determination relational and even physical knowledge.

There is a remarkable confirmation of the continuity of Kant's late thought in the fact that almost exactly this same four-part framework recurs in Kant's discussion of Leibniz in his draft of the *Progress* essay. The major change is that the doctrine of space and time is not listed as just one issue among the others. Rather, it is taken out and appropriately mentioned first as a prior condition for approaching the whole framework, and then at the end the doctrines of preestablished harmony and monadology are separated, so that a four-part structure is still maintained (*Progress*, 20:281–5). Kant's substantive critical points are almost precisely the same as before; there is just a slight change in the tone and focus. The object of criticism is now the whole school of Leibniz and Wolff, and a special theme, now stressed in each of the four points, is that this school violates "common sense," losing itself in the "whimsical" and the "enchanted." The school is also put into an historical context: its four doctrines constitute the "theoretical-dogmatic departure" of metaphysics, which precedes the stage of "skeptical deadlock" uncovered in the Antinomies, and the final stage of "the practically dogmatic completion" (*Progress*, 20:281) of metaphysics in Kant's moral system. Here again, despite his restriction of the principles of general ontology, and his use of antinomies against the tradition, Kant continues to endorse a "rational doctrine of nature," including *a priori* physics and psychology (*Progress*, 20:285–6). His aim is not to eliminate these but to show what form they can take when they are based on the implications of the doctrine of pure forms of intuition rather than on mere concepts. But all this does not yet show that a doctrine such as preestablished harmony is false. In the *Critique*, Kant suggests that it is dependent on the monadology (A 275 / B 331), but he must have known that this cannot settle the issue, for a monadology is compatible with doctrines other than harmony, namely occasionalism, and harmony does not require monadology (Wolff and others had drastically revised the notion of monads while still holding that at least in some contexts nothing better can be found than the doctrine of harmony).

To put Kant's attitude to such traditional alternatives in their fullest context, one should turn to his treatment of Baumgarten's metaphysics. Kant continued to rely on Baumgarten's dogmatic textbook for organizing his own annual lectures[8] even when he had ample opportunity to reorganize his teaching fully in terms of his new Critical philosophy, especially after 1784 when Johann Schultz's Kantian handbook was available. With the recent availability of new data from these lectures, Kant's detailed treatment of Baumgarten can no longer be ignored as a major indication of his own metaphysical views. It can even be argued that the new "system" that Kant calls for in the *Critique* (A 13 / B 27), but never published, is laid out precisely in these lectures, where the categories and their predicables are exposited in some detail.[9]

Although I have been attempting to abstract as much as possible from strictly psychological and theological issues, no treatment of Kant's critique of traditional ontology can wholly ignore substantive views about the mind and God, for it is distinctive of this era that often these impinge very heavily on general ontological issues. This is especially true of the several major discussions of causality in Baumgarten's *Metaphysica* that express the central doctrines of monadology and preestablished harmony. They color the more formal discussions (*Bg* §§19–33, 307f.; cf. *L2*, 28:572), which treat the general notion of a ground and the standard distinctions between primary and secondary causes, concurring and occasional causes and so forth, and they obviously determine the more substantive claims made in the scattered discussions of state and action, succession, and systems concerning substantial interaction (*Bg* §§205f., 297f., 448f., 761f.).

Given all this, it might appear that a short and tempting account of Kant's critique of the tradition could say simply that, given his Paralogisms and Critique of Speculative Theology, the ground under rationalist ontology has been knocked away, and so all the "explanations" of its metaphysics should be dismissed without further ado. Or, similarly, one could contend that the more general epistemological arguments of the Transcendental Analytic already show that all the nontrivial claims of the *Metaphysica* must be hopelessly dogmatic. Kant's own repeated treatments of Baumgarten fortunately did not always take such a quick and high-handed approach – and for good reason. If one looks closely at the *Critique*, it is not easy to show precisely how even on its own terms it has definitely undermined all claims of traditional metaphysics; indeed, from the *Critique* alone it is difficult to find out what all those claims are. To say simply that such claims are illegitimately "transcendent" is to beg a lot of questions about what that means, and it is surely not easy to hold that all of the *Critique*'s own major claims, for example about the eternity of substance, are nontranscendent in an evident sense.[10] Until a specific flaw is exposed in a rationalist argument, it cannot be rejected just on the basis of an unappealing "transcendent" conclusion; as long as there is no other objection, that conclusion could also be taken precisely as a disproof of claims that such conclusions are in general illegitimate. Moreover, there remain a host of specific topics and arguments within traditional metaphysics that deserve individual attention and that are not directly covered by the Transcendental Dialectic's taxonomy of fallacies.

These difficulties for Critical philosophy are compounded by the fact that Kant's own written work hardly presents a thorough treatment of "immanent" ontology. The exact nature of substance, cause, matter, and so forth, remains unsettled on Kant's own admission. Furthermore, we know that Kant was deeply attached to the truth of many traditional metaphysical beliefs (e.g., immaterialism, teleology) even if generally he shifted his views on their manner of justification in favor of only "regulative" or "pure practical" arguments. In the face of these complications, the fact that the Critical Kant did not simply ignore Baumgarten's arguments, but rather discussed them year after year, gains significance. It becomes important to determine what specific flaws Kant stressed here and what options, on balance, he came to favor with respect to the classical issues of ontology. This is a larger task than can be completed in this context, but in what follows I will sketch Kant's lecture treatment of traditional ontology in general and then focus on his discussion of one of its central doctrines, namely preestablished harmony.

In Kant's later lectures, the Critical perspective is laid out primarily in a long modification of the Prolegomena (only three paragraphs in Baumgarten) and the beginning of the Ontology section focusing on "the idea of transcendental philosophy." Unfortunately, from the 1770s we have few samples from that part of the lectures, except for fragments about one notion that is frequently reiterated later – the proposal that metaphysics begin not with the bare concept of a thing in general (*L1*, 28: 172; cf. *L2*, 28: 543, 552, 555; *MM*, 29: 811) but with a consideration of the possibility of knowledge of things, and thus the distinction between merely analytic and "real" or synthetic knowledge. Baumgarten was already known for incorporating episte-mological considerations into his metaphysics,[11] but Kant's point was that Baumgarten's work was largely vitiated by a failure to appreciate the distinction between analytic and synthetic proposi-tions. Kant then moved very quickly from asserting that we need synthetic propositions based on sensible intuition (pure and empiri-cal) to concluding that a study of the conditions of that intuition must be a study of our subjective nature rather than things in themselves – and that such a study is possible prior to any study of things (*L1*, 28: 180).

The standard format for all the later ontology lectures (e.g., *MM*, 29: 793f.; *L2*, 28: 546f.; *K3*, 29: 967f.) thus inserts, in order, prelimi-nary discussions of the distinctions analytic/synthetic, intuition/concept, transcendentally ideal/real (space–time). This leads into a discussion of judgments and categories, and the contention that the determination of "real possibility" ("possibility" being the first con-cept of the old Ontology) and other fundamental concepts[12] rests on what is required by the conditions for our making synthetic asser-tions by applying categories to a spatiotemporal context, conditions that are supposedly accessible as part of our pure subjective nature.

By the 1780s Kant thus prefers to say that metaphysics is not about objects but rather about reason – that is, about the structure of human cognition (*V*, 28: 359, 364; cf., *MM*, 29: 786; *Pure Reason*, A xiv). Hence one should investigate first not the concept of cause but rather the faculty by which it is possible for us to have *a priori* causal knowledge (*MM*, 29: 784). One might well ask why such "subjec-tive" investigations are thought to be easier. Kant sometimes indi-cates that they are so because they involve "self-knowledge" (*MM*, 29: 756; cf., *V*, 28: 392), but this is a casual and misleading way of expressing his view. That is, this expression involves the unfortu-nate suggestion that self-knowledge in some ordinary psychological sense comes first or is more certain, but that is precisely not Kant's Critical view.[13] It becomes clear that Kant really must mean the term "self" here just to be a shorthand reference to "reason," and not the other way around. "Subjective" investigations are privileged for him just insofar as they signify investigations of the elements of "pure thought," such as the forms of judgment. The privilege arises from the fact that Kant believes a complete survey of these forms is accessible (K3, 29: 988; vS, 28: 479), whereas a survey of things would have no closure. One can wonder why these forms are thought to be so easily accessible. Kant suggested that they are implicit in our "common language"; to the question as to how certain these are, he notes that they are "as" certain as experience in general – this is all the certainty he demands (MM, 29: 804). Elsewhere he also argued that the "limits of reason," that is, of items knowable by us, in contrast to things simpliciter, are determinable a priori because they are tied to the forms of our intuition, which are themselves determinable a priori (MM, 28: 781, 831).

All these views exemplify a broadly rationalist perspective. In the lectures, Kant's own metaphysics is repeatedly characterized as "rationalist" or "critical rationalist" (K2, 28: 992; D, 28: 619; K3, 29: 953), for he insists that philosophy must and can rest on a priori knowledge. The new aspect of his thought lies in his claiming to establish the order and limits of this knowledge. The main metaphysical argument that our knowledge must be limited to mere appearance arises from the "dialectical" or "antinomic" character that (he claims) assertions must take on as soon as they transcend the conditions of our sensible intuition and make claims about it as something unconditioned (e.g., D, 28: 620, 658; L1, 28: 187). However, the Critique's Antinomies are notorious for appearing to be question begging, and even in the later lectures there is remarkably little explanation of the crucial antinomic arguments.[14] An adequate consideration of the defense of transcendental idealism would require a closer study of the first two Antinomies, which are supposed to show that it is necessary and not just possible that the spatiotemporal domain is merely phenomenal. For ontology, the Second Antinomy plays an especially crucial and neglected role.[15] On the one hand, it belongs to the first pair of the four Antinomies, for which the "both/and" solution (which says the theses and the antitheses, properly construed, are jointly possible – the first holding noumenally, the second phenomenally) proposed for the second pair is supposedly ruled out. Yet the argument of the text suggests that in fact the Kantian response is to hold both that simple substances are required (A 434 / B 462f.; V, 28: 436; vS, 28: 517–8; D, 28: 663; K2, 28: 731; MM, 29: 850, 859), although they cannot exist as ultimately spatiotemporal, and that all spatiotemporal phenomena are divisible without end, but not absolutely substantial or real.

This result is obscured since the text is set up to shift the topic from the general ontological question of whether there are simple substances to the cosmological issue of whether beings "in the world" consist of simple parts. Kant's view on the explicit thesis and antithesis is actually quite close to Baumgarten (Bg §428), who had asserted both that there must be simple substances and that, for any matter that we perceive, that matter can be further divided. Kant's crucial shift (cf., L1, 28: 209; MM, 29: 827), which is easily missed in reading the Critique, was not categorically to deny this but rather to stress (vs. Bg §§419–21) that simple beings are not literally parts of bodies, not even what Baumgarten called "absolute first" parts. The departure from traditional ontology comes not in a denial of simple beings but in a refusal to allow them to be understood as directly spatiotemporal or as such that spatiotemporal properties can be considered as in principle derivable from the concept of those beings. Given the conclusion of the First Antinomy that the spatiotemporal domain is merely phenomenal, this means not that simple beings are to be dismissed ontologically but rather that they are saved – even if their individual determination is ruled out for us.

Because it is impossible to clarify this issue fully without also going through all of Kant's complex view of substantiality and sensibility, here it will be treated further only insofar as it impinges on the concept of interaction, which is at the center of most of the rest of the Metaphysica (Bg §§19f, 210f, 297f, 307f, 448f, 733f, 761f), and provides the best access to Kant's attitude to the options of traditional ontology.

To appreciate Kant's Critical views on this concept it is important to see their relation to his earliest work and its context. The issue of action in finite substances had been a major controversy in the Leibnizian schools. Bilfinger set the stage for mid–eighteenth-century German discussions by arguing that there are only three basic possibilities here: influx, occasionalism, and harmony.[16] The first system affirms intrasubstantial and intersubstantial action; the second denies both, and the last allows only intrasubstantial action. Baumgarten repeats this taxonomy (Bg §450), and by characterizing the influx theory in terms of an absurd "real" transfer of properties, he limits the discussion in effect to the latter two theories. Occasionalism is then faulted for allegedly also having to rely on an absurd real influx in explaining the action of infinite substance on finite substance (which is crucial because here the infinite substance is the constant source of all action), and, above all, for denying powers within ordinary finite things (Bg §452).

Kant was quite sympathetic to both these points. However, whereas Baumgarten stopped at presenting a version of the preestablished harmony theory (at Bg §§212, 329ff., he tries to show it is equivalent to a harmless "ideal" version of the influx theory that dispenses with literal infusion), Kant clearly was trying to open up some kind of fourth option. At the end of his *Nova Dilucidatio* (1755; see Proposition XIII, "The Principle of Coexistence"), Kant briefly but systematically goes through the traditional three options. The "crude" influx theory is dismissed by being tied to the (here disproven) bad presumption that the "very origin of the mutual connection of things [need not be] sought outside the principle of substances considered in isolation."[17] The preestablished harmony and occasionalist views are criticized as both giving only an "agreement" (on the first view, "conspired" "before"; on the second, "adapted" "during" mundane action) among things, and not genuine dependence.[18] Kant proposes a fourth alternative, the idea of a unifying God who makes things interactive in the very act that makes them what they are.[19] He stresses that on this view the "external" changes of a thing, its interactions with other things, are *just as* immediately attributable to it as any internal changes,[20] and hence there is no extra "artificial" condition, no "occasion" or "preestablishment," that needs to be referred to in explaining action: the interaction of things is revealed directly upon seeing what they are as lawful items based on one creator. This difficult argument foreshadows many themes of Kant's later Critical work: the idea that "inner" attributions are not privileged can be seen as one germ of the Refutation of Idealism, and the centrality of the notion of lawfulness anticipates the Second Analogy.

In the early lectures these views are developed somewhat further. Like Baumgarten, Kant wants to argue from the start that action is always a mixture of spontaneity and reaction,[21] and that in any real action there are always several concurring causes (MH, 28:37). For example, when we listen with attention, outer things are a true ground of the experience, but, in attending, we are also playing a role, so we are active and passive at once (*MH*, 28: 26, 53; cf. *vS*, 28: 513; *V*, 28: 433; and *Pure Reason*, B 157). In particular, Kant stresses that even for God to put a thought into us, there must be a ground within us, a capacity to receive and have the thought; otherwise, there would be no point in saying that it is we rather than God who have the thought.[22]

This is a very significant claim – I will call it the "Restraint Argument" because of how it restrains us from ascribing *all* activity and reality to God – and it balances Kant's early insistence on ascribing the *ultimate* source of all interaction, all true community, to God (*MH*, 28: 51; *Li*, 28: 212–4; *Dissertation* §19, 2: 408). By the Restraint Argument, God *cannot* be solely responsible for that which we know is going on just in us and which is, at least in some significant part, due to us; if that were possible, the admission of God as the unifier of the world could be turned into a Spinozistic monism that makes all apparently distinct individuals into mere aspects of one substance.[23]

At first Kant follows Baumgarten's unusual terminology here in calling influence of this "mixed" kind "ideal" (and also by considering it a kind of preestablished harmony view[24]); "real" influx would be a kind of "miraculous" forcing whereby the patient makes no contribution to the effect[25] and just receives a "transference" of properties from the agent via a kind of literal infusion, an idea already mocked by Wolff.[26] The common presumption here is that neither such transference nor such sheer passivity (given the Restraint Argument) makes any sense.

To try to nail down the absurdity of the vulgar "real" influx theory, Baumgarten added an argument that since the theory treats each patient in causation as sheerly passive, then supposedly all patients, all beings in the world, would be only passive, even the originally presumed "agents," and so there would be nothing active in the world to get action started – that is, ultimately explained.[27] Kant did not repeat this questionable extra argument, and he also soon rejected Baumgarten's terminology. Since it is only "real" causation of a "vulgar" and nonsensical sort that is being excluded, Kant proposed that his system now be called one of "real" or physical influence[28] because in all *other* ways, the only ways that make sense, it does allow interaction. From the beginning, he presumes that although we can't claim to know or directly perceive how causality takes place, we should affirm that it exists rather than fall back into either of the noninteractive and noncommonsensical positions of Malebranche and Leibniz, positions that Kant says have no advantage over sheer idealism[29]

In his *Inaugural Dissertation* (1770), Kant again rejects the vulgar version of the doctrine of real influence for giving the impression that action can be made intelligible simply by viewing things separately (*Dissertation*, §17, 2:407). In discussing the two other theories, he now calls them doctrines of "specially established" harmony, in contrast to the "generally established" harmony of his own theory (*Dissertation*, §22, 2:409). Despite the terminological changes, he claims the same superiority as before for his theory: It alone gives a "primitive bond of substances necessary because [of] a common principle and so . . . proceeding from their very subsistence, founded on their common cause . . . according to common rules," rather than being due merely to individual "states of a substance . . . adapted to the state of another . . . singularly" (*Dissertation*, §22, 2:409). Kant concedes that his view is somewhat like Malebranche's in holding that we get to other things only via God (*Dissertation*, §22, 2:410; cf. *MH*, 28:888),[30] but he says he is unlike Malebranche in not claiming to know this through any privileged vision. His doctrine is now put forth as just the best hypothesis by one who "hugs the shore" of common sense in allowing genuine interaction of finite substances (*Dissertation*, §22, 2:410; cf. *Progress*, 20:282).

The lecture notes from the 1770s are still very much in accord with the *Dissertation:* The mere existence of separate substances is insufficient to make interaction explicable, so a third item must be sought as a ground (*L1*, 28:212). The immediate basis for his own view is the familiar indirect argument against the alternatives. "Vulgar" influx theories[31] are dismissed as providing no explanation (the "original" interaction they posit is simply "blind" and inexplicable), while the "hyperphysical" theories of occasionalism and preestablished harmony are faulted for providing mere agreement rather than genuine interaction.[32] Although Kant agrees with the "derivative" theories in not presuming that finite substances can directly influence each other, he holds to calling his own view one of "real" influence, although not in the vulgar sense.

What does the Kantian view have to offer positively? The crucial points are that, unlike the vulgar view, it involves "laws" (*L1*, 28:213, 215) and, unlike the mere "agreement" views, these are "universal laws of nature," not mere "universal determinations" of a transcendent being.[33] These are points that fit in well with the eventual Critical view, but one can still ask why a direct influence of mundane beings upon each other, without any involvement of a third factor (a being upon whom the laws are based), is being wholly ruled out. Even if one allows Kant's idea that *necessary* beings must be isolated,[34] because any interdependence would have to be comprehensible *a priori* and this would undercut the self-sufficiency necessary to *their* substantiality, it would still seem that nonnecessary beings could have a direct, contingent, and actual interdependence that one would have no reason to expect to be comprehensible *a priori*.

The hidden premise here appears to be a principle that goes back at least to the time of the Herder lectures, namely that "no substance can contain the ground of the accident in the other, if it does not at the same time contain the ground of the substantial power and of the existence of the other" (*MH*, 28:32). Kant seems to understand this to mean that nothing can be the "very origin" of a mode in something else unless it is the ground of existence of the faculty of this mode. Given the Restraint Argument, "the existence of the action of another does not depend simply on one action and one power. Thus all predicates must be produced [in part at least] by one's own power, but since externally an alien power is also required [otherwise interaction is not occurring], then [if the "alien power" is not itself the source of one's being] a third [being] must have willed this harmony [if the "harmony" is to be anything other than mere coincidence]."[35]

Even if this background makes Kant's argument somewhat understandable, there remains the perplexing question of why (by the 1770s) he didn't move on to take the reference to laws to be by itself a sufficient distinguishing characteristic of his theory, that is, why did he continue to bring in a reference to God? The Restraint Argument and the rejection of mere harmony, along with implicit assumptions about the orderliness of the Newtonian world, lead naturally to a theory of interaction expressed in terms of lawfulness, a theory that does not immediately involve any reference to a transcendent being.[36]

Here one might respond that this would leave the great orderliness of interaction an inexplicable given,[37] and thus one would be in a situation just like that of the vulgar influx theory. Kant may well have accepted this response at the time, but if he continued to hold to it, it would have blocked any move to his eventual Critical theory. The crucial step in removing that block was to exploit an extra idea that was not yet developed, namely the idea of a transcendental account of "interaction" which would provide an *a priori* explanation of the need for law-governed relations between physical states as a principle of experience – that is, spatiotemporal cognition. Once Kant believed he had such an explanation, he left out reference to an ultimate source of interaction and focused just on its immanent structure; his general strategy in the Analogies is to construct epistemological arguments concerning *a priori* conditions of time determination[38] that warrant empirical analogues for the metaphysical principles of interaction in traditional metaphysics. There is a hidden aspect to this story, however, for when Kant developed this strategy in his writings, what he did for the most part was to shift the issues rather than to explain exactly his current views on the traditional questions. Here one finds a more detailed approach in the lectures.

In the newly available "Mrongovius" lectures, the issue of interaction is introduced by noting, "this investigation was brought to its height by Wolff . . . and Baumgarten. But now that one seeks mere popularity, and with that gladly abandons thoroughness, this proposition [about how interaction is possible at all] has also been left lying, although it is one of the most important in the whole of philosophy" (*MM*, 29:865). From this one gets a palpable impression of a kind of nostalgia on Kant's part for the controversies of his earlier years. There follows one of the best organized accounts of the traditional options, with Descartes's system presented as the prime instance of occasionalism, and as only trivially distinct from Leibniz's theory. The skeptical "idealist" consequences of the theories are especially stressed: Not only do they dispense with real interaction; they also make separate bodies, as opposed to mere representations of bodies, pointless (*MM*, 29:867).

As before, these theories are rejected because of their idealism, while literal influx is rejected as a nonstarter. But what is put in their place? Once again it is argued that "the world must also have only one cause. The *nexus* of substances is on that account to be thought possible only as derivative [i.e., only via God], but with that not as ideal, but rather concurrently as real." But it is immediately added: "This proof holds, however, only for the *mundus noumenon*. In the *mundus phaenomenon* we do not need it, for it is nothing in itself. Here everything is in *commercium* in virtue of space" (*MM*, 29:868). This reference to space is somewhat misleading, since, as the Third Analogy argues, it is not mere space but rather the conditions for our knowledge of the determination of things in it which is crucial, a determination that in turn is tied to "general laws," the feature that Kant eventually stresses as the crucial one lacking in the idealistic accounts that he rejects.[39]

But even if this is all granted, one surely should still ask about the traditional arguments about interaction (unless one is abandoning "thoroughness" for "popularity"), and in particular about the "proof" that there is "one cause." It is said that this holds (1) "only" (2) "for the *mundus noumenon*." The first part of the claim is easy enough when "only" is taken to mean, "not empirically," but the second part remains difficult; what is it to "hold" *at all* "for the *mundus noumenon*"? The most appealing answer in this particular situation (I do not mean this for all cases of the Kantian phenomenon/noumenon contrast) is that the proof is meant to hold simply for beings knowable by the pure understanding alone. In that realm of hypothetical beings Kant seems to accept the principle that dependent beings require a necessary being,[40] and so if such beings were linked in a world, they would be in connection through God. Hence what he could say here (but, unfortunately, we do not have proof that he does say) is just that although the "proof" is valid, the instantiation of its crucial premise, the preceding principle, is questionable. What it appears he actually stressed (*MM*, 29:868), however, is an additional problem, namely that the "idealistic" theories are inconsistent because they supposedly are meant for an empirical domain, and yet they lack an empirical warrant.

This objection does not resolve the original issue, but it is helpful in reminding us that Leibniz's successors (unlike Leibniz himself) ran into trouble precisely by trying to make their metaphysics "sensible." Just as we can't make empirical sense of decomposing bodies into monads, so also the occasionalist or harmony theorist can't sensibly account for the interaction of the empirical individuals we know. But the lecture text also suggests something that is to be said beyond the empirical level, namely that a dogmatic rejection (e.g., by Leibniz or Malebranche) of the possibility of genuine intersubstantial action would be wrong, and that *if* there is *such* interaction it would be comprehensible to us only with reference to God (and effective finite substances). Unlike before, here Kant cannot utilize a commonsense presumption of interaction, because after the Critical turn he reserves common sense for empirical rather than noumenal claims. Nonetheless, Kant surely continues to *believe* that there is nonempirical interaction (as is clear simply from the implications of his moral theory[41]), so it would be good to know how this belief fits in with his old "derivative" influx theory as well as the new Critical philosophy. Once again, the lecture notes give us the most thorough – and perplexing – evidence on the matter.

Notes from several lectures of the 1790s are now available. In *L2* (28:581), after a reiteration of the theme that interaction in the sensible world creates a whole that is "real, not ideal," it is asserted that "all substances are isolated for themselves," and "the cause of their existence and also of their reciprocal connection is God." But these assertions are unsupported and are preceded by the claim that "The intelligible world remains unknown to us." The assertions come closer to Kant's own earlier views than to Baumgarten's text, so it cannot be presumed that Kant was simply citing someone else's dogmatic views. It is also striking that no specific flaw in these views of substance is cited; the impression remains that *if* we are to think in an *a priori* way about these matters, this is the most appropriate way for us to think about them.

The Dohna notes are slightly more detailed and contain the usual characterization of the occasionalist and harmony theories, as well as the rejection of the "occult" influx theory, which leaves only Kant's old favorite, the "derivative" influx theory.[42] At this point, a somewhat remarkable transition occurs, for there is no direct criticism of this theory but just a note to the effect that, "if we regard space as real, then we accept Spinoza's system. He believed [in] only one substance, and he took all substances in the world to be determinations inhering in the divine."[43] This suggests a *reductio* behind

Kant's reasoning, namely that if one did accept the "interaction" of appearing things as ultimate, as constitutive of a complete and absolutely real system, then this would seem to force one to a kind of monistic and absurd Spinozism. Therefore Kant thought he had to show somehow that the domain of things we take to be interacting, things considered spatiotemporally, is not ultimate but rather "transcendentally ideal." But this leaves unclear what should be said once we abstract from space and time; there Spinozistic monism would still seem to be a significant threat. However, more is in fact said, for rather than simply ignoring the question of whether, absolutely speaking, there is more than one subject, Kant at other places reiterated a version of the Restraint Argument to show that *noumenally* there must be plurality. This argument contends that since the self is given as a finite and separate but dependent subject, not equal to or inherent in any all encompassing being (e.g., Spinoza's God), there must be something in addition to it that exists.[44] However, this argument is conclusive only in a context where it is already conceded that we do know the ultimate extent of the subject we are acquainted with through experience – and after the Critical turn this concession is no longer theoretically grounded and even appears to conflict with the main thrust of the Paralogisms.

The last lecture discussion, $K3$, is very similar to the others, and it still concludes: "If I assume all substances as absolutely necessary, then they cannot stand in the slightest community. But if I assume the substances as existing in a community, then I assume that they all exist through a causality [i.e., the causality of one being]" ($K3$, 29:1008; cf. ibid., 1007_3). In the way of an evaluation of this claim, all that is provided is the usual rejection of alternatives and the remark, "This idea [of derivative influx] has something sublime," followed by the conclusion that "Space itself is the form of the divine omnipresence, i.e., the omnipresence of God is expressed in the form of a phenomenon, and through this omnipresence of God, all substances are in harmony. But here our reason can comprehend nothing more" ($K3$, 29:1008). This is a baffling conclusion, for it would seem that "more" is not really needed, that "reason" has already "comprehended" too much. In particular, here it has been "comprehended" that noumenally there is neither an all-inclusive being nor a sheer plurality of beings but instead a derivative relation such that ultimately there is a plurality of finite substances related through, and only through, being determined by an infinite being, a position that corresponds closely to the pre-Critical view of the *Nova Dilucidatio*, the *Dissertation*, and the early lectures of the 1770s!

Such a result may seem remarkable, but it corresponds to positions repeated in other lectures. Consider the specific issue of mind–body interaction, the major focus of the problem for many philosophers at that time, and one that Kant felt he could handle especially well. His views here only reinforce the "rationalist" impression of his general discussion of interaction. Thus at one point it is said that the action of body on soul need not be said to be "ideal" because it is "just as" genuine as the action of body on body:

The body as phenomenon is not in community with the soul, but rather the substance distinct from the soul, whose appearance is called body. This substrate of the body is an outer determining ground of the soul, but how this *commercium* is constituted we do not know. In body we cognize mere relations, but we do not cognize the inner (the substrate of matter). The extended *qua extensum* does not act upon the soul, otherwise both *correlata* would have to be in space, therefore the soul be a body. If we say the intelligible of the body acts upon the soul, then this means this outer body's noumenon determines the soul, but it does not mean: a part of the soul (a noumenon) passes over as determining ground into the soul, it does not pour itself as power into the soul, but rather it determines merely the power which is in the soul, thus where the soul is active. This determination the author [Baumgarten] calls *influxus idealis*, but this is an *influxus realis*; for among bodies I can think only such an influence.[45]

At other places the special mind–body problem is resolved similarly by being embedded in a treatment of phenomenal interaction in general: "How is the soul *in commercio* (in community) with the body? *Commercium* is a reciprocal influence among substances, however bodies are not substances, but rather only appearances. Thus no actual *commercium* takes place" (*L2*, 28:591; cf. *L1*, 28:204, 209; *D*, 28:682; *K2*, 739). Similarly, in the "Metaphysik Mrongovius": "The primary difficulty that one runs up against in the explanation of the *commercium* with the body is that motion and thinking are so different that one cannot comprehend how the one is supposed to effect the other; but the body is a phenomenon and consequently its properties are as well. We are not acquainted with its substrate. Now how this could be in *commercium* with the soul amounts to the question of how substances in general can be in *commercium,* and the difficulty due to heterogeneity falls away. That bodies are mere appearances follows quite clearly from this because all their properties and powers issue from the motive power."[46]

Thus, the elevating of mind–body interaction to a status "just as" real as body–body interaction goes hand in hand with a debasing of a body–body interaction to a mere phenomenal status, a relation of states. The ultimate explanation of interaction is put off to the noumenal level, where, instead of a positive statement, one gets only the reassurance that there need not be an insuperable problem about "heterogeneity" or any commitment to a literal transfer of properties. But what does it mean to say that there are "connections" of "mere" phenomena[47] that nonetheless do not amount to an "actual *commercium?"*

One explanation here would be to employ a distinction stressed by Kant since the 1760s, namely the idea that we have access only to hypothetical necessities, which provide grounds not of things but of our knowledge (*MH,* 28:37; cf. ibid. 844). This would mean that the synthetic connections of empirical knowledge are distinguishable from mere logical relations but still quite unlike causal connections in an absolute ontological sense. On this view, the causality we speak of in knowledge claims is a relation used just for connecting accidents (representations) but not substances (*D,* 28:647). The obvious problem for this view is then what to make of the *Critique's* Analogies, especially the Third, which surely does appear to assert reciprocal causal relations between worldly substances, indeed all of them. There Kant concludes that if "the subjective community (*communio*) of appearances in our mind" is to "rest on an objective ground . . . objects may be represented as coexisting. But this is a reciprocal influence, that is, a real community (*commercium*) of substances" (A 214 / B 261). In the lectures, on the other hand, appearances and substances in themselves are repeatedly distinguished, e.g.: "*compositio* is the relation of substances insofar as they are in community; but this does not take place with *compositio phaenomenon*" (*MM,* 29:828).

In the end one must decide either that for Kant phenomenal substances truly are ultimate subjects, genuine substances in interaction, as the *Critique* often indicates (but not always: "matter, therefore, does not mean a kind of substance . . . but only the distinctive nature of those appearances"),[48] or that they are not, as the lectures generally say. On balance I do believe that in this instance the lectures give the most accurate indication of Kant's own deeply ambiguous view. The most recent evidence confirms that Kant was unwilling to break away fully from traditional ontology. It is no accident that at one point transcendental idealism was defined as the view that phenomena are not substances but require a noumenal substrate (D, 28:682). While Kant had his differences with his dogmatic predecessors, the appealing epistemological and empirical aspects of the *Critique* should not blind us to the fact that to accept a wholly nonrationalist metaphysics would also have involved giving up on the ontological implications of transcendental idealism, something Kant was not ready to do.

NOTES

1 The following translations of Kant's writings are employed in these pages: *Inaugural Dissertation*, by G. B. Kerferd and D. E. Walford, in *Selected Pre-Critical Writings and Correspondence with Beck* (Manchester, U.K., 1968); the *Nova Dilucidatio*, by John Reuscher, in *Kant's Latin Writings*, ed. Lewis White Beck (New York, 1986); *Lectures on Philosophical Theology*, by Allen Wood and Gertrude Clark (Ithaca, N.Y., 1978); *What Real Progress Has Metaphysics Made in Germany since the Time of Leibniz and Wolff?*, by Ted Humphrey (New York, 1983); and *Critique of Pure Reason*, by Norman Kemp Smith (London, 1929).

2 However, sometimes Kant seems not to challenge that the principle that the conditioned requires the unconditioned *is* valid for things in themselves, but rather to argue that precisely for that reason, since an unconditioned item cannot be found in the domain of spatiotemporal appearances, this shows they must be mere appearances rather than things in themselves (*Progress*, 20: 290; cf. note 40 in this chapter).

3 See my *Kant's Theory of Mind* (Oxford, 1982).

4 Cf. ibid. and Paul Guyer, "The Unity of Reason: Pure Reason as Practical Reason in Kant's Early Concept of the Transcendental Dialectic," *Monist* 72 (1989): 139–67.

5 More specifically, Kant's strategy is to say that the transcendental realist presumes the world has either an unconditioned, i.e., determinately given, finite magnitude or an unconditioned, i.e., determinately given, infinite one. Then it is argued indirectly that because it cannot have such a finite magnitude, it must be said to have the infinite one, and similarly

that because it cannot have such an infinite magnitude, it must have the finite one. Kant's solution is to reject the realist's presumption, and hence the conclusions of the indirect arguments, so that instead of a contradiction, viz., that the world is both determinately infinite and determinately finite, we rather get the result that it is just a continuing series of appearances neither determinately finite nor determinately infinite (cf. A 518 / B 546n.). It is questionable whether Kant's notion of a "determinate infinite" is more than a straw man; therefore, it is not clear that his solution (that we can go on without end in experience) must be incompatible with traditional realism and can fit only (let alone provide an independent basis for) his own idealism; cf. notes 12 and 15. But whatever Kant's problems are here, it is improper to assume, as all too often happens, that he is himself espousing all the various and peculiar arguments reported in the Antinomies. They are rather arguments which he takes to be tempting but dogmatic fallacies (cf. A 521 / B 549 n.). This creates another problem, though, for if the arguments are not accepted in every regard except their last step (drawn on the basis of the original illicit transcendental realist presumption), then there may be other ways, short of transcendental idealism, for escaping contradiction.

The metaphysics of this doctrine is developed further in Kant's *Opus postumum.*

Cf. Allen Wood's essay in this volume, as well as his *Kant's Rational Theology* (Ithaca, N.Y., 1978).

Much of the material in these lectures was made accessible for the first time with *Akademie* volumes 28 (1968) and 29 (1983). A large selection from them will be available in the forthcoming Cambridge translation by K. Ameriks and S. Naragon of *Kant's Lectures on Metaphysics*. In this essay, references to the lecture notes will use the following abbreviations, to which I here add the corresponding dates: *MH* = Metaphysik Herder (1762–4), *L1* = Metaphysik L1 (1770s), *MM* = Metaphysik Mrongovius (1782–3), *V* = Metaphysik Volckmann (1784–5), *vS* = Metaphysik von Schön (late 1780s), *L2* = Metaphysik L2 (1790–1), *D* = Metaphysik Dohna (1792–3), *K2* = Königsberg 2 (1793–4), *K3* = Königsberg 3 (1794–5). All of Baumgarten's *Metaphysica* (4th ed., Halle, 1757) is reprinted in Kant's *Akademie* edition at 17:5–226, except for the Empirical Psychology, which is at 15:5–53. (There is also a useful abridged German translation of Baumgarten by G. F. Meier (Halle, 2d ed., 1783).) I refer to the *Metaphysica* throughout by using *Bg*. Capitalization of "Ontology," etc., refers to a subsection of the *Metaphysica*, just as "Paralogisms" etc. refers to a section of the *Critique*. The quite recent discovery of the *MM* and *K3* manuscripts (vol. 29) is particularly significant because they provide considerable independent confirmation for what is found in the other lecture notes. Although no individual note can be trusted by itself, the striking amount of overlap over the years demonstrates, I believe, that these student notes are in general a very good indication of what Kant taught. But they must be used with caution, especially because there are even problems with their presentation in the *Akademie* edition. See the articles by Werner Stark in *Kant-Forschungen*, vol. I (Hamburg: Felix Meiner-Verlag, 1987).

Here is a brief outline of Baumgarten's *Metaphysica:* I. Prolegomena (§§1–3); II. Ontology (§§4–350), A. Internal Universal Predicates: 1. possibility, 2. connection, 3. thing (including essence and determination), 4. unity, 5. truth, 6. perfection, B. Internal Disjunctive Predicates: 1. necessary, 2. mutable, 3. real, 4. particular, 5. whole, 6. substance, 7. simple, 8. finite – and each of their opposites, C. External and Relational Predicates: 1. identity and diversity, 2. simultaneity and succession, 3. types of causes, 4. sign and signified; III. Cosmology (§§351–500), A. Concepts of World: 1. affirmative, 2. negative, B. Parts of World: 1. simples: in general, and qua spirits, 2. composites: their genesis and nature, C. Perfection of World: 1a. the idea of the best and b. the community of substances; 2. the means: natural and supernatural; IV. Psychology, A. Empirical (§§504–739): 1. existence of soul, 2. faculties, a. cognitive (lower and higher), b. appetitive (in general and qua spontaneous and free), 3. mind–body interaction, B. Rational (§§740–99): 1. soul's nature, 2. interaction with body, 3. origin, 4. immortality, 5. afterlife, 6. comparison of human and nonhuman souls; V. Theology (§§800–1000), A. Concept of God: existence, intellect, will, B. Divine Action: creation, its end, providence, decrees, revelation.

9 See Max Heinze, *Vorlesungen Kants über Metaphysik aus drei Semestern* (Leipzig, 1894), p. 599.

10 This point was stressed already by J. A. Ulrich in 1785. See Frederick Beiser, *The Fate of Reason* (Cambridge, Mass.: Harvard University Press 1987), p. 205.

11 See Max Wundt, *Die deutsche Schulphilosophie im Zeitalter der Aufklärung* (Tübingen, 1945), p. 221. Cf. Lewis White Beck, *Early German Philosophy* (Cambridge, Mass.: Harvard University Press, 1969), p. 285.

12 Kant takes the same line on the "internal universal predicates." Thus the proof of the principle of sufficient reason is rejected as making an unprovable universal claim, and it is denied that we have *a priori* access to a real essence that would provide the explanation of all of a particular thing's actual properties. No argument is allowed from the mere possibility of a thing, i.e., its concept, to the existence of that thing, and unity (in the sense of order), truth, and perfection, are held to apply only to the

structure of knowledge rather than directly to things. The "disjunctive" predicates receive a similar treatment. For example, *a priori* knowledge of necessity and contingency (vs. *Bg* §101) in any absolute sense is denied, and the mutable and immutable are treated (vs. *Bg* §124) as sheerly phenomenal predicates with no relation to absolute necessity. In discussing wholes and parts (vs. *Bg* §155), Kant introduces his distinction beween "real" and "ideal" composites, where in the first case the parts are given prior to the whole, but in the second the whole, as with space and time, is given prior to the parts (as ideal because mathematically infinite). Baumgarten had already distinguished the determinate (maximal, total) metaphysical infinity of the most real thing (*"omnitudo"*), and the mere mathematical infinite of that which is unbounded (*Bg* §248), and he had argued not only that there is an absolute and unalterable infinite thing, but also that any alterable thing must be metaphysically contingent (*Bg* §§257, 131) and finite, even if in various quantitative ways it is mathematically infinite. Kant rejected these arguments, and his theory of space and time also affects his view of the first of external relational predicates: identity (*Bg* §265), simultaneity (*Bg* §280), and succession (*Bg* §297). Unlike the Leibnizians, Kant makes no absolutely necessary connection between simultaneity and extension; instead, he argues for the conditional necessity that, for beings like us, things can be *known* as being at the same time only via a consideration of things that are next to each other. Similarly, in the domain of our knowledge, spatiotemporal differentiation is what settles claims of identity and diversity, rather than vice versa (vs. *Bg* §407). Succession and the other relational predicates all involve causal notions (*Bg* §§307–50) and the remaining "internal disjunctive predicates," which are discussed below.

13 See the Paralogisms and P. Guyer, "Psychology in the Transcendental Deduction," in *Kant's Transcendental Deductions,* ed. Eckart Förster (Stanford, Calif: Stanford University Press, 1989), pp. 47–68.

14 Cf. note 5. The Third Antinomy, which is not fundamental ontologically, is what is stressed at *L2* and *K2*; see Heinze, *Kants Vorlesungen,* p. 572.

15 For many more details on the first Antinomies, see Arthur Melnick, *Space, Time, and Thought in Kant* (Dordrecht: D Reidel, 1989), J. Bennett, *Kant's Dialectic* (Cambridge: Cambridge University Press, 1974), and Carl Posy, "Dancing to the Antinomy: A Proposal for Transcendental Idealism," *American Philosophical Quarterly* 20 (1983): 81–94.

16 Georg Bernhard Bilfinger, *De Harmonia animae et corporis humani maximi praestabilita, Commentatio hypothetica* (1723). See Benno

Erdmann, *Martin Knutzen und seine Zeit* (Leipzig, 1876). The trichotomy goes back at least to Pierre Bayle's "Rorarius" discussion in his *Dictionnaire historique et critique* (1697). Cf. *Pure Reason*, A 390.

17 *Nova Dilucidatio*, 1:416; cf. the argument at ibid., 414. This argument is also noted at Guyer, *Kant and the Claims of Knowledge* (Cambridge, 1987), p. 308.

18 *Nova Dilucidatio*, 1:415. The Reuscher translation of the passage at lines 32–7 (in *Kant's Latin Writings*, p. 104) can give a misleading impression here.

19 *Nova Dilucidatio*, 1:415, "there is a real action of substances that occurs among them, or interaction through truly efficient causes, because the same principle that set up the existence of things shows them to be bound by this law." Cf. *MH*, 28:887, for another early reference to law.

20 *Nova Dilucidatio*, 1:415, "By the same right, therefore, external changes can be said to be produced by efficient causes just as changes that happen internally are attributed to the internal force of a substance."

21 *MH*, 28:96; cf. *MH*, 28:51–2. Thus, judging and sensing aren't opposed as action to inaction; rather, the first is just a "greater" action than the other (*MH*, 28:27). This general ideal may go back to Leibniz's *Specimen Dynamicum* (1695), which claimed that even passion is spontaneous and involves self-activity. Cf. *MM*, 29:723, 823; *MH*, 28:26; *V*, 28:433.

22 *MH*, 28: 52. This argument is nicely complemented by one at *R* 3581, 17:71, which says that while the patient must contribute something, it cannot contribute everything to an action. That is, if everything in us were active, there would be no nature in us for God to act on, i.e., nothing with an enduring identity that goes beyond the different states generated (by "us") at each moment.

23 On Spinoza, see notes 43 and 44. On finite agency, cf. Leibniz, *Theodicy*, §32. Leibniz argued against occasionalism that it did away with the natures of individuals and so could lead to Spinozism.

24 *MH*, 28:26, 52, 888. Cf. *Bg* §§212, 217. B. Erdmann, *Martin Knutzen*, p. 66, notes that similar language is used by G. F. Meier, who translated Baumgarten into German and on whom Kant also lectured.

25 *MH*, 28:53: "If we want to conceive that one power simply suffers from the other, without its own power and thus without harmony, then that is called *influxus physicus* or *realis.*"

26 See Wolff's *Rational Psychology*, §558, cited in Beck, *Kant's Latin Writings*, p. 109, n. 44. Cf. Kant's *Prolegomena*, §9, 4:282; *MM*, 29:823.

27 *Bg* §451. Elsewhere Baumgarten also adds a very weak argument that there must be a plurality of finite substances (*Bg* §§339–91).

28 See, e.g., *Dissertation*, §17, 2:407: "If we free this concept from that

blemish, we have a kind of interaction which is the only one which deserves to be called real." Cf. *K2*, 28:759.

29 *MH*, 28:886–7; cf. *D*, 28:666, 684; *K3*, 29:1008. Here Kant already denies that the heterogeneity of cause and effect is a sufficient reason to deny interaction; thus he was unattracted to the Wolffian compromise of falling back on preestablished harmony for mind–body relations while accepting the influx theory elsewhere.

30 Malebranche, the main advocate of occasionalism (although Kant and others often also attached Descartes to this doctrine – see *L1*, 28:215; *D*, 28:665) was famous for holding that we "intuit all things in God" (*De la Recherche de la Verité*, III, 2, vi).

31 *L1*, 28:213, "*influxu physici originario in sensu crasiori.*"

32 *L1*, 28:215. These theories are still categorized as theories of "derivative" (as opposed to "original") interaction because they do not presume the finite substances can directly influence each other. Cf. Kant's argument (*MM*, 29:932; cf. *D*, 28:664) against Baumgarten's "quite poor" claim (*Bg* §414) that substances (in this case, monads) "next to each other" must be in contact qua "touching," as well as the claim (*Bg* §410) that all action as such involves not just interaction but also reaction qua resistance.

33 *L1*, 28:214: "*harmonia automatica* is when for every single case the highest cause has to arrange an agreement, thus where the agreement does not rest on universal laws, but rather on a primordial arrangement which God put in the machine of the world." However, as Alison Laywine has reminded me, sometimes Kant spoke of Leibniz as stressing the role of universal laws (see A 275 / B 331, but cf. B 167).

34 I.e., such that there cannot be a plurality of them constituting a "world" (*L1*, 28:214). Cf. *Bg* §357, *L2*, 28:581, and *MH*, 28:865, "For by its concept every substance exists for itself, therefore appears to be isolated, and has nothing to do with an other substance." Here, as often in Kant, talk about the "concept of" something is short for talk about what can be *a priori* determinable about it, i.e., what is determinable insofar as it is necessary. Cf. Burkhard Tuschling, "*Necessarium est idem simul esse et non esse,*" in *Logik und Geschichte in Hegels System*, ed. H. C. Lucas and Guy Planty-Bonjour (Stuttgart, 1989), p. 210; and his "Apperception and Ether: on the Idea of a Transcendental Deduction of Matter in Kant's 'Opus postumum'," in *Kant's Transcendental Deductions*, pp. 193–216.

35 *MH*, 28:52–3. All bracketed interpolations are my own interpretive additions. Cf. *L1*, 28:213: "no substance can influence another *originare* except of that of which it is itself a cause."

36 In another passage – arising perhaps from an earlier phase in Kant's

work (since this section may be composed of at least two treatments of the topics, with the second starting at $L1$, 28:214$_{28}$), Kant's theory is characterized simply in terms of "laws of nature . . . it may ground itself otherwise on whatever it wants" ($L1$, 28:213). By calling the hyperphysical theories ones that really do not have laws ($L1$, 28:215; see note 39 below), Kant may have been moving toward a perception of how crucial the reference to lawfulness was to his own theory. J. B. Schneewind has explored a parallel moral dimension of Kant's early interest in a "divine corporation," which gives finite beings a power of self-legislation. See his essay in this volume, and his "The Divine Corporation and the History of Ethics," in *Philosophy in History*, ed. R. Rorty, J. B. Schneewind, and Q. Skinner (Cambridge: Cambridge University Press, 1984), pp. 173–92.

37 For a contemporary view, cf. Ralph Walker, *Kant* (London: Routledge & Kegan Paul, 1978), p. 175.

38 This strategy is detailed in Guyer, *Kant and the Claims of Knowledge*. The concern with time determination already appears in the old notes, albeit in a traditional context, e.g., at $L1$, 28:215, "the actual representation of the conjunction of substances among one another consists in this: that they all *perdure*, that they are all there through one."

39 *MM*, 29:868. "The *influxus physicus* happens according to general laws, but the two systems of the *nexus idealis* do not."

40 *MM*, 29:925; cf. *Bg* §§308, 334.

41 See also *MM*, 29:856, 927–8: "the immediate cause of the sensible world is the *mundus noumenon*."

42 *D*, 28:666, "There must be a being there from which all derive. All substances have their ground in it."

43 *D*, 28:666. Cf. *K2*, 28:732, and *K3*, 29:1008–9. *K3*, 29:977–8 equates Spinozism with transcendental realism.

44 "For if only a single substance exists, then either I must be this substance, and consequently I must be God (but this contradicts my dependency); or else I am an accident (but this contradicts the concept of my ego, in which I think myself as an ultimate subject which is not the predicate of any other being)," from *Lectures on Philosophical Theology*, p. 86 (28:1052); cf. ibid., pp. 74–5 (28:1041f.), and *V*, 28:458; *D*, 28:666; *K3*, 1008f.

45 *K2*, 28:758–9; cf. B 427–8. For such passages it is worth recalling that in German the term for "influence" (*Einfluss*) can be broken down into "pours" or "flows in" (*fliesst ein*). Cf. *L1*, 28:279–80: "But we can no more comprehend the *commercium* between bodies among themselves than that between the soul and the body."

46 *MM*, 29:908. Cf. *K3*, 29:1029, "An unknown something, which is not

appearance, is what influences the soul, and so we obtain in us a homogeneity with things. In this lies the representation that not the phenomenon itself of the body, but rather the substratum of matter, the noumenon, produces in us. The *influxus* on one another thought materially between soul and body, and yet so that both would be outside themselves, and each for itself, is something in itself impossible: and if one assumes it ideally, then this would be nothing but the *harmonia praestabilita*, and would no longer be *influxus*. It must thus be thought as immaterial effect of the noumenon of both, whereupon this means nothing more than that something influences the soul, and then no heterogeneity remains which might raise doubts here . . ." Cf. *D*, 28:684–5, *MH*, 28:886–7. An anticipation of the view that the mind–body relation is not a special problem can be found in Knutzen: see B. Erdmann, *Martin Knutzen*, p. 104.

47 Such connections are also stressed in the lectures: *V*, 28:408, 522–4; *MM*, 29:788, 806–9, 813–18.

48 A 385. For more references, see my *Kant's Theory*, p. 299, n. 79.

9 Vindicating reason

I. THE CRITIQUE OF REASON

Whatever else a critique of reason attempts, it must surely criticize reason. Further, if it is not to point toward nihilism, a critique of reason cannot have only a negative or destructive outcome, but must vindicate at least some standards or principles as authorities on which thinking and doing may rely, and by which they may (in part) be judged. Critics of "the Enlightenment project," from Pascal to Horkheimer to contemporary communitarians and postmodernists, detect its Achilles' heel in arrant failure to vindicate the supposed standards of reason that are so confidently used to criticize, attack, and destroy other authorities, including church, state, and tradition. If the authority of reason is bogus, why should such reasoned criticism have any weight?

Suspicions about reason can be put innumerable ways. However, one battery of criticisms is particularly threatening, because it targets the very possibility of devising anything that could count as a vindication of reason. This line of attack is sometimes formulated as a trilemma. Any supposed vindication of the principles of reason would have to establish the authority of certain fundamental constraints on thinking or acting. However, this could only be done in one of three ways. A supposed vindication could appeal to the presumed principles of reason that it aims to vindicate – but would then be circular, so fail as vindication. Alternatively, it might be based on other starting points – but then the supposed principles of reason would lack reasoned vindication, so could not themselves bequeath unblemished pedigrees. Finally, as a poor third option, a vindication of reason might suggest that reasoning issues in uncompletable regress, so that prospects of vindicating any claim, including claims to identify principles of reason, never terminate: To reason is only to keep the door open to further questioning. In each case the desired vindication eludes. These unpromising thoughts lend some appeal to Pascalian faith, to Humean naturalism or even to postures of postmodernity as responses to the challenge of skepticism about reason.

If the *Critique of Pure Reason* is to live up to its title and its reputation it must deal with skepticism with regard to reason. The whole magnificent and intricate critical structure will have little point if it draws on an unvindicated or unvindicable conception of reason. Yet it is far from clear where or how Kant handles these topics. I shall try here to trace some of his moves, drawing in particular on passages in the earlier sections of the Transcendental Doctrine of Method, but also on widely scattered passages in the prefaces, the Transcendental Dialectic and various shorter writings.[1] I shall try to show that Kant addresses this fundamental topic persistently and with great subtlety, and that he offers an account of what it is to vindicate reason quite different from the foundationalist account that critics of "the Enlightenment project" target, and usually attribute to Kant. Whether his account is wholly satisfactory is a large and complicated question, on which I offer sparse comments.

II. REASON AND LOGIC

It is helpful to begin by asking what sort of thing we expect a vindication of reason to vindicate. One account, with impeccable Cartesian and rationalist ancestry, sees principles of reason as formal principles of logic and method. These principles are to be algorithms for the formation and transformation of simple truths, and to provide axioms that wholly (according to rationalists) or partly (according to many others) constrain acceptable thinking and doing. The vindication of these axioms is problematic. Some boldly insist that they have divine warrant, even that God has installed these principles "whole and complete in each of us";[2] others are discreetly silent.

This is not Kant's view. He insists that principles of reason and of logic are distinct. In the prefaces of the *Critique of Pure Reason* he claims that logic was invented and completed in one stroke by Aris-

totle, that it has precise boundaries and that its success is consequent upon these limitations (B viii–ix). By contrast the prefaces
depict human reasoning as "a merely random groping" (B xv) that
falls repeatedly into contradictions and has yet to find the "secure
path of a science" (B xiii). For Kant logic is abstracted either from the
use of the understanding or from that of reason, and its vindication
would have to be derived from theirs, rather than conversely. However, the fact that logic is derivative in this way allows us to use its
structure as a clue or key to the cognitive structures from which it is
derived.[3] No doubt there are many questions to be raised about
Kant's treatment of logic, but it is at least clear that this is not the
place to look for his vindication of reason.

III. REASON AND UNDERSTANDING

On Cartesian accounts a vindication of reason must be the first of
philosophical tasks. Kant does not treat the matter in this way. The
Critique of Pure Reason begins, in the Aesthetic and the Analytic of
the Doctrine of Elements, with discussion of the "lower faculties of
knowledge," sensibility and understanding. Only in its last and longest section, the Transcendental Dialectic, does Kant turn to questions about reason, the "higher faculty of knowledge." There he
mainly exposes and undermines excessive rationalist claims about
the powers of reason. Vindication of reason is still postponed.

The first pages of the Dialectic stress some differences between
lower and higher faculties of knowledge and acknowledge that investigating the latter raises difficulties that did not arise in investigating the powers of understanding, because we lack all insight
into the supposed real use of reason (A 299 / B 355). This may seem
unsurprising – would not Leibniz have agreed that *we* lack complete insight? – but Kant insists that *no* real use can be vindicated.
The fundamental point of the Copernican turn is that no correspondence of reason to reality be presumed. The use of reason is not
assigned any counterpart to the reduced, empirical realism that
Kant allows the understanding. The parallel that he draws between
understanding and reason is only that both are "faculties of unity";
but the unity the two achieve contrasts sharply:

Understanding may be regarded as a faculty which secures the unity of
appearances by means of rules, and reason as being the faculty which se-

cures the unity of rules of understanding under principles. Accordingly, reason never applies itself directly to experience or to any object, but to understanding, in order to give to the manifold knowledge of the latter an *a priori* unity by means of concepts, a unity which may be called the unity of reason, and which is quite different in kind from any unity that can be accomplished by the understanding.   (A 302 / B 359; cf. A 644 / B 672)

In these "provisional" passages Kant warns his readers that

multiplicity of rules and unity of principles is a demand of reason, for the purpose of bringing the understanding into thoroughgoing accordance with itself. . . . But such a principle . . . is merely a subjective law for the orderly management of the possessions of our understanding . . . [so that] The unity of reason is therefore not the unity of a possible experience, but is essentially different from such unity.   (A 305–7 / B 362–3)

Kant evidently rejects the rationalist claim that the principles of reason can provide a unique and integrated answer to all possible questions. In the Transcendental Dialectic the central objection to rational psychology, rational cosmology, and rational theology is that the rationalist tradition treats each domain as an object of theoretical inquiry, where necessary truths about soul, world, and God are to be reached by intuition or analysis, and where there is no essential difference between the unity achieved by rules and by principles.

A main objective of the Transcendental Dialectic is to show how any view of principles of reason as divinely inscribed axioms or rules of thought, that correspond to reality, leads to contradictions – to paralogisms, antinomies, and impossibilities. Kant rejects the *pièces de résistance* of the whole metaphysical tradition. He deems human reason quite simply incompetent for these illusory tasks. While the Copernican turn was put forward in the prefaces "only as an hypothesis" (B xxii n.), the arguments of the Transcendental Dialectic support the hypothesis that reason does not conform to the real, by inflicting heavy damage on metaphysical systems that assume such correspondence.

IV. IDEAS OF REASON AND STRIVING FOR UNITY

In the introductions of the Transcendental Dialectic we also find suggestions that, as in the case of understanding, logic offers a clue to the structure of the faculty of knowledge from which it is supposedly abstracted. However, in this case the clue is given not by the traditional logic of terms but by syllogistic. This is not because syllogistic is "more abstract" than the logic of terms, but because it links distinct propositions into larger units: It achieves a different sort of unity, and potentially a very extensive, even systematic unity:

From this [discussion of syllogistic] we see that in inference reason endeavours to reduce the varied and manifold knowledge obtained through the understanding to the smallest number of principles (universal conditions) and thereby to achieve in it the highest possible unity.   (A 305 / B 361)

However, the attempt to achieve unity of knowledge is not guaranteed by any really existing unity. There is no metaphysical proof that all aspects of our thinking and doing can be integrated into a single, systematic unity. No principle of sufficient reason, no *ens realissimum* guarantees the principles of reason or the completeness of knowledge. On the contrary, human knowledge is threatened by chaos, while knowledge and action are divided by a "great gulf" that provides the most profound challenge to the possibility of a complete and systematic philosophy. Complete unity can then be no more than "endeavor,"[4] whose success is not guaranteed, and is ultimately shown unattainable.

At the end of the introduction of the Transcendental Dialectic Kant confronts the suspected limitations of reason by posing a dilemma. He asks:

Take the principle, that the series of conditions . . . extends to the unconditioned. Does it, or does it not, have objective applicability [*objektive Richtigkeit*]? . . . Or is there no such objectively valid principle of reason, but only a logical precept [*eine bloß logische Vorschrift*], to advance towards completeness by an ascent to ever higher conditions and so to give to our knowledge the greatest possible unity of reason?   (A 308–9 / B 365)

Either reason has objective validity, and its principles are not essentially different from the rules of the understanding, as these were understood by rationalists, since their real use is underpinned by the objective unity of experience. Or reason is only a *precept* or prescription to seek unity. We know well enough that the upshot of the Transcendental Dialectic is to reject the first horn of the dilemma. It follows then that Kant must understand reason as a precept for the task of achieving "the greatest possible unity." Striving for this greatest possible unity aspires to overcome or dispel the threatened hiatuses of thought and action – with no guarantee of success. Kant does not presuppose that integrated answers to his three fundamental questions "What can I know?" "What may I do?" and "What may I hope?" must be available; he does not assume even that human knowledge must or can form a complete and systematic whole.

V. PRECEPTS AND IDEAS OF REASON

Although the Transcendental Dialectic is so clearly a sustained polemic against rationalism, and against the rationalist conception of reason as guarantor and mirror of reality, there is a good deal in the text that deflects attention from the active, striving (as opposed to passive, mirroring) character Kant ascribes to reason. When Kant speaks of principles of reason in the Dialectic he often uses terms that fit best with conception of reason as mirroring reality. He speaks not of precepts or maxims of reason – which would indicate at once that he thinks of reason as practical principles for guiding thinking and doing – but in traditional rationalist, indeed Platonist, terms of *Ideas of Reason.* He defends his appropriation of this misleading Platonic term, not because but *in spite* of its metaphysical resonance. The term suits not because Kant too wants to endorse a classical, theoretical conception of reason, as correspondence of thought to its real archetypes, but because Plato's Ideas are potent symbols of striving for the most encompassing unity. The Platonic Ideas are an image of the unity of the highest principles that guide a quest for the Good and the Beautiful as well as the True. Kant allows himself this borrowing, which parallels his own three fundamental questions, but rejects the entire Platonic account of the metaphysical basis of unity and success in these quests. He firmly rejects all thought that his Ideas of Reason correspond to any real archetypes, and adopts a position that is irreconcilable with any form of the Platonic vision of Ideas as patterns for knowledge and mathematics.[5] In spite of this unequivocal rejection of any real use of the Ideas of Reason, the borrowed terminology is unavoidably associated with the strongest forms of realism, and masks the quite different Kantian conception of Ideas of Reason, which are conceived as precepts for seeking unity of thought and action, rather than as archetypes that guarantee that unity is to be found.

VI. UNITY OF REASON VS. THE PLURALITY OF ITS PRECEPTS

Granted that the Ideas of Reason are precepts, it is surely puzzling that Kant thinks a plurality of distinct Ideas can create "the greatest possible unity." He introduces a wide range of principles of reason under a variety of labels. There are "Postulates of Reason" and "Maxims of Reason" as well as "Ideas of Reason." All can count as principles of reason, and aim at a single sort of unity, because all are forms or aspects of a single principle, which can be formulated in multiple ways. This explains why Kant speaks both of "the principle of reason," and of many ideas or principles of reason. He says of the underlying principle:

The principle of reason is thus properly only a *rule*, prescribing a regress in the series of the conditions of given appearances, and forbidding it to bring the regress to a close by treating anything at which it may arrive as absolutely unconditioned. . . . Nor is it a *constitutive* principle of reason . . . [but] rather a principle of the greatest possible continuation and extension of experience, allowing no empirical limit to hold as absolute. Thus it is a principle of reason which serves as a *rule*, postulating what we ought to do in the regress, but *not anticipating* what is present *in the object as it is in itself, prior to all regress.* Accordingly I entitle it a *regulative* principle of reason.   (A 509 / B 537)

It is not hard to connect various formulations of this principle to one or another of Kant's own basic questions. Answers to "What can I know?" are guided by Ideas or precepts of scientific inquiry, including

It is a logical postulate of reason, that through the understanding we follow up and extend as far as possible that connection of a concept with its conditions,   (A 498 / B 526)

and

Entia praeter necessitatem non esse multiplicanda.   (A 652 / B 680)

Answers to the question "What ought I do?" are guided by the formulations of the Categorical Imperative, and their more determinate implications (principles of duty, of justice, and so forth). Answers to

the question "What may I hope?" are guided, *inter alia*, by the Postulates of Practical Reason and by maxims of seeking purposiveness,
which provide accounts of various possible "bridges" across the
"great gulf" that would otherwise sunder our grasp of knowable
nature and of free action. Kant maintains that the contradictions to
which the use of reason as a constitutive principle leads can be
avoided by this more modest, regulative conception of reason, in its
various formulations. If we view principles of reason as precepts for
the conduct of thinking, acting, and their coherent connection,
hence as ways of achieving an active grasp rather than a passive
response to the manifold of life, then although we will never regain
the heights that rationalist conceptions of reason claimed to con-
quer, we can unite a wide range of our experience and actions without lapsing into contradiction:

When they [regulative principles] are treated merely as *maxims*, there is no
real conflict, but merely those differences in the interest of reason that
give rise to differing modes of thought. In actual fact, reason has only one
single interest, and the conflict of its maxims is only a difference in, and a
mutual limitation of, the methods whereby this interest endeavours to
obtain satisfaction.   (A 666 / B 694)

Even if we accept Kant's view that the many Ideas of Reason are all
aspects of one striving for unity, reason has not been vindicated.
What is it that shows that striving for unity is fundamental to reason? What shows that such striving has authority for the regulation
of all thought and action? Kant's answers to these questions are
given partly in prefatory remarks and partly in the concluding *Doctrine of Method*.

VII. REASON IN THE PREFACES: DISINTEGRATION OR SELF-DISCIPLINE?

If we go back to the passages in the prefaces in which Kant introduces the theme of reason in the *Critique of Pure Reason*, we can see
that from the beginning of the book he represents human reason as a
form of striving that *both* leads to contradictions, hence is a source
of problems, and yet seeks *unity*, so may be capable of resolving the
problems it has generated. The prefaces depict human reason as
repeatedly frustrated striving for completion and unity, in a being

whose capacities seem inadequate for what it yearns to do, yet also as a capacity to discipline the use of these very powers and so perhaps to resolve its self-inflicted problems. On the one hand Kant's initial diagnosis is that human reason leads to catastrophe, because it

begins with principles which it has no option save to employ . . . rising with their aid to ever higher, ever more remote, conditions. . . . But by this procedure human reason precipitates itself into darkness and contradictions.

(A vii–viii, cf. B xiv–v)

On the other hand Kant repeatedly gestures toward the thought that this same flawed capacity carries its remedy within it:

Reason has insight only into that which it produces after a plan of its own, and . . . it must not allow itself to be kept, as it were, on nature's leading-strings, but must itself show the way with principles of judgement based upon fixed laws, constraining nature to give answer to questions of reason's own determining. . . .   (B xiii)

We have perhaps become so used to reading such turns of phrase as mere personification that we do not sufficiently note that throughout the *Critique of Pure Reason* reason is depicted as an *active* capacity that both *generates and may resolve problems. Reflexive structure* is part of the key to understanding Kant's conception of vindicating reason.

VIII. VINDICATING REASON: A REFORMULATION

If such passages are no mere turns of phrase, but Kant's actual picture of reason, and if reason has no real or objective source or archetype, then the question of the vindication of reason has to be posed anew. To vindicate reason could not be to derive its principles from elsewhere or to show their correspondence to real archetypes. It would be to identify whatever fundamental precept can guide thought and action authoritatively for beings in whom neither is steered by any "alien" reality or by necessity. This does not seem to make the task of vindicating reason any easier. Why should any precept have general authority for such disoriented beings? How could any be vindicated? Why should any have any authority for *us?*

The question is only complicated by the fact that if reason's princi-

ples are precepts for seeking the greatest possible unity, these precepts must apply both to thinking and to doing. Kant often stresses
the basic unity of theoretical and practical uses of reason (e.g.,
Groundwork, 4:391). Yet why should one and the same principle be
authoritative for both tasks? Indeed, if the notorious Categorical
Imperative is the "supreme principle of practical reason," as Kant
insists, then does not practical reason have its own, distinct "supreme principle"? Many doubt whether the Categorical Imperative
can guide practice; even those who think that it can, and that it is
vital for morality, many well doubt whether it could either be or be
closely linked to the supreme principle of reason in general. Further,
Kant's attempts to vindicate the Categorical Imperative remain in
dispute, so do not seem promising models for the vindication of
theoretical uses of reason. The task of constructing a critical vindication of reason seems no less demanding than the rejected task of
vindicating reason within the framework of rationalist metaphysics.

IX. *DOCTRINE OF METHOD:* THE BUILDING OF REASON

So far I have aimed to distinguish Kant's account of reason from
others, without saying anything positive about his approach to the
task of vindication. However, Kant tells us a great deal about the
reformulated task. Numerous passages throughout the *Doctrine of
Method* leave it beyond doubt that he holds that reason's principles
are vindicable, and intends to show how the task must be carried
out.

These texts begin with an extended and deep comparison between
the critical project and a building project:

If we look upon the sum of all knowledge of pure speculative reason as a
building for which we have at least the idea within ourselves, it can be said
that in the Transcendental Doctrine of Elements we have made an estimate
of the materials, and have determined for what sort, height, and strength of
building they will suffice. Indeed it turned out that although we had in mind
a tower that would reach the heavens, yet the stock of materials was only
enough for a dwelling house – just roomy enough for our tasks on the plain
of experience and just high enough for us to look across the plain. The bold
undertaking had come to nothing for lack of materials, quite apart from the
babel of tongues that unavoidably set workers against one another about the

plan and scattered them across the earth, each to build separately following his own plan. Our problem is not just to do with materials, but even more to do with the plan. Since we have been warned not to risk everything on a favorite but senseless project, which could perhaps exceed our whole means, yet cannot well refrain from building a secure home, we have to plan our building with the supplies we have been given and at the same time to suit our needs.   (A 707 / B 735; trans. O. O'N.)

A few preliminary comments on this passage may be useful. First, Kant is drawing on a long tradition of comparisons between building and philosophy, which goes back to antiquity, and had been extended by the rationalists and above all by Descartes. Second, he is also drawing on the darker story of the building of the tower of Babel, whose builders aspired to a splendid tower that exceeded their own capacities, and who were forced into a life of dispersed nomadism after its collapse. Third, it may seem impertinent that after the 700 difficult pages of the *Doctrine of Elements*, Kant should tell his readers that all that he has offered so far is an inventory of the building materials for constructing the edifice of reason. Yet just this would be appropriate if he holds that a vindication of reason is needed, but has not yet provided one.

X. REFLEXIVITY AND THE BUILDING OF REASON

The clue to the late placing of the vindication of reason is that Kant regards it as a reflexive task,[6] which has to assemble certain "materials" before it can begin. This has been signaled from the very first pages of the *Critique of Pure Reason*, where human thinking and doing are depicted as undisciplined striving that leads into tangles and contradictions. Kant's critique of rationalism shows that this striving cannot be disciplined by conforming to some given (outside, "alien") reality. Striving for such conformity would be analogous to the hubris of the builders of Babel: Both projects must collapse.

However, the failure of rationalism – of foundationalism – may not seem enough to require a reflexive approach. Might not the fate of the builders of Babel, giving up the project of building and settlement, provide a more accurate model for human thinking and acting? Once again Kant has signaled from the very beginning of the *Critique of Pure Reason* that this "postmodern" attitude too is untenable. We are in no position to live without reason. The striving that leads us into tangled thought and action is already reasoning, but unreliable reasoning. The question that we must ask ourselves is not "Why should any principles count as those of reason?" but, rather, "Given that we try to reason, how can we mitigate the dangers of the principles on which we unavoidably rely?"

Kant speaks of a critique of reason as a *task* because we are unavoidably committed to thinking and acting, hence unavoidably partially, incipiently reasoning beings, yet with the "peculiar fate" (A vii) that our reasoning constantly falls into difficulty and contradiction. The disasters of metaphysics arise from an unrestricted use of quite common and daily ways of thinking and acting, which we can hardly give up. (For example, the antinomies suggest that contradictions can readily be generated by iterated use of the principle of causality, or of counting or dividing.) Metaphysical hubris is no more than the further extension of the very principles we rely on. Hence any vindication of human reason will have to identify principles for guiding the ways of thinking and doing that we have to hand, and cannot jettison, and must use these very principles both as "material" and as source of a "plan." Neither foundationalism nor postmodernism are genuine options for us. In terms of the humble vocabulary of the building trades, our only feasible option is to ask, What can be built with the materials and labor force available to us?

At this point an objection might be that metaphors of building or construction cannot shed light on a reflexive task. Buildings, it might be said, need foundations, hence metaphors of construction are only appropriate if we accept a foundationalist conception of the vindication of reason – for example, that of Descartes. However, this objection overlooks the possibility of constructions without foundations, such as kites or space satellites, whose components are mutually supporting, although no part of the structure forms a foundation for the rest. Moreover, it also fails to note that even the components of structures that do rest on foundations are and must be mutually supporting in many ways. There is nothing amiss in Kant's strategy of using building metaphors while renouncing the thought that we are given an "absolute" orientation by some external criterion that demarcates "up" from "down," and permits us to identify foundations or axioms for thought or action (*Orientation*, 8). Indeed, in many ways his conception of the building of reason is more prosaic than that of the rationalists whom he criticizes. Kant represents attempts to ground practices of reason as a matter of proceeding with the "materials" and "labor power" that our daily practice of defective reasoning has made available to us, and rebuilding these in ways that reduce dangers of collapse or paralysis in thought or action. The construction of reason is to be seen as process rather than product, as practices of connection and integration rather than as once and for all laying of foundations.

In advancing this conception of the task of vindicating reason, Kant shows nothing about the structure of reason. He merely points to a possibility between rationalism and skepticism – between foundationalism and postmodernism. We may be able to build an adequate account of reason out of available materials and capacities. If we can, we will not, of course, have achieved a presuppositionless vindication of reason. But we would perhaps have shown that the strategies of thought on which we have to rely provide the materials and the plan for constructing an account of some principles that have wholly general authority for thinking and acting. Kant outlines this approach in the opening sections of the *Doctrine of Method.*

XI. THE *DOCTRINE OF METHOD:* WHAT DOES KANT VINDICATE?

Reason is discussed under four headings in the *Doctrine of Method:* The Discipline of Reason, the Canon of Reason, the Architectonic of Reason, and the History of Reason. Here I shall restrict myself to the first of these. Kant discusses the discipline of reason between A 708 / B 736 and A 794 / B 822. He begins with some short but important introductory remarks, which are followed by four sections that include criticism of the philosophical methods of rationalists ("dogmatists") and skeptics. I shall reverse the order and sketch his criticism of supposed alternatives first.

The "dogmatic," or rationalist, conception of reason is modeled on the supposed method of mathematics. Kant regards this method as totally inappropriate. The rationalists made two crucial mistakes. First, they wrongly thought that mathematics consisted of analytic propositions, which form only a small and unimportant part of it; second, they imagined that philosophy could ape the mathematical method of basing proofs on definitions and axioms. It was this second error that led them into the project of building "a tower that should reach the heavens." A more accurate examination of the available building materials and the labor force would have shown them that philosophy has neither definitions nor axioms, and so can produce no proofs, and so to the realization that it is necessary to

cut away the last anchor of these fantastic hopes, that is, to show that the pursuit of the mathematical method cannot be of the least advantage in this kind of knowledge   (B 726 / A 754)

and to the conclusion that

In philosophy the geometrician [*der Meßkünstler*] can by his method build only so many houses of cards.   (A 727 / B 755)

Mathematics cannot be done *more analytico*, and philosophy cannot be done *more geometrico*. Mathematical method provides no wholly general model for reasoning.

The second section on the discipline of reason rejects the skeptical suspicion that reason is really no more than polemic – that is, war. The goal of polemic is victory. Conversation, argument, and writing are often polemicized, in the sense that various sorts of force and pressure can be brought to bear through them, and that they may aim at victory. However, polemic always has the disadvantage that no wider validity can be ascribed to its results. Coerced "agreement" or "understanding" does not outlive the coercion, and does not reach the uncoerced. Polemic can lay no claim to provide a wholly general discipline for thinking or acting. Anybody who seeks an unrestricted audience has to renounce polemic. Kant proposes that a better image of reasoned exchange is that of citizens in free debate:

Reason must in all its undertakings subject itself to criticism; should it limit freedom of criticism by any prohibitions, it must harm itself, drawing upon itself a damaging suspicion. Nothing is so important through its usefulness, nothing so sacred, that it may be exempted from this searching examination, which knows no respect for persons. Reason depends on this freedom for its very existence. For reason has no dictatorial authority; its verdict is always simply the agreement of free citizens, of whom each one must be permitted to express, without let or hindrance, his objection or even his veto.   (A 738–9 / B 766–7)

A debate between citizens can serve as an image for reason, not because it follows given (hence "alien") rules of procedure or order, or because it relies on common presuppositions, but because both are processes with a plurality of participants, whose coordination is not guaranteed or imposed by a ruler or other powers. (Of course, this is not wholly true of actual debates between citizens, but then we do not expect metaphors to work without any restriction whatsoever.) The negative aspect of Kant's criticism of those who construe reason as polemic is easily followed: Thoughts and action that depend on unvindicated authorities will hold only where this authority is accepted, so cannot produce general understanding or agreement or resolve all conflicts of belief and action.

These criticisms of the mathematical and the polemical conceptions of reasoning also support one further, negative conclusion: In the construction of reason it would be no solution to the collapse of rationalism or to the threat of anarchy to appoint some well-organized local "builder" who would erect a more modest version of the project. This solution, the metaphorical counterpart to forms of relativism or communitarianism, once more subjects thought and action to some arbitrary, if less ambitious, power. Its results could have only arbitrarily restricted significance. However, it remains quite unclear what positive conditions a construction of reason must meet.

XII. THE *DOCTRINE OF METHOD:* KANT'S PROPOSALS

Kant's positive proposals are outlined succinctly in the short passages that deal explicitly with the discipline of reason (A 708–12 / B 736–40). These precede the accounts of the failings of the methods of rationalism and of polemic just summarized. His diagnosis, both in the prefaces and in the introductory remarks at the beginning of the *Doctrine of Method*, stressed that we lack not only the materials for the grand projects of rationalism, but more crucially a *plan* for using those that we have.[7] What plan does Kant then propose? And how could any particular plan be justified? Even if we now grasp why a vindication of reason must be a reflexive task that begins with available materials and capacities, still there will surely be a plurality of realizable plans. If we can establish only necessary and not sufficient conditions for reasoned thinking and doing, should we not also suspect that there can be no vindication of reason?

At the beginning of this short section Kant asserts that reason needs "a discipline." A discipline is

The compulsion, by which the constant tendency to disobey certain rules is restrained and finally extirpated.   (A 709 / B 737)

He then notes

that reason, whose proper duty it is to prescribe a discipline for all other endeavours, should itself stand in need of a discipline may indeed seem strange.   (A 710 / B 738)

However, the strangeness of reason's discipline is then promptly explained by pointing out that it is a form of *self-discipline*. Here Kant develops the many earlier passages in which the task of critique of reason has been characterized as a reflexive task.[8] This reflexive discipline is needed because the task is peculiar,

where, as in the case of pure reason, we come upon a whole system of illusions and fallacies, intimately bound together and united under common principles, its own and indeed negative law-giving [*eine eigene und zwar negative Gesetzgebung*] seems to be required, which, under the title of a *discipline*, erects a system of precautions and self-examination out of the nature of reason and the objects of its pure employment.
                                          (A 711 / B 739; trans. emended O.O'N)[9]

What does Kant mean by reason's "own and indeed negative law-giving"? Which plan is the plan of reason? Will it be enough to have only "a system of precautions and self-examination"? Have we been told anything of substance?

There are in fact three substantive points here. First, the discipline of reason is *negative*; second, it is *self-discipline*; third, it is a *law-giving*. That it is *negative* is in any case part of the definition of a discipline and is a corollary of the rejection of "alien" authorities – of foundationalism. Nothing has been assumed from which positive content could be derived; nor can anything of the sort be assumed without begging the question. That it is *self-discipline* confirms that reasoning is a reflexive task, which works on the available material of our incipient and often disastrous practices of reasoning. That the discipline of reason is *a law-giving* entails that it is at least lawlike. Lawlikeness presupposes that a plurality of agents, or at least of cases, may fall under reason's principles.

Any law-giving that is to be both self-imposed and negative – that is, without content – can impose no more than the mere form of law. The discipline of reason can require only that no principle incapable of being a law be relied on as a fundamental principle for governing thought and action. Any other principle, whose content was more determinate, would implicitly subject thought and action to some or other, "alien" hence unvindicated "authority." Hence Kant views the fundamental principle of reason as that of governing both thinking and doing by principles that others too can adopt and follow. We recognize here a more general version of the supreme principle of practical reason, whose best known version runs: Act only on that principle through which you can at the same time will that it be a universal law. (*Groundwork*, 4:421)[10] As in the case of the discussion of practical reason in the *Groundwork*, the fundamental principle of reason in general is without content: It demands simply that thinking as well as acting not violate the form of law.

This conclusion invites the criticism not that Kant's account of reason provides no discipline, but that it does not provide nearly enough. It certainly does not provide sufficient instructions for thinking and doing. This is not inadvertence on Kant's part: He constantly rejects conceptions of reason, such as the Principle of Sufficient Reason, which supposedly give sufficient instructions for all thinking and acting (for example, see A 783 / B 811). His insistence that "reason is no dictator" reiterates the thought that there is no algorithm that fully determines the content of reasoned thought and action. Nor should we "expect from reason what obviously exceeds its power" (A 786 / B 814). Reason offers only necessary conditions for thought and action – in Kant's terminology a "Canon" for thought and action (A 795 / B 823 ff.; *Groundwork*, 4:424). Since the nonspeculative theoretical use of reason has only regulative warrant, we can aim at the systematic unity of knowledge, but only in awareness that the ideal of completeness is not attainable (A 568 / B 596): The regulative principles of reason serve only "to mark out the path toward systematic unity" (A 668 / B 696).

In the case of the spurious speculative employment of reason, we have even less than a canon. Here the discipline of reason can be used only as a dialectical "system of precautions and self-examination" that curbs unwarranted metaphysical speculation. Kant's conception of reason cannot rehabilitate any of the speculative proofs of God's existence, although the idea of a supreme being may still be used to regulate and integrate, indeed may be needed to regulate and integrate, thinking and doing.[11]

It is neither deficiency nor inadvertence that the supreme principle of reason is "only" *the precept of staying within the confines of some possible plan*. This modest conception of reason, which may be rendered in political metaphors as a matter of lawfulness without a lawgiver,[12] is the one presented in the *Doctrine of Method*, and the one that is adumbrated in Kant's earlier and endorsed in his later discussions of what it may take to discipline "our adventurous and self-reliant reason" (A 850 / B 878) without kowtowing to rationally groundless authorities.

XIII. SELECTED CORROBORATIONS OF THE INTERPRETATION

This reading of Kant's approach to the vindication of reason in the *Critique of Pure Reason* can be corroborated by numerous passages in other works. Kant discusses its theoretical import in the essay *What Is Orientation in Thinking?*, and its practical import in many works, including *What Is Enlightenment?*. The topic is handled in another way in the passages on the *sensus communis* in the *Critique of Judgment*. Here I offer only a few illustrations, beginning with some further reflections on Kant's stress on the importance of a *self-imposed plan* in the introductory paragraph of the *Doctrine of Method*.

The chastened builders of the tower of Babel, who cannot wholly turn their backs on building projects, are not forced to settle in some specific new building. Rather they are advised to settle on *some* feasible plan that *all* of them can share. The condition that they must meet if they are to avoid the fate of "nomads" – isolation, dispersal, noncommunication – is to adopt *some* plan, that neither posits unavailable resources nor is unsharable with others. The advice could be rejected, and even if it is followed much will remain open. Unlike Descartes, Kant does not think that there is a unique edifice of reason, or that it could be created by any solitary builder. On Kant's account we think and act reasonably provided we neither invoke illusory capacities or authorities – that is what it is to take account of our actual resources and starting point – nor base our thinking or acting on nonlawlike, hence unsharable, principles.

These constraints allow that innumerable differing ways of thought and of life may meet the constraints of reason.

Nevertheless reason constrains. Kant identifies three recurrent modes of unreason. It is unreasonable to posit capacities, insights, and transcendent authorities that we lack: This is the unreason of transcendental realists, including Platonists and traditional theists. It is unreasonable to assume that thinking and acting can be wholly arbitrary or nonlawlike, as skeptics and postmodernists claim to. It is unreasonable to assume that the fundamental principles of thought and action need reflect only some local authority, as the acolytes of *Schwärmerei* or communitarianism do. His constant insistence that reason is lawlike yet submits to no "alien" authority summarizes his rejection of these three modes of unreason. To think and act reasonably is to make sure that the basic precepts by which both are disciplined are lawlike without accepting spurious authorities.

Second, this reading contributes to an adequate understanding of the well-known 1784 essay *What Is Enlightenment?*.[13] This essay has often been condemned as a shallow defense of freedom of opinion, which endorses "enlightened" despotism. This focus wholly fails to face the central puzzle of the text, which is that Kant equates enlightenment not with reason but with an oddly characterized practice of reasoning publicly. The essay begins by contrasting those who are unenlightened, who submit to others' authority and opinions, and those who are enlightened, in that they speak publicly in their own voice. Kant's conception of a "public use of reason" is highly unusual: It is one that addresses "the entire public" (yet may actually reach only "men of learning"), whereas "a private use of reason is that which a person may make of it in some particular *civil* post or office" (*Enlightenment*, 8:37) – that is, what we would term a position in the *public* service! A "public" use of reason is not defined by its large audience, and cannot take place in the public service, where relations of command and obedience permit only "private" uses of reason. The reason Kant attaches importance to "public" uses of reason is rather that these alone are not premised on accepting some rationally ungrounded – "alien" authorities, (e.g. Frederick II, or the teachings of a church). Hence they alone are full uses of reason, and "private" uses of reason are to be understood as defective, deprived or *privatus*, rather than as sheltered or secluded. Hence the essay points *away* from a conception of "public" reason that is characteristic of public life both under enlightened despotism and in bureaucratized modern states, toward a quite different conception of what fully reasoned communication would be.[14]

No doubt the essay is too vague about the social conditions for fully "public" reasoning. Kant does little more than gesture to two "ideal types" of thinking and acting, in which reason is respectively fully and defectively embodied. However, the essay illuminates Kant's reasons for viewing autonomy, that is, the principle of not submitting to groundless authorities, as the core of reason, hence of enlightenment. Autonomy, as Kant understands it, is not mere self-assertion or independence, but rather thinking or acting on principles that defer to no ungrounded "authority," hence on principles all can follow. For Kant, autonomy is living by the principles of reason; and reason is nothing but the principle that informs practices of autonomy in thinking and doing. He does not reject the view that the Enlightenment is the movement of reason. Rather he recasts and deepens this conventional view by showing that reason, correctly understood, is the principle of thinking and acting on principles all can freely adopt.[15]

A third text that corroborates this reading is the less known essay of 1786, *What Is Orientation in Thinking?*. Here Kant asks not which principles have authority for action, but which have an unrestricted ("orienting") authority for thinking. He claims that only the principle of autonomy in thinking can have any general authority; hence autonomy is all there is to reason. To reason just is to think in a lawlike (principled) way, without deference to any alien "law." It avoids both "lawlessness" (i.e., nonlawlikeness) and "submission" (i.e., to "alien" authorities):

If reason will not subject itself to the law it gives itself, it will have to bow under the yoke of the law which others impose on it, for without any law whatsoever nothing, not even the greatest nonsense, can play its hand for very long.   (*Orientation*, 8:145)

Once again, this essay makes it very clear that Kant does not think reason lives up to rationalist fantasies. Reason is indeed the basis of enlightenment, but enlightenment is no more than autonomy in thinking and in acting – that is, of thought and action that are lawful yet assume no lawgiver. Reason cannot determine everything; it provides a negative discipline for avoiding disoriented thinking but offers no sufficient instructions for thought or action:

To think for oneself is a matter of seeking the highest touchstone of truth in oneself (that is, in one's own reason); and the maxim of thinking for oneself at all times constitutes *enlightenment*. This amounts to less than those who think enlightenment a matter of knowledge imagine. Rather it is a negative principle in the use of one's cognitive capacities; and often those who have a wealth of knowledge are least enlightened in the use of these capacities. To make use of one's own reason means nothing more than to ask oneself with regard to everything that is to be assumed, whether he finds it practicable to make the ground of the assumption a universal principle of the use of reason.   (*Orientation*, 8:146–7 n.)[16]

Finally this minimal account of reason as lawfulness without a lawgiver – as avoiding both anarchy and submission to groundless powers – can be recognized once again in the trio of interconnected maxims that Kant groups together in section 40 of the *Critique of Judgment* (5:293–6) and terms the *sensus communis*. He introduces the term *sensus communis* not simply in connection with taste, but as of far more general import:

We assume a common sense as the necessary condition of the universal communicability of our knowledge, which is presupposed in every logic and every principle of knowledge that is not one of scepticism.

                    (*Judgment*, §21, 5:239)

At a later stage the three maxims of the *sensus communis* are presented as exemplifying the requirements for preserving lawlikeness without assuming a lawgiver. These are not maxims of common sense in the sense that they refer to accepted views. Rather they are maxims

of a critical faculty which in its reflective act takes account (*a priori*) of the mode of representation of everyone else, in order, as it were, to weigh its judgement with the collective judgement of mankind.

                    (*Judgment*, §40, 5:293)

These are maxims for a plurality-without-preestablished-harmony, that is, for a plurality of agents who, like the builders of Babel, can rely on no preinscribed shared plan. The three maxims enjoin such agents to think for themselves, to think from the standpoint of everyone else, and to think consistently (*Judgment*, §40, 5:294). The first maxim proscribes submission to "alien" authorities. Taken alone, refusal of submission might, however, lead to anarchy or to isolation. The second maxim prescribes the antidote to anarchy and isolation by requiring that agents think from the standpoint of others – that is, that their thinking be based on principles that are at least open to others. However, any process of thought or action that is guided by the maxims both of rejecting submission and of sustaining lawlikeness – in other words, rejecting "lawgivers" while maintaining "lawfulness" – will be in constant flux and revision, hence may well generate contradiction and hiatus. Hence the need for the third maxim, which enjoins a process of consistency-restoring review and revision. The third maxim, far from being trivial, is indispensable for any sustained process of thought or action that combines the other two.

The passages on the *sensus communis* differ in many ways from Kant's discussions in other writings of a single supreme principle of reason. They distinguish different aspects of reason's task more sharply; they make more evident that the Kantian vindication of reason presupposes plurality-without-preestablished-harmony.[17] In these passages political metaphors wholly replace the metaphors of construction that predominate in the opening discussion of the *Doctrine of Method*. The political metaphors offer particularly apt ways of characterizing modes of unreason. To reject the first maxim is to submit either to the powers that be or to supposed transcendent realities; it is to fantasize and defer to some "authoritative" lawgiver. To reject the second maxim is to assume that the basic principles of thinking and doing need not be followable by others – that they can be lawless rather than lawlike. To reject the third maxim is to fail to integrate the demands of rejecting illusory lawgivers and of sustaining lawlikeness. Taken in conjunction, the three maxims define constraints for a dynamic process in which the demand for lawfulness without a lawgiver is realized among a plurality. Reason is here sketched not as abstract principle, but as the lawlike guidance of thinking and doing in a dynamic process that neither submits to outside control nor fails to acknowledge differences of opinion and practice, and which treats resulting contradictions and tensions as an indefinitely extended demand for revision.

XIV. CONFIRMATIONS AND OBJECTIONS

This interpretation of Kant's vindication of reason construes reason as the principle of guiding thinking and doing in ways that others too can follow, granted that no coordination with others is given from "outside" by any "alien" authority. Of course, this is only the supreme principle of reason, and it would have to be elaborated in a vast range of more specific principles, which could be embodied in varied social practices. More specific principles could be derived from the supreme principle of reason by showing either that their denials assume some "alien" authority, or that they are not lawlike, so cannot be followed by others. Such principles would have to count as unreasonable; their rejection would constitute the adoption of subordinate principles of reason. This strategy *may* enable Kant to show that principles of logic or of duty, or Ideas or Postulates of Reason, are indeed subsidiary requirements of reason; however, his account of the vindication of the supreme principle of reason cannot establish which derivations along these lines will work, and I cannot go far into the success of his many attempts to identify subordinate principles of reason.

A few more general issues can be dealt with. First, to what extent do the objections that have been raised against supposed vindications of reason hold against Kant's position? Does he invoke arbitrary starting points? Is his attempt at vindication circular? Is it an unending regress?

First, his starting point. Kant does not begin from supposed axioms of reason, of logic or of method, but rather from the unsatisfying character of the most daily attempts to reason. From a supposed divine perspective, these starting points might indeed be arbitrary. However, that perspective is unavailable to us – and nobody who enjoys it has to worry about vindicating reason. We have no choice but to begin from our predicament. However, for Kant *this starting point has the function of posing the problem rather than of providing axioms for its resolution.*

Second, Kant's proposed solution is circular in the sense that he quite deliberately identifies the vindication of reason with a reflexive process, in which the indispensable elements for the *self*-discipline of thought and action are principles that are not "alien," hence groundless, authorities. To become (more fully) reasonable is to discipline available attempts at reasoning by available modes of reasoning. In keeping with this, Kant holds that reason progresses and has a history.

Third, Kant's proposed vindication of reason is indeed open-ended: A discipline is not a proof but a practice, in this case a practice for regulating all thinking and doing. Moreover, because this discipline constrains but does not generate what count as reasoned ways of thought and life, the task of reason cannot be defined in terms of some final product – a completed edifice of reason, comprising a finished system of all truths – but only in terms of a process of subjecting proposed thought and action to the discipline. Reason dictates neither thought nor action; its discipline is construed as process, not as the once and for all discovery of secure foundations.

Kant's vindication of reason may then seem to incur not just one but all three of the catastrophes from which attempts to vindicate reason are said to suffer. However, here appearances mislead. Unvindicated axioms, circular argument, or unending regress would each constitute catastrophe for an attempt to provide foundations for reason; but Kant makes no such attempt. His initial hypothesis, the Copernican turn, repudiates foundationalism. In its stead he offers considerations about ways in which processes of thought and action must be disciplined if they are not to count as unreasoned. To appreciate his alternative vision we have to shed foundationalist expectations and try to assess this account of how we might construct principles that are authoritative for all thinking and doing, granted that such authority can neither be conferred nor imposed.

For anyone who shares Kant's doubts about forms of foundationalism, this program will have many attractions. However, some will fear that the conception of reason that he vindicates, far from being too ambitious – as its rationalist predecessor so plainly was – is so minimal that it can have no significant role. If the whole huge critical undertaking is only going to get us this far, then might not Kant just as well have conceded quite explicitly that he was undertaking neither critique nor vindication of reason and recognized that he was a skeptic – or indeed the first postmodernist? On this point I offer one historical and one systematic thought.

The historical thought is that Kant could hardly have attacked the tradition that had fused Platonist and Christian origins into rationalist metaphysics simply by rejecting its aspirations. If such strategies now seem to be available to Derrida or to Rorty, it is in part because they write as post-Kantians, as Nietzsche already did, and need attack only a profoundly damaged metaphysical tradition.

The systematic thought is that only detailed investigation can show whether and how far principles of knowledge or morality or postulates of hope can be derived from the supreme principle of reason. Even if such investigations can establish some subordinate principles of reason, still these constraints will not fully determine knowledge, action, or hope. To those who expect reason to determine everything, this may seem a deeply disappointing failure. If Kant is right, such disappointment is itself a symptom of undisciplined metaphysical passions (cf. A 786 / B 814). Even if reason is "only" a "system of constraints," these may prove a demanding discipline for thought, for action, and for hope.

Although this cannot be shown without undertaking the detailed investigations, the point may be illustrated by the case of principles of logic. Rationalists expected logic to offer us algorithms for knowing, rules that offer complete instructions for handling every case that falls under them, and that could in principle be used to generate the system of truth. Indeed, it is because formulas of logic and of mathematics are our paradigm algorithms that we may be led to think that this must be where we should look for indubitable foundations for systematic thought and knowledge. However, when we reflect about the standing of such formulas, it becomes clear that they cannot provide indubitable foundations for actual thinking and doing unless not only the abstract formulas, but their application to cases, are algorithmic. However, applications of algorithmic formulas are not algorithms. Kant insists on this as firmly as Wittgenstein does. He points out that "general logic can supply no rules for judgment" (A 135 / B 174). If "general logic" cannot supply rules for judgment, it cannot provide a foundation for thinking, for doing, or for the structure of hope that Kant believes articulates modes of unity between the domains of thought and action.

The first question that we must raise about (general) logic is rather whether actual cognitive processes provide the vindication for its abstract formulas, or the other way round. The question cannot be answered by thinking of the vindication of logical or mathematical formulas as internal to a system of formulas. To do so only raises the question of the vindication of the formal system. However, if we

think of such formulas or systems of formulas as having wider validity, as authoritative for any process of thought or action, we must
either assume that they have the type of vindication foundational-
ists aspire to, or accept that their vindication derives from that
which we can offer for these processes of thought and action. Such a
constructivist vindication of formulas of logic would then have to
begin by seeing which supposed logical principles could be rejected
and which could not, without our thinking and doing precipitating
itself into "darkness and contradiction" and consequent frustrations
(A vii / B xiv). Such a line of thought might reveal the difference
between a Principle of Sufficient Reason, which indeed leads into
problems, and a Principle of Noncontradiction, whose rejection
leads into problems. Only principles of the latter sort could count as
subordinate principles of reason. Only they might point away from
the predicament in which "ever and again we have to retrace our
steps, as not leading us in the direction in which we desire to go" (B
xiv).

The Kantian approach to the vindication of reason is fundamentally a modest affair. It does not disclose any hidden route back to
the Principle of Sufficient Reason. The heroic challenges of rationalist demands to ground reason are rejected, as are their difficulties.
All that is vindicated is a precept of thinking and doing without
relying on any fundamental principle which either presupposes
some arbitrary "authority," or cannot be followed by others. Minimal indeed, but far from empty. Any form of relativism that "submits" to some arbitrary power (state, church, majority, tradition, or
dictator) as the source of reason is rejected. So is any form of rationalism that "submits" to supposed divine or other "necessities." So is
any form of skepticism or postmodernism that equates "reason"
with momentarily available ways of thought. Within these constraints we may be able to work out how far the Kantian conception
of reason guides and constrains what we can know, what we ought to
do, and what we may hope.

NOTES

1 Works of Kant will be cited using the short titles that have been used
   throughout this book and the pagination from the *Akademie* edition.
   The translations used are the following: *Critique of Pure Reason*, trans.

Norman Kemp Smith, 2d ed. (London: Macmillan, 1933); *Kant's Critique of Practical Reason and Other Writings in Moral Philosophy*, trans. Lewis White Beck (Chicago: University of Chicago Press, 1949); *Kant's Critique of Judgment*, trans. James Creed Meredith (Oxford: Clarendon Press, 1952).

2 René Descartes, *The Discourse on the Method* in *The Philosophical Writings of Descartes*, trans. John Cottingham, Robert Stoothof, and Dugald Murdoch, Vol. I, p. 112. For recent discussion of contrasts between Descartes and Kant on these themes, and more generally on the connections between reason and politics in Kant see Reinhard Brandt, "Freiheit, Gleichheit, Selbstständigkeit bei Kant" in *Die Ideen von 1789 in der deutschen Rezeption*, ed. Forum für Philosophie, Bad Homburg (Frankfurt am Main: Suhrkamp, 1989) and Onora O'Neill, "Reason and Politics in the Kantian Enterprise" in *Constructions of Reason: Explorations of Kant's Practical Philosophy* (Cambridge: Cambridge University Press, 1989).

3 The passages where general logic is treated as a key for transcendental logic run across A 67–83 / B 92–109 and A 303–5 / B 359–61. The methodological point is summarized at the beginning of the Dialectic: "Following the analogy of concepts of understanding, we may expect that the logical concept will provide the key to the transcendental, and that the table of the functions of the former will at once give us the genealogical tree of the concepts of reason" (A 299 / B 356).

4 Kant often uses far stronger terms than "endeavor": Reason undisciplined veers between "restless striving" and "passionate desire" (A 786 / B 814).

5 Kant remarks with an odd mixture of animus against and defense of Plato: "In this I cannot follow him, any more than in his mystical deduction of these ideas, or in the extravagances whereby he, so to speak, hypostatised them – although, as must be allowed, the exalted language, which he employed in this sphere, is quite capable of a milder interpretation" (A 314 / B 371 n.).

6 For further discussion of the strategy of postponing the vindication until so late in the work see my "Reason and Politics in the Kantian Enterprise."

7 Cf. "if the various participants are unable to agree on a common plan of procedure" (B vii); "reason has insight only into that which it produces after a plan of its own" (B xiii as well as A 707 / B 735, quoted in the text).

8 See A ix, B xiii, A 747, A 750 as well as various passages cited subsequently in this text.

9 I have emended Kemp Smith's translation here because it imposes a

foundationalist reading. He has it that the "system of precautions and self-examination" is "founded on the nature of reason and the objects of its pure employment." Kant writes that it is erected out of them [*errichtet . . . aus*]. Kant presents the nature of reason and the objects of its pure employment as the material for the self-discipline of reason: Kemp Smith makes them the (unvindicable) foundation.

10 We also recognize a line of argument closely parallel to some by which Kant hopes to vindicate the Categorical Imperative as conformity to law as such, and as unconditional: see e.g., *Groundwork*, 4:402, 421, 431; see also Thomas E. Hill, Jr., "Kant's Argument for the Rationality of Moral Conduct," *Pacific Philosophical Quarterly* 66 (1985): 3–23.

11 Here I skim over a vast range of texts, including particularly bk. II, ch. III, and the Appendix of the *Transcendental Dialectic*, A 642–704 / B 670–732 as well as the *Critique of Practical Reason* and *Religion within the Limits of Reason Alone*.

12 Kant uses this phrase in a different context in the *Critique of Judgment* (5:241), where he speaks of "conformity to law without a law" (*Gesetz-mäßigkeit ohne Gesetz*) and links its role in judgments of taste very closely to the better known formula of "purposefulness without purpose" (*Zweckmäßigkeit ohne Zweck*).

13 For a more extended version of this reading of *What Is Enlightenment?* and of parallels with the slightly later (and less well-known) *What is Orientation in Thinking?*, see Onora O'Neill, "The Public Use of Reason" in *Constructions of Reason* and "Enlightenment as Autonomy: Kant's Vindication of Reason," in *The Enlightenment and Its Shadows*, ed. Peter Hulme and Ludmila Jordanova (Routledge, 1990). For historical background to *What Is Orientation in Thinking?* see Frederick Beiser, *The Fate of Reason: German Philosophy from Kant to Fichte* (Harvard, 1987).

14 Kant's approach here and in the passages on the *sensus communis* (discussed subsequently) are a form of discursive grounding of reason. His approach differs from (at least a standard reading of) Habermas's version of this approach in that he does not invoke an *ideal* of transparent communication, in which all discursive claims can be redeemed, but rather points to conditions for *possible* communication, leaving it open how far this will enable settlement of truth claims, moral claims or other claims.

15 The connection drawn between reason and autonomy in *What Is Enlightenment?* and *What Is Orientation in Thinking?* provide a key to understanding the connections between reason and autonomy that structure Parts 2 and 3 of the *Groundwork*.

16 Compare also the very late *Conflict of the Faculties*, where Kant writes

that "the capacity to judge according to autonomy, that is freely (but in accord with the principles of thinking in general) is called reason" (7:27; trans O. O'N).

17 It follows that, despite long traditions of reading Kant as presenting a "philosophy of the subject," his starting point is rather that of plurality. This raises very large issues about the proper evaluation of Kant's critique of rational psychology and his own account of subjectivity, which must be left aside here. Kant's distinctiveness lies in the fact that his discursive grounding of reason presupposes plurality, and the possibility of community; it does not presuppose "atomistic" subjects, actual communities or ideal communities.

10 Autonomy, obligation, and virtue: An overview of Kant's moral philosophy

Kant invented a new way of understanding morality and ourselves as moral agents. The originality and profundity of his moral philosophy have long been recognized. It was widely discussed during his own lifetime, and there has been an almost continuous stream of explanation and criticism of it ever since. Its importance has not diminished with time. The quality and variety of current defenses and developments of his basic outlook and the sophistication and range of criticism of it give it a central place in contemporary ethics.[1] In the present essay I offer a general survey of the main features of Kant's moral philosophy. Many different interpretations of it have been given, and his published works show that his views changed in important ways. Nonetheless there is a distinctive Kantian position about morality, and most commentators are agreed on its main outlines.[2]

I

At the center of Kant's ethical theory is the claim that normal adults are capable of being fully self-governing in moral matters. In Kant's terminology, we are "autonomous." Autonomy involves two components. The first is that no authority external to ourselves is needed to constitute or inform us of the demands of morality. We can each know without being told what we ought to do because moral requirements are requirements we impose on ourselves. The second is that in self-government we can effectively control ourselves. The obligations we impose upon ourselves override all other calls for action, and frequently run counter to our desires. We nonetheless always have a sufficient motive to act as we ought. Hence no external source of motivation is needed for our self-legislation to be effective in controlling our behavior.

Kant thinks that autonomy has basic social and political implications. Although no one can lose the autonomy that is a part of the nature of rational agents,[3] social arrangements and the actions of others can encourage lapses into governance by our desires, or heteronomy. Kant, as we shall see, found it difficult to explain just how this could happen; but he always held that the moral need for our autonomy to express itself was incompatible with certain kinds of social regulation. There is no place for others to tell us what morality requires, nor has anyone the authority to do so – not our neighbors, not the magistrates and their laws, not even those who speak in the name of God. Because we are autonomous, each of us must be allowed a social space within which we may freely determine our own action. This freedom cannot be limited to members of some privileged class. The structure of society must reflect and express the common and equal moral capacity of its members.

Kant's interest in the social and political implications of autonomy is shown in many places. In the short essay "What is enlightenment?" Kant urges each of us to refuse to remain under the tutelage of others. I do not need to rely on "a book which understands for me, a pastor who has a conscience for me." We must think and decide for ourselves. To foster this, public freedom of discussion is necessary, particularly in connection with religion. An enlightened ruler will allow such discussion to flourish, knowing he has nothing to fear from it (7:35, 40ff / H 3–4, 8ff). Later in "Perpetual Peace" Kant expressed the hope that eventually all states will be organized as republics, in which every citizen can express his moral freedom[4] publicly in political action (7:349ff / H 93ff).

What stands out in Kant's vision of the morality through which we govern ourselves is that there are some actions we simply have to do. We impose a moral law on ourselves, and the law gives rise to obligation, to a necessity to act in certain ways. Kant does not see morality as springing from virtuous dispositions that make us want to help others. He sees it as always a struggle. Virtue itself is defined in terms of struggle: It is "moral strength of will" in overcoming temptations to transgress the law (Morals, 7:405 / 66–7). Law is prior to virtue, and must control desires to help others as well as desires to harm.

It has sometimes been thought that the salience of law and obedience in Kant's view shows that he had an authoritarian cast of mind.
Some unpublished early notes show quite clearly that the moral
stance behind his emphasis on obligation was very different. "In our
condition," he wrote around 1764,

> when universal injustice stands firm, the natural rights of the lowly cease.
> They are therefore only debtors; the superiors owe them nothing. There-
> fore these superiors are called gracious lords. He who needs nothing from
> them but justice and can hold them to their debts does not need this
> submissiveness.[5]

A society built around the virtues of benevolence and kindness is for
Kant a society requiring not only inequality[6] but servility as well. If
nothing is properly mine except what someone graciously gives me,
I am forever dependent on how the donor feels toward me. My independence as an autonomous being is threatened. Only if I can claim
that the others *have to* give me what is mine by right can this be
avoided. Kant makes the point even more plainly in a comment
written a few years later:

> Many people may take pleasure in doing good actions but consequently do
> not want to stand under obligations toward others. If one only comes to
> them submissively they will do everything; they do not want to subject
> themselves to the rights of people, but to view them simply as objects of
> their magnanimity. It is not all one under what title I get something. What
> properly belongs to me must not be accorded to me merely as something I
> ask for.[7]

Kant did not deny the moral importance of beneficent action, but his
theoretical emphasis on the importance of obligation or moral necessity reflects his rejection of benevolent paternalism and the servility
that goes with it,[8] just as the centrality of autonomy in his theory
shows his aim of limiting religious and political control of our lives.

II

Kant's attribution of autonomy to every normal adult was a radical
break with prevailing views of the moral capacity of ordinary people.
The natural law theorists whose work was influential through the
seventeenth and much of the eighteenth centuries did not on the

whole think that most people could know, without being told, every-thing that morality requires of them. The lawyers were willing to admit that God had given everyone the ability to know the most basic principles of morality. But they held that the many are unable to see all the moral requirements implicit in the principles and often cannot grasp by themselves what is required in particular cases. Like Kant later, the natural lawyers thought of morality as centering on obligations imposed by law. For them, however, God is the legislator of moral law, and humans his unruly subjects. Most people are un-willing to obey the laws of nature, and must be made to do so through the threat of punishment for noncompliance. This view was built into the concept of obligation as the natural lawyers under-stood it. They held that obligation could only be explained as neces-sity imposed by a law backed by threats of punishment for disobedi-ence. They would accordingly have thought Kant's view that we can make and motivate ourselves to obey the moral law not only blasphe-mous but foolish.[9] They would also have wondered what kind of account of moral necessity Kant could give, once he refused to ap-peal to an external lawgiver or to sanctions.

A number of philosophers before Kant had begun to reject the natural lawyers' low estimate of human moral capacity, and to pres-ent theories in which a greater ability for self-governance is attrib-uted to people. A brief look at the philosophers whom Kant himself has told us were important in his development will help us see how far beyond them he went.[10]

In deliberate opposition to natural law views, the British philoso-phers Shaftesbury and Hutcheson portrayed virtue rather than law and obligation as central to morality.[11] They argued that to be virtu-ous we have only to act regularly and deliberately from benevolent motives that we naturally approve. Because approval is naturally felt by everyone, and because we all have benevolent motives, we can all equally see and do what morality calls for, without need of external guidance or of sanctions. Christian Wolff, whose philosophy domi-nated German universities when Kant was a student, tried to reach a similar conclusion by a different route.[12] He argued that we can be self-governed because we can see for ourselves what the conse-quences of our actions will be, and can tell which action will bring about the greatest amount of perfection. Since we are always drawn to act so as to bring about what we believe is the greatest amount of perfection, Wolff says we are bound or necessitated to do what we think will be for the best. And this seems to him to explain the necessity we call "moral," or our moral obligation. In political matters we are obligated or obliged to act by sanctions imposed by a political ruler; but in morality we oblige ourselves to act through our perception of perfection. Hence in morality we are self-governed. We need no sanctions to move us to act for the best.[13]

Kant came to hold that neither of these kinds of moral theory was acceptable. They imply that the only necessity involved in morality is the necessity of using a means to an end you desire. If you do not want the end, there is no need for you to do the act that leads to it. But Kant thinks it is just a contingent empirical fact that you have the desires you have.[14] If so, then on these views it is a matter of happenstance whether or not someone is bound by any moral necessity. Obligation becomes a matter of what one wants to do. But true moral necessity, Kant held, would make an act necessary regardless of what the agent wants.

One philosopher prior to Kant, the Lutheran pastor C. A. Crusius,[15] had taken moral necessity to be independent of our contingent ends. There are, Crusius said, obligations of prudence, which arise from the need to act in a certain way to attain one's end. But there are also obligations of virtue, or moral obligations, and these make it necessary to act in certain ways regardless of any of one's own ends. Both the knowledge of these requirements and the motive to comply with them are available to everyone alike because certain laws are incorporated in the structure of our will, and carry their own impetus to action. Because everyone has a will, everyone can always know what morality requires; and when we act accordingly we are determining ourselves to action. Crusius thus explains the idea of moral obligation in terms of an unconditional necessity, and claims that because this necessity binds our will by its own nature we need no external guidance or stimulus to be moral. Crusius's aim in asserting our high moral capacity was in fact to show that we are fully responsible for our actions before God. He took the laws structuring our will to obligate us because they are God's commands; and he believed that obedience is our highest virtue. If Crusius provided Kant with some of the tools he used to work out his idea of autonomy, he was not the inspiration for that idea.

It took a radical critic of society, Jean-Jacques Rousseau, to suggest the idea. Rousseau convinced Kant that everyone must have the capacity to be a self-governing moral agent, and that it is this characteristic that gives each person a special kind of value or dignity.[16] Culture in its present corrupt state conceals this capacity of ours, Rousseau thought, and society must be changed to let it show and be effective. In the *Social Contract* he called for the construction of a community in which everyone agrees to be governed by the dictates of the "general will," a will representing each individual's truest and deepest aims and directed always at the good of the whole. The general will would have to be able to override the passing desires each of us feels for private goods. But, Rousseau said, "the impulse of appetite alone is slavery, and obedience to the law one has prescribed for oneself is freedom."[17] Previous thinkers had frequently used the metaphor of slavery to describe the condition in which we are controlled by our passions, but for them the alternative was to follow laws that God or nature prescribe. Rousseau held that we make our own law and in doing so create the foundation for a free and just social order. This thought became central to Kant's understanding of morality.

III

The problem Kant faced was to show how such law-making is possible. In particular he had to explain how we can impose a necessity upon ourselves. If my obligations arise simply through my own will, how can there be any real constraints on my action? Can't I excuse myself from any obligations I alone impose? Rousseau had nothing to suggest beyond the thought that conscience is a sentiment that moves us without regard for our own interest; and we have already seen why Kant could not accept that suggestion. Someone might not have conscientious sentiments, or might get rid of them. Then on such a view no obligations bind her. Moral necessity could not be explained on that basis. Kant eventually found an explanation by comparing moral necessity to the necessity involved in the laws governing the physical universe. Kant was a Newtonian. He held that the sequence of events in the world is necessary. But its laws involve no commands and no sanctions. Morality, however, is not science. Science shows us how the world has to be. Morality tells us how it ought to be. How can the model of scientific laws help us understand morality?

Kant had read Rousseau and rethought morality before he came to the breakthrough that led to the critical philosophy.[18] In developing his new view of morality he used the tools the critical standpoint gave him. In the *Critique of Pure Reason* he argued that perceptual experience of the world shows only what *does* happen. Since laws say what *has to* happen they must involve a nonexperiential, or *a priori*, aspect, and it must be this that explains the necessity they impart. How is this nonexperiential aspect of lawfulness to be explained? The mind, Kant answered, involves the activity of imposing different forms of order on the perceptual material that its passive receptivity gives it. The forms of order are not externally imposed on the mind. They are an aspect of itself, the aspect through which it makes experience lawful. And they are "pure" or devoid of any empirical content in themselves. Their constitution is independent of their actual forming of perceptions into lawfully ordered sequences.

The question then is whether there is an aspect of the mind that does for action what the mental activities revealed in the first *Critique* do for experience. Thinking in terms of separate faculties of the mind, Kant attributes the initiation of action to the will, responding to desires. Desires, he assumes, are not rational as such. They arise in us because we are finite beings, with bodily and other needs. If there is to be rationality in action, the will must be its source. Kant therefore equates the will with practical reason. Does the faculty of practical reason have an inherent structure in the way that the faculty of pure reason does? If it does, and if it imposes form on the givens we feel as desires, then we have a clue to an explanation of exactly how and why we are autonomous. Taking the activity of practical reason as the source of the necessities that we impose on our willed behavior would show that these necessities are no more escapable than those that give structure to the physical world. They could therefore constitute our morality.

IV

To translate this idea into a moral theory, Kant had to show that the main concepts of morality can be explained in terms of a self-imposed necessity. We can begin to see how he does this by examining the way he relates three ideas central to morality: the ideas of the moral worth of an agent, of the rightness of an action, and of the goodness of the states of affairs that are the goals or outcomes of action.

One way of relating these ideas is to take as basic the goodness of states of affairs that can be brought about by human action. We consider, say, that being happy, or having fully developed talents, is intrinsically good. Then a right act can be defined as one that brings about good states of affairs, or brings them about to the greatest extent possible; and a good agent is one who habitually and deliberately does right acts. In such a scheme, right acts will have only an instrumental value, and we can and indeed must know what is good before we can make justifiable claims about what acts are right. Such a scheme is common feature of the work of Kant's predecessors. Kant rejected it.

He rejected it because it makes autonomy in his sense impossible. Suppose that a kind of state of affairs is intrinsically good because of the very nature of that kind of state of affairs. Then the goodness occurs independently of the will of any finite moral agent, and if she must will to pursue it, she is not self-legislating. Suppose the goodness of states of affairs comes from their conformity to some standard. Then the standard itself is either the outcome of someone's will – say, God's – or it is self-subsistent and eternal. In either case, conformity to it is not autonomy.[19] Conformity would be what Kant calls heteronomy.

An alternative way of relating the three moral concepts became available to Kant through the idea that moral necessity, as embedded in the laws of morality, might have a pure *a priori* status akin to that of the necessity characterizing Newton's gravitational laws. While the mind imposes necessity in both cases, in morality the relevant aspect of mind is the rational will. This leads Kant to take the concept of the good agent as basic. Think of the good agent as one whose will is wholly determined *a priori,* and think of the pattern of that determination as the moral law.[20] Then we can say that it is necessarily true that whatever acts such an agent does are right acts; and whatever states of affairs such an agent deliberately brings about through those acts are good states of affairs. Kant makes it clear in the second *Critique* that this is his position:

the concept of good and evil is not defined prior to the moral law, to which, it would seem, the former would have to serve as foundation; rather the concept of good and evil must be defined after and by means of the law.

(Practical Reason 5:62–3 / 65)

For Kant then the rightness of acts is prior to the goodness of states of affairs, because only outcomes of right acts can count as good states of affairs. We do not discover what is right by first finding out what is good. Indeed we cannot determine what states of affairs are good without first knowing what is right. In order to know what is right all we need to know is what the perfectly good agent would do. Then whenever there is an act that a perfectly good agent could not omit, it is an act anyone in those circumstances has to do.[21]

Kant thinks one more step must be taken before we can obtain a full account of the moral concepts. So far we have considered a will completely determined by its own inner lawfulness. Because this law is a law constituting practical reason, such a will – unlike ours – would be perfectly rational. We finite beings do not have what Kant calls a "holy will," a will so fully determined by its inner lawful constitution that it acts spontaneously and without struggle. Our desires clamor for satisfaction whether they are rational or not. Hence for us the operation of the law in our rational will is not automatic. We feel its operation within us as a constraint, because it must act against the pull of desire. In finite beings, Kant says, the moral law "necessitates," rather than acting necessarily (*Ground-work*, 4:413–14 / 81). The terminology is not helpful, but Kant's thought here is familiar. If you were perfectly reasonable, you would go to the dentist to have that aching tooth looked at; and if you don't go because you fear dentists, you will find yourself thinking that you really ought to go. This is a prudential illustration of something that holds in the purely moral realm as well. When we see a compelling reason to do an act we are reluctant to do, we may not do it; but we admit we ought to.

The term "ought" is central to our moral vocabulary because the tension between reason and desire is central to our moral experience. "Ought" can be defined, on Kant's view, by saying that whatever a holy will, or perfectly rational will, necessarily *would* do is what we imperfectly rational agents *ought* to do (*Groundwork*, 4:413–14 / 81; *Practical Reason*, 325: / 32–3; *Morals*, 6:394–5 / 54–

5). When we speak of our obligation to do something, we are referring to the necessity of a given act, without specifying which act is necessary; and to call an act a duty is to say that it is an action that is obligatory. It is Kant's belief in the importance of struggle in the moral life that leads him to his view that virtue cannot be defined as a settled habit or disposition. God, Kant thinks, necessarily acts morally and for that reason cannot have virtue. Only beings who find morality difficult and who develop persistence in struggling against the temptations can be virtuous. We finite beings will never get to the point at which we do not need the strength to resist desire. We are neither angels nor animals. Virtue is our proper station in the universe (*Morals*, 6:405–9 / 66–71).

V

If we grant Kant his account of the central moral concepts, we want next to know what the moral law is, and how and to what extent it can serve as a principle for showing us what we ought to do. Many critics, from Hegel to the present, have argued that Kant's principle cannot yield any results at all, because it is a formal principle.[22] Are they right?

I have tried to explain why, in order to assure the autonomy of the moral agent, the moral law must be pure and *a priori*. This means, Kant insists, that the law must be *formal*. Like the logical law of contradiction, which rules out any proposition of the form 'P and not-P', the moral law must not itself contain any "matter" or content. Nonetheless Kant thinks form without content in morality is as empty as he thinks it would be in our experience of nature. There must be content, Kant holds, but it can only come from outside the will – from desires and needs, shaped by our awareness of the world in which we live into specific urges to act or plans for action. Our finitude makes the needy aspect of the self as essential to our particular mode of being as is the free will. It takes the two working together to produce morality. But all that the moral law can do is to provide the form for matter that comes from our desires.

Our urges to act come to the will through what Kant calls "maxims." A maxim is a personal or subjective plan of action, incorporating the agent's reasons for acting as well as a sufficient indication of what act the reasons call for. When we are fully rational, we act, knowing our circumstances, in order to obtain a definite end, and aware that under some conditions we are prepared to alter our plans. Because circumstances and desires recur, a maxim is general. It is like a private rule. A maxim might look like this: If it's raining, take an umbrella in order to stay dry, unless I can get a ride. We often don't think explicitly about the circumstances or the contingencies when we are acting, and Kant does not always include them in his examples of maxims. Sometimes we don't even think of the purpose or goal of an action, only of what we are intent on doing. But if we are rational our action always has a purpose, and we are responsive to the surroundings in which we act. A full maxim simply makes all this explicit. A rational agent tests her maxims before acting on them. To do so she uses the laws of rational willing.

Kant thinks there are two basic laws of rational willing. One governs goal-oriented action generally, and is easily stated:

Who wills the end, wills (so far as reason has decisive influence on his actions) also the means which are indispensably necessary and in his power.
(*Groundwork*, 4:417 / 84–85)

This simply says that when a rational agent is genuinely in pursuit of a goal, she must and will do whatever is needed to get it. Otherwise she is not really pursuing the goal. Now whenever there is a law determining a perfectly rational being to action, there is a counterpart, couched in terms of "ought," governing the actions of imperfectly rational beings such as ourselves. Kant calls such "ought" counterparts of the laws of rational willing "imperatives." He uses this term because the laws of rational willing appear as constraining us in the way that commands do. The "ought" counterpart of the law of goal-oriented willing is easily stated:

Whoever wills an end ought to will the means.

Kant calls it the "hypothetical" imperative. It is hypothetical because the necessity of action that it imposes is conditional. You ought to do a certain act *if* you will a certain end.[23]

Given Kant's claim that means–ends necessity is inadequate for morality, it is plain that he must think there is another law of rational willing, and so another kind of "ought" or imperative. The kind of "ought" that does not depend on the agent's ends arises from the moral law; and Kant calls the imperative version of that law "the categorical imperative." The moral law itself, Kant holds, can only be the form of lawfulness itself, because nothing else is left once all content has been rejected. The moral law can therefore be stated as follows:

A perfectly rational will acts only through maxims which it could also will to be universal law.

When this appears to us in the form of the catgorical imperative, it says:

Act only according to that maxim through which you can at the same time will that it should become a universal law.   (*Groundwork*, 4:421 / 88)

We might think of Kant as recommending a two-stage testing of maxims. First test a maxim by the hypothetical imperative. Does the proposed act effectively bring about a desired end? If not, reject it; and if it does, test it by the categorical imperative. If it passes this test, you may act on it, but if it does not, you must reject it. It is not hard to see how to apply the test of prudential rationality. The question is whether the test of morality, the categorical imperative, actually enables us to decide whether or not we may act on a maxim.

Kant gives us a formulation of the categorical imperative that he thinks is easier to use than the one I have already cited:

Act as if the maxim of your action were to become through your will a universal law of nature.   (*Groundwork*, 4:421 / 89)

Now suppose you need money. You think of getting some by asking a friend to lend it to you, but you have no intention of ever repaying him. You plan to make a false promise to repay. Your maxim (omitting circumstances and conditions) is something like this: Use a lying promise to get money I want. Suppose this passes the prudential test. You then consider whether your maxim could be a universal law of nature, whether there could be a world in which everyone was moved, as by a law of nature, to make lying promises to get what they want. It would have to be a world in which it is prudentially rational to make a lying promise to get money. Well, if everyone made lying promises it would be pretty obvious, and people would stop believing promises. But in a world where no promises are trusted, it cannot be rational to try to use a promise in this way. Thus you cannot coherently think a world for which your maxim is a law of nature. You are therefore not permitted to act on it (*Ground-work*, 4:422 / 89–90).

Another example shows a different way in which the categorical imperative works. I pass someone collapsed on the street, and decide not to help him. My maxim is something like this: Ignore people in need of help, in order not to interfere with my plans. Kant says that I can coherently *conceive* of a world of people indifferent to one another's distress. But he believes that I cannot *will* the existence of such a world. Look at it this way. As a rational agent I necessarily will the means to any of my ends. The help of others is often a means I need for my own ends. So it would be irrational to will to exclude the help of others as a possible means when I need it. But if I universalize my maxim, I will to make it a law of nature that no one helps others in need. I would therefore be willing both that others help me when I need it and that no one help others when they need it. This is incoherent willing. Hence I may not act on my maxim (*Groundwork*, 4:423 / 90–91).[24]

When we use the categorical imperative in these cases we suppose that we are examining a maxim embodying the agent's genuine reasons for proposing the action, rather than irrelevancies (such as that the act will be done by a gray-bearded man) that might let it get by the categorical imperative. A vocabulary for formulating our plans is also presupposed (though that vocabulary itself might be called into question, as when we reject racist language).[25] Given these assumptions, the examples show that if maxims of the kind they involve are what the categorical imperative is to test, then the moral law is not empty. There are at least some cases in which we can assess the moral permissibility of a plan simply by considering its rationality, without basing our conclusion on the goodness or badness of its consequences. The Kantian position is a real option for understanding morality.

VI

The categorical imperative can be formulated in several ways. Kant thinks they are all equivalent, and insists that the first formulation, the one we have been considering, is basic. Though the others bring out various aspects of the moral law, they cannot tell us more than the first formula does. It concentrates on the agent's point of view.

The second formulation draws our attention to those affected by our action:

Act in such a way that you always treat humanity, whether in your own person or in the person of another, never simply as a means, but always at the same time as an end.   (*Groundwork*, 4:429 / 96)

Kant is saying that the ends of others – if morally permissible – set limits to the ends we ourselves may pursue. We must respect the permissible ends of others, and we may make others serve our own purposes only when they as moral agents assent to such use, as when someone willingly takes a job working for another. Thus we may not pursue our own ends if they impermissibly conflict with the ends of others.[26] We are also to forward the ends of others, a point to which I will shortly return.

The third formulation instructs us to look at agent and recipient of action together in a community as we legislate through our maxims:

All maxims as proceeding from our own law-making ought to harmonize with a possible kingdom of ends as a kingdom of nature.

(*Groundwork*, 4:436 / 104)

Here we are told always to think of ourselves as members of a society of beings whose permissible ends are to be respected, and to test our maxims by asking whether, supposing the maxims were natural laws, there would be a society of that kind.[27]

Because the richer formulations of the categorical imperative can take us no further than the formula requiring us to test our maxims by asking if they could be universal laws, we must ask how well that principle can serve to show us the way through all of our relations with one another.

The categorical imperative clearly requires a kind of impartiality in our behavior. We are not permitted to make exceptions for ourselves, or to do what we would not rationally permit others to do. But it would be a mistake to suppose that Kantian morality allows for nothing but impartiality in personal relations. The maxim "If it is my child's birthday, give her a party, to show I love her" is thinkable and willable as a law of nature, as are some maxims of helping family members and friends rather than helping others. Of course our actions for those we prefer must be within rationally allowable limits, but within those limits Kantian ethics has nothing to say against the working of human affection.

A broader point is involved here. Although the categorical imperative operates most directly by vetoing proposed maxims of action, it is a mistake to suppose that it does nothing more. It is usually true that from its prohibitions alone no positive directives follow. Whatever is not forbidden is simply permitted. Sometimes, however, a veto forces a requirement on us. Where what is forbidden is *not* doing something – for instance, not paying my taxes – the veto requires me to do something, to pay my taxes, because it is not permitted not to do so. Beyond this, the categorical imperative can set requirements that are not so specifically tied to prohibitions. Kant gives us more detail on this in the *Metaphysics of Morals.*

He there divides morality into two domains, one of law or right (*Recht*), and one of virtue (*Morals*, 6:218–21 / 16–19). The domain of law, which extends to civil law, arises from maxims that are vetoed because they cannot even be thought coherently when universalized. The rejection of such maxims turns out to provide a counterpart to the recognition of the strict rights of others. We may not interfere with their legitimate projects, may not take their property, and so on. The domain of virtue involves maxims that can be thought but not willed as universal laws. Most of what morality requires as action rather than abstention is a requirement of virtue.

We have already seen why Kant thinks we cannot will a maxim of universal neglect of the needs of others, even though such a maxim is thinkable as a law of nature. Now the denial of this vetoed maxim is not the maxim "Always help everyone." It is rather the maxim "Help some others at some times." Kant thinks that further argument from this point will show that it is morally required that one of our own ends be to forward the ends of others. He thinks it can be shown in similar fashion that we must make the perfection of our moral character and of our abilities one of our ends (*Morals*, 6:384–8 / 43–7).

The differences between the domain of law and that of virtue are significant. To be virtuous, I must be acting for the sake of the good of another, or for my own perfection, and viewing these ends as morally required. In the domain of law it does not matter why I do what I do, so long as I abstain from violating the rights of others. Because the motive does not matter in legal affairs, if I do not perform as I ought, I can rightly be compelled to do so. I obtain no moral merit for carrying out legal duties. I simply keep my slate clean. In the domain of virtue, by contrast, there is nothing to which I can be compelled, because what is required is that I have certain ends, and ends must be freely adopted (Morals, 6:381 / 39). Moreover in the realm of virtue there are no requirements about specific actions. It is up to me to decide which of my talents to improve, where my worst moral failings are, and how, when, and how much to help others. Of course I may only do what is permissible within the limits of my legal duties. But the more I make the required ends mine, the more I will do. In the realm of virtue, moreover, I can become entitled to moral praise through my efforts for others. My merit increases as I make their goals my own.

Kant thus makes a place for a concern for human well-being as well as for negative respect for rights.[28] What is to be noted is that he does not base the requirement of concern for others on the goodness of the results virtue brings about. And he does not require us to bring about as much happiness (or as much of our own perfection) as we possibly can. He allows that we will have permissible ends that will compete for time and resources with the morally required ends. Morality does not tell us how to decide between them. It only tells us that we must pursue the required as well as the personal ends, staying always within the limits of justice.

How adequate, then, is the categorical imperative as a moral guide? One might wish to reject the whole vocabulary of law and obligation, and with it Kant's principle, on the grounds that it gives a skewed and harmful portrayal of human relations.[29] But even if one does not wish thus to set aside or subordinate the moral concerns that led Kant to make that vocabulary central, one must allow that there are problems with Kant's claims for the categorical imperative. I note only two.

First, Kant held that his principle leads to certain conclusions that many sensible people do not accept, such as that lying, suicide, and political revolution are always prohibited. If his inferences to these moral conclusions are valid, then his principle is questionable. If he is not right, then a question must be raised about his claim that his principle is so easy to apply that an ordinary person, "with this compass in hand, is well able to distinguish, in all cases that present themselves, what is good or evil, right or wrong. . . ." (Groundwork,

4:404 / 71–2). It is not clear that any single principle can do all that Kant claims for the categorical imperative.

Second, if the adequacy of the categorical imperative for cases involving only relations between two people is hard to determine, its adequacy for helping settle large-scale social issues is even more so. Kant thought that individual decision making would be able to guide people to coordinated action on matters of general concern. This seems extremely doubtful. It does not follow, however, that there is no way of revising the Kantian principle so that it might handle such issues in a way that preserves the intent of Kant's own formulation.[30]

VII

Kant held that the proper way to proceed in moral philosophy is to start with what we all know about morality and see what principle underlies it. The *Groundwork* accordingly begins with an examination of commonsense opinion. From it Kant extracts the motive that is central to morality as well as the basic principle of decision making.

He begins with the claim that we all recognize a kind of goodness different from the goodness of wealth, power, talent, and intellect, and even different from the goodness of kindly or generous dispositions. Under certain conditions any of these might turn out not to be good. But there is another kind of goodness that stays good under any conditions. This is the special kind of goodness a person can have. It is shown most clearly, Kant thinks, when someone does what she believes right or obligatory, and does it just because she thinks it so. Someone lacking kindly feelings, pity, or generosity, and not even caring about her own interest any more, may nonetheless do what she thinks right. The special sort of merit we attribute to this person is the goodness central to morality. It is best thought of as the goodness of a good will (*Groundwork*, 4:393–4 / 61–2).

Reflection on the agent of good will brings out an important point. Her value does not depend on her actual accomplishments. And because she is moved by a desire to do the act or to bring about its results, her value cannot depend on the results she intended either. Her value must depend, Kant says, "solely on the *principle of volition*" from which she acted. And the only principle available, because she is not moved by the content of her action, must be formal.

The agent of good will must therefore be moved by the bare lawfulness of the act. Kant puts it by saying that she is moved by respect or reverence (*Achtung*) for the moral law (*Groundwork*, 4:400 / 68).

Commonsense beliefs about the moral goodness of the good agent show us, Kant thinks, that the categorical imperative is the principle behind sound moral judgment. Kant also thinks he obtains from beliefs about the good agent his view about the motivation proper to morality. Historically the latter was as revolutionary as the former, and systematically the two aspects of the theory are inseparably linked. But the motivational view leads to some new problems for Kant.

The psychological doctrine prevalent in Kant's time held that what motivates us in voluntary rational action is desire for good and aversion to evil. Granting that people often fail to pursue the good either through mistake or through perversity, the view implies that if we do not act from a desire for some perceived good, we are acting wrongly or at least irrationally. Of course it was allowed that people sometimes do their duty just because they ought to. But since doing one's duty was understood to be productive of good – the good of the community – even conscientious action was seen as motivated by desire for the good.[31]

Crusius broke with this tradition when he said that we could obey God's laws simply because they are ordained by him.[32] Kant's assertion that in obeying the dictates of the categorical imperative we could be motivated by what he called respect for the law accepts this decisive break with the older view. Respect, as we have seen, is a concern not for the ends or goods of action, but for the form. So when we are moved by it, we are not pursuing good. But neither are we acting wrongly or irrationally. The central moral motive therefore does not fit the standard pattern.

Respect is unlike other motives in two further ways. First, it is a feeling that arises solely from our awareness of the moral law as the categorical imperative. And it always arises from such awareness. While other motives may or may not be present in everyone at all times, every rational agent always has available this motive, which is sufficient to move her to do what the categorical imperative bids. Second, other motives, such as fear of punishment, greed, love, or pity, can lead us to act rightly. But it is merely contingent if they do. Love, like greed or hatred, can lead one to act immorally. The sole motive that necessarily moves us to act rightly is respect, because it alone is only activated by the dictates of the categorical imperative.

It is easy to see the place of respect in Kant's portrayal of autonomy. Respect provides an answer to the claim, made famous by Hume but probably known to Kant through work by Hume's influential predecessor Francis Hutcheson,[33] that reason cannot motivate us. On the contrary, Kant replies: Practical reason generates its own unique motive. External sanctions, of the sort the natural law theorists thought indispensable to give obligation its motivating power, are unnecessary, at least in principle, because we all have within ourselves an adequate motive for compliance. Respect also makes up for the inequities of nature. Some people are naturally loving, friendly, and thoughtful. Nature has not been so generous to others. If only natural motives were available to move us to do what morality requires, then some, through no fault of their own, would be unable to comply with it. Kant's doctrine implies that no one need be prevented by the niggardliness of nature from attaining moral worth.

If the attractions of the doctrine of respect are plain, it nonetheless gets Kant into difficulties. It leads him to think along the following lines. If I act from any motive other than respect, I am simply doing something I find myself wanting to do. My action may be right, but if so that is merely contingent. Even if it is, I show no special concern for morality when I am moved by my desire. All that is shown by a right act done from a nonmoral motive is that morality and my interest here coincide. Consequently I deserve no praise unless I act from respect. Action from respect is the only kind of action that shows true concern for morality. No other motivation entitles me to count as a virtuous agent.

As critics have frequently pointed out, this seems a paradoxical position.[34] It seems to make almost every aspect of character unimportant to morality, because it denies any moral worth to actions springing entirely from feelings of love, loyalty, friendship, pity, or generosity, and seems to rule out mixed motives as sources of moral worth.[35] Worse, it suggests that kind or loving feelings can get in the way of our achieving moral merit. If merit accrues only when we act from a sense of duty, it seems that human relations must be either unduly chilly or else without moral worth. Did Kant really hold this view? There are passages that suggest he did,[36] and others where he asserts a much more humane view.[37] The most plausible alternative to the extreme position is one that allows conditional mixed motives: I may have merit when moved by the motive of pity, say, if I allow pity to operate only on condition that in moving me it leads me to nothing the categorical imperative forbids, and if respect is strong enough in me to move me were pity to fail. Because the texts show a change of mind, the best interpretation depends on systematic considerations, of which not the least is whether one accepts Kant's belief that there is a unique and supremely important kind of merit or worthiness, the moral kind.

VIII

So far I have tried to explain the principle Kant takes to be central to morality and the motivation he thinks is unique to it. I have said nothing about the justification he thinks he can give for claiming that the principle really holds. We are thus at the point Kant reaches toward the end of the second part of the *Groundwork*. He there says that so far all he has done is to show what ordinary moral consciousness takes morality to involve if there is such a thing. But is there? A parallel question about prudential rationality would be easy to answer. The law of prudence is true by definition, or analytic. To say someone is a "perfectly rational agent" simply means (in part) that she "uses the means needed to attain her goals." But the moral law is not analytic. The concepts "completely good will" or "perfectly rational agent" do not include "acts only through universalizable maxims." And we cannot base the moral law on experience. It is a necessary proposition, and experience alone never grounds such propositions. What basis then is there for the moral law?[38]

The problem as Kant sees it is to discover something through which we can join the subject of the moral law – "perfectly rational agent" – and its predicate – "acts only through universalizable maxims." He sees a possible solution in the idea of freedom of the will. Freedom has a negative aspect: If we are free, we are not determined solely by our desires and needs. But freedom is more than the absence of determination. A will wholly undetermined would be random and chaotic. It would not allow for responsibility, nor consequently for praise and blame.[39] The only viable way to think of a free will, Kant holds, is to think of it as a will whose choices are deter-

mined by a law that is internal to its nature. Such a will is determined only by itself, and is therefore free. But we have already seen
that the only self-determined actions are actions done because of the
universalizability of the agent's maxim. So if we could show that a
rational will must be free, we would have shown that a rational will
acts only on universalizable maxims.[40] We would have proven the
first principle of morality.

Given Kant's Newtonian model of the physical world, a strong
claim about freedom of the will raises problems. Our bodies as physical objects are subject to Newton's laws of motion. If they are moved
by our natural desires, this is unproblematic, because desires themselves arise in accordance with deterministic laws (as yet undis-
covered). Morality, however, requires the possibility of action from a
wholly nonempirical motive. We never know whether real moral
merit is attained, but if it is, the motive of respect must move us to
bodily action, regardless of the strength of our desires. Is this possible?

In the first *Critique* Kant argued that no theoretical proof (or disproof) of free will can be given. In the *Groundwork* Kant thinks he
can give at least indirect support to the claim that we are free. When
we as rational beings act, he says, we must take ourselves to be free.
He means that whenever we deliberate or choose we are presupposing freedom, even if we are unaware of the presupposition or con-
sciously doubtful of it. More broadly, whenever we take ourselves to
be thinking rationally (even about purely theoretical matters) we
must take ourselves to be free, because we cannot knowingly accept
judgments determined by external sources as judgments we ourselves have made. Now anything that would follow about us if we
were really free still follows for practical purposes if we have to
think of ourselves as free. Because freedom entails the moral law, we
must think of ourselves as bound by it (*Groundwork*, 4:447–8 /
115–16).[41]

Can we both take ourselves to be free and believe theoretically in
a deterministic universe? Kant's answer appeals to his first *Critique*.
Theoretical knowledge has limits: It applies only to the world as we
experience it, the phenomenal world. We cannot say that the determinism holding in the realm of phenomena holds beyond it as well,
in the noumenal world. If we think of ourselves as belonging to the
noumenal as well as the phenomenal world, then we can see how in
one respect we may be beings bound in a web of mechanistic deter-

mination, while in another respect we are the free rational agents morality supposes us to be. Our theoretical beliefs and our practical presupposition of freedom do not come into any conflict.

There are many difficulties with this argument. One of them is this. The argument seems to suppose that we are free just when we are acting rationally. But then if we act irrationally, we are not free. Immoral action is, however, irrational. So it seems to follow that we are responsible only when acting as the moral law requires, and not responsible when we do something wicked. Kant might have had a reply to this objection, but if so he did not give it. In his later writings, he introduced a distinction between the will and the power of choice (*Wille* and *Willkür*), which was meant to remove the problem.[42] He held that the will is simply identical with practical rationality and is therefore the home of the moral law, but that we have in addition a power of choice, whose task is to choose between the promptings of desire and the imperatives stemming from the will. It is in the power of choice that our freedom, properly speaking, resides. The will itself is neither free nor unfree.

Kant not only developed his view of free will considerably; he changed his mind about how to argue in support of it.[43] In the *Critique of Practical Reason* Kant continued to hold his earlier view that if we are free we are under the moral law, and if we are under the moral law we are free. But he now argues that what he calls "the fact (*Faktum*) of reason" is what shows us that we are free. There is considerable difficulty in clarifying just what Kant supposes the fact of reason be be.[44] One possible interpretation starts with Kant's claim that the fact of reason is revealed to us through our moral awareness that we are bound by unconditional obligations. Because we know we are bound by such obligations, we know also that we can do what we are obligated to do. This means that we can do it, no matter what the circumstances and no matter what has gone on before. In other words awareness of categorical obligation contains awareness of freedom. But it is awareness of freedom as it expresses itself in imperfectly rational beings. The fact of reason, we might take it, is pure rationality displaying itself as immediately as it can in imperfectly rational beings.[45]

In the *Critique*, therefore, Kant treats freedom as the ground of our *having* moral obligations, and our awareness of categorical imperatives as the ground of our *knowledge* that we are free. He thus gives up

the one attempt he made to support the principle of morals by appeal
to something other than itself – rationality in general – and he uses
our awareness of morality as a foundation from which we can extend
our understanding of ourselves and our place in the universe.[46]

Kant is not here retracting the claims he made in the first *Critique*
about the limits of knowledge. Our justified assurance that we are
free is not theoretical knowledge. While we are entitled to that assurance for practical purposes, we cannot infer from it anything of
pertinence to our theoretical understanding of the world. Indeed
Kant thinks that without the positions established in the theoretical
Critique the moral outlook he aims to defend would be impossible.
Unless we see that knowledge is limited, we will think that the kind
of theoretical knowledge science gives us is all the knowledge there
can be. Then a theoretical understanding of our own behavior will
become inevitable. Kant held that if we think of ourselves solely in
empirical and deterministic terms we will necessarily think of ourselves as heteronomous, as moved by our desires for this or that, and
never solely by respect for law. This thought would be debilitating to
our effort to be moral.[47] But the first *Critique* showed that the deterministic stance of theoretical reason is valid only within the bounds
of experience. Theoretical reason has no jurisdiction over the beliefs
morality requires us to hold.

IX

Kant calls this the primacy of practical reason (*Practical Reason*,
5:119–21 / 124–6). If the categorical imperative requires us to think
of ourselves and the world in certain ways, then the limitations on
speculative reason cannot be used to deny that we have any warrant
for those beliefs. Our nature as rational agents thus dominates our
nature as rational knowers. There are two matters, other than freedom, on which practical reason requires us to accept beliefs that can
be neither proven nor disproven theoretically. One concerns our
hopes for our own private futures, the other concerns our hopes for
the future of humanity. In one case we are led by morality to have
certain religious beliefs; in the other, to have certain views about
history and progress.

In the second *Critique* Kant argues not only that we must think of
ourselves as free moral agents but also that we must see ourselves as

immortal, and as living in a universe governed by a providential intelligence through whose intervention in the course of nature the virtuous are rewarded and the vicious punished. We must have these beliefs, Kant holds, because morality requires each of us to make ourselves perfectly virtuous – to give ourselves a character in which the dictates of the categorical imperative are never thwarted by the passions and desires. And it also requires that happiness be distributed in accordance with virtue.[48] The former cannot be done in a finite amount of time, so we must believe that we each have something like an infinite amount of time available for carrying out the task, or at least for approaching closer and closer to completion. The latter is not possible if the mechanisms of nature are the sole ordering force in the universe, nature being indifferent to virtue and vice. Hence we must believe that there is some nonnatural ordering force that will intervene to bring about what morality requires (*Practical Reason*, 5:122–32 / 126–36).

In his essays on history[49] Kant argues that theoretical reason can never determine whether mankind is progressing or not. War and the innumerable ghastly ways in which people mistreat one another seem sometimes to be waning, sometimes to be increasing, sometimes simply to go through an endless see-saw of more and less. But morality requires us to try to bring it about that there is peace in the world, and that the standing form of government is everywhere one in which individual autonomy is publicly acknowledged and respected. We must therefore believe that it is possible to bring this about, and we must see history as moving, however slowly, and at whatever cost to innumerable individuals throughout countless generations, in this direction. Thus within the world constituted by theoretical reason, practical reason directs us to form a moral world by imposing moral order on the whole of human society as well as on our individual desires.

Kant is not saying that moral agents come to believe these propositions about religion and history through arguments. He is saying rather that each moral agent will find herself acting as if she saw the world as Kant's propositions portray it. Morality, as Kant understands it, makes sense only if certain background conditions are met. Unless these conditions hold, a form of *pointlessness* threatens action dictated by the categorical imperative; and the rational agent cannot act while thinking her action pointless. The belief in freedom is needed first of all, because otherwise we would lack the assurance that we can do what the categorical imperative requires. The other morally required beliefs ward off a different kind of pointlessness.

What is evident in all of these other beliefs to which we are led on practical grounds alone is a concern for human happiness. Kant is often thought to hold that happiness is not valuable, and even to have ignored it wholly in his ethics. This is a serious mistake. It is true that for Kant moral worth is the supreme good, but by itself it is not the perfect or complete good.[50] To be virtuous, for Kant, is to be worthy of happiness: And the perfect good requires that happiness be distributed in accordance with virtue (*Practical Reason*, 5:110–11 / 114–15). Happiness, or the sum of satisfaction of desires, is a conditional good. It is good only if it results from the satisfaction of morally permissible desires. But it is intrinsically valuable nonetheless. It is valued by a rational agent for itself, and not instrumentally.[51]

Atheism and meaninglessness in history threaten to make morality pointless. A holy will necessarily aims at the perfect good, and we imperfect beings therefore ought to do what we can to bring it about. But it seems simply irrational to devote serious effort to bringing about a goal that one believes cannot be brought about. If reason showed the perfect good to be a required but unattainable goal, reason would be at odds with itself. The moral agent, knowing herself required to act in ways that make sense only if certain ends can be achieved, finds herself simply taking it that the world must allow the possibility of success. Since this attitude is not translatable into theoretical knowledge, the agent cannot have any details about *how* her effort will help bring about the ends. All that is needed is the confidence that it will. Philosophy helps, Kant thinks, by showing that nothing can prove the attitude unwarranted.[52]

NOTES

1 Contemporary English-language study of Kant's ethics owes a great deal to the important commentaries of H. J. Paton, *The Categorical Imperative* (London: Hutchinson, 1946), and Lewis White Beck, *A Commentary to Kant's Critique of Practical Reason* (Chicago: University of Chicago Press, 1960), both of which helped stimulate German scholarship as well. John Rawls's widely read *A Theory of Justice* (Cambridge, Mass.: Harvard University Press, 1971) showed one direction in which Kantian-

ism could be revised, and was a major impetus to the use of Kantian insights in developing general ethical theory and in handling concrete current issues.

2 Although Kant did a great deal of thinking about ethics during his early years, he wrote little about it before the publication of the first *Critique*. That *Critique* contains some discussion of moral philosophy, but the major works are the following:

Groundwork of the Metaphysics of Morals (1785), reference to *Akademie* edition volume and page followed by the page number of the translation by H. J. Paton, *The Moral Law* (London: Hutchinson, 1948).

Critique of Practical Reason (1788), references followed by page numbers of the translation by Lewis White Beck (Indianapolis: Bobbs-Merrill, 1956).

Metaphysics of Morals, in two parts, known as the *Doctrine of Right* and the *Doctrine of Virtue*, which were published separately in 1797; references when quotations are from the *Doctrine of Virtue* followed by the page number of the translation by Mary Gregor (Philadelphia: University of Pennsylvania Press, 1964).

Religion within the Limits of Reason Alone (1793), references followed by the page number of the translation by Theodore M. Greene and Hoyt H. Hudson (1934; 2d ed., New York: Harper & Row, 1960).

Kant's essays on history and politics are important sources as well. There are two useful collections: Lewis White Beck et al., *Kant on History* (Indianapolis: Bobbs-Merrill, 1963), and Ted Humphrey, *Perpetual Peace and Other Essays* (Indianapolis: Hackett, 1983). References are followed by "H" and page number from the Beck translation.

Volumes 27 and 29 of the *Akademie* edition of *Kants gesammelte Schriften* contain over a thousand pages of student notes on Kant's classes on ethics, which he taught between twenty and thirty times from 1756–7 to 1793–4 (see Emil Arnoldt, *Gesammelte Schriften* [Berlin: 1909], Vol. V, p. 335). The earliest notes come from 1763–4, the latest from 1793–4. Notes taken in 1780–1 are available in English: *Lectures on Ethics*, trans. Louis Infield (originally 1930) (New York: Harper & Row, 1963).

The student notes offer many insights into Kant's ethical thought, but they also pose several new interpretative problems. In this essay I concentrate on the published works.

3 Not only humans: Kant thinks any rational agents would be autonomous.

4 The term "his" is used advisedly here: Kant had unfortunate views about women. He also thought servants were not sufficiently independent to be entitled to full political status.

5 This is from marginal notes Kant jotted down as he was reading Rous-

seau's *Social Contract* and *Emile* during 1763–4 (20:140–1; I have added some punctuation). It is largely from these notes that we know of the considerable impact that Rousseau had on Kant.

6 20:36, "kindnesses occur only through inequality."

7 *R* 6736, 19:145.

8 See Kant's late remarks on servility in *Morals*, 6:434–6; 99–101; see also Thomas E. Hill, Jr., "Servility and Self-Respect," *Monist* 57 (1973): 87–104.

9 In the essay "On the Common Saying: 'That may be true in theory but it does not work in practice'," Kant says that in connection with our moral self-legislation "man thinks of himself according to an analogy with the divinity" (8:280 n.). The essay is translated in Hans Reiss, ed., *Kant's Political Writings* (Cambridge: Cambridge University Press, 1970).

10 The standard work on the development of Kant's ethics is Josef Schmucker, *Die Ursprünge der Ethik Kants* (Meisenheim am Glan: Anton Hain, 1961). There is no reliable study of the subject in English.

11 For selections from Shaftesbury and Hutcheson, see. D. D. Raphael, *The British Moralists*, 2 vols. (Oxford: Oxford University Press, 1969), and J. B. Schneewind, *Moral Philosophy from Montaigne to Kant*, 2 vols. (Cambridge: Cambridge University Press, 1990). Their works were available in German, and Kant owned the translations of Hutcheson's most important writings.

12 There are no studies of Wolff in English, and little of his work has been translated. Lewis White Beck, *Early German Philosophy* (Cambridge, Mass.: Harvard University Press, 1969) discusses his general philosophy but says little about his ethics. For an excellent study of the early German enlightenment and Wolff's place in it, see Hans M. Wolff, *Die Weltanschauung der deutschen Aufklärung* (Bern, 1949). For selections in English of his ethics, see Schneewind, *Moral Philosophy from Montaigne to Kant*, Vol. I.

13 These views are compendiously presented in Christian Wolff, *Vernünftige Gedancken von der Menschen Thun und Lassen* (1720).

14 Kant holds that it is necessarily true that each of us desires his or her own happiness, and he sometimes equates happiness with the satisfaction of the totality of our desires. But no single desire is a necessary feature of any particular individual. This is a point on which many of Kant's recent critics, particularly those sympathetic to Aristotle, disagree with him. They would argue that some desires or motives or active dispositions are essential to the individual identity of the person. See, e.g., Jonathan Lear, *Aristotle: The Desire to Understand* (Cambridge: Cambridge University Press, 1988), p. 189. Kant would think that if you must have some specific effective desire then you are not free with respect to it. Kant does not

think, as some of his critics believe, that the free will constitutes the whole identity of each individual. But he does think that whatever constitutes individual identity does so only contingently.

15 Crusius was a leader of the anti-Wolffian movement. His moral philosophy is contained in his *Anweisung, vernünftig zu leben* (1744). There is good discussion of his general position in Beck, *Early German Philosophy*. For translated selections, see Schneewind, *Moral Philosophy from Montaigne to Kant*, Vol. II.

16 There is considerable difficulty in interpreting Rousseau's influence on Kant. As indicated above, the most important evidence comes from the notes Kant made when he first read *Emile* and the *Social Contract* during 1763–4 (20:1–192). One of the most frequently quoted notes compares Rousseau's clarification of the hidden aspects of human nature to Newton's uncovering of the hidden aspects of physical nature (20:58–9). Another is more personal: "I am myself a researcher by inclination. I feel the whole thirst for knowledge and the eager unrest to move further on into it, also satisfaction with each acquisition. There was a time when I thought this alone could constitute the honor of humanity and I despised the know-nothing rabble. Rousseau set me straight. This delusory superiority vanishes, I learn to honor men, and I would find myself more useless than a common laborer if I did not believe this observation could give everyone a value which restores the rights of humanity" (20:44).

17 *Social Contract*, I.viii.§4, in *On the Social Contract*, ed. Roger D. Masters, trans. Judith R. Masters (New York: St. Martin's Press, 1978), p. 56.

18 In the 1763–4 notes (see note 5 in this chapter) there are several attempts to formulate the principle behind what Kant later called the categorical imperative. There are also clear indications both of the distinction between it and the hypothetical imperative and of the idea that the former is central to morality.

19 Those who insisted that God laid down the laws of morality by absolute fiat argued that unless that were true, God would be limited by something external to himself. They thought that even eternal moral standards would be an intolerable constraint on God's absolute freedom.

20 Pure theoretical reason is an activity determined *a priori*, and one might think of one of its patterns of activity as embodying the "causal law." The causal law, in this sense, explains why every event must have a cause, but does not alone tell us what event causes what other event; to obtain this knowledge we need data of experience in addition. Similarly, as I explain later, the moral law does not by itself tell us which specific acts are obligatory; we must use it to test maxims in order to learn what we ought to do.

21 Some theorists have taken the rightness of acts as basic, defining a good agent as one who has a conscious habit of doing such acts, and good states of affairs as those intended to be the outcome of right acts. This view tends to go along with intuitionist explanations of how we know what is right. Thomas Reid's *Essays on the Active Powers of Man* (1788) offers one theory of this kind.

22 A brilliant account of Hegelian objections of this kind, as well as other criticisms, is given in F. H. Bradley, *Ethical Studies* (1876; 2d ed., Oxford: Clarendon Press, 1927). ch. 2. The literature on the subject is extensive. The best book in English is Onora (O'Neill) Nell, *Acting on Principle: An Essay on Kantian Ethics* (New York: Columbia University Press, 1975), to which I am much indebted. For a sample of other criticisms of Kant see C. D. Broad, *Five Types of Ethical Theory* (London, 1930), ch. 5. See also the articles by Jonathan Harrison, "Kant's Examples of the First Formulation of the Categorical Imperative," *Philosophical Quarterly* 7 (1957); Julius Ebbinghaus, "Interpretation and Misinterpretation of the Categorical Imperative" (1959), reprinted in Robert Paul Wolff, ed., *Kant: A Collection of Critical Essays* (Garden City, N.Y.: Anchor/ Doubleday, 1967), pp. 211–27; Jonathan Kemp, "Kant's Examples of the Categorical Imperative," *Philosophical Quarterly* 8: 63–71 (1958); Nelson Potter, "Paton on the Application of the Categorical Imperative," *Kant-Studien* 64 (1973): 411–22; Ottfried Höffe, "Kants kategorischer Imperativ als Kriterium des Sittlichen," *Zeitschrift für philosophische Forschung* 31 (1977): 354–84; and the following books: Paton, *The Categorical Imperative*; Marcus G. Singer, *Generalization in Ethics* (New York: Alfred A. Knopf, 1961); Bruce Aune, *Kant's Theory of Morals* (Princeton,N.J.: Princeton University Press, 1979); and John Atwell, *Ends and Principles in Kant's Moral Thought* (Dordrecht: D. Reidel, 1986).

23 The formula given indicates the essential form underlying all particular hypothetical imperatives ("If you want to preserve your health, you ought to go to the dentist"). What makes an imperative hypothetical is not the appearance of an "if" clause in its formulation. Such clauses might appear in categorical imperatives: "If you are asked a question, you ought to answer truthfully." And they need not appear in hypothetical imperatives: "Eat whenever you are hungry." The sole defining feature of a hypothetical imperative is that it obligates the agent to an action only on condition that the agent has desire for something that the action would bring about. For an excellent discussion, see Thomas E. Hill, Jr., "The Hypothetical Imperative," *Philosophical Review* 82 (1973): 429–50.

24 There are many other views about how universalizability or the application of the formula of universal law should be understood. For an excel-

lent discussion, see Christine Korsgaard, "Kant's Formula of Universal Law," *Pacific Philosophical Quarterly* 66 (1985): 24–47.

25 See Barbara Herman, "The Practice of Moral Judgment," *Journal of Philosophy* 82 (1985): 414–35.

26 See Christine Korsgaard, "Kant's Formula of Humanity," *Kant-Studien* 77 (1986): 183–202.

27 Kant seems to assume that those who apply the categorical imperative to their maxims will come out with answers that agree when the maxims tested are alike.

28 He also shows how the basic principles of morality can be extended to handle cases where agents do not comply with the moral requirement of acting from respect for the law. The treatment even of those who are indifferent to morality falls under an extension of the moral law.

29 For strong representations of this point of view, see Alasdair MacIntyre, *After Virtue* (Notre Dame, Ind.: Notre Dame University Press, 1981), and Bernard Williams, *Ethics and the Limits of Philosophy* (Cambridge, Mass.: Harvard University Press, 1985).

30 For an excellent example of an attempt to use the Kantian thinking to deal with a major social issue, see Onora O'Neill, *Faces of Hunger* (Oxford: Basil Blackwell, 1986).

31 If you obey the natural law only because of fear of God's sanctions, you are still motivated by desire for good – the good of avoiding punishment.

32 There are unclear and wavering anticipations of the Kantian move in Pufendorf and Samuel Clarke, but Crusius was the first to make the point central to his moral psychology.

33 See Dieter Henrich, "Hutchenson und Kant," *Kant-Studien* 49 (1957–8): 49–69, and "Über Kants früheste Ethik," *Kant-Studien* 54 (1963): 404–31.

34 The poet Schiller first made this kind of criticism. Schiller's and related objections are discussed at length in Hans Reiner, *Duty and Inclination* (The Hague: Martinus Nijhoff, 1983). A considerable literature has grown up on the subject. For recent discussion of it, see Michael Stocker, "The Schizophrenia of Modern Ethical Theories," *Journal of Philosophy* 73 (1976): 453–66; Richard Henson, "What Kant Might Have Said: Moral Worth and the Overdetermination of Dutiful Action," *Philosophical Review* 88 (1979): 39–54; Barbara Herman, "On the Value of Acting from the Motive of Duty," *Philosophical Review* 90 (1981): 359–82; Marcia Baron, "The Alleged Moral Repugnance of Acting from Duty," *Journal of Philosophy* 81 (1984): 197–220; Judith Baker, "Do One's Motives Have to be Pure?" in Richard Grandy and Richard Warner, eds., *Philosophical Grounds of Rationality* (Oxford: Oxford University Press,

1986), pp. 457–74; and Tom Sorrell, "Kant's Good Will," *Kant-Studien* 78 (1987): 87–101.

35 Kant says that action from any of these desires is heteronomous. This is not because he thinks the desires are not part of the self. It is because through these desires action is governed by something other than the self. In these desires the self pursues good and avoids ill. It is therefore governed by the features of things that make them objects of desire or aversion, and these features are, of course, independent of our wills. Thus in describing heteronomy Kant speaks of the object determining the will "by means of" inclination (*vermittelst der Neigung*) (*Groundwork*, 4:444 / 111).

36 He rejects the feeling of love as a proper moral motive (*Groundwork*, 4:399 / 67); he usually treats the passions and desires as if their aim is always the agent's own pleasure or good (e.g., *Groundwork*, 4:407 / 75); and at one point he says it must be the wish of every rational person to be free of desire (*Groundwork*, 4:428 / 955–6).

37 This is particularly evident in the *Religion*. See 6:28 / 23, where the natural dispositions in human nature leading us to sexual activity and to strive for social superiority are said to be dispositions for good, though they can be misused; and 6:58 / 51: "Natural inclinations, *considered in themselves*, are *good*, that is not a matter of reproach, and it is not only futile to want to extirpate them but to do so would also be harmful and blameworthy."

38 Kant here raises the questions of whether a transcendental deduction of the moral law is possible. The problem differs from that involved in constructing a transcendental argument for, say, the principle that every event must have a cause. We experience a spatiotemporal world of stable and interacting objects, and can therefore ask under what conditions such experience is possible. But we are so far from experiencing a stable moral world that we cannot point with certainty, Kant thinks, to even one case where someone was motivated by respect alone.

39 Freedom of that kind, Kant thinks, would be terrifying, not something to cherish. See 20:91 ff., 27:258, 1320, and 1482.

40 On the thesis that a free will and a will governed by the moral law are one and the same, see Henry E. Allison, "Morality and Freedom: Kant's Reciprocity Thesis," *Philosophical Review* 95 (1986): 393–425, and, more fully, the same author's *Kant's Theory of Freedom* (Cambridge: Cambridge University Press, 1990).

41 For an attempt to unpack this difficult argument, see Thomas E. Hill, Jr., "Kant's Argument for the Rationality of Moral Conduct," *Pacific Philosophical Quarterly* 66 (1985): 3–23; and Allison, *Kant's Theory of Freedom*, ch. 12.

42 See *Religion*, 6:21–6 / 16–21; *Morals*, 6:213–14 / 10–11; 6:225 / 25.

43 For discussion, see Karl Ameriks, *Kant's Theory of Mind* (Oxford: Oxford University Press, 1982), ch. 6.

44 For valuable assistance, see John Rawls, "Themes in Kant's Moral Philosophy," in Eckart Förster, ed., *Kant's Transcendental Deductions: The Three "Critiques" and the "Opus postumum"* (Stanford, Calif.: Stanford University Press, 1989), pp. 81–113; Henry E. Allison, "Justification and Freedom in the *Critique of Practical Reason*," ibid., pp. 114–30; and the discussion of both papers by Barbara Herman, ibid., pp. 131–41.

45 See Dieter Henrich, "Der Begriff der sittlichen Einsicht und Kants Lehre vom Faktum der Vernunft," in *Die Gegenwart der Griechen im neueren Denken*, ed. Dieter Henrich et al. (Tübingen: J. C. B. Mohr Paul Siebeck, 1960), pp. 77–115; and "Die Deduktion des Sittengesetzes," in *Denken im Schatten des Nihilismus*, ed. Alexander Schwann (Darmstadt: Wissenschaftliche Buchgesellschaft, 1975), pp. 55–112.

46 Whether this marks the failure of an attempt to ground morality or a wise realization that morality needs no grounds beyond itself is of course a matter of considerable philosophical disagreement. For extended discussion, see Gerold Prauss, *Kant über Freiheit als Autonomie* (Frankfurt am Main: Vittorio Klostermann, 1983).

47 The second *Critique* is a critique of practical reason generally, and not only of *pure* practical reason, because it examines, among other things, the claim of empirical practical reason – means/end reasoning – to be the only practical reason there is. The establishment through the fact of reason of pure practical reason disproves this claim.

48 "The proposition: Make the highest good possible in the world your own final end! is a synthetical proposition *a priori*, which is introduced by the moral law itself" (*Religion*, 6:7 n. / 7 n.). Kant's argument for this is to say the least unclear. For further discussion see the essay by Allen Wood in the present book.

49 In addition to the collections cited in note 2, see the important essay "An Old Question Raised Again: Is the Human Race Constantly Progressing?" in the *Streit der Fakultäten* (7:77–94); a translation is included in the Beck collection and in *The Conflict of the Faculties*, trans. Mary Gregor (New York: Abaris Books, 1979).

50 Kant repeatedly criticizes the Stoics for making the mistake of thinking virtue the perfect good. The Epicureans, he held, made just the opposite mistake, taking happiness to be the complete good. His view synthesizes the two in the proper way (*Practical Reason*, 5:111–13 / 115–17).

51 A basically virtuous person takes as her fundamental maxim to pursue her own good only on condition that doing so meets the requirements of morality. A basically vicious person reverses the order, and takes as

fundamental the maxim of doing what morality requires only if it is not
in conflict with the pursuit of her own good. See the discussion in
Religion, 6:36–7 / 31–2 and 6:42–4 / 37–9.

52 I should like to thank Richard Rorty, David Sachs, Larry Krasnoff, Paul
Guyer, Fred Beiser, and Richard Flathman, who read this essay at various
stages of its development and made helpful suggestions.

11 Politics, freedom, and order: Kant's political philosophy

Kant's practical philosophy in its entirety comprises ethics and philosophy of right,[1] moral theology, moral anthropology, and the philosophy of history, and combines them into one impressive theoretical structure. The theory of the self-legislation of pure practical reason developed in the *Groundwork of the Metaphysics of Morals* (1785) and *Critique of Practical Reason* (1788) stands at the center of this system. Through this theory Kant provides an entirely new theoretical foundation for justification in practical philosophy. In the previous history of practical philosophy foundations and first principles were sought in objective ideas, in a normative constitution of the cosmos, in the will of God, in the nature of man, or in prudence in the service of self-interest; but Kant was convinced that these starting-points were without exception inadequate for the foundation of unconditional practical laws, and that human reason could only concede absolute practical necessity and obligatoriness to norms that arose from its own legislation. We are subject to the laws of reason alone: With this recognition Kant frees us from the domination of theological absolutism and the bonds of teleological natural law, and likewise elevates us above the prosaic banalities of the doctrine of prudence. Human beings may and must obey only their own reason; in that lies their dignity as well as their exacting and burdensome moral vocation.

In the *Metaphysics of Morals* of 1797 Kant systematically elaborated this theory of autonomous and self-ruling reason and developed a material ethics and a philosophy of right. Besides its foundational part and the realm of the systematic differentiation of the pure legislation of reason into right and ethics, the principles of private and public right on the one hand and the rationally based ends of human action on the other, Kant's practical philosophy also includes anthropology and philosophy of history. Human nature and history constitute the domain for the empirical application of the principles of morality and right. They contain the conditions of realization without attention to which pure practical reason remains powerless, and which must therefore be considered by a practical philosophy that is concerned with the realization of its own principles.

When one looks for political philosophy in the structure of Kant's practical philosophy one finds it in the realms of philosophy of right and the philosophy of history. Kant revoked Machiavelli's separation between morals and politics, and by integrating political philosophy under the authority of pure practical reason re-created the old unity of morals and politics in a revolutionary new conceptual framework and on the basis of a revolutionary new theory of justification. The presentation of Kant's political philosophy requires a task of reconstruction, requires that the arguments and doctrines of his philosophy of right that are essential for political philosophy be put in their internal foundational nexus so that the systematic backbone of the political philosophy can be made clear; that is, it is requisite for us to reconstruct the path of Kant's argument from the concept of right through the foundation of property to the *a priori* principles of the republic of reason. However, Kant's political philosophy also carefully reflects the empirical conditions for the realization of the norms of the rational theory of right and develops an astonishing pragmatism, engaging with relations of political power as they are given in order to discover and exploit possibilities for change free of force and oriented toward principles. This non-Machiavellian but principled pragmatism about reform, which is aimed at a republicanization of relations of domination, is embedded in a philosophy of history that, encouraged by the sympathetic reaction to the French Revolution throughout Europe, expected the historical development of states to be a nonlinear but nevertheless unstoppable progress in right. The utopian vanishing point on the horizon of this practical philosophy of history is the highest political good, perpetual peace.

This brief description of the themes of Kant's political philosophy suggests the course and division of the following exposition. In more detail, I will deal with the elements of the concept of right (Section I); Kant's foundation of private property and his critique of Locke's labor theory of property (II); the connection of the natural condition,[2] property, contract, and state in Kant, in comparison with Hobbes and Locke (III); Kant's *contractus originarius*, the *a priori* principles of the civil condition, and the procedural concept of justice that is grounded on that (IV); the connection between Kant's prohibition of revolution or resistance with his principle of publicity and right-improving reformism (V); and finally, in Section VI, his theory of perpetual peace.

I. ELEMENTS OF THE CONCEPT OF RIGHT

Kant shares the conviction, common to all variants of natural right theory, that there is an objective, timelessly valid and universally binding principle of right, which is accessible to human knowledge, which draws an irrevocable boundary between that which is right and that which is not that obligates everyone, and which contains the criterion with the assistance of which the correctness of human actions can be judged. But in distinction from all his predecessors, in the determination of the concept and principle of right he appeals neither to empirical human nature nor to the nature of a teleological worldview that includes reason, but solely to the legislative reason, purified of all anthropological features and excluding all elements of nature, of a metaphysics of freedom. In the philosophy of right and in the political philosophy that is grounded upon it, exactly as was already done in moral philosophy, the way is thereby barred to every application of natural purposes, human needs and interests, and substantive ethical considerations in Kant's argument. Only the properties of reason itself are available to make determinate the nonempirical concept of right: lawfulness, universality, formality, and necessity. As far as its structure and potential value as a criterion are concerned, the principle of right cannot be distinguished from the categorical imperative: Like the latter, it must contain a universalization argument.

Kant's concept of right states: "Right is . . . the totality of conditions, under which the will [*Willkür*] of one person can be unified with the will of another under a universal law of freedom" (*Morals,* 6:230).[3] The following principle of right correspondingly holds for human actions: "Every action is right which, or the maxim of which, allows the freedom of the will of each to subsist together with the freedom of everyone" (6:230). Because human beings live with others of their kind in space and time, enter into external relations with others of their kind, and influence the actions of others through their own, they are subject to reason's law of right. Kant's concept of right concerns only the external sphere of the freedom of action. Only the effects of actions on the freedom of action of others are of interest to it. Inner intentions and convictions are excluded from the sphere of justice just like interests and needs. That means that no claims of right can arise from one's neediness. Right does not help powerless needs. For Kant a community of right is not a community of solidarity among the needy, but a community for self-protection among those who have the power to act.

The inner world of thoughts, intentions, convictions, and dispositions does not fall under the authority of rational norms of right, and consequently can never be a legitimate realm for control by positive laws. A state that employs the instruments of right for purposes of a politics of virtue and moral education, which punishes unpopular political and ethical convictions and seeks to form people and their thoughts with its laws, oversteps the boundaries of legitimate lawful regulation to which every governmental legislation is confined by the intrinsic meaning of the rational concept of right itself.

Kant's law of right from reason is a universal formal law of the freedom of action. Indifferent to all elements of content in human actions, it is concentrated solely on the question of the formal compatibility of the external freedom of one person with that of others, and thereby limits individual action within the boundaries of its possible universalization. Just as the moral law brings inner freedom into harmony with itself and functions as a principle of consistency for the inner world through its exclusion of all non-universal maxims, so the law of right brings external freedom into harmony with itself and functions as a principle of consistency for the outer world through its hindrance of all non-universalizable uses of the freedom of action.

Because Hegel accused the categorical imperative of being a tautology, both the moral and juridical principles of the Kantian legislation of reason have been repeatedly reproached as empty. But that is a misguided criticism, which fundamentally misunderstands the criterial character of the principles of Kant's practical philosophy and looks at them as if they were meant to be premises from which substantive conclusions could be deductively derived. But a statute book can no more be derived from the universal principle of right than a specific canon of duties can be derived from the categorical imperative. Nevertheless both principles contain criteria that are capable of making important distinctions: Just as the categorical imperative helps to identify parasitic ways of acting,[4] so can the principle of right make every politically inequitable distribution of freedom recognizable as not right. To be sure, the criterial potential of both principles is decidedly less than Kant thought. If no empirical examples of obviously inequitable distributions of freedom in the framework of historical organizations of domination lie to hand, if one directly asks the principle of right how the domain of mutually compatible individual spheres of freedom is to be determined *a priori*, then Kant's principle is an unclear criterion. In any case it does not seem sufficient to base the determination of the right solely on the criterion of formal compatibility. One can take it as a necessary condition of right that different ways of employing freedom not exclude each other. But that cannot convince us that all mutually compatible uses of freedom will be blessed by reason as allowed by right. Certainly the *a priori* framework that is alone philosophically relevant according to Kant takes into account only the formal criterion of compatibility. But if distinctions drawn from this criterion do not suffice, then a relativization of the *a priori* perspective through the addition of empirical considerations is required.[5]

According to Kant right, as the law of external freedom, as the order of coexistence of symmetrical freedom for human beings who live in spatial relations, defines the domain that each may consider his own, occupy as he pleases, and defend against injuries to its boundaries. For right is analytically connected with the authorization of coercion: The authorization of coercion as permission for the defense of universally compatible domains of freedom is a constituent of the concept of right, connected to it "according to the law of contradiction" (6:231). Thus the law of right can also be represented as a universal principle of coercion in the sense of "completely mutual coercion agreeing with the freedom of everyone according to universal laws" (6:232). The order of freedom of rational right and the reciprocal mechanism of coercion demonstrate the same structural characteristics of equality, symmetry, and mutuality. Mutual coercion is the external medium through which the order of freedom of rational right is represented, through which it obtains reality. The justification of defense against deeds that are not right is the philosophy of right's counterpart to the moral necessitation of the categorical imperative.

At the center of Kant's system of practical philosophy is the insight that the unconditional obligation and absolute validity that according to him must be attributed to practical principles could not be grounded if the laws of freedom, the internal laws of freedom of morality as well as the external ones of right, are anchored in theoretical reason and understood in analogy with the categories that are formative for perception as rules of unity of the synthesizing understanding for the internal and external employment of the will. No theory of unconditional obligation could be constructed on the basis of a will connected to understanding alone, on the foundation of instrumental reason. That the concept of right contains coercion as an element valid *a priori*, that persons who themselves lack insight can therefore legitimately be coerced into obedience to the law of right, is not, as many interpreters have asserted,[6] incompatible with Kant's characterization of the law of right as an unconditionally obligatory law of pure practical reason. This law has the status of a synthetic *a priori* practical proposition; and on account of its practical necessity it must presuppose the validity of Kant's doctrine of the fact of reason and the ensuing thesis of the reality of transcendental freedom. The justification of Kant's philosophy of right depends on his moral philosophy. Thus the claim to validity of his political philosophy is also connected to the emphatic concept of reason in his moral philosophy and to the reality of transcendental freedom. The fate of the justification of Kant's philosophy of right and his political philosophy therefore lies precisely where Kant's moral philosophy is most vulnerable. If the concepts of pure practical reason and transcendental freedom should prove to be conceptual chimeras and ethical ghosts, then the whole theory of unconditional practical obligation would also collapse. And the crash of the categorical imperative would then bring down with it the universal law of right with all the corollary principles of the theory of property and political philosophy that depend upon it; the structure of the Kantian practical philosophy, in which reason is dominant, would sink completely into empiricism. Only prudence, which Kant found contemptible, would remain as a basis for the reconstruction of political philosophy, and the meaner task of calculating foundations for the philosophy of right and political phi-

losophy would have to be cashed out with the small change of hypothetical imperatives, good grounds, and shared needs.

II. KANT'S FOUNDATION OF PRIVATE PROPERTY

The universal law of right, the categorical imperative of reason in
the realm of right, limits the freedom of action of everyone in accordance with the criterion of mutual compatibility and assigns to each
person an equally large parcel of freedom in which, as far as right is
concerned, he can do what he pleases. With respect to the use of
objects this universal law of right implies a further principle of the
philosophy of right, which Kant designates as the "permissive law of
practical reason" (§2, 6:247) or the "juridical postulate of practical
reason" (§2, 6:246), and which says that it must be possible in principle for everyone to have a right of property in any object of the
external world and thereby to possess the authority to exclude everyone else from the use of this thing.

The right of reason grounded in freedom demands private property.
The position of radical communism, which advocates the necessary
numerical identity of the physical and the rightful possessor of an
object and can find a criterion for the legitimate application of the
juridical predicate "mine" only in the sensible possession of objects,
is for Kant diametrically opposed to right. Kant developed two anticommunistic arguments. The first argument, which is found primarily in his literary remains,[7] uses the idea for the refutation of idealism
and establishment of realism in the second edition of the *Critique of
Pure Reason*, although to the opposite end, namely to the end of a
juridical refutation of realism and foundation of idealism, for by making the empirical criterion of physical possession absolute, communism becomes a variant of realism in the philosophy of right. Just as a
dogmatic idealist like Berkeley must concede that the inner experience, which is all that he accepts, has its real ground in external
experience and things that are independent of consciousness, so the
communist who purports to understand only an empirical concept of
possession must be taught that the internal and innate possession,
which is all that he concedes, is dependent on the external possession,
which he denies, dependent on the purely juridical possession of external things, which is independent of physical occupancy. The point of
this anchoring of private property in an innate human right is that the

right to property has the status of a generally necessary right. If the original right of freedom finds its external guarantee in property, then every human must have a right to property grounded solely in the right to freedom, which must be ascribed to him merely on the basis of his humanity. Obviously this conception of the right to property calls for a positive politics of distribution by the state.

Kant's second anticommunistic argument is found in section 2 of the *Doctrine of Right.* Here Kant first argues that the things of the world possess no rights, but rather that everything that the human will can ever possess and employ for any end whatsoever is subjected to it. The human being is the lord of the world; the world as the totality of usable nonhuman things is at his disposition. Further, the free will in its use of things can be limited only by the formal law of the right of reason. According to Kant, any juridical regulation that would organize the domination of the will over things on empirical grounds would be opposed to reason, right, and freedom. This would also apply to the communistic regulation of property, which would limit the freedom of the will in its use of things to the duration of the empirical possession of things.

We must keep the radical, aprioristic parsimony of Kant's argument before our eyes. Naturally every intention for the use of objects that goes beyond the end of fundamental self-preservation and tries to plan for the future remains an illusion in a communistic regulation of the use of objects. But it is not its consequence of a fundamental inhibition of civilization that leads Kant to his rejection of communism. Likewise it is not the civilizing efficiency of the domination and exploitation of nature in the framework of an order of private property that leads Kant to argue for the right to exclusive use of things. The ground for his rejection of communism is solely its incompatibility with the pure right of reason that limits the freedom of the will in action as well as use only through formal laws. But by means of this argument Kant at the same time places himself in opposition to the entire tradition of the philosophy of property. From Aristotle to Locke theories of property were always embedded in pragmatic contexts and connected with considerations of human ends, and the needs and ends of natural human beings were always the grounds for the authorization or limitation of the right to property; the conception of a teleologically unqualified freedom of the will not bounded by the needs for preservation and the life-interests of natural human beings would have been profoundly alien to every philosopher prior to Kant. Kant's metaphysics of right, on the contrary, has no regard for human interests and needs. The deontological universalism and anticonsequentialism of pure practical reason is noticeable at every stage of its systematic development and at every step of Kant's argument. The Kantian right to property in the end is also supported solely on considerations of the formal theory of freedom.

Kant's refutation of communism has three positive consequences:

1. Every thing can in principle become and remain the private property of someone.
2. Everyone is allowed to bring masterless things into this possession and to rightfully possess them – that is, to exclude all others from their use in accordance with right.
3. Everyone is obligated so to behave toward others that rights to property can be constituted and an order of private property be established.

Kant's foundation of private property therefore implies the authorization for original acquisition. To be sure, it is at first difficult to see how such an original acquisition can possibly be rightful: Empirical acts of appropriation cannot constitute any right, and unilateral acts of will cannot generate any sort of obligation. If all obligations arose either naturally or through contract or promise, then there would be no way for original acquisition to give rise to any obligation. Kant's solution of this difficulty about *acquisitio originaria* in the theory of right consists in the apparently paradoxical construction of a noncontractualistic theory of consensus, which shares the anticontractualism of Locke's theory of property but, as in the contractualistic foundation of property in Grotius and Pufendorf, is at the same time convinced of the need for consensus in the authorization of exclusion inherent in a right to private property, and which therefore contradicts Locke's thesis that first possession is sufficient to constitute property. Locke's theory of original acquisition through labor is forbidden to Kant for two reasons: first, because empirical actions cannot generate rights, regardless of what features they have; and second, because unilateral acts of will of whatever kind, whether sheer acts of power or expenditures of labor, cannot generate obligations for others. But Pufendorf's contractualism is also excluded for Kant: the voluntarism of such a contract lies beneath the metaphysi-

cal level of unconditional practical obligation to which Kant's philosophy of legislative practical reason is oriented. If it is an *a priori*
presupposition of this legislative reason that everyone is obligated to
do what is requisite to make relations of property possible, then the
individual right to property cannot be left up to the mere choice to
make contracts. The systematic point of the Kantian construction of
the noncontractualistic theory of consensus is that the two ideas of
reason, the idea of the original common possession and of the *a*
priori united will of all, make it possible for the philosophy of right
to interpret the empirically first occupation of a piece of land as an
act of appropriation on the part of the universal will of the ideal
collective possessor of everything that may originally be acquired in
general and thereby to ground an indissolvable obligation for all
others whose freedom of action is affected by this first appropriation
to agree with it for the sake of the erection of a juridical condition
and the establishment of a public system of legislation and rights.
Kant therefore connects the authorization of appropriation with the
obligation to subject the right of property thereby created to juridical
confirmation through the institutionalized legislation of all. To be
sure the *prima occupatio* is legitimate, but in contrast to Lockeian
property grounded in labor, the possession that begins with it is
juridically incomplete. It is only the first move in the game of the
normative justification of rights, the rules of which prescribe the
second move of the universal agreement of all who are affected by
this occupation. This argument rests on the systematically important insight that no empirical act, whatever valuable anthropological or economic properties it may have, can constitute a right and
thereby an authorization for the limitation of the freedom of others.[8]
Locke's conception of property as grounded in labor founders on this
insight; but so does every other theory of original acquisition not
needing consensus. Nozick's entitlement theory of justice also cannot be maintained against Kant's theory of property.

III. THE NATURAL CONDITION – PROPERTY – THE STATE

"From private right in the natural condition there now arises the
postulate of public right: In relation to an unavoidable coexistence
with others, you should make the transition from the state of nature

to a juridical state, i.e., one of distributive justice" (§42, 6:307). Kant understands the *status naturalis* as a condition of natural private right. The natural condition is for him not an anthropological thought-experiment, but one in the philosophy of right. It forms a laboratory for theory, in which the qualification of reason's juridical principles of property for the conflict-free organization of the social use of things can be tested. On the basis of a negative outcome the right of reason itself demands to be made positive, concrete, and institutionalized in a system of distributive justice, which by means of a legislature, judiciary, and executive can determine the property of each in accordance with obligations of right. In other words, in the Kantian philosophy the state is not demanded by prudence and utility, but is called for by reason itself and thus equipped with the property of juridical necessity.

The reason why Kant's philosophy also joins in the chorus of modern political philosophy singing "*exeumdum-e-statu-naturali*"[9] lies in the indeterminacy of the rational principles of right for the appropriation and use of things. "The indeterminacy in regard to the quantity as well as the quality of the externally acquirable object" (§15, 6:266) is the price that must be paid to ground property in the theory of freedom rather than in a connection to purposes and the limits of appropriation. Locke's conception allows for a sufficiently stable order of property in the natural condition, but Kant, on the contrary, must argue for a concretization and differentiation of the implications of rational right through positive right because in the natural condition chaos rules with respect to the concept of right – each person attempts with equal right to fill the emptiness of the natural laws of property with his own interpretation. The result is a war for the monopoly of interpretation over equally justified but incompatible opinions about property and the right of reason. In order to avoid this, reason erects the "postulate of public right": It is juridically necessary to put a universal legislative will in the place of the competing multiplicity of private representations of right and to hand over to it the task of making the natural right to property concrete through unequivocal and adequately determined positive laws.

No philosopher ever connected property and the state as closely as Kant did. For Hobbes property is an institution created by the state, grounded in the sovereign decision of political power. In the framework of Hobbes's political philosophy the question of the practical truth of property makes no sense, for it can be seen only under the guise of the security of peace within the state, as an instrument employed by the leviathan state in its strategy of pacifying the natural condition. In Hobbesian theory the political dimension of the state itself is conceived and grounded entirely independently from property. In Locke's liberal theory things are reversed: Property is not the instrument of the state, but the state is the instrument of property, instituted only for its security. From a juridical and conceptual point of view the Lockean state is external to the concept of property; this concept already attains juridical completion under natural conditions. But in Kant a justificatory interconnection of both property and the state, which sets both conceptions into a relation of mutual systematic dependence, replaces the independence of the state from property in Hobbes as well as the independence of property from the state in Locke. The political and the public dimension is revealed only in the need to create harmony between what is appropriated on the basis of the claim of property on the one hand and the necessity of making the natural private right positive and concrete through universal legislation on the other. Property forms the justificational basis of the state, and the state forms the justificational complement of property.

IV. THE *CONTRACTUS ORIGINARIUS* AND THE *A PRIORI* PRINCIPLES OF THE CIVIL CONDITION

In classical modern political philosophy the path from the natural condition to the civil, juridical, political condition, or the state, leads through the contract of each person with every other. The contract is the place for a simultaneous socialization and establishment of domination. Modern contractualism is the expression of a revolution in the theory of legitimation, in which the traditional teleological and theological justifications in political philosophy have been deprived of power by the sovereign will of the individual. Domination in the modern world is only to be justified through consensus and the freely willed self-obligation of the citizen.

Where, as in the case of Kant, the transition from the natural to the civil condition is conceived of as juridically necessary and commanded by practical reason, and where it is a duty to leave the state of nature rather than something that is merely prudent and in the interest of each person, then, naturally, the presuppositions of a voluntaristic foundation for the state and a recourse to individuals who bind themselves by a contract for the purposes of its legitimation no longer hold. Individuals are already bound *a priori* by their reason to leave the natural condition. Kant has no further use for the idea of a contract in the theory of the legitimation of the state.[10] The voluntarism of the Hobbesian, Lockean, and Rousseauian contract in the theory of legitimation lies beneath the metaphysical level of unconditional practical necessity of Kant's philosophy of right and politics. Kant employs a contract that is conceived as a practically necessary principle of reason and thus stripped of all connotations of voluntarism in order to illustrate the form of the rational state, the state "in the Idea, how it ought to be according to pure principles of right, which serves every real union in a commonwealth as a guideline (*norma*)" (§45, 6:313). Kant therefore transforms the cardinal concept in the theory of legitimation in modern political philosophy into a fundamental norm for both the juridical state and political ethics:

> The act by means of which the people constitutes itself into a state, or properly only the idea of that act, according to which the lawfulness of the state can alone be conceived, is the *original contract*, according to which everyone . . . in the *people* surrender their external freedom, in order to immediately regain it as members of a commonwealth, i.e., of the people considered as a state.   (§47, 6:315)

If history were made by reason alone, then the *contractus originarius*, which has no wish to hide its derivation from the Rousseauian *contrat social*, would be precisely the path taken by humans forming themselves into a society, for only a political organization born out of the contract would agree with the rational concept of right. But history is generally determined by force and injustice, and the history of the origin of states in particular is a history of usurpation and subjection. Kant's contract forms a rational constitution that is equally obligatory for all forms of domination that have arisen from force; as the normative structure of the only juridical condition that can be outlined according to concepts of right, it formulates the ideal of the state of right and political ethics according to which every historical state must be unremittingly measured in its organization as well as exercise of domination. Every empirical legislator is bound by the contract of rational right: He must consider himself to be and behave as a representative of the subject of the contract, the universally united will of all, and that means "that he must give his law as if it *could* have risen from the united will of an entire people" (*Theory and Practice*, 8:297). The norm of the contract is obviously the counterpart to the categorical imperative in political ethics, as it were the categorical imperative of political action. Just as the categorical imperative as a moral principle allows for the evaluation of the lawfulness of maxims, so does the original contract as the principle of public justice serve to measure the justice of positive laws. The application of the norm of a contract requires nothing more than a thought-experiment that is a variant of the test of universalizability that is familiar in moral philosophy. The legislator must examine whether every citizen could subscribe to the law in question. A law will not be acceptable to all if the limitation of freedom that it entails would not affect everyone in the same way, if it distributes freedoms and obligations inequitably, and if the freedom that it makes possible is not universally possible. Public laws would contradict the principle of the contract if they injured the conditions that are constitutive of the state of right grounded in reason, if, therefore, they established relationships lacking the formal characteristics of equality, freedom, and mutuality.

The form of political justice that can be known by means of the contract is procedural. For Kant (and here he follows Rousseau), it is not the agreement of the laws of a commonwealth with material norms of justice that qualifies them as right, but the way in which they arise. The original contract is the model of a procedure of advice, decision, and consensus that guarantees the justice of its results because these are supported by universal acceptance. Kant's proceduralism in the theory of justification makes the democratic formation of the will in a contractual community into the rule for tests of justice. But what is decisive – and here is the difference between Kant's political philosophy and the politicoethical conception of "discourse ethics" that it has inspired in Jürgen Habermas and Karl-Otto Apel – is that for Kant this procedure of a genesis through a democratic plebiscite can be simulated and replaced by the thought-experiment of universalizability. By this means Kant makes it possible for nondemocratic rulers to provide just laws without having to give up power.

The contract is the valid rational constitution of every political community; its structural characteristics are the principles of the form of the right in them. "The civil condition . . . considered merely as the condition of right, is grounded *a priori* on the following principles: 1. the freedom of all members of society, as human beings. 2. The equality of each member with every other, as subject, the self-sufficiency of each member of a commonwealth, as citizen" (*Theory and Practice*, 8:290). According to Kant, the norms of behavior in a positive order of right can concern only the formal criterion of the compatibility of domains of freedom that differ in their content. The political consequence of the right of freedom is the right to be subjected only to laws that are capable of receiving universal assent. Political paternalism and the right of freedom are thereby shown to be incompatible. Kant's political philosophy is decidedly antipaternalistic, rejecting every form of the politics of care for happiness and moral education. This antipaternalism is the political counterpart to the anti-eudaemonism of Kant's moral philosophy. Kant's fundamental insight in the theory of justification, that the goal of universal validity can be reached only if we reject substantive and material aims and restrict ourselves to formal and negative criteria, is manifest in both. All theories of individual and social ethics that are focused on the concept of happiness must capitulate before the ideal of absolute obligation and timeless validity in the theory of justification.

The principles of freedom and equality are two sides of the same coin. Just as freedom requires legislation, so does the principle of equality demand universal laws. The contract's prohibition of any special juridical privileges on the basis of logical grounds alone is sufficient to account for political equality. To be sure, Kant's principle of equality becomes ineffective where requirements of right come to an end; it implies equality before the law and equality of access to all social and political positions, but no economic egalitarianism. The principle of equality is indifferent to the economic structure of society; it does not make the advancement of social equality and economic justice a political goal. Kant's concept of the state of right completely dispenses with a social component. But that is not to say that there is no coherent argument by means of which Kant's philosophy of right can be connected with the principle of the welfare state. The Kantian state is, to be sure, limited to the functions of the realization of right and the protection of freedom, but when one considers the dangers that threaten right, freedom, and the dignity of humans from a marketplace unsupervised by a social state and from radical libertarianism's politics of minimal state restriction, then one sees that the philosophy of right must require a compensatory extension of the principle of the state of right through measures toward a social and welfare state in the interest of the human right of freedom itself. Kant's philosophy of right is thoroughly compatible with the concept of a social state in the service of freedom.[11] But this extension of Kant's philosophy of right by no means revokes its pervasive antipaternalism.

After freedom and equality, self-sufficiency is Kant's third *a priori* political principle. The human being is free and equal *qua* human being, but not self-sufficient as a human being, for the self-sufficient person is someone who has "some sort of property" (*Theory and Practice*, 8:295). Insofar as self-sufficiency defines the citizen and the rational legal competence to be a colegislator is granted to the citizen only as a possessor of property, a contingent economic factor becomes decisive in the assignment of a rational right. In contradiction to his declared goal of a critical foundation for right and politics free of all empirical features Kant elevates a contingent factor to the rank of an *a priori* principle of justification. Kant is guilty here of a serious theoretical error, which by means of an offence against all of the methodological and systematic principles of Kantian philosophy transforms the rational state, which make all humans into citizens, into a state of property owners, which degrades those without property into second-class political beings. But that this political privileging of the lucky owners (*beati possidentes*) is due to prejudice, not argument, is shown by the following consideration. The persons who come together into a commonwealth by means of the original contract are identical with the occupants of the natural condition, who join together in a contract for the purpose of establishing a civil condition and a system of public justice; and these are in turn identical with all of those who feel themselves constrained in their freedom by the acts of appropriation by first occupants, therefore with all of those who are affected by the application of the natural principles of the right to property. The systematic context of Kant's fundamental argument therefore makes it quite clear that the third *a priori* political principle cannot be that of a self-sufficiency requirement that excludes from political participation all those who happen to be without property, but must rather be the potential of property to affect all in principle.[12] For precisely this is the message of Kant's philosophy of property: Everyone's right to freedom is affected by property claims. Consequently political philosophy insofar as it is grounded in the philosophy of property must also recognize the equally justified participation of all in public legislation, which makes the natural laws of property concrete and detailed. Rational right cannot justify placing those who have no possession of property under political tutelage.

V. REPUBLICANISM, REFORM, AND THE PROHIBITION OF REVOLUTION

Kant's political philosophy is characterized by a twofold task. As a metaphysics of right, it derives the purely rational principles of political coexistence from the universal law of rational right and the *a priori* laws of property: freedom, equality, and contract are revealed to be principles upon which an ideal state is based and which determine the political position of citizens and the organization of just domination in an order of reason. This ideal state stands entirely under the auspices of right, right is its foundation and its only purpose; any political objective that, whether directly or indirectly (for example, by employing means of the welfare state), goes beyond the task of ensuring right is illegitimate from the Kantian perspective. (The usefulness of Kantian political philosophy in the context of the contemporary discussion of political philosophy is therefore largely dependent on the answer to the question of to what extent a theory of public goods can be reconstructed as a theory of the insurance of right and – negative – freedom.) Kant's political philosophy, however, is not only a metaphysics of right. It also reflects the problem of the realization of the rational principles of rightful order in history, and in this context becomes a philosophy of compromise and reform.[13]

In Hobbes the contract lends domination within the state a legitimacy compatible with modern individualism but does not establish any normative principles for the limitation of domination. In Rousseau, on the contrary, the contract serves as the mystical founding event of a community of the good life and establishes a theory of just domination. Given Rousseau's concept of material self-determination, just domination can be realized only as the self-government of all, only in the form of democracy as plebiscite. According to Hobbes, as long as the state exists at all then it is whatever it should be. Without any normative or critical distance, his theory agrees with whatever form of state it may come across. Rousseau's social contract, however, can never be connected to any actual political reality. The ideas of a community of life and feeling that are concentrated in it are in irreconcilable opposition to the world of modern politics; they have great critical power, but at the same time they have the lack of obligatoriness characteristic of all dreams and utopias.

As a philosophy of compromise and reform, Kant's political philosophy forms a pragmatic synthesis of Hobbes's sense of political reality and Rousseau's ideal of justice. It neither banishes reason into a utopia beyond the historical world nor identifies it with whatever political reality may be encountered. Kant understands that the realization of right, freedom, and reason can take place only in the historical world and under the conditions of the historical world. A normative political philosophy that is concerned with its own realization must therefore pragmatically engage the extant relations of domination in order to find in them a starting point for nonviolent change, for their republicanization and their reform in accord with the principles of right. The politics of reform are an eternal compromise of transition, and a political philosophy of reform must be simultaneously firm in its principles and pragmatically prudent.

Compromise and reform belong together. Only in that way can right founded in reason come to an understanding with actual political power in order to lead it toward a republicanization of its exercise of domination through public criticism and a philosophical effort at persuasion. Republicanism means a republic in alien form, a simulation of democracy and contract in the exercise of power in states that have arisen in violence and have not been legitimated by democracy. To rule in a republican manner means to grant laws as if they arose from a legislative assembly of the united will of all, and to exercise domination as if a division of powers existed. Kant's concept of republicanism unites experience, prudence, and hope. It gives the citizens the effects of a republic and leaves power to the autocratic rulers, and at the same time assumes that illegitimate domination which has arisen from force cannot resist the spirit of republicanism over the long run and will some day freely give way to a proper republic, a "democratic constitution in a representative system" (23:166). But if the ruler proves to be unwilling to reform and to be influenced through public criticism by citizens and intellectuals – indeed, even if he destroys critical publicity through intrusive measures of censorship – Kant's philosophy can only recommend that the citizens who are so limited in their right to freedom wait for better times, for forceful resistance and revolution are not allowed.

Legalized injustice and a lack of right in the state do not constitute a rightful ground for giving up political obedience. For Kant, a rightful legitimation of resistance and rebellion is impossible; the traditional right of resistance is for him a self-contradictory construction, which on the one hand makes the people the judge in their own affairs contrary to the logic of pacification, and on the other hand implies the institution of a lawless condition, the reinstitution of the natural condition. With every form of resistance, whether it be insurrection, mutiny, or revolution, violence breaks into the order of the state; the continuity of the order that guarantees the possibility of coexistence will be broken. Revolution in particular – which, for obvious reasons, forms the empirical background of Kant's remarks about the right to resistance – is the sin *par excellence* against the rightful state. Progressive violence is unthinkable for Kant. The "state revolutionaries," who, "if constitutions are deformed," believe themselves justified "in reforming them through violence and being unjust once for all so that afterward justice may be all the more secure and blooming" (§62, 6:353), may be driven by the clearest motives of improving right, yet their behavior cannot be justified. An improvement in right can come about only in a way that is itself right, only through reform and republicanization. Improvement in the sphere of political right thus follows different conditions than improvement in the moral realm. The field of morality stands under the law of either-or, an enemy to all compromise; improvement is possible here only as a revolution, as conversion, a leap, and a new beginning. The field of politics, on the contrary, stands under the law of continuity (*lex continui*). The preservation of continuity is the presupposition of any advance in right and justice.

From a contemporary point of view, there are two ways in which Kant's critique of the right to resistance can be misunderstood. On the one hand, Kant's prohibition of resistance does not imply any duty of obedience to a regime that practices state-terror and murders entire groups of the population. A condition that is dominated by mass murderers does not deserve the title of a condition of right. Unjust laws and a constitution with important rights lacking are one thing; terror, violence, and mass-murder, however, are something else. Kant's prohibition of resistance is in the first instance a prohibition of revolution, aimed at the importation of the violent French revolution. One cannot use it to argue for the illegitimacy of resistance against the totalitarian systems of domination of the twentieth century and the mass murder of the Nazis.

Kant's critique of resistance is also misunderstood if one uses it to attack the legitimacy of civil disobedience. Civil disobedience and resistance are two distinct forms of political opposition, the concepts of which must be sharply distinguished. Thanks to Rawls and Dworkin, the theory of civil disobedience has recently become a firm part of contemporary political philosophy. It may be appended without the least difficulty to Kant's philosophy of right as an appendix to the ethics of democracy or the republic.

VI. THE HIGHEST POLITICAL GOOD

The progression of the argument in Kant's political philosophy that we have been following thus far has led from the exposition of the rational concept of right through the rational laws of property to the unfolding of the *a priori* criteria for the constitution of a perfectly just order. In history, this path of thought corresponds to an evolutionary republicanization of forms of domination that have arisen through violence, working toward the establishment of a true republic, by which Kant means a political order characterized by parliamentary democracy, popular representation, and the division of powers. Nevertheless, neither the normative guidance of political philosophy nor the work of reform in history is finished with the attainment of a real republic.

Kant interprets the transition from the natural condition to the civil condition of right and the state as the transition from provisional to peremptory relations of right, thus as the transition from a condition in which right is insecure and conceptually indeterminate and incomplete into one in which right is secured and completely determinate, and therefore one in which all willfulness and violence has been banished from human social relations. For humans to attain this completely rightful condition, they must not only give up the natural condition among individuals, but also overcome the international natural condition, the condition of external lawlessness between states. In view of the unavoidable interdependence of states, "the problem of the erection of a perfect civil constitution . . . is dependent on the problem of the lawful external relation among states and cannot be solved without [a solution to] the latter" (*Universal History*, 8:24). According to Kant, political philosophy must therefore build the theory of the republic into a theory of the international order of right, and the conception of the reformist improvement of right must be enriched with the dimension of a world-historical politics of peace. While Hobbes, Locke, and Rousseau were satisfied with overcoming the interpersonal natural condition and allowed the authority of political philosophy to end at the border of the state, Kant took political philosophy beyond the borders of states and saw its foremost object in the "highest political good" (§62, 6:355) of a just order of world peace.

Given the logical interdependence of the solution of the problem of a just order both within and between states, the idea of the peaceful confederation of states as well as the idea of the republic is anchored in the innate human right to freedom. The individual right to a perfect civil constitution can only be satisfied through an "internally as well as externally perfect constitution of the state" (*Universal History*, 8:27), through a republican "human state" (*Perpetual Peace*, 8:349) or a confederation of republics. Kant's concept of human right obviously goes far beyond the ideas of liberal theory of fundamental rights; insofar as it comprises the conditions of a completely determinate and secure relation of right, it reaches to the utopian dimension of a secured membership in a world republic. If the normative implications of the right that pertains to every human being as such are completely developed, then this right is revealed to be in the end a right to peace and justice both within and between states.

An essential condition of an enduring condition of peace among states is that all states become republics. The internal organization of domination and external political behavior having been firmly clamped together, a constitution must be sought that is pacifist and opposed to war on structural grounds.

Now in addition to the clarity of its origin in the pure spring of the concept of right, the republican constitution also has the prospect for reaching the desired outcome, namely perpetual peace, the ground of which is this. – If (as cannot be otherwise in this constitution) the agreement of the citizens of the state is requisite in order to decide whether or not there shall be war, then nothing is more natural than that those who must decide to bring the terrors of war upon themselves . . . will think very seriously before starting such a bad game.   (*Perpetual Peace*, 8:351)

Kant's concept of peace between nations is noticeably different from Hobbes's model of peace. While Kant will attain peace by overcoming the natural condition among states by means of right, a Hobbesian seeks a strategy for merely managing the natural condition among states. His concept of peace is built on the same elements that also support the individual occupant of the natural condition in his strategy for survival: They can all be brought under the title of armed distrust, whose maxim of rationality is to be found in the acknowledgment of the justifiability of the distrust of the others. The key idea is to stave off war by making any breach of the condition of the absence of war so expensive that no one will rationally be able to find any profit in it. The key thought is therefore the balance of terror, for the stabilization of which a readiness for defensive armament is always necessary which, in turn, in order not to run the risk of being too late, necessarily tends toward a readiness for offensive armament; thus the balance of terror itself drives a spiraling arms race. Kant does not base the order of peace on a balance of terror, but on an order of right. Kant's concept of peace is a secularized version of the traditional connection of *pax* and *iustitia*, peace and justice, which characterizes classical as well as medieval political thought. It asserts a connection between justice within the state and peacefulness between states, and organizes peace as a system for the regulation of conflicts according to the standard of requirements of justice that are acknowledged on all sides.

Perpetual peace, the transformation of all states into constitutionally peace-loving republics, is "of course an unrealizable idea" (§61, 6:350). Kant does not expect that a stable world federation that can always ward off war can ever be attained. Nevertheless, perpetual peace is a necessary guiding idea for politics. Without the doctrine of the highest political good Kant's political philosophy would remain without its keystone. In the demand for perpetual peace practical reason is not being fantastic, but consistent. Just as the subjection of politics to the idea of the republic is practically necessary, so the subjection of politics to the idea of perpetual peace is also a duty. Both demands, the internal political demand of eventual republicanization and the external political demand of the unremitting effort to establish peace, are grounded in one and the same innate human right. The rightful legislation of pure practical reason categorically demands that we work for perpetual peace

and the constitution which seems most fit for that (perhaps the republicanism of all states separately and together), in order to lead to it and to make an end to the abominable making of war, which has hitherto without exception been the ultimate purpose of . . . all states. And if the complete fulfillment of this intention always remains a pious wish, yet we do not deceive ourselves with the maxim of unremittingly working toward it; for this is duty . . . One can say that this universal and enduring establishment of peace constitutes not merely a part but the entire final purpose of the theory of right within the limits of reason alone.   (§62, 6:354–5)

NOTES

1   Kant's noun *Recht* is a perennial problem for translators. The term, Kant's German equivalent for the Latin *ius*, does not connote the moral or legal claim of a particular person or group of persons to a particular benefit or cluster of benefits, as does the contemporary English noun "right" (which, unlike *Recht*, can naturally be used in the plural); rather, like a mass term, it connotes a total situation of external lawfulness (as contrasted to inner morality). For this reason, it is often translated as "justice"; but that can be misleading too, given the compensatory or punitive connotation of many contemporary usages of that English term. For these reasons, I have preferred to follow the precedent of Hegel translators and translate *Recht* by the singular noun "right"; the occasional awkwardness of this translation can serve to remind the reader that Kant's concept of right does not straightforwardly correspond to any single concept in traditional British political philosophy. I will also typically translate the adjective *recht* by the adjective "right," although I will not be able to preserve this correspondence in all derivatives of the

terms. Thus, *"rechtlich"* sometimes has to be translated as "juridical," not "rightful." "Just" and "justice" translate *"gerecht"* and *"Gerechtigkeit"* respectively. [Note by Paul Guyer, who translated this essay.]

2 *Naturzustand.* Following Hobbes's usage, this is usually translated into English as "state of nature." But because the German term *"Zustand"* is clearly distinguished from the term for a political entity, i.e., *"Staat,"* using "state" to translate both confuses a distinction that is clear in the German. In order to preserve this distinction, I will adopt the nonstandard translation of *"Naturzustand"* as "natural condition" [P.G.].

3 Unless otherwise indicated, citations are to Part I of the *Metaphysik der Sitten,* the *Metaphysische Anfangsgründe der Rechtlehre* (*Metaphysical Elements of the Doctrine of Right*), and are located solely by volume and page number of the text in the *Akademie* edition, as well as section number where appropriate. Other Kantian works will be cited by the short titles used throughout this collection. Kant's term *Willkür* is sometimes translated as "faculty of choice" or "elective will," to distinguish it from the *Wille* as the capacity for actually making choices as opposed to the source of rational principles for choice. Because Kant uses the former term almost exclusively in the passages here cited from *Theory of Right,* I have preferred the more natural English translation "will" [P.G.].

4 See Wolfgang Kersting, "Der kategorische Imperativ, die vollkommenen und die unvollkommenen Pflichten," *Zeitschrift für philosophische Forschung* 37 (1983): 404–21.

5 See Peter Koller, "Zur Kritik der Kantischen Konzeption von Freiheit und Gleichheit," in Wolfgang L. Gombocz, Heiner Rutte, and Werner Sauer, eds., *Traditionen und Perspektiven der analytischen Philosophie* (Vienna: Verlag Holder, Pichler, Tempsky, 1989), pp. 54–69.

6 E.g., Hermann Cohen, *Kants Begründung der Ethik nebst ihren Anwendung auf Recht, Religion, und Geschichte,* 2d ed. (Berlin: 1910), p. 403.

7 Kant's *handschriftliche Nachlaß,* or literary remains in his own hand, includes extensive sketches and drafts of the *Metaphysik der Sitten;* the drafts for the *Rechstlehre* to which the author refers are found at 23:207–370 [P.G.].

8 One therefore completely misinterprets the systematic point of Kant's theory of property if one treats *prima occupatio* as an alternative to Locke's conception of first mixing one's labor with an object. It is not possible to play a morally honorable form of property grounded in labor against a morally inferior kind of property grounded in occupation because both labor and occupation are empirical actions, which may serve as signs but which cannot ground a right or call forth normative effects. Kant is not "the most influential philosopher to argue for the

derivation of property rights from first occupancy" (A. Carter, *The Philosophical Foundations of Property Rights* [New York, 1989], p. 79). For the contrast between Locke's and Kant's theory of property see Reinhardt Brandt, "Menschenrechte und Güterlehre. Zur Geschichte und Begründung des Rechts auf Leben, Freiheit, and Eigentum," in Johannes Schwartländer and Dietmar Willoweit, eds., *Das Recht des Menschen auf Eigentum* (Kehl am Rhein, Strassburg: Engel Verlag, 1983), pp. 19–31; Wolfgang Kersting, "Transzendentalphilosophische und naturrechtliche Eigentumsbegründung," *Archiv für Rechts- und Sozialphilosophie* 67 (1981): 157–75; "Freiheit und intelligibler Besitz. Kants Lehre vom synthetischen Rechtssatz a priori," *Allgemeine Zeitschrift für Philosophie* 6 (1981): 31–51; and "Eigentum, Vertrag und Staat bei Kant und Locke," in M. Thompson, ed., *Locke und Kant* (Berlin: Verlag Duncker & Humblot, 1991).

9 "The state of nature is to be left" [P.G.].

10 See Wolfgang Kersting, "Kant und der staatsphilosophische Kontraktualismus," *Allgemeine Zeitschrift für Philosophie* 8 (1983): 1–26.

11 "The antithesis between the state of right and the social state belongs among the numerous erroneous contrasts with which Kant-interpretation is always burdened." Volker Gerhardt, "Die republikanische Verfassung. Kants Staatstheorie vor dem Hintergrund der Französischen Revolution," in *Deutscher Idealismus und Französischen Revolution.* Schriften aus dem Karl-Marx-Haus Trier 37 (Trier, 1988): 24–48, p. 45; see also Gerhardt's review of my *Wohlgeordenete Freihet* in *Allgemeine Zeitschrift für Philosophie* 11 (1986): 79–84, which I have here taken to heart.

12 This idea is taken over from Brandt, "Menschenrechte und Güterlehre" (see note 8).

13 That Kant's political philosophy is a philosophy of reform according to principles has been emphasized in Claudia Langer, *Reform Nach Prinzipien: Untersuchungen zur politischen Theorie Immanuel Kants* (Stuttgart: Klett-Cotta Verlag, 1986).

12 Taste, sublimity, and genius: The aesthetics of nature and art

I. CRITIQUE OF JUDGMENT

With the *Critique of Judgment* (1790), Kant completed his critical enterprise. To this day, however, the third of his three *Critiques* has remained the darkest of Kant's published works and the most inaccessible to the philosophical reader. Its two parts, the *Critique of Aesthetic Judgment* and the *Critique of Teleological Judgment*, are bracketed together by a formidable Introduction – two, in fact: one usually referred to as the First Introduction, and the shorter one Kant substituted for it for publication. Both introductions are relentlessly technical, both rehearse the Kantian scheme as a whole, drawing and redrawing well-known and new distinctions and contrasts; both address themselves to "philosophy as a system." They see the third *Critique* as a culmination and completion of critical philosophy, now enlarged in scope and thus requiring a number of retrospective adjustments to earlier projections of the architectonics of the entire edifice.

There are, broadly speaking, two main ways of approaching the *Critique of Judgment.* One stresses the unity of the work and insists that what Kant has to say in its first part on aesthetic judgments illuminates something important about a more general problem. Those who take this approach consider the two parts of the *Critique of Judgment* to unite aesthetic and teleological judgments in a reasoned progression of thought; they also see the third *Critique* as a kind of bridge between the *Critique of Pure Reason* and the *Critique of Practical Reason.* There is much to be said for this systematic approach, and textual support can be drawn from the two introductions. This approach may also owe something to the perception that the third *Critique* in its entirety addresses in a not altogether clear way a very "deep" problem concerned with the possibility of judgment in general. This problem surfaced first in the Schematism chapter of the *Critique of Pure Reason*. Schematism – part of the first *Critique's* Doctrine of Judgment – has posed problems for interpreters, and many have wondered whether Kant's thought had fully matured at the time he wrote it. The third *Critique* was still to come. Might it not throw some light on the chapter in which Kant speaks of schematism as "an art concealed in the depth of the human soul" (B 182)? What I have called the "systematic" approach to the third *Critique* seems to offer some hope when the problem is construed as that of the possibility of judgment as such. Aesthetic judgments as they are discussed in the first part of the *Critique of Judgment* can then be seen as paradigmatically exhibiting the ground for the possibility of judgment *tout court*.

The other approach concentrates on the first part of the *Critique of Judgment* where, in the *Critique of Aesthetic Judgment*, we find Kant's major contributions to aesthetics – contributions for which he has become known as the father of modern aesthetics. Even if Kant had also other and grander systematic ends in mind when he wrote the third *Critique*, they can be kept in the background and their intelligibility left undecided while issues pertinent to aesthetics are being considered. This is the approach adopted here, as the title indicates.

This approach acknowledges that the *Critique of Aesthetic Judgment* is problematically embedded in a wider theory of Kant's teleology, but it does not engage with the problems addressed specifically in the *Critique of Teleological Judgment*. However, no attempt is made to divorce the first from the second part of the *Critique of Judgment* other than for the sake of gaining elbow room for comments on matters aesthetic. Kant had planned a third *Critique* to complete the critical enterprise for some time. Three years before it actually appeared he had spoken, in a letter to K. L. Reinhold of 28 December 1787, of his hope to publish shortly his "Critique of Taste" (10:513–16). In the few intervening years, that had become the *Critique of Aesthetic Judgment* followed by the second part devoted to teleological judgment. The published Introduction to the whole work ends its formidable overview and rerun of critical philosophy with a schematic table (XI, 5:198) in which a new threefold division of cognitive

faculties makes its appearance. "Judgment" takes the middle position between "understanding" and "reason," and Kant now suggests
that the *Critique of Pure Reason* could be seen as dealing mainly with
the faculty of understanding, the *Critique of Practical Reason* mainly
with the faculty of reason, and the new third *Critique* mainly with
the faculty of judgment. We cannot here concern ourselves with the
complex consequences of this redrawing of the contours of the earlier
work. But we can ask, and indeed have to ask, what Kant now, in 1790,
understands by "*judgment.*"

In the *Critique of Pure Reason*, to judge was to apply a concept or
rule to particulars. Now, rethinking this in the introductions to the
third *Critique*, Kant wishes to call that kind of judgment "determinant" judgment and to distinguish it from "reflective" judgment,
where the particular is given and the rule or concept under which it
falls has to be found or discovered. This is the kind of thinking we
find, according to Kant, in, for example, scientific theory construction, where new "laws" are tried out under which we order and
reorder the wealth of observed particulars. Kant's introduction of the
theory of reflective judgment, in which the movement of thought is
from particular to general, is clearly a widening of the notion of
judgment as employed in the first *Critique* where, as the notion of
determinant judgment, it comes to mean the same as simple subsumption. The *Critique of Judgment* takes the exercise of reflective
judgment at times to be that which links the first to the second part,
for both teleological judgments and aesthetic judgments are treated
as reflective judgments or judgments of reflection. We have to go to
the First Introduction to discover a hint that may help us. There
Kant says that to reflect is "to compare and combine a given representation either with other representations or with one's own cognitive faculties, with respect to a concept thereby made possible"
(*First Introduction*, V, 20:212). This we shall meet again when we
come to the harmony between imagination and understanding as
the general condition of cognition.

There is another connection between the two parts of the third
Critique. In both teleological and aesthetic thought as Kant now
presents it, the notion of purposiveness or finality (*Zweckmäs-
sigkeit*) plays an important part. That judgment in the aesthetic
context and judgment in the context of the systematicity of nature
therefore somehow belong together has much suggestive power, of-

ten exploited by those who wish to press on Kant the view that a principle for reflection on nature can either be carried over into the aesthetic or take its clue from there. Perhaps Kant did have something like this in mind when he discovered a connection that allowed him to treat as akin two otherwise disparate inquiries. That the new idea of reflective judgment opened up a way for Kant to do two separate things in the last *Critique* can readily be admitted. That he wished to present them as unified can also be granted. Whether he succeeded in doing so must be left open.

Here we note only one last point before entering the *Critique of Aesthetic Judgment*. Reflective judgment, when brought to bear on assemblages or aggregates of observed facts, has to assume, taken at its most general level, that nature can be understood, that it is intelligible. Looking for principles by which to comprehend and group natural phenomena is at least very like believing that nature is ordered as if it were designed. Yet there need be no suggestion here of an agent who has done the designing. Looking for order in the world, Kant seems to say, is to assume that nature exhibits on reflection formal purposiveness or finality of form. Remembering that aesthetic judgment is also a species of reflective judgment may help us to understand the difficult notion of "the form of finality" as it is used in the explanation of the judgment of taste. Here, however, we leave the speculations which the two introductions to the *Critique* have invited and turn to the body of the *Critique of Aesthetic Judgment*.

The first book of the Analytic of Aesthetic Judgment is the Analytic of the Beautiful; it is followed by the second book, the Analytic of the Sublime. The Dialectic of Aesthetic Judgment then completes the *Critique of Aesthetic Judgment*. It may come as something of a surprise to find that the theory of reflective judgment is not taken up immediately and developed from where the introductions left off. But Kant begins by taking it for granted that in aesthetic judgment we deal with a "judgment in its reflection" (Note 1, 5:203). Only much later, in the General Remark upon the Exposition of Aesthetic Reflective Judgment, having completed the Analytic of the Sublime, does he return to it.

II. TASTE

We know that at the time of writing the *Critique of Pure Reason*, Kant had not yet reached the position that the third *Critique* takes up. An interesting footnote to the *transcendental aesthetic* (doctrine of sensibility) in the first *Critique* (A 21 / B 36 n.) suggests that Kant then still tended to believe that no more than an empirical approach to the treatment of the beautiful was possible. (In 1764 he had himself, with *Observations on the Feeling of the Beautiful and the Sublime*, contributed an elegant and lively essay to that tradition.) But the main point of the footnote was to reject what the mainly German rationalists tried to do under the name of "aesthetics." Alexander Baumgarten's[1] attempt "to bring the beautiful under rational principles" Kant considered "fruitless"; there could not be a "science of the beautiful," although he admitted that something he called "critique of taste" had already occupied his attention. By 1790, the year in which the *Critique of Judgment* made its appearance, Kant analyzed the judgment of taste as a subjective judgment whose peculiar claim to validity differentiates it from mere avowals. With that move he had effectively distanced himself from empirical aesthetics as well as from what he thought of as Baumgarten's rationalist model of aesthetics.

It is the combination of subjective status with the universality and necessity claim that makes judgments of taste what they are, according to the Kant of the third *Critique*. To anyone who admits that in addition to cognitive judgments and moral appraisals, and over and above expressions of likes and dislikes about which no disputes can arise, there are also judgments which cannot be verified but which nevertheless lay claim to the agreement of other subjects of experience, Kant's analysis will be compelling. What sets the judgment of taste apart from all other kinds of judgment is, according to Kant, that it is the feeling of pleasure alone that determines it. The most subjective and private of human capacities, that of feeling, far from being mute and inchoate, could, Kant now thought, yield the determining ground of the aesthetic judgment. Prior to the third *Critique* no *a priori* principles had been discovered that could bring to feeling what the cognitive and the moral judgment had already been shown to possess in the categories of the understanding and the ideas of reason. That feeling also has a structure that can manifest itself as rational in the widest sense is the "discovery" Kant adds now.

He who has taste shows by his preferences that he values what is beautiful and abhors what is ugly. Having taste is not like having an extra sense, nor like exercising a special intellectual power. It is the ability to respond with immediate pleasure and unclouded vision to beauty in nature and in art, and, further, to communicate this pleasure to others who are capable of sharing it. Communicable pleasure, moreover, informs an attitude of wonder toward the world, and he who feels it does not selfishly seek to possess the objects of his pleasure: He appreciates and appraises them. When we speak thus of aesthetic appreciation and aesthetic appraisal, we encounter the problem central to Kant's inquiry. It is the problem of taste. It might even appear from its outward form as if the *Critique of Aesthetic Judgment* posed only this one question, then let the answer to it emerge in successive stages of argument. What we actually find, however, is not just one long argument about the problem of taste but sprawling clusters of arguments that are by no means all related to judgments of taste. We can ignore this for a while and focus on why the question of taste assumes a pivotal position in Kant's aesthetic theory.

In much eighteenth-century usage, to be a person of taste was to be a person of independent judgment based on individual conviction, not on slavishly following rules. Kant is aware of this usage, and it is part of the aim of his analysis to secure a grounding of the judgment of taste in something that, as the most personal, namely individual feeling, can carry the weight of an implied claim to autonomy. Taste, for Kant, is the ability to "estimate" the beautiful, and the exercise of this ability is the judgment of taste. What taste judgments are and what are the conditions for locating the beautiful are thus aspects or "moments" of the same explicandum. The four moments of the judgment of taste spell out and elaborate what is required for finding something beautiful, or, in other words, the most important characteristics of the judgment of taste. This is perhaps the best known section of the third *Critique*, contained in the Analytic of the Beautiful.

The four moments

Kant presents the four moments of the judgment of taste in terms of his four logical functions of judgment; that is, he explores the judgment of taste in respect of quality, quantity, relation, and modality. This arrangement is somewhat forced and fails to convince in detail. Perhaps one should not place too much weight on this architectonic echo from the first *Critique*. Still, as in the case of distinguishing in the first *Critique* four logical forms of judgment and then four groups of categories, Kant may be indicating here also that the four-fold division is exhaustive. Analysis of each moment yields a partial definition or explication of the beautiful, and the four moments together make up a complex exposition of the judgment of taste. It can be summarized roughly like this: That is beautiful which is felt with disinterested pleasure (first moment). Calling something beautiful we deem it an object of universal delight (second moment). We discern in it "the form of finality perceived without the representation of a purpose" (third moment). And we claim not only that it pleases but that it does so necessarily, and without concepts (fourth moment).

A footnote to the heading of the first moment refers us briefly to what both introductions labor, and to what Kant now takes for granted: When we deal with aesthetic judgment we deal with a judgment of reflection and not with determinant judgment (note 1, 5:203). Also, section 1 of the first moment does not really contribute to the moment of disinterestedness; it makes a more general point, more consonant with the Introductions, quickly reminding us that the judgment of taste is aesthetic and not logical, and firmly linking the aesthetic now to the feeling of pleasure and displeasure, to a "feeling which the subject has of itself and of the manner in which it is affected" (§1, 5:204). This packed little paragraph gives something of a foretaste of much that is still to come. To refer a representation wholly to the subject in its feeling, its "feeling of life" (*Lebens-gefühl*), attempts to capture the essentially subjective nature of the aesthetic and at the same time to distinguish sharply the subjective turn of the aesthetic judgment from the objective reference of the cognitive judgment. Although we gain no knowledge from the exercise of the faculty of discriminating and estimating, Kant seems to say, we feel ourselves engaged when contemplating and comparing a "given representation in the subject with the entire faculty of representations of which the mind is conscious in the feeling of its state" (§1, 5:204). That, in a general statement about how feeling functions in the scheme of the mental life, makes room for the later suggestion that a beautiful thing is one that stimulates the harmonious interplay of understanding and imagination in the act of judging, that is, of appraising it.

The four moments fall into two groups. The first and the third moment specify when an experience qualifies for being an experience of something beautiful, namely when the pleasure felt is disinterested, and when the pleasure is that arising from perceiving in the object the form of finality. These two moments elaborate the criterial conditions under which a particular experience can be allowed as being such that a judgment of taste is in order – that is, as evidence for the object being beautiful. The second and fourth moment deal with universality and necessity respectively, and they concern the claims implied by judgments of the form "This is beautiful." None of the four moments alone provides sufficient conditions for the taste judgment. But together, and working on two different levels – the level of judging in experience and that of the judgment arising from it – they satisfy, Kant believes, the requirements of separating the aesthetic from other modes of experience, and the judgment of taste from other kinds of judgment.[2]

Only when the pleasure felt is disinterested may the object giving rise to that pleasure be called beautiful. That the pleasure should be "apart from any interest" or "independent of any interest" is best understood by contrast with "interested" pleasure, and in this contrast Kant puts pleasure in the agreeable and pleasure in the good over against the pleasure of taste: Only in the latter is there an absence of interest both in the sense of indifference to the real existence of the object and in the sense of its not satisfying or calling forth a want or desire. Kant performs a number of complicated maneuvers contrasting the beautiful with the good, the useful and the agreeable. The differences and relations between them are drawn on repeatedly, so that by the end of the Analytic of the Beautiful, there is something like a map of the leading concepts as they mesh into Kant's map of the mind.

But disinterested pleasure is not the only criterion we are offered. The third moment elaborates another of equal importance. Reflecting on my pleasure, I must not only find it free of all interest and thus take pleasure in the object for its own sake. My pleasure must be that felt in the free play of imagination and understanding that I experience as the form of finality in the object. "The judgment is called aesthetic for the very reason that its determining ground cannot be a concept, but is rather the feeling (of the internal sense) of the concert in the play of the mental powers as a thing only capable of being felt" (§15, 5:228). Imagination and understanding are cognitive powers, but when they are not engaged for the purpose of cognition, their harmony or lack of it is felt as pleasure or displeasure in that which occasions it. The aesthetic judgment that comes about has its ground in the heightened but noncognitive awareness of the fittingness of the object for my enjoyment. Now taking the third moment together with what the second moment suggests as an implied claim in the judgment of taste, we get that the form of finality felt in the experience of the object provides ground for claiming that not only I, but every subject of experience standing in the same relation to the object would feel the same, and, further, have the same justification for having such a feeling in virtue of sharing the same structure of mentality. But with that thought we have reached what Kant saw as his deduction.

Deduction

Kant formulates the need for a deduction in many ways. Analysis of judgments of taste reveals them as laying claim to universal assent, indeed necessarily so. As universality and necessity are marks of the *a priori* and as any alleged *a priori* claim requires legitimization of its title, justificatory arguments will have to be of the transcendental kind. In Kant's terms, what we are looking for is an answer to the question "How are judgments of taste possible?" (§36, 5:288) and thus "This problem of the Critique of Judgment, therefore, is part of the general problem of transcendental philosophy: How are synthetic *a priori* judgments possible?" (§36, 5:289). But such formulations, while reminding us of the wider context of the system, do little to illuminate the specific point.

The judgment of taste as explicated is clearly in need of justification. The need arises because the exposition lays bare an apparent paradox. We rely on our innermost feelings of pleasure alone when estimating the beautiful – an aesthetic judgment "is one whose determining ground *cannot be other than subjective*" (§1, 5:203) – and yet we claim for the deliverances of taste a suprapersonal import. We believe it to be binding for all subjects and not merely for the one on whose experience it is based. This presumption we express in a verdict, "This is beautiful," as if beauty were a quality of the object and as if we could know that this was so. But we do not look for verification, nor for proof, when finding something beautiful; yet we feel ourselves misunderstood when told that it must therefore be merely a matter of private opinion. The judgment of taste, we imply, does not record a cognition, nor is it a private avowal of feeling. Insisting on this seemingly paradoxical feature of the judgment of taste is one of Kant's great and lasting contributions to the theory of aesthetics. Only by showing that the claim to speak with *"a universal voice"* (§8, 5:216) when individual pleasure of the right kind is based on something in human nature that licenses the presumption can Kant justify the aesthetic judgment.

Arguments showing this should, in Kant's context, belong to the deduction and not to the exposition or analysis of the judgment of taste. There is a long and rambling section (§§30–54), titled "deduction of the pure aesthetic judgment" (irritatingly placed, not in the Analytic of the Beautiful where it would seem to belong, but in the Analytic of the Sublime). It does not present one unified argument, nor does it impress by cogency or coherence. And there is no agreement among scholars as to where the deduction begins and where it ends, for a number of arguments from the Analytic of the Beautiful seem properly to belong to the deduction, especially arguments collected for the second and fourth moments, and arguments grounding the form of finality in the harmony of the faculties. Thus different commentators have recommended different routes through the tangled web of the *Critique of Aesthetic Judgment* and offered their own reconstructions of the deduction.[3]

Kant needs an argument from which to conclude that without judgments of taste and their implied claims to universality and necessity, knowledge or cognition in general would not be possible. That is indeed a tall order, and not surprisingly it remains unclear whether Kant has delivered such an argument in the deduction. That he tried to do so, however, is evident in the struggle for a hold on the notion of the subjective conditions of judgment.

In the compressed and cryptic section 38, Kant seems to say that the deduction has been achieved and that we are justified in expecting universal agreement to judgments of taste as we are justified in expecting the pleasure that is felt to be universally communicable. The Remark attached to section 38 speaks disarmingly of the "ease" of this deduction: "What makes this Deduction so easy is that it is spared the necessity of having to justify the objective reality of a concept. For beauty is not a concept of the object, and the judgment of taste is not a cognitive judgment." What exactly is it Kant deems to be easy? Does he really mean no more than that only on the assumption of the fundamental sameness of the conditions of cognition in all men can the claims of taste – provided the judgments are correctly made – be justified? The footnote to the last line of section 38 seems to bear this out. In it Kant repeats an argument that states the assumptions under which the justification can go through. "In order to be justified in claiming universal agreement for an aesthetic judgment merely resting on subjective grounds it is sufficient to assume: (i) that the subjective conditions of this faculty of aesthetic judgment are identical with all men in what concerns the relation of the cognitive faculties, there brought into action, with a view to a cognition in general. This must be true, as otherwise men would be incapable of communicating their representations or even their knowledge; (ii) that the judgment has paid regard merely to this relation (consequently merely to the *formal condition* of the faculty of judgment), and it is pure, i.e., is free from confusion either with concepts of the object or sensations as determining grounds."

Communicability has now moved into a central position. It is shown to be a necessary requirement for cognition. Because all men as subjects of experience are capable of cognition under the same subjective conditions (if this were not so, cognition and knowledge would not be possible), we are justified in assuming these same subjective conditions for the judgment of taste. For the judgment of taste brings into play the very faculties, imagination and understanding, that are engaged in the determinant cognitive judgment; the judgment of taste, however, is a subjective judgment of reflection and arises from the felt satisfaction or pleasure that springs from the achieved harmony of the two faculties in the presence of the beautiful. They are in harmony, balanced out, as it were, not engaged for the sake of gaining knowledge, but for their own sake, for their own mutual enhancement. The beautiful is not cognized – "for beauty is not a concept of the object, and the judgment of taste is not a cognitive judgment" – but appreciated or estimated as that which fosters "the mutual quickening" of the faculties, otherwise employed for the purposes of cognition. In the judgment of taste, it is with pleasure that we experience beautiful objects as if they had been designed for the cooperation of our cognitive powers; to estimate the beautiful is to discern in it the form of finality, or the appearance of having been designed to suit our cognitive capacities.

Soon afterward, Kant speaks of taste as "a kind of *sensus communis*" (§40). The idea of a "common sense" had already figured in the fourth moment (§21), where Kant had argued that the assumption that there are others who can share the pleasures of taste is a necessary ingredient in our thought about subjects of experience. The transcendental argument from which this conclusion is derived is premised on the communicability of cognition: Kant maintains explicitly not simply that cognition or knowledge is in fact possible, but that knowledge that is possible must be communicable to others, or it would not be knowledge. Supplementing the official deduction now with the transcendental argument from section 21, we get the step from the subjective conditions of cognition, when cognition cannot be other than communicable to everyone else, to the subjective conditions of judgments of taste, with the requirement of universal communicability carried over. Section 40 adds a further gloss to this acknowledgment of the nonprivacy of the subjective condition of judgment. Kant speaks of taste not only as a kind of *sensus communis*, but as a kind of *public* sense, a "critical faculty which in its reflective act takes account (*a priori*) of the mode of representation of every one else, in order, *as it were*, to weigh its judgment with the collective reason of mankind." Arguments trying to show that communicability has to be presupposed at a very deep level, at the level of the conditions of experience in general, belong to the very heart of the justification that the deduction of the judgment of taste tries to provide. Unfortunately, though, Kant cannot be said to have succeeded in articulating fully a satisfactory chain of arguments to bring off the deduction. And Kant himself seems to remain doubtful as to whether and when he has completed it.

Dialectic

Kant kept returning to the justification of judgments of taste even after he had moved on to important and new considerations of art and genius in the remaining sections (§§41–54) of the Analytic of Aesthetic Judgment. In the Dialectic, toward the end of the *Critique of Aesthetic Judgment*, he speaks as though the claim to universal agreement that judgments of taste make could receive a full justification only when aesthetic judgments were shown to be linked to, and somehow sanctioned by, moral judgments. A few packed and highly problematic passages attempt to present the beautiful as the symbol of the morally good. This, however, conflicts with the central doctrine of the Analytic of the Beautiful and would seem to be flatly incompatible with the autonomy of the aesthetic as there insisted on.[4] The remarks about beauty as symbolic of morality may have a place in the context of considering why a certain intellectual interest in the representational arts can be defended. But they cannot be seen as contributing to the deduction of the claims of taste. As the Dialectic of the *Critique of Pure Reason* adds nothing to the deduction of the categories, so the Dialectic of the *Critique of Aesthetic Judgment* does not contribute anything new to the deduction of the judgment of taste. Rather, it adds a metaphysical digression from the theory of taste. The attempt to interpret beauty as symbolic of the moral is part of this digression. It can go some way toward satisfying a metaphysical quest for the importance and significance of the beautiful.

A dialectic arises from the recognition of antinomies. There can be little doubt that the Dialectic of Aesthetic Judgment in the third *Critique* is closely modeled on the Dialectic of the first *Critique*, and that Kant set out to find an antinomy of taste because the structure of a critique demanded that a dialectic should follow upon an analytic. (It is this demand for conforming to the requirements of the structure of a critique that so often lends to the text of the *Critique of Aesthetic Judgment* an air of artificiality, and this is noticeably so in its last section, the Dialectic.)

Another discordant feature of the Dialectic, at variance with the theory of the Analytic, enters with the solution offered to the Antinomy of Taste (§57). In section 56 Kant formulates the Antinomy, arising from two conflicting beliefs about taste, in these words:

1. *Thesis.* The judgment of taste is not based upon concepts; for if it were, it would be open to dispute (decision by means of proofs).
2. *Antithesis.* The judgment of taste is based on concepts; for otherwise, despite diversity of judgment, there could be no room even for contention in the matter (a claim to the necessary agreement of others with this judgment).

This antinomy captures once more the tension the Analytic had already elicited from the analysis of the judgment of taste. We believe both that the judgment of taste cannot be proved by being derived from concepts (*thesis*), and that, by laying claim to the agreement of others and thus allowing for debate, the judgment does involve appeal to some sort of concept (*antithesis*).

In order to maintain that the two propositions are in fact compatible and the antinomy only apparent or illusory, Kant in the Dialectic resorts to showing equivocation between two senses of "concept": determinate concept (in *thesis*) and indeterminate concept (in *antithesis*). We know already that no determinate concepts are available for subsumption in judgments of reflection. Thus the thesis is maintained. The indeterminate concept that functions in the antithesis, we might expect to be (in line with the theory so far expounded) the harmony of the cognitive faculties. However, Kant now introduces instead "the supersensible substrate of phenomena," and with it the entire apparatus of his metaphysics of phenomena and noumena – of the latter of which we can indeed know nothing and in that sense have only an indeterminate concept. This postulation of the supersensible as the ground of the judgment of taste comes as a complete surprise to the reader who has so far followed Kant through the *Critique of Aesthetic Judgment* without encountering the doctrine of noumenal reality versus mere appearance. The arguments in the Dialectic for the solution of the antinomy of taste belong to the kind of metaphysical speculation that abandons aesthetic theory in favor of special pleading in Kantian ontology. Their detail therefore need not concern us here.[5]

Kant's formulation of the antinomy of taste (as distinct from the solution proffered) is, by his own admission, a complicated reformulation of certain "commonplaces" and proverbial expressions "at the back of every one's mind" (§56). We do not know whether Kant had read David Hume's essay "Of the Standard of Taste," which antedates the *Critique of Judgment* by thirty-three years and comes remarkably close to asking Kant's question "How are judgments of taste possible?" It has become fashionable to construe many a Kantian epistemological argument as "Kant's answer to Hume." In the context of aesthetics, the casting of the *Critique of Aesthetic Judgment* in the role of such an answer would be most illuminating. There is, unfortunately, no room for it here.[6]

III. SUBLIMITY

Kant, though never leaving the problems of taste far behind, does address himself to more than the issues so far described. Side by side with the Analytic of the Beautiful, there is the Analytic of the Sublime (§§23–8). If we consider the question of taste to be the main issue of the *Critique of Aesthetic Judgment*, the inclusion of the analysis of judgments on the sublime in sections 23–8 must seem a digression from the main theme.[7] If, however, we acknowledge the shift of Kant's interest to fine art and genius in the sections following upon the Deduction in sections 41–54 (yet to be discussed), analysis of the judgment on the sublime may appear less marginal: Considerations of the sublime then reveal many a link with these wider interests that Kant almost reluctantly allows to come to the fore in the closing sections of the second book of this second Analytic. Rather than treat the sections on the judgment on the sublime as of merely historical interest, we can read them as preparatory to that widening of Kant's compass that leads us beyond the issues of taste to those of art and genius. The explicit link between them lies in the introduction of ideas of reason into the analysis of the sublime (ideas belonging not only to theoretical intellect but also to morality). That this link between art and genius and the sublime is also the basis for the contrast drawn by Kant between the beautiful (in which understanding and imagination are balanced out) and the sublime (featuring reason instead of the understanding) complicates matters considerably. We should take this as a challenge to the narrower reading of the *Critique of Aesthetic Judgment* in which the theory of taste and beauty alone held our attention.

Although the analysis of the sublime side by side with that of the beautiful may have been an afterthought in the construction of the *Critique of Aesthetic Judgment* (Kant does not mention it in either Introduction), the conjunction of the beautiful and the sublime is in line with much eighteenth-century thought. Kant himself had used the coupling of the two concepts in his *Observations on the Feeling of the Beautiful and Sublime* (1764). That lively little treatise dates back to the time when Kant did not believe that aesthetic questions could lend themselves to anything other than empirical treatment. Edmund Burke's *A Philosophical Enquiry into the Origin of our*

Ideas of the Sublime and Beautiful (1757) was well known to Kant. In the *Critique of Aesthetic Judgment,* at the end of what he now calls the "transcendental exposition of aesthetic judgments" (277), he contrasts his own critical procedure with that of "Burke and many acute men among us" who gave "a merely empirical exposition of the beautiful and the sublime."

At the beginning of the Analytic of the Sublime, Kant both compares and contrasts the experience of sublimity with that of the beautiful. The comparison finds enough in common to argue for the inclusion of the judgment on the sublime together with the judgment on the beautiful in the class of aesthetic judgments. The contrast, however, differentiates these two forms of aesthetic judgment sharply from each other. Section 23 gives a compressed account of the relation. The beautiful and the sublime both please "on their own account"; both are estimated in judgments of reflection and not cognized in determinant judgments; the delight in both rests on an accord of imagination with the "faculty of concepts that belongs to understanding or reason"; both give rise to singular judgments that claim to be valid for every subject.

But the differences between the beautiful and the sublime are striking. Judgments on the beautiful estimate the object in regard to its form, while judgments on the sublime encounter the object's formlessness or "limitlessness, yet with a super-added thought of its totality." The pleasure in the beautiful is a "positive" pleasure, life-enhancing and joyous, while pleasure in the sublime is of sterner stuff, more like respect, and deserves the name of "negative" pleasure. The beautiful appears to us as if it were designed for, or final for, our powers of judgment, but the sublime may seem ill adapted to our presentational powers and even an "outrage" to our imagination. Strictly speaking, Kant continues, we should not call natural objects "sublime": Sublimity resides in us, in the powers of the human mind to rise above what threatens to engulf or annihilate us. Natural objects may rightly be called beautiful; but no natural object is as such sublime: "All that we can say is that the object lends itself to the presentation of a sublimity discoverable in the mind."

It is difficult to see how Kant can maintain the inclusion of the judgment on the sublime in the class of aesthetic judgments next to, or side by side with, the judgment on the beautiful. For is not that which is said to be similar in the beautiful and the sublime, namely "pleasing on their own account" (§23, 5:244), intolerably stretched when the reference is no longer to that which pleases but rather to that in which a "presentation of sublimity is discoverable," namely the mind? And Kant's "negative pleasure" in the sublime that outrages the imagination, sits ill with the harmony of the faculties. Triumph of reason over imagination rather than an accord between them appears to be responsible for the feeling of the sublime as Kant analyzes it.

If the analysis is to be that of "an aesthetic estimate of objects in respect of the feeling of the sublime" (§24, 5:247), it must yield its explication according to the same four moments as did the analysis of the judgment of taste, Kant says. Regarding quantity it must claim universality; regarding quality, it must be independent of interest; regarding relation, it must exhibit subjective finality; and regarding modality, it must be necessary. Unsurprisingly, this parallel treatment of the sublime and the beautiful in terms of the aesthetic puts a serious strain on the reader of the Analytic of the Sublime. Matters are not made any easier by Kant's further distinguishing between the mathematically and the dynamically sublime. The first confronts us when that which we experience in nature as immeasurably or absolutely great exceeds the power of our imagination; it cannot be grasped as one sensory whole, and we feel helpless until an idea of reason, the idea of a totality, supervenes and "the object is received as sublime with a pleasure that is only possible through the mediation of a displeasure" (§27, 5:260). The second, the dynamically sublime, we confront when nature is experienced as a might so powerful that we feel threatened and crushed, until another idea of reason, the idea of our moral agency, lifts us beyond the sensory to the heights of our own superiority to nature as moral beings. Kant expresses this thought in one of the most eloquent passages of the whole *Critique* (§28, 5:261):

Bold, overhanging, and, as it were, threatening rocks, thunderclouds piled up the vault of heaven, borne along with flashes and peals, volcanoes in all their violence of destruction, hurricanes leaving desolation in their track, the boundless ocean rising with rebellious force, the high waterfall of some mighty river, and the like, make our power of resistance of trifling moment in comparison with their might. But, provided our own position is secure, their aspect is all the more attractive for its fearfulness; and we readily call these objects sublime, because they raise the forces of the soul above the heights of vulgar commonplace, and discover within us a power of resistance of quite another kind, which gives us courage to be able to measure ourselves against the seeming omnipotence of nature.

The point about our own position being secure while contemplating the sublime stresses that the judgment on the sublime is a reflective one and an aesthetic judgment. If we were in real fear of our lives, trying to run away or save ourselves from drowning or from being swept away, we would be involved with the objects and occurrences in their real existence and would be as little capable of the aesthetic stance as a starving man could judge aesthetically the food he craves. Only what pleases independently of all interest, to repeat, pleases aesthetically.

In judgments on the mathematically and the dynamically sublime, ideas of both theoretical and practical reason arise in us and save us, Kant maintains, from being stunned by the greatness and might of nature. Kant's ideas on the sublime have deeply influenced Romantic thought and helped to shape in particular the Romantic conception of imagination. For Kant, though, imagination, in presenting and holding together what sensibility could provide, is unequal to cope with that which cannot be sensed or understood and for which a judgment as to its beauty would be inadequate. Sublimity transcends the bounds of sense and understanding.

Perhaps Kant's struggle to locate the sublime in that which occasions the feeling *and* in the feeling itself can be seen as indicative of a deeper ambiguity. There are passages in which the feeling of the sublime appears like an intimation of noumenal reality. When the human mind encounters itself as sublime, it encounters itself as a moral agent "that from another (the practical) point of view feels itself empowered to pass beyond the narrow confines of sensibility" (§26, 255). This would be the triumph of our rational over our sensible nature, and the pleasure felt in such triumph seems indistinguishable from pleasure taken in the good. This strikes a discordant note within the context of the aesthetic in which Kant wants us to understand the sublime. Despite Kant's protestation to the contrary, the context appears to be more akin to that of morality than to that of the beautiful; many of Kant's arguments read like thinly disguised moral arguments.[8]

In the long "General Remark upon the Exposition of Aesthetic Reflective Judgments" that follows the Analytic of the Sublime proper, Kant grapples with many of the issues that have been raised by the inclusion of the sublime. He adds a wealth of anthropological observations to illustrate the many analogies that can be drawn variously between the agreeable, the beautiful, the sublime, and the good – all objects of pleasure, but only the beautiful and the sublime giving rise to aesthetic pleasure.

Memorable comparisons stand side by side with long excursions into the ways fruitful analogies can be exploited. The beautiful and the sublime are characterized, compared, and contrasted again and again, not always felicitously. On the whole one comes away from the Analytic of the Sublime bewildered rather than enlightened.

What Kant has to say about the judgment on the sublime as an aesthetic judgment remains problematic, though rich in suggestions. The duality of the Analytic of the Beautiful and the Analytic of the Sublime cannot be ignored. Without the second Analytic the Critique of Aesthetic Judgment would certainly have been neater and more manageable; it would have been a Critique of Taste. But it would also have been the poorer in challenging thought and breadth of vision, however imperfectly they may be articulated.

One of the suggestions that remains to be taken up hints at a similarity of the sublime with works of art. Both, unlike the beautiful in nature, make reference to more than perceptual form; they feature ideas – ideas of reason and aesthetic ideas. To the latter we must now turn.

IV. GENIUS

The sections of the Critique of Aesthetic Judgment located between the Deduction and the Dialectic (§§41–54) lack the single focus discernible in the Analytic of the Beautiful and also, though to a lesser degree, in the earlier sections of the Analytic of the Sublime. They are densely packed with detail, but it is not easy to discern in them a progression of connected thought. From the standpoint of the theory of taste, they may appear as no more than a digression, and from the standpoint of the theory of beauty, they may be seen as implementing the investigations that so far have been predominantly (though by no means exclusively) directed to the beautiful in nature. They contain Kant's thought on art and its creation by genius.

The reception of this thought has had a checkered career. The

Romantic conception of creative genius owes much to it, as does an entire tradition of aesthetics in which the artist, the natural genius, takes on the role of originator of art works, and art works come to be seen as the paradigms of aesthetic objects. Philosophers in our time, when approaching the third *Critique* for Kant's contributions to aesthetic thought, have on the whole stressed either the theory of taste or the theory of art and genius, or just listed the contributions disjunctively side by side. As to the last, such an impartial way is not open to the Kant scholar who wants to present and to discuss the views on aesthetics as Kant argued them in the *Critique of Aesthetic Judgment.*

There can be little doubt that Kant wanted his thought on art and genius to be taken seriously; it is less clear whether he believed that these sections followed from the Analytic of the Beautiful, or whether he found it necessary to supplement his thought on beauty with arguments showing that by beauty he meant not only beauty in nature but also in art. It is even less clear that Kant did not shift his ground during the writing of the *Critique of Aesthetic Judgment* and that what he at first almost reluctantly admitted – art and its creation – had moved to center stage by the end of these sections. The present study is already committed to the view that the problem of taste is central to Kant's aesthetics (a commitment mirrored by the prominence given to its elucidation); but it is not thereby committed to holding that the sections on art and genius are of only marginal importance or constitute a digression from the main theme. The analysis of the judgment of taste applies to the beautiful in art as well as in nature (though Kant tends to give examples of natural beauty by preference). The sections 41–54 can be seen as trying to make amends for having apparently downgraded artistic beauty in the Analytic of the Beautiful. But much more importantly, they ask and attempt to answer a totally different question: How does art differ from nature? No answer to *this* question was required for the analysis and deduction of the judgment of taste which had the beautiful univocally as explicandum.

One of the reasons why Kant's thought on art has often met with a puzzled response is that Kant himself apparently admits to a decided preference for natural over artistic beauty. Another reason is that the facts of his life as we know them make it unlikely that he had much acquaintance with works of art. "Kant probably never saw a beautiful painting or a fine statue. . . . His taste in music seems to have been utterly philistine; and only for literature was his critical sense refined and exacting."[9] Knowing this much about Kant, we often hear, can hardly inspire confidence in his theorizing about art. That such observations do not carry any weight in disqualifying Kant's philosophical insights should be obvious. Still, they have often been allowed to get in the way of attending to what Kant has to say.

Kant's preference for natural over artistic beauty seems to be expressed in section 42, where he asks whether an intellectual interest can attach to the beautiful despite the disinterestedness of the judgment of taste which appraises it. Somewhat surprisingly and to the modern ear almost shockingly, Kant declares that an interest in beautiful art "gives no evidence at all of a habit of mind attached to the morally good," while to take an interest in the beauty of nature "is always a mark of a good soul" (§42, 5:298). The distinction that Kant uses here is that between the lover of art and the lover of nature. It shows nothing about whether one kind of beauty is preferable to the other, nor indeed does it show what the real distinction between beauty in art and beauty in nature is supposed to be. The two sections (41 and 42), dealing with empirical and intellectual interest in the beautiful respectively, are concerned with mainly one issue: to demonstrate that although the judgment of taste "must have no interest as its determining ground," it does not follow that "an interest cannot enter into combination with it." In other words, what is felt with immediate and disinterested pleasure can "admit of having further conjoined with it *a pleasure in the real existence* of the object (as that wherein all interest consists)" (§41, 5:296). So Kant admits much more can be said about things of beauty, such as what empirical interest in the existence of beauty comes to: "The empirical interest in the beautiful exists only in society" (§41, 5:297), and what an intellectual interest in the beautiful can tell us about ourselves (§42). It is here that we find the statements about artistic beauty and natural beauty that seem to underrate beauty in art and link an interest in natural beauty with a morally good disposition.

Yet to regard these passages as more than Kant's asides on the analogy between the immediateness of aesthetic feeling and the immediateness of moral feeling on the one hand, and, on the other, the absence of such an analogy in the case of the experience of artistic beauty, would be a mistake. They do not support a ranking of one kind of beauty over the other but follow through the thought that intellectual interest can accompany the pure judgment of taste that is now extended explicitly to encompass the response to beauty in art; and that what can accompany an aesthetic response to nature's forms grows more strongly on ground already cultivated by a sensibility finely attuned to "the moral side of our being" (§42, 5:301). The absence of such an immediate interest in beautiful forms of art is explained by reference to what Kant here conceives art to be. As a first shot, art is sketched into the picture as either imitating nature, or as intentionally directed to our delight. It is thus either once removed from the immediateness of the experience of nature, or of value not for itself, but for the end it serves, that of pleasure.[10] Only then, from section 43 on, does Kant approach directly both the response to art and the creation of art. The distinction between natural and artistic beauty, first introduced rather obliquely in the context of the intellectual interest that may accompany the aesthetic experience, informs the discussions and observations that follow.

That the beautiful in nature and the beautiful in art together form the sphere of the aesthetic, and that both are experienced and judged in the reflective judgment of taste, is taken as established. But that there is a significant contrast to be drawn between beautiful natural objects and beautiful works of art opens up the discussion of "art in general" (§43): "*Art* is distinguished from *nature* as making (*facere*) is from acting or operating in general (*agere*), and the product or result of the former is distinguished from that of the latter as work (*opus*) from operation (*effectus*)" (§43, 5:303). Art is further distinguished, "as a human skill," from science, "as a practical from a theoretical faculty"; and as "free" art from craft, as having a "soul" rather than being a lifeless mechanical contrivance. Only then does Kant's analysis isolate "fine art"; together with agreeable art, it occasions aesthetic pleasure. Kant says of fine art that it is "a mode of representation which is intrinsically final" although devoid of an end (§44, 5:306). And he attempts to explicate the almost paradoxical formulation by equating "intrinsically final" with the essentially intentional nature of products of fine art: Works of art are purposively made, as if there was a concept guiding the execution of a plan. This, however, is dangerous ground, and the reminder that we are dealing here with the beautiful is a timely one: "For, whether we are dealing with beauty of nature or beauty of art, we may make the universal statement: *That is beautiful which pleases in the mere estimate of it* (not in sensation or by means of a concept)" (§45, 5:306). Thus, in recalling the results of the Analytic of the Beautiful with the now explicit acknowledgment of the beautiful in nature *and* in art, Kant can draw back from saying that making something beautiful requires the use of the concept of beauty as guiding the intention. Instead, he gives us the memorable (though also not immediately transparent) formulation of nature appearing as art and art appearing as nature: "Nature proved beautiful when it wore the appearance of art; and art can only be termed beautiful, where we are conscious of its being art, while yet it has the appearance of nature" (§45, 5:306). However, only art's appearing as nature is cashed out in terms of intention, for it is only in art and not in nature that this concept has application: "Hence the finality in the product of fine art, intentional though it be, must not have the appearance of being intentional; i.e., fine art must be clothed *with the aspect* of nature, though we recognize it to be art" (§45, 5:307).

Once more it seems that Kant looks to nature and its beauty as though our experience of it provided the measure also of beauty in art. But then the difference between beautiful natural objects and beautiful artifacts leads to the recognition that a special explanation is required for the intentional making of beautiful things; they do not just happen, they are made by human beings. Normally when something is made with the intention to produce a thing of a certain kind, the agent follows an antecedent concept of the thing he wishes to bring into existence. But there is, as Kant has been at pains to establish, no concept of beauty, and thus no rule according to which to produce a thing of beauty. If there were a concept that could function as a rule for the making of something beautiful, then that concept would also be available for assessing and judging beauty by taste. But Kant's entire discussion so far has ruled that out. Yet we know that beautiful objects are being made, and that at least in some cases they are made with the intention to produce things of beauty. How is this possible? Kant's answer is that there must be a capacity or "natural endowment," a special gift that enables the artist to create artworks. It cannot be a making according to rules that are known in advance, though something like rules or concepts must be presupposed. These latter can only be discerned in the finished product being a thing of beauty, a successful work that stands side by side with natural configurations in which beauty is manifest and con-firmed by the judgment of taste. This special capacity to create beau-tiful artworks, works of fine art, is not an ordinary capacity univer-sally present in all men, but it is something like nature's gift to only a few. It is, Kant says, genius.

"Fine art is the art of genius," he declares in the heading to section 46, and then spells out that it is through genius that nature, as it were, "gives the rule to art." "*Genius* is the talent (natural endow-ment) which gives the rule to art. Since talent, as an innate produc-tive faculty of the artist, belongs itself to nature, we may put it this way: *Genius* is the innate mental aptitude (*ingenium*) *through which* nature gives the rule to art" (§46, 5:307). The rest of the section argues for the necessity of presupposing a rule for something to be art, and then concludes that it must be "nature in the individ-ual (and by virtue of the harmony of his faculties)" that is responsi-ble for giving the rule to art – which comes to saying that "fine art is only possible as a product of genius." So the sense in which nature enters into the production or creation of works of fine art is the sense in which we as human are in our capacities and gifts part of nature. The contrast between natural beauty and the beautiful in art is the contrast between that which is found in the world – in nature outside us – and that which is intentionally created by artists who are especially gifted by nature. The artist does not follow rules he knows or could formulate in advance, nor does he observe guidelines laid out for him by others. He follows his own talent or genius – through which nature gives the rule to art, as Kant has it. It is only thus that Kant can maintain that genius is the special explanation that is needed for the creation of beautiful works of art. If artworks are intentionally made, then there must be a rule or concept accord-ing to which they are made; this rule or concept is not an ordinary rule or concept, based on an ordinary capacity. Genius is "one of nature's elect – a type that must be regarded as but a rare phenome-non" (§49, 5:318), and through it something like a rule, but not a rule or concept in the ordinary sense, is provided according to which creation as the making of a beautiful thing is possible.

Genius, as Kant sees it, is thus always original. Yet "since there may also be original nonsense, its products must at the same time be models, i.e., be exemplary; and consequently, though not them-selves derived from imitation, they must serve that purpose for oth-

ers, i.e., as standard or rule of estimating" (§46, 5:308). The products
of genius are original exemplars, and that means that they can be
followed either by another genius, "one whom it arouses to a sense
of his own originality," or imitated by a lesser mortal. In the latter
case the example "gives rise to a school, that is to say a methodical
instruction according to rules, collected, so far as the circumstances
admit, from such products of genius and their peculiarities. And, to
that extent, fine art is for such a person a matter of imitation, for
which nature, through the medium of a genius, gave the rule." An
original exemplar nurtures and promotes both further originality
and imitative tradition.

In addition to having come about intentionally and exhibiting
original exemplary character, products of genius purvey aesthetic
ideas in the special mode of expressing them. So far, we have met
ideas in Kant's work only as ideas of reason, to which, in contrast to
concepts of the understanding, no intuition can be adequate; they go
beyond all possible experience. Rational ideas are concepts of reason
that cannot be demonstrated in intuition. Aesthetic ideas, qua ideas,
are also contrasted with concepts of the understanding. But while
rational ideas are indemonstrable concepts of reason, aesthetic ideas
are inexponible representations of imagination (§57, 5:343). No concept can be adequate to them, and their introduction is the work of
genius alone. Kant enlarges on the capacity of presenting aesthetic
ideas especially when genius is poetic genius – "it is in fact precisely
in the poetic art that the faculty of aesthetic ideas can show itself to
its full advantage"; but all products of genius alike exemplify something of the mind-expanding power of aesthetic ideas (see all of §49
for more detail).

"In order to estimate a beauty of nature, as such," Kant says, "I do
not need to be possessed of a concept of what sort of thing the object is
intended to be" (§48, 5:311). Its form alone "pleases of its own account." This is a quick reminder of the pure judgment of taste. But it
is also a reminder of the problematic distinction drawn in the Analytic of the Beautiful between free and dependent beauty (§16,
pulchritudo vaga and *pulchritudo adhaerens*). In the third moment,
the distinction of two kinds of beauty to which either the pure or the
impure judgment of taste is appropriate, was briefly introduced and
then passed over; for only the pure judgment of taste, whether on a
natural object or a work of art, received analysis and deduction in the

Analytic of Aesthetic Judgment. Kant entitled his section 16 significantly thus: "*A judgment of taste in which an object is described as beautiful under the condition of a definite concept is not pure.*" In the Analytic, nothing more was made of the "not pure" judgment of taste. The implication, however, was clearly that both natural objects and works of art alike could function as objects of taste judgments, but that only the pure judgments of taste were needed to yield paradigms of the aesthetic judgment.[11] In our present context (§48), where objects as products of genius are contrasted with natural objects, the situation is different: Products of genius, as such, are objects under a certain description, they are works of art. Although their beauty might be judged as purely formal in pure judgments of taste, this would miss the point of their being artworks. To judge them as works of art is to judge them, in the language of section 16, as dependently beautiful; in section 48 Kant does not revive the earlier distinction but puts what is substantially the same point in another way. "If, however, the object is presented as a product of art, . . . a concept of what that thing is intended to be must first of all be laid at its basis. And, since the agreement of the manifold in a thing with an inner character belonging to it as its end constitutes the perfection of the thing, it follows that in estimating beauty of art the perfection of the thing must be taken into account – a matter which in estimating the beauty of nature, as beautiful, is quite irrelevant" (§48, 5:311).

"A beauty of nature is a *beautiful thing;* beauty of art is a *beautiful representation of a thing.*" This is one of Kant's memorable formulations of the contrast between nature and art, and it allows him, in a brief but important aside, to comment on the power of the art of genius to present as beautiful what is actually ugly in nature. "Where fine art evidences its superiority is in the beautiful description it gives of things that in nature would be ugly or displeasing. The Furies, diseases, devastations of war, and the like, can (as evils) be very beautifully described, nay even represented in pictures" (§48, 5:321). It is remarks such as this – and there are many like it that suddenly open up whole vistas for exploration – that convince one of the strength and importance of Kant's philosophy of art. Although no more than roughly and unsystematically sketched in a few sections of the *Critique of Aesthetic Judgment,* many of the problems of modern aesthetics are prefigured, and many of its questions are raised here for the first time.

NOTES

1 *Aesthetica.* 2 vols. (Frankfurt an der Oder, 1750–8).
2 Cf. Paul Guyer, *Kant and the Claims of Taste* (Cambridge, Mass.: Harvard University Press, 1979), ch. 4, pp. 120–33.
3 Cf. especially *Kant's Aesthetic Theory* (Madison: University of Wisconsin Press, 1974) by Donald Crawford, who distinguishes five stages of the deduction spread over the *Critique of Aesthetic Judgment.* In *Kant and the Claims of Taste* Paul Guyer distinguishes between a first attempt at the deduction – with arguments mainly drawn from section 21 – and a second and more successful attempt, concentrating on sections 35–40. Cf. also Anthony Savile, *Aesthetic Reconstructions* (Oxford: Basil Blackwell, 1987), pp. 99–191, and Mary A. McCloskey, *Kant's Aesthetic* (London: Macmillan, 1987), pp. 80–93.
4 Nevertheless, Crawford, in *Kant's Aesthetic Theory*, extends the last stage of the reconstructed deduction to the Dialectic, and R. K. Elliott, in "The Unity of Kant's 'Critique of Aesthetic Judgement'," *British Journal of Aesthetics* 8 (1968): 244–50, has argued that the deduction is complete only with the last paragraph of the Dialectic.
5 Cf. for detail *Kant and the Claims of Taste* by Guyer, who devotes an entire chapter to "The Metaphysics of Taste," pp. 331–50.
6 But cf. Mary Mothersill, *Beauty Restored* (Oxford: Clarendon Press, 1984, ch. 7 and 8) for a detailed comparison between Hume and Kant. Cf. also E. Schaper, "The Pleasures of Taste," in E. Schaper, ed., *Pleasure, Preference and Value* (Cambridge: Cambridge University Press, 1983), pp. 37–56.
7 Guyer omits treatment of the sublime in *Kant and the Claims of Taste*, giving his reasons on pp. 399–40; but cf. also Guyer's "Kant's Distinction between the Beautiful and the Sublime," *Review of Metaphysics* 35 (1982): 753–83.
8 Cf. Paul Crowther, *The Kantian Sublime* (Oxford: Clarendon Press, 1989), pp. 165–6, and Crawford, *Kant's Aesthetic Theory*, pp. 145–59.
9 Lewis White Beck, *Early German Philosophy: Kant and His Predecessors* (Cambridge, Mass.: Harvard University Press, 1969), p. 498.
10 Cf. Paul Guyer, "Interest, Nature, and Art: A Problem in Kant's Aesthetics," *Review of Metaphysics* 31 (1978): 580–603.
11 Cf. E. Schaper, "Free and Dependent Beauty," in Schaper, *Studies in Kant's Aesthetics* (Edinburgh: Edinburgh University Press, 1979), pp. 78–98.

13 Rational theology, moral faith, and religion

I. BACKGROUND

By the middle of the seventeenth century, Lutheran theology had become an ossified and sterile orthodoxy. It was challenged by two currents of thought that were to lead to the eighteenth-century German Enlightenment. The first was *Pietism*, founded by Philipp Jakob Spener (1635–1705). The Pietists regarded Christian faith not as a set of doctrinal propositions but a living relationship with God. They stressed above all the felt power of God's grace to transform the believer's life through a conversion of "born again" experience. Pietism was hostile to the intellectualization of Christianity. Like Lutheran orthodoxy it exalted scriptural authority above natural reason, but for Pietism the main purpose of reading scripture was inspiration and moral edification. The experience of spiritual rebirth must transform the believer's emotions and show itself in outward conduct. Within the universities, the Pietists favored cultivation of piety and morality in life rather than theoretical inquiry. In religious controversy, they urged that the aim should be to win over the heart of one's opponent rather than to gain intellectual victory. The social and political tendencies of Pietism were progressive, even radical. Pietism's Christian ethic was also egalitarian; its emphasis on the immediacy and intimacy of religious experience comported well with a belief in the priesthood of all believers. For Pietism, the visible church was less important than the church invisible, whose membership in principle includes the whole of humanity.

The other current that fed the Enlightenment was *rationalism*, deriving from the philosophy of Christian Wolff (1679–1754). Under the influence of Leibniz, Wolff combined traditional scholasticism

394

with the new science, producing a comprehensive philosophical system. In theology he argued that scriptural revelation was distinct from rational theology, but wholly consistent with it. Wolff's rational theology was founded on the cosmological argument that the contingent world must depend for its existence on a necessarily existent and supremely perfect being. The mid–eighteenth century also witnessed the beginning of critical biblical theology, under the influence of such men as J. A. Ernesti (1707–81) and J. D. Michaelis (1717–91). Under Wolff's influence, H. S. Reimarus (1694–1768) developed a system of rational religion (1754), a German counterpart of English deism, denying the need for supernatural revelation and founding religion on reason (and especially on rational morality). In 1778 Reimarus's so-called *Wolfenbüttel Fragments* were published posthumously by G. E. Lessing. These writings not only rejected all miracles and supernatural revelation, but also attacked the biblical histories as contradictory, fraudulent, and generally unreliable.

Pietism and rationalism were generally foes within the cultural life of eighteenth-century Germany. In 1723 (a year before Kant's birth), Pietists succeeded in persuading Prussian King Friedrich Wilhelm I to dismiss Wolff from his professorship at the prestigious University of Halle. Wolff taught at Marburg until 1740, when he was called back to Halle in triumph by the new king Friedrich II (Frederick the Great). Wolff's philosophy was the medium in which the German Enlightenment grew. Pietism also contributed to it, but the Counterenlightenment thought of Herder and Jacobi also display the lingering influence of Pietist thought and sensibility. Yet it was also possible for Kant's teacher Martin Knutzen (1713–51) to be both a Pietist and a Wolffian. Kant's thought displays the creative interaction between the two movements, but he became more a critic of both movements than an adherent of either.

Kant certainly had a strictly Pietistic education, both at home and in school. His philosophical views did not always please his religious mentors. The influence and financial support of Kant's family pastor F. A. Schultz enabled the poor harness-maker's son to enter the *Collegianum Fredericianum*, Schultz's newly founded Pietist academy in Königsberg. In 1755 Schultz was reportedly disappointed when his former pupil put forward the nebular hypothesis, a purely naturalistic and nonpurposive explanation of the origin of the solar system.

In many matters, Kant's religious beliefs and practices were far from orthodox. Kant was personally opposed in principle to religious ceremonies. He regarded creeds as unconscionable impositions on our inner freedom of thought, almost inevitably productive of a hypocritical frame of mind. Ceremonial praise of the Deity (the "religion of ingratiation") was for him a despicable act of self-degradation. And he saw no possible good in activities whose superstitious aim is to conjure up divine aid for our projects, regarding petitionary prayer (the "wheedling of God") as especially objectionable in this respect (*Religion*, 6:194–200/182–187).[1] In 1775 Kant wrote to J. C. Lavater:

> You ask for my opinion of your discussion of faith and prayer. Do you realize whom you are asking? A man who believes that, in the final moment, only the purest candor concerning our most hidden inner convictions can stand the test and who, like Job, takes it to be a sin to flatter God and make inner confessions, perhaps forced out by fear, that fail to agree with what we freely think. . . . By "moral faith" I mean the unconditional trust in divine aid, in achieving all the good that, even with our most sincere efforts, lies beyond our power. . . . No confession of faith, no appeal to holy names nor any observance of religious ceremonies can help – though the consoling hope is offered us that, if we do as much good as is in our power, trusting in the unknown and mysterious help of God, we shall (without meritorious "works" of any kind) partake of this divine supplement.
>
> (10:176–9 / 79–82)

Later Kant served several times as rector of the University of Königsberg, but was always "indisposed" when his official participation in religious observances would have been required.[2]

Kant's religious views even provoked the hostility of the authorities. The philosopher welcomed Frederick the Great's tolerant (and anticlerical) treatment of religion within the Prussian state (*Enlightenment*, 8:36–37/55). After Frederick's death in 1786, however, he ran afoul of Friedrich Wilhelm II's quite different policies. The new monarch dismissed Kant's patron Baron Zedlitz from his position as culture minister, replacing him with J. C. Wöllner (whom Frederick the Great had called a "deceitful, scheming parson"). In 1788 Wöllner promulgated an edict instituting censorship of all publications regarding their religious content; two years later, he supplemented it with an order that all candidates in theology should be subjected to a rigorous examination to ensure the orthodoxy of their convictions, supplemented by a solemn oath. Kant was outraged by these measures, and commented on them in a postscript to his 1791 essay on theodicy (*Theodicy*, 8:265–71).[3]

The censors did not refuse publication of either *Religion within the Limits of Reason Alone* (1793) or *The End of All Things* (1794). But on October 1, 1794 the king (at Wöllner's urging) wrote a reproving letter to Kant, commanding him to write no more on religious subjects. By this time, Kant's renown was such that he could have disregarded such an impudent and unenlightened command with impunity, as friends urged him to do. But (consistent with his own doctrine of absolute obedience to sovereign authority, even to its unjust commands) Kant regarded himself as bound to obey, and wrote the king a letter pledging himself to do so (*Conflict*, 7:7–11). Yet later (in a spirit more wily than submissive) he chose to interpret this as merely a personal promise to the monarch; immediately upon the latter's death in 1797, he again expressed himself on religious topics in *The Conflict of the Faculties*.[4]

II. RATIONAL THEOLOGY

Kant is famous for his criticisms (which Moses Mendelssohn called "world-crushing" (*Weltzermalmend*)) of the traditional proofs for God's existence. Less well known is the positive side of Kant's rational theology, his argument that the concept of God is natural to human reason, arising necessarily in the course of rational reflection on the concept of an individual thing in general.

In Kant's categories of quality (reality, negation, and limitation), "reality" is presented as admitting of degree, or intensive magnitude (A 143 / B 182; A 273 / B 329). Kant subscribes to the traditional scholastic-rationalist ontology according to which things have different degrees or amounts of reality or being. He also subscribes to the Leibnizian principle that each individual thing differs qualitatively from all others. Following Wolff and Alexander Gottlieb Baumgarten (1714–62), Kant presents this idea in terms of the "principle of thorough determination" (*principium omnimodae determinatio*): Any given thing is determined by one and only one member of every pair of contradictorily opposed predicates, and the complete individual concept of a given thing consists in the precise combination of realities and negations that determines it (A 571 / B 599).[5] Kant holds that when we try to think the conditions for the complete determination of any individual thing, we are led inevitably to the concept of an "all of reality (*omnitudo realitatis*)" (A 575–6 / B 603–4), and thence to the idea of an individual possessing all realities, an *ens realissimum*. This is the "ideal of pure reason," the pure rational concept of a supremely perfect being, or God (A 568 / B 596).[6]

On the basis of Kant's argument, the idea of God is the ground of the concepts of all other things. In his 1763 essay *The Only Possible Basis of Proof for a Demonstration of God's Existence*, Kant used these considerations to argue that God is also "the ground of all possibility" and consequently a necessarily existent being (*Only Possible Basis*, 2:78–9).[7] Although by 1781 he no longer endorses this proof of God's existence, it continues to influence his thinking about rational theology. In the *Critique of Pure Reason* he denies that his 1763 proof justifies a "dogmatic conclusion" that God exists, but he continues to hold that the existence of God as "the substratum of all possibility" is a "subjectively necessary hypothesis" for our reason (A 581–2 / B 609–10).

Kant's conception of God belongs squarely in the scholastic-rationalist tradition. God is the supremely perfect being, extramundane, immutable, timelessly eternal. He is also living, knowing, and willing: omniscient, omnipotent, supremely holy, just, and beneficent. Kant draws a distinction between God's "ontological" predicates, which can be derived from the pure categories, and his "cosmological" or "anthropological" predicates, based on empirical features of the world (especially features of ourselves). Kant defines "deism" as the view that admits only an "ontotheology" or "transcendental theology." For the deist, God is "a blindly working eternal nature as the root of all things" (a single supremely perfect necessarily existent supramundane substance, immutable, impassible, all-sufficient, omnipresent, timelessly eternal), but not a living, knowing, or willing being (*Lectures*, 28:1002/30, 1032–45/62–79). A "theist" is someone who has also a "natural theology," regarding God as a rational and a moral being on the basis of predicates drawn from finite things (especially from our own mental life) (*Lectures*, 28:1046–60/81–99). Regarding such predicates, Kant adopts a theory of analogy. When we ascribe knowledge or volition to God, we cannot mean that he has any property similar to our knowledge and will, but only a supremely perfect analogue, with which we can never be directly acquainted (*Prolegomena*, 4:356–63/105–10; *Lectures*, 28:1023/54).

Kant's discussion of the traditional theistic proofs is based on the view that God is an *ens logice originarium*, whose necessary existence is naturally thought to follow from its status as the root of all possibility. Kant considers proofs for God's existence only as proofs for the existence of a supremely perfect being or *ens realissimum*, and he thinks that a truly adequate proof of the existence of such a being would have to be *a priori*. Kant divides all theistic proofs into three general types:

1. *Ontological* proofs, which argue for the necessary existence of a supremely perfect being from its concept alone.
2. *Cosmological* proofs, which argue for the necessary existence of a supremely perfect being from the contingent existence of a world in general.
3. *Physicotheological* proofs, which argue for the existence of a supremely perfect being from the contingent constitution of the world (e.g., from the teleological arrangements found in it).

Kant argues that a physicotheological proof cannot establish the existence of a supremely perfect being unless it rests covertly on a cosmological proof; and that a cosmological proof cannot establish that a perfect being necessarily exists unless an ontological proof is also sound. In both cases, Kant alleges that the presupposition is involved in inferring the existence of a supremely perfect being (from a necessary being in the case of the cosmological argument, and from a wise world-designer in the case of the physicotheological).[8] His strategy is therefore to show that no ontological proof for God's existence can be given, and thus to defeat the other two proofs as well, by a kind of domino effect. One consequence of this strategy is that Kant in effect mounts no criticism at all of the inference from contingent to necessary existence or the inference from purposiveness in the world to a wise designer. Another consequence is that Kant's entire critique of traditional theistic proofs is made to rest on his critique of the ontological argument, without which Kant's entire critique of rational theology would fall to the ground. (In his 1763 essay, however, Kant had presented independent criticisms of the cosmological and physicotheological proofs. Though he does not repeat them in the *Critique*, he probably did not intend to repudiate them either.)

Kant's critique of the ontological proof may be summed up in the slogan: "Existence is not a real predicate," that is, "it is not anything that could be added to the concept of a thing" (A 599 / B 626). This does not mean that it is a phony predicate, and of course it does not mean that propositions of the form "X exists" add nothing to our information about X. Kant wants to draw a distinction between (1) propositions that "determine" a subject-concept by predicating "realities" or perfections that do not belong to it, and (2) propositions that only "posit" an object corresponding to the subject-concept, without predicating of it anything that might be part of the contents of any concept. "X exists" is a proposition of this latter sort. "When we say 'God is' or 'There is a God', we attach no new predicate to the concept of God, but only posit the subject itself with all its predicates" (A 599 / B 627).

Kant's thesis about existence and predication is famous and influential, but Kant has remarkably little to say in its defense, and its truth is anything but self-evident. The uncontroversial claim is that to say "X exists" is to say that there is some object to which the concept of X corresponds. The point that really needs to be established, however, is that "is" or "exists" is not *also* a reality or perfection, which might belong to the nature of something or be contained in its concept. If this point follows from the uncontroversial claim, Kant never shows us how.

There is a somewhat analogous problem with emotivist meta-ethical theories, which hold that "X is good" predicates no property of X but only expresses the speaker's "commendation" or "approval" of it. There too, it is plausible that "good" normally expresses some sort of commendation or approval of the things to which it is applied. But what really needs to be argued is that "good" cannot *also* refer to natural properties of good things (presumably, the properties making them naturally worth commending). Suppose a philosopher claimed "heavy" is not a real predicate by arguing that the assertion "X is heavy" serves the unique semantic function of "gravitizing" X, or that "blue" is not a real predicate because it merely "azurates" the subject. Emotivists and defenders of Kant's thesis about existence and predication need to show that "commending" and "positing" do not function in their contentions as "gravitizing" and "azurating" do in these.[9]

III. THE MORAL ARGUMENTS

"I had to do away with knowledge," Kant famously declares, "in order to make room for faith" (B xxx). Kant defines "knowledge" (*Wissen*) as the "holding" (*Fürwahrhalten*) of a proposition that is "sufficient" both "objectively" and "subjectively," whereas "faith" or "belief" (*Glaube*) is "sufficient" only "subjectively," not "objectively" (A 822 / B 850). But faith as much as knowledge is justified by reasons that are "valid for everyone"; in this respect, it is distinguished from mere "opinion" (*Meinung*), which is "insufficient" subjectively as well as objectively (A 820 / B 848).[10]

Kant maintains that we can be rationally justified in holding a proposition not only by theoretical ("objective") evidence, but also by practical ("subjective") considerations. He tries to present such considerations in the so-called moral argument for belief in God. Kant thinks I can act rationally in pursuit of an end only as long as I believe that the end is possible of attainment through the actions I take toward it. This means that if I do not believe I can achieve an end E by taking action A, then I cannot rationally do A with E as my end; further, it means that if I do not think any course of action on my part has any possibility of reaching E, then it cannot be rational for me to make E my end at all.

Now suppose there is an end that as a rational agent I am morally bound to set myself. In that case, I can neither rationally abandon this end nor rationally pursue it without believing that it is possible of attainment through the actions I take toward it. Under these circumstances, I have good reason, independently of any theoretical evidence, for holding the belief that my moral end is possible of attainment, and for holding any other belief to which this belief commits me.

Kant's ethical theory does identify such a morally obligatory end, which Kant calls the "highest good" (*Practical Reason*, 5:110–13). Setting this end is bound up with having a morally good disposition and with reason's tendency, in practice as well as theory, to form the idea of an unconditioned totality (A 310 / B367; *Practical Reason*,

5:108). The highest good has two components: the "moral good," virtue of character, and the "natural good," happiness or "well-being" (*Wohl*). The two components are heterogenous; neither's value is substitutable for that of the other. But they do not have equal moral weight; the value of the natural good is conditional upon the moral good. In other words, a person's happiness is valuable to morality, but the value is conditional upon the person's virtue, or worthiness to be happy (*Groundwork*, 4:393; *Practical Reason*, 5:61/110–11). Hence from a slightly different standpoint, the two components of the highest good can be represented as

1. Perfect virtue
2. Happiness proportional to virtue

To pursue the first component is to strive for moral perfection, in the first instance one's own (*Morals*, 6:385), but also the virtue of others, especially through the voluntary moral community that Kant calls a "church" (*Religion*, 6:98, see Sections V and VI of this essay). Pursuit of the second component involves the pursuit of human happiness, others' as well as one's own, to the extent that the pursuit is consistent with moral duty. The pursuit of both components of the highest good involves a rational commitment to believe them possible of attainment. Each thus gives rise to a belief, rationally justified independently of theoretical evidence, in the conditions of this possibility.

Kant maintains that our pursuit of virtue always begins from a state of moral imperfection or, as he puts it in his later writings, a condition of "radical evil," a propensity to choose contrary to the moral law (*Religion*, 6:28–9/23–4). Kant thus argues that our pursuit of moral perfection must consist in an endless progress from bad to better. This, he thinks, gives us a practical ground for belief in an everlasting life after the present one, in which this progress may be carried on. Practical considerations thus lead to faith in immortality of the soul (*Practical Reason*, 5:121–4).[11]

Pursuit of the second component of the highest good is, in effect, beneficence limited by justice. Happiness in accordance with moral desert involves not merely a contingent relation between the two, but a causal connection (*Practical Reason*, 5:111). We ourselves, of course, cannot search the inward heart of moral agents, and do not know the true moral desert of anyone, not even our own (*Ground-*

work, 4:407). But Kant thinks it is plain to us that the possibility of the second component of the highest good depends on the existence of a Providence, which does know each one's desert and ultimately apportions happiness in accordance with it. In other words, the possibility of the second component depends on the existence of an omniscient, omnipotent, just, and benevolent being. Hence pursuit of the highest good rationally justifies belief in a God (*Practical Reason*, 5:124–32).[12]

In the *Religion*, Kant suggests a further object of moral faith, or at least an additional approach to the same objects. The human will must aim at moral perfection, and at a happiness that accords with desert. But, Kant contends, it always begins from a radical propensity to evil, so that its progress is always from bad to better. As moral beings we must seek moral justification, but we begin from a state of evil, the guilt of which we cannot wipe out (*Religion*, 6:72/66). Thus we can conceive the possibility of our moral end only by supposing that if we do all we can, our moral deficiency will be supplemented by a "righteousness not our own" (*Religion*, 6:66/60). Justification requires faith in a divine grace, through which moral perfection can be attained (*Religion*, 6:75–6/70).[13]

IV. MORAL FAITH

Kant is emphatic that morality does not rest on religion, but the other way around: Religious faith is founded on morality. Kant contrasts "moral theology," which bases the concept of God on moral reason, with "theological morality," which superstitiously bases moral conceptions on religious ones (*Lectures*, 28:1001/31). The aim of Kant's moral arguments is to show how morality, which is fundamentally independent of religious belief, nevertheless leads to religion (*Religion*, 6:3–6/3–6). His plain intent is that the moral arguments should serve as a kind of substitute for the theoretical proofs rejected by his theoretical critique; only what they are supposed to justify is a warm and living religious faith, as distinct from dead, abstract theoretical knowledge.

Even if the moral arguments are successful, it is unclear how far they can fulfill this intention. Just because they are not theoretical arguments, they do not provide reasons that directly produce belief in God or immortality. What they show is that morally disposed people are involved in a kind of practical irrationality unless they believe in a future life and a providential and gracious Deity. In other words, Kant's arguments do not show that there is a God and a future life, but only that belief in God and a future life would be very desirable for a moral agent to have, since it would rescue such an agent from a practical paradox. In this respect, Kant's moral arguments are rather like Pascal's wager, which tries to show not that Christianity is true, but that Christian belief would be advantageous to have. Pascal rightly notes that such an argument cannot directly produce belief, but rather gives us reasons to take certain steps (taking holy water, having masses said, acting as if we believe) that are designed to produce belief in us.[14] Kant regards such self-manipulative attitudes as hypocritical and degrading, but he also speaks of moral faith as "belief arising from a need of reason" (*Practical Reason*, 5:141), without saying how reason is capable of satisfying the need. When he describes moral faith as arising from a "voluntary decision of the judgment" (*Practical Reason*, 5:144), Kant seems to suggest that he thinks (what is clearly false) that we have the ability to believe in God and immortality just by deciding to.

Kant often uses the term "belief" or "faith" (*Glaube*) to describe the results of the moral arguments, but he sometimes uses other terms, which may carry weaker implications. His technical term for the result of the moral arguments is "postulate," which he equates with a "practically necessary hypothesis" (*Practical Reason*, 5:11–12). Sometimes Kant speaks of the practical postulates as "assumptions" or "presuppositions" (*Orientation*, 8:146); and he sometimes qualifies moral faith by calling it a "belief for practical purposes" (*Theory and Practice*, 8:279/65). Perhaps such usages indicate Kant's awareness that his practical arguments do not actually yield belief, and involve the (at least tacit) suggestion that they attain to something slightly weaker. If "postulating," "assuming," and "presupposing" are intended to fall short of believing, then "postulating" that God exists or "believing for practical purposes that God exists" may be equivalent (for instance) to hoping that God exists, or just "acting as if" you believe God exists.

Kant is mistaken, however, if he supposes that this would solve his problem. It would be wrong to think that in pursuing an end by means of an action we could do with something less than *belief* that the end is possible of attainment through the action. Granted their premises, Kant's arguments do show that we have a rational need for such beliefs; that need cannot be satisfied merely by hoping or "acting as if." The problem is rather that practical arguments by themselves cannot produce the belief whose indispensability they demonstrate. Such belief requires either theoretical evidence, which Kant regards as unavailable, or else nonrational motivating factors, which Kant wishes to eschew. Kant never entirely faced up to the difficulty for moral faith posed by this dilemma.

Occasionally Kant weakens his conclusion in a different and more defensible way. He suggests that the moral arguments do not necessarily show that we must believe in God and a future life, but are minimally compatible with belief only in their *possibility*. The "minimum of theology," he says, is not that God exists, but only that God is possible (*Religion*, 6:153–4/142; *Lectures*, 28:998/27). Clearly Kant thinks that faith in the actual existence of God harmonizes better with a moral disposition than this agnosticism, but apparently an agnostic can satisfy the minimum demands flowing from the moral arguments. Part of Kant's motivation here is plainly to encourage a tolerant attitude toward people with heterodox beliefs. Kant is emphatic that we cannot have a *duty* to hold any belief; he applies this specifically to the objects of moral faith (*Practical Reason*, 5:149–50). But it is probably no accident that the "minimum of theology" coincides with what Kant thinks can be justified theoretically. For he thinks that we can prove theoretically neither that there is a God nor that there is not. Apparently Kant does not want to find moral fault with anyone whose religious beliefs fall within the range of opinion that is compatible with the theoretical evidence.

Perhaps this minimum may also harmonize with what the moral arguments themselves succeed in proving. For if God's existence is both necessary and sufficient for the actuality of the highest good, then belief in the possibility of the highest good would seem equivalent to the belief that God is possible. Devoted pursuit of one's final moral end might be better served by a confidence that the highest good will at last be attained, but the bare minimum reason requires is belief that it is possible of attainment. Hence Kant thinks morality is compatible with a hopeful agnosticism about God's existence, even though something stronger than this would be preferable.

V. RELIGION

Kant defines "religion" as "the cognition of all duties as divine commands" (*Religion*, 6:153 / 142). This definition is in need of commentary on at least three counts.

1. Kant understands religion as a matter not of theoretical cognition but of moral disposition (*Practical Reason*, 5:129, *Judgment*, 5:481, *Conflict*, 7:36, *Lectures*, 28:998, 1078/27, 122). Hence the definition must be understood in the sense that religion is "the moral disposition to observe all duties as [God's] commands" (*Religion*, 6:105/96).

2. Kant is emphatic that in order for there to be religion, there need not be any special duties to God; religion requires no duties beyond those we owe to human beings (*Religion*, 6:154 n./142 n.; *Lectures*, 28:1101/143).

3. Kant denies that any theoretical cognition of God's existence is required for religion. This is natural enough, because he denies that any such cognition is available to us (*Religion*, 6:153–4 n./142 n.). In fact, for religion it is not even necessary to believe in God's existence. "[For religion] no assertoric knowledge (even of God's existence) is required; . . . but only a *problematic* assumption (hypothesis) as regards speculation about the supreme cause of things." The "assertoric faith" needed for religion "needs merely *the idea of God* . . . only the *minimum* cognition (it is possible that there is a God) has to be subjectively sufficient" (*Religion*, 6:153–4/142).

Religion requires that (a) I have duties, (b) I have a concept of God, and (c) I am capable of regarding my duties as something God wills me to do. I can have religion in this sense even if I am an agnostic, so long as my awareness of duty is enlivened with the thought that if there is a God, then my duties are God's commands.

But why should we think of our duties as commanded by God? Kant's rejection of theological morality makes clear that this way of thinking has no legitimate role to play either in our knowledge of our duties or in motivating us to do our duty (*Religion*, 6:3/3). Kant claims that thinking of duties in this way has something to do with our pursuit of the highest good: "[Our duties] must be regarded as commands of the supreme being because we can hope for the highest good . . . only from a morally perfect . . . will; and therefore we can hope to attain it only through harmony with this will" (*Practical Reason*, 5:129). Because our concept of God's will is supposed to be derived from our concept of morality, we must think of our duties as harmonizing with God's will. But why think of them as divine *commands?*

The answer to this question depends on the fact that Kant regards our pursuit of the highest good as a collective or social enterprise:

> The highest good cannot be achieved merely by the exertions of the single individual toward his own moral perfection, but instead requires a union of such individuals into a whole working toward the same end – a system of well-disposed human beings, in which and through whose unity alone the highest moral good can come to pass.   (*Religion*, 6:97–8/89)

Our moral vocation is a social one, which must be pursued through membership in a *community:*

> [A moral community] is attainable, insofar as human beings can work toward it, only through the establishment and spread of a society in accordance with and for the sake of the laws of virtue, a society whose task and duty it is rationally to impress these laws in all their scope upon the entire human race.   (*Religion*, 6:94/86)

This moral or ethical community must not be confused with a political community, based on coercive laws and aiming at external justice. A community aiming at the moral improvement of its members must be voluntary, and coercive laws will not serve its ends. But it must regard the universally valid moral law as a public law: "All single individuals must be subject to a public legislation and all the laws that bind them must be capable of being regarded as the commands of a common legislator" (*Religion*, 6:98/90). In an external or political community, the people itself is to be regarded as the legislator. But Kant maintains that no group of people could regard itself as legislating universally for all rational beings (*Religion*, 6:96/88). The legislator for a moral community must be someone whose will is in harmony with all moral duties, and someone who "knows the heart" so as to judge each individual's inner disposition. "But this is the concept of God as moral ruler of the world. Hence a moral community can be thought of only as a people under divine commands, i.e., a *people of God, under laws of virtue*" (*Religion*, 6:99/91).

In other words, Kantian morality is communitarian, not individualistic. Religion has a place in human life for him because the moral life is not a purely private matter, in which each of us must merely do our own duty, look after our own inner virtue, and leave others to do the same. Each of us has the vocation of furthering the moral good of others, and each stands in need of the aid of others for our own moral progress. Though membership in a moral community must be noncoercive, each individual has a moral duty to join with others in such a community. Kant describes this as a "duty *sui generis*" because it is not a duty of one individual to others, nor even a duty to oneself, but a duty "of the human race toward itself" to fulfill its common vocation to progress as a species (*Religion*, 6:96–7/88–9). In this way, Kant's philosophy of religion has to be viewed as part of his social philosophy, and his philosophy of history.[15]

VI. THE CHURCH

Kant maintains that it is not possible to decide through experience whether the human race's history shows it to be improving morally, getting worse, or vacillating endlessly between good and evil. But he thinks we can look at this question in light of our vocation to better ourselves (both individually and collectively), and try to form conjectures about the way in which nature or providence might contrive the progress of the human species (*Universal History*, 8:29–31/23–6).

In his 1784 essay *Idea for a Universal History with a Cosmopolitan Purpose*, Kant proposes that the chief goal that nature has set for the human race is the fashioning of a "universal civil society" to protect people's rightful freedom and develop their natural capacities (8:22/16). Nature's means to this end is the human trait of "unsociable sociability," the human passion to "achieve rank among one's fellows, whom he cannot *suffer* but also cannot *leave alone*" (8:21/15). This passion drives people together into societies, where each seeks dominion over others, and all abuse what freedom they have in a struggle to subjugate others. This struggle leads to the founding of states, in which a supreme authority achieves mastery over the lawless wills of its subjects, forcing them to obey a universal law that confines each within its rightful sphere (8:23/17). The problem with this, of course, is that there is nothing to confine the authority itself, which tends to abuse the rights of everyone. Hence in the political realm the human race's remaining task is to establish a constitution where the powers of the state are administered justly. Kant believes this task cannot be completed until states establish a lawful international order, regulating their relations with one another. He also thinks we can discern some definite tendencies in history for this to happen (8:24–6/18–21).

Nearly a decade later in the *Religion*, Kant attempts an analogous historical conjecture as regards the purely ethical society, the "people of God" striving under noncoercive laws to perfect the moral disposition of the human race. As political states are the empirical ectype of a realm of external justice, so the empirical form of the universal ethical community is found in the churches of the various empirical religious faiths (*Religion*, 6:100/91). In the same way that political states have often strayed far from their rational end of establishing external justice, so churches and ecclesiastical faiths have also regularly fallen short of their task. Their chief failing is that in their supposed attempts to please God they have often encouraged not morally good conduct, but rather (morally indifferent) statutory observances or (immoral and degrading) acts of praise and worship, whose ignoble aim is to win special (and undeserved) divine favor through flattery or bribery. Instead of cultivating a disposition to moral freedom, they have promoted cult and prayer, based on the superstitious belief in miracles, fanatical pretensions to supersensible experiences of the divine, or fetishistic attempts to produce supernatural occurrences through ritual acts (*Religion*, 6:53/48; 6:86/81; 6:106/97; 6:174/162; 6:177–8/165–6). Worst of all, they have subjected the conscience of individuals to a hierarchy of priests, enslaving the soul that it is their proper function to liberate (*Religion*, 6:134 n./124 n.; 6:175–80/163–8; 6:185–90/173–8; *Enlightenment*, 8:35–42/54–60).

The historical function of the state is to preserve justice, so that human freedom may flourish and human capacities develop. Analogously, the historical function of the church is to begin the work of organizing a universal ethical community. Thus the function of ecclesiastical faith is to serve as the "vehicle" for pure rational religion; yet ecclesiastical faith is also the "shell" in which rational religion is encased, and from which it is humanity's historical task to free it (*Religion*, 6:121/112; 6:135 n./126 n.). It is not Kant's view that this must involve the abolition of ecclesiastical faith, but only the appreciation of which aspects of it are superfluous: "Not that [the shell] should cease (for perhaps it will always be useful and necessary as a vehicle) but only that it be able to cease" (*Religion*, 6:135 n./126 n.).

The plain intent here is that people should eventually abolish the hierarchical constitution of churches, which puts humanity in spiritual tutelage to a class of priests, who usurp the authority of individuals over their own belief and conscience. The vocation of every adult human being, Kant maintains, is to think for oneself (*Enlightenment*, 8:36/54). When your thinking is subject to the guidance or direction of others, as the thought of children is subject to their parents, then you are in a condition of *Unmündigkeit* ("tutelage" – "immaturity" or "minority"). The greatest human indignity occurs when adult human beings are in such a condition. Religion is not the only form taken by such tutelage, but Kant regards it as the "most pernicious and degrading" form (8:41/59). He defines "enlightenment" as "release from self-incurred tutelage" (8:36/54). Your tutelage is self-incurred if it is due not to the immaturity or incapacity of your faculties, but to your lack of courage and resolve in thinking for yourself. But even those who are in a state of self-incurred tutelage may not be wholly to blame for their condition. Kant describes how ecclesiastical faiths devise highly effective means of filling people with "pious terror" and playing on their propensity to a "servile faith in divine worship (*gottesdienstlich Frohnglauben*)." Such devices undermine people's confidence in their capacities, causing them to feel fear and guilt at their own honest doubts and common sense, preventing them from ever acquiring a faith free of servility and hypocrisy (*Religion*, 6:133 n./124 n.).

Perhaps there was a time when people were on the whole benefited by the paternal guidance of priests, and could do no better than to follow the revealed statutes of a church, handed down by tradition and ascribed to the supernatural authority of divine revelation. But Kant is persuaded that such times are now definitely past. "The leading strings of holy tradition, with its appendages of statutes and observances, which did good service in its time, gradually become dispensable, and finally become shackles when humanity reaches its adolescence" (*Religion*, 6:121/112). He sees the highest vocation of his age as that of putting an end to religious tutelage. Thus he describes his age (cautiously) not as an enlightened age but (optimistically) as an age of enlightenment, in which progressive forces will inevitably liberate people from religious tutelage if only the secular authority safeguards freedom of thought and expression and refuses to "support the ecclesiastical despotism of some tyrants in his state over his other subjects" (*Enlightenment*, 8:40/58).

[At the end of this process] the demeaning distinction between *laity* and *clergy* ceases, and equality arises from true freedom; but there is no anarchy, because each obeys the (nonstatutory) law which he prescribes to himself, and which he at the same time must regard as the will of the world ruler, revealed through reason, combining all invisibly under a common government in one state, already prepared for and inadequately represented by the visible church.   (*Religion*, 6:122/112)

Kant thus looks forward eventually to a time "when the form of a church itself is dissolved, the viceroy on earth steps into the same class as the human being raised to a citizen of heaven, and so God will be all in all" (*Religion*, 6:135/126).

VII. REASON AND REVELATION

In Kant's view, what unites people in a true religious community is not a common cult or creed, but a common devotion to the moral improvement of humanity. Religion, the disposition to observe all duties as divine commands, can therefore exhibit itself in a wide variety of personal faiths. Kant attempts to provide a rational (practical) defense of belief in immortality and in divine providence and grace. But we have seen that he thinks genuine religion is compatible even with an agnostic position on these matters. On the other hand, Kant does not rule out the beliefs of traditional, revealed ecclesiastical faith, so long as they are presented in a spirit that is compatible with a genuine moral religion of reason. The point that matters most to him here is that acceptance of doctrines depending on revelation rather than reason should not be regarded as *morally required* for true religion (*Religion*, 6:153–5/142–3). This is crucial, because true religion aspires to be a universal ethical community embracing all humanity, and this is something no revealed faith can pretend to be.

Pure [rational religious faith] alone can found a universal church, because it is a faith of unassisted reason, which may be communicated with conviction to everyone; but a historical faith, insofar as it is grounded merely on facts, can extend its influence no further than the news of it, in respect of time and circumstances, can acquire the capacity to make themselves worthy of belief.   (*Religion*, 6:102–3/94)

From this passage, it looks as if Kant is arguing that revealed faith cannot be universal because its empirical tidings are bound to be more accessible to people closer to their source than to those more distant from it. That would not be a good argument, since even a morality founded on pure reason must develop through history, and its substance and spirit are also inevitably available more to some than to others.

We understand Kant's argument better if we focus on the point that the issue is not empirical availability, but rational credibility: the capacity of teachings not merely to be disseminated, but to "make themselves *worthy* of belief." Empirical and historical reports have the capacity to do this when the evidence for them is strong enough, even if many people do not have access to them (*Orientation*, 8:141). The problem with supernatural revelation is that because the idea of God is an idea of reason, to which no experience can ever correspond, it follows that no empirical evidence can ever justify the conclusion that some empirical event is a special divine revelation (*Orientation*, 8:142). Consequently, no revealed faith "can ever be universally communicated so as to produce conviction"; so when a church founds itself on supernatural revelation, it "renounces the most important mark of truth, namely a rightful claim to universality" (*Religion*, 6:109/100; cf. *Conflict*, 7:49–50).

Kant does *not* deny that we have supernatural revelation. Such a denial, he thinks, would be just as presumptuous as the claim to know that some particular experience is of special divine origin. Both equally transcend our cognitive capacities (*Religion*, 6:155/143). The point is rather that it is impossible for anyone ever to authenticate any particular putative revelation: "If God actually spoke to a human being, the latter could never *know* that it was God who spoke to him. It is absolutely impossible for a human being to grasp the infinite through the senses, so as to distinguish him from sensible beings and be *acquainted* with him" (*Conflict*, 7:63).

Historically, however, Kant thinks that such (necessarily ungrounded) claims to divine revelation are just as necessary to the foundation of religion as ambition and violence are to the founding of states. It is a "special weakness of human nature" that a church can never be originally founded solely on the religion of unassisted reason but always requires "ecclesiastical faith" based on a putative revelation (*Religion*, 6:103/94). This means that rational religion must not simply assert that there can be no justified claims to empirical divine revelation but needs to take a more positive attitude toward such claims.

Our reason itself, Kant says, counts as an "inner revelation" insofar as it can provide us with a pure rational concept of God and tell us which things a good God would require of us. This "inner revelation" should serve as a touchstone by which all claims to empirical revelation should be measured and interpreted (*Lectures*, 28:1118/60). For although we can never know whether any experience is a divine revelation, we can know of various doctrinal claims whether they are such that a wise and good God *might* have revealed them. In this way, it can correct the concept of God found in the popular cults, which is all too often nothing but "a terrifying picture of fantasy, and a superstitious object of ceremonial adoration and hypocritical high praise" (*Lectures*, 28:1119/161; cf. *Religion*, 6:168–9/156–7). Reason must also serve as the interpreter of traditional revealed doctrines and scriptures, because only it can guarantee that their sense is consistent with the claim that they might have been divinely revealed. Kant is very candid about what this entails:

If [a scripture] flatly contradicts morality, then it cannot be from God (for example, if a father were ordered to kill his son, who is, as far as he knows, perfectly innocent.   (*Religion*, 6:87/82)

Frequently in reference to the text (the revelation) [reason's] interpretation may appear to us forced, it may often really be so; and yet it must be preferred to the literal interpretation if the text can possibly support it.
                                                        (*Religion*, 6:110/100–1)

VIII. KANT AS A RELIGIOUS THINKER

Kant was a man of scientific temperament, concerned with the intellectual development and moral progress of humanity. He was deeply skeptical of popular religious culture, severely disapproving of the traditional activities of prayer and religious ceremonies, and down-right hostile to ecclesiastical authority. He had no patience at all for the mystical or the miraculous.

It may sound paradoxical to claim that such a person was also a deeply religious thinker. But this is nevertheless true, and it is a symptom of the degeneration of religion in our century, and more generally of its decline in human life since the eighteenth century, that we should find it paradoxical. As a man of the German Enlight-enment, Kant regarded the concerns of science and morality as *of course* also religious concerns. In Kant's milieu, there was no war-fare between science and religion, only a conflict between two kinds of religious sensibility: the enlightened religious sensibility, which seeks to reconcile religion with scientific reason, and various forms of contrary sensibility, which mistrust reason, and set religion against it because they prefer either revealed tradition, or mystical experience, or enthusiastic emotionalism.

In our day, unfortunately, the former kind of religious sensibility is all too rare, while the latter is still very much alive and well. It often claims for itself the entire sphere of religion, at the same time advertising itself as the only attitude that properly acknowledges the limits of human reason. But keeping Kant in mind will help to expose the vanity of its pretensions. No thinker ever placed greater emphasis on reason's boundaries than Kant; at the same time, none has ever been bolder in asserting its unqualified title to govern our lives. As Kant sees very clearly, the fact that reason is limited does not entail that there is any other authority or source of insight that might overrule it. This means that although religion is not originally an affair of reason, there can be no true religion at all unless there is also a religion of reason, and the religion of reason must serve as the core, and also the touchstone, of any other kind.

Equally far from Kant's position is the secularist view that treats religion with contempt, and regards it as nothing but a relic of the past or a deplorable refuge for the ignorant and superstitious. Orga-nized religion for Kant is as essential to human destiny as organized political life, and the role of reason in both spheres is equally vital.

Every state arises out of violence in behalf of unjust ambition, none is ever founded on reason alone. But because justice is the only office of the state and the sole source of its legitimacy, practical reason becomes its sole measure, and the development of the state toward the rational idea of justice is the sole human vocation with regard to political life. Analogously, every religious tradition begins in revealed authority, hierarchy, and superstition, but the only legitimate office of religion is to found an ethical community according to universal laws of reason. Thus the human vocation with regard to religion is nothing but the interpretation and development of tradition toward a universal religion of reason. For Kant, a church that clings to religious experience, emotion, or revelation without regard to reason has no more legitimacy than a state whose coercive power is used without regard for human rights. On the other hand, Kant thinks the human race can no more expect to fulfill its collective moral vocation apart from organized religion than it can expect to achieve justice through anarchy.[16]

NOTES

1 All translations from Kant's writings are my own. Standard English translations will normally be cited. In those cases where the *Akademie* edition pagination is not given in the English translation, English pagination will be cited too (English pagination following German pagination, separated by a slash (/)). The following translations are cited:

Critique of Judgment. Trans. Werner Pluhar. Indianapolis: Hackett, 1987.
Critique of Practical Reason. Trans. Lewis White Beck. Indianapolis: Bobbs-Merrill, 1956.
Immanuel Kant's Critique of Pure Reason. Trans. Norman Kemp Smith. New York: St. Martin's, 1965. Cited by A and B edition page numbers.
The Doctrine of Virtue. Trans. Mary J. Gregor. New York: Harper & Row, 1964.
"An Answer to the Question: What Is Enlightenment?" Trans. H. B. Nisbet, in H. Reiss, *Kant's Political Writings.* Cambridge: Cambridge University Press, 1970.
Foundations of the Metaphysics of Morals. Trans. Lewis White Beck. Indianapolis: Bobbs-Merrill, 1959.
"Idea for a Universal History with a Cosmopolitan Purpose." Trans. H. B. Nisbet, in H. Reiss, *Kant's Political Writings.*
Lectures on Philosophical Theology. Trans. Allen W. Wood and Gertrude M. Clark. Ithaca, N.Y.: Cornell University Press, 1978.
"What Is Orientation in Thinking?" In Kant, *Critique of Practical Reason and Other Writings in Moral Philosophy.* Trans. Lewis White Beck. New York: Garland, 1976.

Prolegomena to Any Future Metaphysics. Trans. Carus, rev. Lewis White Beck. Indianapolis: Bobbs-Merrill, 1950.

Kant's Philosophical Correspondence 1759–1799. Trans. Arnulf Zweig. Chicago: University of Chicago Press, 1967.

Religion within the Limits of Reason Alone. Trans. Theodore M. Greene and Hoyt H. Hudson. New York: Harper & Row, 1960.

"On the Common Saying: 'This May Be True In Theory, But It Does Not Apply in Practice'." Trans. H. B. Nisbet, in H. Reiss, *Kant's Political Writings.*

2 See Karl Vorländer, *Kants Leben* (1911) (Hamburg: Felix Meiner, 1986), p. 130.

3 See Ernst Cassirer, *Kant's Life and Thought,* trans. James Haden (New Haven, Conn.: Yale University Press, 1981), p. 376–9.

4 See Lewis White Beck, *Early German Philosophy* (Cambridge, Mass.: Harvard University Press, 1969), pp. 434–6.

5 "The complex of all determinations compossible in a being is its *thorough determination.* Hence a being is either determined thoroughly, or determined less than this. The former is a particular (an individual), the latter is a universal" (Baumgarten, *Metaphysica* (1739) (Halle: Olms, 1963) §148). "The thorough determination inhering in actual beings is their principle of individuation or thisness (*haecceitas*)" (Wolff, *Gesammelte Werke* (Halle: Olms, 1962), 2:3:187–9).

6 Kant's argument for this claim is quite complex. I have discussed it in detail in my book *Kant's Rational Theology* (Ithaca, N.Y.: Cornell University Press, 1978), pp. 25–63.

7 For a discussion of this proof, see ibid., pp. 64–79.

8 Ibid., pp. 96–100.

9 The analogy between Kant's thesis and emotivism was suggested to me by Nicholas Sturgeon. For further discussion of Kant's thesis about existence and predication, and his critique of the ontological proof, see ibid., pp. 100–23.

10 See my book *Kant's Moral Religion* (Ithaca, N.Y.: Cornell University Press, 1970), pp. 13–17.

11 Ibid., pp. 105–24.

12 Ibid., pp. 124–45.

13 Ibid., ch. 6, esp. pp. 226–48.

14 Pascal, *Pensées* (New York: Scribners, 1958), p. 68.

15 See *Kant's Moral Religion,* ch. 5, esp. pp. 187–200.

16 I am grateful for comments by Frederick C. Beiser on a draft of this essay.

14 The first twenty years of critique: The Spinoza connection

I

Defining the limits of a historical period always entails an element of arbitrariness. There are good reasons, however, for setting the conclusion of the first cycle in the reception of Kant's critical program at August 7, 1799, just under twenty years after the first appearance of the *Critique of Pure Reason*. The date marks the publication of Kant's open letter in which he repudiated Fichte's *Wissenschaftslehre* and other attempts at bringing his transcendental philosophy to completion.[1] His own critical work, which in the *Critique* he had claimed to be only of an introductory nature (A 11 / B 25), he now declared to constitute the system of pure reason itself. From that date onward the very reception of Kant became a problem, itself the subject of interpretation and reception. Moreover, at the end of the *Critique of Pure Reason* Kant had predicted that, following the path laid out by his program, one could "secure for human reason complete satisfaction" in regard to all its metaphysical preoccupations, and that this goal could be achieved "before the end of the present century" (A 856 / B 884). By August 1799 the century was only a few months away from its close, and Kant's open letter was itself testimony to the fact that the prediction was not coming true. The date is a good milestone where to stop and take stock of what had happened in the prior twenty years that led from the sanguine expectations of 1780 to the gloomy retrospect of 1799. Finally, 1799 is when Fichte was being driven away from his position as professor of philosophy at Jena because of charges of atheism – and also, unofficially, because he was suspected of Jacobin leanings.[2] The event marks a clear watershed separating the optimism and open-mindedness of the Enlightenment, of which

Kant's *Critique* was a product, and the reactionary conservativism that had already been setting in for some years and which was to dominate the century to come. After 1799 the cultural and political context made it impossible to read Kant in the same spirit in which he had been received in the twenty years before.

But again, the story of Kant's reception in those first twenty years is a very complex one, and how to tell it also entails an element of arbitrary choice. My aim in this essay is to trace the main line of development that connects the *Critique of Pure Reason* with the metaphysics of the past, yet leads directly to the nineteenth century.[3] To this end I shall have to abstract from many parallel plots that in other contexts would be of great philosophical interest. Spinoza will figure prominently in our story – because he is the great representative of the classical tradition in metaphysics, but for other reasons as well that will become apparent in due time. First I must declare, however, certain presuppositions regarding both the context within which Kant's *Critique* was being received, and the nature of critical thought itself.

II

Classical metaphysics was based on the assumption that truth consists in the conformity of the mind to a supposed "thing in itself." The difficulties to which this assumption gave rise are well known, and equally known is how the critical Kant tried to undercut them by removing the assumption itself. He shifted the axis of the relation in which truth consists from the supposed space separating the thing in itself and the mind to a space within the mind (B xvi ff.). The new assumption is that the thing in itself is indeed present to the mind in experience – not however as it is "in itself," but only in the form of "appearances," in virtue of a process that begins with certain passive (and presumably preconscious) states of mind that we call affections or sensations. Knowledge proper is achieved in the subsequent conscious active reproduction by the mind of these states, through a variety of representations that connect them together in the forms of particular determinations of objects whose only reality consists precisely in *appearing* in these determinations (A 50–2 / B 74–6).[4] Such objects are "things" only with reference to us – things of appearance, in other words, rather than things in themselves. Truth in regard to them depends on whether the mind's reflective reconstructions of their being correspond to what is actually exhibited piecemeal in sensation. And since at issue in the reconstructions is the logic and the forms of the presence of an object to the mind – not its being "in itself" – their adequacy can be tested without having to step outside the bounds of experience, as one would have to on the old definition of truth. The idea of the thing in itself is retained, but only as an empty logical space, with reference to which we can keep apart and thereby reconcile otherwise contradictory reflective interpretations of the immediate content of experience (B xxvi–xxviii; A 259 / B 315). Philosophy is redefined accordingly. Its function is not to arrive at entities, or properties of entities, not directly accessible to experience by means of an intricate process of inference, but rather to continue and complete a process of reflection which is part and parcel of all experience. Philosophy's ultimate task is to define precisely the conditions that make experience possible (A 3–5 / B 6–9).

I must stress that, by thus redefining the concept of truth and the task of philosophy, Kant by no means abandoned the classical requirement that science – philosophy in particular – be systematic. On the contrary, he clearly reasserted that ideal. As he says at the conclusion of the *Critique of Pure Reason,*

As regards those who adopt a *scientific* method, they have the choice of proceeding either *dogmatically* [in the manner of Wolff] or *sceptically* [in the manner of David Hume]; but in any case they have the obligation to proceed *systematically*.   (A 856 / B 884)[5]

Nor did Kant modify the architectonics of classical metaphysics. The world, soul, and God are still the pivotal ideas around which the system of knowledge is to be organized. The crucial difference, of course, is that the system is no longer taken to be mirroring a supposed internal unity within the thing in itself. It is now explicitly recognized for what it is, namely the product of the tendency on the part of reflection to achieve completeness. Its unity is a unity of experience rather than the image of a reality transcending it; its ideas, objectifications of the conditions of the reflective unity of consciousness rather than representations of items, so to speak, with an existence of their own (A 327 / B 383 ff.).

However, just because the new critical philosophy inextricably bound truth to reflectivity, it does not follow that it reduced the criteria of truth to the requirements of reflection. Representation through imagination, conceptualization, and idealization does not per se assure that what is thereby brought to reflective consciousness is in fact *given* in experience. Truth requires an existential touchstone, which is provided precisely by measuring reflection against the immediate content of experience. Hence Kant's insistence that there is no knowledge without sense intuition. The senses are the only source of the immediate, existential, element of experience, without which the very notion of truth has no meaning.[6]

For the critical Kant, in other words, the question of truth came down to an issue of the relation in knowledge of intuition to reflection, immediate to reconstructed experience. And to the extent that it posed the question in these terms, the new critical philosophy was drawing inspiration from the mainstream culture of the day. Few periods of history have been as complex – politically, socially, and intellectually – as the one in which critique was born. Yet, if there was a theme that ran through and unified all aspects of the sociophilosophical discourse in the German-speaking lands as well as outside, it was precisely that of the opposition in experience of reflection to intuition, reason to faith. Paradoxically, in an age that gave so much importance to science and reason, the widespread belief was that the reflectivity of reason had somehow upset a more primitive, yet healthier and truer, intuitive relation of man to nature. Though actively pursued in all areas of human endeavor, reason and its works remained suspect nonetheless, as somehow falsifying a more fundamental truth that only the immediacy of feeling and faith could provide. The malaise that affected society at large was directly connected with the disequilibrium that reflection had brought to the otherwise natural balance of human existence.[7] At the end of the century Hölderlin was to give the poetic expression to this theme of lost innocence that influenced Hegel. But long before Hölderlin's *Hyperion* (1797–9),[8] the theme had received its paradigmatic statement from J. J. Winckelman in his *Gedanken über die Nachahmung der Griechischen Werke* (*Thoughts on the Imitation of Greek Works*) (1755).[9] Kant's critical work was itself a contribution to the debate on the theme. And as we shall see, Kant's contemporaries received it precisely in this spirit.

Yet, it is on this very issue of the relation of reflection to intuition that Kant was to present his contemporaries with the most serious difficulty. The pieces of his new system were all put in place only gradually, some of them not before *Religion within the Boundaries of*

Unaided Reason of 1793 and the *Metaphysics of Morals* of 1797. The difficulty was, however, present from the beginning, and had to do with the transition in his account of experience from intuition to reflection. Kant clearly wanted to keep intuition as the final determining factor of knowledge. True knowledge consists in the conceptual representation of an object actually *given* in sense intuition. It was not clear, however, how he could express the conformity of reflective representation to actual intuition without doing so *reflectively* – that is, without assuming as given what is only taken to be given. The difficulty was felt all the more acutely with respect to judgments of existence, where it counted most.[10] In other words, the same problem now faced Kant that had also faced the dogmatic metaphysicians in their attempts to grasp the "thing in itself." The difference is that it now erupted within experience, in the interplay between immediacy and reflection.

Kant had staked the whole success of his critique of reason on the assumption of a strict distinction between the concepts of the "understanding," which he claimed to be intuitively demonstrable, and the purely systemic idea of reason. This is precisely the distinction that he found difficult to maintain. As I have said, the difficulty was manifest from the beginning. Solomon Maimon was the first to detect it, but others made capital of it as well.[11] In the *Critique of Judgment* (1790) Kant himself conceded it quite unwittingly, in a series of paragraphs (§§ 75–8) that Schelling (who was an acute commentator of the age) was later to single out as especially rich in philosophical content.[12] Kant's point in those paragraphs (especially §§ 76–7) is plain enough. It is the function of the understanding to comprehend "real wholes of nature," a function that it discharges by subsuming the particulars in the manifold of nature under the universal by means of concepts and laws. However, for *human* understanding "the particular is not determined by the universal and cannot be derived from it."[13] Hence, although necessary in principle, its accordance with it is in fact "very contingent and without definite principle as concerns the judgement."[14] In an attempt to overcome this contingency, we introduce as principle of subsumption precisely the idea of the whole to be comprehended. This idea is, however, an empty intention that only reflects the requirement on the part of reason to achieve totality of experience. It acquires content only in virtue of the particulars that it helps to bring under laws. Now, what is remarkable about these claims is that although Kant still wants to maintain that truth is only achieved in particular judgments of experience, their clear implication is that no such judgments can ever be made *with necessity* without the mediation of the very systemic intentions that ought to depend for their truth on the particular judgments. But if the idealizing function of reason affects the modality of these judgments, it follows that the system itself is left floating without an existential point of support. As Jacobi was to say, Kant "wanted to underpin reason with the understanding [with its supposed sense-basis], and then pin the understanding on reason."[15]

This difficulty was reflected in an ambiguity that affected the critical project at its foundation. It lay in Kant's attitude toward reason. On the one hand there is no doubt that for Kant reason still reigns supreme in the edifice of knowledge. Its supremacy is due to its power of reflection that makes it the ultimate judge of the validity of any claim to knowledge. Everything is to be brought to its tribunal, reason included.[16] "Critique" is itself the product of reason. On the other hand, in the same section of the *Critique of Judgment* just referred to Kant also tells us that the discursiveness of the human understanding is due to its dependence on the senses – that for an intuitive understanding the very idea of a teleology of nature would make no sense at all. I quote the significant texts in full, because they will be normative for all the immediate followers of Kant:

We must at the same time think of another understanding, by reference to which and apart from any purpose ascribed to it, we may represent as *necessary* that accordance of natural laws with our judgment, which for our understanding is only thinkable through the medium of purposes. . . .[17]

Thus there would be, although incognizable by us, a supersensible real ground of nature [i.e., the thing in itself]. . . . In this we consider according to mechanical laws what is necessary in nature regarded as an object of sense. . . .[18]

Discursiveness is, however, a function of reason. Hence, to say that with reference to an ideal understanding that intuits reality per se it would disappear, is tantamount to saying that the whole realm of reason is in fact only an illusion. But this is precisely what Kant is saying, and the consequences – especially for his moral philosophy, which depends for its validity on reason alone – are disastrous. Kant wanted indeed to retain a place in his system for faith – but a limited place, one clearly delineated by reason. If, however, the whole domain of reason may turn out to be just an illusion, that we should accept it as normative in the first place requires an act of faith. Rather than reason embracing faith, it is faith that ends up now controlling reason. One can say of Kant's reason what Jacobi was to say of the "thing in itself": "[W]ithout that presupposition I could not enter into the system, but with it I could not stay within it."[19]

Such are the difficulties and ambiguities that Kant presented his contemporaries. The mention of Jacobi is important because, as it happens, his *Letters concerning the Doctrine of Spinoza* was published in 1785,[20] four years after the first edition of the *Critique of Pure Reason*, and two years before the second edition. The book was an instant success. It caught the imagination of the literary public and served to remold the current intuition versus reflection debate around the figure of Spinoza. Goethe, whose poem *Prometheus* was first made public by Jacobi in the book as the occasion for Lessing's alleged profession of Spinozism, was in retrospect to describe the events that followed thereupon as an "explosion."[21] The key figures in the first reception of Kant had all read Jacobi, and reacted to the tensions and ambiguities in Kant's critical system with Jacobi's central theses in mind. This circumstance, as I want to show, proved significant for the shape that post-Kantian idealism was to take.

III

This is not the place to document the circumstances under which Jacobi published his *Letters to Moses Mendelssohn concerning the Doctrine of Spinoza* (1785), or the controversy that followed upon it.[22] At any rate, when the book came out, it gave ample evidence that Jacobi had an intimate and accurate knowledge of Spinoza's philosophy – unlike his contemporaries whose acquaintance with it was for the most part by hearsay.[23] It also revealed a complex attitude toward Spinoza, whom he both revered as the greatest philosopher ever, yet decried as the worst corrupter of the human mind. Jacobi's critique of Spinoza was actually intended as a critique of *all* philosophy. It is as if Jacobi felt obliged to defend Spinoza passionately on rational grounds for the sake of rejecting philosophy on the strength of true belief.

In an age of wordy authors, Jacobi was an especially prolix writer. Yet his central theses can be stated briefly.²⁴ The function of reason is to "re-present", through images and concepts, a reality that we must assume as already present to us directly. Knowledge through reason is therefore only second-hand acquaintance – at best "recognition" rather than cognition.²⁵ It follows that rational "knowledge" (if we can call it such), or "science," is a step-by-step regression from one representation of reality to another, along a path that might indeed skirt the intended reality but never touches it. Moreover, because the ground of the bond connecting any two representations lies outside them in the supposed reality, the picture of the world that thus emerges through the representations is necessarily a mechanistic one. It is held together by purely external relations.²⁶ There is no room within it for subjectivity – that is, freedom and spontaneity. A subject who thinks of itself as part of this picture acquires the same distance with respect to its own activities as separates any representation and its intended reality. It must become an observer of its own presumed acts – a pure object unto itself and no longer a subject.²⁷

There were several reasons for Jacobi's fascination with Spinoza. First, more clearly than anyone before him Spinoza had recognized that truth is ultimately its own criterion.²⁸ The apprehension of the Absolute cannot be achieved through any process of ratiocination but must be original and intuitive. This is a thesis with which Jacobi agreed wholeheartedly. But, second, Spinoza had been the victim of the metaphysical tradition in that he had tried to express his intuitively apprehended truth reflectively, through the concept of substance. In this he offered the perfect example of the counterfeit that all philosophy is. Spinoza had failed to see that the universality and necessity of conceptualization is achieved through abstraction. The more universal and necessary a concept, therefore, the greater its distance from reality. Substance, which is the highest concept possible, can only express empty identity – an extreme point of objectification that utterly falsifies the insight into the dynamic and subjective nature of reality with which Spinoza had actually begun.²⁹ Spinoza had been guilty of the original sin of which philosophy is the offspring. Third, once he had made his error, Spinoza had had the intellectual courage of drawing conclusions from it consistently. For this he drew Jacobi's admiration. There is no double-talk in Spinoza (as there is in Herder)[30] about God's personality and God's freedom. God has neither understanding nor purpose. It is sheer power that acts blindly just for the sake of acting, and as it acts the infinite chains of mechanical and logical necessity unfold before our eyes. Purpose and choice, whether on God's side or ours, are just an illusion due to our limited viewpoint.[31] Nor is there an explanation why such chains of necessary finite determinations should appear at all, for every alleged explanation would already presuppose the finite standpoint of these determinations and hence fall short of the sheer indeterminacy or pure identity in which God's being consists. The finite universe is just an illusory display of infinite substance.[32] In the eyes of reason, which is itself part of the display, *that* the universe occurs at all is ultimately a brute fact – the sort that must be dealt with practically just because it is impregnable to theory.

The remarkable thing is that rationality and its products fared the same both when considered from the point of view of Spinoza's God and on the assumption of Kant's "intuitive understanding." In both cases they turn out to be an illusionary phenomenon. Jacobi was later to drive this point home explicitly against Fichte.[33] But so far as it bore upon the nature of philosophy, he had already made it in his controversy with Mendelssohn. Philosophical reason ultimately turns against itself because, by confusing its own abstractions for the real, it becomes incapable of understanding itself. It becomes an irrational phenomenon in its own eyes. Philosophy breeds irrationalism; it is essentially "nihilistic."[34]

Even more remarkable is that in spite of obvious differences, the similarity between Jacobi's and Kant's critique of reason is at times striking. Both men were denying autonomy to reason, and both argued that when left to its own resources it inevitably leads to illusions. With his usual perspicacity Jacobi had even accurately detected where Spinoza's position, Kant's, and his own, met. And that was in the claim that existence is prior to the reflection of thought. As a young man Jacobi had already detected the affinity on the occasion of the publication of *The Only Possible Ground for a Demonstration of the Existence of God*, an essay in which Kant had sought the ground of all possibilities in God's existence.[35] Jacobi was later to recall his reading of the essay as an event laden with emotion.[36] But Kant had then betrayed his own intuition by seeking to establish the existential basis of his system in what

Jacobi considered a pseudo-subjectivity – itself the product of reflection.[37] Jacobi himself had eventually opted for a straightforward realism instead, the kind that we all assume practically. Fortunately we are not just theoretical beings, but moral subjects as well. And in action, through the feelings that accompany it, a whole world is intuitively revealed to us.[38] Since "knowledge" is normally reserved for the products of reason and ratiocination, Jacobi's inclination was to call such intuitive apprehension of reality "faith."[39]

In response to critics, Jacobi even tried at one point to defend this use of the term by appealing to the authority of Hume,[40] but only succeeded (in my opinion) in confusing the issue. At any rate, whether the use of the term was justified or not, the important point is that in faith reality is revealed as irreducibly individual, in direct opposition to the universalizing function of conceptualization. The most fundamental distinctions running through it are those between one subject and another (the "I"and the "Thou"), between a subject and nature, and between the finite "I" and the infinite "Thou" of God.[41] All meaning rests on these distinctions. To deny them is to run up against the absurd – which is precisely what reason does the moment it cuts itself loose from faith. In point of fact reason presupposes faith as its starting point and the matrix within which alone it can function. True knowledge is rhapsodic rather than systematic, descriptive rather than explanatory, or (versus Kant) psychological rather than transcendental.[42] To use Jacobi's most trenchant formula, "philosophy is history."[43]

It is this view of knowledge, grounded in faith, that Jacobi had been trying to force on Mendelssohn since his first letter to him of November 4, 1783, and Mendelssohn could not understand.[44] The correspondence was eventually published in 1785 and, as I have said, it made quite an impact among the contemporaries. When the second edition of the Critique appeared in 1787, the most important changes and additions made to the first edition (notable among them a new Transcendental Deduction and a new Refutation of Idealism) were obviously intended by Kant in response to the charges of psychological subjectivism brought against him in the Feder–Garve review.[45] Yet in the new Preface one can also hear echoes of the Jacobi–Mendelssohn dispute. Although Jacobi is not mentioned by name, the point being made is clear. Whereas Jacobi was destroying "reason" for the sake of

defending "faith," Kant was only *limiting* it and thereby making
room for faith as well (B xxx). Against the *Schwärmerei* of those who
would want to replace the objectivity of science with the subjectivity
of feeling, Kant now pays his respects to Wolff and his tradition by
reaffirming the indispensability of a "thoroughly grounded metaphysics." Kant's intention is not to destroy metaphysics, but only to re-
build it on a new critical basis [B xxxv–xxxvii].

IV

The possibility of exploiting the community of themes in Kant and
Jacobi had however already occurred to others – witness Karl Leonhard Reinhold, whose famous *Letters concerning the Kantian Philosophy* of 1786–7[46] (not to be confused with the much revised and
enlarged version of 1790–2)[47] are widely acknowledged as responsible for the first wide acceptance of the *Critique*.[48]

Reinhold's intentions in the *Letters* are explicit enough. He wants
to show how Kant's critical thought offers a middle ground between
the two extremes of pure faith and pure reason represented by Jacobi
on the one side and Mendelssohn on the other.[49] Not as explicit, but
not any the less clear for that, is how much he relies on Jacobi for the
development of his thesis. Jacobi held that true philosophy always
responds to the needs of an age, and hence finds universal acceptance as a matter of course.[50] Reinhold was now claiming that Kant's
Critique was the natural response to the contemporary crisis of reason and metaphysics. The Protestant Reformation had once defined
itself by the right that it accorded reason to be the ultimate judge in
matters of religious faith. But now that the main battles against
prejudice and superstition had been won, and a spirit of tolerance
had descended upon the land, doubts about its relevance had cropped
up everywhere. The main issue was the extent to which reason
could be said to make a real contribution in matters of religious
concerns, particularly whether it could establish the existence of
God. There were those who claimed that faith is its own guarantee
of truth, and that it has therefore no need of reason. As a matter of
fact, reason can even be dangerous to the cause of faith and good
morals. Pantheism and fatalism are among its notorious offspring.
Others argued instead that without the discipline of reason faith
degenerates into fanaticism. Between the two sides, playing both

against the middle, skepticism thrived. Many took this situation as one of impending catastrophe. Reinhold interpreted it positively instead as the sign that a cultural revolution was in the making. Now that reason was being subjected to the tension of the two most extreme claims about its vocation, it had no choice but to turn upon itself and question in earnest its nature and its capacities. This is precisely what Kant's critique of reason accomplished. Kant's work was the timely response to the problem of an age – the vehicle through which a new culture was being born.[51]

Jacobi had preached the virtue of a "non-knowledge" (*Nichtwissen*) that had nothing to do with skepticism but only sought to recognize the limits of knowledge.[52] Reinhold interprets Kant's "nonknowledge" in a similar vein. It is not the casting of an undifferentiated doubt upon the possibility of knowledge in general, but the precise delineation of what reason can hope to know theoretically. But it thereby reveals another source of evidence, namely the feelings and expectations that a moral man entertains in the pursuit of his moral perfection. This is the evidence that men have in fact always relied on (in virtue of their "common sense," *gesunder Verstand*) for their belief in God. The time has now come for philosophical reason to recognize it officially as the basis of *its* argumentations about God and the supranatural. Reason objectifies the evidence that feelings provide by conceptualizing it.[53]

Finally, according to Jacobi true knowledge is imbued with religious piety. Reinhold now considered Kant's reconciliation of feeling with reflection such a revolutionary achievement that he even drew a parallel (implicitly at least) between Jesus Christ and Immanuel Kant.[54] Just as Christianity led religious belief to moral practice through the medium of a purified heart, so Kant was now leading morality back to religion through critique of reason. The religion of pure reason (with its ideas about God and the supranatural) stands to Christianity (or, which is the same thing, the religion of pure heart) as moral theory stands to moral praxis. The issue is not whether moral theory is a chapter of theology, as one school of thought would have it; or, according to the opposite school, theology a chapter of moral theory. Rather, just as the one is the conceptual expression of certain feelings, so the other is the conceptual expression of a certain praxis. But because the feelings are necessarily connected with the praxis, one cannot have a complete theory of the feelings (theology) without a complete theory of the praxis (moral theory). And the reverse holds as well.[55]

Reinhold's *Kantian Letters* were an instant success. They conveyed in essence a simple message:

In the ground of moral cognition the critique of reason gives theology a first principle such as metaphysics [i.e., the theoretical discipline] could never give to it. . . . And so . . . the notions that ontology, cosmology, and physico-theology supply to the system of pure theology finally obtain content, cohesion, and complete determination.[56]

The consequence, which did not go unnoticed by the school theologians, was that nothing of the old dogmatic system needed be lost once the new source of evidence was identified. Schelling is our witness to this turn of events. In January 5, 1795, writing from his Tübingen seminary, he was to complain to Hegel bitterly:

Here there are Kantians in droves. . . . All imaginable dogmas have been stamped as postulates of practical reason, and wherever theoretical and historical proofs are lacking, the practical Tübingian reason cuts the knot. . . . Before you know it, the *deus ex machina* pops up, the personal individual *being who sits up there in heaven!*[57]

As for Reinhold, spurred on by his success and the requirements of his new position as professor of Kantian philosophy at the University of Jena, he undertook the task of reshaping Kant's critique of reason in such a way that it would become unquestionably acceptable (*geltend*) to everyone.[58] His starting point was the question: Granted that a timely philosophy ought to be accepted by everyone as a matter of course, why was it that Kant's critique of reason, which (as Reinhold believed) answered the needs of the time, had fallen on deaf ears? The question was clearly inspired by Jacobi. For the reply, however, Reinhold now turned to Kant, in direct opposition to Jacobi. Science is by nature systematic, as both Kant and Jacobi knew. But whereas for Jacobi systematization meant that science was an organized kind of ignorance,[59] for Kant it is what confirmed its evidence. But Kant had failed to give systematic form to his own philosophy. He had failed to make explicit the one principle upon which the whole structure of his critique of reason rested. This failure, according to Reinhold, is what accounted for his other failure to win acceptance from his contemporaries. Accordingly Reinhold set out to turn Kant's critique of reason into genuine systematic science in what came to be known as his *Elementarphilosophie.* Just as Jacobi had said that all science is based on representation,[60] so now Reinhold took representation as the basic fact of all consciousness, and the concept of representation as the principle of all philosophy. But whereas for Jacobi science was essentially falsifying *because* it depended on representation, Reinhold now set out to establish its truth on the basis of it – above all to demonstrate apodictically, as Kant had not done, that the "thing in itself" must exist even though we have no knowledge of what it is.

Kant himself felt uneasy about Reinhold's effort. As it happened, its effects were catastrophic so far as the acceptance of the *Critique* was concerned.[61] Reinhold's book precipitated the anonymous publication of *Aenesidemus,* an extended essay in which the author (G. E. Schulze) effectively defended the skepticism of Hume against both Kant and Reinhold.[62] Schulze reiterated and expanded Jacobi's criticism of the "thing in itself." More significant still, he methodically demonstrated that, even within the sphere of the phenomenal, at no point had either Kant or Reinhold shown that their *a priori* conceptual structures actually applied to the content of experience. And Schulze went on to conclude that all that critical philosophy actually amounted to was empty formalism, a charge against which all the pretenders to Kant's succession felt obliged from then on to defend themselves.

This result should not have been surprising. In his naiveté, by countering Jacobi's objections to science with Kant's critique of reason, Reinhold had in fact failed to understand both. He had failed to see the point on which Kant and Jacobi agreed and that put them both squarely on the side of the skeptics, namely that the distance between reflection and existence cannot be bridged reflectively. It does not help, therefore, to identify new sources of existential evidence for the arguments of reason. In all cases, whether it is drawn from feelings, sensations, or elsewhere, the question still remains as to whether, when conceptualized as the premise for an argument, the supposed evidence still has the same existential value as the source from which it is drawn. On this score Schulze's attack had definitely found a target in Reinhold's new *Elementarphilosophie,* and to the extent that in Kant's *Critique* the exercise of the understanding still depended on the reflection of reason, it touched him too. Jacobi had already made the point, before Schulze and without reference to either Kant or Reinhold, when he defended Spinoza for not allowing any transition between the infinite series of finite modes and substance. Both from the standpoint of reflection (which gives rise to the endless series of finite perspectives) and that of absolute existence, the *beginning* itself of reflection is not rationally explicable. In confronting Jacobi with Kant Reinhold had failed to notice precisely the Spinoza connection.

V

It did not escape others however. The *Kantian Letters* had been written without the benefit of the *Critique of Practical Reason*, which was published in 1788, and it is likely that Reinhold's construction of the role of religion in morality was influenced by Kant's own rather naive observations on the subject at the end of the *Critique of Pure Reason*.[63] Quite a different construction would have been required by anyone who had understood (as Reinhold had not) that, short of conceding the day to Jacobi, "God" could not mean the same thing in Kant's metaphysics as it did in scholastic rationalism. The point should have been apparent even with the first *Critique*, but with the second it became compelling. What was required was a more explicit understanding of the function of reason and its ideas within a critical interpretation of experience. As it happened, the innovative move in this direction was made in 1792 (before Schulze's attack) in a book that did not bear the name of the author in its first edition and many at first mistook as the work of Kant. The title of the book was *Versuch einer Critik aller Offenbarung* (*Attempt at a Critique of All Revelation*), and its real author a hitherto unknown Johann Gottlieb Fichte.[64]

The book is written in the transcendental style inaugurated by Kant. It is dedicated to the *a priori* deduction of the idea of a revelation, such as can be derived from the principles of practical reason in abstraction from the content of any historical religion.[65] Presupposed is a distinction between "theology" and "religion." Theology becomes religion when its theoretical propositions about God, the soul, and the world bear practical results in the determination of the will. As theoretical instruments the propositions have no practical consequence, for as such they only express assumptions made for conceptual purposes alone without reference to the requirements of moral existence. Before being capable of determining our will in any respect, the propositions must be subjected to the influence of a moral interest in general for which the will alone is responsible. Once this interest has been established, the propositions can then be used as instruments for generating such particular attitudes in us as the fear of the Lord, reverence, and the like, all of which have moral significance. At this point theology becomes religion.[66]

The influence, however, that theological ideas have on our will varies according as they relate to the two sides of our moral constitution – namely, the sensuous and the intellectual.[67] We can revere God as the creator of nature and the guarantor that the natural happiness of each individual will be commensurate to the individual's moral righteousness. Or we can revere God as the author, through his will, of the very natural laws that allow nature to conform to our transcendent moral ends. Now, religion in its most proper sense arises when the moral law brings with it the added weight of being accepted as God's commandment.

Or finally [theological ideas] have immediate effect upon our will because of the added weight that the [moral] Commandment has by being a Commandment of God; it is then that religion in its *most proper* sense arises.[68]

The concept of revelation is directly connected with this sense of religion. God, as the creator of nature, can also manifest himself to us as the author of the moral law inasmuch as He proclaims himself as such through his causality in the world of the senses.

The concept of revelation is the concept of an effect produced by God in the world of the senses through supernatural causality, in virtue of which he announces himself as the Giver of the Law.[69]

Now, there is nothing in all of this that cannot be found at least implicitly in Kant's doctrine on religion, except for one point that, taken with its two consequences, mark the transition from Kantian critique to post-Kantian idealism. The point is the new importance that Fichte attributes to "pure will" as the faculty of unconditional spontaneous activity. Kant had based moral obligation on the self-legislative nature of practical reason which, when defined in terms of its efficacy, he called "will." But his formula left it open whether it is rationality that constitutes the efficacy of the will or the other way around.[70] In Fichte's discussion of the possibility of revelation it is now clear that it is the power of the will (whether it be God's will or the pure will in us) that first gives rise to morality – that is, to rationality itself.

Two consequences follow. The first is that, since the will's spontaneity transcends the distinctions of moral reason (for morality is only a product of it) one can legitimately ask why we should attribute the law to God and not to the will itself. Fichte's answer is that, materially speaking – that is, so far as the content of moral obligation is concerned – the law is to be attributed to the will in general. But the latter is equally present in every moral being (God included, to the extent that He too is a moral being). Whether the law is therefore presented as the product of man's moral agency, or God's, is a purely formal question. It has to do with *how* the law is promulgated.[71] And because it is clear that the individual man is first motivated by the law because of the will in him, and he would not be able to recognize the same law as promulgated by God without this original motivation, it follows that God (the supposed author of the law and the object of religious worship) has significance for him only because He is an objective projection of his own subjective commitment to morality.

The idea of God (the Giver of Law through the moral law in us) is based on an externalization [*Entäusserung*] of our moral law, by the projection [*Übertragung*] of something subjective in us into a Being outside us; and this projection is the specific principle of a religion instrumental in the determination of the will.[72]

In the century to follow, this notion of religion as an objective projection of a subjective state became canonical for the Young Hegelians (who actually were much more Fichtean then Hegelian). Here we have it explicitly and unequivocally formulated in Fichte's earliest writing, as the first consequence of the asserted primacy of praxis over theory.

The second consequence emerges in response to a further question. Why should the moral individual ever want to project the source of morality that lies within him outside, in a God who is first conceived only as the creator of nature? Or in other words, if the moral law is already within us, and must be there in order for any of its external manifestations to be recognized by us, why should we ever believe in a divine revelation of the same law? why should we ever need any such revelation? Fichte's answer is that revelation has to do with *consciousness* of the law. To *be* a moral being, however, and to *know* oneself to be one, is for practical purposes one and the same thing. Whatever is required for our knowledge of the law is therefore also required for our moral existence. But since we are not just "pure will," but beings of nature as well, the process by which we acquire moral self-consciousness must also be part of nature. And since God is the creator of nature, he must also be responsible for constituting it in such a way that in it we acquire the self-consciousness required for moral life. In this sense God can be said to reveal the law, and the concept of "revelation" is thereby justified.[73]

Fichte's new strategy is clear. It capitalizes on the primacy of existence and intuition over reflection, and on the limitations inherent to reflection, that Kant had already exploited. The difference is that for Fichte it is now clear that the limitations of reflection are essential conditions of all consciousness – not just *human* consciousness – and that existence and intuition must therefore be subjected to them if there is to be any articulated knowledge of them. Thus, although Fichte seems to give new importance to the intuitive moment of experience – indeed, he eventually claimed that we actually have the intellectual intuition that Kant had assumed only as a logical possibility – he is in fact doing away with the myth of an intellect that would have knowledge of the thing in itself without being subject to the limitations of human consciousness that conditions Kant's whole analysis of experience. In this sense, Fichte is actually giving new importance to reflection.[74] After all, *that* one acts and hence exists, and *that* there is an immediate awareness of this existence, is obvious in the very moment of action. And this is all that Fichte will mean by intellectual intuition.[75] But the problem is to determine *what* the active existent is – *what* the anonymous awareness that accompanies any action is the awareness *of* – and for that one needs reflection over and above intuition. An act conscious of itself as act requires, over and above the act itself, a series of secondary reflective acts that transform it into an externalized thing: an object. These particular acts in turn become the objects of further reflections, and so on *ad infinitum*. The eventual result is the emergence of an ideal world of objects, each limiting the rest with its actual or possible presence, and facing this world a subject that both limits it and is limited by it. The *intention* animating the objects, and the subject confronting them, is indeed to represent the original act. But since they are all equally the product of reflection, and reflection is by nature abstractive, they are in fact always posited at a distance from it and as such bound in the end to fail in their intent. This is, however, a necessary limitation of all consciousness (as I have just said) and also the condition to which the original undifferentiated act (which we ex post facto interpret as an act of freedom) must submit in order to become actually conscious of itself. The act must be represented at a distance from itself, so to speak, or projected outside itself. It follows that the connection between the act and its supposed representation or system of representations, although a by-product (so to speak) of the act itself and immediately present to the awareness that accompanies it, necessarily escapes representation. The certainty that we enjoy about it presupposes an existential commitment on our part that transcends the limits of objectivity. It requires faith, in other words, and in this sense *all* knowledge is essentially revelatory. Further, since the greatest distance between an act and its representation – the most perfect objectification – is achieved when the act is experienced as a thing of nature, the whole dynamism of knowledge is directed to interpreting nature precisely as the appearance of acts once freely performed but forgotten in the process of objectification. Nature is the external manifestation of freedom; feeling, the first incarnate awareness of it.[76]

Fichte's *Kritik aller Offenbarung* is significant, not just because it reduces the dynamics of religious revelation to those of objectification in general but because, in doing this, it turns all objectification into a process of revelation. Thus Fichte accepts as a fact of experience the primacy of faith over reflection to which Kant was being pushed by the logic of his critique of reason but which he failed to recognize. In 1794–5, when Fichte produced the first version of his *Wissenschaftslehre* under pressure from the requirements of his new position as the successor to Reinhold at the chair of Kantian philosophy in Jena, the form of the new philosophy reflects the influence of Fichte's long meditations on Reinhold's *Elementarphilosophie* and Aenesidemus's critique of it.[77] Yet the strategy of his new system is still the same as the one inchoate in *Kritik aller Offenbarung*. Sensation and feeling, far from being the amorphous content of consciousness that Kant made them out to be, are complex events that already entail a moment of objectification.[78]

They need interpreting, in other words, and hence cannot provide the existential point of support for the system of reflective thought that Kant expected from them. That point has to be found instead in the immediate awareness of one's existence that accompanies action and the moral faith into which that awareness translates itself. As for the constructs of reason, they are now for Fichte instruments of real knowledge – not because they are any less subjective for him than they were for Kant, but because *all* knowledge is for Fichte interpretation. It consists in an effort to express reflectively an intuition that, by its very nature, constantly escapes it. It is as if Fichte were intent on giving all to reflection in order to give it then back to faith. With Jacobi he could have said that faith is the matrix of all knowledge – that "We are all born in the faith, and we must remain in the faith, just as we are all born in society, and must remain in society."[79] And just as Reinhold had looked upon Kant as the mediator in the dispute between Jacobi and Mendelssohn, so he could now consider himself as standing between Kant and Jacobi.

Yet the similarities were only superficial. In actual fact Fichte had come perilously close to the very Spinoza whom Jacobi had made his vocation to save the mind from.

VI

Fichte had always expressed admiration for Jacobi, whom he once called the "profoundest thinker of our time."[80] And there were indeed enough *prima facie* affinities between the two, such as their common emphasis on action and faith, that when in 1799 Fichte found himself under suspicion of atheism, he could in all sincerity appeal to "noble Jacobi" as one philosopher who could understand him.[81] The truth that Jacobi knew in *lived experience* was the same as he, Fichte, was giving voice to speculatively through the artifice of reflection. Such was Fichte's claim. For his part, however, Jacobi wanted nothing of it.[82] And how could he? When *he* spoke of faith, he meant an immediate certainty regarding such personally important realities as the world outside us, other individuals, freedom, and Providence. In his eyes, Fichte's faith could be no more than a state of mind artificially induced in order to make up for the failure on the part of reason to retrieve its own existence reflectively. It was reason's heroic effort at pulling itself out of the irrationalism to which it is finally led by its own insane attempt at transforming all existence into a product of reflection.

Jacobi found nothing particularly mysterious about Kant's categorical imperative or, for that matter, Fichte's assertion of the "I is I."[83] In both cases we have an extreme yet simple expression of reason's desire to assert itself as the beginning and end of all things – a "logical enthusiasm," a pride of reason, that ultimately leads to reason's own destruction.[84] Hence the strange claims that one hears about an infinite freedom that spurns determination (as if there could be an action in general), or a subjectivity that does not belong to any individual in particular.[85] None of this made any sense to Jacobi. What he found significant, however, was the fact that he had been able to find his way into Fichte's system only by way of Spinoza's *Ethics*.[86] Spinoza's substance plays in Spinoza's system the same role as Fichte's "I" plays in Fichte's. Both are examples of the attempt at building a system using as foundation reflection *as such*. But of course, since the perfect fluidity of absolute reflection shuns all determination, in Fichte's system just as much as in Spinoza's it is impossible to express conceptually the transition from the absolute foundation to the world of real individuals. Hence the latter is interpreted as a mere *epiphenomenon*, which, in the case of Fichte, is invested with the meaning of a manifestation of freedom only through an act of moral faith. But Jacobi also warned Fichte that the same fluidity of thought could support a materialistic interpretation of nature just as well. Spinoza had again shown great wisdom in arguing for two parallel constructions of the Absolute – one according to the attribute of extension, and the other according to that of thought.[87]

As it happened, events were justifying Jacobi's charge that the new idealism born of Kant's critique of reason was only a form of Spinozism. Take for instance the young Schelling, who had just appeared on the literary scene with a flair and enthusiasm all his own. He *sounded* as if he were simply reiterating Fichte. Yet, from the beginning Schelling had criticized the idea of a *moral* God on the ground that it dissipated the aesthetic moment of experience – the "divine in art."[88] His criticism was obviously directed at the scholastic interpreters of Kant. But it also had its implications for Fichte's strict subordination of contemplation to *praxis*. Schelling favored a more aesthetic approach instead. Nature was not to be looked at as just a negative limit, an irrational yet necessary surd that only serves to make us aware of the absolute freedom in us. It is the place rather where we find our freedom already realized; the beauty of its forms attests to the fact.[89] The Spinozistic overtones of the claim were obvious, and Schelling did not fail to make them explicit:

The *first* who, with complete clarity, saw mind and matter as one, thought and extension simply as modifications of the same principle, was *Spinoza*. His system was the first bold outline of a creative imagination, which conceived the finite immediately in the idea of the infinite, purely as such, and recognized the former only in the latter. . . .[90]

But Spinoza shaped his system in the most unintelligible form possible. For on his terms one would have to transfer oneself to the standpoint of Absolute Substance in order to be able to comprehend how and why thought and extension are originally one.

[I]nstead of descending into the depths of his self-consciousness and descrying the emergence thence of the two worlds in us – the ideal and the real – he passed himself by; instead of explaining from our nature how finite and infinite, originally united in us, proceed originally from each other, he lost himself forthwith in the idea of an infinite outside us. . . .[91]

Idealism delves deep into self-consciousness instead, in order to retrieve and express conceptually the very point at which, through a reflective act originating in freedom, a Self is first established, and opposite to it a Nature which is its objective counterpart. It was exactly as Jacobi said. The new philosophy represented an impossible attempt at retrieving reflectively the *fact* of existence. The result was a new Spinozistic view of the universe, not any the less impervious to the presence of genuine individuality for its being arrived at by way of a Kantian detour into subjectivity.

And if Schelling's *Philosophy of Nature* was not enough, Jacobi could have pointed for further evidence to Schelling's discussion of the nature of *Willkür* (*liberum arbitrium*, free choice) in Vol. VII of the *Philosophisches Journal* (1797).[92] Kant had recognized (rather belatedly, a cynic might say) that for all his talk about right and wrong, his moral theory lacked an adequate idea of a moral subject. Reason certainly cannot be said to be either moral or immoral, for as *pure* reason it simply acts out the requirements of rationality spontaneously. It does neither right nor wrong; it simply acts. The same applies to nature, although for directly opposite reasons. In *Religion within the Boundaries of Unaided Reason* (1793; 2d ed. 1794),[93] and again in the *Metaphysics of Morals* (1797),[94] Kant had therefore introduced the idea of a faculty of free choice in virtue of which an individual agent overcomes a supposed original indifference to the commands of the law through an act for which the individual alone is responsible. The individual, thus determined through free choice, is the moral subject. Now, there was nothing particularly new about the idea. It was at least as old as Christian theology. The question was whether it made any sense, and how, in the context of *Kant's* theory of practical reason, or, as Schelling was to put it, whether *Willkür* (or free choice) was an essential element of the freedom of the will or not. Reinhold had taken the stand that it was[95] – indeed, that free choice is the faculty through which the personality of the human individual, and hence its existence as a moral entity, is first established.[96] Quite a different result was obtained, however, if one followed the Fichtean rendition of Kant's theory of *Wille*. For on Fichte's theory pure will is prior to any distinction between subject and object. It has all the features of Kant's intuitive understanding for which the category of possibility could have no meaning. But choice presupposes the definition of alternative courses of action, precisely the sort of distance between subject and object that does not apply to will as such. On the Fichtean interpretation, in other words, choice is a phenomenon of reflectivity. The indifference with respect to any determinate course of action that it presupposes is in fact only an illusion due to the distance established between the subject and its action as the subject becomes reflectively aware of it. Free choice seems to precede action; in truth it only comes ex post facto, in the attempt at retrieving reflectively the effects of the will's spontaneous action. Schelling calls it a "necessary appearance" of *Wille* – necessary because it is implicated in the very process by which *Wille* becomes conscious of itself, but a mere appearance just the same.[97] The implication of course is that the whole domain of moral choice is in fact only an epiphenomenon of a more fundamental activity that goes on anonymously in a putative moral individual. But this is exactly what Jacobi said of moral life in Spinoza's system, and what made this system unacceptable to him because of the denial of personalism that it entailed.

Our last witness to this Spinozistic interpretation of Kant is Friedrich Schiller, whose aesthetic vision of human existence (which clearly influenced Schelling) took its starting point from the *Critique of Judgment*.

[W]hat makes. . . . Man is precisely this: that he does not stop short at what Nature herself made of him, but has the power of retracing by means of Reason the steps she took on his behalf, of transforming the work of blind compulsion into a work of free choice, and of elevating physical necessity into moral necessity.[98]

Man is determined by two kinds of necessity, namely of nature from below, and of reason or duty from above. Neither leaves room for individuality, which finds scope instead in that area of subjective experience where the two opposite pulls meet and, by masking their effects reciprocally, give rise to the semblance of an area of free play. "[A]s soon as the two opposing fundamental drives [of nature and duty] are active within [man], both lose their compulsion, and the opposition of the two necessities gives rise to *Freedom*,"[99] namely the kind of freedom that is dependent on intelligence or free choice. What we call human existence – the domain of individual decision and individual control – unfolds precisely in this area of apparent freedom from compulsion. Schiller calls it the *Staat des schönen Scheins*, the "State of Aesthetic Semblance,"[100] a mere appearance in any event, just like Spinoza's finite world, or Kant's world of discursive understanding when considered from the standpoint of intuitive understanding.

VII

By 1799 the critique movement was thus at an impasse. Clearly Kant did not understand what his would-be followers were up to. We know (though his contemporaries could not) that at the time he was still busily working at a manuscript that has since come to be known, after Erich Adickes's editorial work, as the *Opus postumum*.[101] In this manuscript Kant was trying to perform a transition (*Übergang*) from categorial thought to the science of actual nature. He was still busy, in other words, at the task of building a bridge (*Brücke*)[102] between reflection and immediate experience to which the *Critique of Judgment* had been devoted. But Kant was now reverting to the strategy, already experimented with in the *Metaphysische Anfangsgründe der Natur-*

wissenschaft (*Metaphysical Foundations of Science*) (1786), of using as means of mediation constructs that function like schemata of the imagination.[103] Yet these schemata are also like ideas in the sense that they are *deliberate* constructs of ours. Thus, whereas in the *Critique of Judgment* Kant was being unwittingly forced to the conclusion that the dynamic categories of the understanding are only regulative, in the *Opus postumum* he now falls on the opposite side with the astounding admission that there are "regulative principles which are at the same time constitutive."[104] But to admit this much is either to side with the likes of Fichte and Schelling (whom Kant was repudiating) or concede with Jacobi that the whole critical enterprise is an absurdity – that there simply cannot be a reflective return to immediacy.

But then, this result is not surprising. Kant's intention had been to subject reason to critique. It is not however reason *as such* that he brought to trial, but the reason of classical metaphysics – that of Spinoza – which was based on the assumption that true knowledge is foundational and systematic. The first twenty years of critique helped to expose precisely the irrationalism inherent in this assumption. They were successful at least in the sense that they led to the formulation of the new problem which the nineteenth century – starting with Hegel – went on to explore, namely whether some other assumption is possible that does justice to whatever truth there was to Jacobi's polemic against metaphysics and yet still made room for it.

NOTES

1 Cf. "Erklärung in Beziehung auf Fichtes Wissenschaftslehre," *Kant's gesammelte Schriften, Akademie* ed. (Berlin: 1900 ff.) Vol. XII, *Public Declarations*, § 6, pp. 370–1. Unless otherwise specified, all translations from the German are mine.

2 For a history of the event, cf. Xavier Léon, *Fichte et son temps* (Paris: Armand Colin, 1954; 1st ed. 1902), Vol. I, chs. 12, 13.

3 This essay ought to be read in conjunction with *Between Kant and Hegel: Texts in the Development of Post-Kantian Idealism*, trans. and annotated with two critical studies by G. di Giovanni and H. S. Harris (Albany: State University of New York, 1985), which it supplements. I am deliberately avoiding repeating material already covered there. I am

also abstracting from Kant's controversy with J. A. Eberhard (cf. H. E. Allison, *The Kant-Eberhard Controversy* (Baltimore: Johns Hopkins, 1973)), and from the anti-Kant campaign waged by Friedrich Nicolai and his adepts.

4 I take it that this is, in a few words, the doctrine behind the Transcendental Deduction, whether in the A or B version.

5 Citations from the *Critique of Pure Reason* are from the Norman Kemp Smith translation.

6 Cf. Kant's statement of the Postulates of Empirical Thought, especially the second: "That which is bound with the material conditions of experience, that is with sensation, is *actual*" (A 218 / B 266). The problem is to show how the connections defined by the categories – notably, the "cause–effect" connection that has to do with the actual appearance of an object – can be exhibited in sensations that are *ex hypothesi* rhapsodic. Cf. also Kant's preoccupation with bridging the otherwise heterogeneous poles of "thought" and "sensation" in the Schematism of the Pure Concepts of the Understanding (A 138 / B 177).

7 For the culture of the period, cf. the classic studies, Richard Benz, *Die Zeit der deutschen Klassik* (Stuttgart: Reclam, 1953), and H. A. Korf, *Geist der Goethezeit: Versuch einer ideallen Entwicklung der klassisch-romantishen Literaturgeschichte*, 2d ed., 4 vols. (Leipzig: Köhler & Asnelany, 1955).

8 *Sämmtliche Werke*, ed. Friedrich Beißner, 8 vols. (Stuttgart: Kohlman, 1946–85), cf. Vol. III, pp. 45 (I,9), 153 (II, 112–13). Cf. also, H. S. Harris, *Hegel's Development: Toward the Sunlight, 1770–1801* (Oxford: Clarendon, 1972), pp. xvii, 60–2, 253–4.

9 *Kleine Schriften zur Geschichte der Kunst des Altertums*, ed. Herman Uhde-Bernays, Vol. I (Leipzig: Insel, 1925). Winckelman defined the theme in terms of an opposition between the ancients and the moderns. He sided of course with the ancients (cf. pp. 60–73).

10 Kant seems to concede the point quite unwittingly in his definition of an "analogy of experience": "An analogy of experience is, therefore, only a rule according to which a unity of experience arises from perception. It does not tell us how mere perception or empirical intuition in general comes about. It is not a principle *constitutive* of the objects, that is of the appearances, [as the mathematical principles are] but only *regulative...."* (A 180 / B 222). But if the analogies of experience are only "regulative," the most that they determine is how we must *imagine* the sequence of appearances of an object – not how the object is actually given in sense intuition. Hume would have no objection to this role of the "analogies."

11 Solomon Maimon, *Versuch über die Transcendentalphilosophie* (Berlin:

Voss & Sohn, 1790), pp. 62–3, 182. Cf. also, Ernst Platner, *Philosophische Aphorismen nebst einigen Anleitungen zur philosophischen Geschichte. Ganz neue Ausarbeitung*, Part 1 (Leipzig: Schwickert, 1793), pp. 336–7. The point was also made in the Feder-Garve review of the *Critique* (cf. below, note 46, p. 169 of Appendix II to the Meiner edition of Kant's *Prolegomena*).

12 Cf. F. W. J. Schelling, 'Vom Ich als Princip der Philosophie' (1795), *Werke* (Stuttgart: Frommann-Holzboog, 1971 ff.), Vol. II, p. 175.

13 § 77; J. H. Bernard's translation (New York: Hafner, 1951), p. 255.

14 Ibid.

15 "Er wollte die Vernunft mit dem Verstand unterbauen, und dann den Verstand wieder überbauen mit der Vernunft." Friedrich Heinrich Jacobi, *Von den Göttlichen Dingen und ihrer Offenbarung* (1811), *Werke* (Leipzig: bei Gerhard Fleischer d. Jüng., 1816), Vol. III, p. 370. By "reason" Jacobi means "practical reason," as the context of the passage clearly shows. But for Kant all "ideas" derive their validity from the practical function they play – be it restricted to just scientific praxis.

16 Cf. A xi, and A 751–2 / B 779–80. The ambiguity is expressed in the very expression "critique of reason," where the genitive "of reason" (*der Vernunft*) can be taken in both a subjective and an objective sense.

17 § 77. Bernard's translation, p. 255.

18 Ibid., p. 257.

19 *David Hume über den Glauben oder Idealismus und Realismus, Ein Gespräch* (Breslau: Löwe, 1787), Supplement, p. 289. (Henceforth, *David Hume*). This first edition of the *David Hume* differs in a few but significant places from the edition of 1815.

20 *Über die Lehre des Spinoza in Briefen an den Herrn Moses Mendelssohn* (Breslau: Löwe, 1785). Henceforth, *Spinozabriefe*. The second edition of 1789 (Breslau: Löwe) was much enlarged, practically doubled in size. Unless otherwise stated, I shall be referring to the first edition.

21 *Dichtung und Wahrheit* (1813/1814), *Goethe* (Zürich: Beutler, 1949 ff.), Vol. 10, p. 699.

22 For a handy brief account in English of the events, and a translation of excerpts, see *The Spinoza Conversations between Lessing & Jacobi: Text with Excerpts from the Ensuing Controversy*, trans. G. Vallée, J. B. Lawson, and C. G. Chapple; Introduction by G. Vallée (Lanham, Md.: University Press of America, 1988). Kant contributed to the controversy with his essay, *Was heißt sich im Denken Orientieren?* (1786), in which he clearly showed his sympathy for Mendelssohn without, however, endorsing his dogmatism. In a later letter to Jacobi (#352 [357], August 30, 1789; *Akademie* ed., Vol. XI, p. 74) Kant apologizes for his tone, which he attributes to the need at the time to clear himself of any

suspicion of Spinozism. This need was itself a sign of how influential the *Spinozabriefe* had been. (Cf. in this respect C. G. Schütz's letter to Kant of February 1786, # 240 [259]; *Akademie* ed., Vol, X, p. 407).

23 On the reception of Spinoza in Germany, see David Bell, *Spinoza in Germany from 1670 to the Age of Goethe* (University of London: Institute of Germanic Studies, 1984). This book is marred, in my opinion, by its tendency to turn into an apology for Spinoza – worse still, by its implicit assumption that Spinoza has to be saved from the charge of "atheism."

24 I am not in any way implying that Jacobi's philosophy is of one piece. It reflects many influences and it underwent changes. Later in his life Jacobi deliberately altered his theory of "reason." Whether the nature of the change was as Jacobi himself estimated it, or whether it was a change for the better, does not concern us here. For Jacobi's statement of the change, cf. *David Hume* (1815), *Friedrich Heinrich Jacobi's Werke* (Leipzig: Gerhard Fleischer d. Jung, 1812 ff.), Vol. II, p. 221 n.

25 *Spinozabriefe*, pp. 162–3, 172 and footnote. *David Hume*, pp. 182 ff.

26 Cf. *Spinozabriefe* (1789), pp. 424–5, 429–30.

27 Ibid., pp. 18–19.

28 Ibid., p. 29.

29 Cf. *David Hume*, pp. 65 ff.; 101 ff. *Spinozabriefe* (1789), Supplement VII, pp. 402–4, 408 ff., 419–20.

30 *Spinozabriefe* (1789), Supplement IV, pp. 337 ff; Supplement V, pp. 349 ff.

31 *Spinozabriefe*, pp. 26, 86–107.

32 Ibid., pp. 118–23, 131–2.

33 *Jacobi an Fichte* (Hamburg: Perthes, 1799), pp. 14–23.

34 Cf. *Über das Unternehmen des Kritizismus die Vernunft zu Verstand zu Bringen* (1801), *Werke*, Vol. 3 (1816), esp. 111–12. (By this time Jacobi has assigned to "reason" – newly reinterpreted – a special intuitive function.)

35 *Der einzig mögliche Beweisgrund zu einer Demonstration des Daseins Gottes* (1763) *Akademie* ed., Vol. II, cf. the concluding remarks, pp. 159–62 (§§ 4–5). Cf. *David Hume*, pp. 74 ff., 78 ff. Also, *Spinozabriefe*, pp. 29–32.

36 *David Hume*, p. 85; Letter to Kant, November 16, 1789, #366 [389], *Akademie* ed., Vol. XI, p. 99.

37 Cf. *Jacobi an Fichte*, pp. 31, 33–4.

38 *David Hume*, pp. 35 ff., 40 ff., 102 ff., 107 ff.

39 Ibid. pp. iv–v, 22.

40 Cf. ibid., pp. 29–30.

41 Cf. *Spinozabriefe*, pp. 163–4; *David Hume*, pp. 64–5, 192–3.

42 *Jacobi an Fichte*, pp. 54–5; cf. also *Allwills Briefsammlung* (Königsberg:

Friedrich Nicolovius, 1792), pp. xv ff. (I take it that Jacobi is indirectly talking about himself.)

43 *Spinozabriefe*, pp. 183, 185–6, 197–8.

44 In a letter to Kant of October 16, 1785, Mendelssohn describes Jacobi's Spinoza-book as "a strange mixture, something like a monster: the head from Goethe, the body from Spinoza, and the feet from Lavater." (The book concludes with a long inspirational passage from Lavater.) Letter 228 [248], *Akademie* ed., Vol. X, p. 390.

45 Cf. Letter of Christian Garve to Kant, July 13, 1783 (#184 [205]), *Akademie* ed., Vol. X, pp. 308–12; Kant's reply of August 7, 1783 (#187 [205]), pp. 315–22; and the *Akademie* ed. notes to both letters (Vol. XIII, pp. 122–3, 124). The review was a reworking by J. G. Feder of a manuscript submitted for publication by Christian Garve. It appeared in the *Zugaben zu den Göttingen gelehrten Anzeigen* (January 1782, 3d issue, pp. 40–8). Kant's Appendix to the *Prolegomena to any Future Metaphysics* refers to this review (*Prolegomena zu einer jeden künftigen Metaphysik* (1783), *Akademie* ed., Vol. 4, p. 381). The text of the review can be found reprinted in the Felix Meiner edition of the *Prolegomena* (Hamburg, 1965), pp. 167–74. The full text of Garve's original text was eventually published in the *Allgemeine deutsche Bibliothek* (1783, Appendix to Vols. 37–52, Section II, pp. 838–62).

46 The Letters appeared in *Der Teutsche Merkur*, between August 1786 and September 1787. There were eight of them altogether, in the following order: Volume of 1786, August, pp. 99–127, 127–41; Volume of 1787, January, pp. 3–39, 117–42; May, 167–85, July, 67–88, 142–65, 247–78.

47 *Briefe über die kantische Philosophie*, Vols. I–II (Leipzig: bei Georg Joachim Gosche, 1790, 1792).

48 Cf. *Between Kant and Hegel*, p. 9 and notes.

49 Explicit reference to Jacobi and Mendelssohn is not made until Letter II, p. 137. On the other hand, cf. Letter II, p. 134, and the opening pages of Letter I, with the footnote on p. 102.

50 Cf. *Spinozabriefe*, pp. 184–85, 197–8.

51 This is the substance of Letter I.

52 Cf. *Spinozabriefe*, pp. 29–34. Jacobi will eventually make "*Nichtwissesn*" explicitly the theme of his polemic against Fichte. *Jacobi an Fichte*, p. 1.

53 Cf. Letter II, pp. 127 and 134–7, p. 140; Letter III, pp. 29, 33.

54 Letter III, p. 12.

55 This is the substance of Letter III. Cf. esp. pp. 5, 11–13.

56 Letter III, p. 28.

57 *Briefe Von und An Hegel*, ed. J. Hoffmeister (Hamburg: Meiner, 1961), Vol. I, p. 13.

58 Karl Leonhard Reinhold, *Versuch einer neuen Theorie des menschlichen Vorstellungsvermögen* (Prague: Widtmann & Mauke, 1789). Cf. *Between Kant and Hegel*, pp. 10–19 and notes.

59 "It organizes its non-knowledge. . . ." Jacobi defined science in these words only in 1799. *Jacobi an Fichte*, p. 24.

60 "Representation, *as mere representation*, can and *must* indeed come ahead!. . . . Since our soul is a power of representation, it must start by producing a representation just as representation. . . ." *David Hume*, p. 61. Of course, I cannot prove that *this* passage inspired Reinhold to fasten on "representation" as the first principle of his reformed Kantianism. He could have derived his hint from Kant just as well. Cf. Kant's division of the concept "representation," (A 320 / B 376–7).

61 Cf. *Between Kant and Hegel*, pp. 20–7 and notes.

62 Gottlob Ernst Schulze, *Aenesidemus, oder über die Fundamente der von Herrn Prof. Reinhold in Jena gelieferten Elementar-Philosophie* (N.p.p., 1792).

63 Cf. A 811 / B 839, A 812 / B 840–1. Kant's statements in these passages do not square, in my opinion, with his position in the connection between "faith in God" and the "efficacy of the moral law" in the *Critique of Practical Reason*.

64 Published in Königsberg.

65 Cf. § 1, *J. G. Fichte–Gesamtausgabe*, Vol, I,1, *Werke 1791–1794*, ed. Reinhard Lauth and Hans Jacob (Stuttgart-Bad Cannstatt: Frommann, 1964 ff.), p. 18.

66 §2, pp. 22–3; §3, p. 36.

67 §3, pp. 36–7.

68 Ibid., p. 37.

69 §4, p. 41.

70 Cf. for instance his statements in *Grundlegung zur Metaphysik der Sitten* (1785), *Akademie* ed. Vol. IV, p. 412 (lines 27–30): "so ist der Wille nichts anderes als praktische Vernunft. . . ." Schelling will claim that it is more accurate to say that practical reason is "will." This conversion is significant because it shows how he (and Fichte whom he was commenting on) thought of reason as a determination of will. Cf. *Allgemeine Übersicht der neuesten philosophischen Litteratur* (1797–8), *Werke*, Vol. IV, p. 159 (lines 27–28). In later editions the *Übersicht* was renamed *Abhandlungen zur Erläuterung des Idealismus der Wissenschaftslehre*.

71 §2, pp. 31, 35–6.

72 §2, p. 33.

73 §3, pp. 38–9.

74 Cf. Fichte's strong statements in *Grundlage der gesamten Wissen-*

schaftslehre (1794–5), §8, II and III, *Gesamtausgabe*, Vol. I, 2, pp. 442–5. Also, §4, D, p. 298.

75 Cf. *Über den Unterschied des Geistes und des Buchstabens in der Philosophie* (Lectures given in the summer semester of 1794), *Gesamtausgabe*, II, 3, Lecture II, p. 330 (lines 4–12). Cf. also *Zweite Einleitung in der Wissenschaftslehre* (1797), *Gesamtausgabe*, I, 4, p. 225 (lines 10–13).

76 For an extensive discussion of this point, and further references, cf. my "From Jacobi's Novel to Fichte's Idealism," *Journal of the History of Philosophy*, 27, 1 (1989), esp. pp. 90–7.

77 Cf. the notes that Fichte wrote as he reflected on Reinhold's *Elementarphilosophie*, and the comments on this text by its editor, Reinhart Lauth: *Eigne Meditationen über Elementarphilosophie, Gesamtausgabe*, Vol. III, 3.

78 For "sensation" (*Empfindung*) as requiring interpretation, cf. *Grundlage*, §10, #20, *Gesamtausgabe*, I, 2, p. 437 (lines 27–33); §7, C, p. 419.

79 *Spinozabriefe*, p. 162.

80 Letter 518, to K. L. Reinhold, January 8, 1800, *Gesamtausgabe*, III, 4, p. 180; cf. also, Letters 440, to K. L. Reinhold, April 22, 1799, III, 3, p. 325; 237, to F. H. Jacobi, September 29, 1794, III,2, p. 202; 307, to F. H. Jacobi, August 30, 1795, III, 2, p. 391; 355, to F. H. Jacobi, April 26, 1796, III,3, p. 18.

81 Cf. *Appellation an das Publicum* (1799), *Gesamtausgabe*, I, 5, pp. 415–35.

82 This is the theme of the whole of *Jacobi an Fichte*.

83 Cf. ibid., p. 37 ff.

84 Cf. ibid., pp. 6–7 and 21–3, 14–17.

85 Cf. ibid., 33–4.

86 Ibid., p. 4.

87 Cf. ibid., pp. 3–5.

88 *Philosophische Briefe über Dogmatismus und Kriticismus, Werke*, Letter I, Vol. III, pp. 50 ff.

89 The clearest statement of this position is to be found only later, in 1800. Cf. *System des transcendentalen Idealismus* (1800), *Sammtliche Werke* (Stuttgart: Cotta, 1856–8), Vol. I, 3, p. 627.

90 *Ideen zu einer Philosophie der Natur* (1797), *Sammtliche Werke*, Vol. I, 2, p. 20. English translation, *Ideas for a Philosophy of Nature*, E. E. Harris and P. Heath, trans. (Cambridge: Cambridge University Press, 1988), p. 15.

91 Ibid., p. 36; English translation, p. 27. For Schelling's appreciation of Spinozism, cf. also *Vom Ich als Princip der Philosophie*, §§12, 14; *Dogmatismus u. Kriticismus*, Letters VI, VII, VIII.

92 *Allgemeine Übersicht der neuesten philosophischen Literatur, Werke,* IV, pp. 157–68.

93 *Die Religion innerhalb der Grenzen der bloßen Vernunft, Akademie* ed., Vol. VI, cf. pp. 34–5, 37.

94 *Metaphysik der Sitten, Akademie* ed., Vol. VI, cf. pp. 213 ff., 226.

95 *Allgemeine Übersicht,* p. 161 (lines 15–23).

96 Reinhold was defending what was in fact the old (Aristotelian) scholastic concept of "will" and of its relation to "reason." *Briefe über die Kantische Philosophie,* Vol. II (1792), Letters VI, VII, VIII; *Beiträge* (Jena: Mauke, 1794), "Über das vollständige Fundament der Moral," pp. 206–94; *Auswahl vermischter Schriften,* Part II (Jena: Mauke, 1797), "Einige Bemerkungen in der Einleitung zu den Metaphysischen Anfangsgründe der Rechtslehre von I. Kant aufgestellten Begriffe der Freiheit des Willens," pp. 364–400.

97 *Allgemeine Übersicht,* p. 165 (lines 22–30).

98 *Über die Ästhetische Erziehung des Menschen, in einer Reihe von Briefen, On the Aesthetic Education of Man, in a Series of Letters,* ed. trans. by E. M. Wilkinson and L. A. Willoughby, accompanied by the German text (Oxford: Clarendon, 1967), Letter III, p. 11. These first Letters date from 1793–94. For a history of the text, cf. ibid., pp. 334–5.

99 Letter IX, ibid., p. 137.

100 Letter XXVII, ibid., p. 219.

101 *Akademie* ed., Vol. XXI–XXII; cf. Erich Adickes, *Kants Opus postumum dargestellt und beurteilt* (Berlin: Ergänzungsheft der *Kant-Studien,* 1920).

102 Cf. *Akademie* ed., Vol. XXI, p. 526 (lines 4–13); Vol. XXII, p. 244 (lines 3–6).

103 *Aether, Selbstaffektion,* and *Erscheinung einer Erscheinung,* are the cases in point. For a discussion of the relation of the *Critique of Judgment* to the *Opus postumum,* cf. Vittorio Mathieu, *Kants Opus postumum* (Frankfurt/M.: Klostermann, 1989), pp. 239–46. Kant uses the term "schematism" repeatedly in the *Opus postumum,* e.g., *Akademie* ed., Vol. XXII, pp. 265 (lines 25–6), 487 (lines 18–21).

104 *Akademie* ed., Vol. XXII, p. 241 (line 19: "Regulative Principia die zugleich constitutiv sind."). Cf. Vittorio Mathieu, p. 118.

BIBLIOGRAPHY

The literature on Kant, as might be expected from both the range of his work and his centrality in the history of modern philosophy, is enormous. The following bibliography is necessarily selective. In view of the aims of the present series, it focuses on recent books and collections of articles, although including some older works that have attained classical status. Only very important articles that have not been republished in collections by their authors or anthologies have been listed separately; individual articles in collections that are included are not listed separately. The bibliography also emphasizes works in English, although some of the most important works in German and a few in French have been included. Books that include especially extensive bibliographies are noted. Further bibliographical information can be found in the bibliographical surveys by Rudolf Malter that have been published since 1969 in *Kant-Studien*, the official journal of the Kant-Gesellschaft. More recently, bibliographical surveys prepared by Manfred Kuehn have been published in the newsletter of the North American Kant Society. An annotated bibliography on Kant's ethics is *Kantian Ethical Thought: A Curricular Report and Annotated Bibliography* (Tallahassee: Council for Philosophical Studies, 1984). An extraordinary annotated bibliography of 2,832 items on Kant through 1802 (two years before Kant's own death!) edited by Erich Adickes was published in English in *The Philosophical Review* from 1893 to 1896, and reprinted as *German Kant Bibliography* (New York: Burt Franklin, 1970). This is indispensable for studying the early reception of Kant. Many of the important works by Kant's early critics and admirers catalogued in this work were reprinted in the series *Aetas Kantiana* (Brussels: Culture et Civilisation, 1968–73).

The division of the following bibliography reflects the customary broad divisions in discussions of Kant's philosophy. More specialized works on Kant's philosophy of physical science, politics, and biological science have been listed separately, but some of the more general works in the divisions that they follow also treat of these issues. Many works fit even less neatly

449

into these divisions, which are intended only to help the reader get started in further study of Kant.

KANT'S WORKS: GERMAN EDITIONS

The standard critical edition of Kant's works, the pagination of which is cited by most contemporary authors on Kant, is *Kant's gesammelte Schriften*, edited by the Königlich Preußischen Akademie der Wissenschaften, subsequently the Deutsche Akademie der Wissenschaften (originally under the general editorship of Wilhelm Dilthey). Twenty-nine volumes (twenty-seven thus far published) in thirty-four parts. Berlin: Georg Reimer, subsequently Walter de Gruyter, 1900–. The edition is divided into four parts: *Werke* (volumes 1–9), *Briefe* (volumes 10–13), *Handschriftliche Nachlaß* (volumes 14–23), and *Vorlesungen* (volumes 24–29, no volumes 25 and 26). This edition is widely referred to as the "*Akademie*" edition.

The following twentieth-century editions are also cited:

Ernst Cassirer, ed. *Werke.* 11 vols. Berlin: Bruno Cassirer, 1912–22.

Wilhelm Weischedel, ed. *Werke in sechs Bänden.* Wiesbaden: Insel Verlag, 1956–62. Reprinted in 12 vols. but with the original pagination by Suhrkamp Verlag, Frankfurt am Main, 1968. Unlike the *Akademie* edition, this contains German translations of Kant's several Latin works.

Editions of individual works are also published in the *Philosophische Bibliothek* of Felix Meiner Verlag, Hamburg. These include the standard edition of the *Critique of Pure Reason:*

Immanuel Kant. *Kritik der reinen Vernunft.* Ed. Raymund Schmidt. 2d ed. Hamburg: Felix Meiner Verlag, 1930.

Two other volumes of special note in this series are

Immanuel Kant. *Briefwechsel.* Ed. Rudolf Malter. Hamburg: Felix Meiner Verlag, 1986 (includes letters not in *Akademie* edition).

Immanuel Kant. *Metaphysische Anfangsgründe der Rechtslehre: Metaphysik der Sitten, Erster Teil.* Ed. Bernd Ludwig. Hamburg: Felix Meiner Verlag, 1986 (proposes a new arrangement of some paragraphs of the previously accepted text).

ENGLISH TRANSLATIONS

This list includes only the most important translations currently in widespread use. An undertaking currently in preparation, The Cambridge Edition of the Works of Immanuel Kant, will provide new or revised translations of all of Kant's published works and selections from his correspondence, *Nachlaß*, and lectures. Among the first volumes to appear, beginning in approximately 1992, will be *Pre-Critical Writings, Opus postumum, Lectures on Logic,* and *Correspondence*. Until that edition is completed, the following translations are recommended. Volumes of multiple works are listed first, followed by translations of individual works, listed in alphabetical order of the title of the translation.

Multiple works

Kant: On History. Ed. Lewis White Beck; trans. Lewis White Beck, Robert E. Anchor, and Emil Fackenheim. Indianapolis: Bobbs-Merrill, 1963.

Kant's Critique of Practical Reason and Other Works on the Theory of Ethics. Trans. Thomas Kingsmill Abbott. 6th ed. London: Longmans Green, 1909.

Kant's Critique of Practical Reason and Other Writings in Moral Philosophy. Trans. Lewis White Beck. Chicago: University of Chicago Press, 1949.

Kant's Latin Writings: Translations, Commentaries, and Notes. Trans. Lewis White Beck, Mary J. Gregor, Ralf Meerbote, and John A. Reuscher. New York: Peter Lang, 1986.

Kant's Political Writings. Ed. Hans Reiss, trans. by H. B. Nisbet. Cambridge: Cambridge University Press, 1970.

Perpetual Peace and Other Essays on Politics, History, and Morals. Trans. Ted Humphrey. Indianapolis: Hackett, 1983.

Selected Pre-Critical Writings and Correspondence with Beck. Trans. G. B. Kerferd and D. E. Walford, with a contribution by P. G. Lucas. Manchester: Manchester University Press and New York: Barnes & Noble, 1968.

Individual works

Anthropology from a Pragmatic Point of View. Trans. Mary J. Gregor. The Hague: Martinus Nijhoff, 1974.

The Conflict of the Faculties. Trans. Mary J. Gregor. New York: Abaris Books, 1979.

Critique of Aesthetic Judgement. Trans. with analytical indexes by James Creed Meredith. Oxford: Clarendon Press, 1911.

Critique of Teleological Judgement. Trans. with analytical indexes by James Creed Meredith. Oxford: Clarendon Press, 1928.

[Both of the two preceding texts without indices were reprinted as: *Kant's Critique of Judgement*. Trans. James Creed Meredith. Oxford: Clarendon Press, 1952.]

Critique of Judgment: Including the First Introduction. Trans. Werner S. Pluhar. Indianapolis: Hackett, 1987.

Critique of Practical Reason. Trans. Lewis White Beck. Indianapolis: Bobbs-Merrill, 1956 (now Macmillan).

Critique of Pure Reason. Trans. Norman Kemp Smith. 2d ed. London: Macmillan, 1933.

Dreams of a Spirit-Seer. Trans. E. F. Goerwitz. London: Swan Sonnenschein, 1900.

The Educational Theory of Immanuel Kant. Trans. Edward Franklin Buchner. Philadelphia: J. B. Lippincott, 1904.

First Introduction to the Critique of Judgment. Trans. James Haden. Indianapolis: Bobbs-Merrill, 1965.

The Groundwork of the Metaphysics of Morals (originally *The Moral Law*). Trans. H. J. Paton. London: Hutchinson, 1949 (now Harper & Row). Or: *Foundations of the Metaphysics of Morals and What Is Enlightenment?* Trans. Lewis White Beck. Indianapolis: Bobbs-Merrill, 1959 (now Macmillan).

The Kant-Eberhard Controversy: An English translation together with supplementary materials and a historical-analytical introduction of Immanuel Kant's on a New Discovery According to Which Any New Critique of Pure Reason Has Been Made Superfluous by an Earlier One. Trans. Henry E. Allison. Baltimore: The Johns Hopkins University Press, 1973.

Kant: Philosophical Correspondence 1759–99. Trans. Arnulf Zweig. Chicago: University of Chicago Press, 1967.

Lectures on Ethics. Trans. Louis Infield. London: Methuen, 1930. Reprinted with an introduction by Lewis White Beck. New York: Harper & Row, 1963 (now Hackett Publishing Company).

Lectures on Philosophical Theology. Trans. Allen W. Wood and Gertrude M. Clark. Ithaca, N.Y.: Cornell University Press, 1978.

Logic. Trans. Robert Hartmann and Wolfgang Schwarz. Indianapolis: Bobbs-Merrill, 1974.

The Metaphysical Elements of Justice: Part I of the Metaphysics of Morals. Trans. John Ladd. Indianapolis: Bobbs-Merrill, 1965 (now Macmillan).

Metaphysical Foundations of Natural Science. Trans. James Ellington. Indianapolis: Bobbs-Merrill, 1970

(Reprinted, with *Prolegomena*, in *Philosophy of Material Nature*. Indianapolis: Hackett, 1985).

The Metaphysical Principles of Virtue: Part II of the Metaphysics of Morals.
Trans. James Ellington. Indianapolis: Bobbs-Merrill, 1964.
(Reprinted, with *Foundations of the Metaphysics of Morals,* in *Ethical Philosophy.* Indianapolis: Hackett, 1983.) Or:
The Doctrine of Virtue. Trans. Mary J. Gregor. New York: Harper & Row, 1964.
Observations on the Feeling of the Beautiful and Sublime. Trans. John T. Goldthwait. Berkeley: University of California Press, 1960.
On the Old Saw: That May Be Right in Theory but It Won't Work in Practice. Trans. E. B. Ashton. Philadelphia: University of Pennsylvania Press, 1974.
The One Possible Basis for a Demonstration of the Existence of God. Trans. Gordon Treash. New York: Abaris Books, 1979.
Perpetual Peace. Trans. Lewis White Beck. Indianapolis: Bobbs-Merrill, 1957.
Prolegomena to Any Future Metaphysics. Trans. Lewis White Beck. Indianapolis: Bobbs-Merrill, 1950 (now Macmillan).
Religion within the Limits of Reason Alone. Trans. by Theodore M. Greene and Hoyt H. Hudson, with a new essay on "The Ethical Significance of Kant's *Religion*" by John R. Silber. New York: Harper & Row, 1960.
Universal Natural History and Theory of the Heavens. Trans. W. Hastie, with a new introduction by Milton K. Munitz. Ann Arbor: University of Michigan Press, 1969.
What Real Progress Has Metaphysics Made in Germany since the Time of Leibniz and Wolff? Trans. Ted Humphrey. New York: Abaris Books, 1983.

                    BACKGROUND AND CONTEXT

Beck, Lewis White. *Early German Philosophy: Kant and his Predecessors.* Cambridge, Mass.: Harvard University Press, 1969.
Beiser, Frederick C. *The Fate of Reason: German Philosophy from Kant to Fichte.* Cambridge, Mass.: Harvard University Press, 1987 (contains extensive bibliography of primary sources).
Buchdahl, Gerd. *Metaphysics and the Philosophy of Science: The Classical Origins Descartes to Kant.* Oxford: Basil Blackwell, 1969.
Cassirer, Ernst. *Freiheit und Form: Studien zur deutschen Geistesgeschichte.* 3d ed. Darmstadt: Wissenschaftliche Buchgesellschaft, 1961.
The Philosophy of the Enlightenment. Trans. Fritz C. A. Koelln and James P. Pettegrove. Princeton, N.J.: Princeton University Press, 1951.
Nelson, Leonard. *Progress and Regress in Philosophy: From Hume and Kant*

to Hegel and Fries. Ed. Julius Kraft, trans. Humphrey Palmer. 2 vols. Oxford: Basil Blackwell, 1970–71.

Rosenkranz, Karl. *Geschichte der Kant' schen Philosophie.* Leipzig: Leopold Voss, 1840. Reprint edited by Stefan Dietzsch. Berlin: Akademie Verlag, 1987.

Schneewind, Jerome B. *Moral Philosophy from Montaigne to Kant.* 2 vols. Cambridge: Cambridge University Press, 1990.

Wundt, Max. *Die deutsche Schulphilosophie im Zeitalter der Aufklärung.* Tübingen: J. C. B. Mohr, 1945.

BIOGRAPHIES AND GENERAL SURVEYS

Beck, Lewis White. *Studies in the Philosophy of Kant.* Indianapolis: Bobbs-Merrill, 1965.

Essays on Kant and Hume. New Haven, Conn.: Yale University Press, 1978.

Beck, Lewis White, ed. *Kant Studies Today.* LaSalle, Ill.: Open Court, 1967 (multiple-author anthology; includes extensive bibliography).

Caird, Edward. *The Critical Philosophy of Immanuel Kant.* 2 vols. New York: Macmillan, 1889.

Cassirer, Ernst. *Kant's Life and Thought.* Trans. James Haden. New Haven, Conn.: Yale University Press, 1981.

Rousseau, Kant, and Goethe. Trans. James Gutmann, Paul Oskar Kristeller, and John Herman Randall, Jr. Princeton, N.J.: Princeton University Press, 1949.

Delekat, Friedrich. *Immanuel Kant.* 2d ed. Heidelberg: Quelle & Meyer, 1966.

De Vleeschauwer, H.–J. *La Déduction Transcendentale dans l'oevre de Kant.* 3 vols. Antwerp; De Sikkel; Paris: Champion; and The Hague: Martinus Nijhoff: 1934–37.

The Development of Kantian Thought: The History of a Doctrine. Trans. A. R. C. Duncan. London: Thomas Nelson & Sons, 1962.

Den Ouden, Bernard, and Marcia Moen, eds. *New Essays on Kant.* New York: Peter Lang, 1987 (multiple-author anthology).

Findlay, J. N. *Kant and the Transcendental Object: A Hermeneutic Study.* Oxford: Clarendon Press, 1981.

Förster, Eckart, ed. *Kant's Transcendental Deductions: The Three 'Critiques' and the 'Opus postumum'.* Stanford, Calif.: Stanford University Press, 1989 (multiple-author anthology).

Gerhardt, Volker, and Friedrich Kaulbach. *Kant.* Erträge der Forschung, Band 105. Darmstadt: Wissenschaftliche Buchgesellschaft, 1979 (includes extensive bibliography emphasizing older as well as recent German literature).

Gross, F., ed. *Immanuel Kant: Sein Leben in Darstellungen von Zeitgenossen. Die Biographien von L. E. Borowski, R. B. Jachmann, und A. Ch. Wasianski.* Berlin: Deutsches Bibliothek, 1912.

Gulyga, Arsenij. *Immanuel Kant: His Life and Thought.* Trans. Marijan Despalatovic. Boston: Birkauser, 1987.

Haering, Theodor. *Der Duisburg'sche Nachlaß und Kants Kritizismus um 1775.* Tübingen: J. C. B. Mohr, 1910.

Heimsoeth, Heinz. *Studien zur Philosophie Immanuel Kants.* Kant-Studien Ergänzungsheft 71. Bonn: Bouvier Verlag, 1956.

Studien zur Philosophiegeschichte: Gesammelte Abhandlungen, Band II. Kant-Studien Ergänzungsheft 82. Bonn: Bouvier Verlag, 1961.

Studien zur Philosophie Immanuel Kants II. Kant-Studien Ergänzungsheft 100. Bonn: Bouvier Verlag, 1970.

Heimsoeth, Heinz, Dieter Henrich, and Giorgio Tonelli, eds. *Studien zu Kants philosophischer Entwicklung.* Hildesheim: Georg Olms Verlag, 1967 (multiple-author anthology).

Heintel, Peter, and Ludwig Nagl, eds. *Zur Kantforschung der Gegenwart.* Darmstadt: Wissenschaftliche Buchgesellschaft, 1981 (multiple-author anthology; contains extensive bibliography).

Hinske, Norbert. *Kants Weg zur Transzendentalphilosophie: Der Dreißigjährige Kant.* Stuttgart: Kohlhammer, 1970.

Höffe, Ottfried. *Immanuel Kant.* Munich: Verlag C. H. Beck, 1983.

Kemp, John. *The Philosophy of Kant.* London: Oxford University Press, 1968.

Kennington, Richard, ed. *The Philosophy of Immanuel Kant. Studies in Philosophy and the History of Philosophy, Volume 12.* Washington, D.C.: The Catholic University of America Press, 1985 (multiple-author anthology).

Körner, Stephan. *Kant.* Harmondsworth: Penguin Books, 1955.

Lehmann, Gerhard. *Beiträge zur Geschichte und Interpretation der Philosophie Kants.* Berlin: Walter de Gruyter, 1969.

Kants Tugenden: Neue Beiträge zur Geschichte und Interpretation der Philosophie Kants. Berlin: Walter de Gruyter, 1980.

Oberer, Hariolf, and Gerhard Seel, eds. *Kant: Analysen – Probleme – Kritik.* Würzburg: Königshausen & Neumann, 1988 (multiple-author anthology).

Prauss, Gerold, ed. *Kant: Zur Deutung seiner Theorie von Erkennen und Handeln.* Cologne: Kiepenheuer & Witsch, 1973 (multiple-author anthology).

Riehl, Alois. *Der philosophische Kritizismus.* 3 vols. 2d ed. Leipzig: W. Engelmann, 1908.

Ritzel, Wolfgang. *Immanuel Kant: Eine Biographie.* Berlin: Walter de Gruyter, 1985.

Rotenstreich, Nathan. *Experience and Its Systematization: Studies in Kant.* 2d ed. The Hague: Martinus Nijhoff, 1972.

Schaper, Eva, and Wilhelm Vossenkuhl, eds. *Bedingungen der Möglichkeit: 'Transcendental Arguments' und transzendentales Denken.* Stuttgart: Klett-Cotta Verlag, 1984 (multiple-author anthology).

Vorländer, Karl. *Immanuel Kant: Der Mann und das Werk.* 2 vols. Leipzig: Felix Meiner Verlag, 1924.

    Immanuel Kants Leben. 4th ed., ed. Rudolf Malter. Hamburg: Felix Meiner Verlag, 1986.

Walker, Ralph C. S. *Kant.* London, Henley, and Boston: Routledge & Kegan Paul, 1978.

Werkmeister, W. H. *Kant's Silent Decade: A Decade of Philosophical Development.* Tallahassee: University Presses of Florida, 1979.

    Kant: The Architectonic and Development of His Philosophy. LaSalle, Ill.: Open Court, 1980.

Werkmeister, W. H., ed. *Reflections on Kant's Philosophy.* Gainesville: University Presses of Florida, 1975 (multiple-author anthology).

Whitney, George Tapley, and David F. Bowers, eds. *The Heritage of Kant.* Princeton, N.J.: Princeton University Press, 1939 (multiple-author anthology).

Wolff, Robert Paul, ed. *Kant: A Collection of Critical Essays.* Garden City, N.Y.: Doubleday Anchor, 1967 (multiple-author anthology).

Wood, Allen W., ed. *Self and Nature in Kant's Philosophy.* Ithaca, N.Y.: Cornell University Press, 1984 (multiple-author anthology).

Wundt, Max. *Kant als Metaphysiker: Ein Beitrag zur Geschichte der deutschen Philosophie im 18. Jahrhundert.* Stuttgart: Ferdinand Enke, 1924.

THEORETICAL PHILOSOPHY: EPISTEMOLOGY
AND METAPHYSICS

Adickes, Erich. *Kant und das Ding an sich.* Berlin: Pan Verlag, 1924.

    Kants Lehre von der doppelten Affektion des Ich als Schlüssel zu seiner Erkenntnistheorie. Tübingen: J. C. B. Mohr, 1929.

Al-Azm, Sadik. *The Origins of Kant's Arguments in the Antinomies.* Oxford: Clarendon Press, 1972.

Allison, Henry E. *Kant's Transcendental Idealism.* New Haven, Conn.: Yale University Press, 1983 (includes extensive bibliography).

Allison, Henry E., ed. *Kant's Critical Philosophy. The Monist* 72 (April 1989) (special issue multiple-author anthology).

Ameriks, Karl. *Kant's Theory of Mind: An Analysis of the Paralogisms of Pure Reason.* Oxford: Clarendon Press, 1982.

"Recent Work on Kant's Theoretical Philosophy," *American Philosophical Quarterly* 19 (1982): 1–24 (includes extensive bibliography).

Aquila, Richard E. *Representational Mind: A Study of Kant's Theory of Knowledge.* Bloomington: Indiana University Press, 1983.

Matter in Mind: A Study of Kant's Transcendental Deduction. Bloomington: Indiana University Press, 1989.

Aschenberg, Reinhold. *Sprachanalyse und Transzendentalphilosophie.* Stuttgart: Klett-Cotta Verlag, 1982 (includes extensive bibliography).

Aschenbrenner, Karl. *A Companion to Kant's Critique of Pure Reason: Transcendental Aesthetic and Analytic.* Lanham, Md.: University Press of America, 1983.

Baum, Manfred. *Deduktion und Beweis in Kants Transzendentalphilosophie: Untersuchungen zur "Kritik der reinen Vernunft".* Königstein: Athenäum Verlag, 1986.

Beck, Lewis White, ed. *Kant's Theory of Knowledge: Selected Papers from the Third International Kant Congress.* Dordrecht: D. Reidel, 1974 (multiple-author anthology).

Becker, Wolfgang. *Selbstbewußtsein und Erfahrung: Zu Kants transzendentaler Deduktion und ihrer argumentative Rekonstruktion.* Freiburg: Verlag Karl Albert, 1984.

Bennett, Jonathan. *Kant's Analytic.* Cambridge: Cambridge University Press, 1966.

Kant's Dialectic. Cambridge: Cambridge University Press, 1974.

Bieri, Peter, Rolf-Peter Horstmann, and Lorenz Krüger, eds. *Transcendental Arguments and Science: Essays in Epistemology.* Dordrecht: D. Reidel, 1979 (multiple-author anthology).

Bird, Graham. *Kant's Theory of Knowledge: An Outline of One Central Argument in the* Critique of Pure Reason. London: Routledge & Kegan Paul, 1962.

Brandt, Reinhard. *Die Urteilstafel: Kritik der reinen Vernunft A* 67–76; *B* 92–101. Kant Forschungen, Vol. 4. Hamburg: Felix Meiner Verlag, 1991.

Broad. C. D. *Kant: An Introduction.* Ed. by C. Levy. Cambridge: Cambridge University Press, 1978.

Buroker, Jill Vance. *Space and Incongruence: The Origin of Kant's Idealism.* Dordrecht: D. Reidel, 1981.

Butts, Robert E. *Kant and the Double Government Methodology: Supersensibility and Method in Kant's Philosophy of Science.* Dordrecht: D. Reidel, 1984.

Butts, Robert E., ed. *Kant's Critique of Pure Reason, 1781–1981. Synthese* 47 (Nos. 2 and 3) (1981) (special issues multiple-author anthology).

Carl, Wolfgang. *Der schweigende Kant: Die Entwürfe zu einer Deduktion der Kategorien vor 1781.* Göttingen: Vandenhoeck & Ruprecht, 1989.

Cohen, Hermann. *Kants Theorie der Erfahrung.* 2d ed. Berlin: Dümmler, 1885.

Cramer, Konrad. *Nicht-reine synthetische Urteile a priori: Ein Problem der Transzendentalphilosophie Immanuel Kants.* Heidelberg: Carl Winter Universitätsverlag, 1985.

Dryer, Douglas P. *Kant's Solution for Verification in Metaphysics.* London: George Allen & Unwin, 1966.

Enskat, Rainer. *Kants Theorie des geometrischen Gegenstandes.* Berlin: Walter de Gruyter, 1978.

Erdmann, Benno. *Kants Kriticismus in der ersten und in der zweiten Auflage der Kritik der reinen Vernunft.* Leipzig: Leopold Voss, 1878.

Ewing, A. C. *Kant's Treatment of Causality.* London: Routledge & Kegan Paul, 1924.

A Short Commentary on Kant's Critique of Pure Reason. Chicago: University of Chicago Press, 1938.

Friedman, Michael. *Kant and the Exact Sciences.* Cambridge, Mass.: Harvard University Press, 1992.

Garnett, Christopher B., Jr. *The Kantian Philosophy of Space.* New York: Columbia University Press, 1939.

Gram, Moltke S. *Kant, Ontology, and the* A Priori. Evanston, Ill.: Northwestern University Press, 1968.

The Transcendental Turn: The Foundations of Kant's Idealism. Gainesville: University Presses of Florida, 1984.

Gram, Moltke S., ed. *Kant: Disputed Questions.* Chicago: Quadrangle Books, 1967 (multiple-author anthology).

Gurwitsch, Aron. *Kants Theorie des Verstandes.* Ed. Thomas M. Seebohm. Dordrecht and Boston: Kluwer Academic Publishers, 1990.

Guyer, Paul. *Kant and the Claims of Knowledge.* Cambridge: Cambridge University Press, 1987.

Harper, William A., and Ralf Meerbote. *Kant on Causality, Freedom, and Objectivity.* Minneapolis: University of Minnesota Press, 1984 (multiple-author anthology).

Heidegger, Martin. *Kant and the Problem of Metaphysics.* Trans. James S. Churchill. Bloomington: Indiana University Press, 1962.

Die frage nach dem Ding: Zu Kants Lehre von den transzendentalen Grundsätzen. Tübingen: Max Niemeyer Verlag, 1962.

Heimsoeth, Heinz. *Transzendentale Dialektik: Ein Kommentar zu Kants Kritik der reinen Vernunft.* 4 vols. Berlin: Walter de Gruyter, 1966–71.

Heinrich, Richard. *Kants Erfahrungsraum: Metaphysischer Ursprung und kritische Entwicklung.* Freiburg: Verlag Karl Albert, 1986.

Henrich, Dieter. "The Proof-Structure of Kant's Transcendental Deduction." *The Review of Metaphysics* 22 (1969): 640–59.

Identität und Objektivität: Eine Untersuchung über Kants transzendentale Deduktion. Heidelberg: Carl Winter Universitätsverlag, 1976.

Hinsch, Wilfried. *Erfahrung und Selbstbewußtsein: Zur Kategoriendeduktion bei Kant.* Hamburg: Felix Meiner Verlag, 1986.

Hintikka, Jaakko. *Knowledge and the Known: Historical Perspectives in Epistemology.* Dordrecht: D. Reidel, 1974.

Holzhey, Helmut. *Kants Erfahrungsbegriff.* Basel: Schwabe, 1970.

Hossenfelder, Malte. *Kants Konstitutionstheorie und die Transzendentale Deduktion.* Berlin: Walter de Gruyter, 1978.

Kaulbach, Friedrich. *Die Metaphysik des Raumes bei Leibniz und Kant.* Kant-Studien Ergänzungsheft 79. Bonn: Bouvier Verlag, 1960.

Kemp Smith, Norman. *A Commentary to Kant's 'Critique of Pure Reason'.* 2d ed. London: Macmillan, 1923.

Kitcher, Patricia. *Kant's Transcendental Psychology.* Oxford: Oxford University Press, 1990.

Kopper, Joachim, and Rudolf Malter. *Materialen zu Kants "Kritik der reinen Vernunft".* Frankfurt am Main: Suhramp Verlag, 1975.

Marc-Wogau, Konrad. *Untersuchungen zur Raumlehre Kants.* Lund: Håkan Ohlssons Buchdruckerei, 1932.

Martin, Gottfried. *Kant's Metaphysics and Theory of Science.* Trans. P. G. Lucas. Manchester, U.K.: Manchester University Press, 1955.

Arithmetik und Kombinatorik bei Kant. Berlin: Walter de Gruyter, 1972.

Mathieu, Vittorio. *Kants Opus postumum.* Ed. Gerd Held. Frankfurt am Main: Vittorio Klostermann, 1989.

Melnick, Arthur. *Kant's Analogies of Experience.* Chicago: University of Chicago Press, 1973.

Space, Time, and Thought in Kant. Dordrecht: Kluwer Academic Publishers, 1989.

Meyer, Michel. *Science et Métaphysique chez Kant.* Paris: Presses Universitaires de France, 1988.

Mohanty, J. N., and Robert W. Shahan, *Essays on Kant's Critique of Pure Reason.* Norman: University of Oklahoma Press, 1982 (multiple-author anthology).

Nagel, Gordon. *The Structure of Experience: Kant's System of Principles.* Chicago: University of Chicago Press, 1983.

Parsons, Charles. *Mathematics in Philosophy: Selected Essays.* Ithaca, N.Y.: Cornell University Press, 1983.

Paton, H. J. *Kant's Metaphysics of Experience: A Commentary on the First*

Half of the Kritik der reinen Vernunft. 2 vols. London: George Allen & Unwin, 1936.

Pippin, Robert B. *Kant's Theory of Form: An Essay on the* Critique of Pure Reason. New Haven, Conn.: Yale University Press, 1982 (contains extensive bibliography).

Polonoff, Irving. *Force, Cosmos, Monads and Other Themes of Kant's Early Thought.* Kant-Studien Ergänzungsheft 107. Bonn: Bouvier Verlag, 1973.

Powell, C. Thomas. *Kant's Theory of Self-Consciousness.* Oxford: Oxford University Press, 1990.

Prauss, Gerold. *Erscheinung bei Kant: Ein Problem der "Kritik der reinen Vernunft."* Berlin: Walter de Gruyter, 1971.

Kant und das Problem der Dinge an sich. Bonn: Bouvier Verlag, 1974.

Prichard, H. A. *Kant's Theory of Knowledge.* Oxford: Clarendon Press, 1909.

Reich, Klaus. *Die Vollständigkeit des Kantischen Urteilstafels.* 3d ed. Hamburg: Felix Meiner Verlag, 1986.

Robinson, Hoke, ed. *The Spindel Conference 1986: The B-Deduction.* The Southern Journal of Philosophy 25 Supplement (1987) (special issue multiple-author anthology).

Roussett, Bernard. *La doctrine kantienne de l'objectivité.* Paris: J. Vrin, 1967.

Schaper, Eva, and Wilhelm Vossenkuhl, eds. *Reading Kant: New Perspectives on Transcendental Arguments and Critical Philosophy.* Oxford: Basil Blackwell, 1989 (multiple-author anthology; includes extensive bibliography).

Schneeberger, Guido. *Kants Theorie der Modalbegriffe.* Basel: Schwabe, 1952.

Schwyzer, Hubert. *The Unity of Understanding: A Study in Kantian Problems.* Oxford: Clarendon Press, 1990.

Sellars, Wilfrid. *Science and Metaphysics: Variations on Kantian Themes.* London: Routledge & Kegan Paul, 1968.

Smith, A. H. *A Treatise on Knowledge.* Oxford: Clarendon Press, 1943.

Kantian Studies. Oxford: Clarendon Press, 1947.

Smyth, Richard. *Forms of Intuition.* The Hague: Martinus Nijhoff, 1978.

Srzednicki, Jan T. *The Place of Space and Other Themes.* The Hague: Martinus Nijhoff, 1983.

Strawson, P. F. *The Bounds of Sense: An Essay on Kant's* Critique of Pure Reason. London: Methuen, 1966.

Stuhlmann-Laeisz, Rainer. *Kants Logik: Eine Interpretation auf der Grundlage von Vorlesungen, veröffentlichten Werken und Nachlaß.* Berlin: Walter de Gruyter, 1976.

Thöle, Bernhard. *Kant und das Problem der Gesetzmäßigkeit der Natur.* Berlin: Walter de Gruyter, 1991.

Tuschling, Burkhard. *Probleme der "Kritik der reinen Vernunft": Kant-Tagung Marburg 1981.* Berlin: Walter de Gruyter, 1984 (multiple-author anthology).

Vaihinger, Hans. *Commentar zu Kants Kritik der reinen Vernunft.* 2 vols. Stuttgart: W. Spemann and Union Deutsche Verlagsgesellschaft, 1881–92.

Walker, Ralph C. S., ed. *Kant on Pure Reason.* Oxford: Oxford University Press, 1982 (multiple-author anthology).

Walsh, W. H. *Kant's Criticism of Metaphysics.* Edinburgh: Edinburgh University Press, 1975.

Weldon, T. D. *Kant's* Critique of Pure Reason. 2d ed. Oxford: Clarendon Press, 1958.

Wike, Victoria S. *Kant's Antinomies of Reason: Their Origin and Resolution.* Washington, D.C.: University Press of America, 1982.

Wilkerson, T. E. *Kant's Critique of Pure Reason: A Commentary for Students.* Oxford: Clarendon Press, 1976.

Winterbourne, A. T. *The Ideal and the Real: An Outline of Kant's Theory of Space, Time, and Mathematical Construction.* Dordrecht: Kluwer Academic Publishers, 1988.

Wolff, Michael. *Der Begriff des Widerspruches: Eine Studie zur Dialektik Kants und Hegels.* Meisenheim: Verlag Anton Hain, 1981.

Wolff, Robert Paul. *Kant's Theory of Mental Activity: A Commentary on the Transcendental Analytic of the* Critique of Pure Reason. Cambridge, Mass.: Harvard University Press, 1963.

THEORETICAL PHILOSOPHY: PHILOSOPHY OF PHYSICAL SCIENCE

Adickes, Erich. *Kants Opus postumum dargestellt und beurteilt.* Kant-Studien Ergänzungsheft 50. Berlin: Reuter und Reichard, 1930.

Kant als Naturforscher. 2 vols. Berlin: Walter de Gruyter, 1924.

Brittan, Gordon G., Jr. *Kant's Theory of Science.* Princeton, N.J.: Princeton University Press, 1978.

Butts, Robert E., ed. *Kant's Philosophy of Physical Science: Metaphysische Anfangsgründe der Naturwissenschaft 1786–1986.* Dordrecht: D. Reidel, 1986 (multiple-author anthology).

Forum für Philosophie Bad Homburg, eds. *Übergang: Untersuchungen zum Spätwerk Immanuel Kants.* Frankfurt am Main: Vittorio Klostermann, 1991 (multiple-author anthology).

Gloy, Karen. *Die Kantische Theorie der Naturwissenschaft: Ein Struktur-*

analyse ihrer Möglichkeit, ihres Umfanges und ihrer Grenzen. Berlin: Walter de Gruyter, 1976.

Hoppe, Hansgeorg. *Kants Theorie der Physik.* Frankfurt am Main: Vittorio Klostermann, 1969.

Plaass, Peter. *Kants Theorie der Naturwissenschaft: Eine Untersuchung zur Vorrede von Kants "Metaphysische Anfangsgründe der Naturwissenschaft."* Göttingen: Vandenhoeck & Ruprecht, 1965

Schäfer, Lothar. *Kants Metaphysik der Natur.* Berlin: Walter de Gruyter, 1966.

Tuschling, Burkhard. *Metaphysische und transzendentale Dynamik in Kants opus postumum.* Berlin: Walter de Gruyter, 1971.

Vuillemin, Jules. *Physique et métaphysique kantiennes.* Paris: Presses Universitaires de France, 1955.

PRACTICAL PHILOSOPHY: MORAL THEORY

Acton, H. B. *Kant's Moral Philosophy.* London: Macmillan, 1970.

Allison, Henry E. *Kant's Theory of Freedom.* Cambridge: Cambridge University Press, 1990.

Allison, Henry E., ed. *Kant's Practical Philosophy. The Monist* 72 (July 1989) (special issue multiple-author anthology).

Atwell, John E. *Ends and Principles in Kant's Moral Thought.* Dordrecht: Martinus Nijhoff, 1986.

Aune, Bruce. *Kant's Theory of Morals.* Princeton, N.J.: Princeton University Press, 1979.

Auxter, Thomas. *Kant's Moral Teleology.* Macon, Ga.: Mercer University Press, 1982.

Beck, Lewis White. *A Commentary on Kant's Critique of Practical Reason.* Chicago: University of Chicago Press, 1960.

Bittner, Rüdiger, and Konrad Cramer, eds. *Materialien zu Kants 'Kritik der praktischen Vernunft'.* Frankfurt am Main: Suhrkamp Verlag, 1975 (selections from Kant's *Nachlaß* and early responses to Kant; includes extensive bibliography).

Böckerstette, Heinrich. *Aporien der Freiheit und ihre Aufklärung durch Kant.* Stuttgart: Frommann-Holzboog, 1982.

Broad, C. D. *Five Types of Ethical Theory.* London: Routledge & Kegan Paul, 1930.

Carnois, Bernard. *The Coherence of Kant's Doctrine of Freedom.* Trans. David Booth. Chicago: Chicago University Press, 1987.

Cohen, Hermann. *Kants Begründung der Ethik nebst ihrer Anwendung auf Recht, Religion und Geschichte.* 2d. ed. Berlin: B. Cassirer, 1910.

Cox, J. Gray. *The Will at the Crossroads: A Reconstruction of Kant's Moral Philosophy.* Washington, D.C.: University Press of America, 1984.

Duncan, A. R. C. *Practical Reason and Morality.* London: Thomas Nelson & Sons, 1957.

Düsing, Klaus. "Das Problem des höchsten Gutes in Kants praktischer Philosophie." *Kant-Studien* 63 (1971): 5–42.

Forschner, Maximilian. *Gesetz und Freiheit: Zum Problem der Autonomie bei I. Kant.* Munich: Verlag Anton Pustet, 1974.

Gregor, Mary. *Laws of Freedom: A Study of Kant's Method of Applying the Categorical Imperative in the* Metaphysik der Sitten. Oxford: Basil Blackwell, 1963.

Henrich, Dieter. "Über Kants früheste Ethik." *Kant-Studien* 54 (1963): 404–31.

"Die Deduktion des Sittengesetzes." In Alexander Schwann, ed., *Denken im Schatten des Nihilismus: Festschrift für Wilhelm Weischedel.* Darmstadt: Wissenschaftliche Buchgesellschaft, 1975, pp. 55–112.

"Ethik der Autonomie." In Dieter Henrich, *Selbstverhältnisse: Gedanken und Auslegungen zu den Grundlagen der klassischen deutschen Philosophie.* Stuttgart: Reclam, 1981, pp. 6–56.

Herman, Barbara. "On the Value of Acting from the Motive of Duty." *The Philosophical Review* 90 (1981): 359–82.

"Mutual Aid and Respect for Persons." *Ethics* 94 (1984): 577–602.

"The Practice of Moral Judgment." *The Journal of Philosophy* 82 (1985): 414–36.

Hill, Thomas E., Jr. "Kant on Imperfect Duty and Supererogation." *Kant-Studien* 62 (1971): 56–76.

"The Hypothetical Imperative." *The Philosophical Review* 82 (1973): 429–50.

"Kant's Anti-moralistic Strain." *Theoria* 44–45 (1978–9): 131–51.

"Humanity as an End in Itself." *Ethics* 91 (1980): 84–99.

"Kant's Argument for the Rationality of Moral Conduct." *Pacific Philosophical Quarterly* 66 (1985): 55–76.

Höffe, Ottfried. *Ethik und Politik: Grundmodelle und Probleme der praktischen Philosophie.* Frankfurt am Main: Suhrkamp Verlag, 1978.

Kategorische Rechtsprinzipien: Ein Kontrapunkt der Moderne. Frankfurt am Main: Suhrkamp Verlag, 1990.

Höffe, Ottfried, ed. *Grundlegung der Metaphysik der Sitten: Ein kooperativer Kommentar.* Frankfurt am Main: Vittorio Klostermann, 1989 (multiple-author anthology).

Hutchings, Patrick Æ. *Kant on Absolute Value: A Critical Examination of Certain Key Notions in Kant's* Groundwork of the Metaphysics of Morals *and Of His Ontology of Personal Values*. London: George Allen & Unwin, 1972

Jones, Hardy E. *Kant's Principle of Personality*. Madison: University of Wisconsin Press, 1971.

Jones, W. T. *Morality and Freedom in the Philosophy of Kant*. Oxford: Oxford University Press. 1940.

Köhl, Harald, *Kants Gesinnungsethik*. Berlin: Walter de Gruyter, 1990.

Korsgaard, Christine M. "Kant's Formula of Universal Law." *Pacific Philosophical Quarterly* 66 (1985): 24–47.

"Kant's Formula of Humanity." *Kant-Studien* 77 (1986): 183–202.

"The Right to Lie: Kant on Dealing with Evil." *Philosophy and Public Affairs* 15 (1986): 325–49.

Krüger, Gerhard. *Philosophie und Moral in der Kantischen Kritik*. Tübingen: J. C. B. Mohr, 1931.

Lo, P. C. *Treating Persons as Ends: An Essay on Kant's Moral Philosophy*. Lanham, Md.: University Press of America, 1987.

Mulholland, Leslie A. *Kant's System of Rights*. New York: Columbia University Press. 1990.

Nell, Onora (O'Neill). *Acting on Principle: An Essay on Kantian Ethics*. New York: Columbia University Press, 1975.

Nelson, Leonard. *Die kritische Ethik bei Kant, Schiller, und Fries: Eine Revision ihrer Prinzipien*. Göttingen: Vandenhoeck & Ruprecht, 1914.

Nisters, Thomas. *Kants Kategorischer Imperativ als Leitfaden humaner Praxis*. Munich: Verlag Karl Albers, 1989.

O'Neill, Onora. *Constructions of Reason: Explorations of Kant's Practical Philosophy*. Cambridge: Cambridge University Press, 1989.

Paton, H. J. *The Categorical Imperative: A Study in Kant's Moral Philosophy*. London: Hutchinson, 1947.

Potter, Nelson T., and Mark Timmons. *Morality and Universality: Essays on Ethical Universalizability*. Dordrecht: D. Reidel, 1985 (multiple-author anthology).

Prauss, Gerold. *Kant über Freiheit als Autonomie*. Frankfurt am Main: Vittorio Klostermann, 1983.

Rawls, John. "Kantian Constructivism in Moral Theory." *The Journal of Philosophy* 77 (1980): 515–72.

Reich, Klaus. "Kant and Greek Ethics." Translated by W. H. Walsh. *Mind* 48 (1939): 338–54, 446–63.

Reiner, Hans. *Duty and Inclination: The Fundamentals of Morality Discussed and Redefined with Special Regard to Kant and Schiller*. Trans. Mark Santos. The Hague: Martinus Nijhoff, 1983.

Ross, Sir David. *Kant's Ethical Theory: A Commentary on the Groundwork of the Metaphysics of Morals*. Oxford: Clarendon Press, 1954.

Rossvaer, Viggo. *Kant's Moral Philosophy: An Interpretation of the Categorical Imperative.* Oslo: Universitetsforlaget, 1979.

Schilpp, Paul Arthur. *Kant's Pre-Critical Ethics.* 2d ed. Evanston, Ill.: Northwestern University Press, 1960.

Schmucker, Josef. *Die Ursprünge der Ethik Kants in seinen vorkritischen Schriften und Reflexionen.* Meisenheim: Verlag Anton Hain, 1961.

Schnoor, Christian. *Kants Kategorischer Imperativ als Kriterium der Richtigkeit des Handelns.* Tübingen: J. C. B. Mohr (Paul Siebeck), 1989.

Seidler, Victor J. *Kant, Respect and Injustice: The Limits of Liberal Moral Theory.* London: Routledge & Kegan Paul, 1986.

Silber, John R. "The Copernican Revolution in Ethics: the Good Reexamined." *Kant-Studien* 51 (1959): 85–101.

"Kant's Conception of the Highest Good as Immanent and Transcendent." *The Philosophical Review* 68 (1959): 469–92.

"The Metaphysical Importance of the Highest Good as the Canon of Pure Reason in Kant's Moral Philosophy." *Texas Studies in Language and Literature* 1 (1959): 233–44.

"The Importance of the Highest Good in Kant's Ethics." *Ethics* 73 (1962–3): 179–97.

"Procedural Formalism in Kant's Ethics." *The Review of Metaphysics* 28 (1974): 197–236.

Singer, Marcus G. *Generalization in Ethics.* New York: Alfred A. Knopf, 1961.

Stevens, Rex P. *Kant on Moral Practice.* Macon, Ga.: Mercer University Press, 1981.

Sullivan, Roger J. *Immanuel Kant's Moral Theory.* Cambridge: Cambridge University Press, 1989 (includes extensive bibliography).

Velkley, Richard L. *Freedom and the End of Reason: On the Moral Foundations of Kant's Critical Philosophy.* Chicago: University of Chicago Press, 1989.

Ward, Keith. *The Development of Kant's View of Ethics.* Oxford: Basil Blackwell, 1972.

Williams, T. C. *The Concept of the Categorical Imperative: A Study of the Place of the Categorical Imperative in Kant's Ethical Theory.* Oxford: Clarendon Press, 1968.

Wolff, Robert Paul. *The Autonomy of Reason: A Commentary on Kant's Groundwork of the Metaphysics of Morals.* New York: Harper & Row, 1973.

Yovel, Yirmiyahu, ed. *Kant's Practical Philosophy Reconsidered: Papers Presented at the Seventh Jerusalem Philosophical Encounter, December 1986.* Dordrecht: Kluwer Academic Publishers, 1989 (multiple-author anthology).

PRACTICAL PHILOSOPHY: POLITICAL PHILOSOPHY

Arendt, Hannah. *Lectures on Kant's Political Philosophy.* Edited by Ronald Beiner. Chicago: University of Chicago Press, 1982.

Batscha, Zwi, ed. *Materialen zu Kants Rechtsphilosophie.* Frankfurt am Main: Suhrkamp Verlag, 1976 (multiple-author anthology).

Blumenberg, Hans, Jürgen Habermas, Dieter Henrich, and Jakob Taubes, eds. *Kant/Gentz/Rehberg: Über Theorie und Praxis.* Frankfurt am Main: Suhrkamp Verlag, 1967.

Borries, Kurt. *Kant als Politiker.* Leipzig: Felix Meiner Verlag, 1928.

Brandt, Reinhardt. *Eigentumstheorien von Grotius bis Kant.* Stuttgart: Frommann-Holzboog, 1974.

Brandt, Reinhardt, ed. *Rechtsphilosophie der Aufklärung.* Berlin: Walter de Gruyter, 1982 (multiple-author anthology).

Burg, Peter. *Kant und die Französische Revolution.* Berlin: Duncker & Humblot, 1974.

Busch, Werner. *Die Entstehung der kritischen Rechtsphilosophie Kants 1762– 80.* Kant-Studien Ergänzungsheft 110. Berlin: Walter de Gruyter, 1979.

Deggau, Hans-Georg. *Die Aporien der Rechtslehre Kants.* Stuttgart: Frommann-Holzboog, 1983.

Dulckeit, Gerhard. *Naturrecht und positives Recht bei Kant.* Leipzig, 1932.

Haensel, Werner. *Kants Lehre vom Widerstandsrecht: Ein Beitrag zur Systematik von Kants Rechtsphilosophie.* Kant-Studien Ergänzungsheft 60. Berlin: Pan Verlag, 1926.

Kersting, Wolfgang. *Wohlgeordnete Freiheit: Immanuel Kants Rechts- und Staatsphilosophie.* Berlin: Walter de Gruyter, 1984 (includes extensive bibliography).

Kühl, Kristian. *Eigentumsordnung als Freiheitsordnung: Zur Aktualität der Kantischen Rechts- und Eigentumslehre.* Freiburg: Verlag Karl Albert, 1984 (includes extensive bibliography).

Küsters, Gerd-Walter. *Kants Rechtsphilosophie.* Darmstadt: Wissenschaftliche Buchgesellschaft, 1988 (includes extensive bibliography and review of literature).

Langer, Claudia. *Reform nach Prinzpien: Untersuchungen zur politischen Theorie Immanuel Kants.* Stuttgart: Klett-Cotta Verlag, 1986.

Ludwig, Bernd. *Kants Rechtslehre.* Kant Forschungen, Vol. 2. Hamburg: Felix Meiner Verlag, 1988.

Murphy, Jeffrie G. *Kant: The Philosophy of Right.* London: Macmillan, 1970.

Oberer, Hariolf. "Zur Frühgeschichte der Kantishcen Rechtslehre." *Kant-Studien* 64 (1973): 88–102.

Reich, Klaus. *Rousseau und Kant.* Tübingen: J. C. B. Mohr (Paul Siebeck), 1936.

Riley, Patrick. *Kant's Political Philosophy*. Totowa, N.J.: Rowman and Little-field, 1983.

Ritter, Christian. *Der Rechtsgedanke Kants nach frühen Quellen*. Frankfurt am Main: Vittorio Klostermann, 1971.

Saage, Richard. *Eigentum, Staat und Gesellschaft bei Immanuel Kant*. Stuttgart: W. Kohlhammer, 1973.

Shell, Susan Meld. *The Rights of Reason: A Study of Kant's Philosophy and Politics*. Toronto: University of Toronto Press, 1980.

Symposium on Kantian Legal Theory. *Columbia Law Review* 87 (April 1989).

Van der Linden, Harry. *Kantian Ethics and Socialism*. Indianapolis: Hackett, 1988,

Vlachos, Georges. *La Pensée politique de Kant: Métaphysique de l'ordre et dialectique du progrés*, Paris: Presses Universitaires de France, 1954.

Williams, Howard. *Kant's Political Philosophy*. New York: St. Martin's Press, 1983.

THE THIRD CRITIQUE: COMPREHENSIVE STUDIES AND AESTHETICS

Baeumler, Alfred. *Das Irrationalitätsproblem in der Ästhetik und Logik des 18. Jahrhunderts bis zur Kritik der Urteilskraft*. 2d ed. Tübingen: Max Niemeyer Verlag, 1967.

Bartuschat, Wolfgang. *Zum systematischen Ort von Kants Kritik der Urteilskraft*. Frankfurt am Main: Vittorio Klostermann, 1972.

Basch, Victor. *Essai critique sur l'esthétique de Kant*. 2d ed. Paris: J. Vrin, 1927.

Cassirer, Heinrich Walter. *A Commentary on Kant's Critique of Judgment*. London: Methuen, 1938.

Caygill, Howard. *Art of Judgment*. Oxford: Basil Blackwell, 1989.

Cohen, Hermann. *Kants Begründung der Ästhetik*. Berlin: Dümmler, 1889.

Cohen, Ted, and Paul Guyer, eds. *Essays in Kant's Aesthetics*. Chicago: University of Chicago Press, 1982 (multiple-author anthology; includes extensive bibliography).

Coleman, Francis X. J. *The Harmony of Reason: A Study in Kant's Aesthetics*. Pittsburgh: University of Pittsburgh Press, 1974.

Crawford, Donald W. *Kant's Aesthetic Theory*. Madison: University of Wisconsin Press, 1974.

Crowther, Paul. *The Kantian Sublime: From Morality to Art*. Oxford: Clarendon Press, 1989.

Dunham, Barrows. *A Study in Kant's Aesthetics: The Universal Validity of Aesthetic Judgment*. Lancaster: no publisher, 1934.

Fricke, Christel. *Kants Theories des reinen Geschmacksurteils*. Berlin: Walter de Gruyter, 1990.

Fulda, Hans-Friedrich, and Rolf-Peter Horstmann, eds. *Hegel und die "Kritik der Urteilskraft."* Stuttgart: Klett-Cotta, 1990.

Guyer, Paul. *Kant and the Claims of Taste*. Cambridge, Mass.: Harvard University Press, 1979.

Juchem, Hans-Georg. *Die Entwicklung des Begriffs des Schönen bei Kant: Unter besonderer Berücksichtigung des Begriffs der verworrenen Erkenntnis*. Bonn: Bouvier Verlag, 1970.

Kemal, Salim. *Kant and Fine Art: An Essay on Kant and the Philosophy of Fine Art and Culture*. Oxford: Clarendon Press, 1986.

Krämling, Gerhard. *Die systembildende Rolle von Ästhetik und Kulturphilosophie bei Kant*. Freiburg: Verlag Karl Albert, 1985.

Kulenkampff, Jens. *Kants Logik des ästhetischen Urteils*. Frankfurt am Main: Vittorio Klostermann, 1978.

Kulenkampff, Jens, ed. *Materialen zu Kants "Kritik der Urteilskraft."* Frankfurt am Main: Suhrkamp Verlag, 1974 (original sources and multiple-author anthology).

Kuypers, Karel. *Kants Kunsttheorie und die Einheit der Kritik der Urteilskraft*. Verhandelingen der Koninklijke Nederlandse Akademie van Wetenschappen afd. Letterkunde, Nieuwe Reeks, Deel 77–No. 3. Amsterdam: North Holland, 1972.

Lebrun, Gérard. *Kant et la fin de la métaphysique: essai sur la critique de la faculté de juger*. Paris: A. Colin, 1970.

Macmillan, R. A. C. *The Crowning Phase of the Critical Philosophy: A Study in Kant's Critique of Judgment*. London: Macmillan, 1912.

Marc-Wogau, Konrad. *Vier Studien zu Kants "Kritik der Urteilskraft."* Uppsala Universitets Åarskrift 1938, 2. Uppsala: Lundequistka Bokhandeln, 1928.

McCloskey, Mary A. *Kant's Aesthetic*. Albany: State University of New York Press, 1987.

Menzer, Paul. *Kants Ästhetik in ihrer Entwicklung*. Abhandlungen der Deutschen Akademie der Wissenschaften zu Berlin, Klasse für Gesellschaftswissenschaften, Jahrgang 1950, No. 2. Berlin: Akademie-Verlag, 1952.

Mertens, Helga. *Kommentar zur ersten Einleitung zu Kants Kritik der Urteilskraft: Zur systematische Funktion der Kritik der Urteilskraft für die System der Vernunftkritik*. Munich: Berchmann, 1975.

Mothersill, Mary. *Beauty Restored*. Oxford: Clarendon Press, 1984.

Nivelle, Armand. *Kunst- und Dichtungstheorien zwischen Aufklärung und Klassik*. Berlin: Walter de Gruyter, 1960.

Podro, Michael. *The Manifold in Perception: Theories of Art from Kant to Hildebrand*. Oxford-Warburg Studies. Oxford: Clarendon Press, 1972.

Rogerson, Kenneth F. *Kant's Aesthetics: The Roles of Form and Expression.* Lanham, Md.: University Press of America, 1986.

Savile, Anthony. *Aesthetic Reconstructions: The Seminal Writings of Lessing, Kant, and Schiller.* Aristotelian Society Series, 8. Oxford: Basil Blackwell, 1987.

Schaper, Eva. *Studies in Kant's Aesthetics.* Edinburgh: Edinburgh University Press, 1979.

Schlapp, Otto. *Kants Lehre von Genie und die Entstehung der "Kritik der Urteilskraft."* Göttingen: Vandenhoeck & Ruprecht, 1901.

Uehling, Theodore E., Jr. *The Notion of Form in Kant's Critique of Aesthetic Judgment.* The Hague: Mouton, 1971.

Zeldin, Mary-Barbara. *Freedom and the Critical Undertaking: Essays on Kant's Later Critiques.* Ann Arbor, Mich.: UMI Monographs, 1980.

THE THIRD CRITIQUE: TELEOLOGY AND PHILOSOPHY OF BIOLOGY

Düsing, Klaus. *Die Teleologie in Kants Weltbegriff.* Kant-Studien Ergänzungsheft 96. Bonn: Bouvier Verlag, 1968.

Hermann, István. *Kants Teleologie.* Budapest: Akadémiai Kiadó, 1972.

Löw, Reinhard. *Philosophie des Lebendigen: Der Begriff des Organischen bei Kant, sein Grund und seine Aktualität.* Frankfurt am Main: Suhrkamp Verlag, 1980 (includes extensive bibliography).

McFarland, J. D. *Kant's Concept of Teleology.* Edinburgh: Edinburgh University Press, 1970.

McLaughlin, Peter. *Kant's Critique of Teleology in Biological Explanation.* Lewiston, N.Y.: Edwin Mellen Press, 1990.

Menzer, Paul. *Kants Lehre von der Entwicklung in der Natur und Geschichte.* Berlin: Georg Reimer, 1911.

Stadler, August. *Kants Teleologie und ihre erkenntnistheoretische Bedeutung.* Berlin: Dümmler, 1874.

Zumbach, Clark. *The Transcendent Science: Kant's Conception of Biological Methodology.* The Hague: Martinus Nijhoff, 1984.

PHILOSOPHY OF HISTORY AND ANTHROPOLOGY

Booth, W. James. *Interpreting the World: Kant's Philosophy of History and Politics.* Toronto: University of Toronto Press, 1986.

Galston, William A. *Kant and the Problem of History.* Chicago: The University of Chicago Press, 1975.

Weyand, Klaus. *Kants Geschichtsphilosophie: Ihre Entwicklung und ihr Verhältnis zur Aufklärung.* Kant-Studien Ergänzungsheft 85. Cologne: Kölner-Universitäts-Verlag, 1963.

Van de Pitte, Frederick P. *Kant as Philosophical Anthropologist.* The Hague: Martinus Nijhoff, 1971.

Yovel, Yirmiahu. *Kant and the Philosophy of History.* Princeton, N.J.: Princeton University Press, 1980.

PHILOSOPHY OF RELIGION

Bruch, Jean-Louis. *La philosophie religieuse de Kant.* Paris: Aubier-Montaigne, 1968.

Despland, Michel. *Kant on History and Religion.* Montreal: McGill-Queen's University Press, 1973.

England, Frederick Ernst. *Kant's Conception of God: A Critical Exposition of Its Metaphysical Development Together with a Translation of the Nova Dilucidatio.* New York: Dial Press, 1930.

Henrich, Dieter. *Der Ontologische Gottesbeweis: Sein Problem und seine Geschichte in der Neuzeit.* 2d ed. Tübingen: J. C. B. Mohr (Paul Siebeck), 1967.

Laberge, Pierre. *La Théologie Kantienne précritique.* Ottawa: Éditions de l'Université d'Ottawa, 1973.

Reboul, Olivier. *Kant et la probléme du mal.* Montreal: Presses de l'Université de Montréal, 1971.

Sala, Giovanni. *Kant und die Frage nach Gott.* Kant-Studien Ergänzungsheft 122. Berlin: Walter de Gruyter, 1989.

Schmucker, Josef. *Das problem der Kontingenz der Welt: Versuch einer positiven Aufarbeitung der Kritik Kants am kosmologischen Argument.* Freiburg: Herder, 1969.

Die Ontotheologie des vorkritischen Kants. Kant-Studien Ergänzungsheft 110. Berlin: Walter de Gruyter, 1979.

Webb, C. C. J. *Kant's Philosophy of Religion.* Oxford: Clarendon Press, 1926.

Wood, Allen W. *Kant's Moral Religion.* Ithaca, N.Y.: Cornell University Press, 1970.

Kant's Rational Theology. Ithaca, N.Y.: Cornell University Press, 1978.

REFERENCE WORKS

Eisler, Rudolf. *Kant-Lexikon: Nachschlagwerk zu Kants sämtlichen Schriften, Briefen und handschriftlichen Nachlaß.* Berlin: E. S. Mitter, 1930 (reprinted, Hildesheim: Georg Olms Verlag, 1961).

Martin, Gottfried. *Personenindex zu Kants gesammelte Schriften.* Berlin: Walter de Gruyter, 1969.

Sachindex zu Kants Kritik der reinen Vernunft. Berlin: Walter de Gruyter, 1967.

Mellin, G. S. A. *Encyklopädisches Wörterbuch der kritischen Philosophie.* 6 vols. 1797–1804 (reprinted, Aalen: Scientia Verlag, 1970–1).

Ratke, Heinrich. *Systematisches Handlexikon zur Kritik der reinen Vernunft.* Hamburg: Felix Meiner Verlag, 1929.

Schmid, Carl C. E. *Wörterbuch zum leichtern Gebrauch der Kantischen Schriften.* 4th ed. Jena: Cröker, 1798 (reprinted, Brussels: Aetas Kantiana, 1974).

INDEX

Adickes, Erich, 158n12, n14
aesthetic ideas, 391
aesthetic judgment, *see* judgment
aesthetics, 367–93 *passim; see also*
    beauty; genius; judgment; sublime
affinity, 187–8; principle of, 233, 240–2
Allison, Henry E., 94n21, 99n50,
    100n65, 156n2, 193n7, 195n13,
    197n31, 224n4; on Eberhard, 442n3;
    on moral theory, 339n41, 340n44
Ameriks, Karl, 24, 156n2, 224n3, n4,
    272n3, 279n48, 340n43
Amphiboly of Concepts of Reflection,
    255–6
Analogies of Experience, 14, 56, 127,
    154, 172, 266, 271, 442n10; First
    Analogy, 117, 183; Second Analogy,
    168–73, 262; Third Analogy, 267,
    271, 275n14
analysis, 110–12
analytic and synthetic judgments, 75–6,
    111; in critique of Baumgarten, 259
Anticipations of Perception, 221–2
antinomies of pure reason, 15, 29, 51,
    84, 239, 252–4, 256, 260, 272–3n5;
    First Antinomy, 154, 260–1; Second
    Antinomy, 260–1; Third Antinomy,
    211–12
Antinomy of Taste, 379–80
Apel, Karl-Otto, 355
appearances, 10, 12, 13, 418–19; and
    space, 68–9, 80–91
apperception: in Paralogisms, 252; and
    synthesis, 211; in transcendental de-
    duction, 126–7, 137–8, 140–6, 149–
    54, 206, 208

a priori, meaning of, 62
Aquila, Richard E., 156n2
architectonic: of *Critique of Judgment,*
    267–70, 372–3, 379; of philosophy
    in general, 217–18, 227n18; of Tran-
    scendental Dialectic, 253–4
Aristotelianism, 27
Aristotle on categories, 102, 107
arithmetic, 71–2; as synthetic, 76; and
    time, 80; *see also* mathematics
art, 385–92
Aschenberg, Reinhold, 156n2
Atwell, John, 337n22
Aune, Bruce, 337n22
autonomy, 24, 43; in moral theory, 309–
    18, 342–3; of reason, 299
axioms in mathematics, 78–9

Baker, Judith, 338n34
Baron, Marcia, 338n34
Baum, Manfred, 100n62, 156n2
Baumgarten, Alexander Gottlieb, 6, 8;
    on aesthetics, 371; on cognitive fac-
    ulties, 210, 226n15; on interaction,
    261–3; and Kant's metaphysics lec-
    tures, 256–9, 273–4n8, 274–5n12;
    on rational psychology, 202–3; on ra-
    tional theology, 397, 416n5; on sim-
    plicity of substances, 261
Beattie, James, 55, 61
beauty, 21, 373–5; contrasted with sub-
    lime, 382–3; free and dependent,
    391–2; natural vs. artistic, 386–9,
    392; as symbol of morally good, 379
Beck, Jakob Sigismund, 64

Beck, Lewis White, 59n18, 60n25, n39, n40, 97n37, 274n11, 393n9; on causality, 193n7, 193–4n8, 195n13, 416n4; on Crusius, 336n15; on morality, 333n1; on Wolff, 335n12
Beiser, Frederick C., 24, 274n10, 307n13
Bell, David, 444n23
Benacerraf, Paul, 82
Beneke, F. E., 226n14
Bennett, Jonathan, 121n13, 156n2, 224n4, 225n9, 226n14
Benz, Richard, 442n7
Beth, E. M., 78, 97n36, n38, 97–8n41
Bilfinger, Georg Bernhard, 261, 275–6n16
Bird, Graham, 156n2, 193n7
Black, Joseph, 191, 198n38
Bopp, Karl, 57n4
Boring, Edwin G., 227n20
Boswell, T., 119n3
Bradley, Francis Herbert, 337n21
Brandt, Reinhard, 120n9, 306n2, 366n8, n12
Brittan, Gordon, 193n7
Broad, Charlie Dunbar, 337n22
Brueckner, Anthony, 157n2
Buchdahl, Gerd, 193n7, 194n8, n11, 195n13, n17, 196n18, n20
Buchner, Edward Franklin, 226–7n17
Budde, Johann F., 28, 30, 58n8
Burchardt, Kurt, 224n2, 226n14
Burke, Edmund, 381–2
Buroker, Jill Vance, 95n27

Carl, Wolfgang, 156n2
Cassirer, Ernst, 57n4, 58n10, 61n44, 416n3
categorical imperative, 16, 286, 289, 345–6, 355; conception of, 318–21; formulations of, 321–5, 337n23; and moral motivation, 326–8; see also morality; moral law
categories (pure concepts of understanding), 14; definition of, 109–10, 129–33; and empirical laws, 20–1; and logical functions of judgment, 102–3, 108–10, 116; metaphysical deduction of, 101–19; number of, 133–6; relation of, to objects, 53–4; and schemata, 158n13; transcendental

deduction of, 123–60, 206–9; in Transcendental Dialectic, 252–3
causality, 6, 12, 14, 128, 135, 162–99 passim, 271, 336n20; in antinomies, 253; concept of, 161–4, 192n4; Hume's criticism of, 55, 162–4; and hypothetical judgment, 159n23; Kant's early view of, 35, 47; and natural laws, 161–99; and organisms, 22; universal principle of, 167–70, 170–3
causal laws; metaphysical and transcendental principles of, 181–6; mixed status of, 174; particular vs. general, 164–75; and reflective judgment, 186–91; see also causality
chemistry, 5, 188–92, 236, 239
Christianity, Reinhold on, 428
churches and moral religion, 408–11, 413
civil disobedience, 361
Clarke, Samuel, 29, 338n32
coercion, 4, 346–8
cognitive faculties, 209, 212–14, 226n15; see also reason; sensibility; understanding
Cohen, Hermann, 365n6
communicability, 377–8
communism, 348–51
communitarianism, 294, 298
community, moral, 407–8
concepts: complete, 116–7; content of, 110–13; contrasted to intuitions, 63–4, 117–18; empirical, 230; synthesis of, 110–15; theoretical, 232–3
conservation of matter, 12, 14, 128, 183–5
construction, mathematical, 77–8, 112–13, 120n6, 215; and psychologism, 220–3
cosmological argument, 7, 39, 395, 399
cosmology: Kant's early, 32–3; rational, 252–4, 261
Crawford, Donald W., 393n3, n4, n8
Crowther, Paul, 393n8
Crusius, Christian August, 6, 7, 8; and criticism of Wolff, 28, 30, 55, 58n9; on moral theory, 313, 326, 336n15, 338n32; on psychology, 203, 205, 216

D'Alembert, Jean Le Rond, 28
Darwin, Charles, 22
deduction, *see* metaphysical deduction of categories; transcendental deduction
definitions: in mathematics, 111; in philosophy, 8, 28
deism, 398
Descartes, René, 1, 2, 8, 27, 28, 203, 248n9, 266, 290–1
desire and reason, 315, 317, 327, 335n14, 339n35
Dessoir, Max, 224n3
determinism, 329–30
De Vleeschauwer, H.-J., 58n10, 61n40, 156n2, 225n9
di Giovanni, George, 25, 441n3, 447n76
discipline of reason, 295–7, 302–3
disinterestedness of aesthetic judgment, 374
dogmatism, 36
Dryer, Douglas P., 156n2
dualism, 35, 59
duties and principle of morality, 16

Earman, John, 96n29
Ebbinghaus, Julius, 337n22
Eberhard, Johann August, 94n21, 442n3
Ehrenberg, Hans, 227n17
Elliott, R. K., 393n4
empirical laws, 20–1
enlightenment (*Aufklärung*), 4, 29–30, 280–1, 299, 394–5, 410–11
equality, political, 356–7
Erdmann, Benno, 57n1, 58n5, 60n37, n40, 276n24, 279n46
Erdmann, Johann Eduard, 226n14
ethics, *see* morality
Euler, Leonhard, 29, 58n5, 73, 95n26
evil, radical, 402–3
evolution, 22, 72–3
Ewing, A. C., 99n51
existence and ontological argument, 400–1, 425–6
experience, conditions of possibility of, 56, 129
experiments; in psychology, 222–3; in science, 242–4

faith: Fichte on, 433; and knowledge, 13, 401, 422–3, 426–7; moral, 46, 403–5

Feder–Garve review of *Pure Reason*, 426, 443n11, 445n45
feeling: and beauty, 373–4, 375–6; Reinhold on, 428; in the sublime, 384
Fichte, Johann Gottlieb, 25, 226n14, 417, 425; on critique of revelation, 431–6; and Jacobi, 436–7; and Spinozism, 437; on will, 433, 439, 446n70
forces: attractive and repulsive, 6, 33, 41, 184; Cartesian vs. Leibnizian conceptions of, 28–9, 31–2; in Kant's early metaphysics of nature, 31–2; living, 28–32
foundationalism, 290–1, 295, 303, 305
freedom (external): of discussion, 310; and right, 344–8
freedom (of the will), 2, 4, 6, 12; and aesthetics, 21; in antinomies, 15–16; as basis of moral obligation, 17, 328–31; as evidence of intelligible world, 50; possibility of, 11, 51–2, 328–31; proofs of, 9, 16–20, 23, 328–31; and teleology, 22
free play of imagination and understanding, 374–5, 377
Frege, Gottlob, 121–2n23
Friedman, Michael, 24; on mathematics, 78–9, 95n25, n26, 96n30, n31, 97n34, n35, n38, n40, 97–8n41, 98n45, 122n24, n25, n26; on *Opus postumum*, 197n29, 199n39, n40; on physics, 196n21, n25
Friedrich II (the Great), 395, 396
Friedrich Wilhelm I, 395
Friedrich Wilhelm II, 396–7
Fries, Jakob Friedrich, 226n14

Galileo, 242–3
Garve, Christian, 445n45; *see also* Feder–Garve review of *Pure Reason*
Gauss, Karl Friedrich, 96n30
Gehler, Johann S. T., 227n19
genera, principle of, 233–8, 246
genius, 385–92
geometry, 13, 34, 69–71, 72, 210; basis of, 214–15; non-Euclidean, 216; as synthetic *a priori*, 74–80, 97n37, 98–9n47; and transcendental idealism, 86–7
Gerhardt, Volker, 366n11

Gloy, Karen, 156n2

God: concept of, 253, 398; and faith, 403–5; Fichte on, 431; and interaction, 263, 265–9; moral argument for existence of, 19–20, 50, 332, 401–3; and religion, 406–8; Spinoza on, 425; theoretical arguments for existence of, 6, 7, 15, 38–9, 397–401

Gödel, Kurt, 97n38

goodness, 316–18, 325–6

good will, 325–8

gravitation, law of, 175–80, 188, 191, 241

Guyer, Paul, 60n38, 61n45, 156n2, 159n25, 160n27, 225n9, 272n3, 275n13, 276n17; on aesthetics, 393n2, n3, n5, n7, n10; on causation, 193n7, 194n11, 196n18; on time determination, 278n38; on transcendental idealism, 85–7, 89, 96n31, 99n52, 100n60

Habermas, Jürgen, 307n14, 355

Haering, Theodor, 61n45

Hamann, Johann Georg, 54

happiness: and goodness, 316, 324; and highest good, 20, 333, 402

Harper, William, 94n20, 96n29, 197n30

Harris, Henry S., 441n3, 442n8

Harrison, Jonathan, 337n22

Hatfield, Gary, 24, 226n14, n16

Hegel, Georg Wilhelm Friedrich, 59n19, 107, 120n8, 318, 345, 420, 429

Heinze, Max, 274n9

Helmholtz, Hermann, 216, 226n16

Henrich, Dieter, on deduction, 156n2, 160n32, n33, 225n9, n13; on moral theory, 338n33, 340n45

Henson, Richard, 338n34

Herbart, Johann Friedrich, 226n14

Herder, Johann G., 46–7, 55, 61n42, 395, 425

Herman, Barbara, 338n25, n34, 340n44

Herz, Marcus, 52, 53, 55–7, 127–8

highest good, 20, 50, 331–2; and God, 401–3, 405

Hilbert, David, 78

Hill, Thomas E., Jr., 307n10, 335n8, 337n23, 339n41

Hinsch, Wilfried, 156n2

Hinske, Norbert, 58n7

Hintikka, Jaakko, 64, 66, 78, 92n7, 96–7n33, 97n34, n38, 97–8n41

history, 332

Hobbes, Thomas, 1, 2, 352–3, 358–9

Höffe, Ottfried, 337n22

Hoffmann, Adolf Friedrich, 28, 30

Hölderlin, Friedrich, 420

Hoppe, Hansgeorg, 156n2

Hossenfelder, Malte, 156n2

Howell, Robert, 65, 99n53

humanity as end in itself, 17, 322

Hume, David, 2, 6, 7, 149, 157n8; on causality, 54–5, 128, 162–5, 169–70, 192–3n5; and Jacobi, 425; on motivation, 327; on psychology, 205, 225n10; on self, 150; on taste, 380

Hutcheson, Francis, 8; on motivation, 327; opposition of, to natural law theory, 312

hypothetical imperatives, 319

idealism, see appearances; Refutation of Idealism; space; transcendental idealism

ideal of pure reason, 15, 252, 398; see also God

ideas of reason, 285–6; and aesthetic ideas, 391; in science, 229–30, 232–3, 243–5; and traditional metaphysics, 251–2; transcendental deduction of, 245–7

identity of indiscernibles, principle of, 255

immediacy of intuitions, 64–6, 69–70

immortality: and morality, 9, 19–20, 51, 331–2, 402; and rational psychology, 202–3

impartiality, 322–3

imperatives, 319–21; see also categorical imperative

incongruent counterparts, 9–10, 73–4, 95n27

induction, 163–4, 172–3, 178

inertia, 182

inference, rules of, 37–8

infinitude of space, 69–72

influx, theories of, 261–9, 278n45, 278–9n46

inner sense, 138, 182, 210, 256; and empirical psychology, 222–3; and rational psychology, 201–2, 218–19
instrumentalism, 232
intelligible world, 50
interaction, 6, 12, 14, 128, 135, 185; in Kant's metaphysics lectures, 261–72; mind–body, 270–1
interest in beauty, 387–8
introspection, 211–12
intuition: concept of, 63–6, 92–3n14; as content of concepts, 112–13; inner and outer, 210; intellectual, 66, 93n16, 434; and knowledge, 219–20; psychological status of forms of, 213–14; and reflection, 420–1; space and time as forms of, 13–14, 15, 67–74, 80–91; synthesis of, 105, 110–15; and synthetic a priori judgments in mathematics, 76–80, 215

Jacob, Margaret C., 59n20
Jacobi, Friedrich Heinrich, 25, 395, 422, 438; and controversy with Mendelssohn about Spinoza, 423–5, 437; critique of reason of, 425–7, 443n15, 444n24; and Fichte, 436–7; and Reinhold, 427–9
judgment: aesthetic, 4, 20–1, 367–80; analytic, 111; as a priori, 62; deduction of aesthetic, 375–80; definition of, 120n5; dialectic of aesthetic, 378–90; of experience and of perception, 147; forms or logical functions of, 14, 102–10, 133–6, 146–9; and inference, 38; infinite, 107–8; moments of aesthetic, 372–5, 383; possibility of synthetic a priori, 42, 52, 55; principles of, 12, 14; reflective, 369; singular, 65, 107, 120n10; teleological, 4, 20, 21–4, 368–70; transcendental deduction from concept of, 146–9

Kalter, Alfons, 224n4
Kant, Immanuel, works of:
Attempt to Introduce the Concept of Negative Quantities into Philosophy, 7, 8, 41–2, 48, 128, 192n1

Conflict of the Faculties, 4, 397
Conjectural Beginnings of Human History, 4
Critique of Judgment, 4, 11, 20–4, 57; Analytic of Beautiful, 370–80; Analytic of Sublime, 381–5; Dialectic, 378–80; on genius and art, 385–92; interpretive approaches to, 367–70; on laws of nature, 166–9, 181; on reason, 421–2; on reflective judgment, 187–8; on sensus communis, 300–1
Critique of Practical Reason, 4, 11, 18–20, 21, 209, 317; on faith, 404–5; on freedom of will, 330–1; on highest good, 333; on immortality, 331–2; on practical argument for God, 401–3
Critique of Pure Reason, 4, 11–16, 20, 29, 39, 41, 50, 51, 52, 369; composition of, 54–7; Doctrine of Method, 217–18, 289–97; second edition of, 426; Transcendental Aesthetic, 13–14, 24, 62–100, 153, 210, 214–15, 371; Transcendental Analytic, 14–15, 101–19, 123–60 passim, 163–4, 170–4; Transcendental Deduction, 123–60, 204–9; Transcendental Dialectic, 15–16, 24, 110, 201–4, 229–32, 249–55, 282–6, 329–30
Differentiation of Regions in Space, 9, 73–4
Dreams of a Spirit-Seer, 8–9, 45–52
Duisburg Nachlaß, 52, 56, 61n45
False Subtlety of the Four Syllogistic Figures, The, 37–8, 119n3
Groundwork of the Metaphysics of Morals, 4, 16–18, 317; on freedom of will, 329; on good will, 325–8; on humanity as end in itself, 322; on imperatives, 319–21, 324–5
Ideas towards a Universal History, 4
Inaugural dissertation (On the Forms and Principles of the Sensible and Intelligible Worlds), 9–10, 12, 47–52, 55, 56, 128, 157n10, 159n19; on interaction, 264; Lambert's criticism of, 53; on space, 68, 70–1, 93n17, 94n23, 95n27, 96n31, 99n52
Logic, 63, 64, 91n3, n4, n5, 92n8, 105–

6, 111, 112, 119n3, 120n5, 121n16,
n17, n18, n20
*Metaphysical Foundations of Natural
Science,* 4, 5, 73, 95n26, n27, 123,
254, 440–1; on chemistry, 188–92;
on conservation of matter, 183–4;
on laws of motion and gravitation,
176–8; on psychology, 201, 217,
218–19, 221; on transcendental and
metaphysical principles, 182, 188–
9; on transcendental deduction,
146, 148
Metaphysics of Morals: Doctrine of
Right, 323; Doctrine of Virtue, 318,
323–5; on perpetual peace, 363–4;
on property, 348–51; on right, 344–
7; on social contract, 354
*Observations on the Feeling of the
Beautiful and Sublime,* 42–3, 55,
371, 381
*Only Possible Basis for a Demonstra-
tion of the Existence of God, The,* 7,
15, 38–9, 48, 398; Jacobi on, 425
*On the Clarity of the Principles of
Natural Theology and Ethics,* 7–8,
28, 40–1, 45, 93n14
On the Different Races of Mankind,
52
*On the Old Saying: That May Be
Right in Theory but Does Not Work
in Practice,* 355–7, 404
Opus postumum, 5, 21, 24, 179, 192,
440–1
Perpetual Peace, 310, 362–4
Physical Monadology, 6, 31, 40
*Principiorum primorum cognitionis
metaphysicae nova dilucidatio,* 5,
30, 34–5, 40, 59, 128, 157n7; on systems of interaction, 262
*Prolegomena to Any Future Metaphys-
ics That Shall Come Forth as Scientific,* 4, 13, 158–9n16; on categories,
130, 133–4; on causation, 162, 173–
5; on gravitation, 176; on laws of
nature, 166, 181–2; on rational psychology, 218–19; on space, 81–2,
87, 89, 98n43; transcendental deduction in, 146–9, 152
*Religion within the Limits of Reason
Alone,* 4, 397; on good and evil,

402–3; on organized churches, 408–
11; on religion, 406–8; on revela-
tion, 411–13
*Thoughts on the True Estimation of
Living Forces,* 5, 30–2, 35, 59
*Two Essays Concerning the Philan-
thropic Academy,* 52
*Universal History from a Cosmopoli-
tan Point of View,* 362, 408–9
*Universal Natural History and
Theory of the Heavens,* 5, 31, 32, 39
*What Does it Mean to Orient Oneself
in Thought?,* 4, 291, 299–300, 404,
412
What Is Enlightenment?, 298–9, 310,
410
*What Real Progress Has Metaphysics
Made in Germany since the Time
of Leibniz and Wolff?,* 255–7
Kemp, Jonathan, 337n22
Kemp Smith, Norman, 92n14, 94n22,
95n27, 99n50, 197n32, 225n9, 306–
7n9
Kepler, Johannes, on laws of motion,
175–80, 197n27
Kersting, Wolfgang, 25, 365n4, 366n8,
n10, n11
Kitcher, Patricia, 156n2, 224n2, 225n9,
226n14
knowledge: conditions of possibility of,
137, 214–16; contrasted to faith, 13,
401, 422–3, 426–7; foundations of,
3, 36
Knutzen, Martin, 395
Koller, Peter, 365n5
Korf, H. A., 442n7
Körner, Stefan, 156n2, 248n3
Korsgaard, Christine M., 338n24, n26

Lambert, Johann Heinrich, 28, 46, 53,
57n4
Lange, Joachim, 28, 30, 58n8
Langer, Claudia, 366n13
Lavater, Johann Casper, 396, 445n44
Lavoisier, Antoine, 191–2, 199n39
law, contrasted to virtue, 323–4
Lear, Jonathan, 335n14
Leary, David E., 227n17
Leibniz, Gottfried Wilhelm, 2, 6, 10, 27–
9, 31, 34, 35, 54, 58n11, 128, 203,

Leibniz, Gottfried Wilhelm (*cont.*) 253; on analyticity of judgments, 116–18, 122n26, n28; critique of, 116–19, 255–7; on interaction, 264, 266, 267; on relationist view of space, 67–8, 72–4, 95n26, 255; on substance, 118–19

Léon, Xavier, 441n2

Lessing, Gotthold Ephraim, 295

Locke, John, 3, 205; on property, 350–1, 352–3, 365–6n8

logic: and categories, 101–19, 131–6; general vs. transcendental, 108; Kant's conception of formal, 65, 105–6, 110; and mathematics, 79–80; scholastic, 37; and transcendental deduction, 148; and vindication of reason, 281–2, 283–4

Lovejoy, Arthur, 168–9, 186, 195n12

McCloskey, Mary A., 393n3

MacIntyre, Alasdair, 338n29

magnitude: categories of, 135; extensive and intensive, 14

Maimon, Solomon, 421, 442–3n11

Malebranche, Nicholas, 54, 264, 268, 277n30

materialism, 35, 39, 58–9n12, 204

mathematics: concepts in, 111–15; definitions in, 111–12, 115; foundations and methods of, 8, 27–9, 40–1, 51, 292–3; in Leibnizian-Wolffian school, 28–9; and psychology, 219–23; pure, 96n31, 98n44

Mathieu, Vittorio, 448n103, n104

matter, dynamical view of, 33, 39, 59

maxims, 318–21, 323

Mayer, Tobias, 227n20

mechanics, laws of, 176–7

mechanism, 35, 45

Meier, Georg Friedrich, 276n24

Melnick, Arthur, 193n7, 275n15

Mendelssohn, Moses, 28, 46, 57n4, 397; and Jacobi, 423–6, 436, 445n44; on soul, 202–3, 224n5

Menzer, Paul, 60n37

metaphysical deduction of categories, 24, 38, 101–19 *passim*, 125

metaphysics: critique of traditional, 3, 4, 15–16, 26, 37–46, 249–79 *pas-*

sim; in dialectic of aesthetic judgment, 379–80; divisions of, 218; foundations of, 8, 30–1, 34–5, 38–9; of inaugural dissertation, 49–51; method for, 29, 34, 40–1, 46–7; of nature, 33–4; possibility of, 27, 42–3, 46–8; as science of limits of human reason, 27, 37, 43, 47, 117–18, 259

method, philosophical contrasted to mathematical, 28–9, 34, 36, 40–1, 51, 77–80

Meyer, Jürgen Bona, 224n2, 226n14, n17

mind–body interaction, 270–1

Mischel, Theodore, 227n17

modality: as category, 134–6, 159n24; and laws of motion, 177–8, 180

monadology, 33–4, 255–6

monads, 29, 33–4, 72, 277n32

morality, 309–41 *passim;* and aesthetics, 21; Fichte on, 433–4; foundations of, 2–3, 9, 10–11, 328–31; and freedom, 18–19; fundamental motive in, 325–8; and independence from metaphysics, 44–6; principle of, 4, 8–9, 16–17; and determinism, 23–4; and psychology, 209; *see also* categorical imperative; moral law

moral law: conception of, 318–21; formulations of, 321–5; and intelligible world, 50; justification of, 328–31; and respect, 326–8; *see also* categorical imperative

Mothersill, Mary, 393n6

motion, laws of, 31–2, 176–80, 241

natural law in moral theory, 311–12, 327

nature, laws of, 165–99 *passim;* metaphysical and transcendental principles of, 181–6

necessity: in causation, 162, 165, 171, 174; concept of, 47, 179; as hypothetical, 271; in judgment of taste, 374, 376; moral, 316–18; of spatiality, 73, 86–7; in transcendental deduction, 139–40

Nehrlich, Graham, 96n28

Newton, Isaac, 2, 4, 10, 27, 253; on absolute space, 67, 73, 95n26; on laws of motion, 177–9, 218; on solar system, 32–3

Nietzsche, Friedrich, 304

noumena: knowledge of, 47–9; in negative and positive senses, 18; *see also* things in themselves

Nozick, Robert, 351

objects: and categories, 129–33; concept of, 56, 151; and judgments, 109–10, 115; in transcendental deduction, 124–5, 137, 139–40, 143–6, 151–2

obligation, 310, 312–13; Crusius's theory of, 313; as self-imposed, 314–18; Wolff's theory of, 312–13

occasionalism, 261–6, 268–9

O'Neill, Onora (Nell), 24, 306n2, n6, 307n13, 337n22, 338n30

ontological argument, 6, 15, 36, 39, 399–401

ontology: in inaugural dissertation, 49–50; in metaphysics lectures, 258–61

opposition, real and logical, 7, 41–2, 48, 128, 255

organisms, 22

Paralogisms of Pure Reason, 15, 210–14, 252, 269

Parsons, Charles D., 24, 93n15, 97n40, 98n43

Pascal, Blaise, 404

paternalism, 311

Paton, H. J., 193n7, 193–4n8, 198n38; on morality, 333n1, 337n22

Paulsen, Friedrich, 58n10, 59n14

peace, 361–4

perception, 66

phenomena, *see* appearances

physicotheological argument, 7, 399

physics, 5, 33, 162–99 *passim*, 241; Cartesian vs. Leibnizian, 28–9, 31–2; and non-Euclidean geometry, 75

physiology, 206, 218

Pietism, 28–30, 394–5

Pippin, Robert, 93n18

Platner, Ernst, 443n11

Plato, 54, 285, 306n5

pleasure and taste, 371–2

political philosophy, 4, 342–66 *passim*

Polonoff, Irving, 57–8n4, 58n10, 59n16

possibility, real, 259

postulates, practical, 19–20, 404–5

Posy, Carl, 275n15

Potter, Nelson, 337n22

practical reason, 17–20; and motivation, 327; primacy of, 43–4, 331–2; and will, 296, 315, 330; *see also* reason

Prauss, Gerold, 89–90, 99n52, 340n46

predicates, 110–15; Leibniz's view of, 116

preestablished harmony, 35, 54, 255–7, 261–6, 268–9

Priestley, Joseph, 227n18, n19

progress, 332

property: justification of, 348–51; and state, 351–3

psychologism, 210, 226n14

psychology, 200–27; and mathematics, 219–23; rational, 201–4; scientific status of empirical, 217–24, 233–5; transcendental, 209–17; and transcendental deduction, 204–9

Pufendorf, Samuel, 338n32, 350

purposiveness, 369–70

quantification, 106

Quine, W. V. O., 106, 119n2

rationalism, 6, 7; Kant's critique of, 40–2, 290, 292–3, 303–4; Kant's early, 35–6, 40; in metaphysics lectures, 260; and Pietism, 29–30; in religion, 394–5

Rawls, John, 333–4n1, 340n44, 361

reality in argument for God, 397–8

reason: architectonic of pure, 217–18; and causal laws, 186–91; in contrast with understanding, 421–3; discipline of, 295–7, 302–3; fact of, 330–1, 348; and metaphysics, 15, 425; as practical rather than theoretical, 43–4; public use of, 298–9; Reinhold on, 428–9; and right, 344–8; and science, 228–48; and sensibility, 47–8, 51, 53; and *sensus communis*, 300–1; vindication of, 280–308

reflection, contrasted to intuition, 420–1; Fichte on, 434–5

reflective judgment, 20–4, 369; and empirical causal laws, 186–91, 198n36
reform, political, 358–61
Refutation of Idealism, 6, 14, 99n54, 127, 262; see also transcendental idealism
regulative ideals, 23, 287, 296; in science, 190–2, 228–48
Reich, Klaus, 107, 120n9, 156n2
Reid, Thomas, 337n21
Reimarus, Hermann Samuel, 395
Reiner, Hans, 338n34
Reinhold, Karl Leonhard, 25, 226n14; and Fichte, 435–6; and reconstruction of Kant, 427–31; on representation, 446n60; on will, 439, 448n96
relation, categories of, 135–6, 154
relationism as view of space, 68, 72–4; see also space
religion: concept of, 406–8; and faith, 403–5; Fichte on, 431–6; Kant's personal relation to, 394–7
republicanism, 310, 358–61, 362–4
respect, 326–8
revelation: Fichte on, 431–6; Kant on, 411–13
revolution, 358–61
Riemann, Bernard, 216
right: concept of, 344–8, 364–5n1; justification of, 347–8
rightness, 316–18
Rorty, Richard, 156n2, 227n21, 304
Rousseau, Jean-Jacques: on autonomy, 313–14, 315; influence of, 43–5, 47, 59n22, 334–5n5, 336n16, n17; on social contract, 354–5, 358–9
Rüdiger, Andreas, 28, 30

Satura, Vladimir, 224n2, 226n14, 227n17
Savile, Anthony, 393n4
Schaper, Eva, 25, 156n2, 393n6, n11
Scheele, Wilhelm, 191, 198n38
Schelling, Friedrich Willhelm, 25, 421, 429; philosophy of nature, 437–8; on Spinoza, 438, 447n91; on will, 439, 446n70
Schiller, Friedrich, 338n34, 440
Schmid, Karl C. E., 227n18
Schmucker, Josef, 59n22, 335n10

Schneewind, J. B., 24, 278n36, 335n11
Schultz, F. A., 395
Schultz, Johann, 95n24, 97n37, n39
Schulze, Gottlob Ernst (Aenesidemus), 25, 430, 435
Schwyzer, Hubert, 157n2
science: in Critique of Judgment, 20–3; foundations of, 2–3, 4, 6, 10, 11, 12; and morality, 23–4; and reason, 228–48; see also chemistry; mathematics; physics; psychology
self: identity of, 14; in Paralogisms, 252–4; simplicity of, 15; see also apperception
self-consciousness, see apperception
self-sufficiency, 357–8
Sellars, Wilfrid, 227n21
sensibility, faculty of, 10, 13; and knowledge, 117–18; limits of, 15; and reason, 47–8, 51, 53; and singular intuitions, 66; space and time as forms of, 67–74
sensus communis: and aesthetic judgment, 378; and reason, 300–1
Shaftesbury, Anthony Ashley Cooper, Earl of, 312
Shamoon, Alan, 91n5, 92n6, n12
simplicity of soul, 202–3
Singer, Marcus G., 337n22
skepticism: in Kant's development, 30, 45–6, 48; about reason, 293–4, 298, 305
social contract, 353–8
solar system: Kant's theory of, 32–3, 395; motions of, 177, 241
Sorrell, Tom, 339n34
soul: and rational psychology, 201–4; and transcendental psychology, 213
space: absolute (Newtonian) and relative (Leibnizian) conceptions of, 10, 28, 67–8, 72–4, 95n26; divisibility of, 34, 51, 183–4, 252–3; and geometry, 74–80; magnitude of, 68–72; Metaphysical Exposition of concept of, 67–74; as pure form of intuitions, 13, 15, 62, 67–74; and substance, 182–4; and transcendental deduction, 153–4, 157n2; Transcendental Exposition of concept of, 74–80; transcendental ideality of, 80–91, 255

specification, principle of, 233, 238–40
Spener, Philipp Jakob, 394
Spinoza, Baruch, 418; and Fichte, 437;
    Jacobi on, 423–6; and Schelling, 438
Spinozism, 268–9, 276n23, 278n43
Stahl, Georg, 192, 242–3
state, 4–5; and property, 351–3
Stocker, Michael, 338n34
Strawson, Peter F., 156n2, 225n9,
    226n14; on logic, 120n7, 121n14,
    n15; on reidentification, 109; on
    transcendental idealism, 83
sublime, the, 21, 381–5
substance, 47, 117–18, 135; and categori-
    cal judgment, 118–19; and interac-
    tion, 265; and permanence, 182–5;
    and rational psychology, 202–3; in
    Spinoza, 424
succession, irreversibility of, 168–70,
    195n15
Suchting, W. A., 193n7
sufficient reason, principle of, 6, 34, 36,
    128, 255, 274–5n12, 296, 305
Sulzer, Johann Georg, 61n41
Swedenborg, Immanuel, 8
Swing, T. K., 159n17
syllogisms: forms of, 37–8, 106; in Tran-
    scendental Dialectic, 251–2, 284
synthesis: in metaphysical deduction,
    110–15; and rules, 143–4; threefold,
    138–9; transcendental, 212–13; in
    transcendental deduction, 149–54,
    210–213
systematicity: in knowledge, 20–1; in
    science, 233–45

taste, 370–2; deduction of judgment of,
    375–8; dialectic of judgments of,
    378–80; moments of judgment of,
    372–5; see also judgment
Tetens, Johann Nicolaus, 28, 205
theism, 398
theology: Fichte on, 431–6; Kant's cri-
    tique of rational, 38–9, 397–401;
    Kant's moral, 401–3
things in themselves, 10, 12, 15, 53,
    418–19; and freedom of the will,
    17–18; Jacobi on, 423; nonspatiality
    of, 80–91; Reinhold on, 430; see
    also noumena

Thomasius, Christian, 35
Thompson, Manley, 91–2n5, 92n12,
    97n40, 121n11, n21
time: and arithmetic, 80; in psychology,
    220–1; as pure form of intuition,
    13, 15, 62; in transcendental deduc-
    tion, 138, 153–4
time determination, 14, 127, 154–5, 266
Tonelli, Giorgio, 57n4
Torricelli, Evangelista, 242–3
transcendental deduction: of categories
    of understanding, 14, 54, 110, 123–
    60 passim; in first edition of Cri-
    tique of Pure Reason, 136–46; of
    ideas of reason, 245–7; of judg-
    ments of taste, 375–8; of moral law,
    339n38; objectives of, 124–6; in Pro-
    legomena, 146–9; psychology in,
    204–9; in second edition, 149–55;
    strategies in, 126–7, 133; two stages
    of, 153–4
transcendental idealism, 53, 62, 80–91,
    249–50, 254; and antinomy, 260–1,
    273n5; and interaction, 269
transcendental object, 145
transcendental principles contrasted to
    metaphysical, 181–6, 188
transcendental realism, 272–3n5, 298
truth: Jacobi on Spinoza on, 424; Kant's
    conception of, 418–20
Tuschling, Burkhard, 277n34

Ulrich, J. A., 274n9
understanding, 12; and categories, 102–
    10; contrast with reason, 421–3
unity: in B-deduction, 149–50; in empiri-
    cal knowledge, 233–45; and reason,
    282–5, 287–8; synthetic, 142
universality: in aesthetic judgment, 374,
    376; of causation, 163–4, 165; and
    empirical psychology, 207–9
universalizability, 318–21, 337–8n24,
    345, 355

Velkley, Richard L., 59n22
virtue, 9; definition of, 310, 318; and
    happiness, 20; relation of, to cate-
    gorical imperative, 323–5
Vorländer, Karl, 416n2

Walker, Ralph C. S., 278n37
Walsh, W. H., 156n2, 224n4, 225n9
Ward, Keith, 59n14
Wartenberg, Thomas E., 24
Werkmeister, William H., 60n24
will: Crusius's theory of, 313; Fichte on,
    432–5; Kant's theory of, 315, 317–
    18, 325–8, 328–33, 438–9; terms
    for, 265n3; see also freedom (of the
    will)
Williams, Bernard, 338n29
Wilson, Kirk Dallas, 94n23
Winckelmann, Johann J., 420, 442n9
Wittgenstein, Ludwig, 304
Wolff, Christian, 2, 6, 8, 10, 27–8, 67,
    257, 416n5, 427; on cognitive facul-
    ties, 226n15; on empirical psychol-
ogy, 205, 210; on method, 36,
    59n16; on moral theory, 312–13,
    335n12, n13; and Pietism, 29–30;
    on principles of knowledge, 34; on
    rational psychology, 201–3, 224–
    5n6, 263; on religion, 394–5, 397
Wolff, Hans M., 335n12
Wolff, Robert Paul, 156n2, 193n7, 225n9
Wöllner, Johann Christoff, 396–7
Wood, Allen W., 25, 273n7, 416n6–n13
worth, moral, 316–18
Wundt, Max, 58n8, 274n11

Young, J. Michael, 24, 97n40

Zedlitz, Baron von, 396
Zeno's paradoxes, 239